THE TICKET BOOK
by
ROD DORNSIFE

The author gratefully acknowledges the assistance of Mark Miller in the writing of this book.

THE TICKET BOOK

Published by
THE TICKET BOOK, INC.
P.O. Box 1087
La Jolla, California 92038

First Printing . . . August 1978

Library of Congress Catalog Card Number 78-63037

ISBN 0-9601950-1-7

PRINTED IN THE UNITED STATES OF AMERICA

DEDICATION

To Mom and Dad.
Thanks for all the support and help over the years.

ABOUT THE AUTHOR

Rod Dornsife is well qualified to author a book about traffic tickets. The 27-year-old resident of San Diego served as a police officer for 5 years with a major metropolitan police department before writing *The Ticket Book*. During that time he wrote thousands of traffic tickets and worked in nearly every aspect of traffic enforcement. His police experience includes routine patrol, traffic officer, field training officer, radar operation, special drinking driver details and over 2 years as an accident investigator. He received several official commendations for his exemplary work with the police department, including one of his department's highest honors.

During his final year with the police, Dornsife founded and published *Police Product News*, an entertaining trade magazine for police officers. *Police Product News* was distributed throughout all 50 states and more than 36 foreign countries, and rapidly became the nation's leading law enforcement publication. He also established one of the nation's foremost police equipment supply companies.

Dornsife spent over 2½ years in researching, writing and collecting information and photographs for *The Ticket Book*, traveling coast to coast while conducting interviews and making contacts with State Police officials from each of the 50 states.

PREFACE

As a traffic officer for a major metropolitan police department, I wrote thousands of tickets to people just like you, whether you're a student, a housewife or a lawyer. I couldn't help but notice that the people I stopped were both curious and confused about why they were stopped and why I was giving them a ticket. In the less intimidating environment of social gatherings, when I was off-duty and out of uniform, people wanted to know, "What's the inside story?" It seemed that almost every conversation began with, "I got this ticket . . . ."

Despite the anger that most people felt at receiving a ticket, very few ever took the matter to court to be decided. Those brave souls who did try to defend themselves were usually unprepared; they were clumsy amateurs pitted against legal professionals. Their defenses seemed to be based primarily on rumors, hearsay and TV shows.

These people were so sure of their innocence that they were willing to give up a day at work to fight their ticket. I felt they at least deserved to have enough information to analyze what had happened to them so they could make an intelligent decision about what to do next. A police officer can turn to a wealth of published information and months of training in enforcing traffic laws, but the motorist has virtually no materials available to him that can explain traffic citations and the system from start to finish.

This book was not intended to help anyone "beat" a traffic ticket, but it may help the motorist to determine whether or not he is truly guilty of the offense, and give him the basics of his defense in court. It was written and intended as a complete and informative guide for motorists, aimed at clearing up some of the myths and misconceptions that surround the entire subject of traffic tickets. Of course, not all of the specific information in this book will apply to all 50 states, but you will find that the general principles are the same. Police officers, attorneys and judges will find this book useful and enlightening. It is a frank and accurate discussion of the entire traffic law enforcement system, from the officer's personality to the final verdict of the court. I hope this book will help to strengthen the understanding of traffic officers, laws and the courts, and that it will provide you with entertaining and enjoyable reading

ROD DORNSIFE

IN APPRECIATION

Special thanks to Mark Miller whose many hours of writing and research helped to make this book a reality. Mark is a talented and creative writer who has had numerous articles and short stories appear in national publications. Mark also has an extensive background in advertising and marketing.

Also thanks to Dave Deal, 1651 Monte Vista Drive, Vista, CA 92083 whose superb cartooning appears on the cover and the chapter title pages.

Also greatly appreciated is the work of Gary Porter, 10815 Vista Camino, Lakeside, CA 92040, who did the excellent technical illustrations and graphs appearing throughout the book.

Ed Kessler, 738 West Washington Avenue, Escondido, CA 92025, is the master photographer who was responsible for the photo on the rear cover.

Thompson Type, 3667 Voltaire Street, San Diego, CA 92106, did a tremendous job in the typesetting of the book. Without their superb service and cooperation, the production of this book would have been an impossible task.

Dale T. Smith, a nationally known expert on the subject of radar and radar detection assisted as a technical advisor on the book, and the accuracy of the technical details is largely due to his expertise.

Appreciation is also expressed to the following agencies and organizations for their contributions and cooperation:

AUTOMOBILE ASSOCIATION OF AMERICA,
Falls Church, VA
AUTOMOBILE CLUB OF SOUTHERN
CALIFORNIA, Los Angeles, CA
CALIFORNIA HIGHWAY PATROL, Sacramento, CA
CARLSBAD POLICE DEPARTMENT, Carlsbad, CA
CHULA VISTA POLICE DEPARTMENT,
Chula Vista, CA
FEDERAL COMMUNICATIONS COMMISSION,
Washington, D.C.
NEVADA HIGHWAY PATROL, Carson City, NV
OCEANSIDE POLICE DEPARTMENT,
Oceanside, CA
OREGON STATE POLICE, Salem, OR
SAN DIEGO POLICE DEPARTMENT, San Diego, CA
TIJUANA POLICE DEPARTMENT, Tijuana, Mexico
WESTERN INSURANCE INFORMATION SERVICE,
Santa Ana, CA

and the many manufacturers of both radar and radar detection equipment that were kind enough to provide information and demonstrations of their products.

THE TICKET BOOK
TABLE OF CONTENTS

INTRODUCTION

You're driving along at a comfortable speed, perhaps just a little bit faster than the rest of traffic, nestled in the warm security of your bucket seat and listening to an entertaining program on the radio. Suddenly, your entire mood is shattered by the blinding presence of a patrol car, red and blue lights flashing, high-beams on, spotlights fastened onto your mirrors and the car seems like it's glued to your rear bumper.

You pull over to the side of the road wondering, "Where did that guy come from?" You start thinking of excuses, but you're not really sure why he even stopped you. Shoes crunch on gravel and then he's standing by your door, one hand resting on the butt of his holstered revolver. His face is partially obscured by the brim of his hat and the glare of a flashlight.

"May I see your license and registration?" he says, politely but firmly. He stands motionless as you fumble through your wallet, making excuses. He crouches slightly, fingers clenched on his weapon as you open your glovebox and then he takes both documents back to his patrol car, leaving you to squint into the glare of his lights in your mirrors as you're wondering what is happening to you.

He's back at your door in a few moments. "Sir, I clocked you at 67 miles per hour, which is in excess of the state maximum limit of 55. Sign here."

You sign the citation and then the officer tears out a copy, hands it to you and tells you "Have a nice night and drive carefully." Your tires spit contemptuous pebbles at the patrol car as you pull away wondering, "What did I do wrong? What am I going to do now?"

Now begins a series of tough questions and decisions. The citation seems to follow you around like a lost dog and you find yourself trying to figure all of the angles and possibilities. How do you get rid of the damn thing? Should you just pay the bail and take your lumps on your insurance premiums? Should you go to court and fight it? How strong is the officer's case? Can you win? What's it going to cost you to win? Should you hire an attorney? Are you really guilty of what is written on the citation? There are probably hundreds of questions you're asking yourself, questions that you have no idea where to look to find the answers.

Well, here it is. The answer to all those questions and probably a lot more that you never even considered. In this book we've tried to cover absolutely every facet of a traffic ticket. You'll find all of the answers: Who gave you the ticket, how and why. How to figure out if you're innocent or guilty, whether or not you should go to court and how you should plead. You'll find a lot of information telling you how to prepare your case, how the state is preparing their case against you and what all those terms they use in court really mean. We'll tell you what the verdict is going to mean to you in dollars and cents and how it will affect your driving record, and we'll give you tips on how to avoid being stopped in the future. The traffic law enforcement system is one of the most intimidating systems you will ever encounter in your life, and the officer and the judge are some of the most intimidating people you may ever meet. Going to court inexperienced and unprepared can be a terrifying and disappointing exercise.

We've written this book to tell you absolutely everything you always wanted to know about a traffic ticket, but were afraid to ask. The court system exists to protect you and to give you a chance to tell your side of the story.

After reading this book, you may still fear getting a ticket and going to court, but at least you'll understand the system that you're dealing with. You'll have some practical, realistic insight into everything that's happening to you, and you'll have enough information that you can make an intelligent decision about the alternatives that are available to you. You may even find going to court a challenging, satisfying and enjoyable experience.

WHO IS THIS COP?
Is this guy for real?

WHAT ARE THE DIFFERENT KINDS OF COPS?

There are many, many kinds of cops, covering every imaginable part of our society. There are City, County, State and Federal Police, campus cops, Game Wardens, Park Rangers, Harbor Patrols and Airport Police. There are unpaid Reserve Officers, underpaid regular officers and Private Security "Rent-A-Cops." These cops can be found riding in boats, planes, helicopters, cars, dogsleds, semi-rigs, jeeps, towtrucks, motorhomes, vans, ambulances, buses, trains and subways, or riding on motorcycles, dirt bikes, 3-wheeled scooters, bicycles, snowmobiles, skis and horses.

All these cops look much the same; they all wear uniforms of some kind and wear lots of polished

leather, shiny brass, guns and holsters with chrome snaps and an occasional American Flag lapel pin. All these cops are real, but some are more real than others. This flash of reality tends to occur simultaneously with the flash of lights in your rear-view mirror. The kind of cop who hands you a ticket tends to be the most real of all.

OKAY, WHAT ARE THE KINDS THAT CAN GIVE ME A TICKET?

Generally, we can divide them up as State Troopers and Highway Patrols, County Sheriffs and Constables, and last but certainly not least, your municipal hometown cops. In addition, there are Federal Police like the M.P.'s who can give you memorable tickets on federal property and military reservations, but most of the 82,000 or more tickets written *each day* in the United States will fall into one of the above three categories.

To give some perspective to the number of cops involved, there are approximately 23,000 law enforcement agencies in the U.S., employing between 1 and 35,000 officers per agency. These officers are on the streets 24 hours a day, seven days a week, Sundays and holidays, 365 days a year, ready to give you a ticket.

No matter which kind of cop invites you to traffic court, the principles and methods described in this book will prove to be invaluable in your dealings with the mountains of legal technicalities and rituals in the traffic ticket system. Our traffic courts can be far more confusing than your tax forms, and much less forgiving than the I.R.S. The big difference lies in the fact that you can't turn to an H & R Block to help you with your ticket; this one's between you, the officer and the judge.

HOW DO I KNOW WHO THIS GUY WORKS FOR?

Usually, the officer's agency is painted on the doors and often the trunk of his vehicle, and will also appear on his badge, nameplate and shoulder patches. The most positive method of identification is by reading the fine print on the citation he may hand you. This method is generally regarded as less desirable than the others.

HOW WIDE AN AREA DOES THIS GUY COVER?

The size of the officer's patrol area or "beat" will vary with his particular agency and assignment. The beat may be as small as a single city block, or may cover a set of highways equal in size to one of our smaller states. With many state agencies, the territory will cover a specific section of highway, bordered at each end by specific cross-roads or off-ramps. The size of the territory will usually be determined by the amount of traffic flowing through the area.

HOW MANY TICKETS A DAY DOES THIS COP WRITE?

Once again, the numbers will vary depending on the

Usually the officer's agency can be easily identified from his uniform.

officer's particular assignment. A patrol officer in a residential area may write as few as one each week. The State Trooper, on the lookout all day for moving violations or working a radar car may write 50 or more each day. When you're talking about the daily number of tickets produced by a parking control officer, you may be talking about *hundreds*. On a national average, the average officer produces perhaps 1 to 3 a day for non-traffic officers, 10 or more a day for traffic officers.

DOES THIS GUY HAVE A QUOTA?

Absolutely not, he can write as many tickets as he wants.

WHAT I MEANT WAS, DOES THIS GUY HAVE A *MINIMUM* QUOTA?

That's the one question most citizens will ask an officer. Most officers will answer, "No," . . . but the answer is really, "Yes." The answer will sometimes vary, depending on the rank of the officer and who is asking the question. Up until recent years, many departments had actual quotas, specific numbers of tickets that each officer was expected to write each day. Today, most of these formal quotas have been abolished by public pressure. Most police administrators will assure you there is no form of quota.

However, in most law enforcement agencies, the individual officer's work is judged by his performance within his peer group. If the number of tickets an officer writes falls short of the number written by his peers, his supervisors will take that as an indication that the officer's performance or eyesight is substandard. It becomes a race within a group of officers. Nobody wants to be last, but on the other hand, nobody wants to be first. If you come in first in the ticket race, the other officers in the group will accuse the leader of being a "Hot Pencil" or "Hot Dog" and hold him responsible for raising the average and causing the entire group to work harder to stay "average." Ideally, each officer wants to finish just a little above average, so as a result the actual number of tickets written rises slowly but surely, day after day, until some officers give up and face the fact that they are going to be last. If this happens with more than one, the average starts dropping.

In the ticket race, the guys that come in up front most of the time (although not necessarily first) are often the ones who are promoted into detectives, motorcycles, and other desirable positions. This tends to be one of the incentives for winning in the ticket race.

DOES HE GET THE SAME AMOUNT OF CREDIT FOR ALL TYPES OF TICKETS?

No, but each officer is expected to write a wide variety of tickets. The officer has to write a sprinkling of equipment violations and warnings to prove he still knows all the rules of the game, but the "hazardous" or moving violations are the ones that really chalk up the brownie points in the ticket race.

HOW MUCH TRAINING DOES A COP HAVE IN TICKET WRITING?

Actually, an officer spends very little time learning to *write* tickets, after all, there aren't that many blocks on the form and all of them are labeled. The real training comes in the officer's use of the Véhicle Code, a virtual Sears Catalog of different ways he can give you a ticket. A traffic officer is encouraged to take a copy of the Vehicle Code with him to bed, to meals and when he goes to the bathroom. When they know that book inside and out, they have a tremendous advantage over the unsuspecting motorist who is blissfully unaware of the thousands of ways to run afoul of the law.

The final proving ground for the officer's training is in court. Officer's tend to learn quickly from their mistakes, particularly when they are under the unforgiving eyes of the judge.

DOES THIS GUY USUALLY WORK ALONE?

That will depend on the type of officer and the territory. If you were stopped by a motorcycle officer, the chances are he was working alone. Motor officers feel silly riding double, it's bad for the image and the radio box on the rear of the bike is very uncomfortable. Many traffic officers in cars also work alone, although some agencies always run two-man cars at night. If the territory tends to be particularly hazardous to a single officer's health (due to marauding motorcycle gangs frequenting the area, etc.) two-man units may be used all the time.

Traffic officers sometimes work in pairs, but usually work alone.

Most traffic officers consider themselves lone hunters in the traditional image, stalking the wild motorists through the asphalt jungle.

WHO MAKES SURE HE'S REALLY DOING HIS JOB?

The average traffic officer has more people watching him than a football quarterback on Superbowl Sunday. Just about everybody gets into the act, the citizens of the community, the police administration and the courts.

A traffic officer by the very nature of his profession maintains a high profile in the community. His plainly marked car with its flashing lights readily becomes the center of attention for passing motorists. Often, a citizen will form an opinion that an officer was unfair, too lax, too zealous, or even that he is just lingering in an area too long. The public questions the officer's performance by calling or writing the station, the city council, or even the local newspapers. These are some of the hardest complaints for an officer to respond to, as the complaints are often ambiguous in nature and lacking in detail.

The officer's immediate supervisor, often a sergeant, examines the officer's tickets periodically to determine which areas the officer is covering and which types of violations the officer is writing. The sergeant is usually very good at pointing out little mistakes the officer may have made. Of course, the sergeant is not the one standing on the highway with passing trucks and cars

More than anyone else, the citizens make sure that the police are doing their job.

taking aim at his body, shouting obscenities and blowing the hat from his head and your driver's license from his hands.

The prosecutor is the one that really irritates the officer the most. He's often fresh out of law school and the extent of his knowledge of vehicles was learned pedaling his 10-speed from class to class.

The judge is also very good at finding mistakes. This criticism is the most embarrassing as it's usually in court in front of the violator, the prosecutor, and an audience of other officers and curious citizens. The sergeant, prosecutor and judge are all experts at Monday-morning quarterbacking.

HOW MUCH DOES THIS GUY GET PAID?

Most officers salaries place them in the middle class or lower-middle class of their communities. The actual figures range from a low of $600 per month to a high of $2,000 per month. Many officers work at second jobs or part-time jobs to supplement their incomes, often taking positions as bouncers, security guards or other law enforcement related occupations. The agencies tend to frown on outside work such as this, but the practice is widespread.

Contrary to public opinion, the officer doesn't receive a kick-back or commission on the tickets he writes.

WHY WOULD ANYONE WANT TO BE A COP?

This question probably ranks as #2 on the Ten Most Asked Questions list and is one of the most difficult questions to answer, because the motivations vary so widely from person to person. Some officers are in it for the money, job security and the unique working conditions; a fast car someone else maintains, fresh air and an infinite variety of people and situations. Others see themselves in the lone hunter image, the knight in shining armor out to slay the dragon, or Wyatt Earp up against the bad-guys at the O.K. Corral.

Many officers derive tremendous self-satisfaction from their work, a feeling of achievement and accomplishment. The mere fact that he was accepted out of literally hundreds of candidates boosts the officer's ego. The selection process and the training are very selective and very intense, graduation from the Police Academy is an accomplishment in itself.

Another major factor in the motivation to become a police officer is the excitement of the job. The officers backgrounds are often adventurous in nature, such as fighter pilots or Green Berets. Whatever motivations the officer gives in his application to the agency, it will be carefully examined by department administrators and psychiatrists. Those who have applied for the wrong reasons (I wanna kill! I wanna badge! I wanna shoot and thump heads!), will usually be dropped from the eligible list.

CAN I RIDE ALONG WITH HIM?

Many agencies have a regular "Ride-Along" program. You'll have to inquire and apply at your local Police Department. Most agencies will require you to sign forms releasing them from liability in case you're shot, raped, or otherwise injured while accompanying the officer.

A Ride-Along with a regular officer on routine patrol can be quite enlightening for both of you. If the agency runs two man patrols, you'll have to ride in the back seat, often with a cage (barrier) between the front and rear seats. This can prove to be embarrassing if you happen to be observed by friends or relatives. Their immediate assumption is that either you were just arrested, or that you've switched sides and become a police informant. This may be really awkward to explain.

If your local agency doesn't have a regular Ride-Along program, they may honor your request if you have a specific reason. Allowing citizens to observe police procedure first-hand has proven to be excellent public relations for the law enforcement agencies.

If you do ride along there are two important things to remember. First, always do exactly what the officer tells you to do. Second, don't be afraid to ask questions about *anything* you don't understand. Most officers will be very cooperative in answering all of your questions.

DOES HE REALLY CARE ABOUT TRAFFIC SAFETY, OR IS HE ONLY INTERESTED IN HOW MANY TICKETS HE CAN WRITE?

All officers are concerned about traffic safety from a professional viewpoint, it is part of his job. Whether or not he has any personal feelings about traffic safety will vary between individual officers, depending upon their emotional outlook and their experience. An officer who has seen a large number of accidents caused by bald tires may give tickets to every car he can find with that condition. If his usual beat has a high number of high-speed accidents, he may be on the lookout specifically for speed violations.

As previously discussed, the officer does have an interest in the number of tickets he writes. Whether the officer's motivation stems from an interest in traffic safety or an interest in satisfying his supervisor would be difficult to determine.

IS THIS JUST A GAME TO HIM?

No, traffic enforcement is a profession and his livelihood. However, as with all professions, the officers work games into their daily routines to make the job more enjoyable. Unofficial contests are held, with the winner being the one who wrote the most tickets, the fastest speed, the most impressive car or the most important person. Officers delight in telling tall tales of "the one that got away," of bizarre propositions made by females ("Yeah, when I walked up to the door her skirt was up around her navel!"), or the number of times a single motorist had fallen prey to the officer ("Twenty-second time I've stopped that same Porsche!").

Other officers are into the lone hunter game, hiding in the bushes waiting for the trophy Ferrari to come down to the water hole or on safari, stalking semi-rigs across the empty plains.

These little games are not necessarily a reflection of the officer's maturity, but rather a natural reaction to the type of work. A good analogy is the cowboy working the herd, chasing strays and cutting them back into the flow of the herd. After work, the cowboys would sit around the campfire and entertain each other to break up the tedium of the job. Many officers see themselves in the same way, keeping the herd of cars moving and cutting out the occasional stray.

WHY DOES THE OFFICER ACT AND TALK SO EMOTIONLESSLY AND WITH SO LITTLE FEELING?

Everytime you get a ticket, it's an emotional experience for you. To the officer, there is no reason to get emotional. You represent a number on his daily activity report, one of hundreds, or possibly thousands of tickets he will write that year. In addition, the officer

has a responsibility to be impartial and fair in the way he handles your ticket. When he walks up to the car, his mind is already made up, either you committed a violation for which he will cite you or you didn't.

When the officer is speaking to you, his mind is on many other things. He's watching you to make sure you don't pull a gun, he's watching traffic for other violators, for stolen cars and to avoid being hit, and he's keeping an ear tuned to his radio. The things he says to you ("This is not an admission of guilt, but only a promise to appear.") are well established routine that he may not even think about when he's saying them.

IS HE JUST HAVING A BAD DAY, OR IS HE ALWAYS LIKE THIS?

Chances are, he's just having a bad day. The traffic officer is human like anyone else, he's got a wife and screaming kids, he's got house payments he's worrying about and a sergeant who wants him to bring up his ticket average. He's got to deal with people all day long, and almost no-one is glad to see him.

I DON'T LIKE THE WAY HE HANDLED THE SITUATION. HOW DO I COMPLAIN ABOUT IT?

First, sit down and analyze the situation. Do you have an axe to grind or is this a legitimate complaint? Next, write down all the details, not your impressions but, as Jack Webb was fond of saying "Just the facts." Include any direct quotes from the officer that you recall, and remember, if you had a difference of opinion

A ticket is not an emotional experience for the officer, simply one facet of his job.

with the officer he may have taken notes, too.

With the information at hand, you can either call or write to the agency involved, or to the city council or mayor's office. Perhaps the best way is to write to the Chief's office. Usually, someone from the agency will contact you and discuss all of the details of the incident. If they feel that your complaint is justified, action will be taken and you'll be informed.

Remember, any complaint you make should be outside of the scope of your actual violation. If you disagree with the ticket itself, that should be handled in court.

IF HE TREATS ME WELL, WILL IT HELP TO THANK HIM?

A verbal "Thank you" to the officer may help his ego and make life generally more pleasant, but it doesn't really help the officer much. It certainly won't affect your ticket or the way the case is handled in any way.

A written "Thank You" can make the officer's day. These letters, called "Citizen's Commendations," will often be read at roll call and will be entered as a part of the officer's permanent record. This record contains all sorts of notes and letters, including complaints, from citizens, his peers and his superiors. A good commendation letter is worth big brownie points; it helps his chances of promotion and advancing his career. After all, how many times do people thank him for his type of work?

IS THIS HIS FIRST TICKET? HOW CAN I TELL?

Watch the officer carefully when he fills out the ticket. If he seems unsure of himself, reads all of the blocks, requires repeated coaching from his partner (Who calls the officer "Son"), isn't quite sure of where you should sign and still has price tags dangling from his uniform, there's a good chance that the officer may be lacking in experience. Many citizens just ask the officer, "Is this your first ticket?" and many experienced, veteran officers will say "Yep, it sure is."

Sometimes the cops make little mistakes, too, but usually there's nobody around to recognize them when they occur. Some mistakes are more obvious than others.

DOESN'T THIS GUY MAKE MISTAKES TOO?

No, never. Well, sometimes. Actually, pretty often, but the chances are very slim that the average citizen would ever recognize the mistakes when they do appear. A much repeated phrase at the Police Academy is, "If you don't know what you're doing, at least act like you do." In future chapters we'll discuss how to spot mistakes and what effect they can have on your ticket.

DO COPS GET TICKETS TOO?

Almost never. The law enforcement officers of the United States feel a great deal of brotherhood with each other and extend a so-called "professional courtesy" to other police officers. When an officer is traveling on vacation with his wife and kids and is stopped by the local police, he need only identify himself and what would have been a ticket becomes a friendly warning. Presumably, the stopped officer will reciprocate the goodwill in his own city to officers and citizens from the local in which he was stopped. We won't attempt to rationalize the ethics of professional courtesy, after all, if you're reading this book the chances are you're not a police officer anyway. Claiming to be one will only get you into deeper trouble.

There are certain circumstances in which an officer may receive a ticket. If he has a bad attitude or an insulting manner, he may get the traffic officer mad enough to give him a ticket. In really flagrant violations such a reckless driving or high-speeds, the officer is not cited, but a letter or memorandum is sent to the officer's agency. Complaints of this nature are often

handled by the dreaded head-hunters of the Internal
Affairs Division, and can spell the end to an officer's
career.

DOES HE EVER GIVE BREAKS?

Yes, but it's really unpredictable how the officer will
react to a given situation. If the sun is out, the birds
are singing and he's already the unquestioned leader
in the ticket race, it could be your lucky day.

*"Allright, Sister, out of the car!" Traffic officers might be more
inclined to give a driver a break if there's some special circumstances.*

WHY WOULD HE GIVE SOMEONE A BREAK?

He's human, and as such is subject to all the little subtleties that affect our decisions. They teach him to make his decision before he ever approaches the motorist, but when he's suddenly confronted with a carload of nuns the situation can change. Maybe the officer likes you, maybe he likes your car and just wanted a closer look, or maybe he comes to the realization that his case against you isn't all that strong. Maybe you had a particularly heart-rendering explanation ("My wife's in the back seat giving birth to sextuplets! Look! That one's number five!").

If a traffic officer gives you a break, don't question his motives. Just accept the fact and proceed on your way. But don't be fooled into thinking that because you got away with it once, you'll get away it it again. Under the exact same circumstances another officer might have given you a ticket.

IS HE PREJUDICED?

Webster's Unabridged Dictionary defines "prejudice" as 1) a judgment or opinion formed before the facts are known; preconceived idea, favorable or, more usually, unfavorable. 2) a judgment of opinion held in disregard of facts that contradict it; unreasonable bias; as, a prejudice against Northerners. 3) the holding of such judgments or opinions. 4) suspicion, intolerance, or hatred of other races, creeds, regions, occupations, etc. 5) injury or harm resulting as from some judgment or action of another or others. 6) foresight (Obs.).

We wouldn't want to say that any officer was 'prejudiced,' but you've got to admit that the odds of the officer falling victim to one of the above definitions have to be pretty high.

WHY DOES THIS GUY WANT TO WRITE ME A TICKET?

Don't take it personally now, the officer doesn't want to give *you* a ticket. Many times an officer hears, "But I'm a good driver, twenty-seven years without so much as a warning. Why do you want to give *me* a ticket?"

Well, the officer was out in the field to write violators tickets, and *you* were the one who attracted his attention. If you've made it twenty-seven years without even a warning, it just means that you got away with a lot of violations.

DOES HE KNOW WHO I AM?

Just about every citizen who gets stopped by the police begins with "Do you know my ol' buddy, Officer, ah, can't think of his name right now. Oh yeah, Bill! Do you know Bill? Big fellah with a mustache, always wears sun-glasses?" or "I'm a good friend of Judge Jones," or "Do you know that my husband owns the entire block on the southeast corner of Puckett and Main, and that he pays a lot of taxes, and that makes him a taxpayer and since you get paid with tax money that means that . . ."

Few traffic officers are impressed by the number of your acquaintances on the social register. Traffic officers have written tickets to Governors and the President of the United States. No matter who you are, now's the time to develop a taste for humble pie.

IS HE INTERESTED IN WHAT I HAVE TO SAY?

Usually not, but he'll let you go on talking anyway. Most officers have developed the skills required to carry on a conversation and write out a citation at the same time. If your story's particularly interesting he may even look up from the ticket occasionally. If you're dumb enough to admit you were wrong and then try to explain it all to the officer, he may even take notes on what you say. These words may haunt you again when it's your day in court.

DOESN'T THIS COP HAVE ANYTHING BETTER TO DO?

In the United States, more lives and property are

lost due to traffic accidents than are lost in all other crimes combined. Studies have shown that a direct relationship exists between the number of citations written and the rate of injury and fatality accidents. Usually the cop who writes you a ticket is assigned specifically to traffic law enforcement.

A popular saying is, "There's never a cop around when you want one, but always one when you don't." The truth of the matter is that the one that's "always around" is usually a traffic cop.

GOTCHA!
You get a ticket.

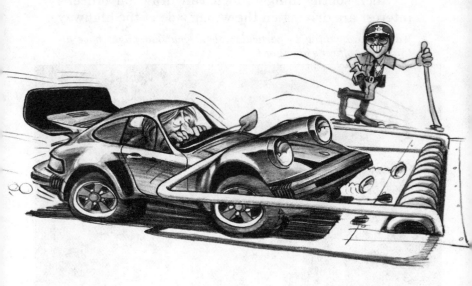

WHY DID THE COP PICK ME?

Chances are, it was something about your car or the manner in which you were driving that attracted the officer's attention. Anything that makes you stand out from the crowd is likely to get you in trouble. If you're moving faster than the rest of the herd, or straying away as you pass and weave through the slower cars you're a dead giveaway to the alert officer.

High performance cars, with fat tires, hood scoops and elevated rear-ends are prime targets, as are most sports cars and just about anything with decent mufflers.

Other subtle things which can draw an officer's interest are driving on the wrong side of the highway

Was there anything in particular about you that might have attracted the officer's attention?

or blowing through a red light. The fact that you broke a law may be the primary reason for stopping you, it's always open season on violators.

WHY DIDN'T HE PICK THE OTHER GUY?

What other guy? Nine times out of 10 the other guy *was* you!

CAN AN OFFICER STOP TWO OR MORE MOTORISTS AT THE SAME TIME?

Yes, depending on the officer's skill and ingenuity. I've had as many as five cars lined up and waiting for tickets when working a two-man radar unit. On the highway, it's a relatively easy maneuver to stop two motorists. As the primary (fastest) target begins to slow and pull over, the officer fades back to the second car and waves him in. A group of trucks, or "convoy" are easy pickings for the experienced officer. His handling of the patrol car could put a cowboy's prize cutting-pony to shame.

DOES HE HAVE TO HAVE A REASON FOR STOPPING ME?

Yes, the law says that he must have a reason for stopping you. This falls under the domain of "probable cause," the reasonable suspicion that you violated the law. Whether you have actually violated the law or not is irrelevant, he need only have that "reasonable suspicion." We won't try and play Perry Mason on this one; the definition and use of probable cause changes daily with almost every court decision. Police officers train extensively in probable cause and get daily updates.

There's a story told at the Police Academy about traffic officers. They claim that if you took two brand new cars straight off the assembly line in Detroit, and dropped them in the middle of the desert, a good traffic officer could write them at least three citations. If the officer doesn't seem quite sure about why he stopped you, don't worry. He'll think of something before he's done.

DO I HAVE TO STOP FOR HIM?

No, but if you don't he may shoot out your tires and ram you repeatedly. "Failure to Yield" as it's known, is something that many officers get real touchy about. It's not a fair move in the traffic game and if you don't play by the rules, neither will he.

One of the most frustrating things that can happen to a traffic officer is to try to pull over an elderly person with a hearing problem, or a van with curtains in the rear windows and the stereo blasting away at the occupants. If the person is proceeding slowly and lawfully, without representing a threat to lives or property, it becomes difficult to justify shooting out the tires or ramming and causing a horrible fiery collision. Often, before the officers manage to get the vehicle stopped, the parade of police cars behind the offender becomes long enough to rival the lighted splendor of the Las Vegas strip.

It should be noted that failure to yield is a violation in itself which the officer will gladly add to your citation. It can also get you arrested and treated like a criminal. A so-called "felony stop," which is jusitified by a failure to yield, is an exciting experience in which you can learn to lie face down and spread-eagled on the asphalt.

HOW DO I KNOW THE GUY THAT'S STOPPING ME IS REALLY A COP?

Unfortunately, you can't *always* be 100% sure. If you were breaking the law; if the car that's behind you is painted identically to other local police cars and has lights and sirens; and if the guy driving the car has a uniform with a badge and a gun; then the chances of him being a real cop are pretty good. If he sounds his

With the special markings, uniform, equipment and license plates most cops are easy to identify.

siren as well as displaying a light, it's a good indication that he's a genuine cop as few criminals would be bold enough to draw so much attention to themselves. If you aren't sure the cop is real, few officers will get excited if you drive a *short* distance to a well-lighted location before stopping.

DOES THE OFFICER HAVE TO BE ON DUTY?

No, but if you're seriously worried about being stopped by an off-duty officer you'd better take a close look at your driving habits. Most officers get enough action during working hours to lose interest in stopping wayward motorists on their off hours. Once he does stop you, he has to get an on-duty cop from the local jurisdiction to borrow his citation book. The traffic cop may sleep with his copy of the vehicle code, but he doesn't necessarily carry his citation book close to his heart at all times.

Many motorcycle officers take their bikes home with them, and will cite you for the really flagrant violations. However, any violation so flagrant as to warrant an off-duty officer to stop you is much more likely to inspire a truck driver to punch your lights out at the next signal.

CAN THE OFFICER BREAK TRAFFIC LAWS TO CATCH ME?

No, most vehicle codes apply to all vehicles, even police cars. The only time police vehicles are exempt from the traffic laws is when they are traveling with lights and siren.

Common sense can tell you that the officer can't catch you unless he's going just as fast as you are. The officers have also found that trying to pace motorists with the lights and siren on just didn't work, most drivers noticed and slowed down before the officer had a chance to pace them. In reality, the officers have to break a few laws in order to catch the average speeder, but after all, that's why he's out there.

HOW FAR CAN THEY CHASE ME?

Generally speaking, an officer in pursuit can chase

They're ready to chase a violator just about anywhere.

you until he catches you. As long as he starts the
pursuit within his own jurisdiction, he can follow you
in continuous pursuit across municipal, county, and
even state boundaries. The ability to cross state lines
depends on whether those particular states have a
mutual agreement regarding "hot pursuit." Anytime
you head for a state boundary, you can almost be assured that law enforcement representatives from the
new state will be on hand to greet you and carry on the
pursuit. Chances are that sooner or later you'll either
stop (for gas, or to go to the restroom) or be stopped (à
la the bulldozer blockade in the movie "Vanishing
Point").

About the only thing beyond the officer's chase
range is another country, like Mexico or Canada. A
police car from the U.S. which ventures into Mexico
will often be impounded by the Mexican authorities,
along with the officer's gun and sometimes the officer
himself. If they treat a fellow officer with such friend-
liness, just think how happy they'll be to see you, the
violator.

WHERE DOES THE OFFICER'S
JURISDICTION END?

Generally, any peace officer of a state has police
powers throughout that state, even though his routine
duties may be confined by the limits of his own city,
county or beat. With the exception of Federal officers,
this jurisdiction usually ends at the state border, and
in all cases at the international border.

One exception is the Tribal Police, established on
Indian reservations under the authority of the Bureau

of Indian Affairs. These agencies function independently in what amounts to an almost sovereign nation. Their jurisdiction is confined to the limits of the tribal reservation.

DO I HAVE TO STOP IN A LEGAL PLACE?

No, but you should make it a point to stop in a safe place. The color of the curb isn't too important, but it's a good idea not to block driveways or traffic lanes, or to pull into a parking lot or other private property. Don't stop too quickly either, as two tons of police car can make quite an impression on your rear bumper.

SHOULD I GET OUT OF THE CAR?

No, just sit still and keep your hands in plain sight. The officer's approach to a vehicle is the most dangerous time for him. He's going to be very cautious and wary of your actions. Do what you can to put him at ease. Now is a good time to sit back, relax, and think up a good excuse.

DO I HAVE TO GET OUT OF THE CAR IF THE OFFICER ASKS ME TO?

This is an answer that changes all the time with various court decisions. The constitutional right to remain in your car has yet to be decided beyond question. Most officers will exercise common sense and won't have you standing out in the pouring rain. If an officer asks you to step out of the car, he's probably got a good reason for it, so play along with him. It's his game, and you've got nothing to lose by humoring him.

If getting out of the car means that much to you, you're probably trying to cover up for a criminal matter beyond the scope of this book. Whether you signed your ticket while sitting or standing may affect your penmanship, but it won't affect your traffic case.

DO I HAVE TO ANSWER THE OFFICER'S QUESTIONS?

No, you don't have to answer any questions, just like it says in the Fifth Amendment of the Constitution. On the other hand, you don't have to yield to an oncoming

Having a pleasant conversation by the side of the road can be difficult, but you're usually better off if you answer the officer's questions.

semi-rig that just blew through a stop sign, but it might be a good idea.

Rather than ignore the question, try changing the subject on him. Comment on his driving skills, his posture and grooming, or how much weight he's lost since the last time he stopped you. Chances are he's not going to actually forget the question, but he may realize that you don't want to answer.

DO I EVEN HAVE TO TALK TO HIM?

Technically, no. Some people just open their windows a crack and slip their license through while staring straight ahead. Rookie officers get very frustrated in dealing with this situation. A seasoned veteran will just slip a lengthy ticket back through the window with a smile on his face, or suddenly notice the striking similarity between you and a bank robbery suspect who should be brought down to the station for questioning.

The silent treatment is a bad tactic in the ticket game. You've got nothing to lose by trying to talk him out of it.

DOES THE OFFICER HAVE TO TELL ME WHY HE STOPPED ME?

Yes, the officer should make his reasons very clear to you why you are being stopped, however, he won't necessarily say anything about it unless you ask him. Proper traffic etiquette for the officer demands that he inform you of his reason for stopping you right after his cheery, "Good morning." If the officer opens with the question, "Do you know why I stopped you?" he is demonstrating very bad technique. He's leaving himself open for the quick comeback, "No, I thought for sure that you would, Officer!"

WHAT DO I HAVE TO SHOW HIM?

A little courtesy helps, but you *have* to show him your license and registration. If your license (or Learner's Permit) specifies that you need glasses, you had better be wearing them or be able to show the officer your contact lenses.

Pull your license and registration out of your wallet, purse, envelope or any other container they may be in. Not only does the officer want to avoid sorting through your pictures of the kids, your old trading stamps and laundry receipts, but he wants to avoid any possible charges of bribery or theft. Handing the officer your wallet is an open invitation to have him take any amount of money he feels would be appropriate for a bribe, and was quite common in the past. Today, most officers will insist that you remove your license from your wallet.

WHAT IF I DON'T HAVE MY LICENSE WITH ME?

It's not a big problem if it's during daylight, if you look like an "honest" citizen, if there's a key in the ignition and if you really have a valid license. Be prepared to tell the officer the name and address of the registered owner, and bear in mind that he may look under the front seat if you've conveniently left your wallet "in my other pair of pants."

Many times a motorist will give the old "other pair of pants" excuse (and often it's perfectly true) and then produce a wallet with all sorts of credit cards when the officer demands some other form of identification.

If you don't produce a license, don't be surprised when this charge is added to your citation. Most courts will dismiss this so-called "Document Citation" if you can present a license in court which was valid at the time of your violation.

WHAT IF I DON'T HAVE
MY REGISTRATION?

How this is handled depends on the officer. If everything else on the car is squared away, the car has current registration tags and if you are the registered owner (or at least can identify the owner) there may be no problem. As with your license, this falls under the category of a Document Citation which can usually be dismissed by presenting the registration in court.

The missing registration is a common occurrence, few people know the exact location of that paper in their cars. Most officers will anticipate the fact that you may have to spend a little time looking for it. Common sense should tell you not to lunge for the glove box or dive under the seat without telling the officer what you are doing and why, before you do it. Don't ask to borrow his flashlight either—that's a common request, but a tacky one. He'll be glad to hold the light for you.

Many officers would rather look in your glove box than have you rummage through it. Ask him if he wants to; he'll appreciate your consideration.

WHY WAS HE SO NOSY ABOUT WHAT I WAS DOING?

He's suspicious about everything, it's his job to be nosy. Primarily, he's trying to determine the true reason why you violated the traffic laws. Is the car stolen, are you speeding away from the scene of some heinous crime or are you just late for work?

Many times, the officer's curiosity can uncover totally unsuspected crimes. Once I stopped a motorist at 3 AM to cite him for bald tires, and ended up arresting him for murder after locating a body in the trunk. There's a reason for being nosy.

CAN HE SEARCH MY CAR?

The law allows the officer to search your vehicle providing that he has the "probable cause" that we previously mentioned. Whether or not a search was legal is something for you and your attorney to work out in your defense. Probable cause is not a subject for amateurs, and most attorneys charge you enough to qualify them as experts.

WHY DID HE TAKE MY LICENSE AND REGISTRATION BACK TO HIS CAR?

He might have returned to his car for any number of reasons, to use his radio, to consult his vehicle code, to get some coaching from his partner or just to get out of the rain. He may have taken your papers with him for two reasons. First, it's unlikely that you'll drive off and leave them behind, and second, he probably wants to

FOR OFFICIAL USE ONLY

run the information on your license and registration through his computer.

Don't worry about the officer going back to his car. He'll be back soon enough.

IS THERE ANY WAY I CAN AVOID BEING RUN ON THE COMPUTER?

Not really. The use of the computer is at the officer's discretion and you've just got to take your chances. You can decrease your chances of being run on the computer by keeping your license and registration updated and by looking as innocent and honest as John-Boy Walton.

On the other hand, if all your papers are already in order, you shouldn't be concerned about being run on the computer.

DOES HE KNOW MY RECORD?

No, not unless he has had a previous experience with you personally. He does have access to your complete record through the use of his radio and the central computer system, but will rarely ever check for complete information. Usually the computer check consists of only a search for warrants and stolen cars.

SHOULD I ADMIT TO THE OFFICER THAT I WAS WRONG?

This is one of the toughest questions of all to answer; it amounts to the choice between the lady and the tiger. Guess wrong and you've had it. If you admit to the officer that you had violated the law, are very cooperative and say, "Gee, Officer, I just don't know what came over me," he may let you off with a warning. On the other hand, if he doesn't let you go, your admission of guilt virtually destroys any hope you had of defending yourself in court.

As a general rule of thumb, always admit as little as possible, and admit nothing at all if you intend to fight your case in traffic court.

WHAT ARE THE CHANCES OF TALKING HIM OUT OF IT?

About 10%. This depends on the nature of the viola-

The chances of talking him out of a ticket are pretty slim.

tion, your attitude and speaking skill, what kind of day the officer has been having and his current standing in the ticket race. Even at 10% odds, it's always worth trying.

DOES IT MATTER IF THE OFFICER IS ALREADY WRITING?

Once he starts writing, you're dead. The citations in his book are issued to the officer by number, and he must account for every one. In order to void out a citation, he has to fill out a lengthy form and do a ton of explaining to his sergeant. The officer can't just rip up a citation and say, "Okay, I'm going to let you off." Once he prints your name at the top of the ticket, it's as permanent as if it were engraved.

Some officers will even tell a citizen, "I'm sorry, but I already started writing." Even though he's committed to issuing the citation, he can still write it up for a lesser violation than the one he originally stopped you for. If you can talk him into changing a speed ticket into a ticket for not having a driver's license it would be a real break for you, one easily dismissed in court by showing up with the valid license.

WHICH EXCUSES WORK?

"I guess my gas pedal stuck." That's one that never works. The only excuses that really, consistently work are the ones which are valid reasons. These reasons include the following:

"My wife's having a baby!" This one's usually good if it's true. If it's not true, you're in a world of trouble

"What do you mean, 'Where's the fire?'" Some excuses are better than others.

because the officer is usually going to either drive or escort you straight to the hospital and your wife's side. If your wife isn't there, or isn't pregnant, you're in for a big ticket.

"I'm a volunteer fireman, and *your* house is burning!" Always good with proper identification and a rising column of smoke in the distance. If your town doesn't have a volunteer fire department, you've got some explaining to do.

"We're undercover police officers and we were tailing a suspect." With badges and a police radio you're home free. Without badges and a police radio it's up the river for impersonating an officer.

"I'm a doctor on my way to the hospital to perform an emergency frontal lobotomy!" Once again, this is a good one if true. The officer may have his dispatcher call your office to check on your story, or may follow you right into the Emergency Room to verify. If they're not waiting for you with a warm body on the table, you're a goner.

Lying to the officer is really dumb, and getting caught is the worst thing that can happen to you. Not only will you get a ticket for the original violation, but you will get an additional citation for providing false information and destroy your credibility in court should you attempt to fight it.

WHAT EXCUSES HAVE OTHER PEOPLE GIVEN?

Just about every excuse you could possibly think of has been given, but unfortunately few of them work. Here's a collection of some of the more common ones that have worked occasionally, but usually fail.

"Do I look like the kind of person who would break the law?"

"The sun was in my eyes and I couldn't see my speedometer."

"I was going down hill and I didn't want to wear out my brakes."

"The kids must have played with my cruise control."

"Isn't that funny? I was just on my way to the Department of Motor Vehicles to take care of that."

"I'm so glad you stopped me officer! I was trying to find a policeman and I thought that if I sped I would find one quicker."

"This isn't my car and it's so powerful!"

"You distracted me, officer. I never would have run that stop sign if you hadn't been parked there."

"But I wasn't going any faster than all those other cars!"

"My kids were playing peek-a-boo and covered my eyes."

"I had a hot pizza on the seat right beside me, and if I hit the brakes it would have been all over the floor."

"I'm late to court for my last ticket!"

"That's a new sign, I just know it! It wasn't there last week!"

"I'm new in town and I didn't know the speed limits."

"Well, I knew it was a school zone but I figured all the kids would be in class by now."

"I just spilled coffee in my lap and burned myself."

"There was a bee in the car!"

"I was looking at the tachometer instead of the speedometer. I thought I was only doing 50 MPH instead of 5000 rpm."

"My wife was nagging me and I got distracted."

"My Saint Bernard just wet on my lap!"

"I just washed my car and I was trying to dry it off."

"I didn't know they gave tickets if you were only 10 over."

"You should give my husband in the other seat the ticket. He's the one telling me how to drive."

"Ever since my brakes stopped working it's hard to slow this thing down."

"I couldn't stop for that sign, my motor would die and I can't get it started again."

"I signaled, officer, it's just that my signals are broke."

Some of these are close, but not quite. The rest aren't even close.

WILL IT HELP IF I CRY?

If you're a male, "no." If you're a female, also "no." After he hands you the ticket, the officer may try to cheer you up with some funny stories, or by asking you out for dinner. Crying just isn't going to help your ticket.

WILL IT HELP IF I'M POLITE?

Maybe not, but it couldn't hurt. Politeness is just one more factor that could help to turn the tide in your favor. Courtesy is contagious, and if you're polite to the officer he may be polite with you. At least you won't have to lay awake at night thinking to yourself, "Maybe I shouldn't have yelled at him."

SHOULD I TRY TO BRIBE THE OFFICER?

Absolutely not, even though you may think this is common in your part of the country. In the past, particularly in the East, bribes were routinely offered and accepted (bribery never caught on as a practice in the Western half of the United States). In some cases, bribes were openly solicited by the officers. This situation has changed considerably in the past decade.

The most common way of offering bribes was to slip a ten, twenty or even a fifty dollar bill (depending on your social status) into the plastic wallet carrier behind your Driver's License. Then, when the officer

Bribery today: Seldom accepted and more than likely you'll be arrested. Definitely not recommended.

removed the license from the carrier, the bribe was removed at the same time.

Today, most officers will smile when they see money offered along with the license. "Is this for me?" the officer will ask. "You see anybody else around here?" you may assure him. The officer's acceptance of the money completes the act of bribery. At that point, he will probably ask you to step out of your car. This makes it easier to handcuff you, after which he will impound the car along with your cash.

Take our word for it, the expenses involved in getting your car out of impound alone (not to mention the costs of your trial and the time you'll spend in jail) will far exceed the cost of your ticket, assuming you're found guilty. Even in the most corrupt police force, there's always a Serpico who's going to bust you for attempted bribery.

CAN HE STOP ME FOR ONE THING AND WRITE ME FOR ANOTHER?

Yes, it happens all the time. Frequently, an officer will stop the vehicle for a moving violation and notice equipment violations after the vehicle has stopped. These will then be added to the ticket.

A lot depends on your attitude. Although the officer's prime reason for stopping you was your excessive rate of speed, if you prove to be particularly obnoxious he may write you for your illegal lane changes and tail-gating violations as well. On the other hand, if you remain pleasant and cooperative he may mention these other violations he has observed, and make you think he's giving you a real break by only writing the one major violation on your ticket.

WILL HE GIVE ME A BREAK AND WRITE ME FOR A LESSER VIOLATION?

He might, but it's nothing you can bank on. Whether or not he's willing to give you a break depends a lot on your attitude, how convincing (or heart-rending) your story is, and the officer's outlook on life on that particular day. Officers tend to give a lot more breaks during their first year of duty, and after that they come to the realization that their job is to give people tickets. Traffic officers tend to be particularly generous with breaks on the day before they retire.

If they don't know the exact speed you were traveling at, they will often write the speed they know you were exceeding (65+).

DO THEY ALWAYS WRITE THE SPEED YOU WERE ACTUALLY TRAVELING AT?

No, they may on occasion write a lower speed than the speed you were actually going. Often, an officer traveling at a certain speed, say 65 mph, will see you pulling away from him in traffic. He doesn't know the exact speed of your vehicle, but he does know for a fact that you were going faster than he was. He may then write the citation as "In excess of 65" rather than the 75 mph you were actually traveling at.

Officers sometimes will reduce a speed to reflect a lower speed than the one he actually clocked you at. He may write the ticket for 85 mph when he actually caught you at 100 mph. His reasons for giving you a break is to reduce the amount of your fine (if he thinks you're a nice guy) or he may be unsure of the higher speed.

WHAT IF THEY DON'T?

When the officer signs the ticket, he is swearing under penalty of perjury that the facts he has written on the ticket are true. If he has written the speed as "In excess of" there is no problem as he has accurately represented the facts as he saw them. If he writes you for a speed lower than that at which you were actually traveling, he has in effect, lied about the facts as he saw them. If this is brought up at trial, it could damage the officer's credibility, and may cast suspicion on the rest of his testimony. This can help establish the fact that the officer is less than accurate in his reporting of the "facts" in your case, and this in turn will effect the "weight" of his testimony.

CAN I ASK HIM QUESTIONS ABOUT HOW HE CAUGHT ME?

Sure, and it would probably be a good idea. Knowledge of the methods he employed in catching you can be invaluable in preparing your defense, especially if what he says at the time of the violation differs from what he says at your trial.

Pay close attention to what he says, and run through his actions in comparison to the facts as you observed them. If the facts seem confusing, contradictory or

downright impossible your case in court starts looking
better and better.

DOES IT MAKE ANY DIFFERENCE HOW HE CATCHES ME?

Yes, the manner in which he caught you can become
very, very important to your defense should the citation go to trial. How he was traveling (on foot, by car,
motorcycle, dogsled or plane), whether he observed the
violation himself, where he was when he observed you
(behind a billboard, in the gas station a mile away or
right on top of your rear bumper) and how much time
he spent between observing you and citing you can
greatly affect the outcome of your trial. After the officer tells you how he caught you, write it down. Remember, he took notes, too.

HOW MANY TICKETS CAN HE WRITE ME?

Most agencies limit the officer to three violations per
citation, primarily because of space limitations. Multiple citations are quite possible, but usually considered
to be in bad taste. If a citizen comes into court with a
citation listing ten or fifteen violations it gives the
appearance that the officer was harassing him.

Usually, the officer will pick out the three most
flagrant violations for the citations. The other violations will be in his notes, so that he can beat you over
the head with them should the case go to trial.

CAN THE OFFICER TAKE AWAY MY LICENSE?

Yes, if you're going to meet with the officer at the court some distance away, the officer will often take your license to ensure that you will be there to reclaim it. This acts much the same as an appearance bond. At the scene of an accident, an officer will often take the licenses of all the drivers, passengers, and even the witnesses to make sure that they all stay around until he has finished his report and recorded all of their statements. If a witness does leave, the officer still can identify him for a followup.

The officer may also take away your license if there

If your license has been forged or mutilated, you may lose it on the spot.

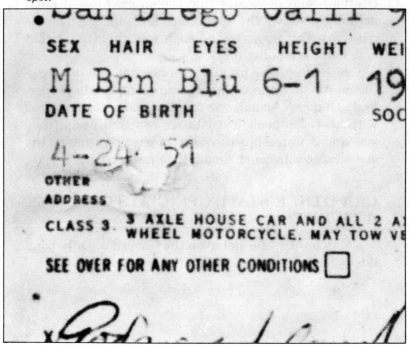

is some irregularity with the license itself. If any part of the license has been altered in any way, if the license has somebody else's name or picture on it, or if you have more than one license, it may be taken away from you. Often the officer will give you the choice of either getting a citation for the improper document (and having it impounded as evidence) or destroying the document on the spot. The wise motorist will rip up his improper or duplicated license.

CAN I WRITE A TICKET?

Unfortunately, no. Almost every driver has had the frustrating experience of seeing a flagrant violation of the law, and being absolutely powerless to do anything about it. The law gives no authority to citizens to issue citations, and stipulates that the officer himself must actually observe the violations for which he issues citations. The only way in which you can give a ticket is to become a police officer.

Some states have provisions for citizens giving parking citations, if the violation occurs on private property. In that case, usually an officer responds to the scene with his ticket book. The citation is actually signed by you and countersigned by the officer, but you're the one who goes to court should the matter come to trial.

CAN OTHER STATE OFFICIALS GIVE ME A TICKET?

No, in most states not even the Governor. Only bona fide police officers can issue citations.

SHOULD I SIGN THE CITATION?

There's really no reason why you shouldn't. Your signature is not an admission of guilt: it doesn't mean that you agree that what is written on the ticket is factual and it doesn't mean that you agree to pay them any money. Your signature is only a promise to appear in court at the time and date specified on the citation.

You do have the option in most states of going immediately to court rather than signing the promise to appear (your ticket). Generally, this won't help your case one bit. The details of your violation are still vivid in the officer's mind, his recollection of the event will

Signing the ticket doesn't admit your guilt . . . and if you don't sign you will usually be arrested.

be virtually unquestionable and you won't have any time to prepare a case.

By signing the citation, you may gain 30 or more days in which to construct your defense (and 30 or more days in which the officer can forget the specific details of your violation). You've got nothing to lose by signing.

Even if you sign the citation, an out-of-state motorist may be asked by the officer to follow him to the nearest judge so that his case can be heard immediately. Justice can be swift for these vacationers. Many cities, particularly those which are tourist oriented, have policies which avoid giving tickets to out-of-state motorists, on the grounds that forcing them to appear on a later date would be unfair. Such cities are trying to avoid any horror stories of speed traps which might hurt the tourist trade.

CAN I STALL FOR TIME BEFORE I DECIDE?

Yes, but not for long. The best way to stall for time is to read the citation very carefully and very s-l-o-w-l-y. Ask him to explain the items you don't understand (or want him to think you don't understand). Usually he'll take the time to talk to you, and perhaps give you enough time and information to make up your mind.

HOW SHOULD I DECIDE?

Take a good look at yourself in your rear-view mirror, and ask yourself the following two questions: 1) Is there any reason whatsoever why I shouldn't sign this ticket? and 2) Am I willing to take the consequences if I don't sign it?

WHAT IF I DON'T SIGN THE CITATION?

In most agencies, the officer will beg and plead with you to sign the citation, basically explaining the same things we've covered in this book and pointing out that there is really no reason at all for you not to sign.

Then another officer, or the officer's supervisor, may come by and beg and plead with you. If that fails, the Watch Commander may even be brought in to take a shot at begging and pleading with you. Usually, each officer becomes progressively more sympathetic with

There are few alternatives to signing the citation and most of them are unpleasant.

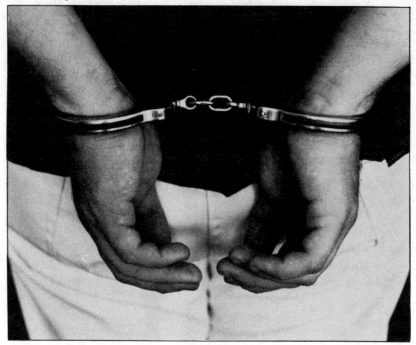

your problems, and progressively more critical of the first officer's tactics which obviously offended you so much that you refused to sign the citation.

After all the begging and pleading fails, the officers will remove you from your vehicle, arrest you and throw you into the local jail until a judge is available to hear your case. The officers aren't just being mean and trying to punish you for not signing the citation; in most cases the officer legally has no choice but to arrest you if you refuse to sign a traffic citation. If you have the misfortune to be arrested at the beginning of a three-day weekend, your stay in jail could be rather lengthy.

DO I HAVE TO SIGN MY NAME?

Yes. Some people try to write "funnies" when they sign their names, putting instead "Go to hell," "I didn't do anything" or the immortal "Mickey Mouse." Attempts at humor of this nature fall under the general category of "Dumb Moves." If the sharp-eyed officer notices that the signature on your citation doesn't match the signature on your license, it gives him reason to doubt your true identity, and a good reason to take you into custody until your identity can be proved.

CAN I TEAR UP THE CITATION?

You can't rip up the officer's copies, but you're perfectly free to destroy your own copy of the citation. Many motorists gleefully turn their copies into confetti or incinerate them with their cigarette lighters right before the officer's eyes. The officer views this kind of activity with amusement, as that copy contains all of the information on when and where you must appear. Some officers find it terribly funny to carefully fold up the motorist's license in the middle of the citation and then casually point out that fact after the motorist has ripped the citation to shreds. There are more constructive ways to vent your hostilities than by destroying an important document which you badly need to prepare your defense.

One word of warning to would-be citation mutilaters. Don't throw the citation (or pieces of the citation) out of the car. All states have litter laws, and the officer will gladly issue another ticket if you violate them.

Other copies of the citation are basically the same as the one you receive, but are routed to various departments.

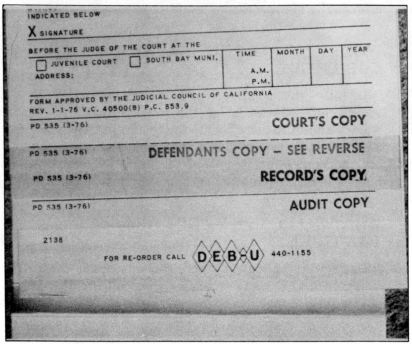

WHAT IS ON THE OTHER COPIES OF THE CITATION? DO THEY SAY SOMETHING DIFFERENT FROM MINE?

The information recorded on the other copies of the citation should be identical to yours. The difference in the copies of the citation lie on the back side. Usually, your copy of the citation will contain information on bail, failure to appear and juvenile procedure (although sometimes a separate copy is allotted purely for juvenile use).

The back side of the officer's copy of the citation may contain blanks for recording his notes and possibly a form for making a diagram. These notes can be very important, and we'll cover them a little later on in the chapter dealing with your defense, *"Fighting the System."* The back side of the other copy(s) of the citation are usually blank.

WHERE DO ALL THOSE OTHER COPIES GO?

Usually, the original copy goes to the court, the second copy stays with the officer and is filed with his agency and third copy goes to the motorist. Don't start ripping out your copy of the violation ("It's okay, officer, this one's mine!") You'd better let the officer do the honors as the distribution of copies may vary.

WHAT IF I LOSE MY COPY OF THE TICKET?

Don't worry about it, there's plenty more copies safely on file. Usually you can either call the agency which issued the citation to find out the date and time of your appearance, or you can appear at the court in person. You'll have to fill out a form, and you'll get the information after they check their computers.

WHEN I LEAVE, IS HE GOING TO FOLLOW ME?

He may follow you, but it is not with the intention of giving you another ticket. Most officers are trained *not* to follow the motorist, it looks too much like harassment in court. If you're traveling on the Interstate with its limited access to sideroads, there may be no other place for the officer to go but behind you. He can't very well pass you by traveling above the speed limit after he had just cited you for doing the same thing.

If the officer is still following you, just kick back and relax. You've already been caught, and chances are he's fishing for other game now.

HOW DID HE GET ME?
You're easier than you think.

The lights on a patrol car (seen here on the overpass) can be one of the easiest things to spot on a hiding patrol car.

WHERE DID THAT GUY COME FROM?

That's probably what the lamb asked himself as the wolf leaped out of the weeds and pounced on him. Chances are he was there all the time, but you were too busy grazing in the fast lane to notice 4000 pounds of illuminated, black and white wolf swooping down the on-ramp into your blind-spot.

When you start feeling real comfortable in your car, and perhaps just a little bored, that's when the lights and sirens jump into sight shouting "Surprise!" in your rear-view mirror. He may have been there the whole time, but you weren't looking for him. He was looking for you.

HOW DO I KEEP FROM GETTING STOPPED IN THE FIRST PLACE?

Avoiding tickets has turned into a multi-million dollar industry, and may soon replace baseball as the national pastime. For many motorists this game is almost as much fun as it is for the traffic officer (except that losing hurts a lot more). Consider the following:

1) Buy a radar detector.
2) Avoid passing police cars on the highway.
3) Get a larger rear-view mirror.
4) Carry a lucky rabbit's foot.
5) Get a master map of your area and a lot of push-pins. Then plot all 'smokey reports' as they come in on the CB.
6) Install a rear-facing seat for a passenger-observer.
7) Don't drive.
8) Trade in your Ferrari for a moped. (Pick a conservative color for the moped. Be sure and wear your helmet.)
9) Don't break any traffic laws.

Of the above list, number 9 has to be the toughest one. Your chances of successfully obeying all of the thousands of traffic laws are almost zero, but there are a few things you can do to decrease your chances of getting stopped. Keep your eyes open for wolves and stay in the middle of the flock. It's always the sheep at the edges of the flock that get picked off. Do your best to look like one of the sheep, too. If the rear end of your car is jacked up so high that it sticks up above a group of traffic, there's a good chance that a traffic cop may be hiding under your bumper the next time you look. Keep a low profile and you'll avoid getting stopped.

CAN HE HIDE?

Sure, there's no law against it, but have you ever tried to hide anything as big and obvious as a police car? Officially, police administrators frown on their officers hiding; it's not considered to be a "fair" method of catching violators. In reality the traffic officer is out there to write tickets. If he parks his car out in plain view on the highway, everybody would slow down and it would be very difficult to find motorists to catch.

The roof mounted lights of a patrol car tend to be a dead-give-away to motorists. Wily traffic officers have been known to hide their lights by leaving the trunk lid open, and when they spot a speeder their acceleration is sufficient to slam the trunk shut. On the open highway, troopers often hide in the traffic flow by staying in the slow lane just in front of a large truck. Even if the motorist slows as he comes alongside the patrol car, it's too late, the officer's visual estimate of speed by watching his mirrors is enough to issue a citation.

Another technique is the "swoop." In the classic swoop maneuver, the officer hides on a freeway on-ramp where he can still observe the highway. As the unsuspecting motorist plows by at 70 mph, the officer swoops down the ramp into his pacing position in the blind spot. The swoop, however, is so well known by most motorists that every onramp gets checked by the experienced driver. Perhaps advertisers should consider placing billboards in these prime locations.

WHERE DO THEY USUALLY HIDE?

It isn't all that easy to hide a patrol car, however,

Now you see it; now you don't. The car that appears to be disabled on the shoulder might be hiding a light bar and a radar unit.

over the years many successful methods have been devised. Favorite spots for working speeders (with radar or otherwise) are in front of other vehicles (trucks, campers and vans) or in front of trees and bushes out of the motorist's sight. The locations are often at the bottom of hills or around curves where the violators never see the patrol car until it's too late.

Officers often watch intersections from nearby alleys and darkened parking lots. Traffic officers soon develop a keen eye and can spot a violation in heavy traffic from as far away as two or more blocks. Intersections tend to be prime hunting grounds for picking up drinking drivers. Officers often "sit" on intersections while doing routine reports or paperwork, a skill which takes a great deal of concentration and practice to master.

Hiding behind billboards is no longer a popular ploy since the advent of the super highways. Most outdoor advertising is now done 50 feet or better above the roadway. Watching traffic from these heights can cause nausea and dizziness, despite the good view.

DO THEY DISGUISE THEIR PATROL CARS?

No, this type of subterfuge is very rare as many Vehicle Codes specify that traffic cars must be of a specific color and marking. Successful anti-speed campaigns have been conducted in some states by radar units using semi-trucks, vans and taxis, but these are few and far between. Most of the stories you hear on the CB about disguised patrol cars are merely the paranoid delusions of the chronic ticket recipient.

For many years, the California highways were dotted with realistic plywood cutouts in the shape of Highway Patrol cars. It was virtually impossible to determine which were real and which were the plywood fakes until you were almost past it. You could always tell the real ones by the red lights that came on as you passed.

Just one of many clever tricks employed by enterprising officers is the "wet towel" trick. In this one, the officer applies a wet towel to one of his headlights, giving it a dim, yellow appearance that deceives motorists who constantly watch their mirrors. The heat from the headlamp quickly dries the towel, which falls away as soon as the car stops moving. This is always good for a laugh when the motorist jumps out of his car and says, "But, officer, I didn't know you were a cop because one of your headlights is out . . . I mean it *was* dim . . . at least I *think* it was dim." The end result is that the motorist looks really dumb.

DOES HIS CAR HAVE TO BE MARKED?

No, although some states require their *traffic* cars to be marked. Some agencies really go overboard in marking their cars, painting "TRAFFIC ENFORCEMENT" or "RADAR" in foot high letters on all four fenders and the trunk. Many agencies even paint the unit's numbers on the roofs of the cars to enable truckers to give accurate smokey reports. (Actually, the roof numbers are for the benefit of aerial units.)

Not all police vehicles are marked, but when they are, they tend to be very distinctive and easily identified.

CAN OTHER CITIZENS REPORT ME TO THE OFFICERS?

Yes, and they do it quite frequently. Most officers will listen patiently, mumble something about "We'll get right on it!" and drive away. The fact of the matter is that the officer is usually just driving around the corner to finish up his coffee and his reports.

The law states that the officer must observe the violation for which he issues a citation, there is absolutely nothing he can do about the car which *you* saw run a red light, unless he saw it too. Citizen complaints of this nature are just a bother for the officer, as he is powerless to take action. A common complaint of traffic officers is that they get asked for directions so often they feel like gas station attendants.

WHY DO THEY ALWAYS WORK THE SAME LOCATIONS?

Police officers tend to be creatures of habit. When the lone hunter finds plenty of game at the watering hole, he returns every night at feeding time. How often do you drive home by the same route (and speed past the same stretch or roll through the same stop)? The hunters congregate where the hunting is the best.

WHAT'S A "CHERRY PATCH"?

A cherry patch is a traffic officer's dream, an intersection or a piece of highway which by its design, or by its very nature, causes a lot of people to violate the law. Working a cherry patch requires little skill on the officer's part—he just waits for a ripe one to come along and then he plucks it. The cherry patch can be a poorly developed intersection (ones marked "No Left Turn" during particular hours are especially good pickings), the downhill stretch of road between a local factory and the middle-class neighborhood, or sections of road fronting on roadside businesses.

Often, a cherry patch develops because the road doesn't change when the rest of the area does. A simulated island (a painted center divider) in front of a newly built drive-in bank is a good example. At five o'clock on a Friday evening it can be a regular picnic ground for a hungry bear.

Technically, officers should report problem areas to their traffic engineering departments to be corrected (or at least examined). In practice, an area which is always good for a few quickies is very valuable and carefully protected. Most officers won't even tell friends in their own squad about these little gold mines, just in case they're running a little behind in the ticket race. It's not unusual for more than one officer to go straight from the barn (police station) to his favorite cherry patch, only to find the officer who was sitting next to him at briefing busily picking cherries.

WHAT'S A "SPEED TRAP"?

There are several definitions of speed trap in common usage, the most popular of which is merely a cherry patch, a good section of highway on which to catch speeders.

Another kind of speed trap is usually a small town located on a major highway. These towns often post ridiculous speed limits through the downtown area, or just rigorously enforce the existing laws. Typical of these operations was Fruithurst, Alabama, a town of 350 residents with six officers working the nearby highway. The police station, courtroom and jail were all in the same building which generated revenues of as much as $20,000 a month. Revenues from citations and appearance bonds paved all of the streets in the town and built a new gymnasium before "The Nation's #1 Speedtrap" was shut down by the joint efforts of the State Attorney General and the Alabama Motorist's Association several years ago. Speed traps such as these are rare today.

Speed trap: A quick change of speed from 35 MPH to 25 MPH, a school zone (the 25 MPH limit applies only when children are around) and a street wide enough to be an Interstate highway.

A third type of speed trap are those which are defined in the vehicle codes of some states. A typical section defines a speed trap as a section of highway which is pre-measured to make speed determinations, or a section of highway with a posted speed which cannot be justified by traffic engineering reports (the posted speeds are far below those at which the average motorist will actually travel).

ARE SPEED TRAPS LEGAL?

Chances are that if your state's vehicle code takes the space to define a speed trap, a speed trap is illegal in your state. The other forms of speed traps range from harassment (in the cases of speed trap towns) to bad-luck (if you're the one caught in a cherry patch), but are rarely illegal.

If you feel that you've been bilked by an illegal speed trap, consider going to your State Attorney General's Office. Most are very good about following up on such complaints, and if the complaints are founded they are very effective in dealing with them.

HOW DOES HE KNOW HOW FAST I WAS GOING?

That depends on what equipment the officer has available to him. He may have used any of a dozen forms of electronic wizardry such as radar or Vascar, a purely mechanical method such as pacing or a stop-watch, or a completely visual means such as aircraft or a visual estimate.

Not all agencies have access to all these methods (for

Sitting in the blind-spot makes it easy for the officer to determine your speed.

instance, the use of Vascar or a stopwatch is illegal in California). Be assured that they'll make full use of whatever methods they have at their disposal. We'll describe all of these methods in detail in this chapter.

CAN HE ESTIMATE MY SPEED VISUALLY?

Yes. Surprisingly enough, many experienced officers (particularly radar officers who have a constant reference to check their estimates) can pinpoint your speed visually within a 5 mph spread. With sufficient experience to back their testimony, these visual estimates are usually accepted in court.

There are factors which can affect the officer's perception of your speed, and these factors can become very important in your defense. Some of these factors are the size, shape and color of your vehicle, the sound of your vehicle, the width of the road and your direction of travel in relation to the officer. Your car's relationship to other cars can be important too. If you were spotted moving through a pack of cars on the highway, the officer's estimate of your speed in comparison to the others is bound to be fairly accurate. A single car moving on a lonely road is much more difficult to estimate.

Traffic officers have a game they play using their speed estimating skills. Two officers will get together in a radar car, cover up the radar read-out and bet coffee and doughnuts over who can estimate closest to the true speed of passing vehicles. In court, it's wise to question the officer's ability to estimate speed. You've got a lot more at stake than coffee and doughnuts.

HOW DO THEY USE AIRCRAFT?

Aircraft are used both for spotting motorists who are in trouble and for catching traffic violators. Often distinctive marks are painted on the highway which allow the aircraft to compute your speed by using the known distance between the marks and sophisticated timing devices in the aircraft. A ground unit is then vectored in to apprehend the motorist.

Often these planes are equipped with C.B. radios which allow them to follow up on citizens' distress calls. One California Highway Patrol pilot near Bakersfield uses the handle "Air Bear" in his small patrol plane.

Getting a bird's eye view of traffic. Warning signs are sometimes posted, and aircraft are usually painted very distinctively.

Helicopters are also used extensively by police agencies, but are used primarily in surveillance and crime suppression, rarely for traffic work.

HOW DID THEY PACE ME?

The officers may have "swooped" into your blind spot from an on-ramp, observed you from a parallel frontage road, or may have been right on your bumper at night.

He may have paced you by driving at the same speed as your vehicle, or by driving at a slower speed and watching your relationship to him. If he was cruising at a steady 65 and you were pulling steadily away from him, he has accomplished a good "pace." Traffic cars often travel along at ten miles over the limit to catch speeders, otherwise they tend to get surrounded by a group of suddenly law-abiding motorists.

Police cars are equipped with special speedometers which make pacing very easy. The dial is broken up into 2 MPH segments rather than the usual 5 MPH segments in most cars. Police motorcycles are often equipped with two speedometers, one which can be locked with a flick of a button, and locks automatically when the pursuit lights are activated.

Once he matches your speed, the pace is complete.

HOW FAR DOES HE HAVE TO PACE ME?

Contrary to popular belief, he need only pace you long enough to get a good estimate of your speed. This may be as little as a hundred feet or over a distance of several miles. He may just cruise along pacing you until you finally notice him, because the longer he paces you the better his case gets. There is no set distance of ¼ of a mile or ½ a mile that he *has* to pace you over.

DOES HE HAVE TO PACE ME?

No, as we mentioned previously, his visual estimate of your speed may be sufficient to issue the citation.

CAN HE PACE ME AT NIGHT WITH HIS LIGHTS OFF?

Technically he has to show lights at night just like you do. In practice, he doesn't mind cheating a little to win the game. (This has been compared to having the Geneva Convention rules of war; after all, the reason for fighting the war is to win.) Patrol cars sometimes cruise dark frontage roads with only a single forward facing spotlight burning. To the motorist overtaking the patrol unit at high speed, the spotlight gives the appearance of being a motorcycle, and it's not until the rest of the lights come on that the driver realizes his mistake.

Of course, the officer who travels at high speed with his lights off at night does so at his own peril. An accident under those conditions would be difficult to explain to his supervisor. This technique is so dumb that any officer who gets caught using it deserves to get hung out to dry. If you're caught by an officer driving with no lights, do him a favor and report it in a letter to his agency, telling them how strongly you feel about this unsafe practice.

IF ONE OFFICER OBSERVES MY VIOLATION, CAN ANOTHER OFFICER WRITE MY CITATION?

No, but it does happen. Particularly with radar cars, one officer may actually observe the speed on the unit and call out to his partner, or call ahead to another unit which will actually issue the citation. This is against P.P.P. (Proper Police Procedure) and can blow an officer right out of the water in court.

When the officer signs the citation, he is swearing that the facts on the citation are true to the best of his knowledge. If he doesn't actually observe the speed himself, the speed told to him by someone else is "hearsay evidence" and is inadmissible in court. To be done properly, another officer can write out the citation, but the officer who actually observed your violation must also sign the ticket.

DO THE POLICE USE C.B. RADIOS?

Yes, the state police and highway patrols of nearly every state either provide C.B.s, or allow their officers to provide a C.B. for their units. Many agencies also operate base stations and monitor continuously for emergencies. A large number of county and municipal

---

Police use the C.B. radio extensively and are often proud of their "handles."

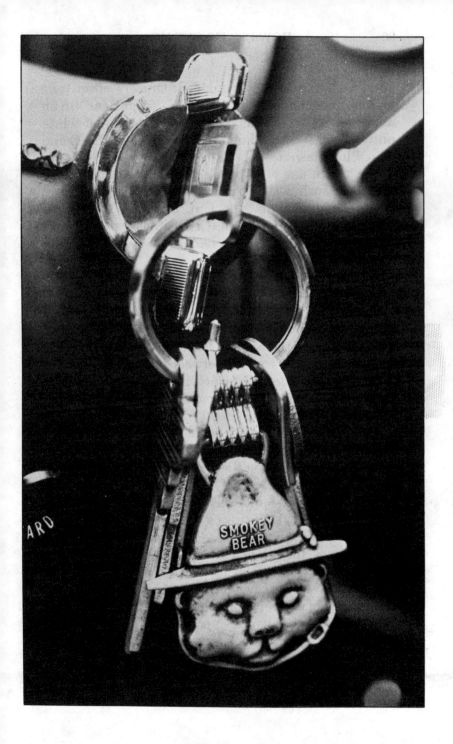

agencies are also C.B. equipped. Officers often take handles relating to their profession, "Polar Bear" (in an all white unit), "Panda Bear" (in a black and white unit), "Pooh Bear," "Mama Bear" (a female officer) and "The Blue Flasher."

The police use of Citizen's Band has been immortalized in such classic country-western tunes as "The White Knight" and "The C.B. Savage." One black California Highway Patrol (CHP) officer with a sense of humor runs under the handle of "The Chocolate Chippie."

HOW DO THE POLICE USE C.B. RADIO?

The C.B. radio was really one of the major catalysts (the other being the 55-mph limit) which turned traffic enforcement into a game between motorists and the traffic cops. It also has turned into a valuable public relations tool which allows motorists to interact with the police on a personal level.

The C.B. allows the officers to get first-hand reports of motorists who need assistance, and also reports from other drivers regarding the locations of flagrant speeders and drinking drivers. C.B. operators quickly turn on drinking drivers and often call for the "smokies" to catch them. The C.B. is also great for giving directions to lost motorists.

Sometimes, the police will appeal to motorists on the C.B. to be on the lookout for a certain type of vehicle that may have been involved in a crime, or to report on the location of accidents or traffic congestion. Response from the citizens is usually very good.

One of the most common types of C.B. transmissions

Most police agencies monitor emergency frequencies with C.B. radio.

are "Smokey Reports" (a report on the location of patrol cars), something that most officers view with a good deal of amusement. Smokey reports tend to serve as a speed deterrent, and the officer would be hard-pressed to duplicate the wide exposure he gets without them. Officers attempting to "hide" while working traffic enforcement soon learn when their tail is showing and will seek better cover, or will intentionally put one officer out in the open for smokey reports while a second cleans up.

Some officers will answer the C.B. call "Break for a smokey report?" with the response, "This is Smokey, what do you wanna report?" Many a trucker has woe-

fully discovered that his "back door" which has been feeding him smokey reports for miles was actually a crafty smokey, intent on trapping the trucker.

WHAT DOES THE SIGN THAT SAYS "SPEED CHECKED BY RADAR" REALLY MEAN?

The sign is put there primarily to slow people down, similar to the sign that reads "Traffic Laws Strictly Enforced." It doesn't necessarily mean that that stretch of roadway is under the watchful surveillance of a radar car night and day; it doesn't even mean that the city even possesses a radar unit.

In some states and jurisdictions, it is required that the signs be posted before radar can be used by the law enforcement agency. This varies widely from region to region and should be checked anytime you get a radar ticket in an unposted area.

When some people see the "Speed Checked By Radar" sign, they get the impression that the entire city's traffic is being monitored by the police from some master control center similar to an airport's air traffic control room. Radar *is* sophisticated compared to other methods of speed detection, but not *that* sophisticated.

ELECTRONIC WIZARDRY
Radar, the battle of the microwaves.

WHAT IS RADAR?

The term "Radar" is an acronym for the phrase "radio detection and ranging." Radar works on the principle that all objects reflect certain types of energy, whether it be light, sound (an echo is an example of reflected sound) or radio waves. Metal objects are particularly good reflectors of radio waves, meaning that trucks, cars and motorcycles are ideal radar targets.

Police use radar to determine the speed of vehicles by transmitting these high frequency radio waves (microwaves) and measuring the difference between the transmitted and reflected signals.

HOW LONG HAVE THEY USED RADAR FOR TRAFFIC PURPOSES?

Radar has been used as a means of measuring the speed of automobiles since the early 1950's. Those first units were huge, filling the entire rear of a station wagon. They had difficult power input arrangements and an open ink well to feed a spring-powered stylus across a sheet of graph paper. The early units were not designed as a traffic enforcement tool, but as a device to compile statistical data for traffic engineering and the like. It only took about 6 months for the usage to change to ticket writing. Because of the open ink well, the car could not be moved while the radar was set up, so the cars had to work in teams with motorcycles or additional patrol cars to give chase to speeders.

As primitive as these early units were, they required the operator to be a highly trained and skilled technician. These units operated on a much lower frequency than modern units. A few (perhaps a dozen) are still in

An early radar unit from the 1960's, many of which are still functional and in use today.

use throughout the United States, but should not be considered as a threat due to their short range and awkward operation. The majority of these units were phased out of operation with the introduction of the first transistorized units in the early 1960's.

WHAT DID THEY DO BEFORE THEY HAD RADAR?

Prior to the introduction of radar, patrolmen had to depend on the tried and accepted methods of pacing, stopwatches and pneumatic hose timers. Setting up a hose timer required nearly half an hour, and alert drivers could quickly spot the timing box and the twin rubber hoses stretched across the street 16 feet apart. Typically, one officer would stay at the box and signal to another officer waiting down the street with a motorcycle or car.

Hose timers, commonly referred to as "snakes" have been dropped for use in traffic enforcement, but similar equipment is still widely used by traffic and engineering departments in making speed and traffic volume surveys.

HOW DOES POLICE RADAR DIFFER FROM AIRCRAFT RADAR?

Typically, aircraft radar is used to locate objects within the radar's field, and to give the location of other aircraft and the surrounding terrain. The radar emits pulses of energy as it sweeps in a full 360° circle with the transmitter displayed as the center of a cathode ray tube. As these pulses strike a target, they are reflected back to the radar antenna and show up on the screen of the cathode ray tube. By watching the movement and position of radar images on the screen, it is possible for pilots and air-traffic controllers to determine the location, speed and direction of travel of the images.

Police radar works within the same frequency spectrum, but its only function is the determination of speed. Rather than sweeping in a 360° circle, the unit is aimed in one direction down a highway or street and it emits a continuous frequency instead of pulses. While the aircraft radar shows images on a cathode ray screen, traffic radar usually shows the speed on an L.E.D. or Numitron gas tube similar to a digital watch or calculator. Sometimes the speed may also be printed out on a tape or a graph. Many radar units from the 1960's show the speed on a dial; a plate drops down and pins the needle against the dial to lock in a violator's speed. Many of these units are still in use today, "pinning" speeders traveling in excess of the 55 mile per hour limit.

HOW DOES TRAFFIC RADAR WORK?

Modern traffic radar is composed of two basic parts: the transmitter and the receiver. Both of these components are mounted in the antenna and activated by the electronic packages in the counting unit which displays the speed.

The transmitter utilizes a solid-state device called a "Gunn Effect Diode." This provides a very stable source of micro-wave energy which is shaped and directed by the antenna horn in much the same way as a

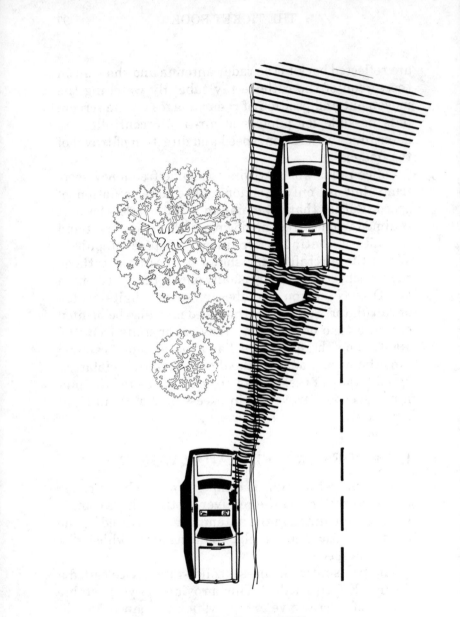

The Doppler Effect

flashlight shapes its beam, although the radar beam is not as sharp or distinct as a flashlight beam.

The antenna also houses the receiver, which collects the micro-wave energy reflected by the target and channels it into the mixer.

The mixer compares the received signal and the transmitted signal to arrive at the difference in frequencies caused by the "Doppler Effect." This "Doppler" (or "Difference") frequency is then transmitted to the counting unit which converts the Doppler frequency into speed in miles per hour. The speed is then displayed by the unit, either digitally in a "Target Speed" window, by a needle on a dial, or on a strip of paper rather like an electro-cardiogram.

WHAT'S A DOPPLER EFFECT?

The Doppler Effect is a fundamental principle of physics discovered in 1842 by Dr. Christian Johann Doppler. His theory shows that when a radio frequency (or a light or sound wave) strikes a moving object, the result is an increase or decrease of frequency directly proportional to the speed of the object.

The most familiar example of this effect is the sound produced by a train whistle. As the train approaches your position, the whistle is high-pitched and shrill; as the train continues past the whistle appears to become lower pitched.

Radar units use the Doppler effect to determine the speed of the target vehicle. If the target is stopped, the radio waves reflect back to the unit at the same frequency. If the target is moving, there is a slight shift in the frequency reflected. As the beam returns to the radar unit, the frequency change is detected and converted to miles per hour for the operator to read.

Some radar units are equipped with an audible mode which also converts the Doppler shift created by the target vehicle into an audible tone. The tone is low pitched as a vehicle comes off a stop and becomes increasingly higher as the speed increases. A group of vehicles traveling at different speeds results in a mixture of tones, even though the radar may be clocking only the lead vehicle. This audible tone is very precise, and officers quickly learn exactly which pitch marks the death note for a speeder. The Doppler tone also lets the officer hear when you hit the brakes and how fast you're slowing, just as surely as if you locked up the tires and slid to a screeching halt.

DOES ALL POLICE RADAR OPERATE ON ONE SPECIFIC FREQUENCY?

No, they operate within a given frequency range, but specifically on three commonly used bands or channels, much like your use of the specific 40 channels allocated for C.B. radio by the F.C.C.

This type of licensing by the F.C.C. is done with all TV stations, radio stations, government agencies and businesses who wish to use the nation's airways, to ensure that broadcasts don't overlap and interfere with each other. If the F.C.C. did not provide for this type of electronic segregation, you might find yourself listening to Johnny Carson on your stereo, or launching a radio controlled nuclear missile the next time you activate your garage door opener.

Police radar's three commonly used frequencies are

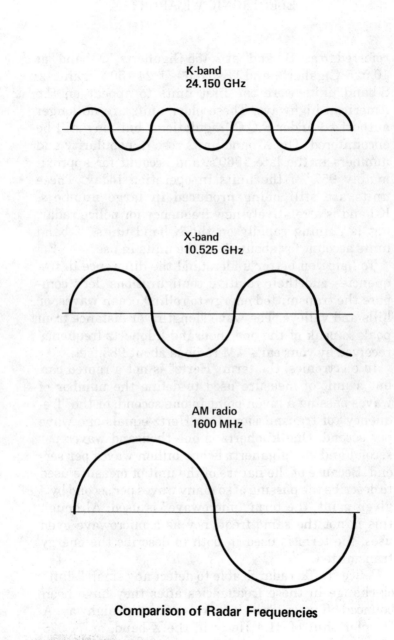

Comparison of Radar Frequencies

referred to as "S-band" at 2.455 Gigahertz, "X-band" at 10.525 Gigahertz and "K-band" at 24.150 Gigahertz. S-band units were the first units to appear on the American highways. These older units are no longer authorized under F.C.C. regulations, but may still be encountered. The X-band units rose in popularity and numbers in the late 1960's, and account for approximately 95% of the units in operation today. These units are still being produced in large numbers. K-band is a relatively new frequency for police radar, but is gaining rapidly on the X-band units. K-band units account for about 5% of the units in use.

To help you better understand the difference in frequencies and their relative configurations, let's compare the transmitted energy to rolling ocean waves, or hills and valleys. The wave "length," or distance from peak to peak of the one thousand kilohertz frequency received by your car's AM radio is about 985 feet.

In electronics, the term "Hertz" is not a rented car, but a unit of measure used to define the number of waves passing a given point in one second, or the "frequency" of transmission. One Hertz equals one wave per second. One kilohertz is one thousand waves per second and one gigahertz is one billion waves per second. Because of the nature of the unit of measure used to describe the passing of so many waves per second by a given point, the term "microwave" is used. Although this is not the same frequency as a microwave oven uses, the term is used in both to describe the energy transmitted.

Police traffic radar is able to detect any small "shift" or change in these frequencies after they have been bounced off your car as it travels down the highway. A Doppler shift of 31.4 Hertz in the X-band, or 72.023

Hertz in the K-band is equal to a relative speed of one mile per hour. The term "relative speed" refers to the speed of the target vehicle as compared to the stationary background.

Many radar manufacturers have constructed their units so as to allow for "fine tuning" of the frequency for peak performance. Some radar technicians have been known to tweak the adjustments, causing the radar unit to operate slightly off frequency and keeping the "good old boys" from complaining about radar detectors picking up their frequency. This procedure is probably against current F.C.C. regulations, but let's face it; how often do you suppose a trooper gets pulled over for a "Federal Frequency Inspection"?

CAN POLICE RADAR AFFECT PACEMAKERS OR CAUSE CANCER?

A rumor circulated through Idaho and California recently about a California man with a pacemaker who supposedly died after passing through a radar monitor. That sparked a U.P.I. headline that screamed, *"Law Enforcement Radar May Interfere With Pacemakers."* The article went on to say that there was absolutely no basis for the rumor, that the western law enforcement agencies had absolutely no record of any such instances, and that in the opinion of one radar expert, "The likelihood of law enforcement radar interfering with cardiac pacemakers is nonexistent." Based on these unquestionable facts, five separate agencies in Idaho banned the use of radar and legislation outlawing the use of radar was introduced into Idaho's Senate.

Studies have indicated that there is no known in-

creased hazard of cancer or other diseases for the officer working in the vehicle with the radar practically in
his lap. If the unit has little effect on him, it certainly
won't affect you in your car as you pass by. The only
health hazards associated with traffic radar are the
shock of getting caught and the pain of parting with
the bail money. If you worry enough about getting
caught, you may develop ulcers without ever passing
through a radar beam.

CAN RADAR CAUSE CATARACTS?

Studies have shown that *heavy* concentrations of
aircraft type radar can cause cataracts, but it has not
been proven yet that police type radar is harmful, or
what concentration of police type radar would be required to become harmful.

Of course, while you are only occasionally bombarded with police radar, the officer operating the unit
is being "zapped" on a regular basis. This matter has
caused quite a bit of concern with some officers, so
much concern that they have demanded special "Hazardous Duty" pay in some cases where they were required to operate a radar unit.

HOW ACCURATE IS RADAR?

When properly used by the officer, most traffic
radars are accurate to within one tenth of a mile per
hour. Many units will even display the speed of the
target vehicle to the nearest tenth of a mile per hour.
However, similar to when you use a pocket calculator,
the answer will be accurate only if the operator has
pushed the right buttons.

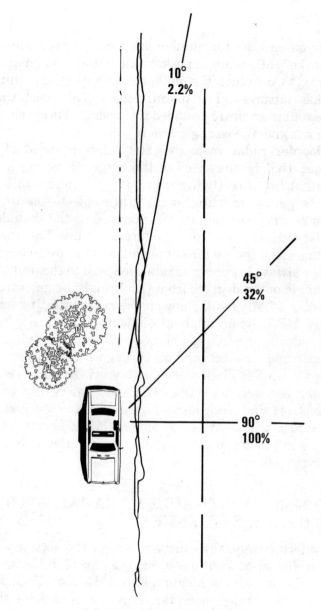

COSINE ANGLE FACTOR

If you consider the number of times you have made a mistake while using a pocket calculator, just imagine trying to convince the manufacturer that the thing makes mistakes. The manufacturer will insist that "the unit is accurate provided it is operated properly. It will not give the wrong answer."

Doppler radar measures the relative speed of a target, that is, the speed of the target traveling in a straight line directly toward or away from the unit. If the target is traveling at a slight angle to the unit, such as when the radar unit is parked on the shoulder of the road, the "cosine angle factor" occurs. This inaccuracy is in the motorist's favor, as the cosine angle factor always lowers your relative speed to the unit. At an angle of ten degrees from the straight beam, a true speed of 45 MPH will show on the radar counting unit as 44 MPH. At an angle of 45 degrees, such as when the radar unit is parked off the roadway on the top of an off-ramp or clocking you through a turn, the true speed of 45 MPH will show as 31 MPH. At an angle of 90 degrees, such as if the radar unit was parked on a side street and clocking you as you passed the end of the street, will show as a speed of 0 MPH. This inaccuracy won't help you at all in court, as it is always in the motorist's favor.

DO THE COURTS ACCEPT RADAR WITH NO OTHER EVIDENCE?

Unfortunately, the courts do accept the accuracy of radar almost without question. The case of the State of New Jersey versus *Dantanio* in 1955 took "judicial notice" (a blanket acceptance by the courts) of the accuracy of radar, established that 1½ to 2 hours of training is sufficient to qualify an operator of radar and stipulated that the radar operator need not understand or be able to explain the internal workings of the device.

A second court case, *Honeycutt* versus the Commonwealth of Kentucky in 1966 agreed completely with the Dantanio decision and further decided that the officer's visual observation of the speed and position of the vehicle was enough to determine which vehicle the radar unit was tracking.

Of course, this doesn't mean that the radar reading is accepted without the officer establishing all of the elements of the violation. In order to successfully prosecute the speeding case, the officer will have to establish the time, place and location of the offense, and show that you were the driver of the offending vehicle. He has to show that the state laws regarding speed limits and radar signs were complied with, and in all states he must prove that your speed was "unreasonable" or in excess of the 55 MPH maximum limit.

The officer must also give his qualifications and training in radar operation and be able to testify that the unit was operating correctly and had been tested for accuracy. Last of all, he should be able to identify the vehicle, and testify that your vehicle was out in front, by itself, and nearest the radar unit when the reading was obtained.

The officer's court testimony is part of the radar training program conducted by the manufacturers. Some manufacturers even provide the officers with check lists to use in court, to make sure that he establishes all of the necessary facts. In all cases, the officer has to make a visual estimate of the excessive speed. The radar is only a tool used to verify the officer's visual observation.

CAN THE OFFICER CHEAT USING RADAR?

Perhaps the most well known example of possible "cheating" with an electronic device is the missing 18 minutes lost from Rosemary Wood's Watergate tapes. Whether the 18 minutes of tape were lost by electronic malfunction, human error, or deliberate action (cheating), we will never know. That is a matter between Rosemary Woods and her conscience.

It is much the same with the officer and his radar unit. If the officer cheats while using his radar unit, you will probably never know it: you have to take the officer's integrity for granted. In any group of humans, including a group of law enforcement officers, there are always a few who cheat. He may be driven by peer pressure, his standing in the ticket race, sheer boredom or frustration at his inability to issue proper, legal citations. Most officers would never consider cheating to catch a motorist (it's easy enough to catch them without cheating) but there's always one officer out there who doesn't play by the rules. If an officer is going to cheat by using radar, there are any number of ways in which he can do it. Here are some of the more common ones:

AUTOMATIC CALIBRATION—Most modern radar units have a method of internal "calibration," a method to check the radar's operation. In most models, a single crystal generates a signal of a known quantity

Two speeds, one bogus and the other authentic. The tiny dot over the "7" indicates a calibration mode, the "50" is the actual speed of a vehicle.

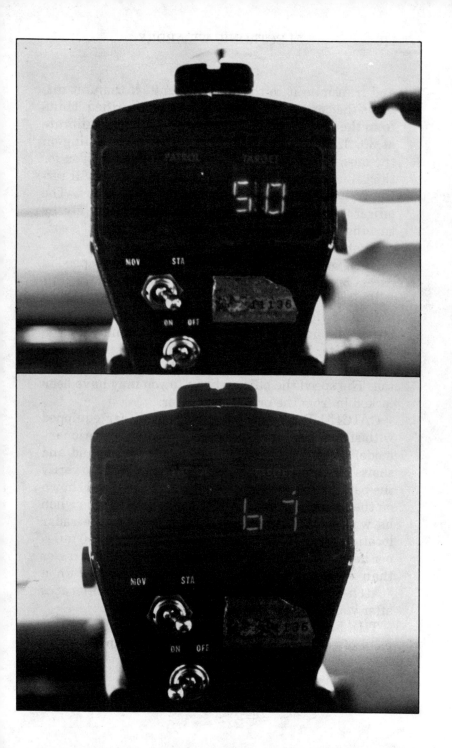

and transmits it to the counting unit. If the unit displays the correct speed, its operation is verified. Units from the various manufacturers of radar will calibrate at 30, 32, 45, 50, 60, 64, 65, 67 and 72 depending on the model. If the officer just happened to write you for the same speed that his unit calibrates at, it will certainly help to create some suspicions in court. The officer can call up this calibration speed merely by turning a knob or pushing a button on the unit's control panel.

LEFTOVERS—When a radar unit detects a speed in excess of the limit given to it by the operator, the unit will alert the operator to the speed with a beep, light or tone. The violator's speed is then locked into the unit, either manually by the operator, or automatically on some units. The speed can also be stored in the unit and not displayed until the operator hits a recall button. The speed the officer shows to you may have been locked in from the previous violator.

CATCH-UP SPEED—When a patrol car equipped with stationary radar (or moving radar in a stationary mode) is moving, the radar picks up the ground and shows the patrol car's speed. This can be used to verify the patrol car's speed when pacing, so the speed shown on the unit may have been locked in at any time when he was driving prior to his setting up at the radar location. If you pass by a parked patrol car at 60 miles per hour, the officer will have to go considerably faster than that to "catch-up" to you. He can lock in a "catch-up speed" at any time as he accelerates after you.

THE FINAL APPROACH—Radar, being a sensitive piece of equipment, is capable of picking up the speed

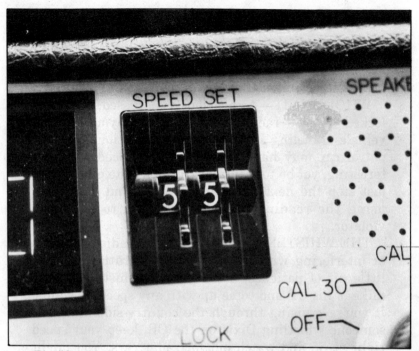

The "Comic Alarm" draws the officer's attention to the radar unit (and away from his comic book) when a radar target exceeds the preset speed.

of any moving object, including trains and aircraft. Small planes land at surprisingly slow speeds (as slow as 50 miles per hour) with larger aircraft landing at speeds well over 100 miles per hour. It is entirely possible for a radar operator to clock a landing or low flying aircraft and leave it locked into the unit. Officers working near airports have been known to clock fantastic speeds well over 100 MPH to use in "war stories" about "the one that got away."

PANNING—The antenna of a stationary unit, or a hand-held radar gun can be panned in a sweeping motion that will cause the radar to read the speed of the landscape as it sweeps by. With a little practice, the officer can sweep up and lock any speed he desires. This is sometimes called "panning for gold."

WHODUNNIT—As previously discussed, the speed locked in on a radar unit may not be your own. A vehicle traveling in the opposite direction from the patrol car may have a high enough speed to be interesting, yet be too far gone to catch. The officer may just stop the next car that comes by and looks fast, using the reading already locked in to show the violator.

THE WHISTLER—A citizen's band radio is capable of interfering with a radar unit's operation. With a little bit of patience, a trooper can whistle into the mike of his CB and come up with any speed he wants. If you're cruising through the country-side and hear someone whistling Dixie on the CB, keep your speed right at 55 and watch out for radar cars. You might have company real soon.

THE TUNE-UP—The most common way radar units are calibrated is by use of tuning forks. These forks are available from the manufacturers in any 5 mile per hour increment from 25 MPH to 100 MPH. When a specific tuning fork is struck, it oscillates at the same frequency as the Doppler frequency for the speed indicated. By holding the fork an inch away from the antenna, the unit would show the proper speed to verify the accuracy of the unit. If you get clocked by radar at a five mile per hour increment, you should ask him how his unit is calibrated and what tuning forks he possesses. To avoid this problem, an increasing number of manufacturers are only supplying 50 MPH forks.

THE HURRY-UP HUSTLE—Many moving radars

will give erratic readings when the patrol car is traveling 65-69 MPH. If the unit is intentionally driven at
those speeds, the officer may lock in one of those inaccurate readings. Most units automatically shut down
and give no reading when the patrol speed exceeds
69 MPH.

THE WIPE—On the older radar units with a needle
and dial face for reading the speed, the operator can
simply wipe the dial once with his hand, causing static
electricity in the plastic dial cover. This will allow the
officer to "wipe-in" a 10 MPH increase, or wipe it back
out with one pass of the hand before demonstrating the
unit to a violator.

THE BAD CONNECTION—On the older dial face
units, a sharp blow to the unit or tapping on the case
while the unit is operating, will cause the needle to
fluctuate as much as 10-20 MPH. The operator can
simply lock in the speed as the needle swings past the
desired mark.

SHIFTING ZONES—With the long range of most
radar units, the unit may be actually clocking you
when you were down the highway in a higher speed
zone. A classic case of this type of error occurred in
1977 in Eau Claire, Wisconsin. A construction worker
was driving down a road marked at 45 MPH. Just as he
made a turn onto another road, his radar detector went
off. At that point, he and his passengers very carefully
watched his speed. 300 feet down the road, they passed
a 25 MPH sign and he drove past that sign at less than
the limit. Less than a fifth of a mile later he was
flagged down by a police officer who charged him with
driving 44 MPH in a 25 MPH zone. In this case, the

man had evidence and witnesses which allowed him to beat the citation in court.

THE SWITCH—Modern radar units may be equipped with optional time and distance functions which allow it to operate like VASCAR. By giving this unit false input, the operator can lock in a false speed and tell the violator that he was really clocked on radar.

SPEEDING FANS—When radar antennas are improperly mounted on the dash or sun visor, or deliberately aimed at the dashboard, they sometimes will pick up the speed of the police car's heater or air conditioning fan. The officer can pick the speed he wants to lock in by choosing between "Defrost" or "High Blower."

KITING—This is just like "kiting" a bank check, the officer simply makes up a conveniently higher figure to write on the ticket if your speed wasn't quite "high" enough. You can pick up on this one by asking to see your speed on the radar unit. If it doesn't match the one on the citation, or if the officer refuses to show you the reading, this will once again cast doubt on his testimony in court.

If Paul Simon, who sang about "50 Ways to Leave Your Lover," had been singing about radar instead, the lyrics might have been:

"Just kite on the cite, Dwight,
   do a little pan, Stan. . . ."

After all, there must be 50 ways to cheat on radar.

HOW DO I KNOW IF THE OFFICER "CHEATED" ON MY TICKET?

In most cases you never will know if the officer cheated. You can only guess, but certain things may help to tip you off to the officer. Ask to see the unit. If the officer refuses to show you the unit, or seems reluctant to show you the unit, you should be on the alert. Most officers are only too happy to show you the radar and briefly explain its operation. This is part of "selling" the ticket to you, making sure that you believe you deserved the citation. Convincing you of your guilt helps to keep the officer out of traffic court.

Take a careful look at the radar unit when he shows it to you. Is the speed displayed the same as he has written on your citation, or are they different? Do all the switches appear to be in the right positions, or is one turned to a "calibrate" position? If he caught you while both you and the officer were moving, and his

A careful look at the radar unit can be enlightening. This unit is in a "Cal 60" calibration mode. Speeds in multiples of 5 and 10 are always suspicious.

unit is a stationary radar, or a moving radar with the switches in the "stationary" position, he may have been cheating.

If your car is equipped with a radar detector which didn't even hiccup when you passed the radar unit, check your detector first. If the unit is plugged in and screams bloody murder with the next radar you pass, you've got to suspect that the officer's radar was not operating when you were caught.

The officer working alone is a lot more likely to cheat than two officers working together. The lone officer may rationalize that you really were speeding and therefore deserve a ticket, even though he was unable to obtain a valid clock on your speed. Like being caught by a pacing patrol car, it's virtually impossible to prove that an officer was cheating. Once the pace car stops rolling the needle returns to 0. It's simply your word against the officer's in court, because by the time of your trial the radar unit has long since been cleared of your speed.

Other officers will be as critical (if not more so) of the cheating officer as you are. Law enforcement agencies and their officers are very sensitive about this type of unprofessional technique. An officer who was known to be cheating on his citations would likely be strung up by his thumbs with the cord of his own radar gun by the other officers.

If you have a valid reason to believe that the officer who gave you a ticket has cheated, go on record by writing to his agency with your suspicions. It's best not to call as there will be no record of your complaint and you may not be talking to the right person. A letter will almost always be referred to the proper official for investigation.

With the current political climate of the country, following some of the biggest political cover-ups and scandals of the century, most agencies are very good in investigating complaints. They may even go so far as to send plainclothes officers past the radar unit to see how they are treated by the officer in question. If an officer is caught cheating, or merely suspected by enough people, his ticket writing days could be over for good.

In all cases in which you suspect foul play on the officer's part, you should bring up your suspicions and reasoning in court. If the reasoning is valid, you may be able to create the "reasonable doubt" that will prevent your conviction.

If you suspect you were the victim of the Automatic Calibration, feel you may have been served up some Leftovers or other such tricks, you can subpoena by number the 5 citations which the officer wrote before and after your alleged violation, or all of the citations issued by that officer on the same day. If several citations have the same speed, you may have a valid defense.

HOW FAR AWAY CAN RADAR CATCH ME?

The average range of most modern radar units is about 4,000 feet; a little less than a mile. Under absolutely ideal conditions (flat terrain, good target, clear weather, etc.) a really good unit can clock a target as far as three miles away. This range seems frightening at first appearance, but you have to remember that in

order to use the reading the officer has to make a
visual observation of your speed and there can be no
other cars between you and the radar. At a distance of
three miles, it's unlikely that the officer will even see
your car, much less be able to identify it, and if you're
the only car on that flat, three mile stretch of road
(you'd have to be towing a houseboat to present a big
enough target), it's rather unlikely that any officer
would pick such a lonely area to work radar. He'll
never make his quota that way.

The common working range of most radar units is
1,000 to 1,500 feet for passenger cars and as much as
2,000 to 2,500 for large trucks. ("Don't fire until you
see the whites of their eyes!" is the rule of thumb.) This
range allows the officer to be close enough to make a
visual identification of the offending vehicle while still
working an area that will present a large number of
targets to choose from. If the traffic is too heavy, however, the area is a poor one for working radar. The
number of targets makes it impossible for the operator
to identify the offending vehicles, and the close bunch-
ing of the cars reads out as an average speed on
the radar.

CAN RADAR "SEE" AROUND CORNERS
OR OVER HILLS?

No, radar is basically a "line-of-sight" device. The
radar energy will continue to scatter in all directions,
and may be detectable around corners and over hills,
however, no readable Doppler shift will return to the
radar unit.

A radar operator can get a good reading by shooting

*An ideal location for working radar, with the target coming down-
hill on a wide street, around a curve, in a residential district and
directly into the path of the radar beam.*

through a curve bordered with a chain-link type fence. Although this reading would probably be accurate, it's validity in court would be very questionable because the officer would have no visual observation to back it up.

Radar is unaffected by glass, as evidenced by the radar units currently in use whose antenna can be mounted in the car rather than mounted externally. Generally, if an officer can see your car, he can "shoot" it. This includes cars he can see in his rearview and side mirrors. By aiming the radar unit directly at the mirror, he can clock any vehicle in the mirror's field. Once again, this technique might be questionable in court, but provides a lot of amusement for the lonely officer working late at night.

HOW MANY TYPES OF RADAR ARE THERE?

Basically, there are four types of radar being produced by the major companies manufacturing traffic radar in the United States.

TRAFFIC SURVEY RADAR is the one type of radar in use on the highways that doesn't represent a direct threat to your driver's license. These units are used by traffic engineers and in some cases law enforcement agencies, to conduct surveys of vehicle speed and volume on highways and surface streets. These X-band units may be mounted on tripods by the roadside, or mounted in an unmarked vehicle "to assure accurate surveys." The radar tabulates all the cars which pass through its field and breaks down their speeds into specific, pre-programmed categories.

A modern, moving radar unit with a small, versatile antenna, remote control unit and "Hold" switch for "defeating radar detectors."

By using traffic survey radar, the traffic engineer can determine how many people are driving above and below the posted limits and make accurate recommendations as to the redesign of the highway, changing the posted limit, or increasing enforcement efforts.

Perhaps the most common type of radar in use today is the STATIONARY RADAR. A patrol car equipped with stationary radar usually sits by the roadside with the antenna facing in the direction in which the officer intends to pick off the next violator. The antenna can be aimed in virtually any direction, but still limits the officer's effectiveness by requiring the unit to be parked while clocking violators.

Keeping the patrol car stationary presents some real

problems. When the engine of the car is started, the voltage drop will often clear the radar unit, losing the violator's speed. Because of this problem, the patrol car is usually kept idling. With gas shortages and the heat produced by modern catalytic converters, idling the engine for any period of time is both against some department's regulations, and virtually unbearable with the heat produced. Having a patrol lurking by the side of the road with a radar unit is also very bad for public relations.

When the patrol car is moving, the stationary radar can only clock the ground speed of the patrol car. This is sometimes used when pacing other cars, as it supplies a very accurate reading of the patrol car's speed.

MOVING RADAR is rapidly gaining in popularity over the older, stationary units. Moving radar is capable of clocking vehicles approaching or traveling away from the patrol car when used in the "stationary" mode, and is also capable of clocking oncoming cars when the patrol car is in motion. One of the newest moving radars gives the operator the option of clocking oncoming vehicles with the radar unit, or switching over to an electronic stopwatch device which is capable of clocking violators moving in the same direction as the patrol car.

HAND-HELD RADAR, sometimes referred to as "speed-guns" are highly versatile moving or stationary radar units housed in a very compact package. The unit is aimed like a gun at the target vehicle which can be picked out of a group of cars. These units may either emit continuously, or only when the trigger is depressed, and may either be wired directly into the

A hand-held moving radar, often mounted on the dash of the patrol car as well.

vehicle's system through a plug, cigarette lighter out-let or powered by a portable battery pack. Their small size allows them to be carried on motorcycles or in patrol cars where it can be aimed in any direction.

These hand-held units are really fun for officers who want to sharpen up on their "quick draw" skills while using some technology straight out of *Star Wars*.

These "radar guns" have occasionally caused misun-derstandings with motorists who were unfamiliar with the technology. The sight of a fully uniformed police officer jumping into view and drawing a bead on your auto with what appears to be a small bazooka can be disturbing, to say the least. Officers are instructed to

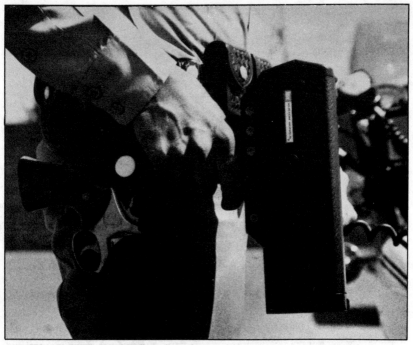

The size of a radar "gun" isn't much bigger than the officer's revolver. Both "guns" can be deadly.

be non-aggressive in the way they use this piece of equipment, but the temptation to over-act is simply too great for some officers.

WHAT IS MOVING RADAR AND HOW IS IT USED?

Moving radar utilizes the same principles of operation as stationary radar, but in a much more sophisticated way. It only detects and displays closing targets in the opposite lane. Moving radar will not compute the speed of targets moving in the same direction as the moving patrol car.

The moving radar's advantage over stationary

radar, is that it allows the officer to patrol his area while using the radar. Thus, in addition to his speed control duties, the officer can assist motorists in distress, investigate abandoned automobiles and perform other routine duties. Moving radar is terribly efficient under most conditions. Because it only detects oncoming traffic, however, it is not usable on divided highways where it is impossible to make a quick U-turn to pursue the violator.

A moving radar measures two Doppler signals. To illustrate this, picture a moving radar equipped patrol car cruising down the highway at 55 MPH. Because there is relative motion between the patrol car and the ground, the microwave energy striking the ground and reflecting back to the antenna undergoes a Doppler shift which the radar converts to the patrol car speed. This is called "low Doppler."

Now, picture yourself as the target, approaching the patrol car at 70 MPH. The radar beam striking your car and returning to the antenna shows the combined speed of both cars, in this case 125 MPH. The computer in the counting unit then subtracts the 55 MPH patrol car speed from the combined speed and displays the result: a 70 MPH target speed. On most newer moving radar units, the patrol car speed is shown as well.

Moving radar can also be used as a stationary radar in the conventional manner, clocking vehicles in either direction while the patrol car is not moving.

One of the newest features appearing on modern moving radars is a sophisticated, VASCAR-like, time-distance computer. This is not a radar device, but only a glorified, electronic stop-watch. This device allows him to obtain speed readings over a measured distance on vehicles traveling in either direction while the patrol car is in motion or stationary. However, the unit has no connection to the speedometer cable, or any other method of measuring the distance used itself. It relies on the operator to input the correct distance, usually based on his estimation. Because it uses the same display and counting unit as the radar, it cannot be used at the same time as the radar. Some agencies equip their cars with both moving radar and a separate VASCAR unit, and do work both lanes simultaneously.

Moving radar, often incorrectly referred to as "New VASCAR," probably constitutes the biggest threat to a speeding motorist. At a closing speed of over 100 MPH you may not even see the officer until you catch him pulling a U-turn in your rearview mirror. Many modern radars are equipped with a "hold" switch which allows them to use the radar intermittently, and transmit a radar beam only when he has visual contact with a target. Even if you're equipped with a radar detector, your first warning may be too late. With the ability to pace you from behind without using the radar (and without alerting your radar detector) and the ability to clock you from the opposite side of the highway, the officer can literally catch you coming and going.

HOW MUCH DOES RADAR COST?

Radar is very expensive. Traffic survey radar which automatically compiles statistics on the vehicles passing through the radar beam costs between $12,000 to $15,000. Stationary radar units start at about $1,000 with a stripped down, no-frills package, and go up to

$3,000 or more for the most sophisticated moving radars. These units are also available with costly options such as fully automatic ticket printers and speed recording instruments. Hand held "guns" are some of the least expensive, with a purchase price of approximately $900 to $1,300. Regardless of what a police agency pays for their radar, they all work quite well.

IF RADAR IS SO EXPENSIVE, HOW DO THE POLICE JUSTIFY THEIR COST?

There is probably no other piece of law enforcement equipment which is easier for them to justify. A really competent (or really incompetent) radar operator may write as many as 50 citations in a single day (this is assuming the guy is a real "hot pencil"). If you assume an average fine of $20, this single officer is generating $1000 in fines per shift. With three shifts per day, even the most expensive unit can pay for itself in 24 hours.

Of course, we've over-simplified this explanation to make a point. If you assume that the officer isn't too excited with his new radar (this is rarely the case, usually they go absolutely nuts like a kid with a new toy) and only wrote 5-10 tickets each day, the unit would easily pay for itself within a month.

As one manufacturer's representative put it, "if they don't pay for the unit within a couple of weeks, they're just not doing their jobs." With the economics involved, it's only public pressure that prevents *every* police vehicle from carrying a radar unit.

WHO PAYS FOR THE RADAR UNITS?

In the past 3 years, most radar money has come from the federal government through the Department of Transportation and Law Enforcement Assistance Administration. This money is often in the form of matching funds, but may sometimes cover the entire cost of the radar program. Whether it comes from the federal government, or out of state or municipal budgets, the expenditure for radar is ultimately paid for by the very taxpayers who will be cited by the use of the devices. It can be a long and hard battle to get the initial expenditure through the town councils and state legislatures. Even today, the California State Legislature has refused to authorize funding for the purchase of radar by that state's highway patrol. To lessen the burden of the initial radar purchase, many manufacturers make their radar units available to the agencies on a lease or rental agreement.

Often when the radar is to be used for a federally funded program, or when the town is located close to a federal reservation such as a military base, the federal government will pay for the cost of the unit (and sometimes the cost of the officer's vehicle and salary) to meet the increased demands on local traffic systems.

Some cities have been provided radar units by private institutions, foundations, large corporations and even service organizations such as the Lion's Club or the Kiwanis. Ultimately, either through taxation or citation fines, you are the one who pays for radar.

HOW MANY STATES USE RADAR?

All 50 states . . . and Guam and Puerto Rico. At this time, the California Highway Patrol is the only state agency which does not have radar. This has proven to be a good thing for the CHP's public relations. Some truckers speak almost fondly of their citations from the CHP, as their non-use of radar makes the whole speed game seem a lot more "sportsman-like." These good "sports" from California wrote 2,297,087 citations last year. Despite their apparent handicap of not having radar, 1,112,913 of those citations were for speed violations, 17 percent of the speeding citations issued in the United States last year.

HOW MANY RADAR UNITS ARE IN OPERATION IN THE UNITED STATES?

Current estimates are that there are roughly 100,000 traffic radar units being operated by the approximately 23,000 law enforcement agencies in the United States today. This gives an average of four radar units to each agency, which may range in size from one officer to well in excess of ten thousand officers. One source estimated that there was one radar unit every 45 statistical miles on the Interstate Highway system. It all adds up to a *lot* of radar units.

DO OTHER COUNTRIES USE RADAR TOO?

Yes, radar is in use in over 20 foreign countries, including Canada and Mexico. However, no other country uses radar so extensively (or zealously) as in the United States.

Radar units age rapidly under their harsh service, but last almost forever.

HOW LONG DOES A RADAR UNIT LAST BEFORE IT WEARS OUT?

Unfortunately, radar units last almost forever with proper care and maintenance. They may look like they were "ridden hard and put away wet" (as cowboys used to say), but they just keep on working. Most of the parts which are susceptible to failure, such as the Gunn Effect diode and the digital displays are easily replaced.

When radar units are replaced, it is usually because the state of the art technology has changed, rather than any failure on the part of the unit. Law enforcement agencies just love anything new, and have bought such recent improvements as the K-band radars, the "hold" switches which are supposed to defeat radar detectors and even a so-called "bionic radar" which speaks, calling out the speed of violators to the officer, even when he is out of the car. Often these new units are used in addition to the old units, rather than actually replacing the old units. Other units are sold off at bargain prices to smaller agencies on limited budgets, or even traded-in to the radar manufacturers as part of the purchase price of the new units.

WHAT HAPPENS TO THE OLD RADAR UNITS?

The majority of the old radar units taken in on trade by the manufacturers end up in warehouses where they just gather dust. Some of these are "remanufactured" with new components and sold into foreign countries, most notably Mexico and South America.

When a radar unit comes to the end of its useful life of patrolling the streets with a law enforcement agency, it is often cannibalized for parts by the technicians. This enables them to keep other units of the same vintage in use much longer.

Some departments have utilized their old radars in an attempt to frustrate radar detectors. Their old units have been mounted on staff cars and other department vehicles, and in one case, two units were mounted fore and aft on a patrol helicopter, just for the purpose of setting off any radar detectors which come within their range. This usage of radar has been declared illegal by the F.C.C., and they are slapping the hands of agencies caught using old radars in that manner.

CAN A CITIZEN BUY A RADAR UNIT?

Yes, many uses for police-type radar units have been found by civilians. One of the most common applications of radar outside of traffic enforcement is in sports, where it has been used to clock both runners and racecars, and is often used to try out aspiring baseball pitchers. With the radar, it's easy for the coach to spot when a starting pitcher's fast ball starts to burn out.

It might prove interesting if a citizen were to use radar to clock police officers, putting the shoe on the other foot. When an officer drives, he doesn't have to keep one eye on his rearview mirror and the other on his radar detector. It would be very rare to find an officer who strictly adhered to the speed limits except when traveling under emergency conditions as required by law. More than one 100 MPH+ run has been made by less responsible officers hurrying to meet fellow officers at a local coffee shop, or rushing to deliver a still steaming pizza back to the watch commander.

DOES THE OFFICER HAVE TO HAVE SPECIAL TRAINING TO OPERATE RADAR?

Yes, the case of *Dantanio* vs. the State of New Jersey decided that the officer had to be trained in the use of radar, but that 1½ to 2 hours training was sufficient. Often this training consists of merely using the unit in the field under a senior officer's supervision. Radar manufacturers usually provide a free "dog and pony show" with the radar units at the time of purchase, which may be as long as 8 hours and include a full presentation of slides and films. This training includes information on the theory of radar as well as its use, but by the time you finish this book, you will probably know far more about traffic radar than most police officers.

CAN I ASK HIM HOW IT WORKS?

Yes, and most times the officer will oblige your request. Most departments' policies require the officer to give you a brief explanation of his radar. Often times this only consists of showing you the unit with your reading, then clearing the unit of your speed and clocking the next passing motorist.

After reading this book, you should understand everything the officer tells you about his unit, as well as

Power/Audio: Dual control for "Power On" sequence and audio volume of the target's Doppler signal.

Target Display: Displays speed of closing or opening vehicle in stationary mode; displays closing vehicle in moving mode.

Patrol Display: Displays groundspeed of patrol vehicle in the moving mode, and may be blanked when the "Monitor" control is activated.

Stopwatch/Range: Dual control which allows the operator to select the stopwatch mode of operation or extend/reduce range depending on terrain or urban interference.

Remote Hold & Lock-Release Control: Allows operator to activate the system's "hold" mode, and to perform the lock-release function from the normal driving position.

Electric Eye: Controls light level of "target" and "patrol" displays, adjusting brightness to suit ambient conditions.

Lock-Release: Locks in or releases target vehicle speed and groundspeed. This function is also available with a remote lock-release button, supplied with the unit.

Highest Speed Lock: Allows the system to track an accelerating vehicle to its highest speed before locking while the system is in the "Automatic Mode" of operation.

Test: Performs, in sequence, light test, calibration and stopwatch test functions.

Stationary-Moving Mode: Selectable switch for determining the mode of operation.

Monitor: Allows the operator to blank the Patrol speed display.

Manual-Automatic Mode: Selectable switch for determining the mode of locking.

A modern radar unit has more features than an all-electric home.

being able to spot anything about the unit or his explanation that seems questionable. Compared to the explanations of radar's workings presented in this chapter, you'll find his explanations to be childishly simple.

DOES THE OFFICER HAVE TO HAVE A SPECIAL LICENSE TO OPERATE RADAR?

No, the only time an officer is required to have any kind of license for radar operation is when he is using moving radar: even then, the only license he needs is a driver's license. An officer operates under a blanket license covering all the officers employed by the agency. Sometimes an officer may have a certificate of completion or other document which states that he received the proper training in the operation of radar.

HOW DO I KNOW IF HIS AGENCY HAS A LICENSE?

You won't have any idea at all unless you ask someone. All agencies using radar are required under Federal Communications Commission regulations to have a valid license (station) for the operation of their units. This license will specify the number of units in operation, and the specific frequency(s) which they are licensed to operate on. Any units which are beyond the quantity listed, or which fall outside of the licensed frequency(s) are illegal units. Often a department will add units, or add K-band units to their existing X-band units, and neglect to update their license as required.

For current information on police radar and state or municipal radar licenses, you can inquire at a local FCC Field Office, or call or write directly to:

Federal Communications Commission
Industrial & Public Safety Facilities Division
Licensing Office, Room 5308
2025 M Street, N.W.
Washington, D.C. 20554
(202) 632-6475

If you only need a copy of a particular law enforcement agency's license, you have to go through a separate office, which is an independent business working under contract to the FCC. Their address and phone number is:

Downtown Copy Center
1114 21st Street, N.W.
Washington, D.C. 20037
(202) 452-1422

The Downtown Copy Center will charge you a "research" fee for locating the information within the FCC's files. This fee can run anywhere from $10 to $300 depending on the information needed. Processing takes a week to ten days, although "expedite" and "same-day" service are available for an extra charge.

When writing to either of these agencies, be sure to mention the specific law enforcement agency about which you are inquiring, and refer to the radar license as a "radiopositioning equipment" license, the FCC terminology for such units.

Another alternative to finding out about an agency's license is to ask the agency itself. Always do this in writing and by certified mail, as this becomes a record of your inquiry which can be used in court if necessary. Basically, the letter should read:

Dear Sirs:

In connection with a pending appearance in the (name of court) on (date of appearance) at (time) I respectfully request the manufacturer's name, serial number, model number and any other identifying symbols for the particular piece of radiopositioning equipment (radar) used on Citation #_____ issued by your agency on (date and time of violation) at (location).

I also need to have as an integral part of my defense, a copy of your agency's Federal Communication Commission radiopositioning (radar) license, showing the license number, date of issuance, date of expiration, authorized frequencies and number of units licensed at the time of my citation. Thank you for your cooperation in this matter.

Sincerely,
(Your signature)

If the agency fails to respond to this inquiry, it can appear in court that the agency was attempting to conceal the information from you.

If you're really serious about taking your case to court and pursuing the issue as far as possible, you will need to explore every possible technical avenue which could conceivably relate to your defense. To do this, you subpoena the agency's FCC license, the actual radar unit which clocked you, the officer's training records (often there are none), the radar unit's calibration and maintenance records, the officer's daily log of activities for the date of your citation, a complete list of the citations issued by that officer for that day (including citation number, location and speed cited), the tuning fork(s) used in the calibration of the radar unit along with their certificates of calibration, and last of all, a complete listing of the makes, models and serial numbers of all radar units in use by that agency. We'll cover how to obtain and use this information in our chapter, "Fighting the System."

CAN THE RADAR UNIT MALFUNCTION?

No, radar has been totally perfected in the last few years and is incapable of making mistakes. At least, that's what the manufacturers and operators of radar would like to have you believe.

Actually, radar is as susceptible to failure and error as any other piece of electronic equipment. They're not any more sophisticated than your color TV or the Skylab space shot, and we all know they never fail either, right? There are numerous ways in which the radar may malfunction and give an incorrect reading, or no reading at all. Often these are due to electrical or mechanical interference rather than the failure of any electronic component in the system.

IS IT TRUE THAT PUTTING TINFOIL IN MY HUBCAPS WILL MAKE THE RADAR GIVE A FALSE READING?

This is a widespread rumor among uninformed people, one that has even found its way into print. In a modern book about "beating police radar legally," the

A radar unit is only as good as its operator.

author says, "The most popular way (to confuse radar) is to place balls of tinfoil under hubcaps and wheel covers. The bouncing and reverberating of the metal globes emits sounds resonant at a specific radar frequency. This can also occur when balls of tinfoil are placed in other cavities within the car's bodywork."

The author continues by saying, "One man I met took the same principle a step further. He keeps a key ring around the rearview mirror and insists that the high-pitched reports caused by the meeting of keys makes the radar ineffective."

Another common belief is that "static straps" defeat radar by grounding the body of the automobile. You should file all of these rumors away with your lucky rabbit's foot and your deed to the Brooklyn Bridge: there is simply no truth to them at all. Many of these rumors may have stemmed from the use of "chaff" or "window" by aircraft in World War II. Chaff are metallic strips that were dropped during air attacks to mask the movements of the aircraft from enemy radar. These strips form a radar "smoke screen" which can confuse aircraft tracking radars. However, an automobile is not an aircraft, and modern police radar bears little resemblance to aircraft radar.

WILL RAPID DECELERATION AFFECT THE RADAR UNIT?

On radar units with digital displays, a rapidly declining speed may be nearly impossible for the operator to read. However, as soon as the officer hears the tone drop on his audible doppler, he knows that the radar unit has been "made" and he'll hit his lock button, preserving your highest speed.

Many radar units have an automatic lock on the highest verified speed of the target vehicle. In order to "verify," older units require at least one second of tracking your vehicle, modern units verify in one-fifth of a second. An erratic in-put caused by a rapid change in speed will be rejected by the unit. An erratic in-put is a change of 3.15 MPH per second for the older units, and 15.75 MPH on the newer models. Assuming that the radar is not already tracking your vehicle (because your reaction time is bound to be longer than the radar's verification time) a rapid deceleration may prevent the unit from locking onto your speed.

The deceleration required to confuse a modern radar unit would require you to brake from 70 MPH to 55 MPH in a little under one second. If you're going to try this one, check your rearview mirror first, otherwise you might end up with a semi-rig in your trunk. Even if the truck following you didn't collide with your car when you hit the brakes, the trucker's fist might collide with your nose at the next truckstop.

WHAT CAUSES RADAR TO MALFUNCTION?

Most radar malfunctions can be attributed to electronic failure, mechanical interference, or electronic interference.

An electronic failure is a failure of one of the components of the radar unit, and rarely affects the speed at which you were clocked. The most common component to fail is the Gunn Effect diode. Typically, the range of the radar unit becomes weaker and weaker until there is no reading at all. Replacement diodes are often supplied free of charge by the manufacturer, and replacing the diode is a relatively simple task.

Another electronic failure occurs when a segment of one of the number displays burns out. Most radars have a test which reads "188" or "888" to check all segments. Usually a burnt out segment will count in your favor, with a 6 possibly reading as a 5, or a 7 reading as a 1. The only number that may read higher with a burnt out segment would be an 8. With two burnt out segments, the speed of 88 MPH could read out as 99 MPH. However, a defense statement of, "But I was only doing 88 MPH!" probably wouldn't go over all that well in court.

One type of mechanical interference with the operation of radar is natural phenomenon such as rain, fog and blowing dust. These tend to shorten the range of radar and cause strange sounds over the audible doppler. Wind-blown tree limbs and signs can also generate false signals. Often, radar units will give a little "beep" and some speed will arbitrarily show on the display; even when the patrol car is parked on an isolated stretch of highway with no other traffic within miles.

Another type of mechanical interference which is limited to moving radar is called "Shadowing." As the patrol car is passed by a truck or other large vehicle moving in the same direction, the radar may read the back of the truck instead of the ground speed. The radar thinks that the truck is the ground, so instead of showing a ground speed of the patrol car as 55 MPH, it sees it as perhaps 10 MPH, the difference in the speed between the truck and the patrol car.

Now the patrol car clocks an oncoming violator who is actually doing 55 MPH. The closing speed between the two cars is 110 MPH, so the unit subtracts 10 and reads 100 MPH on the "violator."

One widely used model of radar from a specific manufacturer suffers from a malady known as "The 715 Error" (in reference to the model number of the unit). When this moving radar is traveling at 55 MPH, it won't read the speed of an oncoming vehicle traveling 53-57 MPH. Instead, it reads right through this first target and shows the speed of the vehicle behind it. If the vehicle following the target is doing 70 MPH, the perfectly legal target may be cited for excessive speed.

"Batching" is another form of mechanical error. While the moving radar follows changes in the target's speed almost instantaneously, it is relatively slow in responding to changes in the ground speed of the patrol car. If the patrol car accelerates suddenly, the radar may immediately read the increased difference between the speed of the patrol car and the target vehicle, without picking up the increase in ground speed. If a patrol car suddenly sped up 5 MPH while closing on a target, the increase would be added to the target speed and a motorist traveling 56 MPH could be cited for doing 61 MPH.

Electronic interference is probably the most common cause of false readings and spurious, phantom speeds. Radar manufacturers used to explain spurious readings to the officers through their instruction manuals, but they were largely eliminated when the public became aware of them and started using them in court. In fact, instruction manuals which are subpoenaed into court often have the pages dealing with interference and spurious readings torn right out of the manual.

Electrical storms, power transformers and transmissions lines, C.B. radios, neon lights and automobile inverters are just a few of the sources of electronic "noise" in the environment. Although these operate at different frequencies than traffic radar, they generate "harmonic" frequencies which may affect the radar. A harmonic is simply a multiple of a base frequency; so a device operating at 500 hertz may create interference at 1000, 1500 and even 10,000,000 hertz, occasionally causing a false number on the radar display. The less expensive radar units are more susceptible to this type of interference than the higher quality units which incorporate special filters to reject these signals.

Many of the latest generation of moving radars mount the antenna inside the car, on the dashboard. The antenna can be aimed in any direction while the car is stationary, allowing the officer to set on an overpass and "shoot" cars in either direction. A little known fact about the units is that spurious readings often occur whenever the antenna is pointed in the direction of the counting unit. This type of malfunction, like most of the others, is rarely understood by the officers who operate the radar units.

CAN YOU CAUSE RADAR TO MALFUNCTION?

Yes, as previous discussed, it's relatively simple for

the unskilled officer or the officer who is purposely "cheating" to misuse his equipment and obtain a false reading from the radar unit.

There are also ways in which the motorist can cause the radar unit to malfunction. Police radar can be caused to malfunction either by intentional or unintentional transmissions of radio or other electronic interference generated by your vehicle. There are even specific devices called Electronic Counter Measures, or ECM's which are designed to give false readings on police radar.

CAN POLICE RADAR BE JAMMED?

Yes, that's what electronic counter measures are all about. ECM's got their start as a system for jet fighters. The ECM detected when enemy radar found the fighter, pinpointed the location of the radar transmitter and sent a missile back to the source to destroy it.

ECM's to counter police radar aren't quite up to the level of pinpointing the patrol car and destroying it with a missile, but the technology is advancing steadily. Radar jammers are becoming available to the public now, being sold under the guise of Amateur Radio equipment or radar calibration devices. The use of these devices for the purpose of jamming a police radar rig are clearly illegal, however, because the equipment can be used for many other completely legal purposes the jammers are available.

Most jamming devices broadcast a signal in the radar frequency range equivalent to a speed predetermined by the operator. The broadcast signal overpowers the much weaker reflection from the radar transmitter and "force-feeds" the false information into the receiver. Even though the reflection says 70 MPH, the much more powerful transmission returns to the unit at 55 MPH or whatever other speed the operator has selected. Jamming devices are currently available at a cost of between $600 and $1000, but often have a very short range. Also, the jamming effort would be very apparent to a police officer using an audible tone; he could literally hear the radar jammer. Of course, these devices have no effect on pacing or VASCAR systems, and a device which jams an X-band unit might have no effect on a K-band radar, or an X-band unit working slightly off frequency.

Anyone foolish enough to use an ECM like this would probably be arrested by federal authorities, if not picked up and lynched by radar detector equipped truckers first, as his jamming transmitter would be setting off every detector within miles.

WHO FIXES THE RADAR UNITS WHEN THEY BREAK?

While the unit is still under the factory warranty (from 90 days to 5 years, depending on the unit) or if the unit is under lease, all repairs to the unit are performed by the factory's trained and FCC licensed technicians.

State police and other large agencies maintain their own radio shops (often shared with all other departments using radios) and licensed technicians who are capable of handling most repairs to the radar units as well. Smaller departments may have one specially trained officer or civilian technician who handles all of the repair and maintenance for all of the agency's radio and radar equipment. A very small town without the equipment, manpower or resources to repair their own units may keep a maintenance agreement with the manufacturer, or have the service performed by a local electronics repair shop authorized by the manufacturer.

HOW IS THE RADAR UNIT CALIBRATED?

All digital radar units are equipped with a self-test function which is commonly referred to as a "calibrate" or "test" mode. When this calibrate or test button is pushed, and internal crystal supplies a signal frequency to the counter in the computing unit. This same signal frequency is then divided to provide a time base or counting period. A typical generated ratio is 64 counts, or cycles, per time period. If the unit's counters are operating properly, this ratio will be displayed as the predetermined speed (64 MPH). It is very important to note that this ratio is the only thing which is tested. If, for example, the crystal itself is off-frequency but the ratio remains the same (as it usually does), the radar will be inaccurate. The officer who performs only this test will have no indication that the radar is furnishing him with inaccurate speed readings. Radar manufacturers commonly label this test function with the word "Calibrate" and this inadvertently misleads even the most well intentioned officer into believing that he has actually "calibrated" his radar unit. It is very important that this point be clarified during any trial involving the use of radar if the officer refers to

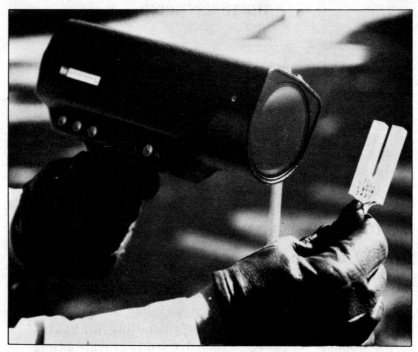
Proper calibration is simple, but often neglected.

"calibrating" his radar with this internal function. The case of *Connecticut vs. Tomanelli* established the *certified* tuning fork as the *only* acceptable test of the radar's accuracy.

When a radar type tuning fork is properly struck, it vibrates at a known frequency, one which can be read by the radar unit and converted to speed. This known "speed" is usually stamped on the side of the fork, along with the operating band it is to be used for and the serial number of that particular fork. Although these tuning forks are fairly durable, they can be bent or otherwise damaged, resulting in an improper frequency. Many officers carry a tuning fork in the patrol car with them for calibration purposes, although some forks are kept in the radio shops and the officers working radar may not have seen them for several years. Most sophisticated radio shops have a signal generator which can also be used to evaluate the accuracy of the radar units. Other equipment allows them to adjust the unit for peak power output and performance, but seldom is any provision made to check the frequency that the unit is operating on.

One test has been described by a leading manufacturer of radar as "perhaps the best indicator of the overall health of the radar." In this test, the radar is directed straight down a roadway as the patrol car is driven through a range of speeds. The radar is compared side-by-side against the calibrated speedometer (even though the radar is capable of much greater accuracy) and gives a good indication of the radar's accuracy throughout the entire operating range. It was suggested by the manufacturer that this test be done on a daily basis.

HOW OFTEN DOES A RADAR UNIT HAVE TO BE CALIBRATED?

Most law enforcement agency's procedure manuals and most manufacturers of radar recommend that the unit be calibrated *by a certified tuning fork* at the beginning and end of *each* shift (six times per day) and that the calibration sequence be performed before and after each violation. However, many officers become lax in this boring and repetitive task and don't bother to perform the required calibrations. Likewise, many departments do not keep accurate records of the cali-

brations and may not even supply their officers with the tuning forks required to conduct a proper calibration.

One of the newest moving radar systems automatically conducts an internal calibration each time the unit is turned on, and calibrates itself again before locking in any violator's speed. Despite all these advanced electronics, the unit must still be calibrated at the beginning and end of every shift by the use of the tuning forks. (With moving radars, two forks are used simultaneously, one to provide ground speed, the other to provide target speed.)

Exactly when the radar unit was calibrated is important to your defense. The rules of evidence require the prosecution to prove the radar's accuracy at the time of your alleged violation. This can only be done by providing evidence that the unit was calibrated *both before and after* the incident and was operating properly both times. Lacking such evidence, the accuracy of the radar unit cannot be established by the prosecution.

SHOULD I ASK TO SEE HIS TUNING FORK WHEN HE STOPS ME?

Yes, anytime you are stopped and cited by a radar unit you should ask to see his tuning fork. If he is unable to show you one, it casts more than a little doubt as to whether he had calibrated the unit before and after your alleged violation.

A certified tuning fork, the only acceptable method of calibration.

WHAT IS A CERTIFICATE OF CALIBRATION?

A Certificate of Calibration is an official looking document provided with the radar unit by the manufacturer. The paper is covered with more printed frills and flourishes than a kindergarten graduation diploma and is about as meaningful.

All this "certificate" really tells you is that the piece of equipment really is a radar unit and that according to some unknown and untitled person's statement, the unit worked when it left the factory. This piece of paper is about as important as the paper in a new pair of pants reading "Inspected by #17."

KUSTOM KR-11
DAILY TEST & CALIBRATION LOG

Date _____

KR-11 Serial No. _____

ON DUTY TEST & CALIBRATION

Time	Forced Seq.	Fork Test Sta.	Mov.	SIGN

TEST & CALIBRATION DURING SHIFT

Time	Forced Seq.	Fork Test Sta.	Mov.	SIGN

OFF DUTY TEST & CALIBRATION

Time	Forced Seq.	Fork Test Sta.	Mov.	SIGN

Instructions:

1. Note time unit is placed in service. Conduct the forced light test and calibration sequence during "power on" or by depressing the "Test" control button. Conduct the stationary and moving tuning fork tests. Check all appropriate boxes in the **On Duty Test & Calibration** column as tests are performed. Initial the "Sign" box when tests are satisfactorily completed.

2. During the shift, conduct the forced sequence and tuning fork tests after each apprehension (noting time of apprehension), check off the appropriate boxes, and initial the "Sign" box in the **Test and Calibration During Shift** column.

3. At the completion of the shift or prior to turning over the KR-11 to another operator, conduct the forced sequence and tuning fork tests, checking appropriate boxes as the tests are performed in the **Off Duty Test & Calibration** column. Initial the "Sign" column box when tests are satisfactorily completed.

4. Use the "Comments" section to note any unusual performance characteristics.

Comments _____

P/N 006-0178-00

IS THERE ANY OTHER RECORD OF THE RADAR'S CALIBRATION?

Many agencies keep absolutely no record of the radar's periodic or daily calibrations, and probably many courts would be surprised to find this out if it were ever questioned in a trial. Most manufacturers recommend that a daily test and calibration log be kept for each unit, with the unit being calibrated before and after the shift, as well as before and after every violation, but these are rarely kept due to the sheer amount of paper work involved.

HOW CAN I TELL IF A POLICE CAR HAS RADAR?

With the huge number of radar units in operation on the highways today, the safest course of action is to assume that any police car you approach may have radar. Today's radar units are becoming more and more compact, and therefore more readily concealed. Radar detectors can help you spot the radar units, but even the detectors are not foolproof with "holding modes" and VASCAR devices. When you see a snake between your feet you don't look to see if he's poisonous, you jump out of the way. It's the same way with patrol cars; if he strikes, it could be deadly to your license. Don't wait until you figure out whether he's poisonous.

ARE ALL RADAR CARS WORKING TRAFFIC ENFORCEMENT?

All radar cars are not necessarily working traffic

Traffic radar takes many forms, both inside the car and out.

enforcement, but most of them are. Radar equipped vehicles are also used in traffic to conduct traffic engineering surveys, and even used by private trucking firms to keep tabs on their drivers. However, with the large number of unmarked and inconspicuous vehicles being used in some states as radar units, it's safe to assume that any car with a radar unit might be a police unit.

CAN THEY USE RADAR FROM AIRCRAFT TO CONTROL TRAFFIC?

No, the previously discussed "cosine angle factor" makes the use of traffic radar from aircraft very impractical. Theoretically, a low flying aircraft cruising at low speeds could track a vehicle target with radar, but it would be really tough trying to pull over the violator. Aircraft are far more effective in their roles as observers, working in conjunction with ground units to apprehend speeders.

At one time, some state agencies had equipped their aircraft with obsolete radar equipment directed toward the highways with the intention of triggering radar detectors. This usage of radar has since been ruled illegal by the F.C.C.

ARE THERE ANY AUTOMATED RADAR UNITS?

No, but there are many non-radar units which are mistakenly identified as radar units. One of the most devious of these is the "ORBIS" system. ORBIS uses sensors buried in the pavement much like the old hose timers. When the ORBIS system senses a speeder, it snaps a picture of the violator's car with infra-red film and special polarizing filters which allow the unit to capture the driver's face through the windshield. The unit also records the date and time of the violation, along with the posted speed and the violator's speed. A photo-ticket is then mailed to the violator's home.

These units are very impractical for a number of reasons. They are very expensive, ranging from $10,000 to $27,000 depending on the options and frills. The units are also highly vulnerable to vandalism, subject to a little midnight target practice by an irate motorist, or just a little spraypaint applied to the lens.

The unit also brings up some truly novel legal problems. Invasion of privacy is an un-resolved question. A picture of a man out for a drive with his lover could be disastrous if mailed to his home and opened by his wife. Also, with the unit being unattended for long periods of time, it would be difficult for anyone to make claims as to the unit's accuracy and calibration. The inability of the unit to speak for itself would seem to make it a little difficult for it to testify or be cross-examined.

DO THEY HAVE TO TELL ME IF THEY USE RADAR?

No, there is nothing that requires the officer to tell you that he used radar, but he almost invariably will inform you that he used radar if he did. Most motorists find radar to be terribly intimidating and are unwilling to even attempt to fight a citation stemming from its use. The officers are well aware of this powerful effect that serves to keep them out of court, but are often as ignorant of the shortcomings of radar as you are.

DOES HE HAVE TO SHOW ME MY SPEED?

Once again, there is nothing that requires the officer to show you your speed, but most officers will show you the unit if the situation seems appropriate. Trying to show the radar to a harried housewife with a car full of kids in the middle of a downpour would be silly, but most officers will be only too happy to show you their units with your speed locked in if the conditions permit. This is an important part of selling the ticket to you. Once you see your speed, most motorists give up their cases on the spot; who can argue with a radar unit?

If the officer is reluctant to show you your speed, or flatly refuses to show it to you, it casts a certain amount of doubt as to the validity of the displayed speed. The officer's refusal can only count in your favor in court.

HOW DOES HE KNOW THE RADAR WAS TRACKING ME AND NOT ANOTHER CAR?

The courts have recognized that the vehicle closest to the radar unit is the "target" vehicle when it is in the radar's beam. Although radar has been known to "skip" over small cars and clock large targets such as trucks coming up from behind, the courts still maintain that the lead vehicle in a pack is the valid radar target. If there is any question about which target is which, most officers will let those cars slip by (unless the speed is really flagrant) and wait for the next clear shot. Veteran radar operators carefully avoid working locations which present poor targets that may be questionable in court.

DOES THE SIZE AND SHAPE OF MY VEHICLE AFFECT THE RADAR?

Yes, the size, shape and even the construction of the vehicle all play an important part in determining the radar's range. About the maximum effective range for any traffic radar is ⅓ of a mile for small, compact vehicles, ½ mile for full size automobiles and ⅔ mile for larger vehicles such as trucks.

Radar always tracks the strongest target, but the courts have maintained that the nearest target is always the strongest.

The shape of the target is very important, too. The huge flat surfaces of the front end of a big truck are just about ideal for reflecting radar waves, while the low, sloping hood of a sports car returns little of the signal to the radar antenna. Metal surfaces tend to be more reflective to the radar energy than fiberglass or plastic panels. None of these factors will make your car "invisible" to the radar, but they do help to reduce the range at which the unit can clock you.

CAN RADAR CATCH ME ON MY BICYCLE?

Yes, and it's not all that uncommon for an officer working radar to issue a citation to a speeding bicyclist who passes through the beam. The range is somewhat limited, but once the radar locks onto the target the reading is valid. In fact, one frustration that radar operators sometimes encounter is having their unit blocked from speeding autos while the unit is locked onto a bicyclist puffing past. A number of campus police agencies at major colleges have invested in hand-held units to combat speeding bicyclists.

HOW WIDE OF A BEAM IS THE RADAR UNIT SENDING?

Depending on the unit, radar manufacturers list their beam spread as 6° to 8°. This is a little deceptive, as their measurement is actually the number of degrees the beam spreads from the exact center of the beam, so the full width of the beam is 12° to 16°. This amounts to a beam roughly 225 feet in diameter at a distance from the unit of 1000 feet.

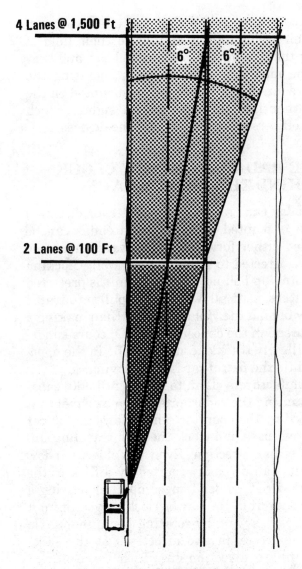

The Width of a Radar Beam

Many officers have found that the effective beam width of their radar unit is similar to their field of vision using the side mirror of the patrol car, and they often use the mirror as a guide when operating the unit. Early radars had a sighting tube mounted on the antenna, rather like the old bazooka sights, which allowed the officers to accurately aim the devices.

DOES THE RADAR UNIT ONLY CLOCK CARS BEHIND THE PATROL CAR?

No, the radar can track cars in whatever direction the antenna is pointed. Almost all antennas can be easily pointed either forward or backward, and some units may be directed to either side as well. Clocking vehicles coming up behind the patrol unit is preferred by many officers, as it allows them to pull into traffic immediately behind the violator rather than making a U-turn to pursue in the opposite lanes. Of course, moving radar will only track oncoming traffic in the opposite lanes while the patrol car is also moving.

Many manufacturers claim to have a full 360° capability by mounting the radar antenna on a swivel that can be rotated by the operator. This allows the officer to work an overpass and clock the cars traveling underneath in either direction. Even the older, window mounted units can be easily rotated by a flick of the adept officer's wrist, so don't speed up after passing a rear-facing radar unit. He may be clocking you in front of the patrol car as well, by rotating his antenna. No radar unit can track in two directions at the same time, only in the direction in which his antenna is facing.

Modern radar units are capable of tracking in any direction while in the stationary mode.

A location offering concealment for the officer, but close to traffic.

WHY DO THEY PICK CERTAIN LOCATIONS TO HIDE IN?

Radar operators usually pick the locations that offer them the best targets. The officers are creatures of habit like anyone else, and work the same locations time after time until the spot is "burned out." These ideal locations are often just over the crest of hills, around curves or on the far sides of dips, anywhere that allows them to catch the motorists by surprise and tends to break up traffic groups into single targets which are easily and clearly tracked by the radar. These prime locations can be worked every day for weeks, and even the same motorist may be caught on three or more consecutive mornings. While the motorists seem a little slow to learn about the location of the radar trap, they're often quick to learn the routine of getting stopped. The second time they spot the radar car, some motorists have even pulled over in front of the patrol car with no action taken by the officer.

Remember that the radar operator is one of the lone hunters, and that certain locations are like a watering hole where speeding motorists gather. You can always expect to find the hunter where the game is most plentiful.

CAN I WARN OTHER MOTORISTS ABOUT THE RADAR TRAP?

Yes, but you do run the slight risk of being arrested for your actions. In the past few years, motorists have been arrested under "Disorderly Conduct" codes for using their CB radio to warn other motorists, and arrested for "obstructing a police officer in the performance of his duties" by erecting a sign saying "Speed Trap Ahead." Both of these cases were dismissed or overturned by a higher court.

The classic warning of one truck driver to another was by flashing the truck's lights to indicate a radar trap ahead. This practice has been largely abandoned with the development and widespread use of CB radio. By warning other drivers about a radar trap, you do stand a very slight chance of being arrested by some overzealous trooper, but your case would probably be dismissed in court.

Some law enforcement agencies publicize the intended locations of radar units. They have gone so far as to publish the dates and locations of radar use in the newspapers to put all the residents on notice. Their philosophy is that the purpose of the radar unit is to improve traffic safety by slowing down the speeds at which vehicles travel in areas where a large number of accidents take place. They seem to feel that they can accomplish this purpose better by warning motorists than by surprising them with a citation.

DO THEY WORK RADAR IN TEAMS?

In the days of radar's infancy, radar was worked almost exclusively in teams. This was due to the limited mobility of the oversized radar units. This is still continued today, despite the low-cost and availability of versatile, modern radar units. Often these take the form of one or more motorcycle officers teamed with an officer in a radar equipped patrol car, or a two car team with the "chase" car positioned down the highway to flag over violators clocked by the radar unit. This has a real shortcoming in that the chase officer doesn't actually observe the radar violation, and by the time he stops the violator the original reading may have been cleared from the unit to allow the operator to clock another vehicle.

Today, radar teams are still found occasionally. One popular team is composed of one officer working speed and the other working drinking drivers. If a speeding motorist is drunk, the one officer handles the arrest, if only a citation is to be issued, the other officer handles it. Another common team is made up of two radar equipped patrol cars. Motorists often speed up immediately after passing a radar car, and may end up speeding directly into the radar beam of a second unit. Two officers can play leapfrog like this all day, each serving as a decoy for the other on every other ticket.

ARE THERE ANY LEGAL RESTRICTIONS ON WHERE RADAR CAN BE USED?

Yes, but radar restrictions vary widely from state to state and even between cities within the same state. Some areas require that a sign notifying motorists of the use of radar be posted in all areas where radar is to be used. If the signs are not posted in accordance with the law which requires them, the evidence obtained by the radar unit will not be allowed into your trial.

In California and several other states whose vehicle codes are modeled after California, evidence obtained by a radar unit is inadmissible in court if it was obtained through the use of a "speed trap." A speed trap is defined in the code as any section of highway with a posted speed limit (other than the state maximum) which has not been justified by a traffic engineering survey within five years before the citation was issued.

WHAT'S A TRAFFIC ENGINEERING SURVEY?

The traffic engineering survey is a survey to examine highway and traffic conditions in order to establish proper speeds in an area. This survey includes a measurement of the prevailing speeds that motorists are actually traveling at, a check on accident records for the area, and an examination of highway and roadside

Traffic engineers use radar to determine the safe speed in a traffic engineering survey.

conditions and potential hazards which may not be readily apparent to the driver.

Some of the conditions the traffic engineer must examine are the incline angles of curves, visibility and sight distances, the volume and movement of pedestrians, the proximity to schools, parks and the like, and the number and density of homes and businesses by the roadside.

The traffic engineer then takes a random sampling of the speeds of 100 or more cars. From this sampling he establishes the "critical speed" and the "pace." The critical speed is the speed at which 85% of the traffic is traveling, or below. If the critical speed for a section of roadway was 45 MPH, only 15% of the vehicles were traveling faster than 45 MPH, with the remainder right at 45 or less. This 85th percentile speed is taken as the speed nearest to the most safe and reasonable limit. For practical purposes, the 5 MPH increment at or immediately below the 85th percentile is the limit selected as a reasonable and enforceable speed limit.

The pace is the 10 MPH range of speeds at which the most motorists are traveling. The upper limit of this range is usually within 2 MPH of the 85th percentile speed. Usually, 70% of all speeds fall within the 10 MPH pace limits, and represent the average speed on the roadway.

To be kept current, these traffic engineering surveys should be taken at least every five years, or whenever conditions in an area change significantly from the time the survey was taken. The survey area should also be re-checked after a new speed limit has been posted in order to verify its appropriateness, relative effectiveness and general acceptance by motorists.

Of course, the requirements for a traffic engineering survey to establish the speed limit do not apply to roadways posted at the state maximum limit of 55 MPH.

IS THERE ANY WAY I CAN SPOT THE RADAR BEFORE THEY SPOT ME?

Yes, there are a few ways to spot the radar unit , some of the ways being more efficient than others. Probably the worst of all methods is the visual identification. You might spot that ominous antenna on the side window, or pick up on the flickering orange glow of the readout at night, but unless there's another

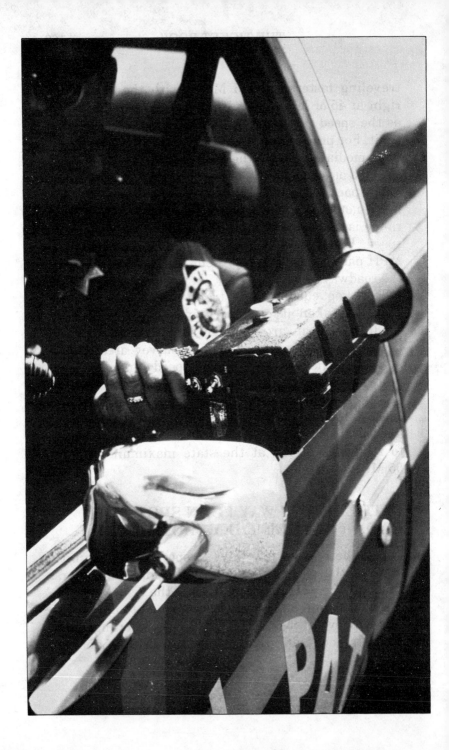

vehicle between you and the radar unit you'd better reach for your license.

Sometimes good Samaritans in the opposite lanes may flash their lights in warning, or wave and shout at you. It's best not to assume that this is a friendly native custom; they may be trying to tell you something. Watch the brakelights of cars ahead of you as they go into curves or over hills. If they start flashing, it's a good indication that something unpleasant is waiting for you on the other side.

Watch for signs by the side of the road as well. Many an officer working radar has suddenly found all the traffic flowing right at the speed limit, and then discovered a hastily constructed warning sign saying "Radar Trap Ahead" half a mile upstream. If you see a sign like this, believe it.

The best ways of spotting radar are the electronic means. CB radio is almost invaluable for this, with motorists continually reporting the location of radar units. The one minor drawback to this system is that the police are often equipped with CBs also, and use it to their advantage. One man with a radar unit and a CB can generate enough "smokey reports" to make himself appear like ten radar units.

The most efficient way of all to spot police radar is through the use of a radar detector. This little device will often tip you off well in advance of the radar being able to spot your car.

WHAT DO I DO WHEN I SPOT A RADAR UNIT?

When you spot a radar unit, the only thing to do is to

Using tricks like reading the radar in the side mirror make spotting a radar unit impossible without a radar detector.

slow down to the posted speed limit as quickly and safely as possible. With the speed and accuracy of modern radar, it may not do any good, but at least you won't lay awake nights wondering, "Maybe I should have slowed down?" If there's another car between you and the radar unit, you're probably safe. However, if you're way over the speed limit and you're the number one lead car, you might as well pull over behind the patrol car and hand him your license.

Most people react incorrectly to spotting a radar unit, and their actions are a dead giveaway to the alert officer. Hitting your brakes too hard is really obvious; as well as hearing the drop in the Doppler tone (if the radar unit is equipped with an audible tone) the officer can't help but notice if you lock up the tires and skid. Use of the emergency brake is as obvious as slamming on your regular brakes. Using the emergency brake may also cause uncontrollable skidding which is the last thing you want. Some people get on the brakes and then stay on them, right on past the officer and over the horizon in an attempt to fool the officer into thinking the car just has bright taillamps. This doesn't fool anybody and is just hell on your brakes. Others stay on the brakes until the moment they are alongside the officer, then release them and try to act innocent.

Some motorists go by with a silly grin and a wave, others extend an unfriendly middle finger. Neither is too effective.

Sometimes the occupants of a vehicle will change places with the driver just after they pass a radar unit, pulling an unlicensed or drinking driver from behind the wheel, hoping that the officer won't notice. Usually the front seat gymnastics are what attracts the officer's attention in the first place, and he has no problem at all following the exchange of places and picking the true driver after a short session of "Twenty Questions" with the occupants.

WHAT'S A RADAR DETECTOR?

A radar detector is the general term given to any of a number of electronic devices designed to warn motorists of radar traps. It is simply a radio receiver which is tuned to pick up the frequencies used by police radar. When the unit receives such a signal, it alerts the motorists by means of a buzzer or light.

The first radar detectors appeared shortly after the

Radar detectors are easy to use, simple to install and highly effective.

first radar surfaced on the highways. These were compact little battery-powered receivers which generally were clipped to the visor of the car. Although largely ineffective against modern radar (totally ineffective against K-band), many of these units are still in use today.

Over a million radar detectors have been sold in the United States in the last three years, as the battle of the microwaves escalates. Every advance that radar manufacturers make is eventually matched by advances in detector design, and detectors continue to be the most efficient method of spotting police radar.

WILL A RADAR DETECTOR SPOT VASCAR?

No, the true VASCAR system does not utilize radar or radio transmissions of any kind, and cannot be detected by a radar detector. There are persistent rumors about the awesome capabilities of some "Super VASCAR," but all such units are simply a sophisticated stopwatch depending on the officer's visual observations for its input information on your speed. Even the new moving radars which incorporate a function similar to VASCAR do not use radar in the "stopwatch" mode and cannot be detected when operated in that mode.

CAN A RADAR DETECTOR HELP ME?

Yes, but how much it will help you depends on the type of driving you do and the nature of the areas you are driving in. If you're a professional driver or salesman spending most of your time on the road, a radar detector is an absolute must. The more exposure you have to police radar, the more likely you are to benefit from a radar detector.

A radar detector is by no means a license to speed. It is intended to allow you to relax and enjoy your driving without suffering from "Ticket Tension." On the highway, especially on longer trips, it's very easy for one's speed to drift up 5 or 10 MPH. The radar detector will alert you to the presence of a radar unit ahead, and give you time to slow down to the legal limit. Of course, this is the entire purpose of operating the radar units, so your use of a detector is consistent with law enforcement's goal of slowing traffic.

ARE RADAR DETECTORS ILLEGAL?

No, a radar detector is nothing more than a radio receiver operating at frequencies above UHF television. As a radio receiver, it comes under the scope of the Federal Communications Act of 1934 which guarantees the rights of all citizens to free radio communications. Radio Free Europe and the Voice of America are examples of the philosophy and intent of the act.

All police and most public agencies are licensed to operate radio equipment by the federal government. Their rights in the area of the use and control of radio communications are limited solely to the terms and conditions of their license. The Act is very specific on this point; providing a one year jail term and a $10,000 fine for any licensee who willfully damages or interferes with another person's radio equipment.

No state has the right to search your car for a radar

detector, to confiscate or destroy your detector, or even to fine you for possession of a radar detector. These actions would constitute a felony under federal statutes, as well as violating your constitutional rights concerning freedom of communication, unreasonable search and seizure, due process of law, confiscation of property and cruel and unusual punishment. Not even the F.C.C. can take away your radar detector, because the congressional intent of the Communications Act of 1934 was to give you the right to receive any electromagnetic signal, even if it came from a police radar unit. Unless fundamental, major changes are made to the Act, there never can be a valid law against radar detectors.

There were several laws passed prior to the Communications Act which banned the use of police frequency radio receivers in vehicles. Most of these laws were repealed or removed from the books, but a handful were not. These were criminal laws (not a part of the Vehicle Code) which were designed to prevent bank robbers and the like from monitoring police activities. When the use of radar detectors became prevalent, local police officials in Michigan, Kentucky and New York dredged up these old laws and attempted to apply them to the radar detectors. Their actions were so obvious that the lower courts in their own states overturned the laws themselves.

Virginia is the only state which ever enacted and attempted to enforce a law specifically aimed at the prohibition of radar detectors. Convictions under this law were voided by their Supreme Court in June of 1978, but the exact status of the law is still unclear at this time. Most knowledgeable observers feel that the law is a dead issue since the police would be required to prove that the radar detector was being used at the time *and* would have to prove that it was being used for an unlawful purpose. Proving these two elements of the violation is virtually impossible in a legitimate court.

Since police officials do not always adhere to the law, it is possible that you may still receive a citation of some sort. Any attempt by the officer to seize your radar detector should be peaceably and courteously resisted, by locking your car and walking away from it. To seize the unit, the officer must now arrest you and secure a warrant (which you should honor). Ask him to read you your rights to make it official. At the very least, you will now have a civil rights case on record. Never permit him to take the unit and steal away into the night. The chances are very good that you won't ever see him or the unit again ... even in court.

The handling of cases involving citations or confiscations for the use of a radar detector are really beyond the scope of this book. If you have such an encounter, send a concise written narrative to the following address. They can usually provide legal guidance and whatever briefs may be required:

ELECTROLERT INC.
Legal Affairs Section
4949 South 25 A
Troy, Ohio 45373

CAN THE USE OF A RADAR DETECTOR HURT ME IN COURT?

It's very unlikely that the use of a radar detector would hurt your case. It's possible that you may be hassled more by an officer who spots your radar detector, particularly if your reactions were a little slow and you earned yourself a ticket. We know of several cases in which the radar detector actually helped a motorist win his case.

In one case, the motorist was able to show that his properly working radar detector (he had witnesses in the car with him) did not respond to the officer's radar unit and therefore the radar had not been actually operating. The case was immediately dismissed.

In a second case, a motorist's radar detector alerted him and the two other occupants of his car to a radar unit ahead. At the time they were in a 45 MPH zone. All of them carefully watched the speedometer, and they stayed just under the limit. The limit changed to 25 MPH and they reduced their speed accordingly. A few hundred feet down the road the motorist was stopped and cited for doing 44 MPH in a 25 MPH zone. Because his radar detector had alerted him to the radar, the motorist was able to show that he was aware of the radar ahead and had stayed right at the speed limit. This case was also immediately dismissed.

HOW DO THE POLICE FEEL ABOUT RADAR DETECTORS?

Frankly, most law enforcement agencies are against the use of radar detectors, with some agencies openly hostile about them. Radar detectors reduce the number of speeding tickets written by an agency, thus eliminating one of the most visible measurements of the efficiency of that agency. They seem to feel that there is something unfair about a motorist being warned that he is about to roll into a radar trap.

It's very frustrating and unnerving for the lone hunter to look back down the trail and suddenly find that he is the one being stalked by the game.

Some agencies have publicly swallowed the bitter pill and come out in favor of using radar detectors as part of an overall traffic safety program within the state. One experiment in Washington was based on the use of solar powered radar decoy units which broadcast continuously over a range of approximately two miles. These units were placed on sections of highway where a large number of accidents had occurred, and ensured that traffic was within the posted speed limits by triggering radar detectors within the broadcast range. Such unmanned "drone" units have since been outlawed by the .F.C.C.

CAN THE OFFICER TAKE AWAY MY RADAR DETECTOR?

According to U.S.C. Title 47 of the federal laws dealing with communications, the individual states do not have the power to confiscate or ban any radio receiver. Of course, the fact that federal law protects your use of a radar detector won't necessarily prevent him from doing so, and you may have to go to court to get your detector back. If the officer does take your detector, or piece of your property, insist that he give you a proper receipt with a full description of the unit, including the serial number. This is the only way that you can be sure to get your own property back again.

SHOULD I DISGUISE MY RADAR DETECTOR?

We don't advise that you attempt to hide your radar detector. There is nothing illegal about the possession and use of the unit, so there should be no reason to hide it. It has as valid a place in your car as your AM radio.

During the height of the radar detector abatement programs in Virginia and other states, cardboard replicas of radar detectors and Kleenex box disguises complete with tissues coming out the top were very popular and widely distributed. However, many officers automatically assume that anything you are trying to hide must be illegal, any attempt at deception will only rouse their curiosity and anger. This is evidenced by the fact that on at least two separate occasions, truckers were arrested and fined in the state of Virginia for possession of cardboard boxes resembling radar detectors. Both of these cases were eventually dismissed in court.

If you feel more comfortable with your radar detector disguised, go ahead and do it, it probably won't hurt. Perhaps a better alternative would be to use a radar detector with a detachable mount, so the unit could be easily removed.

CAN I HIDE MY DETECTOR?

It is next to impossible to hide a regular radar detector. The location of the radar detector is crucial to the

The tissue box was a popular disguise for radar detectors until the development of remote units that could be mounted under the hood.

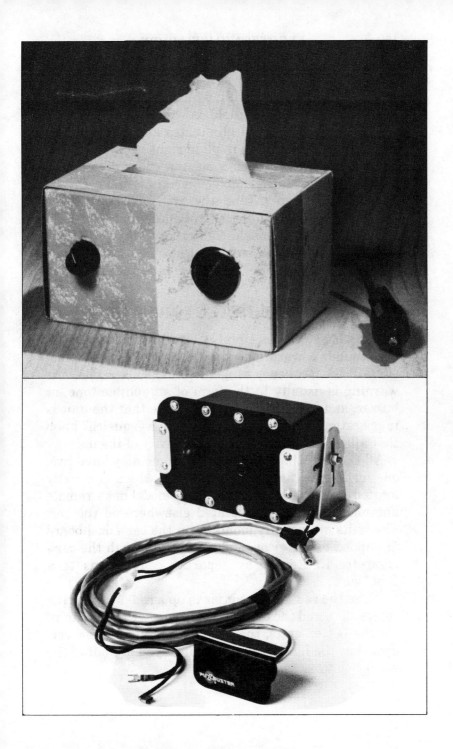

proper operation of the unit: while the radar beam will pass through the windshield, it will not pass through metal. That pretty well eliminates any mounting locations other than those in plain sight.

A recent innovation on some new radar detectors is the "remote mounting" detectors. These units can be effectively hidden behind the grill of a car, while a small, inconspicuous control panel is discretely mounted under the dash. As well as making the unit invisible to a passing smokey, these new radar detectors should prove to be highly resistant to theft.

HOW DO RADAR DETECTORS WORK?

A radar detector is simply a compact radio receiver that sounds a warning whenever it detects transmissions in the frequency range used by police radar. The warning is usually in the form of an audible tone, or buzzer, and usually a light to indicate that the unit is in operation. Most are equipped with a "squelch" knob that allows you to adjust the sensitivity of the unit.

All the units have an antenna (some may have two, one for X-band and one for K-band) which is usually located in the back of the unit. One model has a remote antenna which can be located elsewhere on the car. The units are usually mounted on the car's dashboard or clipped to the visor, and powered through the car's cigarette lighter or by separate connections to a "hot" wire.

When the radar detector picks up a radar signal, the relays click and the buzzer sounds along with the light. On the better units, the buzzer stops after a few seconds, but the light remains lit until you are out of the radar beam.

ARE RADAR DETECTORS ANY GOOD?

That depends on the make and model of detector. Presently there are more than 20 models of radar detectors on the market. The good ones are very good and can easily pay for themselves if you drive fast, or drive a great deal of the time, or drive fast a great deal of the time. The bad ones are counterproductive, and can lull you into a false sense of security that can cost you a good deal of money if you get burned.

The first radar detectors that came out on the market were cheap little battery powered units that were largely ineffective. These units gave radar detectors a bad image that still exists today. Indeed, some of the detectors today aren't much better. A recent survey of radar detectors in a national car magazine rated one widely sold unit as "Strictly a placebo," and another as "Smokey's little helper."

On the other hand, the good units are truly excellent, detecting radar with accuracy and a minimum of false alarms and tipping off the motorist well enough in advance to give plenty of time to slow down.

CAN THEY JAM MY RADAR DETECTOR?

There's probably been more than one officer who has told a motorist he was going to jam their radar detector, but because of the size and shape of the units there are limited physiological possibilities.

However, it is possible to electronically jam a radar detector. Jamming does not mask a true radar signal from the unit, but only triggers the unit with a false signal. This is done with conventional radar units in a number of ways.

We've already mentioned the use of solar-powered decoy units placed in strategic locations along highways to slow traffic in areas where there are a large number of accidents. These may also be used in other areas, solely to aggravate radar detector users. A motorist whose radar detector is continuously triggered by a decoy may eventually ignore the warning and fall directly into a real radar trap.

The officer working either a stationary or moving radar unit may simply leave his unit "on" wherever he goes. Thus he can effectively "jam" any detectors within range, even though he may not be on the prowl for speeders.

Some departments have made use of their old radar equipment for jamming detectors. The outmoded equipment is set up on supervisory cars and even trucks, broadcasting continuously and jamming every detector they encounter. Some agencies have even mounted their old radar units on aircraft, effectively jamming detectors on all roads they fly over.

WHAT'S THE EFFECTIVE RANGE OF A RADAR DETECTOR?

Once again, this depends on how good the unit is. The average radar unit transmits a signal of about one-tenth of a watt. The average radar detector will identify a signal of one millionth of a watt. Of course, not all of the radar signal is directed at the detector, and the sensitivity of the detector varies with the squelch setting.

Under ideal conditions, the range of the better radar detectors is over three miles, almost ten times the

The limitation of Radar Range

normal working range of police radar. While the radar unit works on a line-of-sight principle, and can't "see" around corners or over hills, a good detector is capable of picking up the scattered signal reflecting off the roadway, bridges and other vehicles ahead of you. Any conditions which tend to limit the range of the radar detector will tend to effect the radar unit even more severely; so the effective range of your detector is almost always greater than the range of the radar unit.

HOW MUCH WARNING WILL MY RADAR DETECTOR GIVE ME?

When dealing with radar units equipped with a "hold" or "detector defeat" mode which control the radar broadcast, or when dealing with trigger activated radar-guns, you may have no warning at all. Your detector will light up just in time to say "Surprise! You're busted!" Your only hope with these types of units is that the officer will clock another motorist ahead of you and his beam will trigger your detector when he does.

Moving radar can also result in a really minimal warning. If the patrol car is cruising at 55 MPH while you're doing 70 MPH, you're approaching a ticket at over 125 MPH and your reactions have to be pretty sharp to avoid being clocked.

Stationary radar gives you the best warning of all, and should give you enough time to slow down to a legal speed.

CAN RADAR DETECTORS PICK UP ALL RADAR FREQUENCIES?

No, many of the radar detectors still being marketed will only receive X-band radars. Others are capable of detecting both X and K-band, but are insensitive to radar which has been "tweaked" out of normal operating frequencies and may be broadcasting somewhere in-between.

The best choice is a radar detector which scans across all of the frequencies. One such unit continuously sweeps from 9.4 Gigahertz to 25.0 Gigahertz. None of the units on the market today will pick up the old S-band radar, but few of these cumbersome police radar units are still in use today.

ARE THERE ANY "DETECTOR PROOF" RADARS?

No, any radar transmission within the authorized police spectrum can be detected by modern radar detectors. However, no detector is capable of detecting a radar unit which isn't broadcasting. So-called "Detector Proof" radars are simply equipped with an on-and-off switch on the antenna which allows the operator to broadcast only when he has a target in sight. Many officers find this mode to be cumbersome and awkward to use, particularly with the relatively small percentage of radar detector equipped vehicles on the highway today. About the only time this mode is used, is when the officer is specifically hunting truckers, who are almost always equipped with detectors.

The original detector proof radar is the old "Pie Pan" trick. The officer simply holds a tin plate in front of the antenna of any radar unit, blocking the radar transmission until the target is in sight. Of course, once the officer allows the unit to broadcast, the cat is out of the bag for any radar detector equipped vehicles following the lead target.

DO RADAR DETECTORS GIVE FALSE ALARMS?

Yes, false alarms are common. False triggering can be caused by airport radar, telephone microwave links, military radar, nearby CB units, TV transmitters and more than 25 other users of the same frequency spectrum.

The ability to reject these signals while retaining its

sensitivity to police radar is one of the most important factors to consider when selecting a radar detector. Detectors with metal cases provide more shielding for the unit than those with plastic cases, and most units are equipped with filters of some kind either within the unit itself or at the power connection into the cigarette lighter. With the wide spectrum of microwave frequencies a unit may be sweeping, false alarms are virtually impossible to eliminate.

HOW MANY TYPES OF RADAR DETECTORS ARE THERE?

There are literally dozens of different models of radar detectors on the market today, manufactured by many different companies. Some of these manufacturers have been in business for many years and are well-established, reputable firms. Others are fly-by-night operations which will be formed and will disappear again before this book is published. The models range from truly creative, original designs to blatant copies of other manufacturer's products, but all of the units fall into one of three basic types.

The most common type of radar detector today is the single channel detector which operates on one pre-set frequency, ignoring all other signals. The first radar detectors to appear on the market were single channel units set to receive on the S-band, while today X-band units have become the most popular.

With the recent introduction of K-band radar, the detector manufacturers responded to the challenge and began producing dual channel units capable of receiving both X and K-band radar. These units are also referred to as "stereodyne" or "heterodyne" and often use two separate antennas for the two frequencies. Many of these units are excellent, but poorly designed ones may offer superior detection on one of the frequencies while being totally inadequate on the other. The major drawback with any single or dual channel unit is its insensitivity to radar units that may be operating slightly off frequency.

This drawback, compounded by the radar technician's occasional "tweaking" of the radar units, led to the development of the scanning type detector. These units rapidly scan back and forth across the limits of the entire authorized radar spectrum, thus picking up any radar operating on or near the normal broadcast frequencies. The scanning detectors are undoubtedly the most sophisticated of the radar detectors, but may give a higher number of false alarms by picking up non-radar transmissions on the frequencies it scans in-between the normal police operating bands.

ARE THEY ALL ALIKE?

No, there's a world of difference between the effectiveness, efficiency, esthetics and prices of the different radar detectors on the market.

Some detectors are very sensitive to radar transmission, but don't notify the driver because the lamp is washed out by the sun or the buzzer simply isn't loud enough. Other units can make you jump right out of your seat when they are triggered, but are so insensitive they may not give you a chance to slow down.

The esthetics of the unit vary widely, and usually have little or no relation to the quality of the electronics inside. Today's units range in appearance from black boxes with a krinkle finish, to Flash Gordon like structures of chrome with Lucite rods, and may even incorporate panels of imitation walnut-burl. Some of the worst-looking units may be a far more effective detector than a beautifully packaged unit that doesn't work worth a damn.

When selecting a radar detector, get all of the information you can about the unit. Talk to your detector-equipped friends and some professional drivers; salesmen and truck drivers who are using detectors on a regular basis. Find out which units they are using, and what they like or dislike about the unit you are thinking about buying. The radar detector represents a substantial investment; and the wrong choice may cost you your license.

A radar detector can be bought today for as low as $35 or as high as $175. Single channel detectors are relatively inexpensive, while the dual channel and scanning models are at the upper end of the scale. The price will also vary with where you purchase the unit; it pays to shop around.

WHERE CAN I BUY ONE?

Radar detectors are carried by most automotive parts and equipment stores, as well as electronics stores specializing in C.B. radios and the like, and in some major department stores. Most detectors are also offered directly from the manufacturer, and advertised in the automotive oriented magazines. There are also a number of mail-order and catalogue houses which are distributing detectors. Sometimes the ads are ambiguous about the exact brand being offered, so be certain that the unit is truly the model that you have researched and decided on before ordering the unit.

Buying a used radar detector from a "buddy" may not be a good investment at all. He may already be doing 5 to Life for speeding. If he's really satisfied with his unit, you couldn't buy it from him under any conditions. If someone is unloading a radar detector at a bargain price, there's probably a reason for it.

WHAT'S THE BEST RADAR DETECTOR I CAN BUY?

That would be almost impossible to say, because the technology is changing so rapidly in the field of radar

In overall effectiveness, the best radar detector available today.

and radar detection. We've done a tremendous amount of research and picked one unit we feel is consistently outstanding in its effectiveness and quality. It was a difficult choice, as there are a number of good units and new ones are being introduced on an almost daily basis, but we've selected one which we feel is definitely one of the best. That unit is the Fuzzbuster II® manufactured by Electrolert Inc., of Troy, Ohio.

The Fuzzbuster II® is a scanning detector that sweeps the entire spectrum of police radar, and consistently demonstrates good sensitivity, offering plenty of warning. The unit is also unusual in that a kit is available that permits mounting behind the grill or under the bumper to help discourage theft. While this unit may be a little more expensive than some of its competitors, it is well worth the investment.

WHAT'S VASCAR?

The term "VASCAR" is an acronym (and a trade name for a particular manufacturer's unit) for the phrase "Visual Average Speed Computer And Recorder." VASCAR is merely a very simple time and distance computer. By having the officer measure the time it takes for your vehicle to travel a measured distance, and by feeding that information into the VASCAR unit, the computer determines just how fast you had to be going to cover that distance in the amount of time you did. VASCAR is not a radar device, and depends entirely on the officer observing your vehicle and entering the information into the unit. It amounts to nothing more than a very sophisticated stopwatch.

The VASCAR unit consists of two parts, a control head and a floor mounted computer.

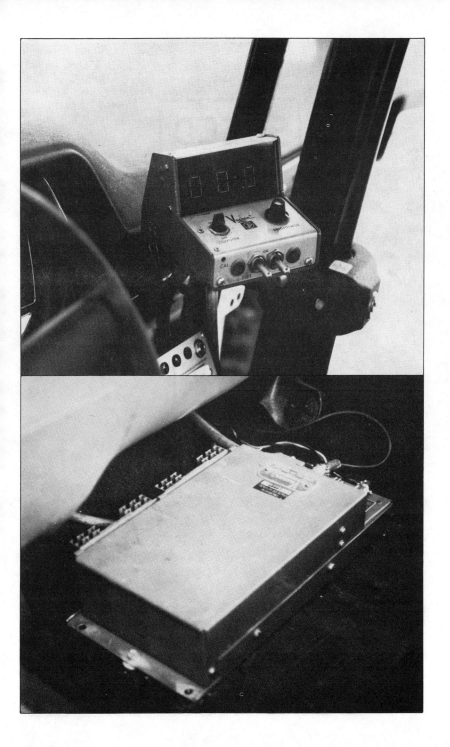

IS VASCAR USED IN EVERY STATE?

No, but it is being used in over 26 states today. There are some states in which VASCAR cannot be used under the existing laws. Typical of these states is California, in which the evidence obtained through the use or maintenance of a "Speed Trap" cannot be used against you in court. One of the definitions of a Speed Trap as defined in the vehicle code is, "A particular section of highway measured as to distance . . . in order that the speed of a vehicle may be calculated by securing the time it takes the vehicle to travel the known distance." Because VASCAR works on the principle of measuring a vehicle's speed over a measured distance, it simply cannot be used in any state with a law such as California's.

Even in those states where VASCAR is used, it may not be in service with every law enforcement agency within that state. VASCAR is used by state police and highway patrols far more than by municipal police, because it is much more effective at highway distances, visibilities and speeds than in the city. Also, some local county or city ordinances may forbid the use of VASCAR.

HOW DOES VASCAR WORK?

The computation of speed by the VASCAR unit is simply a matter of dividing distance by time. The operator has two switches on the unit, one marked "Time" and the other marked "Distance." The distance used in computing your speed is measured by the patrol car through the speedometer cable, and may be

Every patrol car in this state is equipped with both VASCAR and radar, but they only warn you about the VASCAR.

measured at any time before or after the violator is clocked.

In clocking a violator which the officer is following on the highway, the officer flips on the Time switch as the speeder passes a selected point, such as a signpost, bridge abutment, painted line or crack in the asphalt, and flips the switch off when the speeder passes a second selected point. When the patrol car hits the first mark, the officer turns on the Distance switch, and switches it off as he crosses the second point.

The computer then calculates the average speed of the violator to the nearest tenth of a mile per hour, and displays it on numitron tubes in the control module. The reading remains there as "evidence," until the reset button is used to clear the computer for the next reading.

The VASCAR operator doesn't have to be following the speeder, he doesn't even have to be moving. It is a relatively simple matter to clock violators behind the patrol car by observing in the mirror when they pass over the appropriate distance landmarks. Also, the officer may drive across the two selected points, storing the information in his VASCAR computer and then hide well off the highway to clock speeders as they pass over the same points. If the officer stops alongside the highway, the patrol car itself can be used as the second distance point and he can clock your vehicle at precisely the moment you pass his location.

Anytime you spot a patrol car, particularly one parked by the roadside a short distance beyond a major landmark such as a bridge or a sign, you should immediately check your speed and hit the brakes. If he is using VASCAR on a pre-measured section of highway

VASCAR's controls are simple to operate. A typical VASCAR trap, with the patrol car a short distance beyond an easily seen landmark.

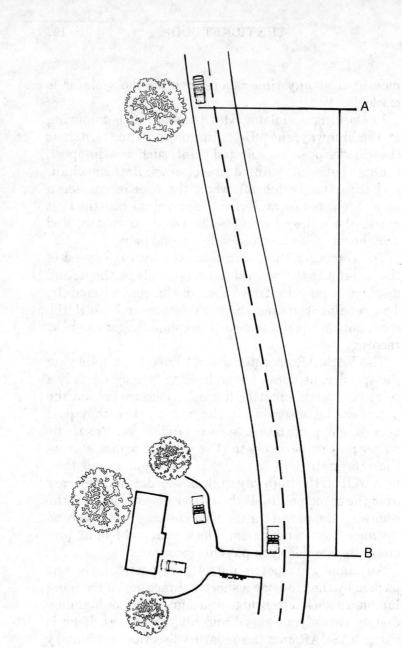

The Principle of VASCAR

Here's how VASCAR works:

1. *The patrol car reaches landmark "A," a roadside tree. The officer then switches "On" the Distance Switch and the VASCAR unit begins measuring the distance through the odometer cable.*

2. *The patrol car reaches landmark "B," the side road, and the officer turns the Distance Switch to "Off." This now locks the distance the patrol car traveled into the VASCAR computer.*

3. *The officer may either park his patrol car at the side of the road, and use the car itself as landmark "B," or pull off the highway to a location in which he can observe both landmarks.*

4. *The target vehicle passes landmark "A" and the officer turns the Time Switch to "On." The VAS-CAR unit begins timing the target.*

5. *The target vehicle passes landmark "B" and the officer turns the Time Switch to "Off." The VAS-CAR unit then has the time the target took to travel an already known distance, and computes and displays the speed of the target in miles-per-hour.*

which you enter at 70 MPH, but you slow to 40 MPH or less before you hit the end point, you may be able to lower your average speed through the two points to an acceptable and safe 55 MPH. Your reactions have to be fast, though, because VASCAR can use two reference points as little as one tenth of a mile apart.

Remember that the VASCAR unit at one time or another has to actually roll over the same section of highway as your car in order for the unit to get an accurate measurement of the distance through the patrol car's speedometer cable. The officer cannot estimate the distance visually and input that distance into the computer.

VASCAR's main fault lies in the fact that it depends entirely on the officer's observations and his input to the computer to determine your speed.

DOES VASCAR HAVE TO BE CALIBRATED?

Yes, VASCAR is calibrated daily by the officers in most agencies, and in the agency's shop at regular intervals determined by them. This calibration is necessary because the tire size and tread wear on the patrol car may change, and all of these may have an effect on the input through the speedometer cable. The VASCAR unit is adjusted through the use of a small, recessed screw setting located on the front panel of the unit.

The officer's daily calibration is conducted by simply clocking the patrol car itself over a selected distance, and comparing the VASCAR's reading to the certified speedometer.

The agency's periodic calibration may incorporate the use of a dynamometer in the shops, or the use of a radar unit to compare against the VASCAR's reading.

HOW MUCH DOES A VASCAR UNIT COST?

A VASCAR unit costs about $900 for the complete package. This is composed of the control head which is usually mounted on the dashboard or the transmission hump, the computer which is mounted on the floor of the patrol car underneath the seats, and an adapter which attaches to the patrol car's speedometer cable.

CAN I ASK THE OFFICER TO EXPLAIN HIS VASCAR TO ME?

Yes, and usually the officer will honor your request and may even demonstrate the unit to you. A brief but convincing explanation of VASCAR's operation is an important part of the officer's "selling" the ticket to you, making sure that you believe your were guilty of the offense so you won't try to challenge the validity of the speed estimate in court.

Although it may be part of a law enforcement agency's policy to have the officer explain their VASCAR to motorists, there is no legal requirement for him to do so.

DOES HE HAVE TO SHOW ME MY SPEED?

No, but he will probably show it to you if you ask him, or if you deny that you were speeding and question what he writes on the ticket. Showing you the speed measured on the VASCAR unit can be another important part of selling you the ticket, but there is nothing which requires the officer to do so. Of course, his refusal to show you your speed on the VASCAR unit may raise doubts in court as to whether the officer actually clocked you at all.

DO THE COURTS ACCEPT A VASCAR READING ALONE AS EVIDENCE?

There are some courts which have a blanket acceptance of all VASCAR readings with no other substantiation of your speed. However, many courts are beginning to seriously question VASCAR evidence, and have begun to reject cases where the speed of the violator is based solely on a VASCAR reading.

CAN THE OFFICER CHEAT USING VASCAR?

Yes, a dishonest officer could use a VASCAR unit to obtain false readings. As with radar, you have to take the officer's integrity for granted, because if he does cheat while using VASCAR, you will probably never be aware of it. VASCAR depends on human input for computing speed. If that input is in error, the readout will be in error.

One way the unscrupulous officer might cheat, is by using the "Short Circuit." To do this, he simply closes the distance switch on his VASCAR unit a short distance *after* he actually passes the second point he uses as a reference point to clock your vehicle with. This means that you are traveling a shorter distance in the same amount of time than the distance actually measured by the patrol car when it passed over the same route. A variation of the Short Circuit is when the officer is a little premature on the Time switch, giving you a much shorter time through the properly measured distance and indicating a much higher speed to the computer.

Another method of cheating, identical to one used with radar, is "Left-overs." To serve you up some Left-overs, the officer simply leaves in the speed of a previous violator without resetting the unit, and then claims that the speed shown is the one he clocked your vehicle with. The "Left-over" reading need not even be from another violator. Because the computer depends on the officer flipping the switches based on his observations, an unethical officer could sit by the side of the road and conjure up any speed he chose, simply by playing with the switches.

IS VASCAR AS ACCURATE AS RADAR?

Yes, VASCAR is capable of a high degree of accuracy when properly used. Most agencies using VASCAR require extensive training and testing of the officer's use of VASCAR, with separate certifications required for daytime and nighttime usage. The final exam for the officer consists of repeatedly clocking another police car under various conditions. The VASCAR student's readings are checked against a radar unit and the certified speedometer, and must be consistently accurate to within three tenths of a mile per hour to be qualified as a VASCAR operator.

A typical VASCAR moving radar combination can be easily operated simultaneously by one officer.

CAN THE OFFICER WORK WITH BOTH VASCAR AND RADAR AT THE SAME TIME?

It's not all that uncommon for a patrol car to be equipped with both systems, and for the two systems to be used at the same time. Typically, an agency which has been equipped with VASCAR in the past and is in the process of converting over to a moving radar system ends up with both units in the patrol car until the VASCAR units break down or are otherwise pulled out of service.

The officer works VASCAR on cars ahead and behind him in his own lane, while working the moving radar on traffic in the opposite lanes. He doesn't have to pay much attention to the radar, as it usually has a tone to alert him to any speed in excess of the limit. An officer who consistently works VASCAR only has to look at the readout when he thinks he has a good violation. Tripping the appropriate switches becomes almost automatic.

A patrol car equipped with both VASCAR and radar can be devastating on the highway, by working traffic in two directions whether moving or stationary. Of course, this is often a case of overkill, as he can generally spot more violators than he could ever hope to catch.

WHAT ARE THE LATEST ADVANCES IN SPEED DETECTION TECHNOLOGY?

The latest advances on the highways today are pretty much limited to radar and VASCAR, and the different variations and combinations that have been developed by the radar manufacturers.

It's just about impossible to determine what may lay ahead in the future, but undoubtedly technological advances will occur and spin-offs from space and military programs will be incorporated into law enforcement traffic control. Work is already being done under military contracts which use lasers and other devices for tracking and determining velocities, and someday these electronic marvels may appear on the highway, strapped to the side of a patrol car to catch another "enemy," the speed violator.

LOOKING AT WHAT YOU GOT
An evaluation of your citation. . . . .

IS THIS A WARNING OR A TICKET?

Warnings often say in large letters, "Traffic Warning," right at the top of the form. There are several types of warnings, verbal warnings (sometimes referred to as 'Holler Stops') where the officer just chews you out or "hollers" at you for your actions; and written warnings which may be parking, equipment or moving violations. Parking and moving warnings usually require no action on your part, although some officers will tell you that receiving more than a given number will cause you to turn into a frog or tell you some other fairy tale to keep you on your best behavior.

Equipment warnings require you to have the violation corrected and certified within a given period of time, usually 15 days. This type of warning is nothing to laugh at, as it may result in an actual ticket if uncorrected. Equipment warnings often have a provision for mailing in the form after it has been corrected. Make sure whether the officer is writing you a ticket or a warning before you bad-mouth him; as many a warning has been ripped up and turned into a citation due to a bad attitude on the part of the motorist.

Some motorists will beg the officer, "Oh, p-l-e-a-s-e, can't you give me a warning?" At that point, some officers have been known to stop writing, stare the driver in the eye and say, "Every time I see you speed I'm going to give you a ticket," and then continue writing the citation. The motorist asked for a warning, but probably didn't expect that kind.

Officers have a quota on the number of warnings they issue similar to the ticket quota. If they issue too few warnings as compared to the number of citations, it is an indication that he's being too hard on drivers; if

The differences between a citation (left) and a warning (right) are subtle but important.

he issues too many, he's being too soft. The major difference between a warning and a ticket is that the ticket will require you to appear in court and the warning will not.

WILL THE WARNING APPEAR ON MY RECORD?

No, warnings are not reported to the Department of Motor Vehicles. However, the issuing agency will keep a copy of the warning in their records for future reference in criminal investigations. Unless you picked up your warning speeding away from the scene of a crime, you needn't worry about the other copy on file with the agency.

NOTICE TO APPEAR

No. Y018802

DATE		TIME		DAY OF WEEK	
	19			M	

NAME (FIRST, MIDDLE, LAST)

RESIDENCE ADDRESS — CITY

BUSINESS ADDRESS — CITY

DRIVERS LICENSE NO.			STATE		CLASS	BIRTHDATE

SEX	HAIR	EYES	HEIGHT	WEIGHT	OTHER DES.
M F					

VEHICLE LICENSE NO.		STATE	PASSENGERS
			M F

YEAR OF VEH.	MAKE		BODY STYLE	COLOR

REGISTERED OWNER OR LESSEE

ADDRESS OF OWNER OR LESSEE

VIOLATION(S)	CODE	SECTION	DESCRIPTION	☐ INFRACTION
				☐ BOOKING REQUIRED

APPROX. SPEED	PF/MAX SPEED	VEH. SPD. LMT.	SAFE SPD.	ACCIDENT YES ☐ NO ☐

LOCATION OF VIOLATION(S)

BUS. ☐   RES. ☐   RURAL ☐   SCHL. ☐   FRWY. ☐

WEATHER	TRAFFIC			CONDITION OF ROAD				NO. OF LANES
RAIN FOG	HEAVY	MED	LIGHT	NARROW	CURVE	HILL	SLIPPERY	

HAZARD TO:	PED. ☐	VEH. ☐	NEAR ACCIDENT ☐	SIGNAL GIVEN YES ☐ NO ☐

☐ OFFENSE(S) NOT COMMITTED IN MY PRESENCE, CERTIFIED ON INFORMATION AND BELIEF.

I CERTIFY UNDER PENALTY OF PERJURY THAT THE FOREGOING IS TRUE AND CORRECT, EXECUTED ON THE DATE SHOWN ABOVE AT   I.D. NO.

ISSUING OFFICER _____ CALIF.
PLACE

NAME OF ARRESTING OFFICER, IF DIFFERENT FROM ABOVE	SERIAL NO.	VACATION

WITHOUT ADMITTING GUILT, I PROMISE TO APPEAR AT THE TIME AND PLACE INDICATED BELOW

X SIGNATURE

BEFORE THE JUDGE OF THE COURT AT THE

☐ JUVENILE COURT ☐ SOUTH BAY MUNI.	TIME	MONTH	DAY	YEAR
ADDRESS:	A.M. P.M.			

FORM APPROVED BY THE JUDICIAL COUNCIL OF CALIFORNIA
REV. 1-1-76 V.C. 40500(B) P.C. 853.9

PD 535 (3-76)

COURT'S COPY

ARE ALL TICKET FORMS THE SAME?

No, they vary from area to area in color, size and the information that appears on the citation. Most state vehicle codes require specific information that *must* appear on all citation forms throughout that state, and while this provides for some standardization within the state, the local agencies remain free to add frills and additional information.

All ticket forms will include your name, address, vehicle description and driver's license number, places for both your and the officer's signature and a brief description of the vehicle code section which you were charged with violating. Ticket forms vary in size from small, multi-part forms that are imprinted with a credit-card type license, to an 8½" x 11" letter-size form.

One officer who works for an agency using this over-size form says that more than one motorist has asked if the extra-large form was provided to allow him to write with his crayons. The size of the form will not affect the size of the fine or the seriousness of your violation, even if it is written in crayon.

WHAT'S A CITATION?

Officially, a citation is a written promise by you to appear in court for an alleged violation on a specific date and time, in lieu of being arrested by the officer. In reality, this is a vastly shortened form which combines an arrest report for your infraction or misdemeanor violation of the vehicle code, and a booking and release slip. Technically, your ticket represents an arrest, and the officer is releasing you from his custody

Tickets vary from region to region, but all contain the same basic information.

on the promise that you will appear in court to face the charges. In many agencies, citations are referred to as "arrests" or "pinches."

IS THERE A DIFFERENCE BETWEEN A TICKET AND A CITATION?

No, whether you call it an arrest, a pinch, a coupon, greenstamp, or invitation; it all means that you got nailed and have an upcoming appearance in court.

The various terms for tickets will vary from region to region, depending where you are and who you're talking to on the C.B. A ticket is a citation and a citation is a ticket. As the poet-playwright William Shakespeare put it, "A rose by any other name would smell so sweet." Well, a ticket by any other name tastes just as sour.

WHAT'S AN INFRACTION?

An infraction is when you break a law (not a leg) for which you cannot be punished with a jail sentence. Many traffic violations fall under this category, and are punishable only by fine, or by suspending or revoking your driver's license. An infraction isn't something you can ignore, however, as you can still go to jail for failure to appear (a misdemeanor) if you don't show up in court.

WHAT'S A MISDEMEANOR?

A misdemeanor is a violation of the law for which you can be punished by up to a year in jail. Only the most serious offenses of the vehicle code fall under the misdemeanor category; reckless driving, driving under the influence of alcohol or drugs, non-injury hit-and-run, exhibition of speed and the like. Driving offenses which result in death or injury to any person are usually felonies, punishable by a year or more in prison.

CAN I GET A TICKET FOR A FELONY?

No, a conviction for a felony requires a trip to "the big house." However, with today's apparent leniency in the court system, many officers joke about citing felons, issuing tickets to murderers and the like on their promise to appear. Some traffic officers complain that when they arrest a felony suspect, it doesn't appear on their monthly activity recap (which shows their standing in the ticket race). These officers will often write the felon a ticket for the traffic violation for which he was originally stopped, and tuck it into his pocket as they throw him into the slammer.

WHAT DID HE SAY I DID WRONG?

Usually, the law which he says you violated will appear in a very abbreviated form somewhere on the citation. He will usually give you an adequate verbal description when he writes the ticket, such as "Sir, I clocked you at 15 miles above the posted speed limit as I paced you for the last 5 miles," or "I observed you making an illegal left turn right underneath that "No Left Turn" sign at the last corner." What actually appears on the description line on the citation is "Speed," "Violation of Signs" or even "Signs."

This ticket describes the violation both by Vehicle Code section and with an explanation.

In addition to the description, somewhere on the citation will appear a vehicle code or traffic code section number. This number indicates the section or the specific law the officer claims you were violating.

HOW DO I KNOW IF I WAS WRONG?

As a general rule for determining the legality of your traffic actions, "If it's rude, it's illegal." Many traffic officers use this rule as a criteria for stopping motorists, and then look up the appropriate "rude" section in the vehicle code. If your driving style is sufficiently rude to cause other motorists to shout vile obscenities in your direction and gesture wildly with their middle fingers, there's a good chance you may have broken the law. If you were caught while speeding, it took only a quick, sickening peek at your speedometer to let you know why you were stopped. Of course, merely being a 'polite' driver still won't keep you from breaking any of the traffic laws.

WHAT IF I DIDN'T KNOW IT WAS WRONG?

Most states have the philosophy that anyone who takes the privilege of driving also assumes the responsibility of obeying all of that state's traffic laws. This doesn't seem all that difficult as you look over the driver's pamphlet with its dozen or so basic traffic laws and take the written test with its 50 or less questions. It's not until you begin trying to track down your

Some state's vehicle laws fill hundreds and hundreds of pages.

traffic violation that you come to the realization that there are thousands upon thousands of traffic laws in the state code, and these don't even begin to take into account the county and city traffic ordinances.

If you didn't know it was wrong, that won't get you out of your traffic ticket. As many judges will routinely tell you, "Ignorance of the law is no excuse."

WHAT DETERMINES IF MY ACTIONS WERE ILLEGAL?

Generally, if your action was in volation of a specific section of a vehicle code, it was illegal. This section could be out of your state's vehicle or traffic code, from a county or city ordinance or even a violation of a "temporary" law such as the order of a traffic officer. If an officer points at your car and then points to your right, your lane just turned into a "Right Turn Only" lane and his instructions carry the force of the law.

WHAT IS A "VEHICLE CODE"?

A "Vehicle Code" or "Traffic Code" is the portion of a state's laws which deal with the use, sale and registration of motor vehicles (in some states the code may cover boats and other forms of transportation also). Typically, these laws are carefully organized by subject into chapters and specific sections. When they talk about "throwing the book at you," this is the book they usually mean.

WHAT'S A VEHICLE CODE SECTION?

A vehicle code section is that particular section of the motor vehicle laws of your state, which deal with a particular action, movement on a highway, or a particular piece of required equipment. These sections are often divided into two or more parts, for instance, the portion of the code dealing with turns might cover left and right turns separately, in different parts of the same section.

HOW DO I FIND OUT WHAT THE VEHICLE CODE SECTION REALLY SAYS?

First, get a copy of your state's vehicle code. Then,

locate the vehicle code section (and sub-section, if given, usually written in the description section of your citation) and look it up in the vehicle code. Carefully read through all of the section with the intent of comparing it to your violation. You may find it necessary to read several surrounding sections to put your section in proper context. Definitions of specific terms used in such codes (like highway and right-of-way) are usually precisely defined in some portion of your state's vehicle code.

HOW DO I GET A COPY OF THE VEHICLE CODE?

This is a question that is all too seldom asked. We spent months cutting through all the red tape to locate this information and probably underwrote Ma Bell's operations for the next year with our long distance charges. With each state we called, it was almost like playing "Twenty Questions" as various officials passed the buck until someone dusted off the file cabinets and came up with the information. Usually these codes are only in demand by police officers, prosecutors and judges; many of the states we called seemed genuinely surprised that anyone had the good sense to ask about how a citizen could obtain a copy of their vehicle code.

We've made it altogether too easy for you, as we have listed by state the correct title, the address from which it can be ordered, the number of pages, type of binding and the cost to you (prices are up-to-date and include postage as of this writing, but are subject to change. Most states prefer money orders as the method of payment). Also given is a phone number you can call for more information on obtaining each state's vehicle code book. If you can't afford your state's vehicle code, write to them and ask about your section. They'll usually send you a xerox copy. If you don't have the time to wait for the mail, your local library will surely have a copy for you to look through. This may be an especially useful source if you are the type of person that files your income-tax return on April 15th and waited until the day of your trial to prepare your defense.

When writing for a copy of your state's Vehicle Code, be sure to mention the exact title of the book and ask specifically for the latest edition and supplements. Some of these codes haven't been revised in over 10 years, and the supplements have more pages than the original book. Also be sure to include your return address, so they know where to ship the document.

DEPARTMENT OF MOTOR VEHICLES LIST

ALABAMA DEPARTMENT OF PUBLIC SAFETY
Accounting Unit
P.O. Box 1511
Montgomery, Alabama 36130
(205) 832-5260
Alabama Motor Vehicle and Traffic Code
$3.50, 250 pages, Loose-leaf

ALASKA DEPARTMENT OF PUBLIC SAFETY
Division of Motor Vehicles
P.O. Box 6188 Annex
Anchorage, Alaska 99502
Alaska Motor Vehicle Laws
No charge, 350 pages, Loose-leaf

ARIZONA DEPARTMENT OF TRANSPORTATION
Directives and Publications Section
206 S. 17th Avenue

Phoenix, Arizona 85007
(602) 261-7325
Transportation Laws of Arizona
$3.00, 437 pages, Soft-bound

**ARKANSAS DEPARTMENT OF FINANCE AND
    ADMINISTRATION**
Motor Vehicle Division
P.O. Box 1272
Little Rock, Arkansas 72203
(501) 371-1885
*Arkansas Motor Vehicle Laws and State Highway Commission
    Regulations*
$1.00, 329 pages, Soft-bound

CALIFORNIA DEPARTMENT OF MOTOR VEHICLES
Division of Administration
P.O. Box 1828
Sacramento, California 95809
(916) 445-6031
California Vehicle Code
$1.00, 824 pages, Soft-bound

COLORADO DEPARTMENT OF REVENUE
Motor Vehicle Division
140 West Sixth Avenue
Denver, Colorado 80204
(303) 839-3757
Colorado Motor Vehicle Laws
$4.00, 382 pages, Loose-leaf

CONNECTICUT DEPARTMENT OF MOTOR VEHICLES
Public Relations Office
60 State Street
Wethersfield, Connecticut 06109
(203) 566-4511
Connecticut Motor Vehicle Laws
No charge, 94 pages, Hard-bound

DELAWARE DIVISION OF MOTOR VEHICLES
P.O. Box 698
Dover, Delaware 19901
(302) 678-4421

Motor Vehicle Laws of the State of Delaware—Title 21 Code Book
$25.00, 245 pages, Loose-leaf

**DISTRICT OF COLUMBIA DEPARTMENT OF LICENSE
    INVESTIGATIONS & INSPECTIONS**
Publications Section
Room 105
D.C. Permit Branch
614 "H" Street, N.W.
Washington, D.C. 20001
(202) 629-3957
Motor Vehicle Regulations of the District of Columbia, Title 32
$4.00, 445 pages, Loose-leaf

FLORIDA HIGHWAY PATROL
Bureau of Records & Training
Niel Kirkman Building
Tallahassee, Florida 32301
(904) 488-7134
Florida Traffic Laws Chapters 316, 318 & 322
No charge, 78 pages, Soft-bound

GEORGIA STATE PATROL
Planning Section
P.O. Box 1456
Atlanta, Georgia 30301
(404) 656-6138
Uniform Rules of the Road (Driving Laws)
No charge, 75 pages, Soft-bound
Driver's License Act (Licensing Laws)
No charge, 45 pages, Soft-bound

**CITY AND COUNTY OF HONOLULU DEPARTMENT
    OF FINANCE**
Purchasing Division
Honolulu Hale
Honolulu, Hawaii 96813
(808) 923-4867
Honolulu Traffic Code
$1.68, 96 pages, Soft-bound
NOTE: The State of Hawaii has no Vehicle Code or Department of
Motor Vehicles. Each island (or county) maintains its own licens-
ing and traffic laws. The above is for the island of Oahu only.

STATE OF IDAHO
Department of Law Enforcement
P.O. Box 34
Boise, Idaho 83731
(208) 384-3635
Idaho Motor Vehicle Laws
$7.50, 350 pages, Loose-leaf

ILLINOIS SECRETARY OF STATE
Vehicle Services Department
Centennial Building
Springfield, Illinois 62756
(217) 785-3000
Illinois Vehicle Code
No charge, 270 pages, Soft-bound

INDIANA BUREAU OF MOTOR VEHICLES
  (For information only)
401 State Office Building
Indianapolis, Indiana 46204
(317) 633-6413
Central Publishing Company (For code book only)
401 North College Avenue
Indianapolis, Indiana 46206
(317) 636-4504
Indiana Motor Vehicle Law Book
$10.50 (Indiana residents add 4% tax), 315 pages, Soft-bound

IOWA DEPARTMENT OF PUBLIC SAFETY
Commissioner's Office
Wallace State Office Building
Des Moines, Iowa 50319
(515) 281-5261
Iowa Motor Vehicle Code
No charge, 168 pages, Loose-leaf

KANSAS DEPARTMENT OF REVENUE
Vehicle Director's Office
State Office Building
3rd Floor
Topeka, Kansas 66626
(913) 296-3601

Kansas Vehicle Laws
$4.50, 450 pages, Loose-leaf

KENTUCKY DEPARTMENT OF TRANSPORTATION
Office of the Commissioner
Bureau of Motor Vehicle Regulation
State Office Building, Room 208
Frankfort, Kentucky 40601
(502) 564-7000
Motor Vehicle Laws of the Com.nonwealth of Kentucky
$3.50, 206 pages, Soft-bound
Or, if trucking or licensing regulations are involved:
Kentucky Administrative Regulations for Motor Vehicles
$15.00, 500 pages, Loose-leaf

LOUISIANA DEPARTMENT OF SAFETY
Louisiana State Police
Research Division
P.O. Box 66614
Baton Rouge, Louisiana 70896
(504) 389-7102
Title 32 of the Louisiana Revised Statutes
No charge, 120 pages, Loose-leaf

MAINE DEPARTMENT OF MOTOR VEHICLES
Court Record Division
Attn: Chief of Driver Improvement
1 Child Street
Augusta, Maine 04330
Title 29, Maine Motor Vehicle Laws
No charge, 154 pages, Soft-bound

MARYLAND MOTOR VEHICLE ADMINISTRATION
Chief of Vehicle Regulations Division
6601 Ritchie Highway
Glen Burnie, Maryland 21062
Maryland Motor Vehicle Laws
$5.59, 751 pages, Soft-bound

MASSACHUSETTS REGISTRY OF MOTOR VEHICLES
  (For information only)
Legal Section
100 Nashua Street
Boston, Massachusetts 02114
(617) 727-3780
Legal Publications (For code book only)
P.O. Box 341
North Andover, Massachusetts 01845
The Handbook of Massachusetts Motor Vehicle Laws
$5.00, 341 pages, Soft-bound

MICHIGAN DEPARTMENT OF STATE
Purchasing and Office Services
Mutual Building
Lansing, Michigan 48918
(517) 373-2570
Michigan Motor Vehicle Code
$2.50, 384 pages, Soft-bound

STATE OF MINNESOTA
Document Section
Room 140
Centennial Building
658 Cedar Street
St. Paul, Minnesota 55155
(612) 296-2874
*Minnesota Motor Vehicle and Traffic Laws: Motor Carrier Laws
  and Motor Vehicle Registration Laws and Supplement*
$6.50, 170 pages, Loose-leaf

MISSISSIPPI MOTOR VEHICLE COMPTROLLER
P.O. Box 1140
Jackson, Mississippi 39205
(601) 354-7414
*Mississippi Motor Vehicle Laws, Tax, Weights, Speed, Titles, Ad
  Valorem and Excerpts from Public Service Laws*
No charge, 202 pages, Soft-bound

MISSOURI STATE HIGHWAY COMMISSION
State Highway Building
Jefferson City, Missouri 65101

(314) 751-4588
Laws of Missouri Relating to Roads, Highways & Bridges
No charge, 200 pages, Loose-leaf

MONTANA DEPARTMENT OF JUSTICE
Motor Vehicle Division
Montana Highway Patrol Bureau
1014 National Avenue
Helena, Montana 59601
(406) 449-3000
Montana Motor Vehicle Code
$3.00, 280 pages, Loose-leaf

NEBRASKA DEPARTMENT OF MOTOR VEHICLES
P.O. Box 94789
Lincoln, Nebraska 68509
(402) 471-2281
Nebraska Motor Vehicle Laws
No charge, 291 pages, Soft-back

NEVADA DEPARTMENT OF MOTOR VEHICLES
Office of the Director
555 Wright Way
Carson City, Nevada 89711
(702) 885-5380
Nevada Motor Vehicle Laws
$5.00 (money order only), 250 pages, Loose-leaf

NEW HAMPSHIRE DEPARTMENT OF SAFETY
Division of Motor Vehicles
Director's Office
James Hayes Safety Building
Haven Drive
Concord, New Hampshire 03301
(603) 271-2484
New Hampshire Motor Vehicle Laws
No charge, 250 pages, Loose-leaf

NEW JERSEY DIVISION OF MOTOR VEHICLES
Public Information Office
25 South Montgomery Street
Trenton, New Jersey 08666
(609) 292-5203

The New Jersey Motor Vehicle and Traffic Regulations, Title 39
No charge, 226 pages, Soft-bound

NEW MEXICO DEPARTMENT OF TRANSPORTATION (Information only)
Secretary's Office
P.O. Box 1028
Santa Fe, New Mexico 87503
(505) 827-2130
The Michie Company (Code book only)
P.O. Box 7587
Charlottesville, Virginia 22906
(804) 295-6171
Motor Vehicle Laws of New Mexico
$10.00 (Projected, estimate only), 439 pages, Hard-bound

NEW YORK DEPARTMENT OF MOTOR VEHICLES
Public Service Unit
Empire State Plaza
Albany, New York 12228
(518) 474-0705
New York Vehicle & Traffic Law
$1.50 (Payable to Commission of Motor Vehicles),
400 pages, Soft-bound

NORTH CAROLINA DIVISION OF MOTOR VEHICLES
Attn: Joe D. Corin
1100 Newburn Avenue
Raleigh, North Carolina 27611
(919) 733-3612
North Carolina Motor Vehicle Laws
$4.00, 490 pages, Soft-bound

NORTH DAKOTA HIGHWAY DEPARTMENT
Supply Division
224 Airport Road
Bismarck, North Dakota 58505
(701) 224-2571
North Dakota Motor Vehicle Laws
$4.00, 250 pages, Loose-leaf

OHIO BUREAU OF MOTOR VEHICLES
Procurement Section

P.O. Box 16520
Columbus, Ohio 43216
(614) 466-7980
Ohio Motor Vehicle Laws
No charge, 300 pages, Soft-bound

OKLAHOMA DEPARTMENT OF PUBLIC SAFETY
Accident and Enforcement Records Services
3600 North Eastern
Oklahoma City, Oklahoma 73136
(405) 424-4011, Ext. 234
Oklahoma Vehicle Laws
$6.00, 275 pages, Soft-bound

OREGON MOTOR VEHICLE DIVISION
Fiscal Section
1905 Lana Avenue, N.W.
Salem, Oregon 97314
(503) 378-6998
Motor Vehicle Laws of Oregon
$2.00, 354 pages, Soft-bound

PENNSYLVANIA DEPARTMENT OF GENERAL SERVICES
Book Store
10th & Market Streets
Harrisburg, Pennsylvania 17125
(717) 787-3130
Pennsylvania Vehicle Code
$2.50, 225 pages, Hard-bound

RHODE ISLAND REGISTRY OF MOTOR VEHICLES
State Office Building
Providence, Rhode Island 02903
(401) 277-2991
Rhode Island Code of Motor Vehicles
No charge, 200 pages, Loose-leaf

SOUTH CAROLINA DEPARTMENT OF HIGHWAYS AND PUBLIC TRANSPORTATION
Division of Motor Vehicles
P.O. Box 1498
Columbia, South Carolina 29216
(803) 758-3204

South Carolina Motor Vehicle Laws
$12.27, 373 pages, Soft-bound

SOUTH DAKOTA DEPARTMENT OF MOTOR VEHICLES
   (Information only)
218 West Capital
Pierre, South Dakota 57501
(605) 773-3541
The Michie Company (Code book only)
P.O. Box 7587
Charlottesville, Virginia 22906
(804) 295-6171
South Dakota Codified Laws, Title 32, Motor Vehicles Pamphlet
$8.50, 400 pages, Soft-bound

TENNESSEE MOTOR VEHICLE DIVISION
Motor Vehicle Warehouse
900 Seventh Avenue North
Nashville, Tennessee 37209
(615) 741-1801
Tennessee Motor Vehicle Law
No charge, 200 pages, Soft-bound

TEXAS DEPARTMENT OF PUBLIC SAFETY
Attn: General Services
P.O. Box 4087
Austin, Texas 78773
(512) 452-0331, ext. 209
Texas Motor Vehicle Laws
$1.05, 400 pages, Soft-bound

UTAH MOTOR VEHICLE DIVISION
1095 Motor Avenue
Salt Lake City, Utah 84416
(801) 533-3311
State of Utah Motor Vehicle Registration and Motor Vehicle
   Business Administration Laws and Regulations
$1.00, 152 pages, Soft-bound

VERMONT DEPARTMENT OF MOTOR VEHICLES
120 State Street
Montpelier, Vermont 05603
(802) 828-2121
Vermont Motor Vehicle Laws

$10.00, 386 pages, Soft-bound

VIRGINIA DIVISION OF MOTOR VEHICLES
  (Information only)
2220 West Broad Street
Richmond, Virginia 23220
(804) 257-0538
The Michie Company (Code book only)
P.O. Box 7587
Charlottesville, Virginia 22906
(804) 295-6171
Virginia State Code, Volume 7
$22.50,448 pages, Hard-bound

WASHINGTON DEPARTMENT OF LICENSING
Highways—License Building
Olympia, Washington 98504
(206) 753-6913
Motor Vehicle Laws of the State of Washington
$5.00, 887 pages, Loose-leaf

WEST VIRGINIA DEPARTMENT OF MOTOR VEHICLES
Supply Division
1800 Washington Street, East
Charleston, West Virginia 25305
(304) 348-3900
West Virginia Motor Vehicle Laws
No charge, 309 pages, Soft-bound

WISCONSIN DEPARTMENT OF MOTOR VEHICLES
Document Sales
P.O. Box 7426
Madison, Wisconsin 53207
(608) 266-1591
Wisconsin Motor Vehicle Law Book
$1.25, 300 pages, Soft-bound

WYOMING HIGHWAY DEPARTMENT
Office of Accounting and Budget
P.O. Box 1708
Cheyenne, Wyoming 82002
(307) 777-7264
Wyoming Highway Laws and Related Statutes
$21.25, 595 pages, Hard-bound

| 22111 | **HAND SIGNALS,** improperly given, (a) left, ~~(b)~~ ri... |
| 22112 | **SCHOOL BUS SIGNALS,** misuse by bus driver. |

SPEED LAWS, CHAPTER 7

22348a	**MAXIMUM SPEED LIMIT,** 55 mph; supersedes 2234... until 6-30-78 or until canceled.
22349	**MAXIMUM SPEED LIMIT,** 65 mph.
2235...	...**SAFE SPEED** for prevailing conditions, use for al... ...ma facie limits: 15 mph, blind intersection... ...sing, or any alley; 25 mph, school zones, ...ential district; otherwise limit posted.
	...**M SPEED LIMIT,** 70 mph when posted.
	...**M SPEED,** (a) impeding traffic; (b) below s... ...**LIMIT** (posted) for condition of bridge, ...

HOW DOES THE OFFICER REMEMBER ALL THOSE LAWS IN THE FIRST PLACE?

Obviously, with thousands upon thousands of state and local laws there is no possible way for the traffic officer to remember them all. Remembering that many traffic laws would be like trying to memorize your city's phone book. Most officers use a reference list they call a "cheat sheet," which is much like your personal list of frequently called phone numbers that you keep by your phone for easy reference. When an officer first observes a violation he can usually recognize one on the basis of the "Rude Rule," that is, if an act on the highway is inconsiderate of another driver or just looks very unusual or unsafe it is probably illegal.

Once the car is stopped, the officer can usually locate the appropriate section of the vehicle code by consulting his "cheat sheet." If a violation is not listed on his cheat sheet it will take him just a few minutes longer to dig out his copy of the vehicle code and look through it or just get on the radio and ask the dispatcher or another officer. The cheat sheet is a handy little card which fits in his ticket book, or on the sun visor of his patrol car and indexes violations by subject matter. Often the description of the violation is extremely brief and vague, like "Max. Speed," or "P.F. Speed" and may not accurately describe your violation. Remember the cheat sheet is not an official vehicle code, but only serves as a ready reference or index. If an officer shows you a cheat sheet while describing your violation, don't accept it as gospel or all inclusive. The vehicle or traffic code for your state is *the* "Bible" of the highways.

Cheat sheets are composed and printed by local or

An officer's "cheat sheet" makes it easy to locate the vehicle code section, but also makes it easy for the officer to miss one of the elements of the violation.

state law enforcement agencies and can contain refer-ence information other than vehicle code violations, so don't be surprised to find that an officer has penciled in a grocery list or has used the corner of the card to write down "Suzie's" phone number from the local diner. The officer may underline offenses that he or his supervisor may want special attention given to such as following too close or violation of right-of-way sections. The cheat sheets used in many agencies have printed what they consider "Hazardous" violations in a different type style so officers are sure which types of tickets the administration considers worthy of citations and not warnings.

DOES THE OFFICER HAVE A COPY OF THE VEHICLE CODE?

Chances are the officer's copy of the vehicle code has been left behind in his locker along with his brass polish and extra shoe-laces. Some traffic officers have been known to carry along a copy in their briefcase as part of their equipment, but often this is several years old and may be out-dated. Really conscientious officers may carry a current copy of the vehicle code, but the likelihood of an officer having a current edition is directly proportional to the number of years the officer has served on the department. Rookies have recent editions, while grizzled veterans still hang on to the copy issued to them in the Spring of '37.

CAN I ASK TO SEE IT?

Of course you can ask to see the officer's copy of the

vehicle code, and the chances are pretty good that he'll show it to you if he has one with him. He will probably be very surprised to be asked for it. (This is kind of like asking to see your family doctor's A.M.A. membership card) and it will give him a good "war story" to tell the other guys at coffee ("You guys won't believe what this dude asked me for!").

The real question is, do you *want* to see a copy of the vehicle code? Your request isn't going to change what he writes (other than to make sure he writes everything very carefully) and will only make you stand out in the officer's mind. Weeks or months later when you appear in court, you won't be "just another speeder" to the officer, you will be remembered as "the guy that asked for the vehicle code." You might be better off waiting until later to look up your violation.

DOES HE HAVE TO SHOW IT TO ME?

No, there is nothing which requires an officer to show his copy of the vehicle code to you. However, most agencies are far more PR oriented than the public generally believes and will go out of their way to accommodate a citizen's reasonable request. If you feel that you absolutely must see a copy of the vehicle code at the time of your citation, try to make it a polite request rather than an aggressive demand. If you make yourself truly obnoxious, the traffic officer's natural defensive reaction is to find additional violations to add to your citation. You'd probably be better off never seeing a copy of the vehicle code at all.

Maximum Speed Limit

22349. Except as provided in Section 22356, no person shall drive a vehicle upon a highway at a speed greater than 65 miles per hour.

Added Ch. 11, Stats. 1959. Effective Sept. 18, 1959.
Amended Ch. 1735, Stats. 1963. Effective Sept. 20, 1963.

Basic Speed Law

22350. No person shall drive a vehicle upon a highway at a speed greater than is reasonable or prudent having due regard for weather, visibility, the traffic on, and the surface and width of, the highway, and in no event at a speed which endangers the safety of persons or property.

Amended Ch. 252, Stats. 1963. Effective Sept. 20, 1963.

Speed Law Violations

22351. (a) The speed of any vehicle upon a highway not in excess of the limits specified in Section 22352 or established as authorized in this code is lawful unless clearly proved to be in violation of the basic speed law.

(b) The speed of any vehicle upon a highway in excess of the prima facie speed limits in Section 22352 or established as authorized in this code is prima facie unlawful unless the defendant establishes by competent evidence that the speed in excess of said limits did not constitute a violation of the basic speed law at the time, place and under the conditions then existing.

Prima Facie Speed Limits

22352. The prima facie limits are as follows and the same shall be applicable

Vehicle codes tend to say the simplest things in the most complicated ways.

NOW THAT I'VE GOT A COPY OF THE VEHICLE CODE, WHAT DOES IT MEAN?

To understand what the particular section of the vehicle code you were charged with violating really means, you must first understand all of the terminology. The words used in the laws often have a very specific meaning, which is usually defined in other sections of the code. The glossary provided in this book will provide you with a close definition of some of the terms used in your state, but if your case is going to hang on the wording of the law you would be wise to check carefully in the code itself.

You might also check in the "Annotated" version of the code, which is available at your city or county law library. This version of the vehicle code will reflect the latest changes in the law and also shows how recent court decisions may have affected those laws. These books are up-dated regularly, and these up-dates may be in the form of paper-bound flyers which should be checked in addition to the hard bound volumes.

Further understanding of the vehicle code section can be gained by listing and examining each of the elements of your violation separately.

WHAT IS AN ELEMENT?

Every violation is made up of a number of separate facts, or "elements." It is only after *all* of the elements have occurred that you have a violation. It's kind of like making a screwdriver. The elements are vodka, orange juice and a glass. If you forget the vodka, you only have a glass of orange juice. If you forget the orange juice, you only have a glass of vodka, and if you forget the glass you have a mess. Leave out any of the elements and you don't end up with a screwdriver.

The elements of your violation are similar: if you don't have all of the elements, you don't have a violation. This can be a mess for the officer, but one which can be easy for you to clean up in court.

WHAT ARE THE ELEMENTS OF MY VIOLATION?

The elements for every section of the vehicle code are

different, and it's up to you to separate and identify the elements of your specific violation. Here are a few examples which should help you in isolating the various elements:

If the law read, "No person shall drive a vehicle upon a highway at a speed greater than 55 miles per hour," you have four elements.

1. You must be a person (your dog can't get a ticket for this);
2. You must be driving a vehicle;
3. The vehicle must be on a highway (not a private road or on a local race-track);
4. And you must be traveling over 55 miles per hour.

A typical law controlling U-turns in a residential area might read, *"No person in a residence district shall make a U-turn when any other vehicle is approaching from either direction within 200 feet, except at an intersection."* The elements of this violation are:

1. You must be driving a vehicle;
2. in a residence district;
3. you must make a U-turn;
4. another vehicle must be approaching;
5. the other vehicle must be within 200 feet;
6. and you must not have been at an intersection when you made your U-turn.

After reading through a few of these sections, they sound almost like they're written in English and the elements become readily identifiable. It's best to list each of the elements on a sheet of paper, so that they can be carefully and individually examined and compared with your violation. If all the elements are present in your violation your only option may be to drop back and punt (See "Fighting the System").

IF I DON'T UNDERSTAND THE VIOLATION, WHO DO I ASK?

For a lot of offenses, particulary violations of local ordinances, you might try calling the agency which issued the citation. These local agencies are usually very cooperative, but be sure you are not talking to an untrained civilian employee who may know little more than you do.

Another option is your family lawyer, who sometimes will give you some quick information without charging for it. If the attorney charges you for his time, the cost of the consultation is likely to be considerably higher than the cost of the ticket.

Your best bet in getting an explanation of your violation might be through your state agency's Public Information Officer. We've cut through all of the red tape for you and compiled a complete list of *the* number to call, usually the desk of a ranking officer who has assured us of cooperation with any callers. (If any of these officers are uncooperative, please drop a note to both his agency and to us; we'll follow up on it.)

STATE POLICE PUBLIC INFORMATION CONTACTS

ALABAMA DEPARTMENT OF PUBLIC SAFETY
Alabama State Troopers
500 Dexter Avenue
Montgomery, Alabama 36130
(205) 832-5095

ALASKA DEPARTMENT OF PUBLIC SAFETY
Alaska State Troopers
Information Officer
P.O. Box 6188 Annex
Anchorage, Alaska 99502
(907) 264-5560

ARIZONA DEPARTMENT OF PUBLIC SAFETY
Arizona Highway Patrol
2310 N. 20th Avenue
Phoenix, Arizona 85005
(602) 262-8011

ARKANSAS STATE POLICE
P.O. Box 4005
Little Rock, Arkansas 72203
(501) 371-2151

CALIFORNIA HIGHWAY PATROL
Office of Public Affairs
P.O. Box 398
Sacramento, California 95804
(916) 445-3908

COLORADO STATE PATROL
Public Information Office
4201 E. Arkansas
Denver, Colorado 80222
(303) 757-9636

CONNECTICUT STATE POLICE
100 Washington Street
Hartford, Connecticut 06106
(203) 566-4054

DELAWARE STATE POLICE
Public Information Office
P.O. Box 430
Dover, Delaware 19901
(302) 734-5973

DISTRICT OF COLUMBIA
Metropolitan Police Department
Public Information Office
300 Indiana Avenue, N.W.
Washington, D.C. 20001
(202) 626-2871

FLORIDA HIGHWAY PATROL
Public Information Section
Niel Kirkman Building
Tallahassee, Florida 32301
(904) 488-7134

GEORGIA STATE PATROL
Public Information Office
959 East Confederate Avenue
Atlanta, Georgia 30301
(404) 656-6140

HONOLULU POLICE DEPARTMENT
1455 South Bertania Street
Honolulu, Hawaii 96814
(808) 955-8111

NOTE: Hawaii has no Highway Patrol or State Police. County law
enforcement agencies handle all traffic enforcement within their
jurisdictions. This agency handles Honolulu City and County,
which is the island of Oahu.

IDAHO STATE POLICE
P.O. Box 34
Boise, Idaho 83731
(208) 384-3851

ILLINOIS STATE POLICE
Public Affairs Section
613 Armory Building
Springfield, Illinois 62706
(217) 782-6637

INDIANA STATE POLICE
Public Information Office
100 North Senate
Indianapolis, Indiana 46204
(317) 633-5674

IOWA HIGHWAY PATROL
Public Information Office
Wallace State Office Building
Des Moines, Iowa 50319
(515) 281-8842

KANSAS HIGHWAY PATROL
Research and Planning Section
Towncite Plaza
Building #2, Suite 130
200 East 6th Street
Topeka, Kansas 66603
(913) 296-3801

KENTUCKY STATE POLICE
Legal Section
Room 305
New State Office Building
Frankfort, Kentucky 40601
(502) 564-4435

LOUISIANA STATE POLICE
Public Information Office
265 South Foster Drive
Baton Rouge, Louisiana 70802
(504) 389-7300

MAINE STATE POLICE
Public Information Office
36 Hospital Street
Augusta, Maine 04333
(207) 289-3038 or 289-3393

MARYLAND STATE POLICE
Public Information Office
Pikesville, Maryland 21208
(301) 486-3101 Ext. 237

MASSACHUSETTS STATE POLICE
State Police Headquarters
Traffic Division
Public Information Officer
1010 Commonwealth Avenue
Boston, Massachusetts 02215
(617) 566-4500

MICHIGAN DEPARTMENT OF STATE POLICE
Public Affairs Section
714 South Harrison Road
East Lansing, Michigan 48823
(517) 373-8349

MINNESOTA STATE PATROL
Information Desk
3800 Dunlap Street
St. Paul, Minnesota 55112
(612) 482-5901

MISSISSIPPI HIGHWAY SAFETY PATROL
Public Relations Bureau
P.O. Box 958
Jackson, Mississippi 39205
(601) 982-1212 Ext. 220

MISSOURI STATE HIGHWAY PATROL
Public Information Section
1510 East Elm Street
Jefferson City, Missouri 65101
(314) 751-3313 Ext. 115

MONTANA DEPARTMENT OF JUSTICE
Montana Highway Patrol Bureau
1014 National Avenue
Helena, Montana 59601
(406) 449-3000

NEBRASKA STATE PATROL
Public Information Office
P.O. Box 94907 State House
Lincoln, Nebraska 68509
(402) 477-3951

NEVADA DEPARTMENT OF MOTOR VEHICLES
Nevada Highway Patrol
555 Wright Way
Carson City, Nevada 89711
(702) 885-5300

NEW HAMPSHIRE STATE POLICE
Traffic Division
James Hayes Safety Building
Haven Drive
Concord, New Hampshire 03301
(603) 271-3296

NEW JERSEY STATE POLICE
State Police Headquarters
Public Information Office
P.O. Box 7068
West Trenton, New Jersey 08625
(609) 882-2000 Ext. 209

NEW MEXICO STATE POLICE
Public Information Officer
Training Section
P.O. Box 1628
Santa Fe, New Mexico 87501
(505) 827-5104

NEW YORK STATE POLICE
Public Relations Supervisor
Building 22
State Campus
Albany, New York 12226
(518) 457-2180

NORTH CAROLINA HIGHWAY PATROL
Public Information office
P.O. Box 27687
Raleigh, North Carolina 27611
(919) 733-5027

NORTH DAKOTA HIGHWAY PATROL
Public Information Section
State Capitol Building
Bismarck, North Dakota 58505
(701) 224-2455

OHIO STATE HIGHWAY PATROL
Planning and Research Section
660 East Main Street
Columbus, Ohio 43205
(614) 466-3120

OKLAHOMA DEPARTMENT OF PUBLIC SAFETY
Public Information Office
3600 North Eastern
Oklahoma City, Oklahoma 73136
(405) 424-4011 Ext. 291

OREGON STATE POLICE
Public Information Office
107 Public Service Building
Salem, Oregon 97310
(503) 378-3723

PENNSYLVANIA STATE POLICE
Public Information Office
1800 Elmerton Avenue
Harrisburg, Pennsylvania
(717) 783-5556

RHODE ISLAND STATE POLICE HEADQUARTERS
Public Information Office
P.O. Box 185
North Scituate, Rhode Island 02857
(401) 647-3311

SOUTH CAROLINA HIGHWAY PATROL
Public Information Section
955 Park Street
Columbia, South Carolina 29202
(803) 758-3315

SOUTH DAKOTA HIGHWAY PATROL
Deputy Director of Field Operations
118 West Capitol Avenue
Pierre, South Dakota 57501
(605) 773-3105

TENNESSEE DEPARTMENT OF SAFETY
Public Relations and Information Office
Room 1225
Andrew Jackson State Office Building
Nashville, Tennessee 37219
(615) 741-2491

TEXAS DEPARTMENT OF PUBLIC SAFETY
Public Information Office
P.O. Box 4087
Austin, Texas 78773
(512) 452-0331

UTAH HIGHWAY PATROL
Public Information Office
Room 304
State Office Building
Salt Lake City, Utah 84114
(801) 533-5621

VERMONT DEPARTMENT OF PUBLIC SAFETY
Vermont State Police
Public Information Office
Montpelier, Vermont 05602
(802) 828-2187

VIRGINIA STATE POLICE
Public Information Office
P.O. Box 27472
Richmond, Virginia 23261
(804) 272-1431 Ext. 269

WASHINGTON STATE PATROL
Public Information Office
General Administration Building
Olympia, Washington 98504
(206) 753-6562

WEST VIRGINIA STATE POLICE
Public Information Officer
711 Jefferson Road
South Charleston, West Virginia 25309
(304) 348-6370

WISCONSIN DEPARTMENT OF
   TRANSPORTATION
Wisconsin State Patrol
Public Information Office
4802 Sheboygen Avenue
Madison, Wisconsin 53702
(608) 266-7744

WYOMING HIGHWAY PATROL
c/o Wyoming Highway Department
Public Information Office
P.O. Box 1708
Cheyenne, Wyoming 82001
(307) 777-7267

SHOULD I BE SATISFIED WITH JUST ONE PERSON'S OPINION?

That depends on who answered it, and how knowledgeable they were. If they sounded like they knew the information and had some kind of background or experience, one person's opinion may be sufficient. In all cases, be sure that *you* have read and understood the section of the vehicle code. Of course, if the opinions you are getting are free, it doesn't hurt to ask.

SHOULD I FIGHT IT?

This is a tough question as many factors will be affecting your decision. Some of these factors are more important than others. One big reason why most people won't fight their traffic tickets is the fact that the system is so imposing. There is no reason for you to fear the system (see "The System") as it's not all that complicated and you have everything to gain by fighting. If you were truly innocent and did not violate the law which appears on your citation, then you should definitely fight it in court.

Another consideration should be the strength of evidence against you. If you were paced with the patrol car kissing your rear bumper for five miles, his estimation of your speed is probably valid. On the other hand, if he clocked you with radar when you were right in the middle of a group of speeding trucks, all of which were traveling faster than you, there might be a reason to question the strength of his evidence and fighting the ticket might be a good idea.

You should also take into account how your violation will affect your driving record and whether it will raise your insurance rates. If this citation may mean losing your license, it's probably worth fighting over.

The convenience of fighting the ticket is another consideration. If the court is located nearby, your traveling time and costs will be minimized. If you can get the time off from your place of employment and the lost time won't cost you too much money, then you may want to fight the ticket.

If you were guilty, but felt you were the unfair victim of a "cherry patch" or some other unfair enforcement technique, you may want to fight the ticket.

You may wish to fight your ticket just for practice and the educational benefits; even if you lose it won't cost you any more than if you mailed the fine in, and if you're lucky the judge may even fine you less. By the time you get into court on a citation that is really vital to you, you may have more accumulated experience in court than the prosecutor.

No book can tell you one way or another whether you should fight your ticket. Of course, there are those people that advocate fighting every ticket, but ultimately you have to evaluate how much fighting the ticket is worth to you. The decision to fight is up to you.

HOW WILL THIS CITATION AFFECT MY RECORD?

The citation's effect on your record will depend on whether or not you are convicted (sending in the fine or pleading "guilty" is the same as a conviction). If you are found "not guilty," or if your case is dismissed, the citation will not appear on your record at all. In California and some other states, a "point system" is

used. To find out whether your state has a point system, check your vehicle code. If you're still unsure, call
or write the state's DMV Public Information Officer as
previously listed in this chapter.

It might prove an interesting experiment if fines
were totally removed, leaving only the point system.
This would remove the revenue incentives for the police agencies, while the driver would still have his
license and insurance rates at stake. Perhaps traffic
enforcement patterns would change drastically under
such a system.

The convictions appearing on your driving record
may also affect the amount of the fine you will be
required to pay. A chronic speeder (as evidenced by his
record) may get a whopping big fine on this third or
fourth conviction and may even lose his license. Your
record can also have a major impact on your insurance
premiums. Compared to your premium, your fine may
look insignificant.

HOW DOES A "POINT SYSTEM" WORK?

Point systems are used to penalize repeat offenders
of traffic laws. A certain number of points are assigned
to each violation, and getting a certain number of
points on your record within a given period of time
may result in the loss of your license.

The California point system is typical of most. In
California, misdemeanor violations count two points
with all other moving violations and accidents where
the driver is at fault counting one point. Getting four
or more points in one year (or six in two years or eight
in three years) may result in the state revoking your

license after a hearing with a special board, or a hearing officer from the Department of Motor Vehicles. Professional drivers (those who drive over 25,000 miles per year) may be allowed two more points each year than the four, six or eight points mentioned above. If another state has a reciprocal agreement with your state, out-of-state violations may add points to your record as well.

HOW WILL THIS CITATION AFFECT MY INSURANCE?

Generally, a single violation in a three year period will have no effect on your insurance. Additional citations can raise your rates by ten to eighty percent *each*. Convictions for driving under the influence of drugs or

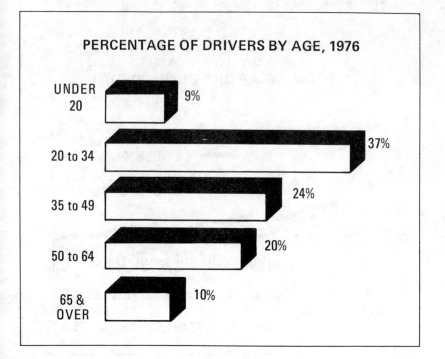

PERCENTAGE OF DRIVERS BY AGE, 1976

UNDER 20 — 9%
20 to 34 — 37%
35 to 49 — 24%
50 to 64 — 20%
65 & OVER — 10%

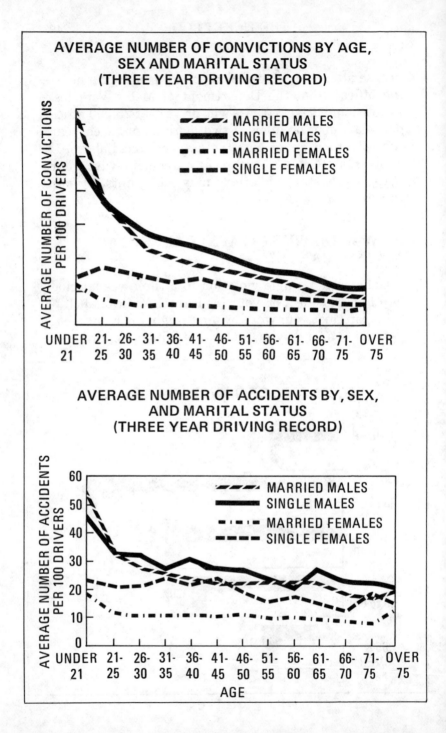

AVERAGE NUMBER OF CONVICTIONS BY AGE, SEX AND MARITAL STATUS (THREE YEAR DRIVING RECORD)

AVERAGE NUMBER OF CONVICTIONS PER 100 DRIVERS

MARRIED MALES
SINGLE MALES
MARRIED FEMALES
SINGLE FEMALES

UNDER 21 · 21-25 · 26-30 · 31-35 · 36-40 · 41-45 · 46-50 · 51-55 · 56-60 · 61-65 · 66-70 · 71-75 · OVER 75

AVERAGE NUMBER OF ACCIDENTS BY, SEX, AND MARITAL STATUS (THREE YEAR DRIVING RECORD)

AVERAGE NUMBER OF ACCIDENTS PER 100 DRIVERS

MARRIED MALES
SINGLE MALES
MARRIED FEMALES
SINGLE FEMALES

60
50
40
30
20
10
0

UNDER 21 · 21-25 · 26-30 · 31-35 · 36-40 · 41-45 · 46-50 · 51-55 · 56-60 · 61-65 · 66-70 · 71-75 · OVER 75

AGE

alcohol, or for reckless driving, are bound to have a major effect on your rates, and possibly cause you to lose your insurance altogether. The effect of citations on your insurance varies widely from company to company, so it's a good idea to shop around for the best price.

The increases in premiums on the basis of citations are justified by several studies. These studies show that most of the population are really good drivers, with 83 percent of the driving population accident free over a three year period. However, the drivers who get the most tickets are the ones who have the most accidents.

Drivers with only one traffic offense in the three year period had almost twice as many accidents as those with no convictions; those with three convictions had more than three times the number of accidents; and those with five convictions had more than four times as many accidents. Drivers with nine or more convictions in three years have over six times the number of accidents as those with no convictions.

If your own insurance company can't supply you with the information on how a ticket will affect your rates, there is a national source of insurance information that may be able to help you. The Western Insurance Information Service is a consumer education service supported by over 35 insurance companies (including Allstate, Farmer's, Montgomery Ward's and others). Its primary purpose is explaining the function and services of the insurance industry, and informing the public about the many factors that regulate the

cost of the protection they buy. They can be reached by
writing or calling:

Western Insurance Information Service
1200 N. Main St. Suite 330
Santa Ana, CA 92701
(714) 558-1052

It's not too uncommon for a traffic officer to have a
motorist come out of his car crawling on his knees and
pleading, "Please, Officer, I can't afford insurance if I
get another ticket." Unfortunately, these guys are
usually the ones driving a Porsche or a Corvette, and
most traffic officers are rather unsympathetic. "Quit
groveling and take it like a man," they answer.

HOW DO THE INSURANCE COMPANIES FIND OUT ABOUT MY TICKET?

When you first apply for insurance, the company
will always run a check on your driving record through
the Department of Motor Vehicles. Other than this
initial check, they will rarely look at your record again
unless you do something to draw their attention; like
having an accident, making a claim or getting behind
on your payments. About the only way they'll become
aware of any new violations is if you call them and ask
about it. This is like calling them up and asking them
to raise your rates.

If you're relatively happy with your present coverage and pick up a few tickets, you'll probably be best
off if you stick with your current company until they
find out about your citations on their own. Renewal
forms from the insurance company are usually for bill-
ing purposes only, and won't even have a place for you

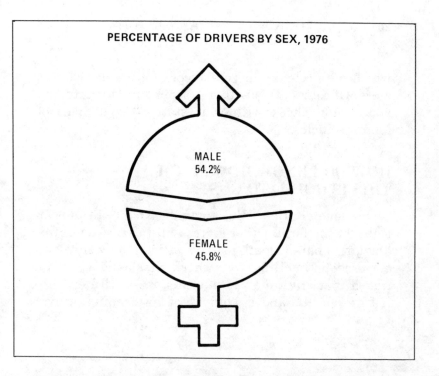

PERCENTAGE OF DRIVERS BY SEX, 1976

MALE
54.2%

FEMALE
45.8%

to mention any new offenses. This isn't hiding anything from the insurance company and under no conditions should you lie to them: they have the means for finding out the truth.

As long as your insurance company is ignorant of your present record, you should stick with them until the violations are cleared off your record.

HOW LONG WILL THIS CITATION AFFECT ME?

In most states, your violation will remain on your record for three years, after which it is expunged (permanently removed) from your record. An exception to this is driving under the influence of alcohol or drugs, which may remain on your record for seven years or more. Of course, this will vary from state to state and you should check with your state's Department of Motor Vehicles.

HOW DO I KNOW HOW MUCH THIS IS GOING TO COST?

On some citations, the amount of bail will appear right on the form. Other states will inform you of the amount of bail by mail, usually with a handy envelope enclosed for mailing your check. It should be mentioned that any time you pay this, it constitutes "forfeiture of bail" and is equivalent to pleading guilty.

Some tickets have the bail clearly indicated.

Paying by mail is most profitable for the state, as there are no court costs involved.

In some cases, you will never know what the bail is until you appear in person at the bail window, or until the moment that the judge's gavel falls.

WHAT ARE THE ODDS OF WINNING IN COURT?

Statistically, your odds of winning are about 30 percent. This doesn't mean that your chances of winning on any given case are about 30 percent, because most of the winning cases are based on there being missing elements of the violation or the violation not occurring at all. Whether or not you can win in court also depends on whether the officer was using radar, on the weather and traffic conditions and on numerous other factors. If you are guilty of the violation, your chances of winning in court are very, very slim.

Nationally, less than ten percent of all persons who are given tickets appear in court for their arraignment; the other 90 percent prefer to send in their bail money. Of the ten percent who appear in court, only one out of ten of those ever end up at trial. It has been speculated by some that if everyone were to go to court on their violations, it would overcrowd the entire court system to the point that it would have to be shut down or totally revised. This seems a little obvious with over 82,000 tickets being written in the U.S. each day. If the courts tried to accommodate a flow like that, there there would be more courtrooms than McDonald's Hamburger stands. The states might set up a chain of

"Fast Trial" Courts, with drive-up windows and a big sign under golden arches reading, "Municipal Court, Over 24 Billion Convicted."

HOW DO I KNOW IF HE USED RADAR?

Usually the officer will tell you that he used radar when he gives you the citation. Some officers will even write "radar" on the ticket, and many states provide check blocks on the citation to show if the officer used radar or VASCAR. There's a good reason for doing this, because if the motorist knows that radar was used he may be less inclined to fight the ticket in court.

For the same reason, the officer will often show the motorist the actual radar unit, by either bringing the unit with your speed locked into it up to the car, or by taking the motorist back to the patrol car.

If you're not sure about it, take a good look at the patrol car. Often the radar antenna is mounted on the left rear window, other times it may be mounted on the dashboard. Appearances can be deceiving, one enterprising smokey in Washington taped a black painted, cylindrical oatmeal box to his rear window and found that most motorists assumed it was a radar unit. Of course, an officer's use of radar will almost always be introduced as evidence in court, but you're much better off if you can find out before then.

WHY DOES THE WEATHER MATTER?

We all know that ice on the roadway, heavy rain, fog and other weather conditions affect visibility, braking distances and the car's handling. When these factors are described on the citation, they usually represent a negative factor in your case, just one more reason why you shouldn't have been traveling at the speed you were.

Weather conditions can be a positive factor in your favor if they could have affected the officer's observation of your violation, or if it may have interfered with the use of his equipment (for instance, heavy rain can generate false readings on some radar equipment).

WHAT DO YOU MEAN BY TRAFFIC CONDITIONS?

Traffic condition usually refers to traffic density and is subject to the officer's interpretation. Usually check

Most citations utilize check-blocks to describe the traffic and highway conditions.

ʾROX. SPEED	PF/MAX SPEED	VEH. SPD. LMT.	SAFE SPD.	ACCIDENT YES ☐ NO ☐
:ATION OF VIOLATION(S)				

BUS. ☐	RES. ☐	RURAL ☐	SCHL. ☐	FRWY. ☐

ATHER	TRAFFIC		CONDITION OF ROAD			NO. OF LANES
N FOG	HEAVY	MED	LIGHT	NARROW	CURVE	HILL	SLIPPERY

ZARD :	PED. ☐	VEH. ☐	NEAR ACCIDENT ☐	SIGNAL GIVEN YES ☐ NO ☐

☐ OFFENSE(S) NOT COMMITTED IN MY PRESENCE, CERTIFIED ON INFORMATION AND BELIEF.

ERTIFY UNDER PENALTY OF PERJURY THAT THE FOREGOING IS TRUE AND CORRECT. :CUTED ON THE DATE SHOWN ABOVE AT

I.D. NO.

ʂUING OFFICER _____ CALIF.
PLACE

ME OF ARRESTING OFFICER, IF DIFFERENT FROM ABOVE	SERIAL NO.	VACATION

THOUT ADMITTING GUILT, I PROMISE TO APPEAR AT THE TIME AND PLACE)ICATED BELOW

SIGNATURE

FORE THE JUDGE OF THE COURT AT THE

☐ JUVENILE COURT ☐ SOUTH BAY MUNI.	TIME	MONTH	DAY	YEAR

boxes are provided for light, medium or heavy traffic. What's heavy traffic to an Arizona Highway Patrol officer in the middle of the desert, might differ quite a bit from the definition used by a New York officer in downtown Manhattan at rush hour.

The traffic condition portion of the citation form is filled out automatically by most officers whether or not it has any bearing on your case. Traffic conditions have the most effect on violations such as illegal lane changes and the basic speed law, but should have little or no effect on equipment citations. Unfortunately, there's no place on the form to mark "No Traffic." Thus, at 3 o'clock in the morning when you and the officer are the only cars on the road, traffic conditions are described as "light."

WHAT DO YOU MEAN BY "NUMEROUS OTHER FACTORS?"

"Numerous other factors" covers a lot of territory which can affect the outcome of your case. One of the most important of these is the severity of your violation. If you were charged with traveling 100 miles per hour through a school zone, it's very unlikely that you will be able to win in court. Merely on the basis of the charge, the judge and jury will have a preconceived notion of you as a homicidal maniac. On the other hand, if you were clocked on a Sunday afternoon at 35 miles per hour in the same school zone, your chances of winning are considerably better.

Another factor is the officer's experience in traffic work. The observations and testimony of a veteran officer are liable to count more heavily against you than those of a nervous rookie.

The accuracy of the officer's observation of your violation is another important factor. If he observed you from a considerable distance, or if his testimony in court is sketchy and lacking in detail, then your chances of winning improve noticeably.

As previously mentioned, the elements of the violation are a very important factor. If all of the elements of the violation aren't presented by the prosecution, you may be home free.

Your dress and grooming are also important, and you should put on your best appearance for the court. Your personality is something else which can help to sway the opinions of the court one way or another. If you get along well with other people, make friends easily and remind people of John-Boy Walton, you may favorably impress the judge and/or jury. Of course, they are not supposed to be influenced by anything other than the facts of the case, but in reality you may remind them of their own son or daughter. (This can be good or bad, depending on how they remember their children.) On the other hand, if you normally have all the tact of Don Rickles, you may be hard pressed to gain the jury's sympathy.

One last thing to consider is your own natural speaking ability. If you are capable of presenting your case well in front of a group of people it can be a tremendous asset to your case. Consider practicing your presentation with a few friends playing the parts of the officer and the prosecutor. However, avoid presenting a "canned" testimony.

Observe a few court cases so you can get a feeling for the type of questions that may be asked and be familiar enough with your material that you can avoid looking at your notes except for dramatic effect. You don't want to present yourself as a budding Perry Mason, but if you can appear to be articulate, sincere and knowledgeable it may count as a big plus for your chances of winning.

TYPES OF TICKETS
There's more than you'd believe. . . .

WHAT ARE THE DIFFERENT TYPES OF TICKETS?

There are more "types" of tickets than we could hope to cover in an entire book based on the subject, but all of them fall under one of the four basic categories of moving, equipment, pedestrian or parking citations.

These four categories cover innumerable types of citations, including tickets for speeding, illegal turns, the manufacture of the vehicle and its ultimate destruction. You can get a ticket for the violation of any one of the thousands upon thousands of vehicle laws which cover absolutely everything having anything to do with the operation of a motor vehicle and the highways on which they operate. The little booklet they hand to you before you take your driver's license test just barely covers the rules of the road, and doesn't even begin to cover all of the laws.

The vehicle code regulates what you have to do if you have an accident, and what you have to do if your car has a bullet hole. It regulates the height of your license plate and the color of the light illuminating it, and specifies how many times per minute your turn signals have to blink. The codes tell you when and where you can or can't turn, the number of sun visors required on a trolley car, what you can drop on the highway without littering (clear water and live poultry feathers in many states), how high your bumper can be and how low your roof can extend. When you buy a car, sell a car, drive a car or build a car from scratch, your every action is regulated by the vehicle code. Failure to comply with those laws can lead to a ticket, or even your arrest. Of course, not all laws apply from state to state.

HOW DO I KNOW WHICH TYPES APPLY IN MY STATE?

The only way to know for sure is to look up the specific subject you're curious about in your state's vehicle code. (See *Looking at What You Got:* An evaluation of your citation.) The codes vary widely from state to state, and some violations may be unique, applying only to your state. In fact, some laws may apply only to your city, or even to a specific part of your city.

DO YOU MEAN THAT I CAN GET A TICKET IN MY STATE FOR SOMETHING THAT'S PERFECTLY LEGAL IN 49 OTHER STATES?

That's right. As an example, in the state of Hawaii in Kauai County a hand signal is required for a U-turn—the arm must be extended outward with a circular motion. One of the most common laws that varies from state to state is the law governing right turns on a red light. For someone driving through a large number of states, it is almost impossible to keep up to date on all of the variations between the vehicle codes of all the different states.

Since collecting all of the vehicle codes of the states you travel through is rather impractical, we recommend that anyone doing a lot of interstate driving pick up a copy of the *Digest of Motor Laws*, an excellent compilation of all of the basic driving laws in the 50 states, U.S. Territories and Canada. It has been compiled and produced by the American Automobile Association. The book, which currently sells for $2.00, can be ordered through:

CREDIT AND ORDER DEPARTMENT
AMERICAN AUTOMOBILE ASSOCIATION
8111 GATEHOUSE ROAD
FALLS CHURCH, VA 22024
(703) 222-6543

This book gives the basic traffic rules affecting passenger cars, trailers, motorcycles and licensing and registration laws. It doesn't quote any specific code sections, but presents the basics of the laws in a straightforward, easily understood manner. This book is an excellent investment for anyone on the interstate driving circuit.

WHAT ARE SOME OF THE TYPES OF TICKETS I MIGHT ENCOUNTER?

The most common types of citations received by today's motorists are moving violations, equipment, parking, pedestrian citations, "documentation" citations and tickets in which the use of alcohol is involved. Typically, municipal departments are the ones who issue parking citations, as these are usually covered under municipal codes rather than the state vehicle code.

Of those tickets given by state agencies, approximately 54 percent of all citations were issued for speeding and other moving violations, 9 percent were given for equipment violations, 20 percent for parking, pedestrian, and other miscellaneous citations, 11 percent for registration and other documentation violations, and roughly 5 percent for driving under the influence of alcohol and related charges.

WHAT'S A "MOVING VIOLATION"?

A moving violation is precisely what it sounds like; any violation of the motor vehicle laws that occurs while the vehicle is moving. The most common of these types of violations are violations of the basic speed law or prima facia limit, exceeding the maximum limit, violation of right of way, failing to obey a traffic control device such as a signal light or a stop sign and the various types of illegal turns.

WHAT IS A "BASIC SPEED" LAW?

A basic speed law is the catch-all law of speeding that basically says that it's illegal to drive faster than it's safe to. This law is in effect in most states, as it covers any speeding situation where the limits may not have been posted, or the conditions make a slower speed advisable. One such typical law states, *"No person shall drive a vehicle upon a highway at a speed greater than is reasonable or prudent having due regard for weather, visibility, the traffic on, and the surface and width of, the highway, and in no event at a speed which endangers the safety of persons or property."*

It is possible to be given a ticket under the basic speed law for traveling at a speed well below the posted speed limit on that roadway. It is also rather confusing to the motorist who receives a citation for doing 30 MPH in a heavy rain, while traveling through a zone posted at 35 MPH.

WHAT DOES THE "PRIMA FACIA" LIMIT MEAN?

A prima facia limit is the speed limit actually posted on the roadway. The mere fact that you were driving above this posted limit is presumed in court to be an unreasonable and improper speed. In court, it's up to you as a driver to prove that this speed was not unsafe when the condition of the highway (traffic congestion, visibility and the like) are considered. If you can prove that the circumstances justified your speed in excess of the prima facia limit, your speed may not be judged as "unreasonable or improper," and it is unlikely that

the speeding charge will stand in court. However, the circumstances have no bearing whatsoever if you were charged with violating the state's maximum speed limit.

WHAT IS THE "MAXIMUM LIMIT"?

The maximum speed limit is the fixed limit which it is unlawful to exceed at any time under any circumstances. Under federal guidelines, the maximum speed limit in all 50 states is presently 55 MPH, lower in some U.S. Territories and Possessions. While some states treat violation of the maximum limit similar to any other speeding violation, others consider it as a "Fuel Law Violation" or an "Environmental Infraction." These states will sometimes not record these "Fuel" violations occurring between 55 and 70 MPH so they will not affect a motorist's insurance rates.

DO THEY REALLY EXPECT YOU TO OBEY THE SPEED LIMIT?

That depends on which "they" you're talking about. If you're talking about "they" of the federal government, then yes, Washington in all its wit and wisdom and bureaucratic glory really expects you to obey the speed limit. Only the feds could expect you to believe in something so unrealistic, and fortunately "they" aren't the ones behind the wheel of a black and white.

In reality, most officers allow a 5 to 10 mile per hour margin on the posted speed limits. Of course, there are those "hot pencils" who zealously write up anyone doing 56 MPH or more on the Interstates, but tickets

giving such slim leeway are frowned upon by most judges and are often automatically dismissed in court.

WHAT IS VIOLATION OF RIGHT-OF-WAY?

Right-of-way is defined in most vehicle codes as "the privilege of immediate use of the highway." This means that the person with the right-of-way has the right to proceed on the highway without interference or interruption from other vehicles. This is the ultimate extension of the "rude rule," and right-of-way exists whether you're walking down a sidewalk or flying in a 747.

Violations of right-of-way occur when you fail to yield the right-of-way to emergency vehicles, to cars already in an intersection, to horses in an equestrian crossing, to pedestrians in a crosswalk and the like. Generally, you are also required to yield the right-of-way to other vehicles when making a left turn, when approaching a "Yield" sign, when turning onto a public road from a driveway or other private road and when entering traffic from an alley. Other forms of right-of-way laws cover stopping for school buses, tobogganing across a highway and hitchhiking.

As a rule of thumb, anytime your actions on a highway interfere with another vehicle's use of that highway, by causing them to brake, swerve, or otherwise avoid your vehicle, you have violated their right-of-way.

Violation of right-of-way is one of the leading causes of accidents (responsible for almost 25 percent of all fatal accidents), and is one of the hardest traffic laws to enforce. While the speeder covers a lot of territory while breaking the law, the violation of right-of-way occurs at one specific location, and then, only for an instant. It is very difficult to ascertain whether or not the violation actually occurred, because many times the pedestrian or driver of the other car may have yielded his right-of-way to you by waving you on or otherwise motioning to you, and this action may have been unobserved by the officer who stops you for the violation. When the other driver has indicated that he is yielding his right-of-way to you, no violation has occurred.

CAN YOU GET A TICKET IF YOU'VE GOT THE GREEN LIGHT?

There are two ways to get a ticket when you've got the green light. The first is by not moving when the light turns green. The law says that when the light turns green, you should proceed; otherwise you're obstructing traffic.

The other way to get a ticket is by entering the intersection when traffic from the cross street is still in it. The law says that you can enter the intersection on the green light only when it is safe to do so, and that you must yield the right-of-way to any vehicles which have already entered. Emergency vehicles have the right-of-way through the intersection no matter what color the signal facing you is.

IS IT LEGAL TO RUN A YELLOW LIGHT?

It is legal to run a yellow light in a vehicle, but not on foot. The yellow light is there simply to caution motorists that the light is about to turn red. Technically, if any portion of your vehicle (the rubber tip of your bumper guard is good enough) enters the intersection before the light turns red, you have the legal right-of-way through the intersection. However, running yellow lights should be treated with discretion, because there are people who like to flash into the intersection from the other direction the second their light turns green, and this could cause a few misunderstandings between several thousand pounds of hurtling metal.

Generally the yellow light is set to show for 1 second for every 10 miles per hour of the posted speed limit. Thus, a yellow light on a stretch of roadway posted at 55 MPH should last 5.5 seconds. It is usually illegal for a pedestrian to enter or cross the roadway after the light has changed to yellow.

DO YOU *ALWAYS* HAVE TO STOP FOR A RED LIGHT?

Yes, if you don't stop for the red light in front of you, sooner or later you'll have to stop for the red light that's following you.

Some states allow a right turn on a red light after the vehicle has made a full stop. At some intersections it may even be posted "No stop necessary for right turn."

CAN A METER MAID WRITE ME FOR A MOVING VIOLATION?

Not unless the meter maid is a sworn police officer with full peace officer powers. Most "meter maids" are

Some cops work both parking and moving violations.

civilian employees of the Police Department, and only have the authority to issue citations for violations of city ordinances. They do not have the power to enforce all of the state's vehicle code any more than the other private citizens of the state.

However, the meter maid should not be ignored in traffic. Her Cushman is often equipped with a radio on which she is capable of summoning a patrol car with officer who can give you a ticket for any violations they observe. There's always a chance that for some reason or another, a sworn officer may be assigned to parking control duty. He's likely to be frustrated at this seemingly menial task, and would probably be more than happy to take a break from his parking chores to give you a citation.

IS IT AGAINST THE LAW TO DRIVE WHILE BAREFOOT?

No, that's a common misconception that's just plain nonsense. Although we do know some people whose feet could be classed as a deadly weapon because of the odor, we are unaware of any laws requiring you to wear shoes in the privacy of your own car.

However, enough people believe in this that it's pretty common to see someone climbing into his car at the beach wearing only a bathing suit and shoes, or scrambling wildly to put their shoes on as you pull them over for some other violation.

WHAT'S AN ACCIDENT CITATION?

An accident citation is a ticket written by a traffic

officer for a violation which was the cause of an accident, or to any driver involved in an accident. This citation isn't based on the officer's actual observation of the accident, but rather on the evidence collected at the scene after the accident has occurred. This evidence may be in the form of statements from witnesses, point of impact (like on the wrong side of the road), the position of the vehicles and the skid marks (or lack of them). One particularly damaging piece of evidence is your own statements to the officer at the accident scene.

In some states, a citation will be issued to you right at the time of the accident. In others, a complaint is filed with the City Attorney's Office and a "Notify Warrant" or "Summons" is sent to you by mail. The summons is usually sent by registered mail and will state a time and place for you to appear in court to answer the charges. If you fail to appear, an arrest warrant may be issued.

If you don't get a ticket at the time of your accident, don't take it for granted that you got away, particularly if you confessed to the officer that you "just didn't see that red light." You had better keep a close eye on your mail box for a few days before you do any celebrating.

If you were ever going to hire an attorney for any citation, the accident citation is the one you need to have professional legal guidance on. With the civil suits that can stem from an accident, and the amount of money that can be involved, you shouldn't depend on the advice of friends and your own instincts. There's a lot more at stake here than points against your license.

IF I CAUSE AN ACCIDENT, WILL I GET A TICKET?

The chances are very high that you might be issued a citation if you were clearly the cause of an accident, but citations are not *always* given in every accident. In some cases the cause of the accident may not be an offense under the vehicle code, and a report giving the cause of the accident will be filed with the Department of Motor Vehicles instead of a ticket.

There are other times when the officer simply doesn't have the time, or doesn't feel that it is necessary to issue a citation. Often, accident citations don't count toward an officer's quota and are neglected as a result. When an officer stops your vehicle for a traffic violation, he's already looking for someone to catch, and he has the time to write it without it interfering with his other activities. On the other hand, when he comes to an accident, it's usually because he was summoned to it by the dispatcher. If he has more "important" things he'd like to be doing elsewhere, he may try to clear up the accident with a minimum of hassle and just ignore writing a citation.

CAN THEY WRITE ME A TICKET IF I'M NOT THERE?

Sure they can. Just because you were hauled away in an ambulance is no reason to believe that you will get out of an accident citation. The officer may even follow you to the hospital, have you sign the ticket while you're waiting for treatment and stuff the citation into your shirt pocket. It doesn't matter to the officer that you've been injured. He's seen lots of injured persons before and it doesn't bother him at all.

If you're not there at the accident scene by choice, you may be in a lot bigger trouble than the accident citation could ever give you. Most states make it a misdemeanor to leave the scene of an accident (it's called "Hit and Run"), and it's a felony if anyone was seriously injured or killed.

WHAT'S AN EQUIPMENT VIOLATION?

An equipment violation is a citation or warning issued to you because of some part of your car being broken, inoperative or simply not meeting the legal requirements established in the vehicle code. Equip-

Some equipment violations are more obvious than others.

ment violations include a noisy exhaust, bald tires, burnt-out lights, overly wide tires, inoperative horns, old windshield wipers and broken windows. Just about anything you do to your car from hanging a garter band on your mirror to putting decals on your windows are regulated by the state's laws, and fall under the general category of equipment violations.

DO EQUIPMENT VIOLATIONS COUNT?

That depends on the type of citation or warning which is issued to you. Many states make a provision for handling equipment violations by having special warning forms. If the equipment isn't corrected within a specified period of time, a citation may be issued, but if you fix whatever is wrong with your vehicle and

have it certified by a police officer, the warning won't count against you or even show up on your record.

However, if the equipment violation is written up on the agency's normal citation form, and if you are required to go to court, the violation will appear on your record. If the equipment has been corrected, usually the court will give you a suspended sentence if no similar violations appear on your record.

CAN THEY GIVE ME A TICKET FOR A CAR I DON'T OWN ANYMORE?

You may receive a citation for an equipment violation on a vehicle which you no longer own, but it is easily dismissed if you have properly transferred the title of the car and have proof. As long as you are the registered owner of a car, you remain responsible for keeping it in proper condition. In court, it's entirely up to you to prove that you are no longer the owner of the vehicle which was cited. Selling the car *after* you get the ticket won't help you at all. After the judge listens to your sad story and gives you a stiff fine anyway, you may have wished you had kept the car.

WHAT'S A PARKING VIOLATION?

First, it's necessary to understand the legal definition of parking. Parking is defined as *"the standing of a vehicle whether occupied or not, otherwise than temporarily for the purpose of and while actually engaged in loading or unloading merchandise or passengers."* A parking violation occurs any time that a vehicle is parked in an illegal place or manner, or is parked at an illegal time.

Parking citations cover such things as abandoned vehicles, double parking, loading zones, curbs and crosswalks, and Fire Station driveways. Typically, a parking citation is issued when you are not in the vehicle. The ticket is issued to the owner of the vehicle, and is written, filed, processed and recorded on the basis of the license plate rather than your driver's license.

If you're parked illegally, and are still in the vehicle, usually a normal traffic citation requiring your signature is issued.

WHAT IF I WASN'T DRIVING THE CAR?

This is the excuse used by almost everybody who appears in court on parking charges, and it just doesn't work. Most states hold the registered owner of the vehicle responsible for the correct parking of the vehicle, regardless of who was driving. The only way to prove that you were not the driver of the vehicle is to show that the vehicle was rented, leased or sold to someone else at the time of the violation.

The judge may consider other valid, provable excuses which would show you were somewhere else at the time of the violation. If you were overseas with the army, on the operating table or serving time in San Quentin at the time the parking ticket was issued, you may stand a chance of having the ticket dismissed.

DO PARKING VIOLATIONS APPEAR ON MY DRIVING RECORD?

No, because they are charged against the registered

Some signs have to be read twice before they make sense.

owner of the vehicle through the license plate rather than through your driver's license. If you fail to appear on the parking ticket, or just ignore the citation and don't pay, this will appear on your record. In fact, failure to appear or pay the fine on a parking ticket may result in a warrant being issued.

One unfortunate person was arrested recently with over 930 parking citations which he had never appeared on. He wasn't guilty of any of them; he just had a personalized license plate that read "NONE," which is what the parking control officer writes on all tickets for cars without license plates.

HOW DO THEY KNOW HOW LONG I'VE BEEN PARKED HERE?

There are two schools of thought in marking cars for timed parking. One is the obvious method, designed to show you that your car has been checked and intended to make you move it. This usually consists of a broad slash of chalk or grease-pencil across the sidewall of your tire. The other method of marking cars is designed to catch the motorist.

To catch motorists, the parking regulation officer usually marks across the tread of the tire with a grease-pencil or one of the new air guns which blow chalk dust, or may simply put a pebble or piece of gravel on the top of one of the tires. Another method used is to write down the license numbers of all the cars on that particular block. When the officer returns at the end of the legal time limit, it's easy to spot the vehicles which were there on his first pass.

Of course, parking control people aren't dumb, and are quite capable of remembering any car with an unusual appearance.

HOW DO THEY KNOW IF I'M LOADING IN A LOADING ZONE?

Usually it's the owner of the store you're parked in front of that tells the local police you're not loading. If your car is left in the loading zone for more than 5 or 10 minutes, and doesn't have commercial plates or other indications that it's being used for commercial reasons, you're likely to get a ticket. Many loading zone regulations fall under city or county ordinances, and are subject to wide variation from region to region.

HOW DO THEY KNOW
I'M NOT HANDICAPPED?

Usually, it's your license plates that give you away on this one. Handicapped persons and disabled veterans in most states are issued special series license plates which identify them as such. Often times they also display the blue and white "H" decal, or a little stick man in a wheelchair that are recognized as handicapped symbols. Persons who have lost the use of a limb frequently equip their cars with special equipment which allow them to operate the vehicle safely, and this is readily apparent to the officer as he looks over your car in the "Handicapped Only" parking space. If your car is a Porsche, and you accidentally left your tennis racquet in the car, you may have some explaining to do in court.

CAN I GET A PARKING TICKET
ON PRIVATE PROPERTY?

Yes, there are usually local ordinances which allow an officer to issue a citation on private property, or even to tow an unauthorized vehicle away. Usually the officer will only take action if a complaint has been filed by the owner of the property, and often the owner must sign the citation along with the officer. Most laws further state that the property must be properly posted, along with the authority to enforce the local ordinance. A typical sign might read, *"Private Property—Parking for customers of Smith's Store only. Violators' cars may be cited or impounded. Per Municipal Ordinance 1234-5."*

Handicapped persons have special permits and often have special equipment in their vehicles.

Some owners of private property take it upon themselves to punish offenders. In some cases, a large notice is pasted across the windshield notifying the driver that he is parked on private property, requiring him to scrape off sticky adhesive before he can leave. Another tactic is the use of a vehicle "immobilizer." This is a large, locking device that looks somewhat like a giant waffle iron. It clamps down over one of the wheels and prevents the wheel from turning. Usually you have to pay $5 or $10 to have someone come out from the business and unlock your car.

Private property is usually well marked.

If you car isn't "authorized," it might not be there when you get back.

WHAT'S PRIVATE PROPERTY?

Private property is simply any piece of land owned by an individual or a company rather than the state. Many private roads, driveways and parking lots are classified as private property. Only a few of the laws governing motor vehicles (specifically reckless driving, noise abatement and the like) apply on private property. It's perfectly legal for an unlicensed driver to cruise on his own driveway, or to run stop signs in his own backyard.

WHY DID THEY TAKE MY CAR?

Usually, cars are towed away and impounded when they are thought to be abandoned or stolen, when they are creating a hazard or an obstruction to other traffic, when it is found blocking a driveway or a fire hydrant, when the driver of the vehicle is injured or sick to the point that he cannot provide for the car's removal from the highway, or when the driver of the vehicle is arrested.

If you park your car in a "Tow-away" zone, you shouldn't be terribly surprised when it is towed away.

WHERE DID THEY TAKE MY CAR?

Vehicles which were abandoned, disabled or found blocking a highway may either be removed to a safe place down the highway, or towed away and stored. The vehicle may be stored at a private towing firm's impound lot, or at an official police garage which is actually run by a law enforcement agency.

If you were unconscious at the time your car was removed, check your pockets, often times the towing receipt or claim check may have been stuffed into your clothing by the officer. If you can't locate your car near the location you left it, call the local police department. They should be able to provide you with complete information on what happened to your car, and where it went. If they don't have any information on your car, then you're already talking to the right people to report a stolen auto.

HOW CAN I GET MY CAR BACK?

Once you locate your car, it's usually only a matter of money. You will probably be charged for the towing plus the mileage, and a daily charge for storage on the car. Even if you catch the tow-truck before he pulls away, you may still have to pay a "hook-up" charge to pay for him coming out to your location. In some cases, you will have to have a signed release from the local law enforcement agency before they will allow you to reclaim your car.

ARE THERE VIOLATIONS I CAN GET WITHOUT BEING IN A MOTOR VEHICLE?

Sure, the vehicle code covers every facet of the use of the highways, including what you can and cannot build next to the highway, what colors can be used when painting the highway and curbs, and covering anything that walks, rolls or crawls on or across the highway.

WHAT CAN THEY DO TO ME IF I'M WALKING?

Other than being run over, a pedestrian may be given a ticket just like the driver of an automobile for violating any one of the hundreds of laws pertaining to pedestrians. These laws include failure to yield to a motor vehicle when crossing outside of a crosswalk, failure to yield to an emergency vehicle when in a crosswalk, starting across the street after the "Don't Walk" sign has already started flashing, walking on a limited-access highway, hitchhiking and jaywalking.

WHAT IS "JAYWALKING"?

Jaywalking is usually defined as a pedestrian crossing a roadway, outside of a crosswalk, and between two intersections which are both controlled by signal lights. Local ordinances may prohibit pedestrians from crossing *any* roadway except at a crosswalk. Crosswalks may either be the plainly marked, painted lines across the asphalt we all think of, or simply an imaginary extension of the sidewalks through an intersection. Thus, in a legal sense, there are crosswalks at almost every intersection whether they are marked or not.

CAN THEY GIVE ME A TICKET ON MY SKATEBOARD?

Very definitely. Since the rise in popularity of skateboards, laws forbidding the use of "wheeled toys" on streets and sidewalks have been enacted in many states. Also, depending on your state's definition of a vehicle, you may receive a citation for speeding, or for failing to obey traffic signals or stop signs. Most of these skateboard laws are municipal or county laws. "No Skateboards" signs are often posted on private property such as shopping malls. While you won't get a ticket for riding your skateboard on property posted like this, you can get thrown off the property by the security guards.

CAN THEY GIVE ME A TICKET ON MY BICYCLE?

Yes, in many states bicycles must be licensed (usu-

You can even get a ticket for walking.

ally through a municipal agency) and are required to obey all of the applicable vehicle code laws that the driver of a motor vehicle would be required to follow. Surprised cyclists have been given tickets for speeding (they can be clocked on radar) and for riding through red lights and stop signs. In most states, it is illegal for anyone to ride a bicycle on a sidewalk.

OKAY, HOW ABOUT A HORSE?

You can get a citation on a horse, too. Often city ordinances will specify places (business districts in particular) where riding a horse is prohibited. You can also be cited on the highway under state vehicle laws if your horse obstructs traffic or causes an accident. You may also get a citation under your state's litter laws if nature follows its course and you are responsible for *"dumping or depositing noisome, nauseous or offensive matter of any kind upon a highway."* Isn't it amazing that the government regulates horse manure.

WHAT IS A "DOCUMENT CITATION"?

Document citations are given to motorists who are not carrying their licenses or registrations, or are unable to show that they have insurance, or a valid license or registration. These citations are often dismissed, or the sentences are suspended when the necessary documents are produced in court, and the dates show that they were valid at the time the citation was issued.

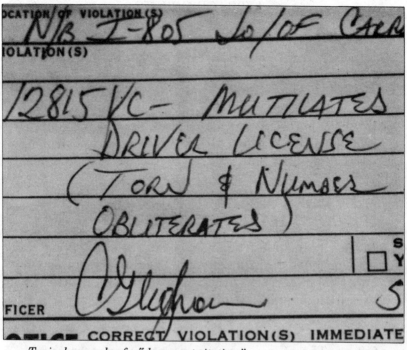

Typical example of a "document citation."

IS IT AGAINST THE LAW TO DRIVE WITHOUT INSURANCE?

At least 11 states to date have compulsory insurance laws, laws requiring you to have insurance. Several other states are now considering it. The bureaucracy required to support an effective compulsory insurance system is huge, and few states can afford to maintain one. As a result, most of the compulsory insurance laws are ineffective, with large numbers of uninsured motorists still operating on the highway.

Operating a vehicle without insurance in the compulsory states is illegal, in non-compulsory states it's merely foolish. Because of the number of vehicles and motorists involved, compulsory insurance is largely unenforceable; people can buy insurance policies, and then cancel them the day after they get their registration. With the potential for lawsuits in automobile accidents, insurance is almost the only way to protect yourself against liability.

HOW DOES THE OFFICER KNOW IF I DON'T HAVE INSURANCE?

Usually, he doesn't have any idea at all whether or not you have insurance. Some compulsory states require the motorist to carry an insurance identification card with them, and to display a decal on the car. These are still ineffective, because they don't show whether or not the insurance policy is still valid and maintained. The officer may not be all that interested in whether or not you have insurance. He isn't the one who may be sued, or the one who's trying to make a claim for repairs.

CAN A PASSENGER DRINK IN MY VEHICLE?

Some states do allow the drinking of alcoholic beverages in a motor vehicle, but these laws vary widely. Other states totally forbid the presence of an open container of alcohol within the vehicle, but may allow it within the living section of a motorhome or camper (check your local laws, sometimes riding in the living section of a trailer may be illegal). Even when legal, drinking in a vehicle is never a good idea. The opportunity and peer pressure is on the driver to drink along with the passengers, and all 50 states have laws against driving under the influence of alcohol.

WHAT ABOUT DRINKING AND DRIVING?

Don't.

THE SYSTEM
A brief introduction to the way things work.

WHAT ARE TRAFFIC LAWS?

Traffic laws are the rules and regulations enacted by the governing bodies of the states to provide an orderly, safe and efficient system of motor vehicle travel while preventing behavior that may result in personal injury, property damage or death.

Driving is not a right; it is a privilege given by the state to the individual who can meet the licensing standards that have been established by that state. Anyone who is found violating the laws of the state is subject to imprisonment or fine, or in the case of driving offenses may have his license suspended or revoked. When a police officer apprehends you in the commission of one of these crimes, he can either arrest you and take you before the first available judge, or he can release you by issuing a citation.

WHAT'S A CITATION?

A traffic citation is not an award they give for good driving techniques, but is a written notification by a law enforcement officer that 1) You broke a traffic law, and 2) You got caught while doing it. The citation advises you of the specific law you were charged with violating, and gives you the time and place that you have to appear to answer those charges. The citation also requires your signature as a "promise to appear" before the officer can release you. Otherwise he has to take you before the first available judge. The citation is also the official record which serves as a formal complaint to the court.

WHAT IS A SUBPOENA?

A subpoena is a document which orders a particular person or object to appear in court at the time and date specified on the document. Subpoenas are usually requested by one of the parties in a trial proceeding, and are issued by order of the court.

HOW IS A SUBPOENA USED?

A defendant in a criminal case is entitled to have witnesses present at the trial to testify in his behalf, and to be confronted by all of the evidence which was used against him. If you feel that the witnesses or articles you wish to have at your trial will not appear voluntarily, you may need a subpoena to ensure that they will be there. To do so, you need only provide the clerk of the court with the names, addresses and phone numbers of the witnesses and the descriptions and locations of the objects at least one week prior to your trial. The expense of issuing and serving (delivering) the subpoenas is assumed by the court and doesn't cost you anything.

However, the court will insist that your requests be reasonable in nature and relevant to the case. You can't subpoena the President of the United States to question him about the 55 mile per hour limit, but you probably could subpoena him if he actually witnessed your alleged violation. Likewise, it would be unreasonable to subpoena the patrol car that was used to apprehend you and expect it to show up in court. However it would be perfectly reasonable to subpoena the certificate of calibration for the car's speedometer, or the unit's portable radar equipment. Any witnesses to the violation, or technical experts to testify about the equipment used by either you or the officer, and any documents or training records that affect you or the officer are fair game for being subpoenaed.

WHAT IF I DON'T APPEAR ON A SUBPOENA?

A subpoena is an *order*, not a request from the court. If you don't show up on a subpoena, the court may find you "in contempt of court" and issue a "bench warrant" for your arrest. In some cases, a Deputy Sheriff or Marshal may be dispatched to your home or business to find you and bring you immediately to court.

WHAT IS A TRAFFIC WARRANT?

A warrant is a written order of the court, directed to a police officer, which demands that the person named on the warrant be brought before the court. Warrants are usually issued by the court when a person fails to appear as promised on a citation, or fails to appear as ordered on a subpoena or summons. A person arrested on the authority of a warrant must be immediately brought before a judge, where he will have the opportunity to answer both the original charges, and the new charges of failure to appear.

Warrants cost the court money to process and execute. If you fail to appear and a warrant is issued, even though you later came to court voluntarily without being arrested, you may be required to pay a fine to cover the expense of the warrant. This can range from $45 to $75 in most states, and is in addition to the fine you have to pay for the original violation.

DO THEY ACTUALLY COME TO YOUR HOUSE AND ARREST YOU?

They may. Often, for minor traffic violations, no direct action will be taken. However, the traffic warrant is entered as "outstanding" on your driving record. Anytime an officer runs your license through a computer check, the computer is going to light up and tell him about the warrant. If you have an outstanding warrant for failure to appear, don't be surprised if you get arrested the next time you are stopped by a traffic officer.

For major violations, and sometimes for minor ones as well, the marshals may actually appear at your house to take you into custody. Often times, the marshal's raids are conducted in the early morning hours to catch you while you're sleeping. In some states, this is prohibited as certain types of traffic warrants can only be executed during daylight hours.

HOW DO I KNOW WHEN AND WHERE TO APPEAR?

The time, date and location of your court appearance are usually specified on the bottom of the citation form. In addition, the officer will usually tell you to make sure that there is no question about when and where you are to appear. Usually, you can appear for arraignment *before* the specified date if you wish.

Usually the time and date of your appearance are clearly indicated on the front of the citation.

WHAT'S AN ARRAIGNMENT?

The arraignment is your first appearance in court on your traffic offense. You will not be asked to present your defense or produce any witnesses at an arraignment, but only to make your "plea" to the court. When you appear at the arraignment, the judge will call your name, read off the charges against you and ask how you plead to each offense. The acceptable pleas are Guilty, Guilty with an Explanation, Not Guilty and Nolo Contendere (or No Contest).

A trial is a separate procedure which follows the arraignment if you plead "Not Guilty." In some states, however, the trial may follow immediately after the arraignment. In fact, the judge may simply tell you what you're charged with and ask you for your side of the story, without even asking your plea. Suddenly you may find yourself presenting your side of the case, before the prosecution's and be almost totally unprepared. This is completely wrong, you have the right to a reasonable amount of time to prepare your case, and proper legal procedure calls for the state to present its case against you first.

An alternative to the arraignment is to pay the bail. Often, the amount of bail is specified on the citation, or may be sent to you in the mail as a separate bail notice. Most minor traffic offenses are bailable and you can merely send the bail money to the court instead of actually appearing. Bail is then "forfeited" at the time of your trial and the offense is recorded on your record the same as if you had plead guilty and paid a fine.

SHOULD I BRING MONEY?

Yes, you should definitely bring enough money to cover any amount that you may be fined. You can check with the clerk of the court in advance to find out what this amount is. If you are found guilty, you must be prepared to pay the full amount of the fine. The judge may not allow you to leave the building without doing so, and you may have to resort to calling a rich friend or a bail bond company before you can be released.

Even if you plead "Not Guilty," you will need to bring money. The court will require you to post a bond equal to the amount of the fine to ensure that you will return for your trial. The bond will be returned to you if you are acquitted at your trial, or if you are found guilty the bond will be used to pay your fine.

CAN I JUST GO TO JAIL
INSTEAD OF PAYING?

Yes, the bail money you pay is used instead of a jail term. If you don't pay the bail, a sentence is your only alternative. Sentences are not always in the county "clink," however. Some judges sentence people to a certain amount of unpaid, volunteer service in an emergency room, or on the crew of an ambulance or wrecker where they can see the results of auto accidents.

DO THEY TAKE CHECKS, MONEY ORDERS
OR CREDIT CARDS?

The vast majority of courts will accept checks from state residents when the bank is also located in that state. Most courts will also accept money orders that are made out with the name of that court. Twenty-seven states currently accept automobile club membership cards of various kinds. The courts bill the club for the amount of bail, and if it is forfeited you are required to pay the club back before your membership card is returned.

No matter how you pay, always be sure to get a receipt for the amount so that you can prove you have paid at a later date.

Many automobile clubs and associations provide members with these "credit cards" which guarantee the member's bail.

WHAT'S A CONTINUANCE?

Following your arraignment, you have a constitutional right to a speedy trial. (This doesn't mean that your trial is going to be a "quickie" but only that the trial date should be scheduled soon, usually within 30 to 45 days.) If you ask for a continuance, you waive the right (kiss it good-bye) to a speedy trial and ask that you be given a longer period of time before appearing. You'll be asked to provide a reasonable explanation for asking for the continuance, such as a witness cannot appear on that date, serious personal or business conflicts and the like. A continuance is only a postponement of the trial proceedings.

A continuance can often be to your advantage. By extending the period of time between your violation and the actual trial, you increase the chances of the officer not being available (he may resign or transfer, or just go on vacation), his memory of the incident fading, and of the evidence being misplaced or lost.

The prosecutor may also ask for a continuance, to give him time to prepare his case or summon his witnesses. This cannot be granted beyond the period within which you are guaranteed a speedy trial unless you waive your rights. An officer failing to show up in response to a subpoena is not a good legal cause for delay of your trial, and often a judge will merely dismiss the case rather than grant a continuance.

SHOULD I ASK FOR A CONTINUANCE?

If you need more time to consider the charges against you, to construct a defense or to hire an attorney, you should definitely ask for a continuance. If you need even more time, you can ask for a further continuance, and multiple continuances are often granted. If you go beyond 3 continuances, the judge begins to suspect you are merely stalling for time and a further continuance may not be granted. Asking for a continuance is very unlikely to hurt your case in any way, and is often of benefit.

WHAT IF AFTER THE ARRAIGNMENT, I DON'T APPEAR IN COURT FOR MY TRIAL?

If you were released from arraignment after paying an appearance bond, there is no big problem. You merely forfeit the bail, and the case is recorded as a conviction against you. If, however, you were released on your "Own Recognizance" (also called O.R., a personal guarantee on your oath that you will appear) then you could be in trouble. The judge may issue a bench warrant for your arrest, and hold you in contempt of court.

CAN I CALL THE COURT TO MAKE EXCUSES?

Many courts will accept a telephone request for a continuance or postponement if the offense is "bailable" and your reason is valid and constitutes an emergency for you. If you suddenly became ill, or were called out of town, you may telephone the clerk of the court you are scheduled to appear in and ask that your arraignment be postponed. If it is granted, be sure and get the name and title of the person you were talking to. Immediately follow up your telephone conversation with a registered letter making reference to the telephone call, and describing the reason for your postponement and your understanding of the new trial date.

If you cannot appear in person, you can often plead "Not Guilty" by mail. The specific procedure is usually printed on the back side of your copy of the citation.

Your letter should state that you waive the right to a formal arraignment and respectfully request that the court accept your plea. You should specify the trial date on which you wish to appear (make it within the "speedy trial" time limit [45 days] and don't waive your right to a speedy trial), specify whether you want a court or jury trial, and ask that you be released until the time of trial on your own recognizance. Most judges will accept this, although many states require that you post a $25 appearance bond in the meantime. You will generally be notified by mail if there are any further forms that have to be completed, or any other problems with your request.

You can also appear by proxy, having your attorney appear at the arraignment to plead on your behalf.

HOW CAN I TAKE CARE OF THE CITATION WITHOUT GOING TO COURT?

If the offense is a bailable offense, the court will inform you what the ticket will cost. You can then mail in a check or money order for the bail amount, and never appear in court at all. In fact, this is what the courts would generally prefer you to do, as it is the easiest way to process your citation through the system while keeping all the expenses to a minimum. Of course, by forfeiting the bail money, your case is treated the same as if you had pleaded guilty to the charge.

WHAT IS A "PLEADING"?

The pleading is just another term for the arraignment,

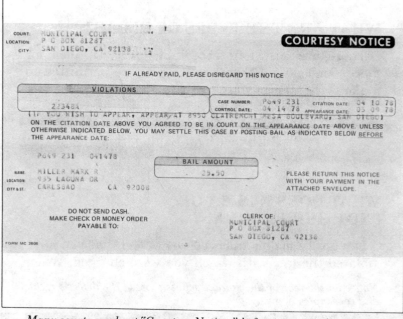

Many courts send out "Courtesy Notices" before your arraignment to make it easy for the driver to plead guilty and pay his fine.

your first appearance in court. The arraignment is usually a separate proceeding, but may be combined with the trial in some courts. There is no reason to be nervous, as it is simply a proceeding in which you can enter your plea, have your bail determined or have a trial date set.

Generally, you should attempt to be pleasant and dignified at your arraignment, as it doesn't hurt to favorably impress the judge. Be neatly dressed and well groomed, be sober, and make any answers or statements polite, respectful and clearly spoken. You can expect the same treatment in return.

WHAT ARE THE TYPES OF PLEAS?

There are only four acceptable pleas (A plea for mercy isn't one of them) which you are permitted to make at the time of your arraignment. Those pleas are:

1. Not Guilty
2. Guilty
3. Guilty with an Explanation
4. Nolo Contendere

WHAT DOES A PLEA OF "NOT GUILTY" MEAN?

Not guilty means that you do not feel that you have violated the law with which you were charged. When

Notice on the rear of the citation waives most of the driver's rights and cops a plea of guilty.

APPEARANCE, PLEA OF GUILTY AND WAIVER

I, the undersigned, do hereby enter my appearance on the complaint of the offense charged on the other side of this citation. I have been informed of my right to a trial, that my signature to this plea of guilty will have the same force and effect as a judgment of court, and that this record will be sent to the Licensing Authority of this State (or of the State where I received my license to drive). I do hereby PLEAD GUILTY to said offense as charged, WAIVE my right to a HEARING by the court, and agree to pay the penalty prescribed for my offense.

_____
(Defendant's Name)

_____
(Address)

_____
(Driver's License Number)

you plead not guilty, you are telling the court that you are innocent of the charge and wish to contest it at trial. The judge will determine the type of trial you wish to have, and then will set a date and time for the trial. He will order you to return at that time, and will caution you that you will receive no further order, notice or subpoena to appear.

If you have not already posted bail prior to your arraignment, he will establish the amount of bail you must deposit with the court to ensure your return before you can be released following the arraignment. Deserving defendants may be released on their own recognizance.

WHAT'S A PLEA OF "GUILTY" MEAN?

When you plead guilty at your arraignment, you are giving up your right to a trial for the offense, and admitting that you committed the offense charged without trying to give any explanation for your misconduct. The plea of guilty goes down on your record just as if you had gone to trial and had been convicted. After pleading guilty to the offense, you are usually sentenced by the judge right at the arraignment.

WHAT DOES "GUILTY WITH AN EXPLANATION" MEAN?

Guilty with an explanation goes on your record just the same as if you had plead guilty. You are still confessing that you committed the offense as charged, but you are offering an explanation of why you committed the offense. If you plead guilty with an explanation, the court will not dismiss your case, but may suspend or reduce the amount of the fine.

Your explanation should be short, concise and to the point. Don't beat around the bush and deny that you committed the violation after making this plea, because the judge will ask you to either withdraw your plea and plead not guilty, or he will just tell you that he has heard enough and give you a sentence. Other than the fact that your sentence *might* be reduced, guilty with an explanation is handled the same as a plea of guilty.

WHAT DOES A PLEA OF "NOLO CONTENDERE" MEAN?

The plea of "Nolo Contendere" means "I'm not admitting that I did it, but I'm not going to argue that I didn't either." As far as your driving record and the court's view of your case are concerned, a plea of nolo contendere is just the same as pleading guilty. However, in a civil suit against you resulting from an accident in which you received the citation, a plea of guilty could be used as an admission by you that you were at fault in causing the accident. The plea of nolo contendere cannot be used against you in that manner.

Nolo contendere is one term that's best left in Latin for the lawyers to use. If you're seriously considering a plea of nolo contendere, you had better consider hiring an attorney to defend you because you may well be in over your head.

Before a case goes to trial, the prosecutor will sometimes want to play "Let's Make A Deal." A not too uncommon trick is the old line, "Rather than prosecute this through to the inevitable verdict of "guilty," I'll let you cop a plea of nolo contendere." If you're approached on this one, don't believe it. Nolo contendere is treated exactly the same by the court as a plea of guilty and your sentence will be identical.

WHAT'S THE DIFFERENCE BETWEEN A COURT AND A JURY TRIAL?

In a court trial, only the judge is hearing your case, and he alone will render a decision as to your guilt or innocence. If the defense of your case is based on some technical point of law, having a judge who understands all about the legal technicalities can really be to your advantage.

In a jury trial, a panel of people from your community (most juries have 12 members, although some may have less) hears your case, and then they privately discuss all of the evidence and come to a conclusion as to your innocence or guilt. The decision of the jury must be unanimous, otherwise the judge has to either declare a mistrial and give you an entire new trial, or dismiss your citation.

The jury trial has some definite advantages, because the prosecutor has to convince all 12 people who are probably drivers like yourself and may be sympathetic to anyone who gets a ticket.

The Constitution gives you the right to a jury trial when you are charged with a crime. Many states have reduced traffic offenses to infractions rather than misdemeanors, so you may not have the right to a jury trial in cases which are classed as infractions. In misdemeanor cases, you will always have the opportunity to have a jury trial. If you desire a court trial, and the prosecutor agrees, then you may waive your right to a jury trial and have your case heard by a judge.

WHAT IF I WANT A DIFFERENT JUDGE?

There are a number of reasons why you might want another judge than the one assigned to your case. If you recently appeared in his court and think he might remember you; if he's widely known as a "hanging judge" with a reputation for being tough; or if you think he might be prejudiced against you for any other reason—you may have your case heard by another judge. This procedure, known as an "Affidavit of Prejudice" *must* be filed before your trial begins, and as soon as possible after you learn which judge has been assigned to your case.

This affidavit may be submitted to the court either verbally or in writing. The basic form for the motion is as follows:

(Your name)
(Your address)
(Your telephone number)
DEFENDANT
              IN THE JUSTICE COURT
       _____ JUDICIAL DISTRICT,
      COUNTY OF _____, (Your State)
Regarding the Matter of)
)   CITATION # _____
People of the State of ___)
)   AFFIDAVIT OF
Plaintiffs, vs.   )   PREJUDICE
(Your name), Defendant)

To the Honorable Justice Court: I, (your name), appearing in propria persona as a party to the within action, believe that the judge before whom the trial of said action is pending is prejudiced against me so that I cannot, or believe that I cannot, have a fair and impartial trial or hearing before such judge.

I declare under penalty of perjury that the above statements are true and correct to the best of my knowledge.

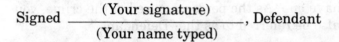

Signed _____, Defendant
        (Your signature)
        (Your name typed)

This document doesn't have to be typed, although it would probably look a lot neater if it were. Just be certain that it is presented to the clerk of the court as soon as you find out who the judge is, and be sure that you would feel better off with some other judge. Be sure to keep a copy for your records too.

WHO IS THE PROSECUTION?

The prosecution is the attorney representing the governmental agency attempting to prove your guilt in court. The prosecution represents the government, and because the government is the representative of the people of your state or city, the prosecution is often referred to as "The People." Depending on which agency is prosecuting you, the prosecution may be variously referred to as the "State," the "Commonwealth," or the "City."

WHO ARE THE "PEOPLE"?

The People is the term used in court to describe the prosecutor, and all of the government. This is because laws are enacted by representatives of the people of that state, and anytime you violate a law, you have committed a crime against the people of that state.

WHO IS THE DEFENSE?

That's you if you get a ticket, and your attorney if you have one. As the person accused of the crime, you will also be referred to as the "Defendant."

SHOULD I HIRE AN ATTORNEY?

If you are charged with any of the really serious offenses like reckless driving, engaging in a speed contest (street racing), hit and run, or driving under the influence, you had better hire the best attorney you can find. Also consider hiring an attorney for minor offenses if your driving record is absolutely horrible and you may lose your license. If you're facing a $500 fine, the few hundred dollars of an attorney's time may be well spent.

For minor traffic offenses, usually the savings in the fine can't justify the expense of an attorney. Often representing yourself can be an advantage, particularly at jury trials. That way it's you as a layman against the prosecutor, rather than a battle between two attorneys. Juries often root for the layman, who they can identify with.

CAN ANYBODY ELSE REPRESENT ME?

In the courtroom, you can either represent yourself, or be represented by an attorney. No one else can represent you.

Sometimes a relative or close friend may be allowed to represent you at your arraignment if you are unavailable. It's up to the judge as to whether your "proxy" will be allowed to speak for you, and usually your representative is only allowed to enter a plea of not guilty, or to ask that the arraignment be postponed until a date when you can appear.

Most states handle juvenile traffic citations in a separate court than the adults.

WHAT IF I'M A JUVENILE?

Most states handle juveniles in an entirely different court than the adults, and often will not even go through an arraignment. Typically the juvenile has to appear in the juvenile court, or a juvenile division of the municipal court building, with at least one of his parents. The case is heard before a referee who will decide your guilt or innocence, and set the fine.

A juvenile is still in the care and custody of his parents or guardians, and doesn't necessarily have the right to have a jury trial.

WHEN I GO TO COURT, SHOULD I MENTION THE OTHER CITATION I PICKED UP IN THE MEANTIME?

It would be unwise (to say the least) to mention any other citations at all unless you are asked directly about it under oath. You shouldn't lie about it if asked, but there's no reason to let the cat out of the bag and face a much stiffer fine. If you have two violations with appearance dates very close together, you should consider appearing in the morning on one violation, and the same day at night court on the other. This way you may avoid facing the same judge twice, and there's a chance that the two sets of paperwork won't ever be correlated before going to the Department of Motor Vehicles.

DOES THE JUDGE KNOW MY PAST DRIVING RECORD?

Part of the procedure when they take your copy of

the citation and put you on the court "calendar" for a particular judge, is to run a copy of your record from the Department of Motor Vehicles and attach it to the other documents associated with your case. If you plead guilty at the arraignment, the judge has the information available to him on which he bases the amount of the fine. For repeat violations, the fines get very large and can go well over $500.

In the court trial, it is improper and illegal for the judge or the jury to consider your past record. The theory is that you are only being tried for the one offense, and anything else has no bearing on the case at hand. However, once your guilt has been established, the judge does have your record with the other documents to consult before sentencing you.

DOES HE KNOW MY OUT OF STATE RECORD?

Yes, most states have reciprocal agreements to exchange information on driving records. A violation by a driver from one state who is cited in another will probably have that information sent back to his own state's Department of Motor Vehicles.

WILL THE OFFICER BE IN COURT?

The officer won't appear at the time of your arraignment, but will usually appear at your trial. As the defendant, you have the right to be confronted by the evidence against you. The most important piece of evidence the "People" have is the officer's own testimony. Without the officer's testimony, it is very un-

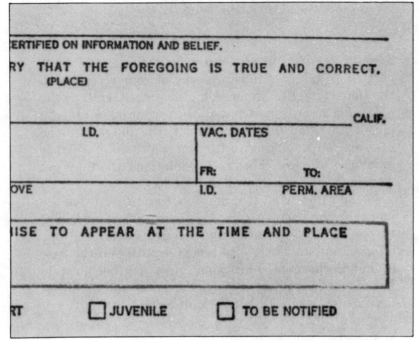

ERTIFIED ON INFORMATION AND BELIEF.

RY THAT THE FOREGOING IS TRUE AND CORRECT.
(PLACE)

CALIF.

I.D.	VAC. DATES	
	FR:	TO:
OVE	I.D.	PERM. AREA

ISE TO APPEAR AT THE TIME AND PLACE

RT ☐ JUVENILE ☐ TO BE NOTIFIED

Many citation forms include a place for the officer's vacation dates, to ensure that the trial won't be scheduled in his absence.

likely that prosecution will be able to prove their case.

If the officer doesn't show up in court, the prosecutor may try to persuade you to go to court and accept the officer's notes, sworn statement or just the citation instead of his actual testimony. It would be very unwise to agree to this, as it is impossible for you to cross-examine a written statement which is likely to be accepted as fact by the court.

If there's a good reason for the officer not showing up (such as he was hospitalized the night before) then the judge might be inclined to grant a continuance to the prosecutor. If the officer doesn't have a reasonable excuse, you can probably move to have your case dismissed and have it granted by the judge. Without

the officer's actual testimony, the chances of a successful prosecution are almost zero, unless there are other
witnesses or physical evidence to support the offense.

WHAT IF THE OFFICER IS UNABLE TO APPEAR?

If the officer is unable to appear, many times the
prosecutor will attempt to get you to agree to a "trial
by deposition." A deposition is the officer's sworn
statement of the facts in a case. A typical deposition
form used by law enforcement agencies is as follows:

CENTERVILLE POLICE DEPARTMENT

Citation Number _____

Defendant's Name _____

Date/Time of Violation_____

Place of Violation_____

V.C. Section(s) Charged _____

DECLARATION OF FACTS
This space is for narrative description. Include the following if applicable:
  1. *Weather conditions.*
  2. *Lighting.*
  3. *Road conditions and type.*
  4. *How was driver identified?*

5. *Where was defendant when first identified?*
6. *Where was the citing officer?*
7. *Essential elements of the violation.*
8. *How and where stop was made.*
9. *Passengers in defendant's vehicle.*
10. *Conversation with defendant.*
11. *Did you have a partner?*
12. *Attach speedometer calibration if speed
    is element.*
13. *Diagram on reverse side of affidavit.*

The form is filled out and then signed by the officer
and witnessed by one of his supervisors. Just remember, you do have a right to be confronted by all of the
evidence (including the officer's testimony) and you
can't cross-examine his notes. We don't recommend
that you agree to a trial by deposition.

WHAT ARE THE CHANCES
THE OFFICER WILL APPEAR?

The chances are very high that the officer will appear at your trial. After all, that's part of his job that
the taxpayers are paying for. However, officers do occasionally miss a trial for various reasons. These reasons include:

1. The officer may have resigned or been fired and is
   no longer working for that agency.
2. The officer may have been transferred to another
   station and be working hundreds of miles away.
3. The prosecutor may have failed to subpoena him
   as a witness.

4. Because of some emergency, the officer may have been required to be on duty the day of your trial.
5. The officer may be on vacation.
6. The officer may be sick.
7. The officer may have simply overslept or forgotten. (Remember, police officers are human too.)

WHAT IF THE OFFICER DOESN'T APPEAR?

If the judge doesn't grant the prosecution a continuance until the officer can show up (the continuance couldn't be beyond your statutory period for a speedy trial), it's just like Christmas time for you. The chances are very good that you will not be convicted, unless the prosecution has other witnesses or evidence that he can enter into the trial to prove your guilt. Because he has to prove your guilt "beyond a reasonable doubt" his chances of doing that are very slim indeed. The mere fact of the officer's absence should be enough to introduce that reasonable doubt in the minds of the judge and/or jury.

IF THERE WERE TWO OFFICERS, WILL BOTH SHOW UP IN COURT?

Very rarely will both officers show up at your trial, unless it is a particularly important trial for a serious violation. If you think that the prosecutor has more than one witness against you, you should move in court to have all witnesses excluded except the one testifying. This is your right, and the court will grant your request. If there is more than one witness, it may actu-

APPROX.	P.F. / MAX.	VEH. LMT.	SAFE				

LOCATION OF VIOLATION (S)

☐ OFFENSE (S) NOT COMMITTED IN MY PRESENCE, CERTIFIED ON INFORMATION AND BELIEF.
I CERTIFY, UNDER PENALTY OF PERJURY THAT THE FOREGOING IS TRUE AND CORRECT,
EXECUTED ON THE DATE SHOWN ABOVE AT   (PLACE)

CALIF.

•ISSUING OFFICER	I.D.	VAC. DATES
		FR: TO:
NAME OF ARRESTING OFFICER-IF DIFFERENT FROM ABOVE	I.D. PERM. AREA	

WITHOUT ADMITTING GUILT, I PROMISE TO APPEAR AT THE TIME AND PLACE
CHECKED BELOW
X   SIGNATURE

☐ MUNICIPAL COURT   ☐ JUSTICE COURT   ☐ JUVENILE   ☐ TO BE NOTIFIED
ADDRESS:

☐ ON THE _____ DAY OF _____ 19 _____ AT _____ M. ☐ WITHIN 15 DAYS

☐ OR YOU MAY APPEAR AT _____ P.M. ON _____ .
TO ANSWER CHARGES OF VIOLATION (S) DESCRIBED ABOVE.
FORM APPROVED BY JUDICIAL COUNCIL OF CALIFORNIA 8-6-76 V.C. 40513 (B) P.C. 853.9
CHP 215 (REV. 8/76)

Separate lines are provided for two officers to sign a citation.

ally be to your advantage. The different witnesses will
often have very different testimonies, and any discrepancies or conflicts between them can all add to
your establishment of reasonable doubt. By contradict-
ing each other the witnesses give the court the impression that their memory of the incident isn't really very
clear (often it isn't).

Because of the conflict that may be generated between two witnesses, it may actually be to your advantage to subpoena both officers to your trial.

DOES THE OFFICER GET PAID FOR HIS APPEARANCE?

If the officer is appearing in court during the hours in which he routinely works, he won't get any extra pay for appearing in court, but will be paid his normal salary for the hours. If he is normally assigned to night duty, he will either be paid overtime, or will be given compensatory hours. (This means that he gets an equivalent number of hours off his normal schedule for the extra hours he puts in during the trial.)

WILL HE APPEAR ON HIS DAY OFF?

Yes, in fact many officers look forward to appearing in court on their day off as a means of generating extra income from the overtime hours. Other officers may want nothing more than to get the heck out of court so they can enjoy their day off. These officers may be quick to pressure the prosecutor to make some kind of deal with you in order to speed things up.

WILL I HAVE A CHANCE TO TELL MY SIDE OF THE STORY?

Yes, after the prosecution has presented, finished and rested its case, you will have an opportunity to present your defense. Your testimony will probably be the key part of your defense.

During the prosecution's presentation, you will also have opportunities to ask their witnesses questions in what is called "cross examination." During that time, you should also be able to point out part of your side of the story by asking some very specific questions.

WILL I BE SWORN IN OR UNDER OATH?

Only if you intend to testify as a witness. Before any witness, including yourself, is allowed to testify, he must face the clerk of the court, raise his right hand and answer the oath given by the clerk: "Do you swear that the testimony you shall give in the cause now pending before this court will be the truth, the whole truth and nothing but the truth, so help you God?"

Before a witness is allowed to testify, he must answer in the affirmative by saying, "Yes." "I do," or something to that effect.

WHAT IF I DON'T BELIEVE IN GOD OR IF I DON'T WANT TO SWEAR ON A BIBLE?

If you object to swearing to God for religious reasons, you can "affirm" that you will tell the truth, but you should tell the clerk of your intentions in advance.

CAN I LIE?

When you are under oath, you are legally bound to tell the truth. Under the Constitution, you can refuse to answer any question that you feel might be used against you in any way, but if you lie and are caught you could end up in jail for perjury.

WILL I BE ABLE TO ASK THE OFFICER QUESTIONS?

Yes, immediately after the officer's testimony you will be given the opportunity to "cross-examine" the witness. You don't have to come on like Perry Mason, but you should be well organized with a complete list of questions you wish to ask the officer prepared well in advance. You can add to this list as he testifies, being sure to note any inconsistencies or conflicts in his testimony. Feel free to take notes on his answers for later use; the court doesn't expect you to memorize everything the officer says.

This is not a time to argue with the officer, or to deny the offense, but only to gather information from the officer's testimony. If you get into a "No I didn't—Yes you did!" type argument with the officer, the judge will give you a verbal slap on the wrist. If you persist, he may even find you in contempt of court and fine you.

You should also be careful not to admit anything in your questions that could be used by the prosecutor in his case. Ask the officer, "Where were you when my vehicle entered the intersection?" not "Where were you when I ran that red light?"

CAN I GET WITNESSES FOR MY SIDE?

Yes, you have the right to have witnesses appear on your behalf, as long as their testimony is relevant to the case.

HOW CAN I GET WITNESSES?

Compile a complete list of all the people you would like to appear at your trial before you go to your arraignment. When you plead not guilty at the arraignment, the judge will set a date for the trial to take place. You should then go to the clerk of the court (one week before the trial at the very latest) and ask him to

Your passengers are often your best witnesses.

prepare subpoenas for those persons. You will have to be able to provide home and business addresses and phone numbers for each of the persons you wish to have served.

If you feel one of the persons you are subpoenaing might not really want to go to court on your behalf, you had better consider dropping him from your defense. He could be hostile to you in court, and do more damage than good.

SHOULD I PAY MY WITNESSES?

Absolutely not. The witnesses are there to present fair accurate information to both sides of the case. If the person testifying has been paid by you (some folks call it bribing a witness) it could be very embarrassing.

Although it may seem too good to be true, the court actually pays the witnesses to compensate them for their loss of a day's work and the cost of transportation. In fact, it is too good to be true, because a typical witness would be paid slightly more than $5 for the day, and perhaps 15¢ per mile.

In civil cases, expert witnesses are often paid for their services, but tactics such as these are best left for the attorneys. You'll have to check with the clerk of the court in your area to find out what the rates for witnesses are, but don't be shocked if they barely cover the bus fare.

HOW MANY WITNESSES CAN I BRING?

You are entitled to bring as many witnesses to your trial as you feel are relevant to your case. Don't do this lightly though, because you will have to swear to the marshal under oath that the witnesses you subpoena are essential to your case. You should also remember that every witness you bring into the trial will be subject to cross-examination by the prosecutor, and he may dig up some answers from your witnesses that you'd rather not have them say.

CAN I BRING CHARACTER WITNESSES?

If you really think you can, you've probably been watching too many late night re-runs. The fact that you got straight A's all the way through kindergarten and always cleaned your plate (even if you ate all your peas and carrots) has absolutely no bearing on whether or not you were doing 85 miles per hour through a playground. Only witnesses who are relevant to the particular incident, in which you are charged, will be allowed to testify.

HOW LONG DOES A TRIAL LAST?

Most trials are surprisingly short; you're lucky if it runs over 15 minutes. However, you will usually have to appear early in the morning to have your case scheduled, and your case might not be called until several hours later. Of course, this time can be to your advantage. Unless yours is one of the first trials scheduled, you'll have a good opportunity to observe how other cases are handled (or mishandled) and may pick up on some useful techniques for your own trial.

DOES A JURY TRIAL LAST LONGER?

A jury trial will often last quite a bit longer than a court trial heard before a judge. A jury trial naturally is slower because of the need to select the jurors for your case, and the need for the judge to give the jury instructions about various points of law. The prosecutor will also be much more careful in the presentation of his case, as he will be trying to convince a group of laymen of your guilt rather than trying to convince a legal professional such as the judge. The prosecutor may also be inclined to object to minor deviations from formal procedure, primarily for the purpose of impressing the jury.

The jury will also take some time in "deliberation." This takes place when they meet privately after the presentation of both sides of the case, to make the final decision as to your guilt or innocence.

WHAT DOES CHALLENGE OF A JUROR MEAN?

When a juror is challenged, he is being "rejected" by either you or the prosecutor as being unsuitable or incompetent to sit on your trial. After the first twelve people are selected for the jury, the judge, the prosecutor and you will all have an opportunity to play "Twenty Questions" with the jury.

Any number of jurors can be challenged "for cause" (a good reason), and will be dismissed and replaced if the judge agrees with you. You also have ten "peremptory" challenges for which you don't have to show a good reason for the juror's dismissal.

Typical reasons for dismissing a juror are because of occupation (you probably wouldn't want an ex-cop on the jury), because of acquaintance or relations (you also wouldn't want a cop's wife or best friend), or because of experience (if the juror just got a ticket, he might be biased in your favor and the prosecutor would reject him).

The challenge of a juror in traffic court usually has little bearing on the outcome of your case and is often unnecessary. Use a little restraint in rejecting jurors, and only challenge them if you really feel that there is a valid reason that would bias your case. If you have too many unreasonable challenges, you may only alienate both the judge, and the remaining jurors.

WHAT DECIDES WHO GETS TO ASK WHO QUESTIONS FIRST?

Your entire case is already planned out. Each testimony and period of questioning has already been determined as a matter of established trial procedure.

WHAT IS TRIAL PROCEDURE?

Trial procedure is the basic format of the trial, quite literally the order in which the trial proceeds. The judge will assist you with any of the little fine points of procedure, because as a layman you aren't expected to know them all. He may also make objections on your behalf, and will prevent the prosecutor from taking unfair advantage of you. The procedural format for a jury trial is as follows (for court trials, all jury activity can be deleted and the judge will give his verdict):

1. The judge calls your case. Both you and the prosecutor should either answer "Ready," or ask the court for a continuance.
2. The jurors will be selected for your case. These are usually selected by a random drawing by the court clerk.
3. The jurors will be questioned about their qualifications by the judge, the prosecutor and you.
4. The jurors are either challenged or approved by the judge, prosecutor and you. The jury is then sworn in.
5. Opening statements are made to the jury by first the prosecutor and then by you. Often the opening statements are waived in a traffic case.
6. The prosecution presents its case, by giving all of its evidence and the testimony of its witness-

es. Then you have an opportunity to cross-examine his witnesses, asking any questions you wish about their testimony. The prosecutor then has a "redirect examination" in which he can clarify any testimony which you brought out of the witness in your questions. Then you can question the witness again on "recross examination." Both sides can redirect and recross examine as many times as is necessary.

7. When the prosecution is satisfied, he will "rest" his case.

8. You present your case, introducing your evidence and having your witnesses testify. The prosecution then has a chance to cross-examine the witnesses, and redirect and recross examinations follow as in the presentation of the prosecution's case.

9. Once you have finished and are satisfied that your case is complete, the defense rests its case.

10. The prosecution "argues" (explains) its case to the jury (or the judge in a court trial).

11. The defense (that's you) "argues" its case to the jury.

12. The prosecution makes any final arguments in reply to any new matters you may have mentioned in your argument.

13. The jury is instructed by the judge about the applicable law. He may also clarify any part of the trial that he thinks may have confused the jury.

14. The jury "retires" into the jury-room to deliberate, and comes to a conclusion about your case.

15. The jury returns and tells the judge what verdict

has been decided. The jury is then dismissed by the judge.

16. If your verdict was "guilty," the judge will pronounce your sentence. If it was "not guilty," you will be excused by the court.

This outline should be carefully studied before going to trial, so that you will know when to ask the appropriate questions on which your defense will be based.

DO THEY ALWAYS FOLLOW TRIAL PROCEDURE?

No, some courts tend to ignore proper trial procedure if they feel they can get away with it. You should never say anything in your defense until the State has presented and rested its case. This is more than just following procedure, this is an important concept of our court system. If a record is kept of the trial proceedings by a tape recorder, or by a transcript made by a court reporter, it will serve notice on the judge and prosecutor that no departures from proper procedure will be allowed.

WHAT'S AN OPENING STATEMENT?

The opening statement is used in advance of presenting any evidence to explain what your evidence is and how it affects your case. The opening statement is very important in criminal cases where the evidence and testimony can be huge and very complex. Most traffic cases are very simple, and the nature and purpose of the evidence will be easily understood. Opening statements are almost never made in court trials (the judge is more familiar with evidence and laws than either you or the prosecutor) and only rarely in jury trials.

Even if the prosecutor does make an opening statement, you as a layman are usually better off if you waive your right to do so. Chances are you'd only be repeating evidence that you will give later in testimony, and there is ample opportunity for you to explain how the evidence affects your case in your closing statements to the court. Because opening statements are so rarely given in traffic cases, don't be too surprised if the judge doesn't ask you if you desire to make one.

WHAT'S "BURDEN OF PROOF"?

Burden of proof is the heavy load that the prosecution has to bear in the trial. Burden of proof is the prosecution's responsibility. It is up to him to *prove* beyond a reasonable doubt that you are guilty of the charges. If he cannot produce enough evidence to prove that you committed the offense before he rests his case, then you are entitled to have the case dismissed by the judge, whether it is a court or a jury trial.

Often the prosecution's case is based solely on the officer's testimony with no other evidence. If the prosecutor just asks for the officer to give a narrative description of your alleged violation, you may find that he failed to establish one of the elements of your violation. (You should have a list of the elements already prepared from when you examined your citation. Check off each element as the prosecution covers it.)

If you do notice any element that the prosecutor failed to establish, be very careful not to establish that fact for him by asking the officer a question that will cover that element. You may even wish to dismiss the witness with no further questions, and move on to your defense, once again without covering the element. This missing element can be brought up in your closing statement to the court along with a request for immediate dismissal.

When the officer testifies, you should also watch to see if he is referring to his notes on the back of his copy of the citation (most officers will have the copy of the citation with them). If you do see the officer looking at some notes when he is asked about the date, time and details of the citation, you should stand and politely ask the judge to inquire if the officer is referring to his notes to refresh his memory. If the officer was doing so, you should ask the judge to instruct him not to unless he absolutely can't remember the details, and to tell the judge or jury when he is actually referring to his notes. Particularly in jury trials, this can throw a lot of doubt on the accuracy of the officer's testimony.

WHAT'S A REASONABLE DOUBT?

The entire purpose of your testimony is to raise a "reasonable doubt" about your guilt. A reasonable doubt is defined as "that condition of mind in which a sincere and well founded doubt is raised as to whether the person charged with a crime is actually guilty." This doubt, which you are trying to implant in the minds of the judge and the jury is the whole purpose of your testimony. You must supply enough concrete information that your guilt is truly questionable.

It's pretty much up to the judge and jury to determine what is a reasonable doubt. However, most of the people on the jury who have doubts of any kind will consider themselves to be reasonable people, and will then consider their doubts to be reasonable as well.

CAN I BRING EVIDENCE?

Yes, you can bring any photos, documents, or subpoenaed items that you think will be of assistance to your defense. After your last witness is excused from the stand, you should ask the judge for permission to have your physical "exhibits" admitted into evidence. This may be done by stating, "Your Honor, may my defense exhibits be admitted into evidence?"

Now you see it, now you don't. Photographs to back your testimony make excellent evidence.

WHAT'S CROSS-EXAMINATION?

Cross-examination is the questioning of the opposing party's witness on the matters to which he testified in his direct testimony. You will have a chance to cross-examine the officer after he gives his testimony for the prosecution, and the prosecution will have a chance to cross-examine you after you give your direct testimony.

Cross-examination is very difficult, and entire books have been written on the subject for lawyers. The court and the jury do not expect you as a layman to come across with the smooth professionalism of Perry Mason and reduce the witness to a weeping, hysterical confession. However, they will be impressed by a well-organized and complete cross-examination.

Your cross-examination should be based on the list of questions you have prepared for the officer well in advance of the trial (we'll talk more about what questions to ask in "Fighting the System") and on any additional questions you may have added during his testimony.

Listen carefully to his answers to your questions, and be sure to note the important ones on a sheet of paper for your reference when making your final argument. It will also help to impress upon the jury the importance of certain answers if you draw their attention by writing the answer down. The judge will probably recognize any relevant facts that you miss in his answers, and may even assist you in your cross-examination.

It is important that you only ask the officer about the facts of his testimony, without becoming argumentative. You can deny his statements later in your own testimony, but if you start in on the officer with "I was not going 65!" you may defeat the entire purpose of your cross-examination. When you are finished asking your questions, you can indicate this to the judge by saying, "No further questions, Your Honor."

WHAT ARE REDIRECT AND RECROSS-EXAMINATION?

The main purpose of the cross-examination is to expose any facts that may have been missed on the direct testimony of the witness. After you are finished with the cross-examination, the prosecutor has a chance to requestion his witness to deny or explain anything that you may have uncovered. This is called the redirect examination. After the prosecutor is finished, you have an opportunity to ask the witness more questions, and this is called recross-examination.

The prosecutor and the defense (that's you) can conduct redirect and recross-examination as many times as is necessary to bring out all of the facts of the case. However, any re-examination of a witness should be avoided unless you really feel that you may uncover some important evidence. Otherwise you will run the risk of boring and alienating the judge and the jury.

DO THEY EXPECT ME TO KNOW ALL THIS RECROSS, REDIRECT AND BURDEN OF PROOF STUFF?

No, the court really doesn't expect you as a layman to know all about courtroom procedures and etiquette. In fact, you'll find that the judge and even the prosecutor will overlook most of your minor mistakes, and may even assist you and instruct you as you go along.

What the court does expect from you, is that you at all times be courteous, respectful and polite. If you remain pleasant and present your material in a logical, organized and tactful manner, you'll generate the respect and sympathy of the judge, jury and the prosecutor.

WHAT'S A CLOSING STATEMENT?

The closing statement is your final opportunity to present your case to the judge and the jury. After both you and the prosecutor have presented and rested your cases, the judge will ask you to give your final arguments, or closing statements.

The prosecutor will give his statement first, and will have a chance at rebuttal to your statement after you are finished. You will not be given an opportunity to respond to his rebuttal.

In your closing statement, you should respond and clear up anything that the prosecutor may have said in his closing statement that may have damaged your defense, and explain once again to the judge and the jury how the evidence which has been presented proves your innocence. Now is the time to demonstrate how the evidence provides a reasonable doubt of your guilt, and to point out any missing elements of the crime with which you are charged.

WHEN DOES THE JUDGE OR JURY DECIDE IF YOU'RE GUILTY OR NOT?

In a court trial the judge usually decides and delivers the verdict immediately after the final argument and the case is completed. Sometimes he may recess the court for a short time while he goes to his chambers (office) to think over the evidence and perhaps to check with some previous cases that were similar to yours. If he is particularly busy, he may take the case "under submission" and notify you of his decision at a later date. Usually the decision is delivered immediately and you are sentenced that same day.

In a jury trial, the jury is taken to another room after your closing arguments and they are left to themselves to come to a decision. The average jury will take 15 to 30 minutes to come to a decision, and the judge will allow them about an hour at the most. If the jury is unable to come to a decision after that amount of time, the judge may declare it a "mistrial." At that time (and if the traffic offense isn't too serious) a motion by you to the judge for dismissal of the charges will usually be granted.

No matter which type of trial you have, if the judge or jury find you not guilty, you have won your case. The citation is then removed from your records and will not appear on your permanent driving record. However, if you are found guilty, the sentence will usually be imposed at that time.

CAN THE JUDGE TAKE
MY LICENSE AWAY?

Yes, he can have the bailiff take it away from you right on the spot. He may also just suspend your license for several days or months, stamping the suspension dates on your license and forbidding you to drive during that period. If the defendant's livelihood depends on the use of his vehicle, the judge may have the clerk stamp the license with special provisions which only allow one to drive the car to and from work.

Even if the judge leaves you with your license, it's no guarantee that you might not lose it eventually. If this conviction is particularly serious, or the latest in a number of similar violations, the Department of Motor Vehicles in your state may revoke or suspend your license for a specified period of time, or even indefinitely.

IF THE JUDGE TAKES AWAY MY LICENSE,
CAN I STILL DRIVE MY CAR?

No, and the judge is going to warn you not to drive after he takes it away. Frequently, the judge will wait until you leave the courtroom, and order the bailiff to follow you out to your car and bring you back to the court if you try to drive it.

If you suspect that you may lose your license as a result of your offense (both the judge and prosecutor will probably warn you of the possibility before you go to trial) you had better get a friend to drive you to the court or perhaps take the bus. If you disobey the judge, he may be *very* unhappy and give you additional fines or even jail for contempt of court.

WHAT DOES A "SUSPENDED" OR "PARTIALLY SUSPENDED" SENTENCE MEAN?

Depending on the severity of your crimes and your past record, the sentences passed in traffic cases may include jail terms and/or fines, along with the possibility of losing your license. In some cases, the judge may penalize you the maximum the law allows, and then suspend all or part of the fine. The suspended amount is an amount you don't have to pay, provided that you meet the conditions set by the court.

Typically, the conditions the judge will impose are that you not have a similar violation for a certain period of time (usually one year). If you violate the terms of this "parole" you are liable for the full amount of the suspended sentence. Often a judge will sentence you to a short jail term and a fine, and then suspend the jail term. This acts as incentive to make you behave on the highways for the period of the suspended sentence.

The suspended sentence will appear on your record just as any other conviction. The judge will often agree to suspend the sentence, or even dismiss the case if you agree to attend traffic violator's school.

WHAT'S THIS "TRAFFIC VIOLATOR'S SCHOOL"?

Traffic Violator's School, also known simply as "Traffic School" is an interesting alternative to a traffic conviction which is currently available in all states except Connecticut, Delaware, Nevada and Vermont. These classes may last anywhere from a single 8 hour

National Safety Council
DRIVER IMPROVEMENT PROGRAM

MARK R. MILLER

Has completed the National Safety Council's
DEFENSIVE DRIVING COURSE as presented by:

SAN DIEGO COUNTY SAFETY COUNCIL
Cooperating Agency

Charles Woods   5/20/78
Instructor   Date

DDC
DEFENSIVE DRIVING COURSE ®

Vincent L. Tofany
President

N⍛ 12945736

Traffic school is a pleasant alternative to a conviction for most people.

session, to 8 weekly 4 hour sessions. The classes are often taught by law enforcement officers. These classes are a valuable opportunity to talk with your local police officers and have your ticket dismissed at the same time.

Typical classes consist of several hours of "catsup movies" depicting the gory results of driving fast and careless, and group discussions on traffic safety. Usually the number of times you can attend traffic school are limited; only once each year, or sometimes only once *ever*, depending on the judge. Once you complete the school, you usually have to take evidence of your completion back to the court to have your citation dismissed.

IF I'M FOUND GUILTY, CAN I MAKE PAYMENTS ON THE FINE?

If you don't have enough money on hand to pay the fine, but you expect to be able to raise the money within a short period of time, you may "appeal to the sympathy of the court." You will have to explain exactly how much money you have, and when you expect to be able to pay the remainder of the fine. The court will often grant your request, provided that they believe you can actually raise the money. Otherwise, you may have to resort to a bail bond company, or even face a jail term in lieu of the fine.

WHAT DO THE COURTS DO WITH MY MONEY?

This varies widely from state to state. Usually the fines and bail forfeitures collected by the courts are turned over to the county treasurer and then paid out to the cities and counties within that court's jurisdiction. These funds are used to support the court itself and the salaries of the police, city attorneys, judges and clerks, and to pay for various equipment.

Roughly half of the money collected goes into Traffic Safety Funds. These funds are used to pay for the purchase, construction and maintenance of traffic signs and lights, for supplies and equipment for traffic law enforcement, for maintenance and construction of public streets, bridges and culverts, and for the implementation of traffic safety programs.

CAN YOU APPEAL A CONVICTION ON A TRAFFIC TICKET?

If you feel that your trial was unfair or prejudiced for any reason, or if you feel that the sentence was excessive for your violation, you may appeal your conviction to a higher court.

The procedures involved in an appeal are quite complex and rather costly, and we strongly advise that anyone considering an appeal hire an attorney. It is possible for you to appeal a case on your own, but it will require a considerable investment of both time and money on your part. The court clerk can assist you with the necessary documents and procedures.

You should also be aware that *very* few of the traffic cases which are appealed each year are reversed by a higher court. You should consider an appeal only if you have suffered a severe injustice.

WHAT IS A "TRIAL DE NOVO"?

A Trial de Novo is the legal term for a new trial, a part of the appeal process in some court jurisdictions. In these jurisdictions, a person does not have the right to a trial before a jury at his initial trial, which is usually in the so-called "General District Court." If you lose this trial, either by going through the entire trial process and being found guilty by the judge or by failing to appear at the trial and being found "guilty in absentia," you have the right to appeal the case to the District Court of Appeals. Generally you have to post an "Appeal Bond" by mailing a check to the court. You can find out how much this bond is by calling the General District Court the day after your case is heard.

Because you did not have the right to a jury at your initial trial, the District Court of Appeals automatically orders a completely new trial. This new trial is the Trial de Novo. Even this trial can be appealed to the next higher court, the Supreme Court of Appeals. The entire Trial de Novo process is available in only a few court jurisdictions, primarily in the eastern United States. You can check with the clerk of the court to find out whether this process is available to you.

DOES THE COURT KEEP ANY RECORD OF WHAT IS SAID IN THE TRIAL?

No, the court rarely bothers to keep transcripts of the proceedings in traffic cases. However, a request that the court keep either a tape recording or a written transcript of the trial will usually be granted, and offers some tremendous advantages to you. First of all, it preserves a record of your entire trial for review by a higher court should you appeal your case. Second, it ensures that the court will follow proper trial procedures, as both the judge and the prosecutor will be aware that any deviations from that procedure will be recorded for posterity with the rest of the trial.

If you ask for a record of your trial to be kept, and are refused by the judge, you may wish to file an appeal if you lose your case. Your appeal to the higher court could suggest the fact that it was because of unusual (and possibly illegal) variations from trial procedure that the judge refused to allow a record to be made of the trial.

FIGHTING THE SYSTEM
The odds aren't   all that bad. . .

WHAT IF I'M GUILTY? SHOULD I STILL FIGHT MY TICKET?

As you probably realize, even though you may be guilty you still stand a chance of not being convicted of the offense. This may be due to lack of prosecution (if the officer fails to show up at your trial), due to a legal technicality such as the prosecutor failing to establish all of the elements of your violation, or because of your own ability to instill a "reasonable doubt" in the minds of the jury.

We do not recommend fighting a citation when you are unquestionably guilty of the offense charged, but this is really a moral decision that each person will have to make for himself. We do recommend that anyone who seriously questions his guilt, in any way, take the time to defend himself against the system.

OKAY, I THINK I'M INNOCENT. HOW DO I FIGHT MY TICKET?

The first step in fighting your ticket is to plead "not guilty" at your arraignment. This is the only plea that allows you to fight your ticket. A plea of not guilty can often be entered by mail instead of actually appearing at your arraignment, but you should read the back of the citation carefully to determine if it will apply in your case. Often, bail money will have to be deposited with the court to ensure your appearance at your trial.

The preparation for your trial should actually begin the moment you get the citation, by carefully noting all of the details of the circumstances, the location, and remembering what the officer said to you and how he caught you. A successful defense is going to require a little research on your part, and quite a bit of preparation before you appear at your trial.

WHERE DO I FIGHT THIS TICKET?

At the time of your arraignment, you will be told where to appear for your trial. (If you plead by mail they will notify you of the trial date and location by mail.) This location, which is not necessarily the same building in which you appear for your arraignment, that may be the "calendar" or "master" court. The judge presiding over the calendar court will ask if both the defense (you) and the prosecution are ready for trial. If both parties are ready, he will assign you to the spe-

The huge number of tickets issued today has lead to the construction of pre-fabricated mobile courtrooms such as this.

cific courtroom in which you will be tried. The schedule
for each different courtroom is called the "calendar."

WILL THERE BE OTHER PEOPLE IN THE COURTROOM, NOT RELATED TO MY CASE?

Yes, there will usually be quite a few other people in
the courtroom. The same court may be hearing a number of other cases, and may hear criminal arraign-
ments, small claims suits and various other actions
besides your traffic case. In addition to those people
involved in the various trials, there may be a number
of spectators attending the court for either educational
or entertainment reasons. Don't be too surprised if you
find your trial is being attended by the sixth grade
class from the local elementary school.

SHOULD I HIRE AN ATTORNEY?

If the offense with which you are charged is a serious
one, such as those involving reckless driving, speed
contests (street racing) or driving under the influence
of alcohol or drugs, you should definitely consider hiring an attorney to represent you in court. You should
also give a lot of thought to hiring professional legal
assistance if a conviction for your offense could cost
you a lot of money, or may result in the loss of your
driving privileges.

A lawyer can nearly always represent you in court
better than you could do yourself. After all, he is a
professional in dealing with the system, and he understands the procedures and protocol of the courtroom.

He will be quick to pick up on the legal implications of the testimonies of the various witnesses, will help to organize your testimony on the witness stand and will know when to make objections and motions. Unfortunately, the lawyer may also cost you a lot of money.

For most people who receive a traffic citation, it just doesn't make sense to spend several hundred dollars to have an attorney represent you for a $25 ticket. In defending most minor traffic offenses, you as a layman can adequately represent yourself.

DO I HAVE THE RIGHT TO A COURT APPOINTED ATTORNEY?

You always have the right to have an attorney represent you in court, but the court is not always required to appoint one for you. Attorneys are very rarely used in cases involving infractions, and only occasionally in misdemeanor traffic offenses. About the only time that a traffic court will provide legal counsel is in cases where the offense is a very serious one and the defendant obviously cannot afford to hire an attorney of his own.

SHOULD I LISTEN TO MY FRIENDS?

That depends on your friend's qualifications. If your friend is a top criminal attorney who has handled hundreds of similar violations, you can probably depend on his advice. However, if your friend is a three-time loser in traffic court, you had better think twice about his advice.

HOW DO I PREPARE MY DEFENSE?

A proper defense begins the moment you are stopped by the officer. A critical part of your defense in court depends on your not making any statements to the officer about your guilt that might be used against you. Anything you say (like, "I was talking to my wife and I thought I was just going with the flow of traffic.") may be included in your officer's notes and may surface again at your trial to haunt you.

As soon as possible after you have been stopped, you should make notes for yourself on exactly what happened. Include when and where you were, which lane you were in, what were the nearest cross-streets or landmarks, what your speed was and what the other cars around you were doing. Try and note where the officer was when he first saw you, how long he had been observing you and exactly what he claimed you were doing. Remember to record the weather and traffic conditions as well.

At your first available opportunity, and a second time immediately before the trial, you should return to the "scene of the crime" to collect further information, and to make sketches and take photographs if necessary.

After checking out the location of your violation, you should check the elements of your violation in the Vehicle Code. Break the offense up into all of its elements and then run through the details of your stop, checking to see whether you truly did violate the Vehicle Code section.

As soon as possible after the violation, you should determine who you want to appear as witnesses for your defense, and what physical evidence (if any) you will need to subpoena. By organizing your information carefully, you will be able to subpoena your witnesses and evidence immediately after your arraignment.

You should think through your defense, particularly in those areas where the officer made his mistakes, or the conditions that led to your "honest difference of opinion." Prepare a list of questions you will want to ask the officer when you have a chance to cross-examine him on the witness stand.

You will also want to organize your own testimony, listing all of the specific points and facts that you wish to uncover. It's not necessary for you to memorize your testimony; in fact, you should avoid delivering a "canned" statement. Organizing your defense into an outline form will insure that you cover all the important facts in some type of logical order. Your testimony should not be read, as direct eye contact with the judge or jury will help you win their sympathy and respect. Glancing occasionally at your notes won't hurt you at all.

If your citation involved the use of radar and your state laws require a Traffic and Engineering Survey, be sure to check with the Engineering Department of your city or county to see if a valid survey exists. If your state, county or local laws require that radar warning signs be posted, make sure that the signs were posted correctly in compliance with the laws.

Be sure to cover every conceivable aspect of your case before you step into the courtroom, and be sure that all of your information is well organized. When you're up on the witness stand, you want to be sure that all of your ducks are in a row.

SHOULD I TALK TO THE OFFICER
IN THE HALLWAY
BEFORE OR AFTER THE TRIAL?

This really isn't a good idea. Before the trial, this will only help to refresh the officer's memory of you and your violation. After the trial, there's really no reason to talk to him. He understands your position from your testimony in court. Seeing him after the trial will only result in name-calling and bad feelings, and there is really no need for that.

Proper procedure calls for the officer to leave the courtroom after he has finished giving his testimony for both sides. The theory is that the officer's job is only to bring you before the judge, and the officer has no interest in the outcome of the case.

In reality, the officer is a curious human being, just like yourself, and he will usually stay to see how you conduct your case and what the final verdict of the court will be.

WILL THEY TRY TO MAKE A DEAL
WITH ME BEFORE THE TRIAL?

Prosecutors often will try to make a deal with a defendant about to go to trial. Deals are often made merely to save the court and the prosecutor time, and are frequently offered when the prosecutor has a weak case or is not yet ready for trial. Usually, the only time a prosecutor will try to make a deal with you is when it is for his benefit.

If you're facing (and contesting) two separate violations, the prosecutor often will offer to drop one offense if you will plead guilty to the other. On a single offense, he may arrange to have the fine suspended ("It won't cost you a thing!") if you will either plead guilty or nolo contendere.

Sometimes a prosecutor may attempt to make friends with you and will try to get you to agree to a continuance. He wouldn't be asking for one if he were fully prepared for trial, and if a continuance is not granted there's a good chance that the judge will dismiss the case.

SHOULD I DEAL?

Not unless the deal is definitely to your advantage. Even if your fine is suspended, it will still appear on your record, costing you driving "points" and potentially raising your insurance premiums. If you agree to a continuance, you will only have to appear in court at a later date to defend yourself. Before making any decision about a deal, take the time to carefully consider exactly what the deal means to you in terms of its effects on your case, and what the deal means to the prosecutor. Don't deal unless the prosecutor is offering what you want out of the trial.

WHY DID THEY DISMISS MY CASE "IN THE INTEREST OF JUSTICE" WHEN I WAS ALL READY TO PRESENT MY DEFENSE?

Prosecutors are not stupid and there may come a time before the trial, in the course of the officer's testimony, or during your initial defense, that he comes to the realization that you are truly innocent of the offense with which you were charged. At that time, he may make a motion to the court that the case be "dismissed in the interest of justice," or that the judge "nolle" (short for 'null process') the case. A motion on this basis is always honored by the judge, so the case will be dismissed and will proceed no further.

WHAT DO I LOOK FOR WHEN I RETURN TO THE SCENE?

The things you should be looking for at the location of your violation, are the specific devices and objects which were involved with your offense, and any other things that might be used in your defense. You'll want to check on the location and condition of traffic signals, stop signs, speed limit signs, road markings, curbs, dividers, islands, intersections, crosswalks and the like. Note any buildings, trees, parking lots, schoolyards and driveways.

Drive through the location as you did at the time you were stopped (but be sure not to repeat your violation). Check for any details that may have caused you to miss a sign, or to be confused about the traffic control devices. Drive through from the officer's viewpoint, too. Could he have observed you in the manner he described to you, or was there something that might interfere with his visibility? For night violations, note carefully the lighting and visibility conditions.

You should also watch the same location, at roughly the same time as your violation and for several hours if possible. Keep track of how many people are violating the same law which you were charged with. If you're lucky, you may be able to observe the same officer apprehending other people for the same thing. He may

---

By returning to the scene you often pick up details you may have missed at the time of your violation.

be working a cherry patch caused by some traffic engineering fault, and rather than reporting it to the Engineering Department, he may be exploiting it to get ahead in the ticket race. Take a look at the section of curb where he usually works. Often times, the curb near a cherry patch will be blackened by exhaust and scorched tire rubber.

If there are businesses or residences nearby, go in and talk to the people there. You may find out that everyone gets nailed by the cop at that location, and he's there like clockwork every day at a certain time.

If you were charged with speeding in a school zone, check the signs limiting the speed. Most stipulate "While Children Are Present." Were children present at the time of your violation? Find out what time school begins and ends. Would a fence or wall make the street inaccessible to the students? Try and note everything that could have any bearing on your case at all.

WHAT SHOULD I LOOK FOR WHEN I RETURN JUST BEFORE THE TRIAL?

On your return visit to the scene, you are specifically looking for anything that may have changed. If the speed limit you were charged under has since been raised, or if any of the things affecting your case have been changed, added or removed, it could count in your favor at the trial. The raised speed limit, for instance, could indicate that your speed at the time was reasonable, and that there was a fault in the engineering of the highway at the time you were cited.

SHOULD I MAKE A DIAGRAM
OF THE SCENE?

Yes, it may serve to refresh your memory during the trial, and may help you to find an element of the offense which you did not violate. The officer will often use a diagram in his testimony, and having your own diagram will help you to spot any discrepancies in his illustration of the scene.

If the prosecutor has failed to prove all of the elements of your violation, you should be very careful in your use of a diagram in your own testimony. You wouldn't want to prove the missing element by demonstrating it with your own diagram.

HOW DO I MAKE A DIAGRAM?

Your diagram should cover the area in which your violation occurred and include all of the elements of the violation. If you were charged with running a red light, your diagram should include the intersection, crosswalks, limit lines and the actual location of the light. The diagram must be kept very simple and be easily read by the jury, very likely from a distance of 20 feet. Your diagram should be no larger than about 3′ x 3′.

You should orient your diagram so that North appears at the top of the paper. The illustration doesn't have to be to scale, but should be proportionate. You should note the approximate width of the streets and lanes involved and show the street markings such as simulated islands, lane dividers and limit lines. Your illustration should not contain any of the moving vehi-

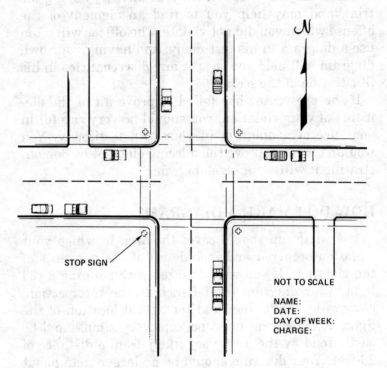

Sample Diagram of the Location

cles, but may include the locations of any parked vehicles. If you bring a few colored markers along with you to court, it will provide an easy method to ask the officer to show the movements of vehicles.

You may wish to bring cardboard cut-outs of vehicles to represent the police car and your own vehicle. Often the court will have magnetic cars to use on their illustration board, but it won't hurt to come prepared. In all cases, you should keep the diagram as simple as possible.

DOES THE OFFICER MAKE A DIAGRAM OF THE SCENE TOO?

Very often the officer actually makes a small and very simple diagram on the back of his copy of the citation at the time of the violation. Usually he makes a larger, more detailed diagram just before the trial, based on the notes on his copy of the citation. If the notes weren't very complete, or no diagram was made at the scene, he may base a lot of his information on his memory of the area and the input from other officers waiting for their trials in the officer's waiting room. The officer may ask, "Does anybody know how many lanes there are at 5th and Main?"

Many prosecutors expect the officer to supply or draw a diagram with every case. If the officer uses a chalkboard or a magnetic board to diagram his side of the story, ask the judge to have the officer make the diagram on paper or photograph the board with a Polaroid camera and ask that the picture be entered into the record as evidence. You can explain to him that you would like to maintain a "complete" record of the trial proceedings.

In driver's license violations, the officers occasionally play a joke on the prosecutor by drawing a large diagram of the license with a little stick-man for a picture and a circle around the expiration date. This is always good for a few giggles in the courtroom until the bailiff or the judge takes a good look at it and has it removed.

SHOULD I TAKE PICTURES OF THE LOCATION?

If your case centers on your visual perception of the area, then photographs could be a very important asset to your defense. Photographs showing a sign blocked by a tree, the faded paint of a simulated island or the sun setting directly behind a traffic light could vividly point out your case.

When making your photos, avoid going overboard with poster size prints. The snapshots from an Instamatic will serve your purpose just as well, as long as the objects in the print are large enough that the judge won't require a magnifying glass. Avoid using wide-angle or telephoto lenses which might distort the perspective of the picture.

When you go to the scene to take pictures, take them at the same time of day if possible, to show representative traffic. Take enough pictures of the area from enough angles to accurately show the area with the distances involved.

Green, yellow and blank. If you didn't see the red light, maybe it wasn't there.

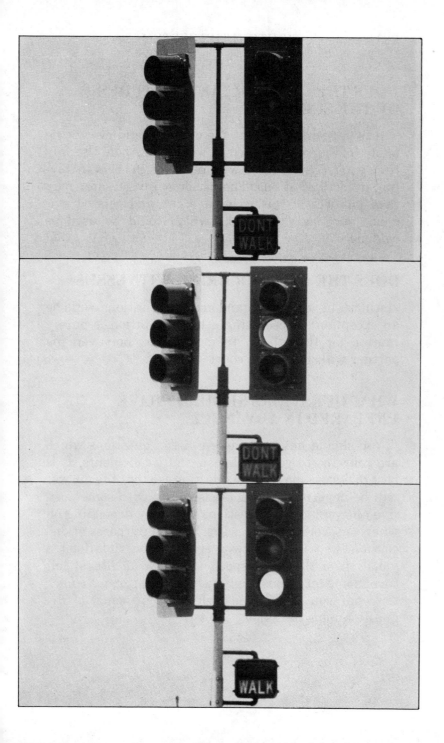

DOES THE OFFICER TAKE PICTURES OF THE SCENE?

It is very unlikely that the officer would ever bring photos of the location to court with him. About the only time you might be faced with photos is in cases involving accident citations. The accident investigator may take pictures of the accident scene and related evidence such as skid marks which could be used as evidence.

DOES THE OFFICER BRING WITNESSES?

Almost never (once again, accident citations could be an exception). Prosecuting a traffic citation is purely routine for the officer. In most cases, not even his partner will show up in court.

WHAT QUESTIONS SHOULD I HAVE PREPARED IN ADVANCE?

You should have a complete list of questions which are relevant to your violation and its elements. It is best to phrase most of the questions so that the answer will be negative, broken occasionally with some positive answers. These questions will vary depending on what you were charged with. For the purposes of discussion, we will cover two very common violations, a violation of the basic speed law, and an illegal left turn. Some questions apply to both violations. No matter what you are charged with, the principal of the questioning is the same.

1. ESTABLISH THE LOCATION OF THE OFFICER AT THE TIME HE FIRST OBSERVED YOUR VEHICLE. THIS WILL APPLY TO BOTH VIOLATIONS.
   A. Officer, where were you when you first observed my vehicle?
   B. Where was my vehicle at that time?
   C. What kind of vehicle were you using at that time?
   D. Was your vehicle parked or moving at that time?
2. ESTABLISH THE CONDITIONS UNDER WHICH HE OBSERVED YOU.
   A. What were the weather conditions at the time? (If the weather was poor, it may have affected his vision. However, it would also make your speed more likely to be unsafe. Figure out whether the question will help or hurt you before asking.)
   B. Officer, what were the traffic conditions at the time, with regard to my vehicle and other vehicles and persons on the roadway?
   C. (If the officer was parked) Officer, was your engine running or off?
      1. (If off) What did you do to start your vehicle?
      2. Did you fasten your seatbelt?
      3. Did you use your radio? (The more he did, the less he was watching what you were doing.)
   D. (If he started the engine) Did you start your engine before, after, or during your observation of my alleged violation? (If before, you can argue that he started to chase you before he thought

you had done anything wrong. If during, you can show that he was doing two things at once.)

E. (If he was moving) Officer, how fast were you traveling?

   1. What lane was your vehicle in?

   2. What was the position of the sun in relation to your vehicle?

   3. How far away from my vehicle were you at that time?

3. ESTABLISH HIS OBSERVATION AND MEMORY OF THE LOCATION.

A. Officer, during the time you were following my vehicle, did you have a clear view of the roadway?

B. Were you observing the roadway and traffic carefully?

C. As a police officer, your powers of observation and your memory for such details are quite good, aren't they?

D. And your memory is clear as to the roadway and traffic conditions on (the street you were stopped on) at the time and date of my alleged violation?

E. (Now you question him about every conceivable detail and hazard of that particular stretch of road. Avoid hazards that may have been there. That's the prosecutor's job.)

   1. What was the width of the highway?

   2. What kind of area was it, residential, industrial or vacant land?

   3. Was there an island or divider strip down the center of the highway?

   4. What was the posted speed limit in that area? (Only use if the officer has already

Your questions may include the details of weather, traffic and road conditions.

stated in his testimony. Otherwise, you establish the element for the prosecution.)

5. Where were those speed limit signs posted?
6. Is that speed limit still in effect?
7. What was the speed of the flow of traffic?
8. How fast would you estimate the speed of my vehicle? (Omit if you were going faster than the flow.)
9. Now, in relation to that roadway, were there any sharp curves?
10. Were there any railroad crossings?
11. Were there any dips or hills?
12. Was the pavement under repair?
13. Were there any fallen trees?
14. Was there anything at all obstructing the roadway?
15. Was there a soft shoulder on the road?
16. Was there any water on the pavement?
17. Was there any gasoline on the pavement?
18. Was there any oil on the pavement?
19. Did you notice any foreign objects on the pavement at all?
20. Were there any pedestrians on the roadway?
    a. How many and where were they?
    b. Were there any pedestrians waiting to cross the roadway?
    c. Were there any blind pedestrians in the roadway?
21. Were there any animals in the roadway?
22. Were there any children on bicycles in the roadway?
23. Were there any adults on bicycles in the roadway?

24. Did you observe my vehicle passing any others?
25. Did you observe my vehicle passing more than (two or three or more, pick a number that's accurate) vehicles?
26. And what lane were those other vehicles in?
27. Were there trucks?
28. Were there any other emergency vehicles other than yours on the the highway?
29. Were there any vehicles waiting to enter the roadway from parking lots?
30. From driveways?
31. From side streets?

4. ESTABLISH HIS OBSERVATION OF YOUR ALLEGED VIOLATION.

A. For speeding.
1. Officer, how many cars were there in the lane in which I was traveling?
2. How close were the cars in front of and behind me?
3. What was the speed of those vehicles?
4. What were the conditions in the lanes to the right and left of my vehicle?
5. And did you clock my vehicle with your speedometer, by a casual visual estimate or by some other means?
6. Was that a calibrated speedometer?
7. When was it last calibrated?
8. Who calibrated the speedometer?
9. What are their qualifications to calibrate?
10. Do you have a Certificate of Calibration?
11. What are your qualifications to estimate speed in this manner?

12. Did you have any special training to do this?
13. How long did you pace my vehicle?
14. How fast were you traveling to catch up to my vehicle?
15. And did you display your red (or blue) light as required by law when you first began disregarding the speed limit to catch up to my vehicle?
16. Did I pull over immediately?
17. How long did you pursue me before I pulled over?
18. Do you recall the reason you gave me when you first approached my vehicle, as the reason for stopping me?
19. Do you recall the speed you claimed I was traveling at that time?

B. For illegal left turn (violation of right-of-way).

1. Officer, did I come to a complete stop in the intersection before attempting to turn left?
2. Was my turn signal in use and correctly operating?
3. How far before reaching the intersection did I begin signaling?
4. How close was the nearest oncoming vehicle?
5. At what speed was the oncoming traffic approaching?
6. Did you notice the driver of the nearest oncoming vehicle motioning to me?
7. Did any vehicle swerve to avoid my vehicle?
8. Did any vehicle have to lock up its brakes to avoid a collision?

9. Were there any traffic control devices operating in the intersection?
10. Was there in fact, an arrow to indicate a
right of way for my vehicle?
11. Did any vehicle sound its horn during my
turn?
12. Isn't it true, that the main basis of your
evaluation of my turn as unsafe was based
on the fact that oncoming traffic slowed?
13. In your experience, haven't you found that
vehicles often slow when approaching an
intersection, particularly when another vehicle is turning in the intersection?
14. And haven't you found that this is often due
to common sense and caution rather than
there existing an actual or immediate
hazard?

This list was presented to give a general idea of the
scope and nature of questions you can ask, all of which
should be oriented toward your goal of establishing a
reasonable doubt of the officer's observation of your
violation, and of the existence of all of the elements of
your violation. In preparing your list, you can begin by
listing the elements of the violation, and using them as
general headings on which to base your questions.

You can formulate an entire list of questions covering nearly every conceivable facet of your violation
and the environment in which it occurred with a little
imagination, and perhaps some additional input from
your family or friends. You should also note the answers you expect to get.

When the officer deviates from the answers you expect to hear, you should either pursue the question to

get the whole truth of the matter, or else drop that particular line of questioning. If the answers seem to be headed toward revealing some damaging information, you may want to shift gears and go to a different line of questioning.

ARE RADAR VIOLATIONS HANDLED DIFFERENTLY?

As we discussed in our chapter, "Looking At What You Got," the prosecution will have to prove all of the elements of your violation. In the case of radar citations, there are some very special elements which the prosecution should prove. If these are not brought out in the officer's testimony, these missing elements are vulnerable to your attack. You should select those elements which you feel are most vulnerable in your particular case.

Whether or not you expose these vulnerable points through questioning the officer on cross-examination (and thereby give the prosecutor a chance to clear them up the best that he can on the recross), or whether you choose to bring them up in your closing statement (and let the prosecutor cover up to the best of his ability), is up to you. Depending on the nature of the case, you will probably want to do some combination of the two, along with any other evidence you may have.

Here are some of the elements of a radar citation which should be considered, elements which arise out of the law itself and from the rules of evidence:

A. THE BASIC ELEMENTS
1. The date, time and location of the alleged violation.
2. The fact that he was an on-duty police officer.
3. The officer was operating radar.
4. It was legal to operate radar at that location and that any required signs were posted and required surveys conducted.
5. A speed reading was present on the radar unit.
6. That speed was in violation of the law.

B. THE FACT THAT THE RADAR WAS OPERAT-*ING* PROPERLY
1. Unit calibrated before and after violation (shows unit was accurate at time of arrest).
2. The calibration was performed correctly with a certified tuning fork.
3. The fork was accurate (need certificate from manufacturer).

C. THE FACT THAT THE RADAR WAS OPERAT*ED* PROPERLY
1. The officer's qualifications (training, experience) were adequate.
2. The radar unit was properly installed.
3. The radar unit was in the proper operating mode.
4. The radar was responding to your car and not to electronic interference.
5. The radar unit was properly aimed.
6. The patrol car (if moving) had maintained a constant speed to prevent "Batching" error.
7. The officer did not move the antenna prior to arrest (to prevent sweeping or panning errors).

8. There were no fans in operation, or windblown objects which could generate a false radar signal.

9. There was no traffic adjacent to the path of the radar beam (frontage or service roads along highway).

10. There were no other vehicles in the radar unit's beam.

11. The unit had been cleared of the previous violator's speed.

12. There was no other radar operating nearby to cause interference.

13. That the unit was operated legally and was properly licensed with the unit's description and serial number on the station license.

D. THE RELIABILITY OF THE OFFICER'S VISUAL TESTIMONY (Radar alone is insufficient)

1. Establish whether the officer's view was direct or reflected in his mirrors.

2. Establish whether the officer observed the alleged speed first visually or by radar.

3. Establish the officer's ability to judge speed and distance.

E. THAT IT IS VALID TO ASSUME THAT THE SPEED SHOWN ON THE RADAR UNIT WAS THE SPEED OF YOUR VEHICLE

1. Establish the fact that radar beams cannot be seen.

2. Establish the connection between the speed of your vehicle and the speed shown on the radar unit.

WHAT'S THE PURPOSE OF THAT ASSUMPTION?

It is a fundamental concept of our legal system that there has to be a necessary connection between the already proven fact (the number on the radar display) and the fact that has been presumed (that the number accurately represents the speed of your vehicle). This is part of what is called "Due Process."

It's up to the prosecution to prove that this connection exists in your particular case. The court usually relies on outdated legal cases and routinely assumes this connection. However, this assumption is wrong, and is something that you should force the prosecution to prove. If they don't, be sure to point this out in your closing argument to the court. You can also go on the offensive and set about disproving this connection yourself.

HOW CAN I DISPROVE THAT ASSUMPTION?

You can basically disprove that assumption by demonstrating to the court that the radar reading the officer observed may have arisen from one or more non-vehicular sources. There are three demonstrations that can be conveniently performed in the courtroom. All that is needed is a charged-up 12 volt car battery, a CB radio and antenna, the radar unit which you have hopefully subpoenaed into court and a "Y" connector with two cigarette lighter plugs attached.

Plug the radio and the radar unit into the "Y" connector and connect it to the battery. Now you are ready for your demonstration.

1. If you mistakenly reversed the polarity on the wires, you will blow up the radar unit, demonstrating that it is inoperative and therefore your innocence is undeniable. (This method is not recommended.)

2. Operate the calibrate control. If it doesn't calibrate properly, you have once again shown that the radar was not operating correctly. If it does operate, respectfully ask the judge to point out the vehicle in the courtroom which is traveling at the speed indicated on the unit. (If this number happens to be the same speed you were cited for, you're home free!)

3. You might also point out to the judge that there is considerable difference between the reading on the radar unit and his visual observation (which showed nothing moving, thus a speed of 0 MPH).

4. Place the radar unit in either automatic or manual mode. Key the CB mike and whistle into it in a *clear* and *steady* tone until a number appears on the radar unit (usually takes at least 3 seconds). The higher the pitch of your whistle, the higher the number that will appear. This procedure demonstrates both radio and electrical interference. Once again you should ask the judge to point out the vehicle in the courtroom traveling at the speed indicated on the radar, and once again you should mention that there seems to be another difference of opinion between the two observations.

5. Turn up the audio on the radar and aim the antenna directly at the display from a few inches away, until you hear a steady tone. Point it steadily at the display until you get a reading. This demonstrates a

sweeping error which often occurs when the antenna is mounted inside the patrol car, or when the officer is pointing it around in different directions past the counting unit. Again, you can ask the judge if he observes any car in the courtroom traveling at that speed. By now, he should be catching on.

6. At this point move for a dismissal based on a demonstrated lack of due process connection. It should be honored by the court. If you are denied, you have established excellent grounds for a judicial review (an appeal) in a higher court.

HOW CAN I CHALLENGE THE OFFICER'S ABILITY TO VISUALLY ESTIMATE SPEED AND DISTANCE?

The classic method of testing the officer's ability to estimate distance is to ask him to estimate the dimensions of the courtroom. Unfortunately, this is one that they often teach the officer in the police academy and he may well have the dimensions of the courtroom memorized. You can still use this one though, but you should throw the officer a curve. Instead of asking the width or length of the courtroom, ask him the distance diagonally from corner to corner. Be sure to bring either a yardstick or a tape measure so the bailiff will be able to check the distance.

To disprove the officer's ability to visually estimate speed, take out a hard-boiled egg you have brought for the purpose and ask the officer to watch it carefully. (The whole courtroom will probably go silent as everybody focuses their attention on the egg expecting it to splatter on the floor). Drop the egg from a height which you have already measured (it's best to use your shoulder height or your furthest reach over your head, as you can measure this accurately in advance and easily duplicate the same height in court). Then ask the officer the approximate speed of the egg when it hit the floor. Depending on the distance it was dropped from, here are the speeds of the egg when it hits the floor:

DISTANCE (FT.)	M.P.H.	FT. PER SEC.
2.5	8.624	12.649
3.0	9.447	13.856
3.5	10.204	14.966
4.0	10.909	16.000
4.5	11.570	16.970
5.0	12.196	17.888
5.5	12.792	18.761
6.0	13.360	19.595
6.5	13.906	20.396
7.0	14.431	21.166
7.5	14.937	21.908
8.0	15.427	22.627
8.5	15.902	23.323
9.0	16.363	24.000
9.5	16.812	24.657
10.0	17.248	25.298
10.5	17.647	25.922
11.0	18.090	26.532
11.5	18.497	27.129
12.0	18.895	27.712

The interesting thing about the "Egg Trick" is that it can work in both directions. If the officer is unable to "guess" the correct speed of the egg within a few miles per hour, you can tell the officer the correct speed and will have successfully demonstrated his inability to visually estimate speed. If however, he does come pretty close you can just thank the officer and go on to your next question without telling him whether he is right or wrong. Usually neither the judge nor jury have any idea how fast the egg may have been traveling, and will also doubt the officer's ability to judge that speed.

WHY DOES IT MATTER IF HE SAW MY CAR OR THE RADAR READING FIRST?

The order in which he observed the speed shown on the radar unit and the visual observation of your car can be a vulnerable point in the prosecution's case, and once again it is something that you can use to your advantage no matter which order he followed.

If he observed the speed on the radar unit and then looked at your car, you can argue that the reading he observed on the radar unit prejudiced his observation of your vehicle and prevented him from fairly and accurately estimating your speed.

On the other hand, if he claims he visually estimated the speed of your vehicle before looking at the reading on the radar, he is claiming that the range of his visual powers are greater than that of the radar unit. If he has already given some ridiculous distance as the range of his radar unit, it casts a lot of doubt on the credibility of his testimony.

IS THERE A SPECIAL LINE OF QUESTIONS I SHOULD ASK IN RADAR CASES?

If you were caught by a radar unit, there are some very special questions you will want to cover in addition to the preceding questions dealing with the road, traffic and weather conditions. These questions should generally be phrased so they tend to generate a "No" answer from the officer, as every "no" helps to erode his credibility as an "expert witness" and helps lend support to establishing a "reasonable doubt."

Presented here are only a few of the many questions you may wish to ask the officer about radar. This list is by no means complete, or even organized into the best order for your particular case. With a little time and imagination, you should be able to come up with many more questions. Before you go into court, be sure that you are very familiar with our chapter on radar, *Electronic Wizardry*. That way you'll know what answers to expect and will be able to recognize incorrect responses from the officer.

A. QUESTIONS REGARDING THE BASIC ELEMENTS OF A RADAR CITATION.
   1. Officer, were you using radar at the time of my alleged violation?
   2. Where was your patrol car located?
   3. Were you hidden from traffic?
   4. Would you agree that the purpose of traffic safety radar is to slow traffic down?
   5. Don't you feel that hiding defeats that purpose?
   6. Does hiding allow you to surprise a lot of motorists?

7. How many motorists did you cite on the day of the alleged violation?

8. How many radar citations do you write on an average day?

9. Do you know if that is about average for a traffic officer in your agency?

10. How many officers does your agency employ?

11. So that works out to roughly (# of citations) per day that are issued by your agency: is that correct?

12. Now, if you write an average of (# of citations) on an average day, am I correct in assuming that you have written several hundred citations since you stopped my vehicle.?

13. But you feel that you can still remember my vehicle and my alleged violations out of all those others?

14. Is it legal to use radar in the city of (where you were stopped)?

15. Is it required by law to have signs posted regarding the use of radar?

16. Were those signs posted at the time of the alleged violation?

17. Where were those signs posted?

18. Does this state require a Traffic Engineering Survey on all highways where radar is in use?

19. Has such a survey been conducted on the highway at the specific location involved in my alleged violation?

20. When was that survey conducted?

21. What did that survey show as a safe speed for that highway?

22. Who conducted that survey?

23. What type of radar were you using?
24. What was the make and model of that unit?
25. Is that a stationary or a moving radar?
26. (If a moving radar) What mode was the unit in at the time of my alleged violation?
27. Did you show me a speed reading on your radar unit at the time you stopped my vehicle?
28. What was the speed displayed at that time?
29. What was the speed posted on that highway?
30. I know you weren't clocking any vehicle at the time you showed the unit to me, so how was that speed displayed?
31. Can you preserve any violator's speed merely by using this "lock" button?
32. How do we know that the reading you showed me at the time I was stopped was not another violator's?

B. QUESTIONS REGARDING THE OPERATING CONDITION OF THE RADAR UNIT.

1. Officer, can you tell us basically how radar works?
2. Are you familiar with the term "calibration"?
3. Would you tell us what the purpose of calibrating the radar unit is?
4. Was the unit you were using calibrated at the time of my alleged violation?
5. How was that unit calibrated?
6. When was the last time it was calibrated *before* my alleged violation?
7. When was the first time the unit was calibrated *after* my alleged violation?
8. Who calibrated the unit?
9. What method was used to calibrate the unit?

10. Is your unit equipped with a so-called "internal calibration" feature?

11. So by merely pushing a button or turning a knob this speed appears on the display?

12. Do you know what a certified tuning fork is?

13. Have you ever seen a radar tuning fork?

14. Did you bring such a fork to court with you?

15. Did you calibrate your radar with a fork at the beginning of your shift on the day of the alleged violation?

16. Did you calibrate your radar unit with a fork at the end of your shift?

17. Did you calibrate your radar with a fork immediately before you first observed my vehicle?

18. Did you calibrate your radar with a fork immediately after citing my vehicle?

19. Are you aware of the manufacturer's recommendation that the radar operator calibrate his unit with a fork at the beginning and end of every shift and before and after every violation?

20. The manufacturer also recommends that careful records be kept of all these calibrations. Does your agency keep such a log?

21. Do you have this calibration log with you today?

22. Now, officer, about this tuning fork. Could you explain how it is used to calibrate the radar unit?

23. By merely striking the fork and holding it near the unit it will display a speed reading, is that correct?

24. Are you aware that those forks are available from the manufacturer in every 5 mile per hour increment from 25 to 100 miles per hour?

25. Was the fork you used certified as accurate by the manufacturer?

26. Do you have a Certificate of Calibration for that fork?

27. Did you bring that certificate with you today?

28. The manufacturer of the radar unit recommends that your agency maintain a regular program to inspect and calibrate your tuning forks, as they may be bent or damaged and drift off the frequency. Do you have such an inspection program?

29. When was the fork you used last calibrated?

30. Do you have a record of that calibration?

31. Did you bring that record with you today?

32. Did your radar unit come from the manufacturer with a Certificate of Calibration and Type Acceptance?

33. Did you bring that certificate with you today?

34. Are you the only officer who uses that radar unit?

35. How many other officers use that same radar unit?

36. To the best of your knowledge, has that radar unit ever malfunctioned or required repair in any way?

37. Approximately how many times in the last year has that particular unit been into the shop for service of any kind?

38. Are maintenance records kept on that radar unit?

39. Have you ever read through those records?
40. Did you bring those records with you today?

C. QUESTIONS REGARDING THE CORRECT OPERATION OF THE RADAR UNIT.

1. Have you ever had any training in the use of radar?
2. Where did that training take place?
3. What were the approximate dates of that training?
4. How long did that training last?
5. By whom were you trained?
6. What were their qualifications to train you?
7. Did they at any time determine your abilities by testing your use of knowledge of radar?
8. Have you had regular proficiency tests since that time?
9. Have you had any proficiency tests in the use of radar at any time since that training?
10. On any tests on the use of radar that you have taken, was your proficiency rated as Good, Fair, or Unacceptable?
11. How would you rate your proficiency in the use of radar today?
12. Do you have any record of your radar training?
13. Did you bring that record with you today?
14. Were you given a diploma, certificate, or anything at all to indicate that you are qualified to operate a radar unit?
15. Did you bring that with you today?
16. Officer, what was the weather like on the day of the alleged violation?
17. Are you aware that direct sunlight and temperature can effect the reading of your radar unit?

18. Is your radar unit equipped with a device which allows you to check all of the segments of the speed display?

19. Are you aware that one or more unlit segments of that display could mislead you by showing a false number, for instance, by showing a 6 as a 5, or a 7 as a 1, depending on which segments were burned out?

20. Had you made a check of all those segments on the day of the violation?

21. Had you made a check of all these segments immediately before clocking my vehicle?

22. Was your patrol car running or was the engine off?

23. Did you know that when starting the patrol car, the voltage drop may cause a spurious reading?

24. Was the radar unit electrically attached to the car by means of a cigarette lighter plug or through direct wiring?

25. Have you ever checked that connection?

26. Are you aware that a poor, faulty or dirty connection may result in a spurious reading?

27. Was your radar unit in operation immediately before clocking my vehicle?

28. How long had it been since the unit was turned on?

29. Do you know that many radar manufacturers specify a lengthy warm-up period before their unit can be used?

30. Do you know what the specified warm-up period for your radar unit is?

31. Have you ever used your stationary radar in a

pacing mode, to establish the patrol car's speed while pacing a possible violator?

32. Can you lock in the patrol car's speed for future reference?

33. So the speed you show to the motorist could just as easily be the patrol car's catch-up speed as the speed you clocked the motorist at?

34. Have you ever had an unexplained, spurious signal appear on your radar unit when there were no vehicles within radar range?

35. Isn't it true that a wind-blown tree limb or sign can also generate spurious signals?

36. Isn't it true that rain, fog and blowing dust all have an effect on your radar unit's operation?

37. Was your patrol car equipped with a Citizen's Band radio?

38. Was there any CB traffic present at the approximate time of the alleged violation?

39. Are you aware that by whistling into the microphone of a CB radio, you may often generate a false radar signal?

40. Are you aware that nearby radio transmissions of any sort may cause a spurious radar reading?

41. Do you know what a harmonic frequency is?

42. Are you aware that harmonic frequencies can generate false signals on a radar unit?

43. Are you aware that electrical storms, power transformers and transmission lines, neon lights and automobile invertors are all capable of generating harmonic frequencies which can affect radar?

44. Are you aware that you can clock trains or aircraft with your radar unit?

45. Are there any airports or railroad tracks near the location of the alleged violation?

46. How was your radar antenna mounted on the vehicle?

47. How easy or difficult is it to change the position of that antenna to face a different direction?

48. Are you aware that by sweeping the antenna around it may read the relative ground speed of the scenery going past and lock onto that false reading?

49. At any time in your operation of that radar unit, was the antenna pointed at the counting unit?

50. Are you aware that by aiming the antenna at the counting unit, even briefly, you may generate a spurious reading?

51. Have you ever aimed the antenna of your radar unit toward the dashboard of your car?

52. Are you aware that by doing this, you may actually be clocking the heater or air conditioner fan?

53. Is it true that your radar unit tends to track the strongest signal?

54. Are you aware of the fact that a large vehicle behind a smaller vehicle, which is actually closer to the radar unit, may generate the strongest signal?

55. What frequency does your radar unit broadcast on? (He may tell you the band, but press for the frequency.)

56. Does your agency have a license to broadcast

on that frequency in accordance with the current Federal Communications Commission Rules and Regulations, Volume 5, Part 89?

57. Is the frequency you state your radar operates on one of those authorized on your FCC station license?

58. Are you familiar with that license?

59. Do you know whether the operation of your radar unit is legal?

60. How many radar units does your agency operate?

61. Do you know how many units are authorized on your license?

62. Is there any record of which unit you used for this particular citation?

63. Do you know the serial number of that unit?

64. Is this one of those covered and listed on your FCC license?

D. QUESTIONS REGARDING THE RELIABILITY OF THE OFFICER'S TESTIMONY

1. Officer, what is the width of your radar unit's beam? (He will usually answer by telling you the number of lanes it covers.)

2. Can you tell us your beam width in degrees?

3. When you actually made the speed estimate, were you watching the radar unit or my vehicle?

4. (If watching the radar unit) So when you observed my vehicle, you had already formed an opinion of my vehicle's speed, is that correct?

5. (If watching your car) So you saw my vehicle and estimated its speed visually *before* it was picked up by your radar unit?

6. Were you watching my vehicle directly or in your rearview mirror?

7. Doesn't your mirror have a much wider angle of view than what you have previously testified was the width of your radar beam?

8. How do you know the radar beam was aimed at my vehicle?

9. Do you aim the unit down the roadway everytime you set up the radar units?

10. Do you re-aim the unit after every citation?

11. Was the radar unit aimed *exactly* at my vehicle?

12. Roughly how many degrees off dead-center was it?

13. Are you aware of the term "Cosine Angle Factor" as it applies to traffic radar?

14. Did you know that a cosine angle factor can cause an error in the radar's accuracy in determining the speed of an approaching vehicle by as much as 32% at an angle of only 45° and that the error begins and increases as the radar unit varies from other than a direct path with the violator?

15. How fast do you claim I was going? (Let's use 65 as an example.)

16. Why did you stop me for allegedly doing 65 MPH? (Usually he will answer, "Because you were violating the law.")

17. Would you have cited someone traveling 56 MPH?

18. How about 57?

19. 58? 59? 60? 61? 62? 63? 64? (At some point he will respond.)

20. But that's only a one (or whatever) MPH difference between my alleged speed. They were
violating the law. If radar is as accurate as you
say, why don't you stop everyone whom the
radar shows is violating the law?

These few sample questions can represent a real
challenge to most officers and are sure to raise more
than a few doubts in the minds of the judge or jury
about the accuracy of the radar reading and the proficiency of the operator. These questions were only presented as an example on which you can build and base
your own questions to suit your own defense. Most of
these questions could easily be adapted to cases involving VASCAR and stopwatches as well. It is very important that you organize your questions so that one
builds on the foundation of the previous question and
the whole line of questioning is presented in a logical,
easy-flowing manner which is designed to lead both
the judge and jury to the conclusion you want.

You should be sure to keep track of the officer's
answers and be prepared to use those answers and
benefit from them in your closing statement.

ARE THERE ANY OTHER APPROACHES?

Yes, as we have previously stated, radar lacks the
necessary due process connection, and its admission as
evidence without establishing all the other subele-
ments constitutes a violation of the 14th Amendment
of the Constitution. If your case is really blatant, you
can file a civil action in a federal court naming anyone
involved (like the officer, prosecutor, judge, etc.). A

lawsuit such as this should be filed by a competent attorney pursuant to 42 U.S.C. Section 1893.

The purpose of this lawsuit is not to collect damages, but rather to do damage to the offenders. A prosecutor confronted with a federal suit will plea bargain in earnest since *his* only advantage now lies in *your* acquittal.

This suit can be filed prior to your trial based upon your knowledge that the particular radar used lacks the required connection and citing the discrepancy between your speed and the cited speed. The suit can also be filed after your initial trial by citing additional specific grounds for the suit. This approach is more viable, and the effort is more in line with the stakes involved.

These lawsuits are serious business that will take up a considerable amount of your time and money, but if you're serious enough about your tickets, it's something that you may want to consider.

DOES THE PROSECUTION HAVE QUESTIONS PREPARED TO ASK ME?

Usually the prosecutor's office supplies him with a manual outlining the steps necessary for a successful prosecution of all the various offenses. Included with a description of the offense is a list of questions that should be asked for the prosecution to prove all of the elements of the crime. Sometimes on routine traffic matters, the prosecution may relax and ad-lib his way through the case without bothering to refer to the manual. This is why it is important for you to keep track of the elements the prosecutor covers.

The prosecutor's first contact with the officer is often just moments before the trial. If the offense is a serious one, he may jot down a few quick questions to ask you in court. The majority of times, the prosecutor is basically unprepared to present his case, and will depend on his "superior" professional knowledge and experience to present a successful prosecution.

WHAT KIND OF EXPERIENCE DOES THE PROSECUTOR USUALLY HAVE?

In smaller jurisdictions, one prosecutor may handle all of the city's cases, from traffic to serious criminal matters. In that case the prosecutor may have a considerable amount of experience.

In very large cities, the turnover rate within the prosecutor's office is usually very high. (A lot of the attorneys move to a private firm after getting a start in the prosecutor's office). Traffic cases are often considered the bottom of the ladder, and are frequently assigned to the most inexperienced rookie in the office. Prosecutors who appear in the traffic courts of the larger jurisdictions will frequently have very limited experience.

HOW DO I KNOW THE OFFICER'S EXPERIENCE?

You can usually determine the officer's experience by the degree of composure he can maintain on the stand under direct testimony and cross-examination. Rookies tend to stammer and may seem unsure of some of their answers and often present beautifully detailed diagrams.

Sometimes the notes on the back of the officer's copy of the citation may be very extensive.

LIGHT / MODERATE / HEAVY   CLEAR / CLOUDY   WET / DRY

(MODERATE circled)   (CLOUDY circled)   (DRY circled)

ON I-805 (N/B)

9346

4-5-78

YR. MAKE 77

3, 4, 50, 62 67 73 83

I-805 (N/B)

N/B I-805 S/o = CARROLL CYN. RD.

OF

APPROX. 6 VEHS.
1 MI. PACE
6 CAR LENGTHS N-2 LN.

I WAS N/B I-805 FROM
GOVERNOR DRIVE. OBS. SUBJ. IN N-1
LANE PASSING TRAFFIC, ON MY
ENTERING FWY. I IMMED. BEGAN
A PACE, WITH SUBJ. PULLING AWAY
@ IND. 68 MPH (ACT. 70 MPH)
FOR 1 MI.

STATED HE WAS TALKING
WITH HIS WIFE & WASN'T
WATCHING HIS SPEED — THOUGHT
HE WAS JUST KEEPING UP WITH
TRAFFIC.

On the other hand, veteran officers tend to nod off asleep in the back of the courtroom until they're called on to testify, are cool and collected under fire (even when they're really unsure of themselves), and present simple, crudely drawn (but complete) diagrams.

If you think the officer's experience might be of benefit to your defense, ask him about it in cross-examination. In fact, the prosecutor may establish the officer's qualifications as part of the officer's direct testimony.

HOW DOES THE OFFICER REMEMBER WHAT I DID?

The officer's memory of your violation is usually pretty faint, unless you did something unusual that really stands out in the officer's mind. For the most part, the officer will base his testimony on the citation and his notes.

DOES THE OFFICER HAVE TO TELL THE TRUTH?

The officer is sworn to tell the truth the same as any other witness, and any failure to do so could be considered as perjury (a felony). The officer's driver's license isn't riding on the outcome of the case, and he really has no motivation that would cause him to lie in court. However, some officers may tell little "white lies" or half truths. You shouldn't expect the officer to tell an outright lie, but you shouldn't expect him to volunteer damaging information either. As an example, the officer may testify that a street has been surveyed for speed, but fail to mention that the last survey was conducted in 1902.

This question, like many other facets of the officer's testimony, depends almost entirely on the integrity of the officer. If you've made the citation into a grudge match between you and the officer, he might be tempted to give some misleading or incomplete answers, but the vast majority of officers would never even consider any form of outright deception on the witness stand.

DOES THE OFFICER EVER ASK ME QUESTIONS DURING THE TRIAL?

The officer will never ask you a question directly, other than asking for clarification of any question he

Your own statements at the time of the violation may be brought up again in court.

@ IND. 68 MPH (ACT. 70 MPH) FOR 1 Mi.

STATED HE WAS TALKING WITH HIS WIFE & WASN'T WATCHING HIS SPEED — THOUGHT HE WAS JUST KEEPING UP WITH TRAFFIC.

might not understand when you cross-examine him. However, when the prosecutor is cross-examining you, the officer is usually sitting at the prosecutor's table, slipping him questions and whispering in his ear.

CAN I ASK TO SEE HIS NOTES?

The officer is probably basing his testimony on his notes, and you should definitely ask to see them. His notes may be confined to the back of his copy of the citation, or he may have additional notes on a separate piece of paper. Either one is fair game and may prove very upsetting to the officer. If you demand a "sneak preview" of the officer's testimony, be sure not to give him the opportunity to expand on any damaging information that might be mentioned in his notes. If the information in his notes appears to benefit your case, you should ask the judge to enter them into evidence.

If the officer testifies to anything during the trial that is not written on the front of the citation or in his notes on the back, you should challenge that testimony. He has written several hundred citations since yours and any testimony he gives regarding facts not documented at the time of the violation will be viewed as questionable by the judge or jury. Remember, you've probably had just the one citation since that day and your memory of the event and its specific details will be far better.

Have the officer explain his notes, you might not be interpreting correctly.

LIGHT   CLEAR   WET
MODERATE   CLOUDY   DRY
HEAVY

CHP VEH NO. ROLLING. ON I-805 (N/B)

D/R E.S.W. LANE 1 2 3 4 5 OTHER 77

CHP VEH NO. 9346 YR. MAKE 77

DATE 4-5-78   30 40 50 60 65 70 80

        30 40 50 62 67 73 83

RED LIGHT SIREN HORN HAND

ON I-805 (N/B)

N/B I-805 S/p = CARROLL CYN. RD.

O F

APPROX. 6 VEHS.

1 MI. PACE

6 CAR LENGTHS N-2 LN

ENGLISH? YES

I WAS N/B I-805 FROM

GOVERNOR DRIVE. OBS. SUBJ. IN N-1

LANE PASSING TRAFFIC, ON MY

ENTERING FWY. I IMMED. BEGAN

A PACE, WITH SUBJ. PULLING AWAY

@ IND. 68 MPH (ACT. 70 MPH)

FOR 1 MI.

IF I CAN'T READ HIS NOTES, OR DON'T UNDERSTAND WHAT HE HAS WRITTEN, CAN I ASK HIM TO EXPLAIN THEM?

Absolutely, in fact, even if you think you *do* understand them you should still have the officer give his explanation. Many times the officer will have a place to comment on your attitude on the back of the citation. You can really jump on a comment like this ("Did you write the ticket because of my driving or my attitude?"). You should also look for any comment like "C.B." or "Radar Detector" that could indicate he wrote you out of prejudice for persons using this type of equipment rather than because of any alleged violation of the vehicle code. You should also question the officer about any apparent erasures on his copy of the citation.

WHAT IF HE DOESN'T HAVE ANY NOTES?

Occasionally, the officer won't have any notes at all. If this is the case at your trial, ask the officer why there are no notes. After he explains, ask him again about his recollection of the day of the alleged violation, and ask him if he is absolutely sure that he is not confusing you with some other violator.

WHAT ELSE DOES THE OFFICER BRING INTO COURT?

About the only thing that the officer may bring to court with him are his copy of the citation, a diagram of the location of your alleged violation, and possibly

the speedometer calibration sheet from his patrol car
(if your speed was established by pacing).

WHAT IS A SPEEDOMETER CALIBRATION?

A speedometer calibration is a verification of a patrol car's speedometer accuracy which is conducted at
periodic intervals (usually every few months, but this
will vary from agency to agency). This is usually done
by placing the patrol car on a dynamometer or by
checking the speedometer against the readings from a
radar gun. This calibration is usually carried in the car
for the officer's reference and may be duplicated on the
back of the citation for later use in court.

The speedometer calibration merely shows that the
speedometer was accurate at the time it was calibrated, and proves nothing about its accuracy at the
time of the violation. To prove this, the car would have
to be calibrated both *before and after* your violation. If
the officer brings any calibration document to court at
all, it will usually show only the calibration prior to
your violation and will not show any calibration that
may have been performed since that time.

A motorist who is clocked by a pacing patrol car
often gives up all hope of fighting their case in court.
There's a feeling among laymen that the pace is absolutely irrefutable evidence. Here's a few sample questions that you might ask the officer who claims he
paced you at a certain speed:

1. Officer, were you riding alone, or with a partner at the time of the alleged violation?
2. Were you or your partner driving?
3. (If partner was driver) Despite the fact that you were not driving the vehicle, is it true that you wrote the citation?
4. Did you actually observe the speedometer yourself?
5. What was the speed indicated on the speedometer?
6. Was that a calibrated speedometer?
7. What date was that speedometer calibrated on?
8. What were the results of that calibration? (Most will give an error factor.)
9. Did you have a certificate or other record of calibration in the patrol car on the day of my alleged violation?

DEPARTMENT OF CALIFORNIA HIGHWAY PATROL

SPEEDOMETER CALIBRATION CHART

DATE 12-30-77	VEHICLE NUMBER 9346
MILEAGE 29	TEST EQUIPMENT SERIAL NUMBER 66783

NAME(S) OF PERSON(S) MAKING CHECK

VEHICLE READS	30	40	50	55	60	65	70	80	90
ACTUAL SPEED	31	41	51	56	61	66	71	82	

CHP 227 (REV 10-74)   USE PREVIOUS EDITION UNTIL DEPLETED

10. Did you bring that document with you today?
11. Do you drive only this particular patrol car?
12. Is it possible that you remembered the error from another patrol car while you were determining my speed?
13. Who performed the calibration of your speedometer?
14. What were the qualifications of the person who performed this calibration?
15. Was a calibration performed after my alleged violation which indicated that the speedometer was accurate then?
16. Was a record or certificate made of that calibration?
17. Did you bring that document with you today?
18. Is it true that these routine calibrations are performed because of tire size variance and other possible mechanical changes which might affect the speedometer reading?
19. What was the tire size of your patrol car?
20. Is your patrol car equipped with a spare tire?
21. What is the size of that spare tire?
22. Are you aware of the fact that changes in the tire pressure will cause variances in the circumference of a tire?
23. Were your tire pressures checked on the day of the alleged violation?
24. Were those pressures the same when your speedometer was calibrated?
25. Officer, when was the last time that the patrol car you were using had a flat tire, a tire replaced, or the tires rotated?
26. Is it true, Officer, that you computed my speed

based solely on your speedometer reading and only checked your error factor after issuing the citation?

27. Is it likely that the speedometer in my vehicle could also have a certain percentage of error?

28. Isn't it true that the combination of the two error factors could amount to a substantial difference in the apparent speed?

WHERE DOES THE OFFICER GET HIS SPEEDOMETER CALIBRATED?

Similar to his radar unit, the patrol car's speedometer is calibrated by police mechanics in the police

A police car's speedometer is designed to make pacing easy.

garage facility. A relatively small staff (perhaps as small as a single mechanic) is responsible for testing and keeping the records on hundreds of patrol cars in addition to their routine maintenance duties. This has been compared to leaving the fox to guard the chicken coop. And in this case there's a lot of chickens in the coop.

SHOULD I HAVE MY SPEEDOMETER CALIBRATED ALSO?

If the speed of your vehicle was established by the patrol car pacing you and your speedometer didn't agree with the officer's, then having your speedometer calibrated could be a good idea. If it's a question of your word versus the officer's, having your own calibration performed can add a lot of credibility to your testimony.

WHERE CAN I HAVE MY SPEEDOMETER CALIBRATED?

Many automotive repair facilities, particularly those maintained by large automobile dealers, have dynamometers which can be used to calibrate your speedometer. In addition, many small auto radio repair and speedometer repair shops have complete facilities for speedometer calibration. These can be located in the Yellow Pages of the telephone directory, listed under "Speedometer."

Many businesses specialize in nothing but speedometer repair and calibration.

HOW MUCH DOES IT COST?

Speedometer calibrations are simple to perform and rather inexpensive. A typical calibration will cost from $7.50 to $25.00 depending on how they correct the problem (if any). This may consist of actually changing the gear drive of the unit, to merely pasting a sticker on the face of the speedometer telling you what the error is. However it is done, be certain to get a ceritificate of calibration, a letter or other document certifying that the speedometer was checked and showing the results of that calibration. This document should be brought with you to court.

WHAT'S THIS TRAFFIC ENGINEERING SURVEY YOU MENTIONED?

The traffic engineering survey is the engineering study which examines highway and traffic conditions in order to establish the proper speed limit in an area. This survey includes a measurement of the prevailing speeds that motorists are actually traveling at, a check on accident records for the area, and an examination of highway and roadside conditions and potential hazards which may not be readily apparent to the driver.

HOW CAN THE TRAFFIC ENGINEERING SURVEY AFFECT YOUR CASE?

The traffic engineering survey is the only justification that the city has for posting the speed limit (other than the state maximum limit). If conditions have changed significantly since the survey which established the speed limits was conducted, that posted speed may no longer be valid and would be a reason for arguing your case.

In many states, a traffic engineering survey which is no more than five years old is required on any street on which radar is used. These states make the evidence from a radar unit operating on an un-surveyed street inadmissible in court, and can be a reason for having your case immediately dismissed.

WHERE CAN I FIND THE TRAFFIC ENGINEERING SURVEY?

The traffic engineering surveys are part of the records maintained by the Engineering Department of

CUMULATIVE SPEED CURVE

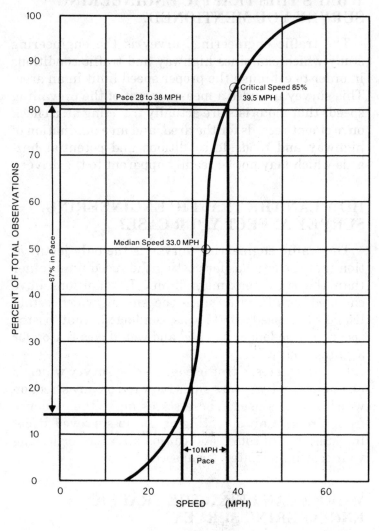

LOCATION_____   TIME _____TO _____

DIRECTION_____   PRESENT SIGNED ZONE _____MPH.

DATE _____   NUMBER OF VEHICLES____100____

your city or county. These records are usually available at City Hall (in a large city the Engineering department may have a separate office) or County Operations Center.

HOW DO I PREPARE MY TESTIMONY?

Your own testimony is very simple to prepare, it's simply your version of the story. You should practice this presentation by telling it to your friends and family a few times until you are familiar with the material, but avoid memorizing the testimony as a speech. You should make notes, outlining briefly the points you wish to cover in the order you think best presents your viewpoint. Since you are representing yourself, the judge will allow you to take the witness stand and state in a narrative form your version of the alleged violation.

You are not required to testify, in fact, it is one of your constitutional rights. The prosecutor can't use your failure to testify against you in any way, although it might cause a few raised eyebrows among the jury. However, if you feel you have adequately established your defense through the cross-examination of the prosecutor's witness(es), and you fear that the prosecutor may uncover something when he cross-examines you, you may wish to avoid testifying. If you had other witnesses in the car at the time of the alleged violation, you may wish to establish your case entirely through the examination of your witnesses.

SHOULD I TRY TO COME ON
LIKE PERRY MASON?

No, your testimony should be *un*professional, sincere and conversational in nature. You want to generate sympathy with a jury of laymen, and acting like a legal professional isn't the way to do it. If you try to act the part of a lawyer, you may find the rest of the court expecting you to know and follow all of the proper procedures. Appearing to be an inexperienced (but well-informed) layman is usually to your benefit.

WHAT SHOULD I SAY IN MY TESTIMONY?

The only thing you should say in your testimony is a narrative description of the details of the incident as you saw them. You should not attempt to be argumentative, but should just present the facts as you see them, in the order in which they occurred. The notes for a typical testimony for an alleged violation of the maximum speed limit might be as follows:

1. Alleged violation occurred at 1:00 a.m.
2. Virtually no other traffic on freeway.
3. Driving in #3 of four lanes.
4. No other traffic within half a mile.
5. Weather was dry and clear and the freeway was well lighted.
6. My speed was a steady 55 to 60.
7. I noticed the headlights of the patrol car immediately as he came down the on-ramp after me.
8. I immediately reduced speed to exactly 55 miles per hour.
9. He pulled me over after less than one quarter

of a mile and charged me with doing 65 miles per hour.

10. He stated at the time that he had paced me for over a mile.

11. He also stated that he had clocked me as high as 70 miles per hour, but would give me a "break" by only writing me for 65.

You can then state in your argument that you feel the officer misinterpreted what he saw, and that he had no opportunity to accurately observe your speed. Your entire attitude should not be that the officer was lying about the facts of the case (even if he were), but that he had merely made an honest mistake.

WHAT SHOULD I AVOID SAYING IN MY TESTIMONY?

Don't say anything that could be used as an admission that you actually violated the law. If you were to say, "I didn't see the officer at all when I ran the red light, so I don't understand how he could have seen me," the prosecutor will be sure to extract your statement, "I ran the red light" and use it against you in his final argument. A proper way to phrase the statement would be, "I didn't see the officer at the time of the alleged violation."

You should also avoid any statements which don't relate to the specific incident. Your past driving record and present driving habits are not on trial and have no bearing whatsoever on the case. If you bring up your past driving record as part of your testimony, you open yourself up to questions about it from the prosecutor during cross-examination. Anything you mention in your testimony can be later questioned by the prosecutor.

Your testimony should be based only on your observation of the facts and evidence. Your opinions about the officer's powers of observation, the legitimacy of his birth or the validity of the 55 mile per hour speed limit have no place in the courtroom.

CAN I LIE ABOUT IT?

Don't even think about lying during your testimony. Perjury (lying under oath) is a felony, and the courts frown on it very much. Bear in mind that anything you say in your testimony can be questioned by the prosecutor, and he may already have information about the truth that will make you look very bad in front of the judge or jury.

WHAT IF I HAD A GOOD REASON FOR VIOLATING THE LAW?

The court will usually recognize valid reasons for breaking the law. Speeding is understandable in a medical emergency and few people would question it if you weren't driving like a madman. However, this should be brought up at your arraignment rather than going to trial. You aren't disputing the fact that you broke the law, you are only stating that you had a good reason for doing so. The proper way to handle this is by pleading "guilty with an explanation" at your arraignment. Occasionally, a judge may dismiss your case with a valid explanation, but more often the plea of guilty is accepted and the sentence is suspended.

The fact that everyone else was doing it just means that everyone else was guilty too.

IF EVERYONE ELSE WAS DOING IT, IS THAT A VALID EXCUSE?

The fact that you were just "driving with the flow of traffic" doesn't mean that you weren't driving above the legal speed limit, and is not an acceptable reason for having your case dismissed. It may, however, raise a valid question as to why the officer selected you out of all the other violators. If you testify that "Everyone else was doing 85 and I was just keeping up with them," this constitutes an admission by you that you were speeding. The prosecutor will be sure to catch any such statement.

CAN I BLAME MY VIOLATION ON THE OFFICER'S PRESENCE?

The courts recognize that the patrol car can be a very distracting factor for many drivers. It is not uncommon for a police officer to pull up behind a motorist at a signal and then have the motorist look at the police car in his rearview mirror and proceed right on through the red light. If you choose to use this as a defense, you should plead "guilty with an explanation" and tell the judge about it at your arraignment.

IS IT A VALID DEFENSE ON EQUIPMENT VIOLATIONS IF I'VE SOLD THE CAR SINCE THE VIOLATION OCCURRED?

No, the fact that you no longer own the car may relieve you of your obligation to correct the equipment violation, but doesn't change the fact that you were caught driving the car with the equipment in that condition when you did own it. In some states, you may be required to repair the violation before you can legally sell the car to anyone else, other than a bona fide scrap disposal yard.

WILL THE JUDGE OR JURY GET MAD AT ME FOR DEFENDING MYSELF LIKE THIS?

There's no reason why they should get mad at you if your case is presented sincerely and logically without wasting the court's time. Pay attention to what is happening in court, follow the judge's instructions on procedure and do the best job you can and you will generate both the sympathy and the respect of the judge and jury.

The entire purpose of the court system is to provide a place for you to defend yourself. The fact that you are defending yourself is the only thing that justifies the judge's salary and the very existence of the court itself. If people didn't defend themselves against traffic citations, the whole system could consist of nothing but cashier's windows and traffic cops would carry changemakers on their belts like the hot dog vendors in a baseball stadium. It's your court system, and it's your right to use it. Nobody will get mad at you for exercising those rights.

WILL THE OFFICER TRY TO GET BACK AT ME IF I WIN?

If you win, the chances are the officer will just leave mumbling to himself and shaking his head in amazement. That officer will probably never even see you

"Be out of town by sundown or I'll come gunning for you." Few officers would ever try to take revenge.

again, much less write you another ticket. The officer would have nothing to gain by trying to get back at you, and would have everything to lose. Both his supervisors and the judge deal very harshly with any attempt by the officer to harass you.

WHEN I WIN, DO I GET BACK THE MONEY I POSTED AT THE ARRAIGNMENT?

Yes, you are entitled to a full refund on any bond that you may have posted to insure your appearance at trial. However, don't expect the court clerk to fork over cash or a check right on the spot. It often takes 30 days or longer for the refund check to be processed and mailed to you. Be sure to ask the court clerk about the return of the bond before you leave the court for the day.

IF I LOSE, CAN I APPEAL IT?

You can appeal your conviction in traffic court if you are convinced that the prosecution's evidence was truly insufficient to convict you, or if you feel that the sentence was overly harsh or any part of the trial was prejudiced against you. You should know, however, that few traffic cases are ever overturned on an appeal, and that the appeal will take a lot of time and money.

Because of the time and expense involved, we strongly recommend that anyone considering an appeal hire an attorney to represent them, or at the very least take the time to consult with a competent legal professional about the course of action you are considering. You will probably find that the attorney can handle your appeal far more easily, and in many cases more economically than you can.

You generally have 10 days from the time of your judgment in which you can appeal your traffic case. If you intend to appeal your case, you must file a written "Notice of Appeal" with the clerk of the court that heard your case.

If you intend to file the appeal yourself, there are numerous documents, copies and records which have to be filed at specific deadlines. The court clerk will probably be willing to assist you in selecting and filling out the appropriate forms, but be prepared to spend a lot of time with paperwork. For the normal person who works, the time element makes an appeal almost out of the question.

ALTERNATIVES TO FIGHTING
Other than walking.

WHAT'S AN "INSTANT TRIAL"?

The instant trial is a new program that has been started in some parts of the country as an option to a jury or court trial. It takes place immediately after the arraignment and disregards the normal trial procedures. In order to have an instant trial, the defendant has to waive his right to a jury trial and thus waives any right to appeal the case to a higher court. If the arraignment was conducted by a commissioner, he will usually conduct the trial as well and you will have to waive your right to be heard by a judge.

In an instant trial, the judge has only the court's copy of the violation to use as testimony of your alleged offense. Anything it says on that ciation is liable to be taken as the truth by the judge.

We don't recommend that *anyone* ask for this instant trial option as we don't see a benefit to you in any type of case. The program was started as an effort to help the courts deal with the huge burden of cases they hear, and probably does help them with that load. You should remember, that you have a right to be confronted with all the evidence against you (including the officer's testimony) and you can't cross-examine a citation. We feel that the instant trial requires you to give up too many of your rights to be fair and impartial.

CAN MY FRIEND, THE COP, FIX IT FOR ME?

No, there's no way that a police officer can make your ticket disappear. There's too many records of the violation in existence to have it removed, with a copy going to the police department (along with the officer's daily log which lists the violation) and one to the court. Any attempt by the officer to "fix" your ticket would probably get him fired, if not thrown in jail.

Sometimes, when an officer has a "friend" who just won't take "No" for an answer, the officer will take his friend's ticket and tell him that he will take care of it for him. Usually, he just goes down to the bail window and pays the bail, resulting in a conviction for the "friend." This is the only way that an officer can "fix" a ticket for you.

CAN MY FRIEND, THE JUDGE, FIX IT FOR ME?

If your friendly judge was hearing your case, he could dismiss the citation and effectively "fix" the ticket for you. However, proper procedure requires a judge to disqualify himself from any case in which he knows either party, or any case which he feels he could not fairly hear without prejudice.

If a judge is caught fixing tickets, it's very likely that the other judges he works for will "fix" him. A dishonest judge could be thrown off the bench, disbarred (forbidden to work as an attorney) and even tried and sentenced to a jail sentence.

HOW ABOUT THAT CUTE FILE CLERK I MET AT THE D.M.V.?

Nope, there's nobody who can effectively "fix" your ticket without taking a chance of getting caught and penalized.

Thurman "911" Porsche
23109 Indianapolis Avenue
Mumpsie, Indiana
August 30, 1978

The Chief of Police
Mumpsie Police Department
Mumpsie, Indiana

Dear Chief,

Last night (August 29) at 11:30 P.M. I happened to meet one of the officers from your department, Clarence T. Puckett (Badge #3) out on Highway 13. In the course of our conversation, he mentioned the fact that he had observed me keeping up with the flow of traffic, which consisted of a Corvette that got away. I really don't know why the officer chose me out of all that traffic and I don't really mind the ticket I got for doing 127 MPH (the officer said I was going faster than that before his Rambler's engine blew, but that was where the speedometer pegged out). What I really felt I should mention was what could possibly be construed as an unprofessional attitude on the part of the officer.

Specifically, during the conversation that followed my pulling over, the officer mentioned the names "Homicidal Maniac, Mental Defective, Moron, Idiot, Snot-nosed Punk, Dip, Reprobate, Jerk, Numbskull, Simpleton, Ninny, Bedlamite, Nerd, Speed Freak, Lunatic and Chicken Thief". I really resented having been called a "Chicken Thief", and I thought I should make this formal complaint.

Please feel free to contact me regarding this matter. I want to know if it.is your policy to allow your men to go around calling honest citizens "Chicken Thief".

Sincerely,

Thurman "911" Porsche

P.S. Sorry about his Rambler.

I DON'T MIND THE TICKET, BUT WHAT ABOUT HIS ATTITUDE?

Unfortunately, there's very little you can do about an officer's attitude, because attitude is such a subjective thing which really gives you few facts to complain about. If you really feel that you have a legitimate complaint about the officer's attitude, and perhaps some direct quotes which are representative of that attitude, you can make a complaint to the agency involved, the city council or the mayor's office.

The best way to do this is to write directly to the Chief of Police's office. Usually, someone from that agency will contact you to discuss all of the details of the incident. If they feel that your complaint is justified, action will be taken and you'll be informed.

Remember, any complaint you make should be outside of the scope of your violation. If you disagree with the ticket itself or have an axe to grind with the officer, you should handle that in court.

WHAT CAN I DO IF I THINK I WAS THE VICTIM OF A "CHERRY PATCH"?

If you think you were the victim of a fault in the engineering of the roadway, you should write a letter of complaint to the City Engineer describing why you feel that there is an error in the design of the roadway and asking him to correct that situation. If the design of the roadway is changed, or if you receive a letter of agreement from the engineering official, you have a very good chance of proving your case in court. You also will have the pleasure of having plucked one more cherry out of the officer's cherry patch.

WHAT IF I THINK THE LAW IS WRONG?

If you think a law is wrong, because of constitutional or other reasons, you may be able to get the law overturned in court. Any action like this is almost sure to get into the higher courts either through "judicial review" or on your own appeal. If you're considering a defense based on the illegality of a law, you really should consider hiring an attorney to represent you. The chances are that any such trial would be based on a lot of legal technicalities and details which would be beyond your abilities as a layman.

If you think the law is legally correct, but still a stupid law, then you might put pressure on your legislators by writing letters or circulating petitions to have the law removed.

WHO SHOULD I WRITE?

Because your traffic ticket falls under state laws, you should write to your state representatives (rather than your federal senator or representative). The state senator and assemblyman for your district should be listed in your telephone directory. In addition, you may wish to write to your city council, mayor, county supervisors and possibly the governor of your state.

IF I MOVE TO ANOTHER STATE, CAN I JUST FORGET ABOUT IT?

No, the long arm of the law extends across state boundaries, and the various Department of Motor Vehicles regularly exchange information on the drivers in their states.

The first time you are stopped by the police, or try to reregister your vehicle or apply for a license in the new state, they'll likely locate your old traffic warrant from the previous state. While they may not arrest you, they will probably refuse to issue you any new documents until the warrants are cleared from your original state's records.

RED TAPE
Dealing with the paper machine.

I LOST MY COPY OF THE CITATION, NOW WHAT DO I DO?

If you remember the time and date you were supposed to appear, there's no problem. Just appear at the court, report your presence to the clerk and they should put you on the calendar. They have a copy of the citation, and should have all the information there already.

If you don't remember when you are supposed to appear, you can call the court. With your name, they should be able to tell you when to appear. If you don't remember the court in which you were to appear, you can call the law enforcement agency which issued the citation. If you tell them the location of your alleged violation, they should be able to tell you which court to call for arraignment information.

CAN I JUST IGNORE THE CITATION?

When you signed the citation, you gave your promise to appear in court on or before the date specified on the ticket. If you just ignore it, it won't go away. Failure to appear is a separate crime (usually a misdemeanor) from that of the violation. If you fail to appear in court, they will issue a warrant for your arrest. If they don't come to your residence and arrest you, you will very likely be arrested the next time you are stopped for a routine traffic violation.

I FORGOT TO APPEAR: NOW WHAT SHOULD I DO?

Your best course of action is to go immediately to the

court to surrender yourself, and explain to the judge why you failed to appear. Often there are several days grace given before a warrant is issued by the court. If you are willing to go into the court and pay your fine, it will usually be accepted without any further penalties. However, if you allow more than a week to go by, the warrant is sure to be issued and you will face an additional fine, and possibly a jail term.

HOW DO I FIND OUT IF THERE'S A WARRANT OUT ON ME?

If you failed to appear on a traffic citation, you're probably aware of it, and more than likely there's a warrant out for you. It's virtually impossible for you to find out any warrant information without directly confronting a police officer who may arrest you. If you call the County Marshal's Office, they'll usually tell you, "Oh, just come in any day, 8 a.m. to 5 p.m. and we'll be glad to tell you." (Said the spider to the fly.) They usually will not give this type of information over the phone.

About the only way to find out if you have a warrant, is if you have a friend (a really good friend) on the police department. He'll be able to run your name through the computer to determine if you have a warrant.

Of course, the warrant won't show up in the computer right away. The judge will usually give a few days grace in which you can appear before the warrant is issued, and then it may take another 10 days before it appears in the computer.

Usually the only people that can tell you about a warrant are the ones that will arrest you if you have one.

DO TRAFFIC WARRANTS EVER EXPIRE?

Some do, and some don't. It is usually the judge who establishes any expiration date on a traffic warrant. (A traffic warrant is actually a misdemeanor violation for failure to appear, and is completely separate from the actual charge of the traffic violation.) The judge may allow the warrant to exist indefinitely (or until you are arrested), or may set a specific expiration date, often 5 or 10 years from the date it was issued.

WILL THEY RENEW MY LICENSE, EVEN THOUGH THERE'S A WARRANT OUT ON ME?

No, although they may give you the 60 day extension on your old one when you apply. Usually, your license comes by mail a month or so after you renew. All renewals are checked for warrants before they are sent, and if you've got warrants you don't have a license.

This is one reason why officers always check the expiration date on your license, and often issue citations for an expired license. They catch a lot of people with "outstanding" warrants in this manner.

DO I HAVE TO TELL THE DEPARTMENT OF MOTOR VEHICLES EVERYTIME I MOVE?

Yes, most states require you to report any change in residency within 10 to 30 days after moving.

HOW DO I GET A COPY OF MY DRIVING RECORD?

You can usually get a complete copy of your driving record through your local office of the Department of Motor Vehicles. Usually, a small fee (50¢ to $3.00) is charged for this service.

CAN ANYONE OTHER THAN THE COURTS TAKE AWAY MY LICENSE?

Yes, your license can be suspended or revoked on the basis of your driving record by the Department of Motor Vehicles. This usually happens when you accu-

mulate a number of points through citations and/or accidents. By law most states are required to warn you when you are getting close to a suspension and will allow you to attend a procedure called a "hearing" in which you will have a chance to argue your side of the story before your license is suspended. Your license can also be revoked for medical reasons (epilepsy, blindness, etc.).

HOW DO I KEEP FROM GETTING PARKING TICKETS ON A CAR THAT I'VE SOLD TO SOMEONE ELSE?

In order to avoid these annoying citations, be sure that you complete all of the necessary paperwork and properly report it to the Department of Motor Vehicles when you sell the car. The fact that you're receiving parking citations means that the Department of Motor Vehicles records still show you as the registered owner of the car. You still have to appear in court for these violations, but they will be dismissed when you present properly completed papers (bill of sale, etc.) that show you no longer own the car.

The officer may take away your license to make sure that you'll follow him back to the court.

GLOSSARY OF TERMS
You've got to know the language.

ACCIDENT—Whenever your vehicle meets something other than the asphalt.

ACCIDENT CITATION—A traffic ticket given to the driver who caused or contributed to an accident by violating a vehicle law.

ACQUITTAL—A court verdict of "Not guilty."

ACTIVITY RECAP—A weekly or monthly report card on the officer's standing in the ticket race.

AFFIDAVIT OF PREJUDICE—A legal document requesting the court to schedule a different judge for your trial than the one previously scheduled.

AGENCY—The organization which employs a law officer. This may be a federal agency (the F.B.I.), a state agency such as a State Police or Highway Patrol, a county agency such as a Sheriff or Constable's Office, or a municipal agency such as a city police department.

ALLEGED VIOLATION—A violation of the law which has been claimed by the officer (usually in the form of a traffic ticket), but has not been proven in court.

ALLEY—A narrow (usually less than 25 feet wide) minor street, usually used for access to the rear of a property or business.

AMERICAN FLAG LAPEL PIN—Piece of frequently worn jewelry for law enforcement officers. Many officers feel this adds to their sincerity and credibility. Not an official piece of equipment.

ANNOTATED VEHICLE CODE—Vehicle code which contains updates on the most current court decisions and definitions by the Attorney General in addition to the complete text of the law.

APPEAL—A request by a person who has been found

guilty, to a higher court to review the correctness of the lower court's decision.

ARRAIGNMENT—The proceeding by which a person is called before the court to be advised of the charge(s) against him and to enter his plea.

ARREST—The apprehension and taking into custody of a person who is charged with a crime. A traffic ticket is a release from custody for a person technically under arrest.

ATTABOY—Any commendation from either a citizen or the officer's agency. Attaboys become a part of the officer's personnel file.

ATTORNEY—A person who is legally appointed by another to act in his behalf. Also, LAWYER.

AUDIBLE SIGNAL—The tone emitted by a radar unit to alert its operator to the speeds of vehicles the unit is tracking.

AUTHORIZED EMERGENCY VEHICLE—Generally, those vehicles which are engaged in law enforcement, fire or lifesaving services. Emergency vehicles are equipped with warning lights and sirens which require other vehicles to yield the right-of-way when they are in operation.

AUTOMATIC LOCK—Special feature on some radar units which allows the unit to automatically lock onto the highest speed the unit detects.

BAD CONNECTION—A term used to describe one of the ways to cheat with radar, specifically tapping on the case of the older needle type radars, causing the needle to fluctuate.

BAIL—Security (usually cash) given to the court in exchange for the release of a person in custody, to assure his presence in court later.

BAIL FORFEITURE—The act of giving up the bail money to the court instead of appearing as promised.

BAILIFF—A minor officer of the court who is responsible for controlling prisoners, guarding the judge and jury, and for maintaining order in the court.

BASIC SPEED LAW—A law which generally forbids the operation of a vehicle at a speed faster than is safe, considering the weather, traffic and roadway conditions.

BEAM WIDTH—The spread of energy projected by a radar unit, usually 12-16° wide.

BEAR—Any police officer.

BEAT—The area which an officer patrols, in some cases a particular section of highway.

BEST INTEREST OF JUSTICE—A term used when the prosecution requests a motion for dismissal of a court case when it is felt that the case cannot be successfully prosecuted.

BIG HOUSE—Any state or federal prison.

BIONIC RADAR—Manufacturer's description of a radar unit with an electronically synthesized voice which calls out the speeds it observes.

BLIND SPOT—The area on the right rear of most vehicles in which the driver cannot see with his mirrors. This is where officers like to "hide" to pace a vehicle.

BOND—Any amount of money or guarantee given to the court as bail.

BRIBE—Anything given or promised to influence another person's judgment or conduct.

BURDEN OF PROOF—The legal principal that it is the duty of the complaining party (the prosecution) to present sufficient proof to establish the validity of the charges.

BURNED—Describes a radar or VASCAR operation whose location has been discovered by the motoring public.

BURNED OUT—Used to describe an area which has been overworked by traffic officers to the point that it no longer generates traffic tickets.

BUSINESS DISTRICT—Any area in which more than half of the property is occupied by commercial businesses.

CALENDAR—The list of cases established by the court to determine the order and dates in which they will be handled.

CALENDAR COURT—The court which conducts scheduling for all the other courts in a jurisdiction. Also MASTER COURT.

CALIBRATE MODE—A position on the function control selector of a radar unit which allows the operator to determine if his unit is correctly operating by producing a known, predetermined reading.

CALIBRATED SPEEDOMETER—A speedometer which has had its accuracy verified by external means.

CALIBRATION LOG—A written record of calibration dates and procedures.

CANNED TESTIMONY—Testimony which is memorized and sounds stale.

CATCH-UP SPEED—Term used to describe one of the ways of cheating with radar, specifically by clocking the patrol car's speed when pursuing the violator rather than the violator's actual speed.

CB RADIO—Any Class D, 27 Megahertz transceiver used by individuals to communicate with each other.

CERTIFICATE OF CALIBRATION—A document from the manufacturer of a radar unit or radar tuning fork certifying its specifications and accuracy.

CERTIFIED TUNING FORK—A tuning fork used for radar calibration which is registered by serial number and guaranteed by the manufacturer to produce a specified speed on the radar unit.

CHAFF—Any of a number of scattered materials used to mask a radar image. (Applies only to aircraft radar.)

CHALLENGE OF JUROR—The right of either party in a trial to object to a juror during the process of jury selection.

CHANGE OF VENUE—The transferring of a court case to another court. In traffic cases changes of venue are only allowed to move the case to a county seat.

CHARACTER WITNESS—A witness who has knowledge of the person's character, personality and background, but no actual knowledge of the case being tried.

CHEAT SHEET—A simplified reference card used by officers to look up the vehicle code sections for various violations.

CHERRY PATCH—A particular stretch of roadway in which a lot of traffic citations are issued for dubious reasons.

CHP—The California Highway Patrol. Also CHIP or CHIPPIE.

CITATION—A written, official notice to appear in a court and answer a charge against you.

CITIZEN'S COMMENDATION—A letter of praise for a law officer from a citizen.

CITIZEN'S COMPLAINT—A letter of complaint about a police officer from a citizen. Usually requires investigation by his agency.

CITIZEN'S ARREST—An arrest made by a private person.

CLOCK—The act of observing and recording the speed of a vehicle. A clock may be performed with a stopwatch, radar, VASCAR or speedometer.

CLOSING STATEMENT—The final arguments made in a trial.

COMMERCIAL VEHICLE—Any vehicle which transports people or cargo, and charges for that service. Commercial vehicles are usually issued special license plates by the state.

COMMISSIONER—A person (usually an attorney) appointed by the courts to perform some of the functions of a judge.

COMMUNICATIONS ACT OF 1934—The act of Congress which guarantees a U.S. citizen the right to receive radio communications, including police radar signals.

COMPENSATORY TIME—Time off from work given to a law officer to make up for the time he spends in court.

COMPULSORY INSURANCE—Insurance coverage which is required under state or federal law.

CONSTABLE—A police officer, usually employed by a county or municipality.

CONTEMPT OF COURT—Showing disrespect for the authority or dignity of the court by disobedience or disorderly conduct.

CONTINUANCE—The postponement of a trial or proceeding to another scheduled date.

CONTRIBUTORY NEGLIGENCE — Carelessness which helps to bring about an accident, and usually prevents the person from collecting damages from the person who was primarily responsible.

CONVICTION—A verdict of guilty.

CONVOY—A line of CB-equipped vehicles (usually trucks) moving together on the highway.

COP—Any policeman. Believed to have been derived from Constable On Patrol.

COSINE ANGLE FACTOR—An error in radar's detection of speed which occurs whenever the radar target deviates from a straight alignment with the radar unit.

COUNTING UNIT—The part of the radar unit which processes the Doppler signals and computes and displays the speed.

COUNTY CLINK—Any jail facility maintained by a county.

COUNTY MOUNTIE—Any law officer employed by the county, specifically a deputy sheriff or constable.

COUPON—A CB slang term for a traffic ticket.

COURT—Any place in which justice is administered and trials are held. Also, the persons who conduct such proceedings.

COURT TRIAL—A trial held without a jury. The judge alone determines the verdict of the trial.

COURT APPOINTED COUNSEL—An attorney appointed by the courts to represent a defendant who is otherwise unable to afford one. Usually not available to persons charged with minor violations.

CRASH AND DASH—Another term for hit and run.

CRITICAL SPEED—The speed at or below which 85% of the traffic on a particular highway is moving. Also the 85th PERCENTILE SPEED.

CROSS EXAMINATION—The questioning of a witness who has already been questioned by the opposing side to determine the validity of his answers.

CROSSWALK—Any area designated for a pedestrian's

use in crossing a street. The crosswalk may be marked, or may be an imaginary extension of the sidewalks or curb lines.

DAILY ACTIVITY REPORT—A count of all of the officer's tickets and arrests for the day.

DAILY LOG—The complete record kept by the officer of all his activities for the day.

DEFENDANT—The person charged with a crime.

DEFENSE—Your justification in court for the actions with which you were charged. Also, the defendant and his attorney are referred to as the defense in court.

DETECTOR DEFEAT MODE—An option on some radar units which allows the operator to selectively control when his unit broadcasts. Basically, an On-Off switch for the antenna.

DEUCE—A drunk driver. A term originally derived from the old California Penal Code Section "502." The drinking driver law in that state is now in the Vehicle Code under Section "23102 A."

DEWEY—Common reference for a drunk driver by law officers. Derived from the term *Driving While under the Influence, DWI*, or *Driving Under the Influence, DUI* Officers speak of looking for "DEWEY" and how easy he is to find.

DIAGRAM—A map like sketch of an area used to demonstrate the positions of vehicles during an accident or alleged violation.

DISMISSAL—The act of throwing a case out of court or dismissing the charges.

DISPOSITION—The arraignment and outcome of a trial.

DOCUMENT CITATION—A ticket given for violations involving a vehicle's registration or a driver's license.

DOPPLER EFFECT—The apparent change in the frequency of a reflected radio wave, which varies with the speed of the source.

DOPPLER FREQUENCY—The difference between the frequency of the radio waves projected by a radar unit, and the waves reflected by a moving object.

DOPPLER TONE—The audible tone produced by some radar units which represents the speed of the vehicle being clocked.

DRIVER—The operator of any motor vehicle.

DRIVER'S LICENSE—The permit issued by the state which allows a person to legally operate a motor vehicle.

DRIVING RECORD—The record maintained by the state of your name, description, address, driving violations and accidents.

DUI—Commonly used abbreviation for Driving Under the Influence, specifically under the influence of alcohol or drugs.

DWI—Abbreviation for Driving While Intoxicated or Driving While under the Influence.

85th PERCENTILE SPEED—The speed at which 85 percent of all traffic is traveling at or below.

ELECTRONIC COUNTER MEASURES (ECMs)—Any electronic device used to defeat police radar.

ELEMENTS—The basic parts of a crime, all of which must have occurred in order for it to be classified as a crime.

EQUIPMENT VIOLATION—Any ticket given for illegal or inoperative equipment on a vehicle. Also, FIXIT TICKET.

EVIDENCE—Anything legally presented in court,

such as the statements or testimony of a witness, or an object, which tends to prove the point in question.

EXCLUSION OF WITNESS—The right of any party in a trial to have witnesses removed from the courtroom while any other witness is testifying.

EXHIBIT—Documents or other objects used in a trial as evidence.

EXPUNGE—The act of having all records of a violation totally removed from the records.

FAILURE TO APPEAR—A misdemeanor crime of violating a promise to appear in court.

FAILURE TO YIELD—Not stopping for a police car displaying its lights and sounding its siren.

FATAL ACCIDENT—An accident that results in the death of another person within one year of the date of the accident.

FCC—The Federal Communications Commission, the federal agency responsible for the licensing and regulations governing police radar.

FELONY—Any crime punishable by a term in the state prison.

FELONY STOP—The procedure used by law officers when they believe they may be stopping a vehicle involved in a felony. May consist of removal of the occupants from the vehicle at gunpoint.

FENDER BENDER—Any minor automobile accident.

5th AMENDMENT—The amendment to the U.S. Constitution which gives a person the right not to testify against himself.

FINAL APPROACH—A method of cheating with radar, specifically by clocking and locking the speed of aircraft near an airport.

FINE TUNING—The act of adjusting a radar unit to a frequency outside those authorized by law.

FIXIT TICKET—An equipment violation which requires the equipment to be repaired.

FLY BY NIGHT—Term used to describe many manufacturers of radar and radar detection equipment.

FIX—Any attempt to influence the issuance, action or outcome of a traffic ticket.

FREEWAY—A limited access high-speed highway without tolls.

FREQUENCY SHIFT—The change that occurs in the frequency of the broadcast radar beam and the beam reflected back to the radar unit from a moving object.

GIGAHERTZ—A frequency of a billion waves per second.

GREENSTAMP—A CB slang term for money. Also, a traffic ticket which requires you to pay a fine.

GUILTY—A verdict by the court or jury, or a plea at an arraignment, that an offense had been committed by a defendant as charged.

GUILTY WITH AN EXPLANATION—An admission at arraignment of guilt, with an attempt to justify the violation through an explanation to the judge.

HANDICAPPED ZONE—A parking area legally reserved for only those persons with handicaps.

HANGING JUDGE—A judge with an established reputation for finding defendants guilty and assessing harsh penalties.

HARMONIC FREQUENCY—Any multiple of a frequency which may effect a radar unit operating on that frequency.

HAZARDOUS VIOLATION—Any violation which might possibly cause an accident.

HEAD-HUNTERS—Any officer working for the

Internal Affairs Division of a law enforcement agency.

HERTZ—A measurement of frequency equal to one cycle per second.

HIGH DOPPLER—The frequency used by a moving radar unit to track the speed of the target.

HIGHWAY—Generally refers to any publicly maintained roadway which is open to any member of the public for vehicular travel.

HIT AND RUN—A driver who leaves the scene of an accident in which he was involved without leaving the required information or notifying authorities.

HIT AND SPLIT—Same as Hit and Run.

HOLD SWITCH—A cut-off switch on the antenna of some radar units. Also known as a Radar Detector Defeat Mode.

HONEYCUTT vs. THE COMMONWEALTH OF KENTUCKY—Court case involving a radar ticket which determined that the radar operator's visual observation of a vehicle was sufficient to identify it as the one clocked by the radar unit.

HOSE TIMER—Outdated device used to determine the speed of motorists.

HOT DOG—Any law officer who is very aggressive. Also "Cowboy."

HOT PENCIL—An officer who writes a large number of tickets.

HOT PURSUIT—A fresh chase in which the officer is continuously behind the violator, without losing sight of the car he is chasing.

HUNGRY BEAR—A traffic officer who is low on his quota and ready to feed on a passing motorist.

HURRY-UP HUSTLE—A method of cheating with radar, specifically by driving a moving radar equipped patrol car at higher speeds than the radar is capable of computing.

HYDROPLANING—A phenomena which occurs when the tires of a car lose contact with the road and ride up on a layer of water.

IGNORANCE OF THE LAW—Something you may have suffered from before reading *The Ticket Book*.

IMPLIED CONSENT—A provision in every state that makes your agreement to a chemical test for alcohol automatic by the fact that you have a driver's license.

IN PRO PER—Short for In Propria Persona meaning appearing in person on your own behalf.

INTERNAL CALIBRATION—A check of a radar unit's accuracy through the use of a crystal or other electronic means. Actually, it only checks the unit's ability to analyze a frequency ratio, and does not use the radar itself.

INFRACTION—A minor violation of the law, usually punishable only by a fine.

INSTANT TRIAL—New and somewhat questionable procedure currently being tested in selected areas. Consists of a quickie trial at the time of the arraignment without the officer's presence.

INTERNAL AFFAIRS DIVISION—The department of a law enforcement agency responsible for investigating charges and accusations against police officers.

INTERSECTION—The area formed where two or more highways meet, generally defined by an imaginary extension of the curb lines.

INTERSTATE—Any of the national system of highways which may cross state boundaries.

INTRASTATE—Any of an individual state's highways.

JAYWALKING—Walking across a street without regard to the traffic or laws.

JUDGE—An elected or appointed public official authorized to hear and decide civil and criminal cases in a court of law.

JURISDICTION—The area in which a law officer has authority to operate.

JUROR—Anyone serving on a jury.

JURY—A body of citizens who are selected to hear and decide a case in court.

JURY TRIAL—Any trial which is decided by a jury.

JUSTICE COURT—A court with limited power to hear cases within a specific region. Usually presided over by a Justice Of The Peace.

K-BAND—A frequency of 24.150 Gigahertz, one of the three bands currently authorized for police radar.

KILOHERTZ—A frequency of a thousand cycles per second.

KITING—A method of cheating with tickets, specifically, indicating a speed on the ticket higher than that which the motorist was actually clocked at.

LANDMARK CASE—A case which is so important that it establishes a precedent for future cases.

LAW ENFORCEMENT AGENCY—Any national, state, county or municipal organization with the responsibility for enforcing that authority's laws.

LEARNER'S PERMIT—A temporary driver's license given to a person who otherwise would not be qualified to operate a motor vehicle. Learner's permits often require a licensed driver in the same vehicle.

LEFTOVERS—A method of cheating on radar, specifically, failing to clear the unit of a previous violator's speed.

LESSER AND INCLUDED VIOLATION—A traffic violation which is part of a much larger violation. Example: Running a stop sign and speeding might be lesser and included violations in a reckless driving charge.

LET'S MAKE A DEAL—A game prosecutors play when it's to their advantage.

LIMIT LINE—A line painted on the roadway or imaginary to indicate the point at which vehicles are required to stop at a sign or a light.

LOADING ZONE—Any area designated for the specific purpose of loading or unloading persons or materials.

LOW DOPPLER—In a moving radar unit, the frequency which is used to determine the patrol car's speed.

MAGISTRATE—A minor official with the authority to hear minor cases in a limited region.

MARSHAL—A law officer empowered to carry out the orders of the court. Also, a police officer in some small towns.

MASTER COURT—The court responsible for scheduling cases for the other courts within a jurisdiction.

MAXIMUM SPEED LIMIT—The highest speed that a vehicle may legally travel, even if it is safe to go faster.

MAY—When a law says "may" it gives the person permission to act as the law states. If the code uses "shall" instead, that is an indication a citation would be issued for violating that section.

MEDIAN—The center of the highway.

MEGAHERTZ—A frequency of a million cycles per second.

MERGING—The process by which two separate traffic streams combine to form a single stream.

METER MAID—Obsolete term referring to a female parking regulation officer.

MIRANDA DECISION—Court decision requiring a law officer to inform a suspect of his constitutional rights before the results of the officer's questioning are allowed as evidence.

MISDEMEANOR—A crime punishable by imprisonment in a county or municipal jail for less than a year, but cannot result in imprisonment in a state or federal prison.

MISTRIAL—A trial which is made void through some mistake in the trial proceedings, or because of the jury being unable to come to a decision.

MOTORCYCLE—Generally defined as any vehicle having no more than three wheels.

MOTOR-DRIVEN CYCLE—Definition varies between states, usually any motorcycle, scooter or bicycle with less than 15 brake-horsepower, or with wheels less than 18 inches in diameter.

MOTOR VEHICLE—Any vehicle which is self propelled.

MOVING RADAR—Any radar unit capable of clocking a target while the vehicle the radar unit is mounted in is in motion.

MOVING MODE—The mode which allows a moving radar to operate while the vehicle is in motion.

MOVING VIOLATION—The violation of any law which regulates the safe movement of vehicles or pedestrians.

MUNICIPAL COURT—The court representing any local government.

MUNICIPAL ORDINANCE—Any law enacted by a city government.

NCIC—The National Crime Information Center, the nation's clearinghouse for information on all criminal activities.

NEW VASCAR—A common term erroneously used to describe moving radar.

NEW YORK vs. DANTANIO—The landmark case on radar, in which the court accepted the fact of radar's accuracy and set the guidelines for the operator's training and understanding.

NO FAULT INSURANCE—Insurance in which each party bears responsibility for the repairs to their own vehicles.

NOLO CONTENDERE—A plea which does not admit guilt, but does not deny it either. Used primarily in cases involving accidents, it counts the same as a plea of guilty. Also NO CONTEST.

NOT GUILTY—A verdict by the court or jury, or a plea at arraignment, that an offense had not been committed by a defendant as charged.

NOTIFY WARRANT—A notice to a citizen that he or she has been charged with a crime.

NUMITRON GAS TUBE—A device which electronically displays any digit from 0-9, two or three tubes are used frequently to display the speed on a radar unit.

OATH—A declaration or promise to tell the truth.

OFFICIAL TRAFFIC CONTROL DEVICE—Any sign, signal, marking or device designed to regulate, warn or guide traffic and placed in accordance with law.

OFFICIAL TRAFFIC CONTROL SIGNAL—Any device that alternately signals vehicles to stop and proceed.

OPENING STATEMENT—The initial remarks made to the jury in a trial.

OPERATOR—The driver of any motor vehicle.

ORBIS—A sophisticated hose-timer type system which photographed offenders and automatically processed the citations.

ORDINANCE—Any law or regulation established by a government.

OWN RECOGNIZANCE—A release from custody without posting bail on a defendant's promise to appear. Also, O.R.

PANNING—One of the ways to cheat with radar, specifically by sweeping a stationary radar so that it reads the background rather than the target vehicle.

PANNING FOR GOLD—Same as panning.

PARKING—The standing or halting of a vehicle, whether occupied or not, for anything longer than a temporary period while loading.

PARKING CONTROL OFFICER—An officer whose primary duty is the enforcement of parking regulations.

PARKING VIOLATION—Any citation issued for violation of parking regulations.

PASSENGER VEHICLE—Any self-propelled vehicle designed for the transportation of persons.

PATROLMAN—Obsolete term for a male Patrol Officer.

PATROL OFFICER—Base rank for a law enforcement officer primarily engaged in patrol work.

PATROL SPEED—The speed of the patrol car.

PEDESTRIAN—Any person traveling on foot.

PENAL CODE—The laws of a state dealing with various crimes and their penalties.

PEOPLE—General title used to describe the prosecution, as in The People vs. You. Technically, any violation you commit is against the people of your state.

PEREMPTORY CHALLENGE—An arbitrary objection to the selection of a juror which cannot be denied by the court. Usually, both parties have a limited number of peremptory challenges.

PERJURY—The willful telling of a lie when under oath to tell the truth.

PERSON—As used in vehicle codes, person usually refers to any individual, partnership, business or corporation.

PHYSICAL EVIDENCE—Any object or materials submitted to the court to lend support to the claims of either party.

PICTURE TAKER—A CB slang term for a police officer in a radar equipped patrol car.

PIE PAN TRICK—The original anti-radar detection device, consists of holding a pie pan in front of the radar antenna until a target is within clocking range.

PLAINCLOTHES UNIT—An unmarked police car.

PLEA—A statement made by the defendant in response to a charge.

PLEAD—The act of presenting your plea.

POINT SYSTEM—A system used in some states in which traffic violations and accidents are assigned points. Accumulation of a specific number of points can result in suspension or revocation of your license.

POLICE IMPOUND—The holding in custody of a vehicle by a law enforcement agency.

POSTED LIMIT—The speed limit which appears on signs near or on the roadway. Also PRIMA FACIA LIMIT.

PPP—An abbreviation for Proper Police Procedure, the policies and guidelines under which officers of a law enforcement agency operate.

PRIMA FACIA SPEED LIMIT—The speed limit posted on or near the roadway other than the state maximum.

PRIVATE IMPOUND—The holding in custody of a vehicle by a private person or company by the authority of a law enforcement agency.

PRIVATE ROAD OR DRIVEWAY—Any highway which is not owned, regulated or maintained by the state, but is owned by an individual.

PROBABLE CAUSE—Reasonable grounds or suspicions that a person is guilty of a crime.

PROCEDURE—The specific protocol and organization of the trial in a formal court.

PROFESSIONAL COURTESY—The practice of giving special consideration to members within the same profession.

PROLONGATION OF CURB LINES—The imaginary extension of the curbs where two roadways meet to form an intersection.

PROMISE TO APPEAR—A written agreement on most citations which guarantees your appearance to answer the charges and must be signed before the officer can release you.

PRO SE—Appearing in person, also PRO PER.

PROSECUTION—The party (usually an attorney employed to represent the state) which initiates the proceedings in any criminal trial.

PROSECUTOR—The attorney who represents the government in a trial.

PROXY—A person authorized to represent another person.

PUBLIC ROAD—Any highway owned, operated and maintained by a city, county or state for the use of the general public.

QUOTA—A specific number of tickets which must be issued by an officer to demonstrate adequate performance.

RADAR—Short for "radio detection and ranging," an electronic device used by law enforcement agencies to determine the speed of vehicles on the highway.

RADAR DETECTOR—Any radio receiver designed to receive police radar frequencies.

RADAR DETECTOR JAMMER—Any device designed to broadcast on police radar frequencies for the purpose of triggering radar detectors.

RADAR GUN—A hand-held radar unit shaped somewhat like a pistol.

RADAR JAMMER—Any device designed to interfere with the operation of police radar.

RADAR TRAP—General term for any location in which radar is frequently in use.

RADIOPOSITIONING EQUIPMENT—The technical name for radar used by the Federal Communications Commission.

RADIOPOSITIONING LICENSE—The permit issued to law enforcement agencies by the Federal Communications Commission which allows them to use radar.

RAMP—General term referring to any exit or entrance to a limited access highway.

REASONABLE AND PRUDENT—A phrase frequently used in laws to describe the actions of a logical and ordinarily cautious individual.

REASONABLE DOUBT—A sincere disbelief that a person is guilty of a crime.

RECROSS EXAMINATION—The second round of the questioning of a witness in a trial, following the redirect examination.

REDIRECT EXAMINATION—Questioning of a witness in a trial in response to cross examination of the witness' initial testimony.

REFEREE—A person appointed by the court to hear testimony and evidence and render decisions on minor cases.

REFLECTED FREQUENCY—The frequency of the radio wave reflected off a moving object.

REGISTRATION—The official record of a vehicle's technical and licensing information.

REGISTERED OWNER—The person recognized by the state as the owner of a vehicle for licensing purposes. Not necessarily the legal owner of the vehicle. Banks are often legal owners and you are the registered owner.

RENT-A-COP—Any private security guard.

RESERVE OFFICER—A volunteer part-time police officer. While on-duty and in uniform most reserve officers have the same powers as a regular police officer.

RIDE-ALONG—A program which allows citizens to ride with a police officer and observe him as he goes about his duties.

RIGHT-OF-WAY—The privilege of immediate use of the highway.

ROADWAY—The part of the highway used by vehicles.

ROOKIE—Any new, relatively inexperienced officer.

RUDE RULE—A basic principle of traffic laws, generally, if an action on the highway is rude, it is probably illegal.

S-BAND—A frequency of 2.455 Gigahertz, one of the three bands currently authorized for police radar, and the first frequency to be introduced and used.

SCANNING DETECTOR—A radar detector which scans all of the possible frequencies used by radar, rather than being tuned to just one or more individual frequencies.

SECTION—The individual specific laws within a vehicle code.

SELLING A TICKET—The technique of an officer convincing a motorist that he really deserved a citation.

SERVICE—The legal process by which official documents such as subpoenas are served.

SHADOWING—A form of moving radar malfunction in which the unit reads a large moving vehicle instead of the ground speed.

SHALL—When a law says "shall," the action described is mandatory and is a citable offense.

SHIFTING ZONES—A way of cheating with radar, by clocking vehicles in a higher speed zone with a radar unit operating in a lower speed zone.

SHOOT—The act of clocking a motorist with a radar unit.

SHOULDER—Either edge of a road or highway.

SIDEWALK—The part of the highway other than the actual roadway which is designated by curbs or markings for pedestrian travel.

SLAMMER—Any place of incarceration.

SMOKEY—A CB slang term for any member of any

law enforcement agency, especially a member of a state police or highway patrol. Also SMOKEY THE BEAR.

SMOKEY REPORT—A CB radio report on the location of a police car.

SNAKES—A hose timer.

SPEEDING FANS—A method of cheating with radar, specifically by clocking the speed of a heater or air conditioning fan instead of a motorist.

SPEED TRAP—A location which is designed to catch motorists, either by the design and posted speeds on the highway or the manner in which the laws are enforced.

SPEEDY TRIAL—One of a person's constitutional rights, the right to have a trial within a short period after the arraignment.

SPURIOUS READING—A false reading which sometimes appears on a radar unit with no apparent cause.

SQUELCH—The control that adjusts the sensitivity of a radar unit or radar detector.

STATE OF CONNECTICUT vs. TOMANELLI—The court case which established the tuning fork as the recognized method of calibration for radar units.

STATE TROOPER—Any member of a state police or highway patrol.

STATIONARY MODE—The mode which allows a moving radar to operate while the patrol car is not in motion.

STATIONARY RADAR—A radar which does not have the capability of clocking other vehicles while the patrol car is in motion.

STEREODYNE—Term used by some manufacturers

to describe the operation of a radar detector capable of receiving two frequencies.

STOPPING—The cessation of movement of a vehicle on a roadway, whether occupied or not.

STOPWATCH MODE—An option on some modern radar units which allows the unit to operate as a time-distance computer without using radar.

SUBPOENA—A legal document requiring a witness to attend a trial.

SUBPOENA DUCES TECUM—A legal document requiring a person to bring records or other specified evidence to court.

SUPERIOR COURT—The highest court on the local government level, usually responsible for hearing cases involving felonies.

SUSPENDED SENTENCE—A penalty from the court which is temporarily or indefinitely postponed, rather than carried out immediately.

SWITCH—One method of cheating with radar, specifically by using the radar in a time-distance mode and telling the motorist he was clocked with radar.

SWOOP—A favorite technique for catching speeders on the highway, consists of rapid acceleration down an on-ramp and into the motorist's blind spot.

TARGET—The vehicle being clocked by radar.

TARGET SPEED—The speed of a vehicle being clocked by radar.

THROUGH HIGHWAY—A highway which extends between two points without stopping, and whose side roads are controlled by stop signs or signals.

TICKET—Any citation issued for a violation of the law.

TICKET RACE—The unofficial competition that

exists between law officers in the quantity of citations which are written.

TICKET TENSION—The acute anxiety suffered by some motorists whenever they sit behind the controls of a motor vehicle.

TIME DISTANCE COMPUTER—An electronic device which determines the speed of a vehicle based on the amount of time required for that vehicle to travel a known distance.

TRAFFIC—Automobiles, trucks, buses and other vehicles, pedestrians, and herded or ridden animals which are using the highway for the purpose of travel.

TRAFFIC AND ENGINEERING SURVEY—An official study of a section of highway to examine the prevailing speeds, accident records, and other roadside conditions.

TRAFFIC CITATION—Any ticket issued for a violation of a traffic law.

TRAFFIC CODE—The laws governing the operation of a motor vehicle. Also, VEHICLE CODE.

TRAFFIC CONDITIONS—Usually refers to the number, density and speed of vehicles in an area.

TRAFFIC OFFICER—Any law officer whose main duty is the enforcement of traffic laws.

TRAFFIC SAFETY INDEX—The ratio between injury and fatal traffic accidents and issued citations, serves as an indication of a traffic enforcement program's efficiency.

TRAFFIC SAFETY RADAR—Radar used by law enforcement agencies to enforce speed laws.

TRAFFIC SURVEY RADAR—Radar used for statistical purposes only, usually capable of storing information on the numbers of vehicles traveling at specific speeds.

TRAFFIC VIOLATOR'S SCHOOL—Educational program conducted by some courts as an alternative to a conviction.

TRAFFIC WARNING—A written notice of a violation which does not require an appearance in court or a fine.

TRIAL—The formal examination of the facts of a case to determine the guilt or innocence of a person in a court of law.

TRIAL BY DECLARATION—A trial in which the prosecution presents no witness, but only a written statement from a witness.

TRIAL BY DEPOSITION—Same as Trial by Declaration.

TRIAL DE NOVO—A new trial sechedule by a District Court of Appeals.

TUNE-UP—A method of cheating with radar, specifically by using a tuning fork to generate a false reading on a radar unit.

TWEAKING—The illegal adjustment of a radar unit to operate outside of the bands licensed by the FCC.

UNDER SUBMISSION—The period of time in which the court is considering the case in order to make a decision.

UNIFORM VEHICLE CODE—The model law recommended by the National Committee on Uniform Traffic Laws and Ordinances for adoption in all states.

UNITED STATES CODE—The federal laws established by Congress. Also U.S.C.

U-TURN—The turning of a vehicle so as to proceed in an opposite direction.

VASCAR—Short for "Visual Average Speed Computer and Recorder," VASCAR, a trade name, is simply a time-distance computer.

VEHICLE—Any device which is capable of transporting persons or property upon a highway.

VEHICLE CODE—The laws governing the use and operation of a motor vehicle.

VERBAL WARNING—A spoken warning of a traffic violation by a law officer. Also, HOLLER STOP.

VIOLATION—The failure to observe or obey a law.

VISUAL ESTIMATE—Observation of a vehicle's speed by merely seeing the vehicle on the roadway and estimating its speed.

WARRANT—An authorization from a court for the arrest of an individual.

WAR STORY—Any funny story or tall tale told by a law officer, usually to other officers at social gatherings.

WATCH COMMANDER—The person in charge of a particular agency or station at any given time. Usually a sergeant on a small agency, or a captain or lieutenant with a larger agency.

WEATHER CONDITIONS—Any weather that affects the road surface or visibility on the highway.

WEIGHT OF TESTIMONY—The amount of credibility given to a witness.

WET TOWEL TRICK—Technique used by some officers to sneak up on speeders at night. Consists of placing a wet paper towel over one headlight to give the car a poorly maintained appearance at night.

WHISTLER—One method of cheating on radar, specifically by whistling into a CB radio to generate a false signal.

WHODUNNIT—A method of cheating on radar, specifically by clocking a vehicle traveling in the opposite direction from the one the officer has stopped.

WIPE—A method of cheating with radar on the old needle indicator types, specifically by generating static electricity on the needle face to affect the reading.

WITNESS FOR THE PEOPLE—Any witness who testifies for the prosecution, usually the officer who stopped you.

WORKING RANGE—The distance at which the use of radar is practical, usually less than 2500 feet.

X-BAND—A frequency of 10.525 Gigahertz, one of three bands authorized for the use of police radar by the FCC.

THE END

WE NEED YOUR HELP!

The Ticket Book is an ongoing project that needs your contribution. If you feel that any part of our book contains inaccurate information, or if you've uncovered information you'd like to see included in future editions, please let us know. We're also keeping tabs on law enforcement agencies and courts that are abusers of the system. If you were given a ticket or convicted under questionable circumstances, we'd like to hear about it. Although we do not give legal advice, and can't answer every individual letter, we are very interested in your experiences, questions and comments on traffic tickets and on *The Ticket Book* itself. Please be sure to include a return address on your letter or postcard and write to us in care of:

THE TICKET BOOK
Reader Service Bureau
P.O. Box 1087
La Jolla, CA 92038

NEED ANOTHER TICKET BOOK?

You can order a copy of *The Ticket Book* for yourself or a friend by using one of the handy coupons on the opposite page. Simply fill out the coupon, enclose a check or money order for $6.95 (California residents add 6% sales tax) and send it to:

THE TICKET BOOK, INC.
P.O. Box 1087
La Jolla, CA 92038

Need a lot of *Ticket Books?* We have special programs which allow car clubs and other organizations to earn extra income by selling *The Ticket Book* to their members. If you're interested in receiving a full information packet on our club program, just send a description of your organization to:

THE TICKET BOOK, INC.
Promotional Sales Division
P.O. Box 1087
La Jolla, CA 92038

NAME _____

ADDRESS _____ APT. NO.____

CITY _____ STATE_____ ZIP____

SEND ONLY $6.95 IN CHECK OR MONEY ORDER TO:
THE TICKET BOOK, INC., P.O. BOX 1087, LA JOLLA, CA
92038 *(Calif. Residents Add 6%. No C.O.D.s Please)*

- -

NAME _____

ADDRESS _____ APT. NO.____

CITY _____ STATE_____ ZIP____

SEND ONLY $6.95 IN CHECK OR MONEY ORDER TO:
THE TICKET BOOK, INC., P.O. BOX 1087, LA JOLLA, CA
92038 *(Calif. Residents Add 6%. No C.O.D.s Please)*

- -

NAME _____

ADDRESS _____ APT. NO.____

CITY _____ STATE_____ ZIP____

SEND ONLY $6.95 IN CHECK OR MONEY ORDER TO:
THE TICKET BOOK, INC., P.O. BOX 1087, LA JOLLA, CA
92038 *(Calif. Residents Add 6%. No C.O.D.s Please)*

Discovering Popular Culture

ANNA TOMASINO
Hunter College, City University of New York

PEARSON
Longman

New York San Francisco Boston
London Toronto Sydney Tokyo Singapore Madrid
Mexico City Munich Paris Cape Town Hong Kong Montreal

Other readers featured in the "Longman Topics" series include:

To Peter and John,
whose love, support, and encouragement
helped make this book a reality.

Publisher: Joseph Opiela
Senior Marketing Manager: Sandra McGuire
Production Manager: Savoula Amanatidis
Project Coordination, Text Design, and Electronic Page Makeup:
    GGS Book Services
Cover Design Manager: Wendy Ann Fredericks
Cover Photo: © Sion Touting/Corbis
Senior Manufacturing Buyer: Mary Fischer
Printer and Binder: R. R. Donnelley & Sons Company—Harrisonburg
Cover Printer: Phoenix Color Corporation

For permission to use copyrighted material, grateful acknowledgment is made to the copyright holders on pages 249–251, which are hereby made part of this copyright page.

Library of Congress Cataloging-in-Publication Data

Discovering popular culture/ [edited by] Anna Tomasino.
    p. cm.—(Longman topics)
    ISBN 0-321-35596-2
    1. Popular culture—United States. 2. United States—Civilization—
1970- I. Tomasino, Anna. II. Series.

E169.12.D57 2006
306.0973'09045—dc22

                                                    2006043201

Visit us at http://www.ablongman.com

ISBN 0-321-35596-2
    7 8 9 10—DOH—10 09

CONTENTS

CHAPTER 6   Consumerism   **210**

"It has become more true than ever that our understanding of the larger world ... comes to us through popular culture."

—Bernard Beck (from Chapter 4)

"(People) are reading our material and realizing that movies and 'new history' and music and fast foods ... are the things that shape and drive American culture. They may not be loved, but they have to be understood."

—Ray Browne quoted in Trussell (from Chapter 5)

Popular culture students and scholars often encounter accusations that their courses are not valid. Critics question how analysis of entertainment can be vital, meaningful, and serious academic work. The above observations are the first line of defense: "Our understanding of the larger world ... comes to us through popular culture," and we study popular culture because it is a rich depository of "the things that shape and drive American culture."

From *The Simpsons* to *The Sopranos*, *American Beauty* to Victoria's Secret, from malls to theme parks, advertising to sports, slang to blogging, the selections in this book cover a range of topics that will keep readers interested. The diverse popular culture mediums covered in the text include television, film, advertising, space (malls), books, and cyberspace. From gender studies to linguistics, psychology to sociology, political science to music, art to literature, this book introduces a variety of academic disciplines as well as a variety of writing contexts including academic articles, excerpts from scholarly and popular books, articles from popular newspapers and magazines such as the *New York Times* and the *New Yorker*, personal essays by well-known composition favorites—Richard Rodriguez, Brent Staples, Barbara Ehrenreich—as well as Congressional testimony, and others. The timely and timeless selections in this book are engaging, relevant, intellectually challenging—and fun!

Discovering Popular Culture is divided thematically into six chapters: Chapter 1, "American Character and Image"; Chapter 2,

"Gender Roles: Images of Masculinity and Femininity"; Chapter 3, "Children and Family"; Chapter 4, "Race and Ethnicity"; Chapter 5, "Education: Popular Culture and the Academy"; and Chapter 6, "Consumerism." The selections represent different voices and encourage classroom debate about American popular culture as well as a greater understanding of that culture—of our values and priorities.

Half the size and cost of typical readers, *Discovering Popular Culture* can be used alone or paired with other Longman Topics titles. Special features of *Discovering Popular Culture* include:

- 28 readings in six units, providing both focus and flexibility.
- Coverage of diverse cultural media including television, film, advertising, photography, writing, radio, magazines, music, comics, and the Internet.
- Readings that represent a variety of points of view on contemporary and timeless icons like Andy Warhol, the Marlboro cowboy, *The Simpsons*, *The Sopranos*, Michael Jordan, Harry Potter, and Disney, and cultural forces like Victoria's Secret, hip hop, blogging, MP3 players, and many more.
- Readings that reflect a variety of styles and disciplines that students will encounter in courses across the curriculum.
- Essays of varying lengths that can be covered in a single lesson.
- Chapter introductions that highlight the themes, topics, and relationship between selections.
- "Getting Started with Definitions: A Refresher List," which follows this Preface, provides some useful definitions and usages for the study of popular culture from the *Oxford English Dictionary Online*.
- Concise author biographies at the beginning of each selection.
- Questions for Discussion and Writing, following each reading, that provide excellent starting points for class discussion and writing assignments and encourage post-reading reflection.
- Questions for Making Connections at the end of each chapter that encourage students to explore the relationships among the readings and to conduct further research on the issues raised.
- A point of view that encourages serious exploration of entertainment, forms often dismissed as passive and trival.

Discovering Popular Culture provides an excellent basis for courses including introduction to writing, freshman composition, block courses that focus on a single topic, and introduction to popular culture studies.

ANNA TOMASINO

GETTING STARTED WITH DEFINITIONS: A REFRESHER LIST

At times, academics intentionally begin their analyses with definitions of familiar words. Why would an established academic writing for an intellectual audience begin an essay with the definition of a word that is clearly part of our universal word base (masculinity, femininity, culture)? What is to be gained?

One reason would be to establish a common understanding, since various connotations (implied meanings) often exist. Beginning with the simple dictionary meaning can provide an excellent starting point to then expound on the larger cultural implications of the term. For example, in Chapter 2, "Gender Roles: Images of Masculinity and Femininity," Ralph Donald begins his essay, "From 'Knockout Punch' to 'Home Run'" with several definitions of manhood (paragraphs 1–5, page 20) quoting from various authorities to illustrate what it literally means for boys to enter manhood. Donald establishes the definition and usage of the term and then explores how constructions of masculinity are revealed in sports metaphors and war films.

Although you are no doubt already familiar with most of the following words, the refresher list of definitions and usages below from the *Oxford English Dictionary Online*[1] is provided to establish common ground. For a more comprehensive list, please visit http://www.oed.com. The comprehensive list of usage is illuminating.

Culture: "The cultivating or development (of the mind, faculties, manners, etc.); improvement or refinement by education and training."

Some Examples of Usage:

1651 HOBBES Leviath. II. xxxi. 189 The education of Children [is called] a Culture of their mindes.

---

[1]Entries reprinted from *Oxford English Dictionary Online*. Copyright © Oxford University Press, 2006.

1752 JOHNSON Rambler No. 189 12 She . . . neglected the culture of [her] understanding.

"The training, development, and refinement of mind, tastes, and manners; the condition of being thus trained and refined; the intellectual side of civilization."

1876 M. ARNOLD Lit. & Dogma xiii, Culture, the acquainting ourselves with the best that has been known and said in the world.

1948 T. S. ELIOT Notes Def. Culture ii. 41 Culture is not merely the sum of several activities, but a way of life. Ibid.

Mass: "Relating to, involving, or affecting large numbers, or the majority, of people or things (examples of which are very common in 20th-cent. use), as mass appeal, art, audience, behaviour, circulation, communication, communicator, consciousness, consumer, -consumption, culture . . . "

Popular: "Affecting, concerning, or open to all or any of the people; public; esp. in action popular; of, pertaining to, or consisting of the common people, or the people as a whole as distinguished from any particular class; constituted or carried on by the people; designating (aspects of) art and culture whose forms appeal to or are favoured by people generally; esp. in popular art, music, song, etc."

Some Examples of Usage:

1866 C. ENGEL Introd. Study National Mus. v. 168 The peculiar character of the popular music of a nation appears to be in great measure determined by the climate of the country, by the occupation and habits of the people, and even by the food upon which they principally subsist.

1898 G. B. SHAW Plays Pleasant & Unpleasant I. p. v, I had no taste for what is called popular art, no respect for popular morality, [etc.].

High: "Of exalted rank, station, dignity, position, or estimation. (Of persons or their attributes; also, with emphatic force, in high God, high heaven.) Freq. in high life, society."

Some Examples of Usage:

1920 D. PARKER (title) High society.

1895 G. B. SHAW Our Theatres in Nineties (1932) I. 106 After the exasperatingly bad acting one constantly sees at the theatres where high comedy and 'drama' prevail, it is a relief to see even simple work creditably done.

1964 HALL & WHANNEL Popular Arts I. ii. 55 These popular arts . . . were not objects of contemplation like the works of high art, but communal artifacts.

Semiotics: "The science of communication studied through the interpretation of signs and symbols as they operate in various fields, esp. language."

Some Examples of Usage:

1964 T. SEBEOK et al. Approaches to Semiotics: Margaret Mead proposed semiotics . . . as a term which might aptly cover 'patterned communication in all modalities'.

1973 D. OSMOND-SMITH tr. Bettelini's Lang. & Technique of Film: Some talk of a universal semiotics, capable of including within itself all aspects of the film as sign-system.

"Of or pertaining to semiotics or the use of signs."

1923 H. G. BAYNES tr. Jung's Psychol. Types i. 82, I say 'semiotic' in contradistinction to 'symbolic'. What Freud terms symbols are no more than signs for elementary instinctive processes. 1957 Publ. Amer. Dial. Soc. XXVIII. 4 It is an utterance that 'craves' a verbal or other semiotic (e.g., a nod) response.

1973 AKHMANOVA & MAR ENKO Meaning Equivalence & Linguistics Expression 7 The Morse code is a semiotic system par excellence, for in it every unit of content and every unit of expression are in regular one-to-one correspondence . . . The same applies . . . to all the other semiotic systems such as, for instance, notation in music, or chemical formulae, or mathematical signs.

Connotation: "The signifying in addition; inclusion of something in the meaning of a word besides what it primarily denotes; implication. That which is implied in a word in addition to its essential or primary meaning."

Some Examples of Usage:

1867 LEWES Hist. Philos. II. 6 The very word heresy, which simply means private judgment, has in all times borne an opprobrious connotation.

1877 Athenæum 21 July, That adjective [un-english] possesses a somewhat uncomplimentary connotation.

Denotation: "The action of denoting; marking, noting; expression by marks, signs, or symbols; indication; A mark by which a thing is made known or indicated; a sign, indication; and, a term employed to denote or describe a thing; a designation; and, the meaning or signification of a term."

Some Examples of Usage:

1614 SELDEN Titles Hon. 341 Time hath brought the word knaue to a denotation of ill qualities.

1893 F. HALL in Nation LVII. 450/1 The term ârya . . . may have a wider denotation than that which was long attached to it.

CHAPTER 1

American Character and Image

Regardless of regional distinctions and ethnic diversity, cultures around the world recognize a distinct American identity. Symbols such as the American Flag, the Statue of Liberty, and the American bald eagle represent the idea of America that is imbued with optimistic notions of freedom, progress, riches, and success.

How is this shared understanding of American culture conveyed both to its citizens and to people around the world? How is that image transmitted?

Before reading, examine your own point of reference: Where are your ancestors from and where did you grow up? What does the word *America* connote for you? Who influenced your concept of America? What did adults and educators lead you to believe about America? What are your expectations of success? Also consider the shadow self. What accounts for unfulfilled dreams and betrayed expectations?

Reflect upon your vast history of popular culture: specific television programs, movies, musical lyrics, advertising, and goods. In what ways has popular culture influenced your idea of America?

The selections in this chapter focus on the distinctive American character and image reflected in various mediums of popular culture: television, goods, products, beverages, food, movies (Warhol); advertising (Rufus); film (Deneen); and advertising (Gertner).

Warhol is given the coveted first place because, as Patrick S. Smith observes: "Warhol acutely understood and used the icon-making effects of mass media in art."[1] Warhol's prophetic musing "In the future, everyone will be world famous for 15 minutes"[2] seems to be more true than ever in this era of reality TV, game shows, and interactive audience participation for shows like *American Idol.*

Popular culture artist and icon Andy Warhol comments on equal access to goods. He writes, "Sometimes you fantasize that people who are really up there and rich and living it up have something you don't have. . . . But they drink the same Cokes and eat the same hot dogs . . . all of this is really American" (paragraph 3). Is Warhol correct? Can you think of any goods that are not available to all Americans?

Clearly, one of the most famous images transmitted to all people is the cowboy. In "Marlboro Country: Advertising," Anneli Rufus writes that the cowboy "represents for millions around the world America itself" (paragraph 7). The cowboy is brave, individualistic, and "victorious" (paragraph 7). Ironically, Rufus's celebration of the cowboy's American loner image is conversely denounced by Richard Rodriguez: "Americans are so individualistic, they do not realize their individualism is a communally derived value. . . 'You Americans are not truly individualistic, you merely are lonely'" (paragraph 12). Rodriguez challenges readers to question their identities.

Is Rodriguez right that we are merely lonely? Rodriguez's sentiments are echoed in Patrick Deneen's analysis of three films entitled "Awakening from the America Dream: The End of Escape in American Cinema?" Deneen's analysis of three films "captures an aspect of this ingrained feature of American character, the dream of escape." Deneen writes "Always searching for the better choice of locale and lifestyle, this restless quality of the American character also threatened tranquility of mind, undermined stability in communities, and gave rise to the possibility of the perpetually unsatiated soul" (paragraph 3). Deneen's analysis of three films from the 1940s and 1990s raises important questions about the distinctive American character. Is there a lonely "unsatiated soul" beneath the image of the prosperous nation which, according to Warhol, offers equal access to goods?

Are the majority of Americans sincerely and truly happy? Gertner writes, "you are wrong to believe that a new car will make you as happy as you imagine. . . . we might believe that a new BMW will make life perfect. But it will almost certainly be less exciting than we anticipated; nor will it excite us for as long as predicted" (paragraph 4). Although individuals clearly have their own personal definition of happiness, the image of a distinctive American identity is transmitted around the globe in various popular mediums: television programs, films, books, advertising, music, and cyberspace.

Pre-Reading Chapter 1

1. Understand your point of view before reading. Write down your answers to the questions posed in this introduction so that you have a record of your initial responses. Later on, before class discussion and writing assignments, you will have documentation of your thought process: from pre-reading to post-reading.

2. Survey the titles of the essays and authors in Chapter 1: "What's Great About This Country"/Andy Warhol; "Marlboro Country: Advertising"/Anneli Rufus; "The American I"/Richard Rodriguez; "Awakening from the American Dream: The End of Escape in American Cinema?"/Patrick Deneen; and, "The Futile Pursuit of Happiness"/Jon Gertner. Write down your expectations for each of the titles. Are you familiar with any of the topics or authors, for example, Andy Warhol? Keep a record of your brainstorming session.

3. For the duration of assignments from Chapter 1, keep an idea log and scrapbook of advertisements. The purpose is to identify parallels between topics and diverse mediums so that when you get ready for class discussion and writing assignments you have already generated ideas and perhaps identified a topic you are interested in further exploring. Keep a list of music lyrics, television shows, and movies that are topically connected with the idea of America. Let's say you turn on the television: the Eddie Murphy film *Coming to America* may be on. If so, after reading Deneen's film analysis you may decide to write about the idea of America presented in the movie of your choice. Alternately, you may decide to analyze patriotic music lyrics of your favorite musician.

Endnotes

1. Smith, S. Patrick. "Andy Warhol." *www.galenet.galegroup.com/servlet.*
2. "In the future, everybody will be world famous for 15 minutes" (slightly misquoted as ". . . will be famous for 15 minutes" or "Everyone will have their fifteen minutes of fame"). This quote became common enough during his lifetime that later, for fun, he amended it to "In fifteen minutes everybody will be famous." *http://en.wikiquote.org/wiki/Andy_Warhol*

What's Great About This Country
ANDY WARHOL

*Award-winning popular culture icon and artist Andy Warhol was
born of humble immigrant parents. His own life story exemplifies
the American dream. Warhol is best known for his artistic depictions of celebrities and everyday mass-produced items like Camp-
bell's soup cans. In addition, he was an award-winning filmmaker
and author of several books, including* Andy Warhol's Index *(1967),*
POPism: The Warhol '60s with Pat Hackett *(1980) and* The Philosophy of Andy Warhol (From A to B and Back Again) *(1975), of
which the following is an excerpt.*

Pre-Reading

As mentioned in the biographical sketch, Warhol's life is a success
story for the American Dream. Before you read, define the American Dream. Write a one-page explanation of what you believe is
"great about this country."

———————— ◆ ————————

What's great about this country is that America started the
tradition where the richest consumers buy essentially the
same things as the poorest. You can be watching TV and see
Coca-Cola, and you can know that the President drinks Coke, Liz
Taylor drinks Coke, and just think, you can drink Coke, too.
A Coke is a Coke and no amount of money can get you a better
Coke than the one the bum on the corner is drinking. All the
Cokes are the same and all the Cokes are good. Liz Taylor knows
it, the President knows it, the bum knows it, and you know it.

In Europe the royalty and the aristocracy used to eat a lot
better than the peasants—they weren't eating the same things at
all. It was either partridge or porridge, and each class stuck to its
own food. But when Queen Elizabeth came here and President
Eisenhower bought her a hot dog I'm sure he felt confident that
she couldn't have had delivered to Buckingham Palace a better
hot dog than that one he bought her for maybe twenty cents at
the ballpark. Because there *is* no better hot dog than a ballpark
hot dog. Not for a dollar, not for ten dollars, not for a hundred
thousand dollars could she get a better hot dog. She could get one
for twenty cents and so could anybody else.

Sometimes you fantasize that people who are really up-there and rich and living it up have something you don't have, that their things must be better than your things because they have more money than you. But they drink the same Cokes and eat the same hot dogs and wear the same ILGWU clothes and see the same TV shows and the same movies. Rich people can't see a sillier version of *Truth or Consequences*, or a scarier version of *The Exorcist*. You can get just as revolted as they can—you can have the same nightmares. All of this is really American.

The idea of America is so wonderful because the more equal something is, the more American it is. For instance, a lot of places give you special treatment when you're famous, but that's not really American. The other day something *very* American happened to me. I was going into an auction at Parke-Bernet and they wouldn't let me in because I had my dog with me, so I had to wait in the lobby for the friend I was meeting there to tell him I'd been turned away. And while I was waiting in the lobby I signed autographs. It was a really American situation to be in.

(Also by the way, the "special treatment" sometimes works in   5 reverse when you're famous. Sometimes people are mean to me because I'm Andy Warhol.)

Questions for Discussion and Writing

1. What is Warhol's main idea and where is it located in the excerpt? What evidence does he include?

2. What assumptions is Warhol making about equal access to goods? Consider whether or not you believe his assumptions are oversimplified. Give specific examples to support your response.

3. Explain how you believe the word choice and examples would change if Warhol had been asked to revise this excerpt for publication in an academic journal.

4. "A lot of places give you special treatment when you're famous, but that's not really American" concludes Warhol (paragraph 4). He adds " 'special treatment' sometimes works in reverse" (paragraph 5). What is "special treatment"? Write an essay explaining whether or not celebrities should receive "special treatment."

5. "Warhol acutely understood and used the icon-making effects of mass media" writes Patrick S. Smith in "Andy Warhol" (*www.galenetgroup.com/ servlet*). Select any other individual you believe understands (or understood) "the icon-making effects of mass media." For example, you could select Madonna, Elvis, or Marilyn Monroe. What caused this individual to become an icon? What were the consequences for the individual and society?

Marlboro Country: Advertising
ANNELI RUFUS

Writer and journalist Anneli Rufus is currently literary editor of the East Bay Express. Her publishing credits include Salon, *the* San Francisco Chronicle, *and the* Boston Globe. *"Marlboro Country: Advertising" is from her most recent book* Party of One: The Loners' Manifesto *(2003); Rufus's other books include* California Babylon *(2000),* Weird Europe *coauthored with Kristen Lawson (1999), and* Magnificent Corpses: Searching Through Europe for St. Peter's Head, St. Claire's Heart, St. Stephen's Hand, and Other Saintly Relics *(1999).*

Pre-Reading

Take a blank piece of paper and draw two columns. In one column, make a list of descriptive adjectives of a cowboy. In the other column, write the connotation of each of your descriptions. After you have finished, explain whether or not you believe the cowboy represents a distinct American image.

———————————— ✦ ————————————

Corporations battle hard to create brand loyalty, to make vast numbers of consumers prefer, for instance, one cola over another even though blind taste tests regularly show that there is little distinguishable difference between major brands of coffee, soda, beer, and cigarettes. Such items, dubbed "parity products" by industry insiders because, for all intents and purposes, the items are identical, must be hawked not on the basis of any tangible distinction. Instead, their success depends on the advertisers' claims that each has its own *personality*, individuality, its own message, and that certain brands speak for certain sectors of the population. Lifestyle, sport, gender—the bigger the sector, the better. Thus Virginia Slims were pressed on female smokers in the early 1970s, during the first big wave of feminism, as the "women's cigarette." Again, the lure and implications are all about inclusiveness. Clothes emblazoned with product logos are all, in a way, team uniforms. Wearing a Nike shirt or Red Bull hat is a declaration of membership. *I'm part of something big.* Such displays, replicated a hundred times over in any street scene or school hallway, reveal the nonloner bias. Brand loyalty means *Hey, I'm not a loner.*

• • •

This rule has its exception. Cowboys sell.

And cowboys are, in the public imagination, loners. Independent. Inviolate. Like America. Rugged individuals who speak the truth, shoot from the hip.

The advertising cowboy, like the cinematic cowboy, eludes all those prejudices leveled against loners in the real world. Behind the wheel of a Ford Bronco, he is not seen as a loser or a lonely pervert or a nerd. He is not seen as secretive. The opposite: without saying a word, he is meant to convey an openness like that of the big blue Western sky. 5

As such, the cars he hawks are not compacts, but behemoths with Wild-West names like Forester, Pathfinder, Rodeo, Range Rover. Sinewy hands gripping the wheel, he races across plateaus and down mountain roads. In his deadpan gaze is a look of quiet victory.

He sells cigarettes too, pimp that he is. *Real* cowboys smoke. Any day at a rodeo proves that. But tobacco is not *unique* to the Wild West. Faced with the challenge of promoting a parity product, Marlboro might just as easily have chosen any other archetype—a sailor or a hipster or an English lord. Yet the cowboy, the loner, was chosen. In the 1950s, just when the real Wild West was breathing its last, the Philip Morris company introduced its cowboy icon. Designed by the Leo Burnett advertising firm, the "Marlboro Man" was a ploy to broaden the appeal of a brand whose promotions, until then, had wimpily called the cigarettes "mild as May." Burnett's new ads, featuring the cowboy, promised that Marlboro "delivers the goods on flavor"—alluding to actual cowboys' work of delivering herds cross-country to slaughterhouses but also packing a subtle sexual punch. When the ads went national in 1955, sales skyrocketed, reaching $5 billion that year: an increase from just one year earlier of 3,241 percent.

Are the fragrant glowing leaves in every cigarette a small personal campfire, signifying the loner's dominion over all he surveys? In 1964, the ad agency gave a name to the mythical "Marlboro Country," whose sunsets mirrored the crimson in the brand's logo. After cigarette commercials were banned from TV in 1971, the solitary figure lent itself to print ads and billboards so perfectly that, one year later, Marlboro was the world's best-selling tobacco product.

How ironic that the Marlboro Man is, today, the most famous cowboy in the universe and practically the only one still in the public eye: a true loner, the sole survivor of his genre. (And how sad that he is held responsible for countless lung-cancer deaths—including, most famously and ironically, that of the male model who portrayed him for years: Wayne McLaren died in 1992 at age fifty-one. In his wake, Camel cigarettes' icon, "Joe Camel," has been similarly blamed for spawning a new generation of teenage smokers. Perhaps indicative of loners' ever-descending public image, Joe is a social animal, usually depicted amongst a clutch of cool camel pals.) Unlike the cinematic cowboy, the Marlboro Man is not a figure from the past, clad in a vintage costume. He is a contemporary cowboy, his prairies crisscrossed with paved super-highways. He brings those old values right into the present. As such, as the most famous cowboy in the universe, he represents for millions around the world America itself. Thus the arguably most famous aspect of America around the world is its loner aspect. America the individualist, the victorious and eternal loner.

10   As such, the cowboy has now been co-opted to sell cigarettes to Eastern Europe. Where better to press the macho loner into service than a place where, as Ayn Rand could have told you, individualism has for millions been only an uncatchable dream? Cowboys bow down to no authority. Cowboys do what the hell they want. Nobody spies on cowboys.

Eastern Europeans were already die-hard smokers by the time Philip Morris arrived. While nearly forty years of public-health campaigns in the United States had lowered the proportion of adult smokers here to some 25 percent by the mid-1990s, the World Health Organization determined that Eastern and Central Europe were at that time home to the world's highest proportion of adult smokers—some 60 percent of men and 30 percent of women. And that's not counting the kids. Offering higher-quality cigarettes than the locally produced ones to which Eastern Europe was long accustomed, Philip Morris leaped at the chance when restrictions were lifted on advertising in those countries. As Radio Free Europe reported in 1997, cinemagoers in Prague regularly saw the Marlboro Man in lengthy ads preceding films: "The mythic character's chiseled features are accompanied by displays of fine horsemanship, incredible scenery from the American West, and a soundtrack suggesting high adventure. . . . And in the Russian capital as throughout the East, the Marlboro Man stares down at passersby from innumerable billboards." Not only did "his" cigarettes taste better, they also symbolized the just-now-possible good things that come with being a loner: privacy, independence, discernment. It has been estimated that

Philip Morris's exports to the region soared by more than 400 percent within four years in the mid- to late 1990s.

Questions for Discussion and Writing

1. If Rufus is correct that "blind taste tests regularly show that there is little distinguishable difference between major brands of coffee, soda, beer, and cigarettes" and that "for all intents and purposes, the items are identical" then how, according to Rufus, are corporations able "to create brand loyalty"? (paragraph 1). What do you believe are the consequences for consumers?
2. Rufus observes, "Marlboro might just as easily have chosen any other archetype—a sailor or a hipster or an English lord. Yet, the cowboy, the loner, was chosen" (paragraph 7). Do you think that any other icon would have worked? If so, which one and why? If not, then what, in your opinion, makes the cowboy icon effective?
3. Locate the different adjectives Rufus uses to describe the cowboy icon. Does she create a vivid image in the minds of readers about the symbolism of the cowboy? Refer to your list of adjectives in the Pre-Reading exercise. If you were editing this chapter, what adjectives and descriptions would you add or remove?
4. The image of the loner is mentioned throughout the excerpt. In fact, Rufus observes that "the advertising cowboy, like the cinematic cowboy, eludes all those prejudices leveled against loners in the real world" (paragraph 4). In your opinion, what are several "prejudices leveled against loners in the real world"? Write an essay defending the loner image using evidence from your personal experience, observations, and views.
5. Rufus's understanding of the cowboy icon is very clear. Consider whether or not you believe that other interpretations of the cowboy are also possible. Write an essay analyzing what you believe the cowboy icon represents. You do not necessarily have to focus on "Marlboro Man" and advertising; you can focus on an alternative medium (for example, the cowboy icon in western films).

The American "I"

RICHARD RODRIGUEZ

Writer and journalist Richard Rodriguez is best known for his critically acclaimed award-winning autobiography Hunger of Memory: The Education of Richard Rodriguez *(1982). In this excerpt from*

Brown: The Last Discovery of America *(2002), Rodriguez ponders the American identity. His publishing credits include* American Scholar, New Republic, Wall Street Journal, Los Angeles Times, Harper's, *and* Washington Post. *He has contributed to* King's Highway *(1999), written a foreword to* American Soul *by Franz Schurmann (1995), and written the autobiographical* Days of Obligation: An Argument with My Mexican Father (1992).

Pre-Reading

How important is it for you to feel connected to a group: your family, a community, school, a team? What are the benefits and drawbacks of joining an organization, a team, a club, a group? Do you think that Americans are less communal than other cultures with strong traditional bonds?

————————— ✦ —————————

I am the observer.

Every American comes upon the "I," awakens to it. The prow of the ship. The top of the tree. The hilt of the sword. The animate eye. The quick. The reader of the card pertaining to the sword. Very interesting, but now I need to go to the bathroom. The American I. As in, *I believe, I take Jesus Christ as my personal savior. I am sorry for the earthquake victims. I will have tuna on rye. I love you.* The I does not impose solitude, though it is lonely; the I is alive. The I may be an instrument of connection, but even as such it is an assertion of will. *I have my rights.*

As so often happens in America, the I attached to me at school: You!

5   Who? I was no longer my brother's brother, my sister's brother, my mother's son, my father's son, my backyard's potentate. I was alone. I . . . I had to go to the bathroom, what should I do?

Go to college, become a man different from your father. It's up to you. Don't go to college, become a man different from your father.

The American I is as old as the Boston Tea Party, as old as the document of Constitution: "We the People . . ."

We? But I am a royalist. As the son of immigrants, I do not remember America seeming like a choice, though Americans were always and everywhere talking about choices.

They talked about black beans or refried. Presbyterian or Methodist. Ford or Chevrolet. Cinema One or Cinema Two. Gay or straight. CBS or NBC. Paper or plastic. Diet or regular. Regular or decaf. Plain or buttered. White or whole wheat or sourdough or English muffin. Every lighted window, every court, every slug of type, every knuckle of America strained to accomplish my assertion: I am innocent.

I may be unwise, I may be mistaken, I may be guilty. But the essence of the American I is that I am irreducible.

I can be punished for my crime, in other words. Isn't that odd? My body can bear the weight of punishment for a crime weighed in the apprehension of others who did not see, who do not know what I know.

Americans are so individualistic, they do not realize their individualism is a communally derived value. The American I is deconstructed for me by Paolo, an architect who was raised in Bologna: "You Americans are not truly individualistic, you merely are lonely. In order to be individualistic, one must have a strong sense of oneself within a group." (The "we" is a precondition for saying "I.") Americans spend all their lives looking for a community: a chatroom, a church, a support group, a fetish magazine, a book club, a class-action suit.

But illusions become real when we think they are real and act accordingly. Because Americans thought themselves free of plural pronouns, they began to act as free agents, thus to recreate history. Individuals drifted away from tribe or color or 'hood or hometown or card of explanation, where everyone knew who they were. *That's Victoria and Leo's son, isn't it?* Americans thus extended the American community by acting so individualistically, so anonymously.

Questions for Discussion and Writing

1. Summarize Rodriguez's observations of the American "I." Explain whether or not you agree with his observations.

2. "You Americans are not truly individualistic, you are merely lonely. In order to be individualistic, one must have a strong sense of oneself within a group" states Paolo (paragraph 12). What do you believe Rodriguez is assuming when he says "the 'we' is a precondition for saying 'I'" (paragraph 12)?

3. Why does Rodriguez, the son of immigrants, repeat the phrase "become a man different from your father" (paragraph 6)? What effect is he trying to create?

4. In paragraph 8, Rodriguez observes "Americans were always and everywhere talking about choices." In paragraph 9, Rodriguez lists "either/or" choices. Evaluate his list. Write a personal essay exploring the positive and/or negative

consequences attached to one of your personal choices (for example, education, job, car, etc.).

5. Do you think that too many Americans, in the pursuit of the American dream, lose the collective "we" in favor of the individualistic "I"? Do immigrants need to be concerned about losing their culture as they assimilate? Write a research paper about the challenges facing any group of immigrants that have lost (or are at risk to lose) their culture as they assimilate into America. At some point in your essay, include several suggestions to help the group preserve their heritage.

Awakening from the American Dream: The End of Escape in American Cinema?

Patrick J. Deneen

Educator, historian, and political theorist, Patrick Deneen teaches at Princeton University. In this analysis from Perspectives on Political Science *(Spring 2002), Deneen examines what he believes to be the distinctly American dream of escape in three films. He has been published in numerous academic journals, including* Political Theory, Social Research, Polity, Polis, Society, *and* Commonwealth. *He is the author of several books, including the APSA 1995 Leo Strauss awarding-winning book* The Odyssey of Political Theory: The Politics of Departure and Return, Democratic Faith *(2005), and* Awakening from the American Dream: Escape in American Cinema *(2005).*

Pre-Reading

Generally, are the people you know satisfied with their lifestyle? Conduct a systematic random sample of the people you know (friends, family, classmates). Select every third person you see and ask each of them two questions: Are they satisfied with their lifestyle? What do they believe would bring them greater happiness?

✦

THE DREAM OF ESCAPE

"**W**hat, then, is the American, this new man?" The question, posed in 1782 by the French aristocrat turned Pennsylvania farmer Hector St. John de Crèvecoeur, answers itself: The American is a new man, a creature yet unseen, unknown in the annals of history. He is a being defined by his newness—self-created, unbound, indefinable. It is the newness of this new man that astounds Crèvecoeur: "He is an American, who, leaving behind him all his ancient prejudices and manners, receives new ones from the new mode of life he has embraced. . . . Here individuals of all nations are melted into a new race of men, whose labours and posterity will one day cause great changes in the world . . . The American is a new man, who acts upon new principles; he must therefore entertain new ideas and form new opinions."[1] The American sheds all that once defined him in an old and intentionally forgotten world. Most promising, perhaps, is the fact that reinvention does not cease upon arrival in the new world but remains an ever-present possibility as long as new avenues of escape from the limits and impositions of both the Old and New Worlds alike remain available to the New Man. And, for Crèvecoeur, it is precisely that possibility of escape to new potentials, new freedoms, and new self-definitions that stands so invitingly and inexhaustibly in the American's future: "[W]e are the most perfect society now existing in the world. Here man is free as he ought to be, nor is this pleasing equality so transitory as many others are. Many ages will not see the shores of our great lakes replenished with inland nations, nor the unknown bounds of North America entirely peopled. Who can tell how far it extends? Who can tell the millions of men whom it will feed and contain? For no European foot has as yet traveled half the extent of this mighty continent!"[2]

It is hardly surprising that a people who left various native lands seeking a new start should define itself as a nation seeking ever-new avenues of re-creation. It is a part of the American soul, a creed in its national devotions as old as its first moments and captured indelibly by some of its ablest spokespeople. At the moment of America's direst early crisis, self-creation became part of America's official national definition as described by Thomas Jefferson in his 1774 pamphlet to a despised king. In "A Summary View of the Rights of Americans," Jefferson recalled that "our ancestors, before their emigration to America, were the free inhabitants of the British dominions in Europe, and possessed a right which nature has given to all men, of departing from the country in which chance, not choice, has placed them, of going in quest of new habitations, and of there establishing new societies, under such laws and regulations as to them shall seem most likely to promote public happiness."[3] Inasmuch as all humans are born into circumstances not of their own choosing, Jefferson proposed a revolutionary new justification for universal mobility, the desire for infinite improvement of circumstance, and a presumed suspicion for those who accepted their unbidden circumstance without reflection and choice. Jefferson, in revolutionary prose, articulated what untold millions of subsequent Americans would cite as their rationale for "pulling up stakes," "moving out," "starting over," "leaving town," and countless less-articulate but implicitly theorized declarations of independence from accidental circumstance and dedication to a life in the pursuit of happiness.

Always searching for the better choice of locale and lifestyle, this restless quality of the American character also threatened tranquillity of mind, undermined stability in communities, and gave rise to the possibility of the perpetually unsatiated soul: Happiness pursued, after all, may preclude happiness achieved. Alexis de Tocqueville identified a universal "restlessness" as one of the central characteristics of the American psyche some fifty years after Jefferson's articulation of the right to uproot oneself and discerned the oppression of spirit that infinite physical and psychic freedom could entail. Dreaming constantly of "the goods they do not have," Americans "show themselves constantly tormented by a vague fear of not having chosen the shortest route that can lead to [them]." Tocqueville perceived that the American constantly reaches for the next best thing, exhibits perpetual discontent with what he or she has achieved and thus "grasps them all without clutching them, and he soon allows them to escape from his hands so as to run after new enjoyments." Tocqueville described a people who, rather than achieving ever greater levels of bliss with each perceptible improvement in circumstance, suffered from a kind of frenzied dissatisfaction: "In addition to the goods that he possesses, at each instant he imagines a thousand others that death will prevent him from enjoying if he does not hasten. This thought fills him with troubles, fears, and regrets, and keeps his soul in a sort of unceasing trepidation that brings him to change his designs and his place at every moment."[4]

Tocqueville identifies a terrible contradiction in the American soul: In their unique craving for "newness," for the infinite possibility of the better, greater, more perfect possibility, Americans are impelled to pursue a happiness ever out of reach. Incapable of

rest and satisfaction with what they have achiev
effect fall into a form of enslavement—enslaven
without end. In their restlessness they are endles
out hope of contentment. Unable to restrain thei
promise of what lies around the next corner, they p
find satisfaction with what they have come to know   ... own
street. The imperative of choice may itself result in the inability to
choose no longer to choose, to accept a limitation on choice itself,
but instead rather incline individuals toward feelings of dissatisfaction at choices not yet offered and not yet taken. By declaring
what they are not, Americans preclude discovering what they are;
by insisting on what they will not have, they prevent themselves
from keeping anything.

What follows is an analysis of three popular films dating   5
from the 1940s to the 1990s. Each captures an aspect of this ingrained feature of American character, the dream of escape. In *It's
a Wonderful Life*, we witness the endearing story of George Bailey,
a man who desperately craves to escape the limiting life of the
small town of Bedford Falls. *Avalon* points to the cost of realizing
escape, particularly the loss of community, and with it the loss of
collective memory, a loss that leads to the triumph of amnesia
over memorial for the dead. Lastly, *American Beauty* portrays the
fruits of escape, the entrapment of the modern bourgeois American, and yet suggests a new form of escape in the rejection of the
traditional American dream of escape, a form of escape that,
ironically, only further embraces the solipsistic trajectory of
American escape.

IT'S A DESTRUCTIVE LIFE

Frank Capra's *It's a Wonderful Life* portrays the decent life of a
small-town American, George Bailey (Jimmy Stewart), an everyman who saves his community from an evil Scrooge—Henry F.
Potter (Lionel Barrymore)—and who only comes to realize his accomplishments by witnessing what terrors might have occurred
had he never lived. George Bailey represents all that is good and
decent about America: a family man beloved by his community
for his kindness and generosity.

Yet, if there is a dark side of America, the film quite ably captures that as well—and contrary to popular belief, it is found not
solely in Potter. One sees a dark side represented by George
Bailey himself: the optimist, the adventurer, the builder, the man
who deeply hates the town that gives him sustenance, who craves

nothing else but to get out of Bedford Falls and remake the world. Given its long-standing reputation as a nostalgic look at small-town life in the prewar period, it is almost shocking to suggest that the film is one of the most potent, if unconscious, critiques ever made of the American dream that was so often hatched in this small-town setting. For George Bailey, in fact, destroys the town that saves him in the end.

Undoubtedly viewers have come to adore this film in part because it portrays what Americans intuitively sense that they have lost. Among the film's first scenes is an idyllic Bedford Falls covered in freshly fallen snow, people strolling on sidewalks, a few cars meandering slowly along the streets, and numerous small stores stretching down each side of the tree-lined streets. It is an America increasingly unknown and unseen: wounded first by Woolworths, then Kmart, then Wal-Mart; mercilessly bled by the automobile; and finally drained of life by subdivisions, interstates, and the suburbs. Americans admire this movie because it portrays Mr. Gower's drug store as a place to meet neighbors over a soda or an ice cream, not merely a place to be treated as a faceless consumer buying painkillers; similarly, like the bar in Cheers, Martini's bar is somewhere that everybody knows your name, a place to spend a few minutes with friends after work before one walks home.

George Bailey hates this town. Even as a child, he wants to escape its limiting clutches, ideally to visit the distant and exotic locales vividly pictured in *National Geographic*. As he grows, his ambitions change in a significant direction: he craves "to build things, design new buildings, plan modern cities."[5] The modern city of his dreams is imagined in direct contrast to the enclosure of Bedford Falls: it is to be open, fast, glittering, and kaleidoscopic. He craves "to shake off the dust of this crummy little town" to build "airfields, skyscrapers one hundred stories tall, bridges a mile long. . . ." George represents the vision of postwar America: the ambition to alter the landscape to accommodate modern life, to uproot nature and replace it with monuments of human accomplishment, to re-engineer life for mobility and swiftness, unencumbered by permanence, a life no longer limited to a moderate and comprehensible human scale.

10   George's great dreams are thwarted by innumerable circumstances of fate and accident: most of the film is a retelling of various episodes of George's life for the benefit of a guardian angel—Clarence Oddbody (Henry Travers)—who will shortly be sent down to earth to attempt to save George during his greatest test.

Despite all of George's many attempts to leave the town of Bedford Falls—first as a young man with plans to travel to Europe, later to college, and then still later, and more modestly, to New York City—various intervening events prevent him from even once leaving Bedford Falls. Over his life, however, we discover that George has helped innumerable people in the community over the years; these countless seemingly small interventions will later be discovered to have amounted to the salvation of the entire town. Despite George's persistent desire to escape the limitations of life in Bedford Falls, he becomes a stalwart citizen of the town he claims to despise.

However, if George's grandiose designs, first to become an explorer and later to build new modern cities, are thwarted due to bad fortune he does not cease to be ambitious and does not abandon the dream of transforming America, even if his field of design is narrowed. Rather, his ambitions are channeled into the only avenue that life and his position now offer: he does not create airfields or skyscrapers or modern cities, but remakes Bedford Falls itself. His efforts are portrayed as nothing less than noble: he creates "Bailey Park," a modern subdivision of single-family houses, thus allowing hundreds of citizens of Bedford Falls to escape the greedy and malignant clutches of Potter, who gouges these families in the inferior rental slums of "Pottersville." George's efforts are portrayed as altogether praiseworthy, and it is right to side with him against the brutal and heartless greed of Potter. However, such sympathies serve also to obscure the nature of Bailey's activities and their ultimate consequences. In particular, it is worth observing the nature of "Bailey Park," not merely by contrast to "Pottersville"—in comparison to which it is clearly superior—but also in contrast to downtown Bedford Falls, where it may not compare as favorably by some estimations.

Bedford Falls has an intimate town center and blocks of houses with front porches where people leisurely sit and greet passers-by who constantly amble on the nearby sidewalks. Bedford Falls is a town with a deep sense of place and history. When George's car crashes into a tree, the owner berates him for the gash he has made: "My great-grandfather planted this tree," he says. He is the fourth generation to live in his house, and the tree's presence serves as a living link to his ancestors.

It is especially worth noting the significant role of the front porch in the film. Numerous scenes take place in the intermediate space between home and street. While apparently serving as a backdrop for the action on the screen, the porch points up the way of life that Bedford Falls permits. In a discerning essay entitled "From Porch to Patio," Richard H. Thomas notes that the front porch—built in part for functional purposes, especially to provide an outdoor space that could be used to cool off during the summer—also served a host of social functions as well: it was a place of "trivial greetings," a spot from which an owner could invite a passer-by to stop for conversation in an informal setting, a space where "courting" could take place within earshot of parents or the elderly could take in the sights and sounds of passing life around them. The porch "facilitated and symbolized a set of social relationships and the strong bond of community feeling which people during the nineteenth century supposed was the way God intended life to be lived."[6]

By contrast, Bailey Park has no trees, no sidewalks, and no porches. It is a modern subdivision, the trees have been plowed under to make room for wide streets and large yards with garages. Compared to Bedford Falls—which is always filled with strolling people—the development is empty, devoid of human presence. The residents of this modern development are presumably hidden behind the doors of their modern houses or, if outside, relaxing in back on their patios. The absence of front porches suggests an alternative conception of life that will govern Bailey Park—life is to be led in private, not in the intermediate public spaces in front that link the street to the home. One doubts that anyone will live in these houses for one generation, much less four. The absence of informal human interaction in Bailey Park stands in gross contrast to the vibrancy of Bedford Falls.

15 The patio—successor to the front porch—embodies as many implicit assumptions about how life is to be led as does the porch. Thomas notes that the move from urban centers into suburban enclaves in the years following World War II led to the creation of "bedroom communities" in which one did not know one's neighbors and where frequent turnover made such stable community relationships unlikely, where privacy and safety were dual concerns leading to the creation of the patio space behind the house, most often at the expense of a porch in the front. Thomas contrasts the two:

[T]he patio is an extension of the house, but far less public than the porch. It was easy to greet a stranger from the porch but exceedingly difficult to do so from the backyard patio. . . . The old cliché says, "A man's home is his castle." If this be true, the nineteenth-century porch was a drawbridge across which many passed in their daily lives. The modern patio is in many ways a closed courtyard that suggests that the king and his family are tired of the world and seek only the companionship of their immediate family or peers.[7]

Bailey Park is not a community that will grow to have a form of life and communal interaction similar to that in Bedford Falls; instead, George Bailey's grand social experiment in progressive living represents a fundamental break from the way of life in Bedford Falls, from a stable and interactive community to a more nuclear and private collection of households that will find shelter in Bailey Park but little else in common.[8]

We also learn something far more sinister about Bailey Park toward the end of the film. George contemplates suicide after his uncle has misplaced $8,000 and George comes under a cloud of suspicion. At this point the recounting of George's life for the benefit of Clarence the angel ends, and Clarence enters the action to dissuade George from taking his own life. Inspired by George's lament that it would have been better had he never lived, Clarence grants his wish—he shows what life in Bedford Falls would have been like without the existence of George Bailey. George's many small and large acts of kindness are now seen in their cumulative effect. Particular lives are thoroughly ruined or lost in the absence of George's efforts. Furthermore, the entire town—now called "Pottersville"—is transformed into a seedy, corrupt city in the absence of George's heroic resistance to Potter's greed.

Attempting to comprehend what has happened, and refusing to believe Clarence's explanations, George attempts to retrace his steps. He recalls that this awful transformation first occurred when he was at Martini's bar and decides to seek out Martini at home. Martini, in the first reality, is one of the beneficiaries of George's assistance when he is able to purchase a home in Bailey Park; however, in the alternative reality without George, of course the subdivision is never built. Still refusing to believe what has transpired, George makes his way through the forest where Bailey Park would have been, but instead ends in front of the town's old cemetery outside town. Facing the old gravestones, Clarence asks, "Are you sure Martini's house is here?" George is dumbfounded. "Yes, it should be." George confirms a horrific suspicion: Bailey Park has been built atop the old cemetery. Not only does George raze the trees, but he commits an act of unspeakable sacrilege. He obliterates a sacred symbol of Bedford Falls's connection with the past, the grave markers of the town's ancestors. George Bailey's vision of a modern America eliminates his links with his forebears, covers up the evidence of death, supplies people instead with private retreats of secluded isolation, and all at the expense of an intimate community, in life and in death.

20   George prays to Clarence to be returned to his previous life, to suffer the consequences of the seeming embezzlement, but to embrace "the wonderful life" he has lived and has in turn created for others as well. His prayer granted, George returns home to find that a warrant for his arrest awaits him, as do reporters poised to publicize his shame. However, his wife Mary has contacted those innumerable people whose lives George has touched to tell them of George's plight. In one of the most moving scenes on film, George's neighbors, friends, and family come flocking to his house, each contributing what little they can to make up the deficit until a pile of money builds in front of George. Trust runs deep in such a stable community of long-standing relationships: As Uncle Billy exclaims amid the rush of contributors, "They didn't ask any questions, George. They just heard you were in trouble, and they came from every direction." George is saved from prison and obloquy, and Clarence earns the wings he has been awaiting.

Despite the charm of the ending, a nagging question lingers, especially when we consider that many of the neighbors who come to George's rescue are ones who now live in Bailey Park. If the tight-knit community of Bedford Falls makes it possible for George to have built up long-standing trust and commitment with his neighbors over the years, such that they unquestioningly give him money despite the suspicion of embezzlement, will those people who have only known life in Bailey Park be likely to do the same for a neighbor who has hit upon hard times? What of the children of those families in Bailey Park, or George's children as they move away from the small-town life of Bedford Falls? A deep irony pervades the film at the moment of its joyous conclusion. As the developer of an antiseptic suburban subdivision, George Bailey is saved through the kinds of relationships nourished in his town, which will be undermined and even precluded in the anomic community he builds.

NOSTALGIA AND THE INESCAPABILITY OF REGRET

Barry Levinson's *Avalon* (1991) is both a paean to the cohesive immigrant culture of early twentieth-century Baltimore and a lament for the "lost city" in the wake of the automobile, the suburbs, and television. While acknowledging the temptations and even the inevitability of escape in a nation with abundant land populated by the offspring of the restless spirits who settled it, Levinson indulges in nostalgia for erstwhile networks of extended family, the obligations and trust that such commitments engendered, and the intimacy and slowness of everyday life that allowed for remembrance of the past through storytelling and inherited memory. Yet, while sometimes cloying, the nostalgia never overbears. Levinson is attentive to all of the limitations that immigrant urban life entailed, including the absence of private space, the resulting fraying of familial nerves, and the unfulfilled cravings for the outward signs of success that postwar Americans increasingly sought to display.

Avalon centers on the story of two generations of the Krichinsky family of Poland. The film opens with the wizened voice of Sam Krichinsky (Armin Mueller-Stahl) telling about the day when he arrived in America, 4 July 1914, amid the explosions of fireworks, endless red, white, and blue bunting, and streams of citizens on the streets of Baltimore celebrating with sparklers. We discover that he is telling this story to an entranced group of children on Thanksgiving, many decades after his arrival, above the background din of silverware and the complaint of his wife, who berates him for telling the story yet again. He continues with his story nevertheless, insisting that "if you stop remembering, you forget."[9] Avalon marks the passing of years by successive portrayals of Independence Day and Thanksgiving, unquestionably the two most "American" of American holidays, and reveals the transformation of civic and familial structures and practices over time. Independence Day 1914 could not be portrayed more patriotically, and Thanksgiving several decades later, depicted in the film's opening scenes, is the occasion for an enormous gathering of extended family who live in a small world of row houses in Baltimore. Both holidays change markedly with the passing years.

The world of Baltimore in the years preceding World War II is settled, predictable, and comfortable. The children of the Krichinsky brothers benefit from this settled world, growing up in close proximity, with two cousins in particular, Gabriel and Izzy (Aidan Quinn and Kevin Pollack) sharing a closeness resembling that of brothers. After World War II that world becomes increasingly unsatisfying to the subsequent generation. Gabriel and Izzy work as door-to-door salesmen at the beginning of the film. Like their parents they are willing to work hard to earn a modest living that allows them to share space with parents and siblings in the crowded row houses of the old neighborhood. For all the charms of city living, life there is constraining for the ambitious younger generation. Gabriel's wife, Ann (Elizabeth Perkins), lodges a standing complaint about the overcrowding of the house, which they share with Gabriel's parents, Sam and Eva Krichinksy, as well as their own son Michael: "The problem is we never have a moment's privacy. Everyone is on top of everyone; we need our own place." Izzy and Gabriel—who continue to live across the street from one another, presumably in the houses they grew up in, though now with their spouses and children as well as their parents—grow discontented with the limits of this comfortable but confining existence.

25   This discontent is symbolized most starkly during a flashback as Sam tells his grandchildren—Michael, as ever, among them—about the marriages of Gabriel and Izzy. They have both married American women (not women from their own neighborhoods and similar ethnic backgrounds), opting not for a family wedding but instead eloping without knowledge and approval of their elders. As Sam reads their marriage licenses he discovers that each Krichinsky son has changed his surname as well—they are now Gabriel Kaye and Izzy Kirk. Sam is furious: "What are you, a candy bar? How can we be a family?" he asks them. And although he eventually forgives them, his question lingers: How can the family persist when its most outward sign—a shared name, the inherited accident of birth that shows that one belongs to a community unchosen but inextricably one's own—has been intentionally abandoned? Both Gabriel and Izzy join that oldest of American attempts at escape from the past, the creation of a new identity, the sloughing off of an unchosen inheritance and arbitrary past for a chosen future, echoing that ancient right claimed by Jefferson when justifying the right of all people to leave the unchosen home of birth for a chosen place of destination.

Increasingly, choice comes to dominate the film and is shown to be the natural inheritance of America's immigrant families. The successive generations merely assume the same right to opt out of their inherited communities, just as their elders did when they emigrated to America—but in so doing, they threaten the new communities that were built as refuges of belonging in the New World. *Avalon* portrays a Baltimore as lost as the Chicago that Alan Ehrenhalt described in his seminal study, *The Lost City*, in which he observes that contemporary nostalgia for community often neglects the costs that necessarily accompany the cohesiveness of such settings, primary among which is the absence of choice in many aspects of daily life:

> To worship choice and community together is to misunderstand what community is all about. Community means not subjecting

every action in life to the burden of choice, but rather accepting the familiar and reaping the psychological benefits of having one less calculation to make in the course of the day.[10]

People in the old neighborhood are increasingly bombarded by the choices resulting from the prosperity of the 1950s, choices that are viewed warily by the older generation even as they are embraced by their children and grandchildren. Detecting and seeking to capitalize on this restlessness and increased craving for the novel, Gabriel and Izzy, having chosen new identities, forswear their careers as door-to-door salesmen and open a store that sells televisions—with numerous different brands and dozens of styles. The logic of choice culminates in their opening of a warehouse department store—now no longer in the center of the city, but at the outskirts, reachable only by automobile, presumably because the cost of rent and overhead allows for cheaper prices, greater sales, and ever more expansion of choice as consumer demand and expectations grow. They open their new warehouse store on the Fourth of July, many years after Sam Krichinsky's arrival in America, amid the patriotic effusions of Baltimore's citizens. Now, instead of marking America's founding, innumerable shoppers are lined up outside the store awaiting its grand opening. The consumer replaces the citizen; novelty replaces memory.

Gabriel and Izzy also choose to leave the urban community in which they were raised, mimicking that choice made by their parents when they journeyed to the New World in search of freedom. When told they will be leaving Baltimore for the "suburbs," Michael asks his mother, "What does it mean, the suburbs?" She replies, "It's a nicer place to live—it's got lawns and big trees." Yet, despite this description of the external qualities of the suburbs, life there comes to center inside, rather than outside, the home. In Baltimore, daily life is depicted as unfolding largely outside, on the stoops and on the streets of the neighborhood. The discomfort of row-house living is not ignored, particularly during the summer months when the absence of air conditioning and the enclosure on two sides by other houses could make interior life stifling and unbearable. Yet, solutions to the absence of air conditioning are also in evidence: one Fourth of July, Sam takes Michael and other children to a local lake where they watch fireworks and then, along with many other families in the neighborhood, remain on the shore to sleep for the night. Sam tells the children stories and also imparts the ancient wisdom of outdoor sleeping during the summer. "[W]ith the breeze, you can sleep." As Sam falls asleep with the children, the camera pans back to reveal hundreds of temporary campers by the water, reposed securely together as they seek the breeze. The scene of a sleeping neighborhood ably captures that lost world of public life described by Ehrenhalt, when people "considered the streets to be their home, an extension of their property, whereas today the streets are, for many people, an alien place. A block is not really a community in this neighborhood anymore. Only a house is a community, a tiny outpost dependent on television and air-conditioning, and accessible to other such outposts, even the nearest ones, almost exclusively by automobile."[11]

As Ehrenhalt's comments suggest, the film, also about a lost city, increasingly features the automobile and the television. With the move to the suburbs, it becomes essential for each of the adult family members to drive to reach other family members or to purchase the essentials of life, in contrast to the Baltimore neighborhood which they left, where a large open-air market is full of people making their daily purchases, all walking and min-gling informally. Eva regards Ann's driving skills with suspicion, but the film implicitly shows that Ann must learn to drive if she is to run a household in the suburbs, even as Eva must increasingly come to rely upon others for transportation.[12] While the move to the suburbs from the city involved an act of definite choice, it also removes the choice of whether to learn to drive or not, or whether one will increasingly depend on the automobile for one's daily life. One choice leads to the removal of other choices, but that re-moval is obfuscated by a growing consumer culture that offers myriad choices of models of automobile, even as people grow un-aware that they have the lost the choice whether to own and oper-ate one in the first place.[13]

30   Television becomes the other star of the film. After they move to the suburbs, the family's life comes to center around the televi-sion for leisure and is the place where life unfolds, in contrast to the streets and stoops of Baltimore where they formerly retreated in the evening. The family begins to eat in front of the television, even abandoning their meal when the *Milton Berle Show* comes on. They eventually put a television in nearly every room, includ-ing the kitchen and the bedroom. Toward the film's close, in stark contrast to the opening scene of a chaotic but lively Thanksgiving holiday, Gabriel and Ann Kaye eat their Thanksgiving dinners silently seated on the living room couch with their two children, each facing the television as they shovel food into their mouths

without remark. While perhaps an overstated example of contemporary American trends, Levinson rightly reminds us of the extent to which television has come to be associated with a central family holiday like Thanksgiving, with entire families often gathering after dinner to watch specially scheduled football games or popular movies.

By the end of the film, television comes to dominate the domestic landscape and aptly serves as a symbol of the innumerable choices that allowed the dissipation of the urban community and added to the isolation of suburban life. Television has come increasingly to mirror and accommodate a lifestyle dominated by a central desire for endless choice, the avoidance of long-term commitments, and an unwillingness to remain in settings that could prove demanding, if ultimately rewarding. Ehrenhalt finds television the perfect symbol for this culminating obsession with choice over stability:

> Channel surfing is not exactly a metaphor for life, but it isn't a bad caricature of the larger predicaments for the 1990s. . . . Too many of the things we do in our lives, large and small, have come to resemble channel surfing, marked by a numbing and seemingly endless progression from one option to the next, all without the benefit of a chart, logistical or moral, because there are simply too many choices and no one to help sort them out. We have nothing to insulate ourselves against the perpetual temptation to try one more choice, rather than live with what is on the screen in front of us.[14]

Television obscures certain forms of memory even as it imparts new memories. As Sam insisted, "If you stop remembering, you forget"; however, Levinson implies that, in addition, when one loses the capacity to speak and listen there are no memories to recall. *Avalon*'s last scene portrays an adult Michael visiting his grandfather Sam in a nursing home with his son, also named Sam. Michael has grown up in a world of extended families that are not yet completely dissipated, before the dominance of television, and steeped in Sam's stories related at countless Thanksgivings and in the semipublic places of presuburban life. Young Sam, however, grows up in a world where those institutions have almost ceased to exist in the wake of the escape of families from both the encroachments and the richness of urban life. The movie ends as it began, with Sam telling about the day he arrived in America, 4 July 1914. But unlike the previous generation, trained in listening and using their imaginative resources to paint an inner picture based on another's words, young Sam's attention wanders quickly to the television, where the flickering images supplant the need to listen, where words cease to guide and vision is divorced from meaning and memory.[15]

Sam relates that he tried to find Avalon, which is the name of the apartment house in which he lived with his brothers when he first came to America. America, however, has moved on, uprooting the old to be replaced by the new, obliterating memory in the pursuit of the novel and stylish. Avalon is gone, and Sam's fruitless search to find the physical evidence of his lost past leads him to admit that "for a minute, I thought I never was." Close to death, silently wondering about the continuities of existence, Sam recognizes that obscurity and amnesia about the past are the results of a culture of escape.[16] If George Bailey literally plows over the graves of the dead to erect his subdivision, Avalon suggests that the move from the "lost city" to the suburban idyll echoes this burying of the past, if not as swiftly and obviously as the bulldozer, nevertheless, over the long term and with help of the automobile and the television, just as thoroughly.

AMERICAN BEAUTY: END OF ESCAPE?

American Beauty portrays a world in which Bailey Park is ascendant and where the fancy of Ann Kaye to have her "own place" in the suburbs is achieved. Yet in this film one finds none of the progressive hopes for the future of *It's a Wonderful Life*. The suburbs are a trap, not an escape, a place where life has become predictable, stale, and without wonder or enchantment. However, the film also contains none of the nostalgia of *Avalon* for a better place in the distant past, before the exodus from the vibrancy of the cities and the move into an unstable present peopled by strangers. There is no fantasy of escape to a particular place, as from the small town to the city or city to suburbs. Yet escape remains as fond a dream as ever, even if it is no longer evident to where one can escape, or even if escape remains possible.

35 *American Beauty* centers on the life of Lester Burnham (Kevin Spacey), a suburban husband who longs to escape the deadening existence of modern American conformity. The film opens with a long shot above an unnamed town, one more affluent than Bailey Park but composed of houses built along a similar design, though larger and more comfortable. As the camera zooms in to reveal a tidy suburban street lined with trees and neat

houses, Lester intones in a voiceover: "This is my neighborhood. This is my street. This is my life." He then tells us, "In less than a year I'll be dead. In a way, I'm dead already."[17] The film centers on the brief period between Lester's observation and his actual death and describes how he comes to embrace life even as death approaches.

Lester's existence is portrayed as sterile, predictable, and wholly uninteresting. He detests his job, and his family appear to detest him. The sterile neighborhood represents nearly the full extent of life for the Burnham family, aside from stultifying work, clique-driven school, and a dissatisfying family life inside the home. In the neighborhood are a gay professional couple named Jim and Jim and a new family that moves into the house next door to the Burnhams'. Like the Burnhams, the new neighbors are a small nuclear family: a father—Colonel Frank Fitts—a mother who appears to be autistic, and a son, Ricky Fitts (Wes Bentley). Colonel Fitts is a homophobic autocrat who collects Nazi paraphernalia, tests his son's urine for drugs, and beats Ricky when he disobeys. Ricky, in turn, puts on an act of abject obedience for his father but in fact sells drugs throughout the town.

That which is usually shown to be "normal" in most American television shows and movies—the suburban nuclear family—is portrayed in *American Beauty* as a repository of deceit, conformity, materialism, marital—and especially sexual—discontent, selfishness, anxiety, psychological disorder, substance abuse, and even outright violence and hysteria. Indeed, the only well adjusted and traditionally "normal" family that appears during the course of the film is the gay couple, Jim and Jim, who appear at the Fitts' door with a generous housewarming gift and maintain informal neighborly contact with the Burnhams.

Lester is suddenly awakened from his conformist slumber one evening while attending a basketball game. There, watching his daughter's friend Angela perform a cheerleading routine, Lester becomes nearly obsessed with the promise of youth. Into his disenchanted world explodes a fantasy of color, texture, sight, and sound, represented by deep red rose petals that continue to appear in any fantasy involving Angela. Later that evening, envisioning Angela surrounded by rose petals, we hear him realize that he's been in "a coma . . . for twenty years, and I'm only now waking up."

In the theme of "sleeping" and "awakening" one hears echoes of that classic American tract of nonconformity, Henry David Thoreau's *Walden*. As Thoreau describes, one must will wakefulness against the temptations of conformist sleep: "We must learn to reawaken and keep ourselves awake, not by mechanical aids, but by an infinite expectation of the dawn, which does not forsake us in our soundest sleep."[18] Almost as if describing Lester before his epiphany induced by the cheerleaders, Thoreau writes that "by closing the eyes and slumbering, and consenting to be deceived by shows, men establish and confirm their daily life of routine and habit everywhere, which still is built on purely illusory foundations. Children, who play life, discern its true law and relations more clearly than men, who fail to live it worthily, but who think that they are wiser by experience, that is, by failure."[19] As Lester rebels against the unreal life he leads, he adopts more and more the perspective of a child, attempting to recapture his own youth by reliving various experiences of his adolescence. He quits his job by means of his rebellious "job description" for management; he begins smoking marijuana supplied by Ricky; at Angela's suggestive prompting, he begins lifting weights and eventually sets up a combination weight room/drug den in his garage. He takes a job at a "Smiley Burger" franchise, where he works at the drive-through window. He seeks to relive the freedom of his youth, a time when "all I did was party and get laid. I had my whole life ahead of me. . . ."

40   Lester seems to follow the teachings of Thoreau in *Walden* through his rejection of civilization's expectations and his disdain for materialism. Yet Lester's rebellion seems in many respects a pale shadow, even a laughable parody, of Thoreau's move away from civilization. If there is any "place" that resembles the retreat that Thoreau's Walden Pond represents, it is Lester's garage. Hardly a repose of natural solitude, his garage—that architectural feature that gained prominence at the time of developments such as Bailey Park—is a place that is both not his home, therefore representing a place apart, yet still attached to his home, still within the bounds of what is safe, predictable—apparently nonconformist even as his mortgage covers the costs.

Similarly, although Lester quits his job in an act of apparent bold confrontation with the inanities of management, he succeeds in extorting a full year's pay and benefits from his immediate boss when he threatens him with false charges of sexual harassment. His rebellion will be financed by corporate America, including his health and retirement benefits. One detail of Lester's town we discover later is that he lives on Robin Hood Trail, a telling irony since he steals from the rich to give to himself; he is hardly poor but wishes to pretend to disregard material possessions without the discomforts that poverty would entail. In a late scene in which he tries to seduce his wife, Carolyn, by reminding her of how vivacious and fun she was as a younger woman, she breaks the spell by warning him that he is about to spill beer on the living room sofa. Infuriated at this petty observation, Lester explodes at her. "So what, it's just a couch. This isn't life. It's just stuff. It's become more important to you than living." One marvels at Lester's accusation of Carolyn's materialism here, for the scene began with Lester declaring to Carolyn that he has just purchased a 1970 Pontiac Firebird, "the car I've always wanted. And now I have it. I rule." Lester's rebellion is financed by corporate America, comprised of adolescent retreat into the garage (where, for generations, teenagers have gone to practice in their makeshift bands) and prurient fantasies about underaged girls, and symbolized by the purchase of youthful muscle cars.

Lester is awakened from his "awakening" when he finally has the opportunity for a sexual liaison with Angela. As he disrobes her, he discovers that, notwithstanding her braggadocio, she is what she appears to be, a vulnerable, sexually inexperienced girl. Lester suddenly awakens—again—and appears to recognize the shallowness of his rebellion. As he contemplates a picture of his family, in which each member smiles unassumingly at some point in the obscured past, Lester is shot from behind by Colonel Fitts, a man contorted by his own homoerotic longings, which Lester has rejected. In the moments before death, Lester engages in a nostalgia for a purer past, a past that symbolized the true happiness of his life—picturing himself as a boy scout, his grandmother's hands, his cousin's Firebird, Jane as a girl, and Carolyn as a young woman. One can only relive the past through memory, not through the literal attempt to recapture an adolescent past as an adult.

Achieving a kind of clarity at the moment of death, Lester imparts to us the wisdom of that moment. As his soul rises above the town, his voiceover intones:

> I guess I could be pretty pissed about what happened to me, but it's hard to stay mad when there's so much beauty in the world. Then I remember to relax, and stop trying to hold onto it. Then it flows through me like rain. I can't feel anything but gratitude for every single moment of my stupid little life. You have no idea what I'm talking about I'm sure. But don't worry—you will, someday.

Lester's soul flies above the city into the clouds, and we have a final image of the only form of actual escape in an age when all other avenues are closed—the gratitude for a lived life that comes at death. It is knowledge that we cannot have now—we have "no idea" what Lester is talking about—but will come someday, since death comes to us all.

45   However, one wonders if Lester has in fact gained a special kind of wisdom at the film's end, whether death has given him insight into human happiness. For, in keeping with that oldest feature of the American character, it is only through escape— literally pictured as he ascends above and away from his town— that Lester realizes the abiding value of the events of his now passed life. In a revelation comparable to that of George Bailey, Lester understands that he led "a wonderful life," but one that looks wonderful in retrospect, not as it's lived. The disdain for the conformity and sterility of late-twentieth-century American sub-urban life is not dismissed, only obscured by the distance that the camera provides as it pans outward and away. The film finally does not pose any potential remedies for the anomic life of the nuclear American family, seemingly trapped in the place to which so many, for so long, sought escape. In contrast to the other films under examination, there is no evidence of an extended family in *American Beauty*, no network of familial bonds or friendships built over time in an intimate and stable community. Lester's ap-parently profound concluding remarks are in fact revealed to be wholly facile when one considers the film's concluding recom-mendation for how to live in a setting that it so obviously dis-dains. Cynicism is still the order of the day, until the moment of death when redemption will be provided at the moment of final escape. The frontier is closed; return to Eden is forestalled; com-munity is quaint, impossible, and finally too limiting. Political remedies are nonexistent, as politics is as entirely absent as grandparents or trusted neighbors. All that remains is the hope of escape in the future and the willful disdain of our American pres-ent. Awakening from our American dream of escape we discover that it was a nightmare all along, a fond wish that brought us to the point of hating what we so desperately craved, of despising what we have become, and of no longer seeing how we can find a way to escape from the interminable vision of escape.

Endnotes

1. J. Hector St. John de Crèvecoeur, *Letters from an American Farmer* (New York: Penguin Books, 1983), 69; 70.
2. Crèvecoeur, 67–8.

3. Thomas Jefferson, "A Summary View of the Rights of British America," in *Thomas Jefferson: Writings* (New York: Library of America, 1984), 105–6.
4. Alexis de Tocqueville, *Democracy in America*, trans. Harvey C. Mansfield and Delba Winthrop (Chicago: University of Chicago Press, 2000).
5. *It's a Wonderful Life*, produced and directed by Frank Capra, Liberty Films, 1946. All subsequent quotations are from this version of the film.
6. Richard H. Thomas, "From Porch to Patio," *The Palimpsest* (August, 1995); 123.
7. Thomas, 126–7.
8. People in such communities cease to lead a common life, but increasingly share common interests that are based on similar socioeconomic backgrounds. Such self-selected "communities" result in a decline of interaction between people of different classes, backgrounds, ethnicities, and experience, even as it gives the outward appearance of commonality through concurrence of interests. See Robert B. Reich, "The Politics of Secession," in *Work of Nations* (New York: Vintage Books, 1992), 282–300; and Christopher Lasch, *The Revolt of the Elites and the Betrayal of Democracy* (New York: W. W. Norton and Co., 1995), 25–49.
9. *Avalon*, produced by Mark Johnson and Barry Levinson, directed by Barry Levinson, TriStar Pictures, 1990. All subsequent quotations are from this version of the film.
10. Alan Ehrenhalt, *The Lost City: Discovering the Forgotten Virtues of Community in the Chicago of the 1950's* (New York: Basic Books, 1995), 23.
11. Ehrenhalt, 255.
12. Eva believes her suspicions are justified when a street car jumps its tracks and destroys Ann's car. Ironically, while the film explicitly portrays a moment when a public transportation vehicle destroys a privately-owned automobile, the true tendency proved to be the opposite—the popularity of automobiles would eventually lead to the dismantling of many systems of urban and suburban public transportation. This dynamic is delightfully explored in the live action/animated film, *Who Framed Roger Rabbit?*
13. As Benjamin R. Barber writes, "the American's freedom to choose among scores of automobile brands was secured by sacrificing the liberty to choose between private and public transportation, and mandated a world in which strip malls, suburbs, high gas consumption, and traffic jams (to name just a few) became inevitable and omnipresent without ever having been the willed choice of some

democratic decision making body—or for that matter the individuals who liked driving automobiles and chose to buy one. This politics of commodity . . . offers the feel of freedom while diminishing the range of options and the power to affect the larger world. Is this really liberty?" *Jihad vs. McWorld* (New York: Random House, 1995), 220–1.

14. Ehrenhalt, 271–2.
15. On the way that visual media obliterates context and memory, see Neil Postman, *Amusing Ourselves to Death: Public Discourse in the Age of Show Business* (New York: Penguin Books, 1985), esp. 99–113.
16. Hannah Arendt describes cohesive political communities as a form of "organized remembrance" in *The Human Condition* (New York: Doubleday and Company, 1959), 176. Such a city "assures the mortal actor that his passing existence and fleeting greatness will never lack the reality that comes from being seen, being heard, and generally appearing before an audience of fellow men . . . " (176–7). See also my discussion on the connection between the embrace of limits, human community, and the possibility of memorial for even the most obscure of humanity in *The Odyssey of Political Theory: The Politics of Departure and Return* (Lanham, Md.: Rowman and Littlefield, 2000), ch. 5.
17. *American Beauty*, produced by Bruce Cohen and Dan Jinks, directed by Sam Mendes, DreamWorks SKG, 1999. All subsequent quotations are from this version of the film.
18. Henry David Thoreau, *Walden and Other Writings* (New York: Random House, 1965), 81.
19. Thoreau, 86.

Questions for Discussion and Writing

1. In your own words, summarize Deneen's observation of how the dream of escape is depicted in *It's a Wonderful Life*, *Avalon*, and *American Beauty*.
2. What, according to Deneen, are the various motivations that drive Americans toward escape? What do you believe are the deeper issues involved?
3. Why does Deneen include support from several historians and historical figures such as Jefferson and Tocqueville? In your own writing, how adept are you in incorporating primary sources?
4. Deneen writes "self-creation became part of America's official national definition" (paragraph 2). Write an essay arguing whether or not you believe the statement is true.
5. Watch any one of the three films mentioned in the article and then write your own analysis. Does your analysis differ from Deneen's? If so, why? If not, why not?

The Futile Pursuit of Happiness
JON GERTNER

Journalist Jon Gertner has been a senior editor at Money *since 1999. Previously, he was senior features editor for* The American Lawyer. *This very engaging article on happiness, published in* New York Times Magazine *on September 7, 2003, captured the attention of readers across the country. Gertner's other prestigious magazine and newspaper publications include* New York Times Magazine, New York, Audubon, *and* The New York Observer.

Pre-Reading

List five achievements and material possessions that you currently have. Did the achievements and material possessions make you as happy as you thought they would? Explain why you believe they did or did not live up to your expectations of happiness.

———————— ✦ ————————

If Daniel Gilbert is right, then you are wrong. That is to say, if Daniel Gilbert is right, then you are wrong to believe that a new car will make you as happy as you imagine. You are wrong to believe that a new kitchen will make you happy for as long as you imagine. You are wrong to think that you will be more unhappy with a big single setback (a broken wrist, a broken heart) than with a lesser chronic one (a trick knee, a tense marriage). You are wrong to assume that job failure will be crushing. You are wrong to expect that a death in the family will leave you bereft for year upon year, forever and ever. You are even wrong to reckon that a cheeseburger you order in a restaurant—this week, next week, a year from now, it doesn't really matter when—will definitely hit the spot. That's because when it comes to predicting exactly how you will feel in the future, you are most likely wrong.

A professor in Harvard's department of psychology, Gilbert likes to tell people that he studies happiness. But it would be more precise to say that Gilbert—along with the psychologist Tim Wilson of the University of Virginia, the economist George Loewenstein of Carnegie-Mellon and the psychologist (and Nobel laureate in economics) Daniel Kahneman of Princeton—has taken the lead in studying a specific type of emotional and behavioral prediction. In the past few years, these four men have begun to question the decision-making process that shapes our sense of well-being: how do we predict what will make us happy or unhappy—and then how do we feel after the actual experience? For example, how do we suppose we'll feel if our favorite college football team wins or loses, and then how do we really feel a few days after the game? How do we predict we'll feel about purchasing jewelry, having children, buying a big house or being rich? And then how do we regard the outcomes? According to this small corps of academics, almost all actions—the decision to buy jewelry, have kids, buy the big house or work exhaustively for a fatter paycheck—are based on our predictions of the emotional consequences of these events.

Until recently, this was uncharted territory. How we forecast our feelings, and whether those predictions match our future emotional states, had never been the stuff of laboratory research. But in scores of experiments, Gilbert, Wilson, Kahneman and Loewenstein have made a slew of observations and conclusions that undermine a number of fundamental assumptions: namely, that we humans understand what we want and are adept at improving our well-being—that we are good at maximizing our utility, in the jargon of traditional economics. Further, their work on prediction raises some unsettling and somewhat more personal questions. To understand affective forecasting, as Gilbert has termed these studies, is to wonder if everything you have ever thought about life choices, and about happiness, has been at the least somewhat naïve and, at worst, greatly mistaken.

The problem, as Gilbert and company have come to discover, is that we falter when it comes to imagining how we will feel about something in the future. It isn't that we get the big things wrong. We know we will experience visits to Le Cirque and to the periodontist differently; we can accurately predict that we'd rather be stuck in Montauk than in a Midtown elevator. What Gilbert has found, however, is that we overestimate the intensity and the duration of our emotional reactions—our "affect"—to future events. In other words, we might believe that a new BMW will make life perfect. But it will almost certainly be less exciting than we anticipated; nor will it excite us for as long as predicted. The vast majority of Gilbert's test participants through the years have consistently made just these sorts of errors both in the laboratory and in real-life situations. And whether Gilbert's subjects were trying to predict how they would feel in the future about a plate of spaghetti with meat sauce, the defeat of a preferred political candidate or romantic rejection seemed not to matter. On average, bad events proved less intense and more transient than test participants predicted. Good events proved less intense and briefer as well.

Gilbert and his collaborator Tim Wilson call the gap between what we predict and what we ultimately experience the "impact bias"—"impact" meaning the errors we make in estimating both the intensity and duration of our emotions and "bias" our tendency to err. The phrase characterizes how we experience the dimming excitement over not just a BMW but also over any object or event that we presume will make us happy. Would a 20 percent raise or winning the lottery result in a contented life? You may predict it will, but almost surely it won't turn out that way. And a new plasma television? You may have high hopes, but the impact bias suggests that it will almost certainly be less cool, and in a shorter time, than you imagine. Worse, Gilbert has noted that these mistakes of expectation can lead directly to mistakes in choosing what we think will give us pleasure. He calls this "miswanting."

"The average person says, 'I know I'll be happier with a Porsche than a Chevy,'" Gilbert explains. "'Or with Linda rather than Rosalyn. Or as a doctor rather than as a plumber.' That seems very clear to people. The problem is, I can't get into medical school or afford the Porsche. So for the average person, the obstacle between them and happiness is actually getting the futures that they desire. But what our research shows—not just ours, but Loewenstein's and Kahneman's—is that the real problem is figuring out which of those futures is going to have the high payoff and is really going to make you happy.

"You know, the Stones said, 'You can't always get what you want,'" Gilbert adds. "I don't think that's the problem. The problem is you can't always know what you want."

Gilbert's papers on affective forecasting began to appear in the late 1990's, but the idea to study happiness and emotional prediction actually came to him on a sunny afternoon in October 1992, just as he and his friend Jonathan Jay Koehler sat down for lunch outside the psychology building at the University of Texas at Austin, where both men were teaching at the time. Gilbert was uninspired about his studies and says he felt despair about his failing marriage. And as he launched into a discussion of his personal life, he swerved to ask why economists focus on the financial aspects of decision making rather than the emotional ones. Koehler recalls, "Gilbert said something like: 'It all seems so small. It isn't really about money; it's about happiness. Isn't that what everybody wants to know when we make a decision?'" For a moment, Gilbert forgot his troubles, and two more questions came to him. Do we even know what makes us happy? And if it's difficult to figure out what makes us happy in the moment, how can we predict what will make us happy in the future?

In the early 1990's, for an up-and-coming psychology professor like Gilbert to switch his field of inquiry from how we perceive one another to happiness, as he did that day, was just a hairsbreadth short of bizarre. But Gilbert has always liked questions that lead him somewhere new. Now 45, Gilbert dropped out of high school at 15, hooking into what he calls "the tail end of the hippie movement" and hitchhiking aimlessly from town to town with his guitar. He met his wife on the road; she was hitching in the other direction. They married at 17, had a son at 18 and settled down in Denver. "I pulled weeds, I sold rebar, I sold carpet, I installed carpet, I spent a lot of time as a phone solicitor," he recalls. During this period he spent several years turning out science-fiction stories for magazines like *Amazing Stories*. Thus, in addition to being "one of the most gifted social psychologists of our age," as the psychology writer and professor David G. Myers describes him to me, Gilbert is the author of "The Essence of Grunk," a story about an encounter with a creature made of egg salad that jets around the galaxy in a rocket-powered refrigerator.

10 Psychology was a matter of happenstance. In the midst of his sci-fi career, Gilbert tried to sign up for a writing course at the local community college, but the class was full; he figured that psych, still accepting registrants, would help him with character development in his fiction. It led instead to an undergraduate degree at the University of Colorado at Denver, then a Ph.D. at Princeton, then an appointment at the University of Texas, then the appointment at Harvard. "People ask why I study happiness," Gilbert says, "and I say, 'Why study anything else?' It's the holy grail. We're studying the thing that all human action is directed toward."

One experiment of Gilbert's had students in a photography class at Harvard choose two favorite pictures from among those they had just taken and then relinquish one to the teacher. Some students were told their choices were permanent; others were told they could exchange their prints after several days. As it turned out, those who had time to change their minds were less pleased with their decisions than those whose choices were irrevocable.

Much of Gilbert's research is in this vein. Another recent study asked whether transit riders in Boston who narrowly missed their trains experienced the self-blame that people tend to predict they'll feel in this situation. (They did not.) And a paper waiting to be published, "The Peculiar Longevity of Things Not So Bad," examines why we expect that bigger problems will always dwarf minor annoyances. "When really bad things happen to us, we defend against them," Gilbert explains. "People, of course, predict the exact opposite. If you ask, 'What would you rather have, a broken leg or a trick knee?' they'd probably say, 'Trick knee.' And yet, if your goal is to accumulate maximum happiness over your lifetime, you just made the wrong choice. A trick knee is a bad thing to have."

All of these studies establish the links between prediction, decision making and well-being. The photography experiment challenges our common assumption that we would be happier with the option to change our minds when in fact we're happier with closure. The transit experiment demonstrates that we tend to err in estimating our regret over missed opportunities. The "things not so bad" work shows our failure to imagine how grievously irritations compromise our satisfaction. Our emotional defenses snap into action when it comes to a divorce or a disease but not for lesser problems. We fix the leaky roof on our house, but over the long haul, the broken screen door we never mend adds up to more frustration.

Gilbert does not believe all forecasting mistakes lead to similar results; a death in the family, a new gym membership and a new husband are not the same, but in how they affect our well-being they are similar. "Our research simply says that whether it's the thing that matters or the thing that doesn't, both of them matter less than you think they will," he says. "Things that happen to you or that you buy or own—as much as you think they make a difference to your happiness, you're wrong by a certain amount. You're overestimating how much of a difference they make. None of them make the difference you think. And that's true of positive and negative events."

Much of the work of Kahneman, Loewenstein, Gilbert and Wilson takes its cue from the concept of adaptation, a term psychologists have used since at least the 1950's to refer to how we acclimate to changing circumstances. George Loewenstein sums up this human capacity as follows: "Happiness is a signal that our brains use to motivate us to do certain things. And in the same way that our eye adapts to different levels of illumination, we're designed to kind of go back to the happiness set point. Our brains are not trying to be happy. Our brains are trying to regulate us." In this respect, the tendency toward adaptation suggests why the

15

impact bias is so pervasive. As Tim Wilson says: "We don't realize how quickly we will adapt to a pleasurable event and make it the backdrop of our lives. When any event occurs to us, we make it ordinary. And through becoming ordinary, we lose our pleasure."

It is easy to overlook something new and crucial in what Wilson is saying. Not that we invariably lose interest in bright and shiny things over time—this is a long-known trait—but that we're generally unable to recognize that we adapt to new circumstances and therefore fail to incorporate this fact into our decisions. So, yes, we will adapt to the BMW and the plasma TV, since we adapt to virtually everything. But Wilson and Gilbert and others have shown that we seem unable to predict that we will adapt. Thus, when we find the pleasure derived from a thing diminishing, we move on to the next thing or event and almost certainly make another error of prediction, and then another, ad infinitum.

As Gilbert points out, this glitch is also significant when it comes to negative events like losing a job or the death of someone we love, in response to which we project a permanently inconsolable future. "The thing I'm most interested in, that I've spent the most time studying, is our failure to recognize how powerful psychological defenses are once they're activated," Gilbert says. "We've used the metaphor of the 'psychological immune system'—it's just a metaphor, but not a bad one for that system of defenses that helps you feel better when bad things happen. Observers of the human condition since Aristotle have known that people have these defenses. Freud spent his life, and his daughter Anna spent her life, worrying about these defenses. What's surprising is that people don't seem to recognize that they have these defenses, and that these defenses will be triggered by negative events." During the course of my interviews with Gilbert, a close friend of his died. "I am like everyone in thinking, I'll never get over this and life will never be good again," he wrote to me in an e-mail message as he planned a trip to Texas for the funeral. "But because of my work, there is always a voice in the back of my head—a voice that wears a lab coat and has a lot of data tucked under its arm—that says, 'Yes, you will, and yes, it will.' And I know that voice is right."

Still, the argument that we imperfectly imagine what we want and how we will cope is nevertheless disorienting. On the one hand, it can cast a shadow of regret on some life decisions. Why did I decide that working 100 hours a week to earn more would make me happy? Why did I think retiring to Sun City, Ariz., would please me? On the other hand, it can be enlightening.

No wonder this teak patio set hasn't made me as happy as I expected. Even if she dumps me, I'll be O.K. Either way, predicting how things will feel to us over the long term is mystifying. A large body of research on well-being seems to suggest that wealth above middle-class comfort makes little difference to our happiness, for example, or that having children does nothing to improve well-being—even as it drives marital satisfaction dramatically down. We often yearn for a roomy, isolated home (a thing we easily adapt to), when, in fact, it will probably compromise our happiness by distancing us from neighbors. (Social interaction and friendships have been shown to give lasting pleasure.) The big isolated home is what Loewenstein, 48, himself bought. "I fell into a trap I never should have fallen into," he told me.

Loewenstein's office is up a narrow stairway in a hidden corner of an enormous, worn brick building on the edge of the Carnegie-Mellon campus in Pittsburgh. He and Gilbert make for an interesting contrast. Gilbert is garrulous, theatrical, dazzling in his speech and writing; he fills a room. Loewenstein is soft-spoken, given to abstraction and lithe in the way of a hard-core athlete; he seems to float around a room. Both men profess tremendous admiration for the other, and their different disciplines—psychology and economics—have made their overlapping interests in affective forecasting more complementary than fraught. While Gilbert's most notable contribution to affective forecasting is the impact bias, Loewenstein's is something called the "empathy gap."

Here's how it expresses itself. In a recent experiment, Loewen- 20
stein tried to find out how likely people might be to dance alone to Rick James's "Super Freak" in front of a large audience. Many agreed to do so for a certain amount of money a week in advance, only to renege when the day came to take the stage. This sounds like a goof, but it gets at the fundamental difference between how we behave in "hot" states (those of anxiety, courage, fear, drug craving, sexual excitation and the like) and "cold" states of rational calm. This empathy gap in thought and behavior—we cannot seem to predict how we will behave in a hot state when we are in a cold state—affects happiness in an important but somewhat less consistent way than the impact bias. "So much of our lives involves making decisions that have consequences for the future," Loewenstein says. "And if our decision making is influenced by these transient emotional and psychological states, then we know we're not making decisions with an eye toward future consequences." This may be as simple as an unfortunate proclamation

of love in a moment of lust, Loewenstein explains, or something darker, like an act of road rage or of suicide.

Among other things, this line of inquiry has led Loewenstein to collaborate with health experts looking into why people engage in unprotected sex when they would never agree to do so in moments of cool calculation. Data from tests in which volunteers are asked how they would behave in various "heat of the moment" situations—whether they would have sex with a minor, for instance, or act forcefully with a partner who asks them to stop—have consistently shown that different states of arousal can alter answers by astonishing margins. "These kinds of states have the ability to change us so profoundly that we're more different from ourselves in different states than we are from another person," Loewenstein says.

Part of Loewenstein's curiosity about hot and cold states comes from situations in which his emotions have been pitted against his intellect. When he's not teaching, he treks around the world, making sure to get to Alaska to hike or kayak at least once a year. A scholar of mountaineering literature, he once wrote a paper that examined why climbers have a poor memory for pain and usually ignore turn-back times at great peril. But he has done the same thing himself many times. He almost died in a whitewater canoeing accident and vowed afterward that he never wanted to see his runaway canoe again. (A couple of hours later, he went looking for it.) The same goes for his climbing pursuits. "You establish your turn-back time, and then you find yourself still far from the peak," he says. "So you push on. You haven't brought enough food or clothes, and then as a result, you're stuck at 13,000 feet, and you have to just sit there and shiver all night without a sleeping bag or warm clothes. When the sun comes up, you're half-frozen, and you say, 'Never again.' Then you get back and immediately start craving getting out again." He pushes the point: "I have tried to train my emotions." But he admits that he may make the same mistakes on his next trip.

Would a world without forecasting errors be a better world? Would a life lived without forecasting errors be a richer life? Among the academics who study affective forecasting, there seems little doubt that these sorts of questions will ultimately jump from the academy to the real world. "If people do not know what is going to make them better off or give them pleasure," Daniel Kahneman says, "then the idea that you can trust people to do what will give them pleasure becomes questionable." To Kahneman, who did some of the first experiments in the area in the early 1990's, affective forecasting could greatly influence retirement planning, for example, where mistakes in prediction (how much we save, how much we spend, how we choose a community we think we'll enjoy) can prove irreversible. He sees a role for affective forecasting in consumer spending, where a "cooling off" period might remedy buyer's remorse. Most important, he sees vital applications in health care, especially when it comes to informed consent. "We consider people capable of giving informed consent once they are told of the objective effects of a treatment," Kahneman says. "But can people anticipate how they and other people will react to a colostomy or to the removal of their vocal cords? The research on affective forecasting suggests that people may have little ability to anticipate their adaptation beyond the early stages." Loewenstein, along with his collaborator Dr. Peter Ubel, has done a great deal of work showing that nonpatients overestimate the displeasure of living with the loss of a limb, for instance, or paraplegia. To use affective forecasting to prove that people adapt to serious physical challenges far better and will be happier than they imagine, Loewenstein says, could prove invaluable.

There are downsides to making public policy in light of this research, too. While walking in Pittsburgh one afternoon, Loewenstein tells me that he doesn't see how anybody could study happiness and not find himself leaning left politically; the data make it all too clear that boosting the living standards of those already comfortable, such as through lower taxes, does little to improve their levels of well-being, whereas raising the living standards of the impoverished makes an enormous difference. Nevertheless, he and Gilbert (who once declared in an academic paper, "Windfalls are better than pratfalls, A's are better than C's, December 25 is better than April 15, and everything is better than a Republican administration") seem to lean libertarian in regard to pushing any kind of prescriptive agenda. "We're very, very nervous about overapplying the research," Loewenstein says. "Just because we figure out that X makes people happy and they're choosing Y, we don't want to impose X on them. I have a discomfort with paternalism and with using the results coming out of our field to impose decisions on people."

Still, Gilbert and Loewenstein can't contain the personal and 25
philosophical questions raised by their work. After talking with both men, I found it hard not to wonder about my own predictions at every turn. At times it seemed like knowing the secret to some parlor trick that was nonetheless very difficult to pull off—when I ogled a new car at the Honda dealership as I waited for a new

muffler on my '92 Accord, for instance, or as my daughter's fever spiked one evening and I imagined something terrible, and then something more terrible thereafter. With some difficulty, I could observe my mind overshooting the mark, zooming past accuracy toward the sublime or the tragic. It was tempting to want to try to think about the future more moderately. But it seemed nearly impossible as well.

To Loewenstein, who is especially attendant to the friction between his emotional and deliberative processes, a life without forecasting errors would most likely be a better, happier life. "If you had a deep understanding of the impact bias and you acted on it, which is not always that easy to do, you would tend to invest your resources in the things that would make you happy," he says. This might mean taking more time with friends instead of more time for making money. He also adds that a better understanding of the empathy gap—those hot and cold states we all find ourselves in on frequent occasions—could save people from making regrettable decisions in moments of courage or craving.

Gilbert seems optimistic about using the work in terms of improving "institutional judgment"—how we spend health care dollars, for example—but less sanguine about using it to improve our personal judgment. He admits that he has taken some of his research to heart; for instance, his work on what he calls the psychological immune system has led him to believe that he would be able to adapt to even the worst turn of events. In addition, he says that he now takes more chances in life, a fact corroborated in at least one aspect by his research partner Tim Wilson, who says that driving with Gilbert in Boston is a terrifying, white-knuckle experience. "But I should have learned many more lessons from my research than I actually have," Gilbert admits. "I'm getting married in the spring because this woman is going to make me happy forever, and I know it." At this, Gilbert laughs, a sudden, booming laugh that fills his Cambridge office. He seems to find it funny not because it's untrue, but because nothing could be more true. This is how he feels. "I don't think I want to give up all these motivations," he says, "that belief that there's the good and there's the bad and that this is a contest to try to get one and avoid the other. I don't think I want to learn too much from my research in that sense."

Even so, Gilbert is currently working on a complex experiment in which he has made affective forecasting errors "go away." In this test, Gilbert's team asks members of Group A to estimate how they'll feel if they receive negative personality feedback. The impact bias kicks in, of course, and they mostly predict they'll feel terrible, when in fact they end up feeling O.K. But if Gilbert shows Group B that others have gotten the same feedback and felt O.K. afterward, then its members predict they'll feel O.K. as well. The impact bias disappears, and the participants in Group B make accurate predictions.

This is exciting to Gilbert. But at the same time, it's not a technique he wants to shape into a self-help book, or one that he even imagines could be practically implemented. "Hope and fear are enduring features of the human experience," he says, "and it is unlikely that people are going to abandon them anytime soon just because some psychologist told them they should." In fact, in his recent writings, he has wondered whether forecasting errors might somehow serve a larger functional purpose he doesn't yet understand. If he could wave a wand tomorrow and eliminate all affective-forecasting errors, I ask, would he? "The benefits of not making this error would seem to be that you get a little more happiness," he says. "When choosing between two jobs, you wouldn't sweat as much because you'd say: 'You know, I'll be happy in both. I'll adapt to either circumstance pretty well, so there's no use in killing myself for the next week.' But maybe our caricatures of the future—these overinflated assessments of how good or bad things will be—maybe it's these illusory assessments that keep us moving in one direction over the other. Maybe we don't want a society of people who shrug and say, 'It won't really make a difference.'"

"Maybe it's important for there to be carrots and sticks in the   30
world, even if they are illusions," he adds. "They keep us moving towards carrots and away from sticks."

Questions for Discussion and Writing

1. In what ways does the title of the article, "The Futile Pursuit of Happiness," reflect the theme?

2. In your owns words, explain what Gertner means by "affective forecasting."

3. Stylistically, examine Gertner's use of the second person "you." If you were editing the article, would you ask Gertner to change or remove the references to the second person? Why or why not?

4. Evaluate Gilbert's statement: "Things that happen to you or that you buy or own—as much as you think they make a difference to your happiness, you're wrong by a certain amount. You're overestimating how much of a difference they make. None of them make the difference you think. And that's true of positive and negative events" (paragraph 14). Use your responses to the pre-reading exercise as a starting point and write a narrative essay about a past event or purchase that did or did not meet your expectations.

5. Write an essay about the correlation between financial success and happiness. You could research lottery winners and write an essay about whether or not sudden fortune increased happiness. Alternately, you can research a celebrity who has had instant success and write an essay about whether or not fame, in your opinion, increased his or her happiness.

Questions for Making Connections

1. Warhol, Rufus, Deneen, Rodriguez, and Gertner explore the idea of America by examining different aspects of popular culture. Warhol writes: "The idea of America is so wonderful because the more equal something is, the more American it is" (paragraph 4). Rufus connects the image of the cowboy to the idea of America, "And cowboys are, in the public imagination, loners. Independent. Inviolate. Like America. Rugged individuals who speak the truth, shoot from the hip" (paragraph 3). Write an essay in which you compare and/or contrast how any two writers in this chapter depict the idea of America. Which of the two writers presents the most persuasive argument? Include support from both readings.

2. How do you believe Rodriguez, who laments the loss of the collective "we" (for Rodriguez the "I" is lonely), would respond to Rufus's celebration of the individual "I" (a celebration of the loner aspect)? What assumptions do you believe each of the writers makes?

3. In your opinion, who fits the description of the American hero? Write an essay describing the ideal American hero. For example, your hero could be a sports celebrity icon such as Michael Jordan (if so, you may want to read ahead to Chapter 4) or firemen, who emerged as national heroes after 9/11. In your response, consider how you believe others would respond to your selection.

4. Do the findings in Gertner's "The Futile Pursuit of Happiness" contain any useful answers regarding Deneen's concerns about the "restless quality of the American character"? Write an essay in which you describe whether or not the findings in Gertner's article provide any solace to the concerns raised in Deneen's article.

5. Several of the writers in this chapter refer to cola: Warhol ("Coke" paragraph 1); Rufus ("cola" paragraph 1); and Rodriguez ("choices" paragraphs 9–10). Why do you think that a beverage such as cola would be mentioned in these diverse selections? Conduct research on the history of the beverage cola in America. Write a documented essay about the beverage and its popularity in American culture.

Gender Roles: Images of Masculinity and Femininity

Gender: "**Usage Note:** *Traditionally, gender has been used primarily to refer to the grammatical categories of "masculine," "feminine," and "neuter," but in recent years the word has become well established in its use to refer to sex-based categories, as in phrases such as* gender gap *and the* politics of gender. *This usage is supported by the practice of many anthropologists, who reserve* sex *for reference to biological categories, while using* gender *to refer to social or cultural categories. According to this rule, one would say* The effectiveness of the medication appears to depend on the sex (not gender) of the patient, *but* In peasant societies, gender (not sex) roles are likely to be more clearly defined. *This distinction is useful in principle, but it is by no means widely observed, and considerable variation in usage occurs at all levels."*

From http://dictionary.reference.com/search?q=gender

As indicated in the usage note above, gender is used "to refer to social or cultural categories." For many of us, our familiarity with gender roles began even before we could speak our first words: boys are dressed in blue, girls in pink; princes are warriors possessing physical strength; princesses have beauty, grace, and charm. Although progress has clearly softened the once bold lines separating femininity and masculinity, expectations still exist.

Societies as well as personal cultural traditions transmit ideologies about what it means to be a man and what it means to be a woman. Before reading, consider your personal history: What did the male and female role models teach you about gender roles? Did the personal knowledge you received about how to be a man or woman resonate with popular culture mediums (for example, did the television programs you watched present women and men whose values represented your own role models)? Use your recollection of music, television programs, comics, toys, and lyrics to reminisce about the various notions of masculinity and femininity that you observed in popular culture. As a child, which toys did you desire to play with? Which toys were you discouraged from playing with? Are any of your cultural gender expectations in conflict with personal desires? (For example, if you would like to focus on career rather than family life, is that a conflict because of cultural expectations to marry and have children?) Also consider the challenges facing individuals who defy gender roles. What is your opinion of people who defy gender roles? What specific conflicts and challenges do you imagine they face by defying gender categories?

How are images of masculinity and femininity socially constructed? Does popular culture shape, reinforce, modify, or challenge them? The selections in this chapter focus on gender roles—images of masculinity and femininity as they appear in various popular culture mediums: advertising and fashion (Dove); advertising, fashion (Smith); film (Donald); and film (Ehrenreich).

How is femininity socially constructed? How is the feminine beauty ideal reinforced? In "Only Two Percent of Women Describe Themselves as Beautiful," researchers explore "the implications of a global society that narrowly defines beauty by the images seen in entertainment, advertising and fashion runways and the startling impact this has on women" (paragraph 1). Unfortunately, but not surprising, "the result" reveals that "only two percent of thousands of women from 10 countries around the world consider themselves beautiful" (paragraph 1). In the report, researchers question: "Does this mean that we live in a world where women are not beautiful or does it mean that women around the world are calling for a broader definition of beauty?" (paragraph 1). Is it realistic to hope for a "broader definition of beauty" to replace current views? Could a "broader definition of beauty" dramatically alter the current beauty market?

Victoria's Secret clearly has a tight hold on the current beauty market. In "Decoding Victoria's Secret: The Marketing of Sexual Beauty and Ambivalence," Marie D. Smith writes: "Much as Ford or GM pushes its latest car models with enticing new names, so VS models the ultimate female body, improved annually by the invention of buzzwords such as 'miracle bras,' water and gel-filled bras, 'seamless body,' 'a body for your body'" (paragraph 3). What do you make of the fact that "Like most other women's apparel ads, VS ads are apparently based on three assumptions: (1) a woman's physical body is an instrument for selling any product, including herself; (2) a woman is always struggling to get or hold onto the right man in order to give meaning to her life; and (3) a woman's self-image is largely based on a male perception of her physical beauty" (paragraph 3)? Do you agree with the three assumptions?

What about men and social constructs of masculinity? In "From 'Knockout Punch' to 'Home Run': Masculinity's 'Dirty Dozen' Sports Metaphors in American Combat Films," Ralph Donald examines the "culturally prescribed construction" of masculinity as reflected in combat films and suggests: "if all the world is changing and adapting, perhaps the macho, uncommunicative, unemotional, pseudo-athletic misogynists America seems intent on turning out should also consider some fundamental alterations" (paragraph 59). Alternations are difficult to see, especially in a culture where social constructs of masculinity are reinscribed in popular culture mediums.

It's not surprising that Barbara Ehrenreich encourages readers to relinquish ideals and accept real physical human bodies. Ehrenreich laments the destruction of human flesh in her personal essay, "Why Don't We Like the Human Body?" Is she correct that "at this particular historical moment, we have come to hate the human body." Lamenting the loss of sex (paragraph 6) and then "food" (paragraph 7), she says that "human flesh" has been "a big disappointment" (paragraph 8)! Perhaps, she suggests "Hollywood could help by promoting better uses for the body, like real sex, by which I mean sex between people who are often wrinkled and overweight and sometimes even fond of each other" (paragraph 10). But would audiences pay to see films with real people? Is Hollywood to blame or are consumers to blame? What does popular culture reveal about ingrained attitudes toward gender? Can you imagine a time when there will indeed be "fundamental alterations" in images of masculinity and femininity? If so, will these new definitions and images become immortalized in television, film, advertising, music, and other popular culture mediums?

Pre-Reading Chapter 2

1. Write your answers to the questions raised in this introduction. In your response, be honest about your upbringing and the ideas you received about gender. You can later draw on your recorded observations of your autobiographical experience before class discussion and writing essays.

2. In this chapter, you'll read the following: "Only Two Percent of Women Describe Themselves as Beautiful"/Dove, StrategyOne, Nancy Etcoff, Susie Orbach; "Decoding Victoria's Secret: The Marketing of Sexual Beauty and Ambivalence"/Marie D. Smith; "From 'Knockout Punch' to 'Home Run': Masculinity's 'Dirty Dozen' Sports Metaphors in American Combat Films"/Ralph Donald; and, "Why Don't We Like the Human Body?"/Barbara Ehrenreich. What perspectives do you expect to encounter? Which of the titles capture your attention?

3. In your idea journal and scrapbook, pay attention to popular culture references to gender. Keep copies of advertisements you see in magazines, for example *Cosmopolitan* and *GQ*. Record your observations. If you hear music lyrics that address gender issues, keep a notation of the song, artist, and theme. Pay attention to parallels. For example, although Smith writes about marketing sexual beauty in Victoria's Secret, you might see a music video that uses sexuality in a provocative manner. Later on, if you decide to write a paper on sexual beauty, you might consider sexuality in music videos before further narrowing your topic to a particular artist and even motive—misogynistic attitudes toward women in a particular video by a particular artist.

Only Two Percent of Women Describe Themselves as Beautiful

DOVE, STRATEGYONE, NANCY ETCOFF, AND SUSIE ORBACH

As mentioned in paragraphs one and two of this press release by Dove/Unilever, "Dove partnered with Dr. Nancy Etcoff, Harvard University professor and author of Survivor of the Prettiest, *and Dr. Susie Orbach, London School of Economics, visiting professor and author of* Fat is a Feminist Issue, *to develop 'The Real Truth About Beauty: A Global Report,' which explores the relationship women have with beauty." The press release was published by Dove/Unilever on September 29, 2004.*

Pre-Reading

How many women do you know who would "describe themselves as beautiful"? Describe a family member or friend you believe is beautiful. Explain whether or not your choice coincides with the beauty ideal as presented in the advertisements you see on television and in magazines.

—————— ✦ ——————

NEW GLOBAL STUDY UNCOVERS DESIRE FOR BROADER DEFINITION OF BEAUTY

NEW YORK, Sept. 29/PRNewswire/—Dove® unveils a groundbreaking new study today that discusses the implications of a global society that narrowly defines beauty by the images seen in entertainment, advertising and fashion runways and the startling impact this has on women. The result: only two percent of thousands of women from 10 countries around the world consider themselves beautiful. Does this mean that we live in a world where women are not beautiful or does it mean that women around the world are calling for a broader definition of beauty?

Dove, as a global beauty brand and responsible marketer, wants to investigate these issues and understand women's views on beauty. With these concerns in mind, Dove partnered with Dr. Nancy Etcoff, Harvard University professor and author of "Survival of the Prettiest," and Dr. Susie Orbach, London School of Economics, visiting professor and author of "Fat is a Feminist Issue," to develop The Real Truth About Beauty: A Global Report, which explores the relationship women have with beauty. Specifically, Dove's mission is to determine how women define beauty; their level of satisfaction with their own beauty; and its impact on their sense of well-being.

"The Real Truth About Beauty: A Global Report makes it clear that it is time to lift the quota system on images of beauty," says Etcoff. "This study uncovers that beauty is never going away and has enormous power. Beauty should not be reduced to a political or cultural problem but understood as a basic human pleasure."

Beauty: The Eye of the Beholder

The Real Truth About Beauty: A Global Report uncovers startling information about how women physically perceive and define their look. Supporting the current and narrow definition of beauty, the respondents are hesitant to claim ownership of the word "beauty," with more than 40 percent strongly agreeing that they do not feel comfortable describing themselves as beautiful.

5   Furthermore, only five percent feel comfortable describing themselves as pretty and a mere nine percent feel comfortable describing themselves as attractive. Additionally, just 13 percent of women say they are very satisfied with their beauty; 12 percent say they are very satisfied with their physical attractiveness; 17 percent are very satisfied with their facial attractiveness; and only 13 percent are very satisfied with their body weight and shape. In fact, in a society captivated by diet and makeover programs, a third of women around the world are very or somewhat dissatisfied with their body weight. The women of Japan have the highest levels of dissatisfaction at 59 percent—followed by Brazil (37%), United Kingdom (36%) and the United States (36%), Argentina (27%) and the Netherlands (25%).

Pop Culture's Beauty Mark

Having assessed how women think about as well as evaluate their own beauty and appearance, the study asks women about social issues emerging from mass media and pop culture. From Brazil to the Netherlands to Argentina—across cultures, ages, ethnicities and race—women make it clear they believe there is a one-dimensional and narrow, physical definition of beauty. The findings show that the ideas of beauty and physical attractiveness are largely synonymous, and although both are highly valued by society, both are rendered almost impossible to attain.

Respondents said they felt pressure to try and be that "perfect" picture of beauty:

- Sixty-three percent strongly agree that women today are expected to be more attractive than their mothers' generation.
- Sixty percent strongly agree that society expects women to enhance their physical attractiveness.
- Forty-five percent of women feel women who are more beautiful have greater opportunities in life.

- More than half (59%) strongly agree that physically attractive women are more valued by men.

The study explores the degree to which mass media has played a role in portraying and communicating a narrow definition of beauty:

- More than two-thirds (68%) of women strongly agree that "the media and advertising set an unrealistic standard of beauty that most women can't ever achieve."
- Well over half of all women (57%) strongly agree that "the attributes of female beauty have become very narrowly defined in today's world."

Women Around the World Unite

The traditional definition of beauty, based only on physical appearance, is powerfully communicated through the mass media and has been assimilated through popular culture. It is this ideal that many women measure themselves against and aspire to attain. However, women around the world would like to see media change in the way it represents beauty.

For example, women feel they are surrounded and bombarded with images that are unrealistic: 10

- The majority (76%) wish female beauty was portrayed in the media as being made up of more than just physical attractiveness.
- Seventy-five percent went on to say that they wish the media did a better job of portraying women of diverse physical attractiveness, including age, shape and size.

The Real Truth About Beauty: A Global Report uncovers that women recognize beauty is more than just physical—it includes character, passion and presence. And, in order to influence a cultural shift in popular culture and mass media, it is necessary to come together and stake a claim to redefine beauty.

"What women in this study tell us is that a sense of legitimacy and respect is wrapped up with beauty in today's world. Whether this sentiment dismays or delights us, it poses a serious challenge," says Orbach. "And it is this in the first instance: For the idea of beauty to become truly democratic and inclusive, then beauty itself must be revitalized to reflect women in their beauty as they really are rather than as portrayed in the current fictions that dominate our visual culture."

So What Is Beautiful?

How are the women of the world defining beauty and what do they really want to see as society continues to evolve? The study finds two-thirds of women strongly agree that physical attractiveness is about how one looks, whereas beauty includes much more of who a person is. Women rate happiness, confidence, dignity and humor as powerful components of beauty, along with the more traditional attributes of physical appearance, body weight and shape, and even a sense of style. The respondents also see beauty in many different forms:

- Seventy-seven percent strongly agree that beauty can be achieved through attitude, spirit and other attributes that have nothing to do with physical appearance.
- Eighty-nine percent strongly agree that a woman can be beautiful at any age.
- Eighty-five percent state every woman has something about her that is beautiful.

Not only do women agree that happiness is the primary element in making a woman beautiful, but they strongly agree that they themselves feel most beautiful when they are happy and fulfilled in their lives (86%). Furthermore, 82 percent of women agree that, "If I had a daughter, I would want her to feel beautiful, even if she is not physically attractive."

15   In conclusion, the study demonstrates that authentic beauty is a concept lodged in women's hearts and minds and seldom articulated in popular culture or affirmed in the mass media. As such, it remains unrealized and unclaimed—an idea of beauty that is a narrower, functional definition of "physical attractiveness."

However, this study clearly outlines women's views about the true components of beauty and affirms that, while they include physical attractiveness, they also include happiness, kindness, wisdom, dignity, love, authenticity and self-realization. Through this study, the possibilities for the beautiful to be known, found and represented have been infinitely extended and the ways in which female beauty can be defined have been profoundly deepened.

The Campaign for Real Beauty

Sparked by the results of the global study, Dove is launching a major initiative designed to provoke discussion and encourage debate about the nature of beauty. The Campaign for Real Beauty asks women to give serious thought to a host of issues surrounding beauty, such as society's definition of it, the quest for "perfection," the difference between beauty and physical attractiveness, and the way the media shapes our perceptions of beauty.

The Campaign for Real Beauty uses various communication vehicles to invite women to join in the discussion about beauty and share their views of it with women around the world:

- Advertising: A global advertising campaign, launching October 2004, will question whether "model" attributes, such as youth, slimness, and symmetrical features, are required for beauty— or are completely irrelevant to it. Each ad presents an image of a woman whose appearance differs from the stereotypical physical ideal, and asks the reader/viewer to judge the woman's looks by checking off a box.

  —"Wrinkled? Wonderful?" features Irene Sinclair, 95, of London, England with a wrinkled face and asks: "Will society ever accept old can be beautiful?"
  —"Gray? Gorgeous?" features Merlin Glozer, 45, of London, England with a natural mane of gray hair and asks: "Why aren't women glad to be gray?"
  —"Oversized? Outstanding?" features Tabatha Roman, 34, of New York, NY, a plus-size woman, and asks: "Does true beauty only squeeze into a size 6?"
  —"Half empty? Half full?" features Esther Poyer, 35, of London, England, with small breasts and asks: "Does sexiness depend on how full your cups are?"
  —"Flawed? Flawless?" features Leah Sheehan, 22, of London, England, with freckles and asks "Does beauty mean looking like everyone else?"

  Each ad will direct readers/viewers to a special web site (http://www.campaignforrealbeauty.com) where they can cast their votes.

- Web site: At http://www.campaignforrealbeauty.com, women can cast their votes on the questions raised in the ad campaign and engage in an ongoing dialogue about beauty by posting to discussion boards, hearing what women around the world are saying, and downloading research studies about beauty.

- Billboards: Mobile billboards will be placed in major cities challenging women's notions of beauty by encouraging them to cast their votes. A featured interactive billboard, located in New York's Times Square, highlighting the "Wrinkled? Wonderful?" ad will keep a running tally of the vote submitted for that issue.

- Panel discussions:

  —The Campaign for Real Beauty launches in New York City on September 29 with a kick-off panel discussion about beauty, co-hosted by American Women in Radio and Television®, and featuring Dr. Nancy Etcoff of Harvard University; Mindy Herman, former CEO, E! Entertainment Television; Andi Bernstein, Vice President, Special Projects, Oxygen Media and additional media and beauty industry leaders, moderated by Jamie Colby, Correspondent and Anchor, Fox News Channel.

  —Dove is furthering the panel discussions on a grassroots level by partnering with the Woodhull Institute for Ethical Leadership, a not-for-profit educational organization that provides ethical leadership training and professional development for women, for two special weekend workshops to be held in Atlanta (October 8–10) and Chicago (November 12–14).

- The Dove Self-Esteem Fund: Dove has established the Dove Self-Esteem Fund to raise awareness of the link between beauty and body-related self-esteem. The new initiative continues an ongoing effort by Dove to fund programs that raise self-esteem in girls and young women. The Dove Self-Esteem Fund is working through the Unilever Foundation to sponsor uniquely ME!, a partnership program with Girl Scouts of the USA that helps build self-confidence in girls ages 8–14 with resources and program activities. The Dove Self-Esteem Fund also supports Body Talk, an educational program for schools in the United Kingdom and Canada.

About The Real Truth About Beauty: A Global Report

The Real Truth About Beauty: A Global Report was conducted by research firm StrategyOne in collaboration with Dr. Nancy Etcoff and the Massachusetts General Hospital/Harvard University, and with the expert consultation of Dr. Susie Orbach of the London

School of Economics. The study is based on quantitative data collected from a global survey of 3,200 women from Argentina, Brazil, Canada, France, Italy, Japan, Netherlands, Portugal, United Kingdom, and the United States.

About Dove

Dove, manufactured by Unilever, is the No. 1 personal wash   20
brand nationwide. One in every three households uses a Dove product, which includes bar cleansers, body washes, face care, anti-perspirants/deodorants and hair care. Dove anti-perspirant/ deodorant is the No. 2 female-oriented anti-perspirant/deodorant brand in the United States. Dove is available nationwide in food, drug and mass outlet stores. The Dove mission is to make women feel more beautiful every day by challenging today's stereotypical view of beauty and inspiring women to take great care of themselves. Visit http://www.dove.com.

Questions for Discussion and Writing

1. What exactly do the findings of this global study reveal about women, beauty, and happiness? Which of the arguments do you agree or disagree with?
2. Researchers reveal, "This study uncovers that beauty is never going away and has enormous power. Beauty should not be reduced to a political or cultural problem but understood as a basic human pleasure" (paragraph 3). What "political or cultural problem[s]" do you believe they are referring to? Explain.
3. This selection is a press release by Dove, a manufacturer of beauty products for women, and only a portion of the report was cited. What additional information do you imagine the full report will provide?
4. Take an informal poll of your friends and/or classmates. How do your findings compare with the findings in the report? Write an essay comparing your own findings to those in the selection. Does your poll support, refute, or modify their claims?
5. Select an advertisement of any beauty product and write an essay on the "beauty idea." Is it represented in the advertisement? If so, how? In your response, describe the ad in detail. The following questions may help: Who is depicted? How are the people positioned? What colors and designs are used? Do you believe they are symbolic? What do the words denote and connote? What idea(s) are being sold? What is not stated but implied? Does the beauty ideal presented in your advertisement perpetuate gender stereotypes?

Decoding Victoria's Secret: The Marketing of Sexual Beauty and Ambivalence

MARIE D. SMITH

Marie D. Smith is a retired college professor of French and Spanish. Her main interests are languages, literature, pop culture, and travel. During her career, she received several awards for her teaching and related interests from the Florida Association of Community Colleges, the Florida Foreign Language Association, and the Union Teacher Press Association, among others. Her article on Victoria's Secret from Studies in Popular Culture *(October 2002) was first published by the* Popular Culture Association of the South, *for which she and her husband regularly present papers. She resides with her husband, Claude Jay Smith, in Jacksonville, Florida, and has two sons.* [*]

Pre-Reading

How many women (or men) do you know who actually purchase Victoria's Secret products? Do you think that Victoria's Secret has been effective at "marketing sexual beauty"? Explain why or why not.

———————— ✦ ————————

Since the 1977 opening of a single store in San Francisco by Roy Raymond, the underwear business dubbed "Victoria's Secret" has evolved into a chain of about nine hundred stores, achieving a phenomenal financial share of the $12 billion women's lingerie market and transforming the image of intimate apparel on a wider scale than any other retail operation. Like many other successful businesses, its long-term success was based on a timely idea: to induce women themselves to replace their girdles and plain, practical white cotton bras and to indulge on a regular basis in the glamorous lingerie supposedly reminiscent of the frilly, fancy undergarments of the Victorian Era. True, this was

---

[*]Biography contributed by Professor Marie Smith.

what men had been buying for them all along, but only as the occasional Christmas, Valentine, or birthday gift. Although Raymond opened his original store in 1977 as an environment catering to *male* buyers, this vision was rejected by Leslie Wexner, who bought the chain (which had grown to six stores) for $4 million in 1982. According to Dan Finkelman, senior vice president at Intimate Brands, Victoria's Secret's parent company, Wexner geared his strategy toward women—the sex that buys more than 90% of intimate apparel in the form of underwear, but that, he believed, secretly aspires to buy lingerie. Finkelman asserted that "If we gave women a chance to make themselves feel sexy in a wonderful, romantic environment, they'd prefer that to going to a mass merchant to buy a three-pack" (McGinn 1–2).

A change in image was what was needed—new colors, patterns and styles that promised sexiness packaged in a tasteful, glamorous way and with the snob appeal of European luxury. Catalogs listed VS's headquarters as London, even though it was really Ohio. The up-scale tone was carefully fostered, thus avoiding the raunchy sexual image of Victoria's "naughty" rival, Frederick's of Hollywood. Currently the bordello elements in VS's decor are being de-emphasized even more in hopes of appealing to women from teen-agers to mothers and grandmothers. According to Lauri Brunner, retail analyst for the banking firm Dain Rauscher Wessels, "They're getting out of hot-pink wallpaper and using pale pink and beige wallpaper. . . . Fixtures will be of higher quality and signage will be much better" (Christie 1). Robin Burns, president and chief executive officer of Intimate Brands' beauty products division, describes the new look as "residential." The new stores, such as the posh 18,000 square foot store in New York, will have "crystal chandeliers and mahogany furniture set in a colonnaded interior" (Burns 1).

Although VS's parent company, Intimate Brands, also owns Bath & Body Works and White Barn Candle, VS accounted for more than half of IB's $4.5 billion revenue in 1999. Capitalizing on this success, VS has further expanded its glamorous image into a total body image, including a line of fragrances and makeup, now sold in about five hundred Victoria's Secret Beauty Stores (McGinn 2). VS generated $2.9 billion in the year 2000 (Burns 1) with purchases from the 380 million catalogues distributed annually accounting for one-third of the company's revenue (Christie 2). Additionally, VS has aggressively promoted its image concept through communication technology: in 2000, the virtual store grossed $135 million, tripling sales over fiscal year 1999. Seven to nine percent of these were international sales (Christie 1). The May, 2000, Webcast drew two million viewers (Howell 1). Television advertising, on-line marketing, and webcast lingerie runway shows feature supermodels displaying the latest product or image tweak. Much as Ford or GM pushes its latest car models with enticing new names, so VS models the ultimate female body, improved annually by the invention of buzzwords such as "miracle bras," water and gel-filled bras, "seamless body," "a body for your body." Aggressive, wide-scale promotion of the right image at the right time might seem to account for VS's success. Like most other women's apparel ads, VS ads are apparently based on three assumptions: (1) a woman's physical beauty is an instrument for selling any product, including herself; (2) a woman is always struggling to get or hold on to the right man in order to give meaning to her life; and (3) a woman's self-image is largely based on a male perception of her physical beauty. But a closer look at the contents of the typical VS image, and the language used to sell it, will reveal hidden messages based on these assumptions that are at least as powerful as the obvious ones mentioned above. It can be argued that VS's marketing is more effective than that of other companies because these hidden messages play into the ambivalence, insecurity, and contradictions, both inherent and society-based, which characterize male/female sexual relations.

The first assumption, that a beautiful female body can sell any product, is based on the idea that men respond first to a woman as a visual object and only later as a person, that is, "the male gaze," said to objectify a woman as a commodity for the pleasure of an absent male spectator. When this arguably "natural" male response is overlaid with societal norms which say that sex is bad, wrong, or dangerous except in very restrictive conditions, then the visual attraction takes a strong swing in the direction of the "voyeuristic": the vision takes on added enticement because it is forbidden and prurient.

5   Consider, for example, this description of the February 1999 VS fashion show webcast by Edward Rothstein in the *New York Times:*

> The medium has met the message: delay, provocation, unpredictability, furtive flickers of something hidden—these elements of the Webcast are also part of the appeal of Victoria's Secret. Gazing at this Webcast was like watching a striptease through a keyhole, catching glimpses of a fuller world that one squints at, trying to imagine in fleshy glory. . . . Sex as partial disclosure: sounds like Victoria's secret. (Rothstein 2)

This same mysterious dream world of seductive images is created in VS's catalogs, the facial expressions of the female models being anything but expressions that females would direct at other females (barring lesbian attraction). The models are above all cool and mysterious, closed lips slightly pouting or smiling, or lips parted slightly but rarely smiling openly. The look is inaccessible à la Grace Kelly, sometimes even defiant à la Marlene Dietrich. The looks and poses may be variously described as mysterious, pensive, secretive, knowing, seductive, sultry, dreamy, confident, teasingly indifferent, vaguely dissatisfied, demure, enclosed, and private. The sheer number of these descriptors suggests the ambiguity of the poses, but they all convey sexual allure and careful preparation in anticipation of a male's admiration. The allure and potential accessibility to the unseen male spectator are further heightened by the fact that the model is almost always featured alone, in a private world with borders of lines or solid color which isolate her. It is rare to see anything which would suggest that she has any relationships. Unlike many other fashion catalogs, there are no other women, men or children shown with her to suggest that she is a wife, a companion, or a mother. She is completely anonymous—without even the name, statistics, or brief life history accorded a Playboy Bunny. She is all possibility.

The second and third assumptions evident in female intimate apparel ads are that a woman is struggling to get or hold on to a man to give meaning to her life, and that her self-image is largely determined by a male perception of female beauty. These assumptions are substantiated by the fact that ads featuring females are designed to attract *men*, but sell primarily to women who presumably are drawn to them to find out what men want or desire in a woman. An article entitled "Victoria's Not-So-Secret Strategy" by Marisa Kula, cites Renee Redd, director of the Women's Center at Northwestern University, who asserts that

> This culture has an . . . incredible focus on women's bodies. . . . [W]omen' self-esteem . . . rests on how attractive they are to men. And while VS may not have created the standards of female desirability, its mass-marketing both nurtures the existing stereotypes . . . and fertilizes their future growth. Worst of all, it is a very specific . . . stereotype that is presented as "sexy." Put it this way: Do you look like a Victoria's Secret model? No? Then you don't look sexy (Redd 3).

As deplorable as promoting a stereotyped image may be, it is obviously enormously successful in reaching the female consumers that VS has targeted. Redd's article does concede that

"The models are not the anorexic type that women tend to idealize. The image of the curvaceous woman is therefore healthier, but the underlying effect is that women are sensing this is what men want" (Redd 2).

Unlike the anorexic or boyish-looking models in most magazines, wearing clothes that fit them like sacks, the typical VS model reveals her curves in undergarments or clothes that typically mold to the body, a button or two discretely undone, a thumb perhaps tucked into her bikini bottom or jeans—as if to ask, "Wouldn't you like to take this off?" Curves are much more in evidence than bones, and there is actually more variety of shape—at least bust shape—than the usual assumptions about stereotypes would suggest. The one restriction is that the customer be a size fourteen or under. For the small-breasted woman, VS has small-breasted models who succeed in being erotic and provocative, their cleavage emphasized by gel, airlift, underwire, or removable push up pads. These supports are mentioned only in small print, while the large, attention-getting letters—often printed on the upper chest—proclaim that the cleavage-producing bra is simply a "Miracle." The VS models, fifteen of whom were listed on a web site called "Who2 Loop," represent types from sultry/exotic to cool/savvy to angelic/divine. Like a well-stocked dessert tray, there is something to suit any taste in the international array of beauties with a variety of nationalities: Australian, Czech, Polish, Belgian, Dutch, British, American, French, Brazilian, German, and so on (Who2 Loop 1). The conclusion must be that VS wants to garner as many women as possible, worldwide, who are small or medium-sized and who want to look like what men presumably want. Indeed, VS's latest sales pitch is "A body for your body," which is apparently meant to suggest to women that VS can remodel whatever they've got.

10   So, Victoria's surprising secret, according to this writer's interpretation, is that she has based her huge success with *women* upon being the best at giving *men* what *they* want visually. In contrast to the varying degrees of graphic sexual display in *Playboy, Penthouse,* or *Hustler*, the pubic area as well as the nipples and areola, are never on view in VS. In spite of this lack of graphic display, men apparently love to look at the women in Victoria's Secret. A sampling of magazines and web sites catering to men corroborates this fact. An anonymous article posted in <formen.ign.com> entitled the "Babes of Victoria's Secret" contains descriptions of six of the models from the male point of view. The following description captures the flavor of all six: "Tyra Banks just simply rules the

planet. . . . [H]er body could melt my hypothalamus gland in two seconds flat. . . . [H]er majestic breasts . . . rival any other set I've ever seen. They're as close to perfection in boobs as can be hoped to achieve" (<Formen>3). Here is another male point of view, also from an article at the <Formen> web site, this one entitled "Flesh Merchant: Victoria's Secret Catalog": "From the confused and horny teenager to the husband whose wife is out of town, the Victoria's Secret Catalog is perhaps the most tasteful way to get your rocks off without feeling like a scumbag" (Douglas 1). The only slightly dissatisfied male comment that I found in a horde of enthusiastic male reviews was in an article deploring the digital removal of nipples in Victoria's Secret. The article was entitled "How to Draw the Nipples Back on Victoria's Secret Catalogue Models Using Adobe Photoshop 4.0" (Ronzoni 1).

This comment aside, part of Victoria's secret attraction for men may actually lie in the possibility that, in addition to loving the sight of beautiful female faces and bodies, men actually find a degree of visual mystery, uncertainty, and secrecy to be more provocative and stimulating than complete sexual exposure. This may be particularly true in a society characterized by sexual repression, ambivalence, and guilt. According to Michel Foucault in his study *The History of Sexuality*, this repression began at the beginning of the seventeenth century and reached its height during the Victorian regime. The prevailing view was that only married heterosexual sex was normal. All other forms of sexuality were treated with "an injunction of silence" except when referred to in a "clandestine, circumscribed, and coded type of discourse" (144).

Sexual repression still exists, in spite of the erosion of belief in Protestant authority as well as the sexual and feminist movements. In fact, modern advertising, according to Jackson Lears, fills the void left by the erosion of belief in divine authority: "[T]he advertiser [is] a modern replacement for the priest . . . permit[ting] the individual to consume and still be absolved of guilt and sin" (Quinóy 1).

Mirroring this repression, the reaction to Victoria's Secret seems enthusiastic and, at the same time, slightly guilt ridden. Among the typical chatroom comments that I encountered on the Internet, both male and female reactions were ambivalent. One male reviewer enthusiastically described his favorite VS models and then, in an abrupt about-face, ended his article with the following acknowledgment of his un-liberated maleness: "Notice I have been a very good boy and did not refer to these women as chicks although I treat them like objects which I appoligize [sic] for" (O'Collegian 1). In a similar vein, a female fan of VS had this to say about her conflicted attitudes: "I don't think I'm a fan of the Miracle Bra. Sure, it's . . . a cool thing to . . . strap it on and ta-da, have instant cleavage." But she follows this up with the disclaimer: "I'm pretty comfortable with my average cleavage, thank you very much, and I don't feel I must increase my bust to look . . . more 'womanly.' 'Cause after all, breasts are not what being a woman is really all about" (Abbagirl 1).

VS catalogues cater to and reassure both men and women who want to be "good" and "bad," safe and daring, at the same time. To accomplish this, a strange, oxymoronic language is used that simultaneously strokes the id and soothes the super-ego. Accompanying the all-important image, the very infrequent but prominent messages have a double appeal to the reality of a woman's actual body and to the miraculous transition that VS will help her achieve: women who want to be "more" are promised a "natural miracle," "bare solutions," "glamorous support," "beyond basics," "new classics," and a "second skin." An interesting example of VS's play on the divine/earthy dichotomy is the marketing of its "Dream Angel Series" of perfumes, lotions, and body powder. The model's facial expressions and body postures, which are sultry or provocative, sharply contrast with the innocent pink and white of the background color and giant angel wings. The message which accompanies this medium is "Dream angels divine—the third scent from heaven." The arms deftly cover the "forbidden" portions of the breast while simultaneously holding one of the large, luxurious wings over the pubic area. The result is ethereal beauty, a platonic ideal of sensuality without any suggestion of the scatological aspects of sex. Not since the 'Fifties TV shows *Bewitched* and *I Dream of Jeannie* have the vixen and the angel been so tantalizingly fused. Nostalgia for a "purer," more discrete time when SEX did not proclaim itself so blatantly is a large part of VS's appeal also.

15   The conclusions then, that I have reached, are essentially three. (1) Most women, in spite of the consciousness-raising effects of the Women's Liberation movement, have thoroughly internalized the belief that a narrow, male-constructed image of female sexuality and beauty defines their self worth. (2) This male-constructed image is accompanied by feelings in both sexes of ambivalence, confusion, and guilt, resulting in a need for sending and receiving conflicting sexual messages. (3) A large part of Victoria's Secret's enormous marketing success has been achieved through a consistently glamorous, flawless portrayal of this ambivalent, hyper-real version of the female body.

Works Cited

Abbagirl. "Victoria's Secret/Thongs." (12/28/97) *http://www.abbagirl .com/ravel.html*

Burns, Robin. Quoted in "Victoria's Secret Wants New Look." (7/16/01) *http://www.celebritytrendz.com/community/news/vs_newlook.html*

Christie, James. "Victoria's Secret Reveals Skimpy Web Strategy." (10/12/00) *http://www.redherring.com/indez.asp?layout*

Douglas, Adam. "Flesh Merchant: Victoria's Secret Catalog." (11/3/99) *http://formen.ign.com/news/11795.html*

Foucault, Michel. *The History of Sexuality, Vol. 1: An Introduction.* Trans. Robert Hurley. New York: Vintage/Random: 1980.

Howell, Donna. "Victoria's Secret Trusses Up Webcast History." (2001) *http://netculture.about.com/library/blvictoriassecret.html*

IGN For Men. "Babes of Victoria's Secret." (12/06/00) *http:// formen.ign.com/news/28672.html*

McGinn, Dan. "Case Study: Victoria's Secrets." (2/00) *http://www .mbajungle.com/main*

O'Collegian Staff. "What is Victoria's Secret?" (7/16/97) *http://www.ocolly.okstate.edu/issues/1997_Summer/970716/html*

Quinõy, Luisa. "Therapeutic Ethos." *http://www.lclark.edu/~soan370/ modernity.te.combo.html*

Redd, Rene. Quoted in "Victoria's Not-So-Secret Strategy." (9/27/99) *http://www.societypolitics.chickcick.com/articles/570pl.html*

Ronzoni, Tony. "How to Draw the Nipples Back on Victoria's Secret Catalogue Models Using Adobe Photoshop 4.0." *http://www .zug.com/ad-html/secret.html*

Rothstein, Edward. "A Sex Metaphor, by Victoria's Secret." (2/5/99) *http://www.nytimes.com/library/tech/99/02/biztech/articles/05roth.html*

Victoria's Secret. "Christmas Dreams and Fantasies." (Christmas 2000) *www.Victoria'sSecret.com*

Who2 Loop. "The Girls of Victoria's Secret." (2001) *http://www.who2 .com/victoriassecret.html*

Questions for Discussion and Writing

1. According to Smith, what are the leading factors that account for Victoria's Secret success?
2. Explain whether or not you agree with three assumptions listed in paragraph 3. What other assumptions can be made about the advertisements?
3. Why does Smith include so much financial information?
4. In paragraph 7, Renee Redd is cited as saying: "This culture has an . . . incredible focus on women's bodies . . . [W]omen's self-esteem . . . rests on how attractive they are to men. And while VS may not have created the standards of female

desirability, its mass-marketing both nurtures the existing stereotypes... and fertilizes their future growth." Do you agree with this statement? What are the consequences and deeper issues involved in "existing stereotypes"? Write an essay about "existing stereotypes about women" in which you explore the consequences and deeper issues involved. Use examples from your own observations.

5. Regardless of where you stand on the issue, write a research paper in support of Victoria's Secret. What arguments can you make in favor of their marketing and success? Be specific.

From "Knockout Punch" to "Home Run": Masculinity's "Dirty Dozen" Sports Metaphors in American Combat Films

RALPH DONALD

Professor Ralph Donald has taught and professionally worked in various aspects of broadcasting, journalism, and film. His extensive research interests include film and television propaganda, motion picture history, and gender-related studies, such as this analysis on masculinity and film published in Film and History *(2005). He has presented numerous papers at academic conferences and has been published in books and academic publications including* Race/Gender/Media: Considering Diversity Across Audiences, Content, and Producers, *Rebecca Ann Lind, ed. (2003),* The Masculinities Reader, *edited by Stephen Whitehead and Frank Barrett (2001),* Fundamentals of Television Production *(2000),* Communicator, Film and History. *He currently teaches at Southern Illinois University at Edwardsville.*

Pre-Reading

What lessons did the boys you grew up with learn about how to become men? Which sports activities were they encouraged to participate in? In what ways do sports activities prepare boys for manhood?

✦

L ucy Komisar says that "Little boys learn the connection between violence and manhood very early in life... Boys play cowboys and Indians with guns and bows and arrows... They are gangsters or soldiers interchangeably ... They are encouraged to ... fight back,' and bloodied noses and black eyes become trophies of their pint-sized virility" (202).

This may help to explain why war films, especially combat films, and westerns are so popular among American boys; they are bred for it. After all, as Molly Merryman writes, the process of proving oneself a man is "... a culturally-prescribed construction in which men are willing to risk danger, dismemberment and death to prove their masculinity" (Creedon 1). And if, at the time, there is no war handy for American males to prove themselves, sports such as football, baseball, hockey or boxing provide another social venue, complete with the opportunity for selfless team effort, the thrill of conquest and the chance for glory as well as physical injury—everything needed to transform a boy into a full-fledged warrior-man in our culture. Pam Creedon argues that anxiety over having no war to provide an opportunity to achieve this manly status causes American boys and men to turn to football, for example, an excellent substitute for armed conquest (13–14).

Sally Jenkins describes football in terms a general would understand: "... bullying the opposition into retreat with mob action" (Creedon 8). There is even a pecking order for comparing sports to war. George Carlin put it this way, in contrasting football with baseball:

> Baseball and football are the two most popular spectator sports in this country. And as such, it seems they ought to be able to tell us something about ourselves and our values... The objectives of the two games are completely different: In football, the object is for the quarterback, also known as the 'field general,' to be on target with an aerial assault, riddling the defense by hitting his receivers with deadly accuracy, in spite of the blitz, even if he has to use the shotgun. With short, bullet passes and long bombs, he marches his troops into enemy territory, balancing his aerial assault with a sustained ground attack that punches holes in the forward wall of the enemy's defensive line.
>
> In baseball, the object is to go home! And be safe! (Carlin 52–53)

So an American boy can prove his readiness for manhood in two principal ways: If there is a war handy, he can become a soldier and fight bravely for his team. In the absence of a war, he can become an athlete and fight bravely for his team. For young men who have witnessed hegemonic masculinity and the subjugation and trivialization of women throughout childhood and adolescence, the continuation of their male-favored status in life is at risk unless they can find a way to "step up to the plate," "take their cuts" and "win one for the Gipper." The alternative, say the mainstream voices of American socialization, is too dreadful to consider: life as, at best, an un-manly male, or at worst, a suspected homosexual.

5   The social construction by which boys become men, then, seems pretty simple, no more sophisticated than Native American rituals involving being hung by their pectorals to prove the endurance of a brave, or counting coup in combat against an enemy of the tribe.

In modern America, the war film, especially the combat film genre, often blurs the distinction between war-making and sports participation, effectively melding these two contemporary constructions of masculinity. One hand washes the other in the sports-war continuum: Sports metaphors inserted into the vocabulary used by soldiers in war prime the combatants to recall the conventional behavior expected of them in their boyhood socialization on the playing fields. They are cued to recall that above all, doing their duty for the team is required, and that they must complete all other requirements necessary to "get the job done." And, after all, man *is* what he does: his *work*. So as we heard in Carlin's recitation of football combat jargon, Hollywood's combat films stress most of the key values leading to success in sports, and, not surprisingly, vice-versa. Here are, excuse the pun, a "dirty dozen" of them:

1. Call the plays right.
2. Come in for the big win: take your turn at bat.
3. Do a good job of work.
4. Appreciate your interference, don't hog all the glory, and sacrifice for the team.
5. "Americans love a winner and will not tolerate a loser."
6. Be bold, never too cautious.
7. To win, don't always face the enemy head-on: be both strong and clever.
8. Females are losers.
9. Know the score.

10. The enemy team is inferior, so learn how to exploit their weaknesses.
11. Don't give up: fight on to victory, and finally,
12. You gotta play hurt.

In an ongoing textual analysis of 67 combat films produced in the United States from the 1940s to the present, I have identified 28, or 41 per cent, that contain one or more sports metaphors that directly refer back to the conduct of warlike activities. Here are some examples.

CALL THE PLAYS RIGHT.

In *Flying Leathernecks* (1951), in Col. Kirby's last advice to "Griff," the officer who will replace him as squadron commander, he states that Griff will do the same thing all commanders do every night, "wondering as you stagger into your bunk, whether you called every shot right today." Later, Griff responds, "I'll try to call the plays right: I had a good coach." The theme of this movie is also important because it portrays the conflict between the macho, "tough guy" approach to becoming the warrior versus the cultured, humanistic man who tries to keep a sense of humanity amid the chaos of war. Along with many post-World War II war films, *Flying Leathernecks* stipulates that a man had to be tough to be a commander—or to be a real soldier, for that matter. John Wayne, as Col. Kirby, is tasked with toughening up his squadron's executive officer Griff, played by Robert Ryan, for the rigors of command (read "manliness"). When Griff's previous commander was wounded and sent stateside, Griff and his men expected him to be promoted to squadron commander. But Kirby was given the command, because in the Marines, Griff was not tough enough. Griff, among many similar characters in post-World War II films, does not come naturally to the tough guy persona that Kirby embodies: he finds it impossible to order men to their death while maintaining a cool isolation from the friendships that develop between comrades in his unit. Likewise, John Agar's Pfc. Conway, a member of Wayne's squad in *Sands of Iwo Jima* (1949), was also too much of a humanist—too sensitive and caring an individual— to be deemed manly enough for war. Like Griff, Conway required the Duke's toughening-up process. But at the end, both Griff and Conway "get with the program," adopt the tough, John Wayne persona, "saddle up," grit their teeth and "lock and load" for victory.

The football metaphor of the quarterback calling the right plays is found 35 years later in *Full Metal Jacket* (1987), when a newly-appointed squad leader, appropriately named "Cowboy," gets as argument from an overly-aggressive Marine nicknamed "Animal Mother." Cowboy orders his squad to pull out, leaving behind two Marines wounded, but probably dead: "Back off, Mother," Cowboy shouts. "I'm calling the plays. I say we're pulling out."

10   Similarly, a submarine captain in *Up Periscope* (1959) is concerned about a tough command decision he made on his last patrol. His judgment may have assured that the boat would not be detected and sunk by Japanese destroyers, but it may have cost a wounded sailor his life. Wrestling with the same humanism vs. macho-ism issue as Griff in *Flying Leathernecks*, the captain asks his executive officer, "If you had been in my shoes and you were calling the signals, how would you have played it?" The honest exec says that frankly he would have done things differently. But, the exec adds, playing things according to the Navy book (read playbook) is why they made him captain.

COME IN FOR THE BIG WIN: TAKE YOUR TURN AT BAT.

In *Full Metal Jacket*, an outlandish, *gung-ho* Marine colonel is outraged by Pvt. Joker's wearing of a peace symbol on his fatigue jacket while his helmet is decorated with the words, "Born to kill." Joker tries to explain this contradiction as "the duality of man, sir, the Jungian thing." But the colonel, who sounds more like a football coach that a battalion commander, is having none of this ambiguity, which he considers wishy-washy: "How about getting with the program?" barks the officer. "Why don't you jump on the team and come on in for the big win... It's a hardball world, son. We've gotta try to keep our heads until the peace craze blows over."

In *American Guerilla in the Philippines* (1950), Ensign Palmer spends two years organizing Filipino and American guerilla actions against the Japanese. An American submarine has just arrived, full of supplies, guns and ammunition. Palmer knows that General MacArthur's return to retake the Philippines is imminent, and it is time to go in for the big win: He contacts his people to spread the word that "The football has arrived, and the game is on as scheduled."

The notion of having to step up to the plate to bat has a twofold meaning in both baseball and war: batting is perhaps the most individualistic act one does in this team sport, yet one's actions can sometimes be strictly for oneself or in others, a pure sacrifice for the team. This will come up again in some of the other sports metaphors.

As in sports, the motion of "momentum," piling success on after success, is significant. The first time up to bat can set the tone for the rest of the game. This is not lost on Gen. Omar Bradley in *Patton* (1970). Bradley and his aide survey the aftermath of the American defeat in the battle for the Kasserine Pass in North Africa. There are dead Americans lying all about, amid destroyed U.S. tanks and other vehicles. "For the American Army to take a licking like that the first time at bat against the Germans . . . " (he shakes his head in disgust). The American Army has struck out.

In *The Enemy Below* (1957), an American destroyer captain is still recovering from his last mission, but must step up to the plate again (play hurt) to command his ship in a desperate game of cat and mouse with an enemy submarine. The ship's doctor describes this dilemma to the ship's executive officer: "He's weak as a kitten. A man that gets his ship torpedoed and spends 25 days on a raft in the North Atlantic oughtn't have to hit the ball again with only a few weeks in the hospital."

DO A GOOD JOB OF WORK.

There is an old adage about the difference between men and women in terms of their self-image: "A woman is what she looks like, and a man is what he does." Fortunately for women, new personal options have been added to the social construction of female identity that allow them additional, more substantial, ways to establish themselves. But for men, nothing much seems to have changed since the age of the Neanderthals: once boys become established as men, securing a job and succeeding at it defines their potency. Both in sports and in war, there is a job of work to be done: As Captain Collins explains in *The Sand Pebbles* (1966), a warrior's job of work is ". . . the give and take of death." Men are uneasy unless they feel confident in their jobs. Men may not like it, but in war, Captain Collins' definition becomes their job description, and most men are task-oriented. Sports metaphors clarify the task at hand.

Mixing a number of messages about their jobs in one statement, the Admiral in *They Were Expendable* (1945) tries to explain to Cmdr. Brickley why he cannot permit the eager skipper the chance to prove the effectiveness of his P.T. boats in action against a task force that is headed their way. The Admiral explains it this way: "Listen, son: you and I are professionals. If the manager says, 'sacrifice,' we lay down a bunt and let somebody else hit the home runs...Our job is to lay down that sacrifice (fighting a delaying action against the Japanese in the Philippines). That's what we're trained for, and that's what we'll do."

In *Full Metal Jacket*, we observe that the idea of doing a job of work even has a shorthand: The sergeant assigns his men a risky plan of attack for the difficult objective facing them, and then shouts, "Let's go: Let's get it [implying that "it" is their job of work] done." However, most GIs excel in griping, and the sergeant in *Battleground* (1949) often allows his men the opportunity to complain about the job *en masse*. After explaining to the men that they must once again risk their lives to achieve an ambiguous objective in a strange, unknown location, he barks, "It's a stinkin' situation, right?" And the men, in unison, shout, "Right!" Tension is relieved, and the men proceed to do their job of work.

APPRECIATE YOUR INTERFERENCE, DON'T HOG ALL THE GLORY, AND SACRIFICE FOR THE TEAM.

In these films, one of the most important connections made between combat and sports is the importance of teamwork, subordination of personal ambition and sacrifice for the good of the team. The word "teamwork" is mentioned in some context in every film in this study.

20   Among the American Volunteer Group pilots in *Flying Tigers* (1942) is Woody, a lone wolf character who never seems to understand the concept of teamwork. After listening to Woody brag about his latest exploit in shooting down a Japanese plane, another pilot, Blackie, finally has enough: "How does it feel to be a one-man team?" Blackie asks. "You aren't the first ball carrier that didn't appreciate his interference." But sacrifice for the sake of the team is not in Woody's playbook. Since AVG pilots receive cash bonuses for each Japanese plane they shoot down, Woody had become greedy. Blackie continues, explaining, "Twice I've been on the trail of the Nakajima (Japanese aircraft) when you cut in for the kill—and the credit." Later in the film, Woody finally learns—the hard way—the lesson repeated in so many war films—subordinate your own needs and desires for the good of the team, or dire consequences occur. Two other AVG pilots are arguing about who should fly a mission as the skipper's (John Wayne's)

wingman in place of Woody, who has gone AWOL with a pretty nurse. Hap explains to Alabama that he has considerable experience as Wayne's wingman, and that he works as an offensive lineman to block for his skipper: "I know every one of his quirks, every one of his moves. We're a team, don't you understand? It's like he was the bait carrier and I was his interference." Hap flies the mission but is killed. Afterwards, Woody, disgraced and repentant, redeems himself by flying a suicide mission—for the team.

Likewise, in *They Were Expendable*, a feisty young lieutenant, a P.T. boat commander named Rusty, decides he wants to transfer out. Rusty wants to make a name for himself in the Navy on board a destroyer, so he is writing a letter to request a transfer. But Rusty's boss, Cmdr. Brickley, asks, "What are you aiming at, building a reputation or playing for the team?" That night, the men hear an announcement that Pearl Harbor has been bombed. Hearing this, Rusty crumples up the letter and, for the rest of the picture, unselfishly devotes himself to his work in the P.T. squadron.

And in *A Wing and a Prayer* (1944), a squadron commander chastises a pilot who becomes jealous of another pilot's Navy Cross: ". . . Remember," the commander says, "you're part of a team, and you'll play as the team plays."

So it becomes the job of every team member to subjugate personal wishes and desires to the final strategic goal. Typical of this ethic is a scene in *Task Force* (1949). Admiral Richard and Commander Scott, his air operations officer, are sweating it out, waiting for word on how their aircrews are faring in the battle of Midway. Scott is frustrated and hates having to stay behind and do his supervisory job on the aircraft carrier. He wishes he were flying this crucial mission, leading his young pilots on an attack against Japanese aircraft carriers. The admiral reminds Scott, "You think things would be different if you were up there? Nobody's the whole team, Scotty. It takes the whole Navy to make up a team. I'm bettin' on the boys that are carrying the ball."

In *Run Silent, Run Deep*, (1958), after a sub captain dies on a mission, his replacement, who lost his own sub a year earlier, takes command. But the new captain's executive officer thought that *he* was in line for the command. The exec was told that because of his experience, he is to play "backstop" to the skipper for this mission. Eventually, as in most of these kinds of films, the exec overcomes his personal disappointment and selfish attitude.

When the captain is injured, the exec fulfills his backstop role and completes the mission.

25   In the address to his troops in the beginning of *Patton*, the general touches on a number of subjects, including the importance of teamwork: "Now an army is a team," Patton says. "It lives, eats, sleeps, fights as a team. This individuality stuff is a bunch of crap. The bilious bastards who wrote that stuff about individuality for the *Saturday Evening Post* don't know anything more about real battle than they do about fornicating."

Object lessons in avoiding individuality abound in many of these films. In *Eagle Squadron* (1942), a new pilot named Coe dies because he acts independently and does not follow squadron procedure. Pilot Brewer mourns his friend's loss, but is told that Coe might not have been killed if he had followed procedure and not gone off as a lone wolf to strafe a target of opportunity. There, he was set upon by three Messerschmitts and was shot down. Brewer learns that teamwork is the key to success in the Battle of Britain.

In *The Purple Heart* (1944), captured Doolittle raiders vote to include a Chinese man who gave them aid as an honorary member of their bomber crew. Team membership—"making the team"—is one indicator of athletic success. After all, one cannot excel in sports if he is cut from the squad. So "making the team" is an ultimate indicator of manly acceptance. The captain announces, "I'd have him on my team any time."

However, not everyone wants to be on the team, and, in these films, such a man requires "counseling." In *Air Force* (1943), the captain of the B-17 bomber, the *Mary Ann*, has a crewman named Winocki who presents such a problem. Because Winocki washed out of flight school and was re-assigned to the less glamorous job of machine gunner, he says that he plans to quit the Army Air Corps in a few weeks. In the meantime, he displays a considerable amount of bad attitude. But the captain makes it clear to Winocki that sports teamwork is expected on the *Mary Ann*, regardless of the crewman's feelings: "You've played football, Winocki. You know how one man can gum up the whole works? You've got to play ball with us and play the game or I'll have to get rid of you." This is not exactly a Knute Rockne oration, but the point has been made: play ball with the rest of us or you are off the team.

After the attack on Pearl Harbor, Winocki is a changed man. He rededicates himself to his job, but still has bouts of non-team-sanctioned individualism. On one occasion, the *Mary Ann* must set down on a remote landing strip. Japanese begin firing on the aircraft, and the captain orders everyone back inside the plane, and plans to take off. But Winocki ignores the order and starts to run into the jungle, shooting angrily—and wildly—at the Japanese, hidden in the jungle. The crew chief forcibly restrains Winocki, knocking him unconscious and carrying him to the ship. Once airborne and Winocki is awake, the crew chief, who always wears a Cincinnati Reds baseball cap, explains his actions in strictly baseball terms: "They'd have cut you down before you got to first base." Incidentally, *Air Force* and *Patton* contained more individual sports metaphors than any other films in this study.

"AMERICANS LOVE A WINNER AND WILL NOT TOLERATE A LOSER."

This key sports value is a direct quote from that famous open-   30
ing speech in front of the huge American flag in *Patton* and speaks directly to the socialization of American boys in sports, the importance of successful competition and the need to win.

> When you were kids, you all admired the champion marble shooter, the fastest runner, the big league ballplayers, the toughest boxer. Americans love a winner, and will not tolerate a loser. Americans play to win all the time. I wouldn't give a hoot in hell for a man who lost and laughed. That's why Americans have never lost, and will never lose a war, because the very thought of losing is hateful to Americans.

If one agrees that films are cultural artifacts, and that popular feature films can be said to mirror contemporary societal mores and culture, consider the preceding words in *Patton*, which was released in 1970, written by screenwriter Francis Ford Coppola at the height of the killing and American protests over the unwinnable war in Vietnam.

As previously mentioned, in *Sands of Iwo Jima*, Sgt. Stryker's job is to turn his squad of losers into winners. But in these films, there seems to always be one soldier in a squad who poses a particularly thorny problem. One of Stryker's men is particularly clumsy and uncoordinated on the bayonet course. The platoon leader sarcastically asks the private what he thinks he is doing: "Running the bayonet course, sir," he replies. "Not in this league you're not," the lieutenant quips. In this officer's eyes, the

Marines are the big leagues, and the soldier's work on the bayonet course is definitely bush-league. Later, after other unsuccessful attempts to turn this Marine into a winner, Stryker finds a way, using music, to teach the Marine some rhythm and improve his performance with the bayonet.

Boxing is a game of punches, but also counterpunches. And in the sports metaphor-rich *Air Force*, screenwriter Dudley Nichols manages to get in a few jabs: The crew of the *Mary Ann* talk with the commander of Hickam Field in Hawaii, just after the Japanese attack. Commenting on the initial Japanese success, the commander makes it clear that the next time the result will be different: "They took the first round, but there'll be others," he says resolutely.

BE BOLD, NEVER TOO CAUTIOUS.

Again in *Patton*, the importance—at least to the general—in moving boldly and decisively is brought home to viewers in the contrast between the studied caution of Gens. Lucien Truscott and Omar Bradley vs. the impulsiveness of Patton. Truscott warns his commander that he needs an extra day to prepare for the amphibious "end run" Patton requires in his quest in Sicily to take the city of Messina ahead of Field Marshall Montgomery. "You're too old an athlete to think that you can postpone a match that's already been scheduled," Patton says to Truscott. Responding, Truscott says, "You're an old athlete yourself, sir: you know matches sometimes are postponed." Gen. Bradley then chimes in, saying, "George, if Lucien's right and we can't back him up by land, our end run could be a disaster." Later in the argument, Patton, irritated, gets formal with Truscott: "General," Patton says, "if your conscience will not permit you to conduct this operation, I'll relieve you and find somebody who can." Truscott replies, equally formal, "General, it's your privilege to relieve me any time you want to." Backing away from that kind of confrontation, Patton concludes this argument by saying, "Well, this match will not be postponed."

35   In the comedy-drama *Kelly's Heroes* (1970), ironically released the same year as *Patton*, an equally impulsive, Patton-like general is listening in at his headquarters to radio traffic in what he assumes to be a bold incursion across German lines by some units under his command. Actually, there is an incursion in progress, but it is Kelly's, undertaken for the purpose of stealing millions in German gold bullion from a bank behind German lines. The general leans over the radio set as his orderly arrives with coffee on a tray. The general, as enthusiastic as a football fan, dismisses the

orderly saying, "Get the hell outta here, Barnes! We've got the game on!" Later, the general hears Bellamy, a sergeant in the engineers, radioing Kelly that they cannot bridge a river because the bed is too soft. "So what do we do?" Bellamy asks. The general, by this time frothing at the mouth like a true football fanatic and hoping his team will not meekly fall back, shouts, "Go, team, go!"

TO WIN, DON'T ALWAYS FACE THE ENEMY HEAD-ON: BE BOTH STRONG AND CLEVER.

Success in sports is not always about brute strength: Manliness not only requires an encyclopedic knowledge of sports rules, but also sports strategies and tactics. Winning in a sport such as football does not always mean a frontal attack, regardless of what the general in *Kelly's Heroes* thinks. And there are lessons in the sports metaphors found in combat films to make this point. As he does often in *Patton*, the general explains to his chief of staff that understanding the history of warfare is essential to success in the present. To solve the post-D-Day problems the allies are experiencing in French hedgerow country, the American command should simply look to the past—but in sports terms. He explains, "What they should do now is pivot the way von Schlieffen planned it in the First World War. Then we might get a chance to do some real broken field running." Shortly after this scene, Gen. Bradley explains "Operation Cobra" to Patton, a plan similar to von Schlieffen's, which Bradley calls "a sweeping end run," which he has assigned to Patton's Third Army.

In *Thirty Seconds Over Tokyo* (1944), reciprocity in boxing is compared to the United States' bold strike on the Japanese mainland. Rather than attempt an open attack when the U.S. was still reeling from its losses in Pearl Harbor, another, more clever, approach is used. In the film, Lt. Col. Doolittle refers to this daring raid as "Uncle Sam's first counterpunch of the war."

FEMALES ARE LOSERS.

To men, winning is everything, and in the socialization of American boys, the way women and girls would behave or react is often cast as the undesirable, lesser alternative to acting in a manly way. Consider what fathers tell their sons: "Don't cry: only girls cry." Or, when boys are not measuring up to the manly goals set for them, another male might sarcastically classify them as "girls" or "ladies." When a boy plays golf with his dad, he is likely to hear someone in the group whose putt stops short of the hole referred to as an "Alice," a reference to the weakling sister in James Fenimore Cooper's *Last of the Mohicans*. In *The D.I.* (1957), a company commander thinks that a drill instructor is pampering a recruit. He tells the D.I. to toughen up the recruit himself or ". . . I'll trim the lace off his panties." Komisar writes:

> Boys are encouraged to rough-house; girls are taught to be gentle ("ladylike"). Boys are expected to get into fights, but admonished not to hit girls. . . Men are aggressive as they "take" or "make" women, showing their potency ("power") in their conquest. Women, on the other hand, "submit" and "surrender," allowing themselves to be "violated" or "possessed." (203)

Until quite recently, in sports, women were considered to be inferior weaklings, due to the strength differential. It is a little-remembered fact that in the 1950s, there was a rule in schoolgirl basketball that prevented them from dribbling the ball all the way down the court, since it was assumed that females were too weak to stand the strain of a run all the way down the court. Girls were limited to dribbling three steps before having to stop and pass the ball.

40   In the testosterone-laden *Top Gun* (1986), the entire training setup at the Top Gun school for advanced aerial combat training is analogous to a men's athletic competition: Points are earned for victories over opponents in mock aerial dog fights. Scoring is announced with the regularity of a sports stadium P.A. Early in the competition, while examining the prize, the Top Gun trophy, Slider, a flyer/competitor, quips, "The second place trophy is down the hall, in the ladies' room."

In *A Guy Named Joe* (1943), Pete, the ghost of a World War II bomber pilot killed in action, becomes guardian angel to another pilot, Ted, helping him learn to fly and coaching him (although Pete cannot be heard or seen). Eventually, the young pilot becomes an ace. Pete's former girlfriend, Dorinda, also a pilot, is not allowed into combat, despite her expert flying ability. She is allowed only to shuttle planes back and forth for the men. As the screenplay would have it, Dorinda falls in love with Ted. She overhears plans for Ted to fly what may be a suicide mission to bomb a Japanese emplacement. Out of love for Ted, Dorinda steals his plane and flies the mission herself. Of course, this is 1943, so the ghostly Pete flies along as Dorinda's coach, assisting her in accomplishing the mission.

To bolster his male ego, a male must feel superior to some-one. The female provides this "inferior" comparison. That is one of the reasons so many American men fought so hard against per-mitting women to vote. Let suffragette Alice Duer Miller's 1915 re-joinder to male arguments against the vote for women—complete with views on men and sports and war—complete this section:

Why We Oppose Votes for Men

1. Because man's place is in the army.
2. Because no really manly man wants to settle any question otherwise than fighting about it.
3. Because if men should adopt peaceable methods, women will no longer look up to them.
4. Because men will lose their charm if they step out of their natural sphere and interest themselves in other matters than feats of arms, uniforms and drums.
5. Because men are too emotional to vote. Their conduct at base-ball games and political conventions shows this, while their innate tendency to appeal to force renders them particularly unfit for the task of government. (David and Brannon 215)

KNOW THE SCORE.

This precept is voiced in many ways in these films, but it usually adds up to the importance of understanding what is going on, what is at stake in war. Again, to be successful in sports or war, real men "know the score," know what is happening and what must be done at all times. In *Bombardier!* (1943), knowing the score for a tough bombing raid for which they have been training for months, is a simple statement of fact: training is over, and it is time to commence the football game. So right before the big raid, the group commander and his flyers gather in a football-like hud-dle, place their right hands on top of his in the middle of the hud-dle, and listen to the commander/quarterback's words: "Of course, you've all played football: This is the kickoff." Of course, the commander/quarterback was Pat O'Brien, who played the fa-mous football coach in *Knute Rockne, All American* (1940).

In these combat films, clever players can use American sports terms to confuse the enemy. In *American Guerilla in the Philip-pines*, the Japanese have been listening to American radio trans-missions. So Ensign Palmer uses football and baseball terms in a coded report on enemy shipping: "Two large wolves on the

20 yard line, going down center field." Likewise, in the Vietnam War film, *Bat-21* (1988), Air Force officers use golf terms for map references to locate a downed flyer, because they were sure that the Viet Cong did not comprehend the game.

45   Sports terms in combat films are not limited to those tactical words used during a game, but are also utilized to describe war as a kind of grand spectator sport. Manliness, it seems, extends beyond a player's active role in the game to the role of fan (short for fanatic, which best describes some men's allegiance to the games of their youth). As mentioned before, the general in *Kelly's Heroes* listened to "the game" on his radio, and acts every bit as fanatic as any tailgate party participant. In *A Walk in the Sun* (1945), one soldier gripes about only being able to hear the fighting from the gully in which he and a sergeant are hiding. "You get a grandstand seat, but we can't see nothing." In *One Minute to Zero* (1952), from high ground, American soldiers watch as U.S. planes bomb a column of enemy tanks. "This time we got box seats," one officer says.

Sometimes, "knowing the score" simply means, in 1940s slang, to "get wise" to the situation. In *They Were Expendable*, a sportsman to the end, a dying crewman asks, "What's the score?" It is somewhat unclear for a moment whether he is asking his shipmates how well the squadron did on their mission (incredibly, two P.T. boats sank *both* a destroyer and a large cruiser in torpedo attacks), or whether he was asking if his wounds were mortal. But his honest shipmate's answer is, "Ninth inning, kid." The crewman turns his head and dies.

THE ENEMY TEAM IS INFERIOR, SO LEARN HOW TO EXPLOIT THEIR WEAKNESS.

This characteristic, in which the enemy, the Indians (vs. the cavalry), the villains (vs. James Bond), etc., are incapable of the manly skills of shooting straight or waging an intelligent battle, is found in many kinds of action/adventure films. Virtually all combat films made during World War II made it clear to U.S. audiences that the enemy was inferior to Americans in all aspects of war-making, and, by inference, were not as manly as the Yanks.

In *A Walk in the Sun*, a soldier makes a sportscaster's appraisal of the enemy's accuracy after an artillery shell misses the platoon's landing craft: "Ball one, too high...At Messina they pitched a few strikes. But here, no control, no control."

In *God Is My Co-pilot* (1945), Gen. Chenneault describes the imminent Japanese air strike in boxing terms: "The old one-two. Lead with six [planes] from the east and cross with 12 from the west." Of course, because the enemy never changed their playbook, the Flying Tigers were able to shoot down most of the Japanese planes.

DON'T GIVE UP: FIGHT ON TO VICTORY.

Sports jargon is used regularly to remind soldiers in these films to stay the course, that the manly course is not to be dissuaded by discouraging events. In *Bombardier!* when the bomb school commandant asks a cadet how his studies are going, the cadet says that it is tough, but he will be all right. The commandant replies, "That's right: keep punching." As previously mentioned, in *Air Force*, the gunner Winocki had a bad attitude, which he discusses with a young, inexperienced crewman. The gunner advises the youngster not to consider making the Army Air Corps his career. The crew chief hears this, and tells the youngster not to listen, and to "Stay in the box, son, and keep on pitching." Later in the film, the captain of the bomber is told that unless their disabled B-17 can get off the ground in a few hours, it must be destroyed, to avoid it falling into the hands of the enemy. "Can you get that engine [that you are working on] running right?" the captain asks. The enthusiastic crew chief boasts, "We'll have her hitting home runs in 90 minutes flat!" Likewise, in this film, the Marine air commander at Midway Island asks the crew of the *Mary Ann* that if they see his old boss, General MacArthur, to "Tell him that we'll be in there pitching until they strike us out." The oxymoronic metaphor here is because the Marines on Midway thought that it was only a matter of time before they would be overrun by the Japanese.

One general's pep talk to his men, pinned down on Omaha Beach on D-Day in *The Longest Day* (1962), is simple and a direct assessment of the situation, and an exhortation to do their manly jobs: "I don't have to tell you men the score, you all know it: Only two kinds of men are going to *stay* on this beach, those who're already dead and those who're gonna die. Now get off your butts!"

YOU GOTTA PLAY HURT.

First of all, it should be understood that in sports talk, playing hurt is not exclusively about toughing out an injury. As Dan Jenkins writes, "*You Gotta Play Hurt* takes its title from an old saying among athletes. Sportswriters use it to sum up problems in their

50

daily lives. Mostly, they use it as they stare at their writing machines, on deadline, hung over."

But in most references in war films, it refers to the manly art of ignoring pain and injury to carry on for the team. Most readers are aware of John Wayne's ability to withstand pain and punishment in his war films. In *The Longest Day*, Wayne's character, Lt. Col. Benjamin Vandervoort, suffers a compound leg fracture in a parachute jump, but this undaunted alpha male still marches along using a rifle as a crutch.

This is not pure military sacrifice: it is the ethic of the athlete, who, although injured, will continue on for the sake of victory. In *The Purple Heart*, this "play hurt" ethic is also lionized. P.O.W. Sgt. Skvoznik is led away from his cell by the Japanese, almost certainly to be tortured. The rest of the crew are not worried that Skvoznik will talk, because, as one flyer points out, the sergeant is a former college football star, and once "played the best game of his career with three broken ribs."

CONCLUSION

55   Gen. Patton is credited with saying that the problem with wars is that they are not always there when you need them. Between armed conflicts, and oftentimes coinciding with America's smaller, less popular brushfire wars, American males participate in and cheer fanatically for sporting events. These events become alternative rites of passage that are close analogs to wars for a male population that needs war to provide them with opportunities to perform manly acts. To fit into male society, young, impressionable boys are taught to adopt this same fanaticism. Komisar characterizes this as "the masculine mystique":

> The masculine mystique is based on toughness and domination, qualities that once may have been necessary in a time when men felled trees and slew wild animals. Now they are archaic and destructive values that have no legitimate place in our world, but continue to exist as idealized standards for some lofty state of "masculinity." The mystique has characterized many nations, but it is particularly dangerous in contemporary America because of our distinctively high levels of internal violence, our "Bonnie and Clyde" tendencies toward its glorification, our enormous capacities for mechanized warfare, and our virtual obsession with being Number One. (202)

So to become a successful sports hero-warrior, and therefore measure up as a man, there is a danger. In becoming a disciplined, self-controlled *übermensch* who keeps his feelings to himself and plays hurt, never cries out and abhors any demonstration of weakness, much of the rest that life has to offer may be missed. Perhaps there is virtue in compromise, perhaps even to the point of feeling OK about a fight well-fought, but lost, effort. Perhaps there is room for other than a complete and devastating victory in life and in relationships.

But as shown earlier, an imperative in sports in America, and equally significant in its analog, war, is the primacy of *winning*. Shatan says, "In the United States, winning is the central theme in the making of a boy's self-image. Boys learn early that 'any boy can win.'" Does not every stadium loudspeaker system have on permanent disc storage the rock group Queen's ballad, "We Are the Champions"?

Corporations teach their employees to revere Hall of Fame Green Bay Packer coach Vince Lombardi's motto, "Winning isn't everything. It's the only thing." But the male fixation with winning has its dangers: Fear of showing weakness by backing down in a schoolyard fight can result in at worst a bloody nose: But Presidents Johnson and Nixon's refusal to back down from the debacle of Vietnam—and be branded a loser—killed 57,000 American soldiers. Consider Joan Mellen's statement concerning film heroes she describes as "indomitable males":

> . . . the stereotype of the self-controlled, invulnerable, stoical hero who justifies the image of unfeeling masculinity as a means of winning in a world that pounces on any sign of weakness . . . Male heroes pontificate platitudes such as that invoked by an elderly John Wayne in *The Shootist:* "I won't be wronged, I won't be insulted, I won't be laid a hand on. I don't do these things to others, and I require the same of them."

Winning has become much too important in our culture. In *Heartbreak Ridge* (1986), Clint Eastwood's character, Marine Gunnery Sergeant Highway, characterized his entire career as if it was a won-lost statistic on the sports page: When the film ended, he was satisfied, and finally ready to retire, now that his war record (read sports won-lost record) was evened out at "1-1-1": one win (Grenada), one loss (Vietnam) and one tie (Korea).

Perhaps this obsession with winning is the most serious and most potentially dangerous of all the absurd notions that American

60

war films and sports fixations inflict upon the psyches of young boys. Unfortunately, this "John Wayne" attitude is the most out-moded and the least helpful value in a contemporary world in which the peoples of all nations must learn to adapt, change and become more tolerant of diversity. If century-old governments and political philosophies can give way, if all the world is changing and adapting, perhaps the macho, uncommunicative, unemotional, pseudo-athletic misogynists America seems intent on turning out should also consider some fundamental alterations. After all, life is much more than a game.

Works Cited

Carlin, George. *Braindroppings*. New York: Hyperion, 1997.
Cooper, James F. *The Last of the Mohicans*. New York: C. Scribner's Sons, 1919.
Creedon, Pam. "The Super Bowl and War: Theater for the Masculine Myth in Democracy." A paper presented to the Sports Interest Division, International Association of Mass Communication Research, Port Alegre, Brazil. 2004. 1, 8.
Jenkins, Dan. *You Gotta Play Hurt*. New York: Simon and Schuster, 1991. 1.
Komisar, Lucy. "Violence and the Masculine Mistique." D.S. David and R. Brannon eds. *The Forty-Nine Percent Majority: The Male Sex Role*. Boston: Addison-Wesley, 1976. 202, 203.
Mellen, Joan. *Big Bad Wolves: Masculinity and the American Film*. New York: Pantheon, 1977. 5.
Miller, Alice D. "Why We Oppose Votes for Men." D.S. David and R. Brannon eds. *The Forty-Nine Percent Majority: The Male Sex Role*. Boston: Addison-Wesley, 1915. 215.
Shatan, C. "Happiness is a Warm Gun: Militarized Mourning and Ceremonial Vengeance." *Vietnam Generation* 1(1989): 127–151.

Filmography

1943	*Air Force:* Director: Howard Hawks
1950	*American Guerilla in the Philippines:* Director: Fritz Lang
1988	*Bat-21:* Director: Peter Markle
1949	*Battleground:* Director: William Wellman
1943	*Bombardier!:* Director: Richard Wallace
1957	*The D.I.:* Director: Jack Webb
1942	*Eagle Squadron:* Director: Arthur Lubin

1957   *The Enemy Below:* Director: Dick Powell
1951   *Flying Leathernecks:* Director: Nicholas Ray
1942   *Flying Tigers:* Director: David Miller
1987   *Full Metal Jacket:* Director: Stanley Kubrick
1945   *God is My Co-pilot:* Director: Robert Florey
1943   *A Guy Named Joe:* Director: Victor Fleming
1986   *Heartbreak Ridge:*Director: Clint Eastwood
1970   *Kelly's Heroes:* Director: Brian Hutton
1940   *Knute Rockne, All-American:* Director: Lloyd Bacon
1962   *The Longest Day:* Director: Ken Annakin (Brtish exteriors);
        Andrew Marton (American exteriors); Bernhard Wicki
        (German scenes); Darryl F. Zanuck (uncredited)
1952   *One Minute to Zero:* Director: Tay Garnett
1970   *Patton:* Director: Franklin Schaffner
1944   *The Purple Heart:* Director: Lewis Milestone
1958   *Run Silent, Run Deep:* Director: Robert Wise
1966   *The Sand Pebbles:* Director: Robert Wise
1949   *Sands of Iwo Jima:* Director: Allan Dwan
1949   *Task Force:* Director: Delmex Daves
1945   *They Were Expendable:* Director: John Ford
1944   *Thirty Seconds Over Tokyo:* Director: Mervyn LeRoy
1986   *Top Gun:* Director: Tony Scott
1959   *Up Periscope:* Director: Gordon Douglas
1945   *A Walk in the Sun:* Director: Lewis Milestone
1944   *A Wing and a Prayer:* Director: Paul Wendkos

Questions for Discussion and Writing

1. In your own words, what is Donald's key argument?
2. Throughout the essay, Donald includes a comprehensive list of films as evidence to support his main idea. Which of the films are you familiar with, if any? Does that add to your understanding? Does unfamiliarity with films place readers at a disadvantage? Explain why or why not.
3. Evaluate Donald's "dirty dozen" list in paragraph 6. Which of the key values do you agree with most?
4. Donald writes, "So an American boy can prove his readiness for manhood in two principal ways: If there is a war handy, he can become a soldier and fight bravely for his team. In the absence of a war, he can become an athlete and fight bravely for his team" (paragraph 4). Do you agree with this statement? Write an essay exploring the ways in which boys in your community are trained to "prove [their] readiness for manhood." You may want to refer to your pre-reading responses.

5. Select any television show (*The Apprentice,* for example) and write a short essay entitled "Sports Metaphors in _____." View one episode of the show and use Ralph Donald's "dirty dozen" list from paragraph 6 to write an analysis illustrating whether or not his sports metaphors are relevant to the show. In your essay, credit Ralph Donald's ideas and include a "Works Cited" page.

Why Don't We Like the Human Body?

BARBARA EHRENREICH

Award-winning essayist, columnist, and writer, Barbara Ehrenreich is well known for her weekly columns in Time *and the* Guardian. *She has published numerous articles in periodicals such as* Esquire, The Nation, Vogue, New York Times Magazine; *she is a contributing editor for* Mother Jones *and* Ms. *magazine. Ehrenreich has written seventeen nonfiction books (several of which she co-authored), including* Global Woman: Nannies, Maids, and Sex Works in the New Economy *(2003);* Nickel and Dimed: On (Not) Getting by in America; Blood Rites: Origins and History of the Passions of War *(1997);* The Snarling Citizen: Essays *(1995), of which the following is anthologized. The essay originally appeared in 1991 in* Time *magazine.*

Pre-Reading

In your opinion, do you think that most of the people you know are satisfied with their bodies? Explain why you think they either have or do not have a positive body image. Has anybody you know ever taken steps to alter their bodies (for example, plastic surgery, diets, exercise program, hair straightening, extensions, replacement, etc.)? What was the result?

———————— ✦ ————————

There's something wrong when a seven-dollar movie in the mall can leave you with posttraumatic stress syndrome. In the old days, killers merely stalked and slashed and strangled. Today they flay their victims and stash the rotting, skinless corpses. Or they

eat them filleted, with a glass of wine, when there's time to cook—
or live, with the skin still on, when there's only time for a snack.
It's not even the body count that matters anymore. What counts is
the number of ways to trash the body: decapitation, dismemberment, impalings, and (ranging into the realm of printed word) eye
gougings, power drillings, and the application of hungry rodents
to some poor victim's innards.

All right, terrible things do happen. Real life is filled with
serial killers, mass murderers, and sickos of all degrees. Much
of the twentieth century, it could be argued, has been devoted
to the ingenious production and disposal of human corpses.
But the scary thing is not that eye gougings and vivisections
and meals of human flesh may, occasionally, happen. The scary
thing, the thing that ought to make the heart pound and the
skin go cold and tingly, is that somehow we find this fun to
watch.

There's no shortage of theories to explain our addiction to violence and horror. In what might be called the testosterone theory, a congenital error in the wiring of the male brain leads to a
confusion between violence and sex. Men get off on hideous
mayhem, and women supposedly cover their eyes. Then there's
the raging puritan theory, which is based on the statistical fact
that those who get slashed or eaten in the movies are usually
guilty of a little fooling around themselves. It's only a tingle of
rectitude we feel, according to this, when the bad girl finally gets
hers. There's even an invidious comparison theory: we enjoy seeing other people get sautéed or chain-sawed because at least it's
not happening to *us*.

The truth could be so much simpler that it's staring us in the
face. There has always been a market for scary stories and vicari-
ous acts of violence. But true horror can be bloodless, as in Henry
James's matchless tale *The Turn of the Screw*, and even reckless violence, as in the old-time western, need not debauch the human
form. No, if offerings like *American Psycho* and *The Silence of the
Lambs* have anything to tell us about ourselves, it must be that, at
this particular historical moment, we have come to hate the human body.

Think about it. Only a couple of decades ago, we could con-   5
ceive of better uses for the body than as a source of meat or
leather. Sex, for example. Sex was once considered a valid source
of thrills even if both parties were alive and remained so throughout the act. Therapists urged us to "get in touch with our bodies";
feminists celebrated "our bodies, ourselves." Minimally, the body

was a portable personal habitat that could be shared with special loved ones. Maximally, it was a powerhouse offering multiple orgasms and glowing mind-body epiphanies. Skin was something to massage or gently stroke.

Then, for good reasons and bad, we lost sex. It turned out to spread deadly viruses. It offended the born-again puritans. It led to messy entanglements that interfered with networking and power lunching. Since there was no way to undress for success, we switched in the mid-1980s to food. When we weren't eating, we were watching food-porn starring Julia Child or working off calories on the StairMaster. The body wasn't perfect, but it could, with effort and willpower, be turned into a lean, mean eating machine.

And then we lost food. First they took the red meat, the white bread, and the Chocolate Decadence desserts. Then they came for the pink meat, the cheese, the butter, the tropical oils, and, of course, the whipped cream. Finally they wanted all protein abolished, all fat and uncomplex carbohydrates, leaving us with broccoli and Metamucil as the only official food groups. Everything else, as we now know, is transformed by our treacherous bodies into insidious, slow-acting toxins.

So no wonder we enjoy seeing the human body being shredded, quartered, flayed, filleted, and dissolved in vats of acid. It let us down. No wonder we love heroes and megavillains like Robocop and the Terminator, in whom all soft, unreliable tissue has been replaced by metal alloys. Or that we like reading (even in articles that are, of course, deeply critical of the violence they manage to summarize) about diabolical new uses for human flesh. It's been, let's face it, a big disappointment. Might as well feed it to the rats or to any cannibalistically inclined killer still reckless enough to indulge in red meat.

But it's time for a truce with the soft and wayward flesh. Maybe violent imagery feeds the obsessions of real-life sickos. Or maybe, as some argue, it drains their sickness off into harmless fantasy. But surely it cheapens our sense of ourselves to think that others, even fictional others, could see us as little more than meat. And it's hard to believe that all this carnage doesn't dull our response to the global wastage of human flesh in famine, flood, and war.

10 We could start by admitting that our 1970s-era expectations were absurdly high. The body is not a reliable source of ecstasy or transcendent insight. For most of our lives, it's a shambling, juryrigged affair, filled with innate tensions, contradictions, broken springs. Hollywood could help by promoting better uses for the

body, like real sex, by which I mean sex between people who are often wrinkled and overweight and sometimes even fond of each other. The health meanies could relax and acknowledge that one of the most marvelous functions of the body is, in fact, to absorb small doses of whipped cream and other illicit substances. Then maybe we could start making friends with our bodies again. They need nurturance and care, but, like any friend, they should be good for a romp now and then, by which I mean something involving dancing or petting, as opposed to dicing and flaying. But even "friends" is another weird and alienated image. The truth, which we have almost forgotten, is that Bodies "Я" Us.

Questions for Discussion and Writing

1. How does Ehrenreich answer her question "Why Don't We Like the Human Body?"
2. In what context are food and sex mentioned? Explain whether or not you believe the analogy is effective.
3. What effect did her list of "the number of ways to trash the body" have on you as a reader (paragraph 1)? What effect do you think she was trying to achieve?
4. Do you agree with her assumption "surely it [violent imagery] cheapens our sense of ourselves" (paragraph 9). Are there any ways that violent imagery can have a positive effect? Write an essay agreeing, disagreeing, or modifying her claim.
5. Using Ehrenreich as a model, write an essay of similar length entitled "Why We Like the Human Body." In your essay, use contemporary examples from entertainment (television, film, music, etc.) to illustrate your point.

Questions for Making Connections

1. When you look around your daily life, what expectations of masculinity and femininity do you witness? In what ways do expectations of masculinity and femininity differ? How do your observations (at home, in school, at work) compare with the information presented by any two authors in this chapter?
2. Imagine that the researchers who conducted "The Real Truth About Beauty: A Global Report" have been asked to help Victoria's Secret create a new advertising campaign. What recommendations do you believe researchers would suggest to Victoria's Secret? In your essay,

utilize evidence from Dove and Smith to support your specific suggestions about product recommendations, marketing campaigns, and choice of models.

3. Donald analyzes masculinity in American combat films. Conduct your own analysis of masculinity in another genre (for example, men's magazines, music videos, etc.). Write an essay comparing your findings to Donald's analysis. Does your research support, refute, or modify his claims?

4. Donald writes, "Hollywood's combat films stress most of the key values leading to success in sports" (paragraph 6). Select three out of the twelve values on the list (for example, 1. Call the plays right, 9. Know the score, and 11. Don't give up: fight on to victory), and write a focused essay illustrating how your selections apply to femininity. Use at least one film in your analysis.

5. Ehrenreich writes, "Then maybe we could start making friends with our bodies again" (paragraph 11). What assumption does Ehrenreich's statement make about people's satisfaction with their bodies? Do you agree with Ehrenreich? Write an argumentative essay defending or blaming any aspect of the media (advertising, film, television) for perpetuating unrealistic images of female beauty and/or male attractiveness. In order to narrow your topic, focus on either female beauty or male attractiveness and a specific medium (a specific issue of a magazine, a specific episode of a television program, a specific scene in a movie), and use evidence to support your argument. In your essay, also offer solutions to create a positive body image.

Children and Family

The arrival of children is greeted with great joy and festivities. Parents spend time and money amassing great stores of photographs, mementos, and memorabilia. Within this treasure trove are clues to a child's popular culture influences: Imagine looking at a photograph of a child holding a favorite toy. In the background is a still of their favorite movie captured on the television screen. Beside the child is a blanket decorated with Sesame Street characters. The toy, movie, and blanket each provide clues to the popular culture influence at that time.

Before reading, reflect on your own childhood and family life. Did you grow up in a traditional family? In what ways did the television shows and films you watched echo your personal experience? What toys, books, and comics did you enjoy as a child? What values did they represent? Did your family censor you from watching any movies or television programs? Why? Did they give you reasons why they banned you, for example, from watching a particular movie or playing with a particular toy?

How are children and the family represented in television, fashion, comics, books, space? What types of activities do families usually do together? How is the family influenced by popular culture? How is popular culture influenced by family?

The selections in this chapter focus on children and the family and representations in diverse mediums, including television, advertising, Internet (McIntyre); television (ACLU and Garrison); space (mall) and advertising (Loh).

It is not surprising of course that the most controversial popular culture debates center around the media's impact on children. Indeed, the question of popular culture and its effect on children is a serious societal concern. It is so serious that the

United States government is involved. Jeff J. McIntyre, on behalf of the American Psychological Association (APA), gave testimony before the United States House of Representatives about "the effects of repeated exposure of children to violence" (paragraph 3). He testified that "hundreds of **studies have confirmed** that exposing our children to a steady diet of violence in the media makes our children more violence prone. The psychological processes here are not mysterious. Children learn by observing others. Mass media and the advertising world provide a very attractive window for these observations" (paragraph 8) [emphasis mine]. The American Civil Liberties Union (ACLU) disagrees, stating "**Research has not proven** that watching violence on television causes watchers to commit violence" (ACLU, paragraph 3) [emphasis mine].

How can two very reputable organizations like the APA and the ACLU arrive at very different conclusions about the effects of media violence on children? Whom should we believe?

Does violence influence children's behavior? According to congressional testimony by Jeff McIntyre on behalf of the American Psychological Association, ". . . repeated exposure to violence in the mass media places children at risk for increases in aggression; desensitization to acts of violence; and unrealistic increases in fear of becoming a victim of violence" (paragraph 5). Is it true? The opposing point of view is clearly held in the American Civil Liberties Union comments to the Federal Communications Commission regarding violent television programming and its impact on children: "Research has not proven that watching violence on television causes watchers to commit violence" (paragraph 3). In addition they astutely point out that "Defining 'violence' presents great constitutional difficulties" (paragraph 23). Although there may be "constitutional difficulties," public figures, organizations, and individuals do not seem to have any difficulty at all expressing personal opinions about popular culture's impact.

Even President George Bush said in the 1990s that "*The Simpsons* is a bad influence on children" (paragraph 2). Are the Simpsons a bad influence? Or, is it just fun, harmless entertainment? In "*The Simpsons:* A Reflection of Society and a Message on Family," Eric Garrison writes that the family is "the driving force of the main message of the show" (paragraph 9). What does the show reflect? The answer to the question is at the heart of the show's controversy: According to Garrison, "many of the general public see it as subversive and ultimately harmful" (paragraph 2). What does this statement assume about the values of the general public?

What happens when families turn away from potentially destructive television programs and venture outdoors to spend quality family time together? In "Shopworn: Like the Valley Girls Who Made It Famous, the Suburban Mall Is Now on the Wrong Side of Forty," Loh writes: "the mall has gotten into the very gut, the very psyche, of the American family . . . what safer harbor for families than a big, beige, temperature-controlled box?" (paragraph 6). What does her statement reveal about the impact of the mall on family life? Do the families in your neighborhood spend time at the mall? What do they do when they go to the mall? What does it reveal about their values? Is it realistic to imagine that families can effectively monitor children's programming and activities?

Pre-Reading Chapter 3

1. Write your answers to the autobiographical questions so that you can examine the personal experiences of your childhood and family life. This will set a foundation of where you have been so that as you read the essays you can further reflect on how similar or different your ideas are from the authors.

2. As you survey the titles and authors in Chapter 2, note your first reactions to key words: "APA Congressional Testimony on Media Violence and Children: Testimony of Jeff J. McIntyre on Behalf of the American Psychological Association"/Jeff J. McIntyre; Violent Television Programming and Its Impact on Children/American Civil Liberties Union (ACLU); "*The Simpsons:* A Reflection of Society and a Message on Family"/Eric Garrison; and "Shopworn: Like the Valley Girls Who Made It Famous, the Suburban Mall Is Now on the Wrong Side of Forty"/Sandra Tsing Loh. Brainstorm on these topics and note your first impressions. Are you familiar with any of the authors or organizations? For example, the ACLU is often in the news. What do you already know about the organization?

3. In your idea journal and scrapbook, be observant to the way children and the family are reflected in the popular culture mediums you encounter in your daily life today: from the songs you enjoy to the newspapers you read, from television shows and movies you watch to toys and games you see advertised or in store windows. This list will come in handy later on when you decide to write an assignment. For example, after reading about violent television programming, you may want to explore a similar theme but in a different medium (a recent video game you spotted in a storefront at the mall).

APA Congressional Testimony on Media Violence and Children: Testimony of Jeff J. McIntyre on Behalf of the American Psychological Association

JEFF J. MCINTYRE

The American Psychological Association (APA) is dedicated to promoting the health and well-being of society by conducting research studies and by focusing on professional development of its more than 150,000 members. On May 20, 2004, Jeff J. McIntyre testified on behalf of the APA. Notice that in paragraph 2, he lists his credentials before proceeding to give his testimony before the United States House of Representatives, Committee on the Judiciary, Subcommittee on Courts, the Internet, and Intellectual Property before the Honorable Lamar S. Smith, Chairman.

Pre-Reading

Do you think that congressional hearings are necessary and/or effective in censoring television programs, movies, and music lyrics? Explain why or why not. Do you think that the government should get involved? If so, why? If not, why do you believe the government should not?

────────── ✦ ──────────

Good morning, Mr. Chairman and Members of the House Judiciary Subcommittee on Courts, the Internet, and Intellectual Property. I am Jeff McIntyre and am honored to be here to represent the American Psychological Association.

I have conducted years of work related to children and the media as a negotiator for the development of a television ratings system, as an advisor to the Federal Communications Commission's V-Chip Task Force, as a member of an informal White House Task Force on Navigating the New Media, as a member of the steering committee for the Decade of Behavior Conference on Digital Childhood, and most importantly, as a representative of the research and concerns of the over 150,000 members and affiliates of the American Psychological Association.

At the heart of the issue of children and the media is a matter long addressed by psychological research—the effects of repeated exposure of children to violence. The media violence issue made its official debut on Capitol Hill in 1952 with the first of a series of congressional hearings. That particular hearing was held in the House of Representatives before the Commerce Committee. The following year, in 1953, the first major Senate hearing was held before the Senate Subcommittee on Juvenile Delinquency, then headed by Senator Estes Kefauver, who convened a panel to inquire into the impact of television violence on juvenile delinquency.

There have been many hearings since the 1950's, but there has been only limited change—until recently. Media violence reduction is fraught with legal complications. Nevertheless, our knowledge base has improved over time, with the publication of significant and landmark reviews. Based on these research findings, several concerns emerge when violent material is aggressively marketed to children.

Foremost, the conclusions drawn on the basis of over 30 years of research contributed by American Psychological Association members—including the Surgeon General's report in 1972, the National Institute of Mental Health's report in 1982, and the industry funded, three-year National Television Violence Study in the 1990's—show that the repeated exposure to violence in the mass media places children at risk for:

- increases in aggression;
- desensitization to acts of violence;
- and unrealistic increases in fear of becoming a victim of violence, which results in the development of other negative characteristics, such as mistrust of others.

If this sounds familiar, it is because this is the foundation upon which representatives of the public health community—comprised of the American Psychological Association, the American Academy of Pediatrics, and the American Medical Association—issued a joint consensus statement in 2000 on what we absolutely know to be true regarding children's exposure to violence in the media.

Certain psychological facts remain that are well established in this debate. As APA member Dr. Rowell Huesmann stated before the Senate Commerce Committee, just as every cigarette you smoke increases the chances that someday you will get cancer, every exposure to violence increases the chances that, some day, a child will behave more violently than they otherwise would.

Hundreds of studies have confirmed that exposing our children to a steady diet of violence in the media makes our children more violence prone. The psychological processes here are not mysterious. Children learn by observing others. Mass media and the advertising world provide a very attractive window for these observations.

The excellent children's programming (such as *Sesame Street*) and pro-social marketing (such as that around bicycle helmets) that exists is to be commended and supported. Psychological research shows that what is responsible for the effectiveness of good children's programming and pro-social marketing is that children learn from their media environment. If kids can learn positive behaviors via this medium, they can learn the harmful ones as well.

10   The role of ratings systems in this discussion merits attention. There continues to be concern over the ambiguity and implementation of current ratings systems. It appears that ratings systems are undermined by the marketing efforts of the very groups responsible for their implementation and effectiveness. That, Chairman Smith and members of the Subcommittee, displays a significant lack of accountability and should be considered when proposals for industry self-regulation are discussed.

Also undermined here are parents and American families. As the industry has shown a lack of accountability in the implementation of the existing ratings system, parents have struggled to manage their family's media diet against misleading and contradictory information. (For instance, marketing an R rated film to children under 17.) While the industry has made some information regarding the ratings available, more information regarding content needs to be made more accessible. As with nutritional information, the content labeling should be available on the product and not hidden on websites or in the occasional pamphlet.

Generally speaking, most adults see advertising as a relatively harmless annoyance. However, advertising directed at children, especially at young children, that features violence generates concern. The average child is exposed to approximately 20,000 commercials per year. This is only for television and does not include print or the Internet. Much of this is during weekend morning or weekday afternoon programming. Most of the concern stems not from the sheer number of commercial appeals but from the inability of some children to appreciate and defend against the persuasive intent of marketing, especially advertising featuring violent product.

A recent Federal Trade Commission report on the Marketing of Violence to Children heightens these concerns. As a result of the "Children's On-Line Privacy Protection Act" the Federal Trade Commission has ruled that parents have a right to protect their children's privacy from the unwanted solicitation of their children's personal information. We would argue that, based on the years of psychological research on violence prevention and clinical practice in violence intervention, parents also have the right to protect their children from material that puts them at risk of harm. With the considerations in place for children's privacy, the precedent for concern about children's health and safety is well established.

Decades of psychological research bear witness to the potential harmful effects on our children and our nation if these practices continue. Chairman Smith and Subcommittee members, thank you for your time. Please regard the American Psychological Association as a resource to the committee as you consider this and other issues.

Questions for Discussion and Writing

1. What is the APA? Conduct research and learn about the organization. What does their mission statement reveal about their motivations and priorities?
2. Evaluate the three bullet points highlighted in paragraph 5. Do you agree with them? If so, explain why. If not, explain why not.
3. Stylistically, why does McIntyre list his credentials in paragraph 2? Whenever you read a book or article, do you read "about the author"? Explain why it is helpful to know an author's credentials. Is there any information missing from the author's credentials?
4. Why does McIntyre include an analogy to smoking (paragraph 7) and nutritional labeling (paragraph 11)?
5. In paragraph 8, McIntyre states: "Hundreds of studies have confirmed that exposing our children to a steady diet of violence in the media makes our children more violence prone." Write an essay supporting, refuting, or modifying his claim.

Violent Television Programming and Its Impact on Children
American Civil Liberties Union (ACLU)

Established in 1920, the American Civil Liberties Union (ACLU) is a nonprofit, nonpartisan organization dedicated to protecting the rights of all citizens. This letter to the Federal Communications

Commission is dated September 15, 2004, and is referenced as *"Re: Comment on Notice of Inquiry, MB Docket No. 04-261; In the Matter of Violent Television Programming And Its Impact on Children."*

Pre-Reading

Why do you believe the ACLU would get involved? Conduct research on the ACLU; you may want to go to their website. What groups do they support? Why? What do you imagine are some cases they would get involved in?

———————— ✦ ————————

The ACLU submits these comments in reference to MB Docket No. 04-261. In the Matter of Violent Television Programming And Its Impact on Children. The Notice of Inquiry is long and fairly complex, seeking comment on many issues regarding violence and its effect on children, as well as the constitutionality of regulating depictions of violence. Our comments are limited to two issues: (1) the adequacy of research demonstrating the effects of violent programming; and (2) the constitutional issues in government regulation of violent programming.

The Notice of Inquiry is a response to a letter from thirty-nine members of the House of Representatives, Committee on Energy and Commerce, dated March 5, 2004. Congressional concern over media effects on children is hardly new. Each new medium is greeted with concern and efforts to regulate it on behalf of the children. The Internet is one of the most recent forms of information and entertainment causing Congressional concern, spawning several attempts to regulate the information that can reach children. Thus far, those attempts have failed, because they failed to adequately address constitutional concerns. Attempts to regulate violence in the broadcast medium are likely to meet the same fate.

Research has not proven that watching violence on television causes watchers to commit violence.

Congress often calls witnesses in hearings on media violence that opine their certainty that media violence causes violence. A dispassionate review of the data, however, demonstrates something far different.

5   The causes of violence are many and varied, and watching violence on television is not the sole, or even the most important factor. In September 2000, the Federal Trade Commission issued

a report entitled "Marketing Violence Entertainment to Children: A Review of the Self-Regulation and Industry Practices in the Motion Picture, Music Recording & Electronic Game Industries." In Appendix A of that report, the FTC reviewed the available research on the impact of violence in the entertainment media. Regarding causation, the FTC noted that "[m]ost researchers and investigators agree that exposure to media violence alone does not cause a child to commit a violent act, and that it is not the sole, or even the most important, factor in contributing to youth aggression, anti-social attitudes, and violence."

The FTC noted that "[b]roader research into the causes of youth violence has identified interacting risk factors, such as genetic, psychological, familial, and socioeconomic characteristics. Severe antisocial aggressive behavior appears to occur most often when more than one of these factors is present. The typical profile of a violent youth is one who comes from a troubled home, has poor cognitive skills, and exhibits psychological disorders such as anxiety, depression and attention deficit hyperactivity."

Intuitively, the conclusion that media violence causes actual violence is incorrect. While violent media is allegedly on the rise, violence, and in particular youth violence, has declined according to FBI statistics. If media violence is a causative factor, one would expect to see a rise in violent crime, rather than a decrease.

Attachment 1 to these comments is an *amicus* brief filed on behalf of thirty-three media scholars in the case of *Interactive Digital Software Ass'n v. St. Louis County* in 2002, and is submitted with the permission of the authors.

The brief analyzes the studies and data in the area. Quoting psychologist Guy Cumberbatch, it notes, "If one conclusion is possible, it is that the jury is not still out. It's never been in. Media violence has been subjected to lynch mob mentality with almost any evidence used to prove guilt." The brief additionally discusses the positive benefits of fantasy violence, and concludes that "[c]ensorship laws based on bogus claims that science has proved harm from violent entertainment deflect attention from the real causes of violence and, given the positive uses of violent fantasy, may be counterproductive."

Courts that have examined the data have likewise not been impressed with the proponents of causation. Most recently, a federal district court in Washington struck down a law dealing with violent video games where the violence was perpetrated against a law enforcement officer. The proponent of the law was confident that it would be upheld because it was allegedly supported by

10

research that showed that watching violence produces violent activities. The court, however, was unimpressed, and held the law unconstitutional. [*Video Software Dealers Ass'n v. Maleng*, No. C03-1245L (D.Wash. July 15, 2004)]

Assumptions about the negative effects of viewing violence ignore the positive societal value of violent programs that teach us important lessons about history or call attention to problems that society must address. "Roots" was a national television event of enormous educational value that necessarily showed the brutality of the institution of slavery. The made-for-television movie "The Burning Bed" was credited with bringing about reform of existing spousal-abuse laws and included what some would call disturbingly violent scenes. "Saving Private Ryan" was a powerful movie about the horrors of war, and included many disturbing scenes to illustrate that point.

While those who wish to censor violence claim "[h]undreds of studies over decades document the harmful impact that exposure to graphic and excessive media violence has on the physical and mental health of our children," the fact remains that the basis for regulating media violence rests more on wishful thinking than hard data.

Regulating television violence is unlikely to survive constitutional scrutiny.

The Supreme Court has repeatedly stressed that "above all else, the First Amendment means that government has no power to restrict expression because of its message, its ideas, its subject matter, or its content." *Police Department v. Mosley*, 408 U.S. 92, 95 (1972). Moral and esthetic judgments are "for the individual to make, not for the Government to decree, **even with the mandate or approval of the majority.**" *United States v. Playboy Entertainment Group, Inc.*, 529 U.S. 803, 818 (2000). [Emphasis added.]

15   The overriding justification for regulation of television violence "is the concern for the effect of the subject matter on young viewers." *Id*. at 811. Clearly, any such regulation by the government would be content-based. Content-based speech restrictions are subject to strict scrutiny. *Id* at 813.

Strict scrutiny requires that any content-based speech regulation must be narrowly tailored to promote a compelling government interest. If a less restrictive alternative would serve the Government's purpose, it must use that alternative. *Id*.

The fact that the studies do not generally support the thesis that media violence causes actual violence has important implications for strict scrutiny analysis. To the extent that these studies provide the "compelling government interest" in regulating television violence, they are woefully inadequate. As the FTC noted, media violence is not the sole, or even the most important factor in youth violence. Thus, there is no compelling government interest in regulating such content.

The fact that a proposed regulation may not impose a complete prohibition on that show does not save the regulation.[1] "The distinction between laws burdening and laws banning speech is but a matter of degree. The Government's content-based burdens must satisfy the same rigorous scrutiny as its content-based bans." *Id.* at 812.

It is also unavailing to claim that the speech at issue is of minimal value. "The history of the law of free expression is one of vindication in cases involving speech that many citizens may find shabby, offensive, or even ugly. It follows that all content-based restrictions on speech must give us more than a moment's pause." *Id.* at 826.

"Material limited to forms of violence is given the highest degree of First Amendment Protection." *Sovereign News Co. v. Falke,* 448 F.Supp. 306, 394 (N.D. Ohio 1977), *remanded on other grounds,* 610 F.2d 428 (6th Cir. 1979), *cert. denied,* 447 U.S. 923 (1980). In *Winters v. New York,* 333 U.S. 507 (1948), the Supreme Court invalidated a law that prohibited the distribution to minors of any publication "principally made up of . . . accounts of criminal deeds, or pictures, or stories of deeds of bloodshed, lust or crime." *Id.* at 508. Even though the Court saw "nothing of any possible value to society in these magazines," the justices held that the material was "as much entitled to the protection of free speech as the best of literature." *Id.* at 510.

The First Amendment not only protects expression that depicts violence; it also protects speech that advocates the "use of force or violence." *NAACP v. Claiborne Hardware Co.,* 458 U.S. 886, 927 (1982). In *Brandenburg v. Ohio,* 395 U.S. 444 (1969) (*per curiam*), the Supreme Court held that the government may not "forbid or proscribe advocacy of the use of force or of law violation except where such advocacy is directed to inciting or producing imminent lawless action and is likely to incite or produce such action." *Id.* at 447. The Court further stated that "[a] statute which fails to draw this distinction impermissibly intrudes upon the freedoms guaranteed by the First and Fourteenth Amendments. It sweeps within its condemnation speech which our Constitution has immunized from Government control." *Id.* at 448.

Applying *Brandenburg,* it is clear that television entertainment fails to meet this stringent test. Nothing in the data supports the conclusion that watching media violence will incite imminent violence. In the context of song lyrics thought to advocate minors to commit suicide, courts have found that expression enjoys full First Amendment protection. *Walker v. Osbourne*, 763 F.Supp. 1144 (M.D. Ga. 1991), *aff'd*, 958 F.2d 1084 (11ᵗʰ Cir. 1992) (*per curiam*). *cert. denied*, 113 S.Ct. 325, 121 L.Ed.2d 245 (1992). *See also, Zamora v. Columbia Broadcasting System*, 480 F.Supp. 199 (S.D. Fla. 1979); *DeFilippo v. National Broadcasting Co.*, 446 A.2d 1036 (R.I. 1982); *Olivia N v. National Broadcast Co.*, 126 Cal. App. 3d 488, 178 Cal. Rptr. 888 (1981), *cert. denied*, 458 U.S. 1108 (1982). The same result is likely for television violence.

The foregoing discussion makes it clear that (1) violent material is protected under the First Amendment; (2) because regulation of violent content is a content-based regulation, it must endure strict scrutiny; (3) there is no compelling governmental interest in regulating media violence, and therefore, any such regulation will fail under the strict scrutiny standard.

Defining "violence" presents great constitutional difficulties. For the FCC to regulate violence, it must define what constitutes permissible and impermissible depictions of violence. The law favors bright lines when regulating speech, so it is clear what is and is not permissible.

Vague laws and interpretations create traps for broadcasters and speakers because they are unsure, in the absence of a bright line, what conduct constitutes permissible depictions of violence from impermissible depictions of violence. Rather than have broadcasters act at their peril, the law prefers reasonable notice of what conduct will give rise to legal consequences, so that the speaker or broadcaster may act accordingly. Vagueness results in chilling of communications that may well NOT be impermissibly violent, simply because the cost to the speaker or broadcaster of being wrong is too great. Vagueness encourages silence rather than robust debate. "Uncertain meanings inevitably lead citizens to 'steer far wider of the unlawful zone' . . . than if the boundaries of the forbidden areas were clearly marked" *Grayned v. City of Rockford*, 408 U.S. 104, 109 (1972). Thus, any vagueness in the definition of permissible violence serves to chill protected speech.

As noted above, violence can often teach us important historical lessons, and illustrate societal problems existing today. Thus, the FCC would first have to define "violence," then proceed to define what are permissible and impermissible depictions of violence. Just defining violence can be a daunting task. For example, the FTC in its report of September 2000 noted that researchers who study the effects of media violence are not even consistent in their definitions of "violence." If researchers are unable to concur on an objective definition of "violence," it is unlikely the FCC will be able to make such decisions in a way that will withstand constitutional scrutiny.

Assuming the FCC can provide an objective definition of "violence," it must then proceed to the task of defining what is and is not permissible. For example, "The Magnificent Seven" is a movie about seven men who protect a village from violent marauders. Is their defense of the village "good" violence (allowable)? Is the depicting of violence of the marauders therefore not allowed? If so, then how does one place the violence committed by the Magnificent Seven in context? Prohibiting showing the violence of the marauders would seem to make the violence committed by the seven valiant warriors unreasonable. Or, is the movie left to only show a debate between the marauders and the seven warriors with no violence whatsoever? (And probably, no audience.)

While proponents of regulating media violence often claim they are only seeking to prohibit "gratuitous" or "excessive" violence, defining that is a lot like "knowing it when you see it," which is insufficiently precise for constitutional purposes.

Endnote

1. The Notice of Inquiry discussed the possibility of a "safe harbor" in which violent shows would be aired only at certain times at which children were not likely to comprise a significant portion of the viewing audience. Thus, the material would not be absolutely prohibited.

Questions for Discussion and Writing

1. What prompted the ACLU to write this letter to the Commissioner?
2. What evidence does the ACLU include to support its assertion that "Research has not proven that watching violence on television causes watchers to commit violence" (paragraph 3)? Do you disagree with the conclusions presented by their research?
3. Examine the way the argument is constructed. List the order in which key ideas appear. Is there any rationale behind the organization of the argument?
4. Write an essay that examines the causal connection between a particular television program and violent behavior. Select any episode of a television show, scene from a movie, or lyrics from a song that has stirred controversy in the news. Conduct your own research to support your thesis and observations.
5. Write a research paper agreeing with, refuting, or modifying the ACLU's argument that "Regulating television violence is unlikely to survive constitutional scrutiny" (paragraph 13).

The Simpsons: A Reflection of Society and a Message on Family

ERIC GARRISON

Shortly after graduating with a communications degree from Sonoma State in 2002, Eric Garrison began analyzing other trends of media related to satire, and even worked in the medium itself. Today, Garrison brings his expertise to an interactive marketing agency in San Diego but still finds the time to write freelance reviews and stories. Garrison's analysis on The Simpsons *is available on* The Simpsons Archive website, *snpp.com, a fan-based comprehensive guide to* The Simpsons.

Pre-Reading

How familiar are you with *The Simpsons*? What is your favorite episode of *The Simpsons*? Explain the topic of the show and why you enjoy that particular episode. Alternatively, if you have never watched *The Simpsons*, conduct research by visiting one of *The Simpsons'* many websites maintained by fans. What do fans have to say about the show?

◆

In December of 1989, Matt Groening had a new idea that differed from all the other show ideas at the time. While the other shows on ABC, CBS, and NBC consisted of dreary soap operas such as *General Hospital* and other instantly forgettable shows, Groening decided to go into another direction, animation sketch comedy. It was a rare formula that hadn't really been done in the years since *The Flintstones*. The result was the new jewel of Fox's prime time lineup: *The Simpsons*. It started out as a few shorts on the *Tracy Ullman Show* and quickly earned enough of a following to develop itself into its own time slot on Sunday nights.

It's been about 12 years since then, and *The Simpsons* doesn't look like it'll be stopping for years. To understand such a phenomenon and its own effect on the general public, one must look at the general messages and morals of the show. In the heart of things, *The Simpsons* is a satire first and foremost. But despite any good intentions that the show may offer "in the spirit of good fun," many of the general public see it as subversive and ultimately harmful to their own well being. President George Bush at the time was heard as saying "*The Simpsons* is a bad influence on children." Some critics even think that where the show once had decency and clear-cut values, it is now a sloppy mess that should be taken off the air. To analyze these problems and to find a solution to them, the Potter Box must be applied to the whole Simpsons phenomenon. The problems will be identified; the values of the show will then be looked at along with some of the guiding principles. Finally, who gains to benefit from *The Simpsons*, the viewers or the show's producers?

When it started out, *The Simpsons* was a picture of the modern American nuclear family. Homer was "the lovable oaf," as described by the show creator Matt Groening. A well-meaning Dad, Homer had his ups and downs in the following years. Then there was Marge, the well-to-do housewife. She was at the start, and is currently, the only restraining voice of the household. Lisa is the shy but inquisitive genius of the household. She started out as any normal genius child would; she would constantly analyze every situation in the Simpson's household, and attempt to try to find a solution for it. Bart was every boy child in America. A modern day Dennis the Menace with no clear inhibitions. Maggie was the silent infant of the household, and would only make sounds from her pacifier.

IDENTIFYING THE PROBLEM

Already, the show had a few stereotypes, or portraits of the modern American family. The first few seasons of *The Simpsons* pointed fun at many American issues and provided their own ethical solutions to many moral dilemmas. In the seasons to come, more characters would enter the show, and the show itself would grow from a small cast to a cast of hundreds. One of the main issues that some of the public would begin to hold against the show was stereotyping.

Apu started out in concept as a simple convenience store   5
clerk. According to show writer Mike Reiss, though, when Hank Azaria (the voice of Apu) started to voice act the script, Azaria couldn't help but give Apu an Indian accent. "We couldn't help it," says Reiss, "Once Apu was given an Indian accent, Apu Nahasapeemapetilan was born." In the following seasons, Apu is given many stereotypical jokes and situations. In one such episode,

an indignant Apu approaches a calm Reverend Lovejoy for calling his religion "miscellaneous":

> "You know Hindu isn't a small religion. There are 7 hundred million of us." "Aw, that's Super." (Owen)

Not only does Lovejoy smile and nod at what Apu says, but also it's in a condescending way. It's here where the dividing lines between stereotyping and religion itself come into question.

Christianity is one that is constantly mocked through some of the show's back characters, both Ned Flanders and Reverend Lovejoy. Reverend Lovejoy pictures God as harsh and vengeful in the weekly town church meetings. In one episode Lovejoy points out Ned Flanders as "the fallen one" for a mere traffic offense (Sohn). In the seasons to come, many of the show's creators found themselves being pushed by the Fox Network to not make fun of one religion: Catholicism.

The show's creators were furious about the whole matter. The show's writer Mike Scully says the following thing about the topic:

> "People can say hurtful things to each other about their weight, their race, their intelligence, their sexual preference . . . but when you get into religion, some people get very nervous." (Rosenberg)

In excluding Catholicism, the whole show's values were put at stake. After all, *The Simpsons* has always been making fun of everybody. By excluding someone, the show's own morals and values were put at risk.

10   The whole problem involving Catholicism resulted from a *Simpsons* episode that depicted the family watching the Super Bowl. Spoofing an old ZZ Top video, the commercial in the show showed a car pulling up in front of a gas station. An average guy then honks the horn, as nobody is there to serve him gas. Suddenly, dancing to rock music, three scantily clad attractive women emerge from the station and take the nozzle from the gas pump and insert it in a very seductive way into the man's car. They then open the hood of the car and one of the other girls bends in front of him and the guy can't help but look at her sizable cleavage. Hanging in front of it is a cross. The narrator of the commercial then says:

> "The Catholic Church: We've made a few . . . changes." (Rosenberg)

With such criticism against them, how can the show continue to operate as it is?

IDENTIFYING THE PRINCIPLES

Behind all the satire, though, is the driving force of the main message of the show: family.

While religion itself has been scrutinized under a watchful eye, it also has been shown as a force to be reckoned with in time of family crisis. In one episode, religion is being scrutinized again, but in a more friendly way. Homer approaches God in a dream about his own crisis of faith:

HOMER: I'm not a bad guy. I work hard and I love my kids, so why should I spend half my Sunday hearing about how I'm going to hell?

GOD: Hmm, you've got a point there. You know, sometimes I'd rather be watching football. Does St. Louis still have a team?

HOMER: No. They moved to Phoenix. (Mullin)

God isn't shown as a vengeful God; here he is shown as a caring father to one of his own children. Homer mentions his own family values, and God praises him for it. The show itself says here, religion shouldn't be what it's all about; it should basically be about being a good person and taking care of your family.

While the show may go in many different directions, show creator Matt Groening has a lot to say on the subject:

. . . "There's sort of an unspoken rule that we have on the show, which is we can do humor as dark as we want to, but the show itself is a celebration of the family." (Figueroa)

Family is supposedly one of the driving forces of the show in   15
the early seasons. But somewhere along the line, the show seemed to lose a little focus. There isn't an exact point, but the show dropped its own family focus and decided to stretch its own boundaries into an all-out satire. In the earlier seasons, Bart was constantly seen as the protagonist of the show. Many fans fondly remember when Bart did all the crank calls to Moe's tavern. While then it was Bart's antics that were applauded, now it's Homer's antics. The main brunt of the later changes in the show now occur through the now main character, Homer Simpson.

In the first few years, Homer was the well-to-do dad. In the very first episode, "Simpson's Roasting on an Open Fire," Homer takes a job as a department store Santa to help pay for the family's Christmas. It is Bart's own use of the family Christmas money for getting a tattoo that causes the lack of funds in the Simpson family. At the end of the episode, through a sheer force of accident, they find the new family Christmas present, the dog, Santa's Little Helper, at the racetrack. Marge lovingly looks at Homer and says "God bless him." Once again, the mottos of religion and family are tied together to present the show's own morals. Christmas is saved through Homer's good will or random luck of the moment.

Fast-forward a couple years. Homer is transformed from a hard working Dad to a spur of the moment oaf in the blink of an eye. Gone is the Dad who works hard to pay for the family's debts: replacing him is Parody Homer. By about season 7 the transformation has been made complete. In the often-panned "Frank Grimes episode," we find the new worker around the Power Plant, Frank Grimes, being disgusted by just how lazy Homer is. Near the end of the episode he carelessly says to Homer, "You are what's wrong with America, Simpson."

Homer is the lazy oaf riding on the shoulder of the average working man, Frank Grimes. At the end, though, Grimes can't stand it anymore; he goes nuts and kills himself in a "Homer-like" situation. He messes with the plant's power and electrocutes himself. At Grimes' funeral, Homer is sleeping soundly and says, "Turn the channel Marge." The rest of the town then laughs at Homer's antics, and the side character Lenny says "that's our Homer."

Where are the messages of family that had once been in the show? Instead we just find a parody of the average American worker. Don't bother working, the episode suggests, there will always be a Homer to cut you off. Be lazy! It was a funny episode, but gone were the warm messages that *The Simpsons* once had in yesteryear. Through "Parody Homer," all of society is being scrutinized, but underneath it all there are no family values or ethics of those values being used today.

20

George Meyer, referred to by many other Simpsons writers as the real writer of the show, has this to say about the "evolution" of Homer: "Homer has become a lot more volatile and mercurial. He will go from sentimentality to furious rage and then fall asleep all in the space of 10 seconds." Mike Reiss agrees with what Meyer says. "Absolutely, Homer has become a sort of paradox of sorts. Do we know anybody like him in real life? He has to be like he is; we have no one else to make fun of in the real world. If anybody in real life was made fun of all the time like he is in the show, they'd have killed themselves multiple times over by now."

Here we stand shocked—the actual creators of the show basically admit one of the show's more long-standing problems. They're running out of ideas. Reiss is once again the first to admit. "We've been going on for 10 years plus! Every topic you can imagine has already been covered. Next season Lisa will be becoming a Buddhist, if the show keeps on going on after that, who knows? We might have to make her a lesbian." Despite the deadpan humor shown above, one thing is getting true. The show has already covered all it has been able to in issues of family. Through Homer they have mocked government, sex, gender, and bias. Parody and family issues have now been covered.

WHO BENEFITS?

For about 12 years now, *The Simpsons* has been chugging along through parody and morals of family. Now that the show seems to be losing its edge, shouldn't it be put out of its misery? The creators seemed to be divided on the matter. In one interview with *Newsweek*, Groening had this to say about the show's content:

> "You know, we can just sit around, and make the show run another couple of years. Or, we can actually make a 10-year plan. Jim said, 'Ten years.' So, if we can keep the show fresh, sure. But everyone agrees that if we lose our direction, we should give it up." (Figueroa)

The interview was made 2 years ago; since then, the show has been renewed to 2003.

Here is where the real factor of the *The Simpsons* comes in: money. In a recent interview with Dan Castellaneta (Homer's voice), the following fact was revealed: the voice actors received a $1,000,000 signing bonus to stay on the show for another 2 years. In addition to that, the actors would be paid $100,000 per episode (Johnson). There are no obvious complaints coming from the actors about the question of the show's longevity.

Groening had this to say in a later interview about the "dilemma" that the voice actors were facing. "I have sympathy. They are incredibly talented, and they deserve a chance to be as rich and miserable as anyone else in Hollywood . . . Hold out for as much money as you can get, but make the deal" (Chocano). Where are the ethics that Groening previously voiced about the show running out of ideas? It has been reported that the producers would stop the show—once it was out of ideas. In recent years, episodes of *The Simpsons* have been more episodic than anything. Even the infamous Grimes episode had more plot than some of the more recent episodes.

25   In a recent episode, dated in mid-December 2001, Moe the bartender had the dilemma of being sick of running a hole in the wall bar. With the advice of his old schoolteacher, Moe decided to run a ritzy new version of his tavern. Homer and his buddies were kicked out of the bar, and Moe found himself yet again unhappy about the new changes to his bar. Meanwhile, Moe's teacher revealed to Moe that he was dying of cancer.

In front of Moe, the teacher then walks into a pool to drown himself. There was no visible reaction from Moe to help the teacher; instead, Moe was caught up in his own troubles and went back to his bar dilemma. The conclusion of the episode ignores the teacher's death and has Moe still bored with his bar life. He ends up going back to the status quo, and has Homer and his friends once again enter the bar.

Already, the episode shows too much of a convoluted plot. While the Grimes episode had a general message about the workforce, this episode of the show seemed to have no general message. Fans in recent years have criticized *The Simpsons* for its lack of plot and lack of story depth. The TV Internet Newsgroup Alt.TV.Simpsons.com reveals that many people are against the direction in which the show is headed.

One of the lead protestors of the group is Ondre Lombard, who says *The Simpsons* has "turned into a cold, cynical, anything-for-a-joke series with one-dimensional characters" (Weinman). The show's creators have recently funded their own private war with these protestors through their character, the Comic Book Guy. It started in a 1997 episode, where the Comic Book Guy, seeing a bad Itchy and Scratchy episode, says:

COMIC BOOK GUY: "Last night's 'Itchy and Scratchy' was, without a doubt, the worst episode ever. Rest assured that I was on the Internet within minutes, registering my disgust throughout the world. . . . As a loyal viewer, I feel they owe me."

BART: "What? They've given you thousands of hours of entertainment for free. What could they possibly owe you? If anything, you owe them."

COMIC BOOK GUY: "Worst episode ever."

This passage sums up well the writers' own contempt for how scrupulous fans can be in analyzing the show. It obviously annoys the writers that their episodes are being received poorly, but despite any misgivings, *The Simpsons* franchise looks like it'll keep plunging ahead. A conclusion must be made. Do the writers of the show actually hold any responsibility to the series fans?

PHILOSOPHIES AND CONCLUSIONS

Out of all the philosophies out there, two philosophies can be   30
used to apply both to the creators and the fans themselves. One
that applies to the show's creators thus far is that they're egoists.
That is, they have really used the show as a vehicle for maximum
benefit for themselves. From the beginning of the show, the creators have been quite vocal about how the show really is just for
themselves. If they heeded every complaint about the show, *The
Simpsons* would just become another sub par, boring, politically
correct television program.

But despite any vocal assertions that the show is for the
creators themselves, *The Simpsons* always has been a creation
of many. Matt Groening may have created the concept, but it is
other writers such as George Meyer and Mike Reiss who have
given the show its own originality. So where does responsibility to
the fans come in? The writers do bear a responsibility in that the
show should be entertaining. It hasn't been for quite a while. Parody Homer, while fresh a few years ago, is an old staple of the
nineties. If *The Simpsons* wants to remain on the cutting edge, it
will have to adapt for the upcoming "2Ks."

The philosophy that bears this in mind is Relativism. That is,
the writers should still write what they think is right for the show,
but they shouldn't be egotistical about it. They deserve much of
the money that has come to them so far; they don't deserve the
money, though, for making a mediocre show. Like in the case of
Catholicism, there has been much censorship of the show itself
that has prevented it from reaching the full potential that it once
had. Gone are any simple messages or sharp satire; instead, the
show has become a vehicle for mediocre, outdated ideas. New
blood should be hired to keep the show fresh.

Another reason the show has become stale is the staple of
money. Greed in some cases has prevented them from searching
for any kind of new status quo for the show. George Meyer had
this to say about the program's beginnings:

> "When I first got to *The Simpsons*, we were still kind of figuring
> it out. The characters were pretty much limited to the family and
> a few neighbors. We could pretty much do whatever we wanted
> to and create characters when we needed them." (John Bonne)

With new restrictions by the networks and greed among some
of the writers, *The Simpsons* has entered a rut. What it needs is

new blood, or an end to its present syndication. That is the responsibility that *The Simpsons* will have to its viewers.

35   While many people have been offended by some of the show's often scathing humor, one must remember that *The Simpsons* is a satire. No one is disincluded, and that's what keeps it one step ahead of most shows in its competition time slot. If the show's writers actually listen to what some of the fans are saying, then maybe the show can return to its former glory. If not, it's time for *The Simpsons* to make a fond farewell.

Works Cited

John Bonne
"The Simpsons Has Lost Its Cool"
MSNBC, October 2, 2000
Carina Chocano
"Matt Groening"
Salon.Com. January 30, 2001
http://www.salon.com/people/bc/2001/01/30/groening/
Ana Figueroa
"Life in Hell"
Newsweek (via MSNBC), October 27, 2000
Allan Johnson
"Dan Castellaneta: Actor comes home . . . alone"
Chicago Tribune, June 5, 2001
Bret Mullin
"The Simpsons, American Satire"
Simpsons Archive
http://www.snpp.com/other/papers/bm.paper.html
David Owen
"Taking Humor Seriously—George Meyer, the Funniest Man
  Behind the Funniest Show on TV"
The New Yorker, March 13, 2000
Howard Rosenberg
"Fox Does Have Standards—and Double Standards"
Los Angeles Times, June 2, 1999
John Sohn
"Simpsons Ethics," *The Simpsons* archive
http://www.snpp.com/other/papers/js.paper.html
Jaime J. Weinman
"Worst Episode Ever"
Salon.Com. January 24, 2000
http://www.salon.com/ent/tv/feature/2000/01/24/simpsons/

Questions for Discussion and Writing

1. Garrison writes, "*The Simpsons* is a satire first and foremost" (paragraph 2). What is a satire? Look up the definition of the word and consider whether or not you agree with Garrison's assessment.

2. In what context is the issue of religion raised? Why is it that "some people get very nervous" when it comes to topic of religion?

3. The article is divided into four sections: "Identifying the Problem," "Identifying the Principles," "Who Benefits?," and "Philosophies and Conclusions." Evaluate each of the four sections. Which one do you think has the most persuasive argument? Do you think it was necessary to have the divisions? Explain why or why not.

4. Select an episode of *The Simpsons* or an episode of another television show depicting family life. Write an essay comparing Garrison's observations of family life as depicted in *The Simpsons* to your own observations of family life depicted in the episode you select. What type of family relationship does the episode depict? Do the characters experience the same anxieties and concerns? To what extent does Garrison's analysis of *The Simpsons* coincide with your own analysis of the episode you selected?

5. Imagine that you have been asked to write a proposal for a new television show about family life. In one page, describe your show and the main characters, and give a synopsis of the family life of your characters.

Shopworn: Like the Valley Girls Who Made It Famous, the Suburban Mall Is Now on the Wrong Side of Forty

SANDRA TSING LOH

Writer and performance artist Sandra Tsing Loh is a commentator on National Public Radio (NPR), Morning Edition, and Market-place. Loh's review of Paco Underhill's book Call of the Mall *is from the* Atlantic Monthly *(June 2004). A contributor to numerous anthologies, Loh is the author of* Depth Takes a Holiday: Essays from Lesser Los Angeles *(1996);* Aliens in America *(monologue) (1997);* If You Lived Here, You'd Be Home by Now *(novel) (1997); and* A Year in Van Nuys *(2001). Her work has also appeared in the* New York Times, Elle, Vogue, *and* Harper's Bazaar.

How frequently do you visit the mall? When was the last time you visited the mall? What are the obvious and not so obvious reasons why people go to malls? What are the possible positive and negative consequences of visiting a mall?

———————— ✦ ————————

"Increasingly, cities are becoming the province of the rich, the childless, or the poor. I love cities. But America hasn't lived there for a long time . . . If you really want to observe entire middle-class multigenerational American families, you have to go to the mall."

But, we might ask the self-described Envirosell "research wonk" Paco Underhill, whose above contention appears in *Call of the Mall*, do we really want to? Underhill's most recent foray into the rich, potpourri-and-candle-scented field of retail anthropology (his first was *Why We Buy: The Science of Shopping*, published in 1999) addresses such tough questions as Are we really interested in spending an entire book inside the mall? Why is mall architecture so ugly? and Exactly what is an Aqua Massage? Underhill's answers turn out to be fascinating (mostly), and when they aren't, they're boring in a sort of exquisitely bleak, existential way, just like the mall.

For those who argue that sometimes a Cinnabon is just a Cinnabon, Underhill opens his mall jaunt by invoking the spirit of the French historian Daniel Roche, author of *A History of Everyday Things* (2000). "It's not as though studying people as they congregate to buy and sell things is a totally frivolous or small-minded endeavor," he writes.

> Consider the history of our species, a fair swath of which has been propelled by merchants or their emissaries traveling to the far reaches of the planet, sometimes at great risk, in order to bring back stuff to peddle to the rest of us. As any schoolchild can testify, the romance of the ancient world teems with spice routes and trade winds and trafficking in silks and precious metals, frankincense and myrrh, gunpowder and fur.

For Underhill, the history of retail is a grand adventure that entered a new phase in the glittering emporiums of America's burgeoning cities.

The merchant princes were nineteenth century men, driven by ambition and muscle and determination to succeed in the brick-and-mortar vocabulary of the era. Their stores were their alter egos, and these titans of retailing all had serious edifice complexes. The great department stores of the day bore their owners' names—Gimbel, Macy, Wanamaker, Neiman Marcus, Marshall Field.

5

At first blush it would appear that the suburban car culture's rise triggered just another exciting phase in the journey. After all, since its inception, in Edina, Minneosta, in 1956, the mall has in many ways proved a wonderfully successful retail invention. In the boom years of the 1970s and 1980s a new mall opened somewhere in the United States every three or four days. Studies suggest that 30 percent of adults living in a county with the kind of mall that Underhill describes in his book will have visited it at least once in a given three months. Malls currently account for 14 percent of all U.S. retailing (excluding cars and gasoline), about $308 billion in annual sales.

More telling than those mere facts and numbers is how the mall has gotten into the very gut, the very psyche, of the American family. What is a family, after all, but a collection of not quite independent, somewhat less than completely ambulatory people? And what safer harbor for families than a big, beige, temperature-controlled box? It's not just the mall-rat teens, marooned at the octoplex on Friday nights because they cannot drive. It's the packs of seniors who began exercise programs of "mall walking" on the advice of doctors who didn't want them to slip in snow and ice. It's the mothers looking to kill time with very small children (because mall customers literally shop slower than their urban counterparts, and are more patient in line, pushing a couple of tots in a stroller to get a new spatula at Lechter's can fill an entire cloud-free afternoon).

The problem, Underhill argues, is that there's rot in the mall's very DNA. Mall owners, far from being merchants who want to creatively engage our acquisitive urges, are simply real-estate developers trying to maximize every rental dollar, mostly by minimizing their overhead. Which is not a good thing. To begin with, the resulting architecture is a horror ("A big wall with a little mouse hole" is the way one top mall designer describes it). And now these blank, lifeless exteriors are gradually decaying, with an almost Michael Jackson–like weirdness. For instance,

> Mall of America, the biggest in the United States and the most potent tourist attraction in all of Minnesota, may have looked good on the drawing board. But it has aged badly since it opened in August 1992. You can see stains on the outside of the building, and grass has begun to poke through the asphalt of the parking lots. It is huge and unsightly. You can't imagine Disney World or the Statue of Liberty being allowed to decay this way. Yet this mall has more visitors than Disney World, Graceland, and the Grand Canyon combined.

And further,

> Next time you're at a mall, instead of going directly inside, stroll around the perimeter of the place. It will be one of the more joyless promenades you'll ever make. You'll be very alone out there, on a narrow strip of sidewalk, assuming it has a sidewalk—many malls don't—with maybe a security guard or two to keep you company ... There will almost certainly be shrubbery, neatly clipped, but it's greenery of the most generic kind. Nobody thought you'd ever look too closely at it. Its only job is to be green.

And that disorientation, that disconnect in form and space, reaches to the inside of the mall—which Underhill describes as being, like television, a "totally fake environment that attempts to pass itself off as a true reflection of who we are and what we want." There's a video arcade, a rock-climbing wall, a food court, and "a Cinnabon stand, four cookie stands, three pretzel stands, three ice-cream stands, and no place wheresoever to buy an apple." It's a pastel-hued town—or, at least "town-like"—square that actually resists true civic discourse. (Many states have had to legislate out certain kinds of retail-unfriendly free-speech activity: irritants over the years have included political candidates, Klansmen, and anti-war activists distributing leaflets.) Underhill labors to suggest a connection between malls and racism, because so few of them are near public transportation.

But for this reader, *Call of the Mall*'s unique contribution to the field—if not exactly its pleasure—is less the sociological analysis than the shock of personal recognition Underhill provokes as he lasers in on some unexamined moments in modern life. Only a retail specialist could be so attuned to the human condition in all its shabby, formless boredom. Underhill, again in the spirit of Roche, relentlessly tracks the violent shifts in our emotional landscape as we look for parking and find somewhat better (nearer to the Sears end) or somewhat worse (nearer to the Bloomingdale's) than we had expected. Once inside, he rails,

> Do all mall maps stink? In our studies of people in shopping centers, we've timed how long they spend staring at those big, lighted board mall directories. In one study the average was twenty-two seconds. That's a very long time to study a map . . . The directories in most malls look like they were designed for electricians—like wiring guides.

Only Underhill would take time to observe.

> To the extent that muggings do occur in malls, they may take place in rest rooms, which are usually hidden down some lonesome corridor away from the main thoroughfare. In fact, that's the best way to find the bathroom in an unfamiliar mall—look around for the least inviting hallway, the narrow one where the lighting is dimmest.
>
> See? Here's just such a passage radiating off the promenade. It's gloomy and unwelcoming—if the mall were an urban setting, this would be an alley. Come on, let's go inside.

And finally,

> There's something Fellini-esque about a department store cosmetics section. You stand here on a Saturday morning, dressed in the standard mall-casual suburban wardrobe, gazing at a chamber glittering with chandeliers, populated by saleswomen wearing makeup and hair dramatic enough for opening night at La Scala. Their faces are like masks of pale, poreless skin, ruby-red lips, smoldering eye treatments—positively kabuki-like . . . The purchase of cosmetics is as public as a private art form gets. It isn't quite a massage, but it is an intimate act between two consenting adults.

It's here that perhaps the most telling bit of retail absurdity 10 lies. Up above the cosmetics counter, Underhill points out, you'll typically find a gigantic image of Elizabeth Hurley, from an ad you saw in *Vanity Fair*, now blown up and ringed with glowing spotlights. Down below, the rest of the female species shuffles around, barely able to find a decent mirror in decent light to try out the lipstick.

Underhill quotes a fellow retail expert:

> "The companies don't design these departments to make the shopper the star. To them, the star of this counter is the supermodel or the celebrity who's in the ad campaign. After all, they paid her a ton of money—she must be the star. After her, the secondary star is the lady who is selling the product. Then, in last place, comes the customer. It's totally wrong."

Ah, the eternal gap between Madison Avenue and, if not Minnesota exactly, the Minnesota that lurks within our souls. Speaking of the Gap, I myself remain haunted by that television commercial several years ago of Gap swing dancers. That was the Gap promise, in thirty seconds: just pull on these magic khaki pants and you'll know freedom from all life's cares—your spirit will be buoyant, gravity-defying, fairy-light! Consider the actual Gap experience: wrestling with too-tight pants in a too-tight dressing room in the middle of a three-hour trip to a stained, aging mall with bleak, gloomy bathrooms and horrible parking.

To say that Underhill is our bard of the suburbs is not to say that The City—or, at least, its image—is absent from *Call of the Mall*. Indeed, mall landscapes obliquely reflect and refract what seem to be fleeting, romantic, impossibly distant group memories of The City. Witness the pet store, a little area set aside for the rude life forms—and their droppings—that are only too familiar to urban shoppers but otherwise completely absent from the mall. And while teens toss a Frisbee in a lifelike play environment way up on the top floor, one girl yearningly muses: "I don't know if you've ever been to Washington Square in New York . . . but it's this park, and they have these tables with like built-in checkerboards on top?"

Then there's the Tiffany store window, tiny and boxlike, which displays just one thing: a beautiful black-and-white photo of a rainy Central Park–like landscape, a miniature diorama capturing part of our—or at least someone's—past life. Underhill says, "It sells the romance of Central Park in the rain, and being very near to Tiffany, to people who are walking around a mall." ("Hey," his shopping companion adds, "there's a smudge on the window.")

And of the mall's future?

Today, when most American malls are over twenty years old, the question of what to do about aging centers will soon be upon us.

If the buildings themselves had any intrinsic value, we'd be more likely to restore or salvage ones that need it. We restore and repurpose many public structures, such as former post offices, hotels, libraries, even churches. But most malls are too ugly and banal to warrant such effort. They've been designed to be serviceable, nothing more, and once they no longer can serve they'll have to be razed, and replaced with ... I don't know. Maybe something even worse.

I think of ghosts of retail past and retail future in my own Los   15
Angeles. I think of how our Sherman Oaks Galleria—that's right, the very Galleria made famous in "Valley Girl"—is no more. This makes me remember my own teen life, in the 1970s, in southern California. I can still feel the exciting pulse of nascent adulthood as I and my best friend, Mary Robertson, whizzed along the freeways in her tiny new Chevy Chevette. I can still envision each green-and-white exit sign, each raggedy palm tree, the malls sprawling just beyond like big pink hatboxes of promise. As with Barbie play makeup, the mall offered a vision of glamorous, cosmopolitan adulthood, an adulthood that now lay much nearer at hand. Instead of a real Sin City, Mary and I had impulsive and daring visits to the Cheesecake Factory, where the whole sensual world lay before us in over-twenty-one flavors: Amaretto, Grand Marnier, piña colada.

Today my southern-California retail world is a grid of Target (the standard), Tarjhay (uptown, lattes), and, of course, Targhetto (of the tattered parking lot, where you find yourself thinking, So this is where gang members buy their Tupperware, the better to neatly organize their important gang items). It's a colorful mélange of strip malls that advertise dry-cleaning in five different languages, and almost always feature a "USA #1 DONUTS." I think of my sixty-two-year-old Manchurian stepmother's first trip to the Van Nuys Costco—how her eyes widened in alarm, and excitement, at the sight of a fifty-foot tower of Bounty paper towels, how her white tennies flashed and pattered as she ran. Never mind Christopher Columbus and his precious spices; when it comes to retail excitement, Alice truly was beholding a brave new world.

What is a family, after all, but a collection of not quite independent, somewhat less than completely ambulatory people? And what safer harbor for families than a big, beige, temperature-controlled box?

Questions for Discussion and Writing

1. According to Loh, "the mall has gotten into the very gut, the very psyche, of the American family" (paragraph 6). Evaluate the veracity of this statement. Explain whether or not you believe that to be the case.

2. Loh asks, "And what safer harbor for families than a big, beige, temperature-controlled box?" (paragraph 6). Describe the tone of this question. What does this question imply about the structure and space of malls?

3. This appears in the "Books and Critics" section of the magazine. What sense do you get of Loh's impression of the book? Is it favorable? Stylistically, Loh includes many excerpts from the book. Do you think it is appropriate?

4. Go to a local mall and observe family dynamics. Who is there (for example, a mother holding the hand of a child)? What are they doing? Are they eating in the food court? Do the family members seem happy? Are they smiling? Is the child crying? Document your observations and then share them with your classmates. What conclusions do you draw about why the family was in the mall? What type of experience do you believe they had? Are your observations similar to the claims made in Loh's article?

5. Obtain a copy of Underhill's book *Call of the Mall* and write a book review of similar length. How does your review compare with Loh's review?

Questions for Making Connections

1. The American Civil Liberties Union (ACLU) and McIntyre, on behalf of the American Psychological Association (APA), disagree about the impact of violent television content. The ACLU maintains "Research has not proven that watching violence on television causes watchers to commit violence" (paragraph 3) while the APA insists that "Hundreds of studies have confirmed that exposing our children to a steady diet of violence in the media makes our children more violence prone" (paragraph 8). Write an argumentation essay examining both sides of the debate concerning violent television programming and its impact on children. Formulate a clear thesis on your position supporting, opposing, or modifying the claim. In the essay, include reference to both McIntyre and the ACLU.

2. In paragraph 15, Loh writes "the mall offered a vision of glamorous, cosmopolitan adulthood." Select any film, advertisement, or episode of a television program and write an essay about the "vision" (or fantasy) you believe is being offered.

3. Loh asks, "And what safer harbor for families than a big, beige, temperature-controlled box" (paragraph 6)? Select any space you believe serves as a "safe harbor" or escape for families (for example, a movie theater, an amusement

park, a park, the circus, etc.). Compare the allure of that space to the allure of malls expressed in Loh's article. In your response, you may want to refer to one of the other essays in the text. For example, you could cite the statistics by the APA to illustrate that one of the factors motivating parents to find a "safe harbor" is to get away from the television set. Theaters are a controlled environment because parents can choose which films to see.

4. How does your relationship with your family compare to the relationship of your favorite television family? The creator of the *The Simpsons*, Matt Groening, shares that "There's sort of an unspoken rule that we have on the show, which is we can do humor as dark as we want to, but the show itself is a celebration of the family" (quoted in Garrison, paragraph 10). Select one episode of any television program and compare how your personal relationship with your family coincides or differs from the television family. Does the show "[attempt] to pass itself off as a true reflection of who we are and what we want" (Underhill quoted in Loh, paragraph 8)? In your essay, you may also want to consider whether or not it is important to you to watch a show that is a mirror of your actual experience.

5. The ACLU notes "the positive societal value of violent programs that teach us important lessons about history or call attention to problems that society must address" (paragraph 11). Write an essay in defense of the positive social values of violence in entertainment. In your response, consider using evidence from any of the selections in this chapter to support your claim.

Race and Ethnicity

From African Americans to Italians, Latinos to Asians, the writers in this chapter examine images of race and ethnicity transmitted through various popular culture mediums: films and television (Beck); television and film (Navarro); film (Tucker); sports and advertising (Kellner); and music (Staples).

Music, advertising, sports, television, and film on one level often appear to be harmless and enjoyable forms of entertainment. But are these merely insidious pleasures transmitting dangerous myths? The writers in this chapter offer illuminations about popular culture, race, ethnicity, relations, and stereotypes. There are a variety of ethnicities represented including Italian, Latino, and African American. Commonly threaded throughout each of the selections is documentation of the relentless spirit of resistance: each group rises and rallies against negative stereotypes.

Any examination of race and ethnicity requires a truthful examination of stereotypes. In *Hamlet*, Polonius advises his son "This above all, to thine own self be true." In the spirit of truth seeking, take time to review your personal attitudes about race and ethnicity. The purpose of understanding personal private history and popular culture references is to better understand our own assumptions. If you feel more comfortable, keep journal entries (for your own eyes only) exploring the following: What was your first experience of difference? What is your earliest recollection of either perceiving "other" or of perceiving yourself as "other?" What attitudes about race and ethnicity did you experience at home or in school? What pictures and images did you see in popular culture? In what ways has the portrayal of race and ethnicity in popular culture reinforced or challenged your assumptions?

In "The Myth That Would Not Die: *The Sopranos*, Mafia Movies, and Italians in America," Bernard Beck points out that shows like *The Sopranos* have "been criticized by several Italian American individuals and organizations as the latest installment in the never ending offensive story of the Italian gangster world" (paragraph 10). Clearly, Beck is correct that indeed "the efforts of actual Italian American people and organizations to adjust their terms of image and identity in America are limited by the refusal of the public-as-movie-audience to abandon their beloved, cherished Mafia images" (paragraph 9).

From the mafia to maids, it truly seems that no group escapes the media's convenient packaging. In "Trying to Get Beyond the Role of the Maid; Hispanic Actors Are Seen as Underrepresented, with the Exception of One Part," Mireya Navarro, likewise, laments that although "the role of maid has belonged to different ethnic groups at one time or another in the history of film and television, . . . these days it seems to be a niche for Hispanic actresses" (paragraph 5). She argues "Hispanic actors and media watchdogs argue that stereotypical roles loom disproportionately large because there are not enough alternatives" (paragraph 23). This sentiment is echoed by Chris Tucker in his personal essay "Different Stories," where he pleads for the absolute necessity of more alternatives for African American actors and comedians like himself: "We need to tell the stories from back then . . . Tell the story of Frederick Douglass. The guy came from nowhere and was one of the most brilliant minds of all time" (paragraph 22).

Are there stories that escape stereotypes?

In Douglas Kellner's scholarly analysis "Sports, Media, Culture and Race—Some Reflections on Michael Jordan," he notes, "Jordan thus presents a figure who mobilizes many fantasies (i.e., athletic greatness, wealth, success, etc.) . . . though his Blackness too has conflicting connotations" (paragraph 15). Staples more harshly rants against a similar negative connation. Staples' "Editorial Observer" column rants at the current violent nature of hip-hop and the negative messages the hip-hop music industry is transmitting to teenagers. Staples begins: "African-American teenagers are beset on all sides by dangerous myths about race. The most poisonous one defines middle-class normalcy and achievement as 'white,' while embracing violence, illiteracy and drug dealing as 'authentically' black" (paragraph 1). Think about the various "myths about race" that you received. Were they dangerous?

Will we ever be able to eradicate "dangerous myths about race"? Will we ever be able to eliminate stereotypes? Will there be a time when popular culture mediums transmit to audiences the "different stories" behind the colorful mosaic of our diverse lives?

Pre-Reading Chapter 4

1. Write down all your responses to the questions raised in paragraph 3. Have the opinions you held as a child and young adult evolved? Explain whether or not you believe your ideas and opinions are "politically correct."

2. As you survey the titles and authors in this chapter, note your first reactions to the titles and any key words that capture your attention: "The Myth That Would Not Die: *The Sopranos*, Mafia Movies, and Italians in America"/Bernard Beck; "Trying to Get Beyond the Role of the Maid; Hispanic Actors Are Seen as Underrepresented, with the Exception of One Part"/Mireya Navarro; "Different Stories"/Chris Tucker; "Sports, Media Culture, and Race—Some Reflections on Michael Jordan"/Douglas Kellner; and "Editorial Observer: How Hip-Hop Music Lost Its Way and Betrayed Its Fans"/Brent Staples. Before reading, jot down word associations, for example, "mafia," "monk," "hip-hop." Are you familiar with the topics?

3. In your ideas journal and scrapbook, maintain a list of topics and parallels across mediums. For example, after reading about "hip-hop," you can write your own parallels with other musical genres, such as punk. After reading about Jordan, you can write down your own observations about another sports hero (for example, Tiger Woods).

The Myth That Would Not Die: *The Sopranos*, Mafia Movies, and Italians in America

BERNARD BECK

A distinguished professor and social critic, Bernard Beck has written numerous articles on welfare, films, and theater covering such diverse topics as "On the Politics of Speaking in the Name of Society," "The Military as a Welfare Institution," "The Limits of Deinstitutionalization," "Welfare as a Moral Category," "Talking Violence Blues," "Cooking Welfare Stew," "Joe: American in Blue-Collar Drag," "Toward a Poor Classroom," and "Ghost in the Family," for journals including Social Problems, Contemporary Sociology, American Sociologist, *and* Multicultural Perspectives. *Many of his articles, such as the following, from* Multicultural Perspectives *(2000), have been reprinted in numerous academic books. Beck currently teaches at Northwestern University.*

Pre-Reading

Beck writes, "Of course, every immigrant group was associated . . . with some stereotyped occupation" (paragraph 2). List five immigrant groups and the "stereotyped occupation" associated with each group. What are the best ways to challenge stereotypes? Provide at least three suggestions.

✦

THE RETURN OF COLUMBUS

Everyone knows that Italian explorers began the European transformation of the New World. When masses of Italians immigrated to America at the end of the last century, however, they arrived in an English-speaking country in which they were strangers. The mainstream culture of that America had not come from those early Italian arrivals; the Americans and the Italian immigrants were strangers to one another. Over the course of a century, both the host society and the incoming group got an idea of one another and of the peculiar new way of living, which was emerging here and transforming both of them: the crowded, multicultural, industrial city. Among the many new features of urban life that appeared were modern crime, criminal business, and the organized forces intended to deal with it. We got a new form of cops and robbers. We also got new ways of understanding crime and how it works in a modern society. It is not surprising that the new activity and the new members of society came to be thought of together.

For more than 100 years, American culture has nurtured a peculiar theme, defining modern criminal business as an Italian invention and finding the Italian version most interesting, if not always the most alarming. The Greeks ran restaurants, the Chinese ran laundries, and the Irish were policemen. Every new group in turn was also associated in the minds of respectable citizens, at least for a while, with disreputable activities such as crime, sports, and manual labor. These were often the most accessible ways of making a living and achieving social mobility. So many groups trying to define their ethnic pride must live down some gangsters and can boast of famous athletes.

However, Italians were and are especially identified with organized crime, even as they have grown and prospered as an American group. Success, respectability, and familiarity have not freed them from the taint of the Mob. This enduring image has become a staple of the American commercial culture and folk consciousness. Through the dissemination of American ideas in movies and popular culture, Italians have come to stand for organized criminality all over the world.

BRAVE NEW WORLD

Several new developments have occurred during the last two centuries. Together, they produce this contemporary cultural monolith—the Italian movie gangster world. In America, the worldwide movement of industrialism and big cities happened quickly and without significant interference. The institutions of urban living had to evolve quickly and uncontrollably. These cities were not ancient centers changed by modern conditions. They sprang virtually from the American landscape, leaving the inhabitants, almost all of them newcomers to city life, to figure out the rules afterward.

5   A large industrial labor force was needed immediately, and great numbers of peasants and other traditional people from other parts of the world were recruited for the jobs. These newcomers were strangers not only to city life and industrial organization, but also to America itself, with its foreign language, history, culture, and (usually) religion. They came from places now identified as large countries, but in many cases those countries were very recent packages of formerly separate regions. So those who came from the various parts of Italy were more likely to be self-defined by local rather than national origin. In America, as a result, they undertook the difficult task of becoming Italians in unconscious collaboration with a multitude of strangers who were now to be called their compatriots.

Finally, modern conditions and capitalist values created the possibility of large-scale organizations devoted to illegal enterprises. Crime, like manufacturing, was transformed by the scale and openness of modern society into a complex activity requiring and making possible the coordination and management of large numbers of workers. Simultaneously, large and complex systems of what we now call the criminal justice system appeared, including modern police forces, court systems, and penal institutions. To further complicate the picture, the diverse cultures and values of the immigrants produced conflicts over many of the laws that were enacted for the regulation of American life but having their inspiration in the beliefs of the dominant and narrow group of the native born. This emergent multiculturalism was no secret to the pillars of the American community. Their constant fear over this period of change was the deleterious and immoral effect of the strangers who were necessary for economic development but abhorrent to respectable communities. It was a neat ideological trick to attribute the origin of the new, modern forms of crime to the newly arrived immigrants. In fact, both appeared as a consequence of the basic and irresistible growth of the most modern of modern societies.

LIFE COULD BE A DREAM

Another ingredient of this modern American stew was the rise of popular culture. A growing accompaniment to the new realities of modern life was a burgeoning industry of ideas and images mass produced with modern technologies and distributed through the marketplace as a bonus of urban life. The concentration of population and the organization of large scale enterprise made it possible and necessary to create culture that would be shared by a large American population. Otherwise, there would be no mechanism for Americans to share common values and sentiments. Except for their common reception of this kind of culture, they could not affirm their common membership in a moral community. The demands of modern living were increasingly palliated by a stream of culture whose hyper-reality often mattered more than the concrete reality of daily life. It has become more true than ever that our understanding of the larger world is more important to us, and that understanding comes to us through popular culture. Therefore, our images and understandings of immigrants, of subcultures, and of the human nature of diverse peoples are heavily influenced by what we receive through that culture.

On the other hand, that culture is received and used by us for a variety of thinking and feeling tasks. It is a popular insight that in the modern world, information and entertainment are no longer distinct. Our use of entertainment requires that cultural products follow the rules of cultural convention. Nowhere is this iron law of popular narrative more evident than in movies and television. The fate of diverse subgroups in our society depends on the roles assigned to them in such popular dramas, and those roles are assigned in accordance with the needs of plot construction more than the needs of accuracy.

In consequence, the cultural role of the Italian American community and its identification with organized crime are dictated by literary even more than by sociological principles. The changes in Italian American lives are reflected in the popular culture only as variations on this basic theme. The efforts of actual Italian American people and organizations to adjust their terms of image and identity in America are limited by the refusal of the public-as-movie-audience to abandon their beloved, cherished Mafia images. All of the serious concerns that subcultural groups have in a modern society, such as the limits of assimilation, the relevance of maintaining separate identity, and the value of preserving traditional culture, are affected for Italian Americans by the looming presence of the organized crime image. And as with other groups, their own understandings of themselves are subject to those images, just as the understandings of the general public are. Most problematic is the fact that the characteristics attributed to Italian American people and culture in those images are felt by them and by others to be admirable as well as deplorable, fascinating as well as terrifying, endearing as well as off-putting. Those characteristics include some that Italians are happy to identify with, such as warmth, family closeness, loyalty, courage, eloquence, humor, and concern for personal honor. In fact, as the most recent vehicles show, the movie images of Italian Americans in organized crime are used by Italian Americans as sources of amusement and models of personal style.

IS THIS THE END OF RICO?

10   *The Sopranos* (Landress & Chase, 1999), which began in 1998, is a weekly dramatic series made for cable TV and shown on Home Box Office. It has been critically applauded and nominated for a number of Emmy Awards. It has also been criticized by several Italian American individuals and organizations as the latest installment in the never-ending offensive story of the Italian gangster world. This kind of movie or television show has been wildly popular with audiences in America and around the world since the 1930s, if not earlier. Although Italians were pictured in them

from the very beginning, as in *Scarface* (Hawks, Hughes, & Rosson, 1932), other immigrant groups have also been highlighted in gangster movies from that period until the present. Another 1930s classic, *Angels With Dirty Faces* (Bischoff & Curtiz, 1938), dealt with Irish gangsters, as does *State of Grace* (Dowd, Ostrow, Rotholz, & Joanou, 1990) from the 1990s. Other groups include Jews, as in *Once Upon a Time in America* (Milchan & Leone, 1984) and *Bugsy* (Beatty, Johnson, & Levinson, 1991); Chinese, as in *Year of the Dragon* (DeLaurentiis & Cimino, 1985) and countless Triad movies; Japanese, as in *Rising Sun* (Kaufman & Kaufman, 1993) and countless Yakuza Movies; African Americans, as in *Kansas City* (Altman, 1996) and *Hoodlum* (Mancuso & Duke, 1997); Hispanics, as in the most recent *Scarface* (Bregman & DePalma, 1983); and even White South Africans from the Apartheid era in *Lethal Weapon 2* (Donner & Silver, 1989). Although these other groups may have had to suffer under temporary reputations for organized criminality, they have been able to move on in American life, leaving those images behind them. There has been no such escape for Italians.

One of the most interesting features of the continuing survival of the Italian movie gangster, so deplored by Italian American advocates, is the centrality within the genre of the present generation of distinguished Italian American filmmakers—directors including Francis Ford Coppola (*The Godfather;* Ruddy & Coppola, 1972, and its sequels), and Martin Scorsese (*Goodfellas;* Winkler & Scorsese, 1990); actors, including Marlon Brando (*The Godfather;* Ruddy & Coppola, 1972; *The Freshman;* Lobell & Bergman, 1990), Robert DeNiro (*The Godfather: Part II;* Coppola, 1974; *Goodfellas;* Winkler & Scorsese, 1990; *Once Upon a Time in America;* Milchan & Leone, 1984; *Analyze This;* Rosenthal, Weinstein, & Ramis, 1999), Al Pacino (*The Godfather;* Ruddy & Coppola, 1972; *Scarface;* Bregman & DePalma, 1983) and Joe Pesci (*Goodfellas;* Winkler & Scorsese, 1990; *Lethal Weapon 2;* Donner & Silver, 1989); and writers, especially Mario Puzo, author of *The Godfather. The Sopranos* (Landress & Chase, 1999) has already raised James Gandolfini, Lorraine Bracco, and Edie Falco to prominence for their performances.

The growing interest in exploring the Italian character of organized crime that these film artists demonstrate is evidence of its deep meaning to Italian Americans, to their sense of identity, and to the unresolved issues this community faces in negotiating its role in American society. Moreover, the content of the movies has changed over time to reflect the changing matters that concern successive generations of Italian Americans. From the problems of working class immigrants in the first generation to the quandaries of suburban middle class life in the third and fourth, movies about gangsters turn out to be movies about being Italian. Violence, legality, and respectability remain central issues, but they are found side by side with questions about preserving traditional loyalties, family bonds, and a distinctive national culture that ranges from cooking to emotional displays. These are not the concerns imposed on this culturally embattled ethnic group by a mainstream culture that is derogatory and repressive. They are the concerns raised from within that community by its most accomplished children.

After reviewing the history of gangster movies, Italian and non-Italian, a student might think that the enduring association of Italians with organized crime in the American popular imagination reflects recognition of the peculiar interest that the Italian version has, in the positive and attractive qualities it highlights. These qualities are seen as peculiarly and admirably Italian by members of the group and by outsiders. It is certainly not necessary to be involved in organized crime to be authentically Italian. However, that corner of the Italian American experience may be a landmark for those exploring ethnic identity without accepting the cultural judgments of the overwhelming generic American culture. In the fictional world of the Italian gangster movie, there is a foundation for someone who would resist becoming altogether too "Merigan."

References

Altman, R. (Producer & Director). (1996). *Kansas City* [Film]. (Available from the Fine Line Cinema, Los Angeles, CA)

Beatty, W., Johnson, M., & Levinson, B. (Producers), & Levinson, B. (Director). (1991). *Bugsy* [Film]. (Available from Columbia TriStar Pictures, Los Angeles, CA)

Bischoff, S. (Producer), & Curtiz, M. (Director). (1938). *Angels With Dirty Faces* [Film]. (Available from Warner Bros., Los Angeles, CA)

Bregman, M. (Producer), & DePalma, B. (Director). (1983). *Scarface* [Film]. (Available from Universal Pictures, Los Angeles, CA)

Coppola, F. F. (Producer & Director). (1974). *The Godfather: Part II* [Film]. (Available from Paramount Pictures, Los Angeles, CA)

De Laurentiis, D. (Producer), & Cimino, M. (Director). (1985). *Year of the Dragon* [Film]. (Available from MGM/UA, Los Angeles, CA)

Donner, R., & Silver, J. (Producers), & Donner, R. (Director). (1989). *Lethal Weapon 2* [Film]. (Available from Warner Bros., Los Angeles, CA)

Dowd, N., Ostrow, R., & Rotholz, R. (Producers), & Joanou, P. (Director). (1990). *State of Grace* [Film]. (Available from Orion Pictures, Los Angeles, CA)

Hawks, H., & Hughes, H. (Producers), & Hawks, H., & Rosson, R. (Directors). (1932). *Scarface* [Film]. (Available from United Artists, Los Angeles, CA)

Kaufman, Peter (Producer), & Kaufman, Philip (Director). (1993). *Rising Sun* [Film]. (Available from Twentieth Century Fox, Los Angeles, CA)

Landress, I. S. (Producer), & Chase, D. (Director). (1999). *The Sopranos*. New York: HBO.

Lobell, M. (Producer), & Bergman, A. (Director). (1990). *The Freshman* [Film]. (Available from TriStar Pictures, Los Angeles, CA)

Mancuso, F., Jr. (Producer), & Duke, B. (Director). (1997). *Hoodlum* [Film]. (Available from MGM/UA, Los Angeles, CA)

Milchan, A. (Producer), & Leone, S. (Director). (1984). *Once Upon a Time in America* [Film]. (Available from Warner Bros., Los Angeles, CA)

Rosenthal, J., & Weinstein, P. (Producers), & Ramis, H. (Director). (1999). *Analyze This* [Film]. (Available from Warner Bros., Los Angeles, CA)

Ruddy, A. S. (Producer), & Coppola, F. F. (Director). (1972). *The Godfather* [Film]. (Available from Paramount Pictures, Los Angeles, CA)

Winkler, I. (Producer), & Scorsese, M. (Director). (1990). *Goodfellas* [Film]. (Available from Warner Bros., Los Angeles, CA)

Questions for Discussion and Writing

1. According to Beck, what is the Italian gangster image portrayed in film, television, and the media? In what ways does your personal image coincide or differ from his interpretation? In your response, include specific examples from his essay and your own observations.

2. Why do you think that "success, respectability, and familiarity have not freed them [Italians] from the taint of the Mob" (paragraph 3)? What do you believe accounts for "the refusal of the public-as-movie-audience to abandon their beloved, cherished Mafia images" (paragraph 9)?

3. In paragraphs 10 and 11, Beck includes a comprehensive list of films and television programs. What purpose does the list serve? As a reader, how helpful was the list in supporting Beck's thesis? Are there any additional gangster films that you would add to the list?

4. Watch an episode of *The Sopranos* or rent an Italian gangster film. Analyze the extent to which the episode or movie scene perpetuates the stereotype. In your response, consider the following questions: Who are the main characters?

What are they wearing? How do they speak? What groups are not included in the episode (for example, women or children)? Are your conclusions similar to or different from Beck's conclusions?

5. Beck writes, "the fate of diverse subgroups in our society depends on the roles assigned to them . . . in accordance with the needs of plot construction more than the needs of accuracy" (paragraph 8). Select any group of immigrants (for example, Italian, Irish, Chinese, Greek, etc.) and write an essay supporting, modifying, or refuting Beck's claim.

Trying to Get Beyond the Role of the Maid: Hispanic Actors Are Seen as Underrepresented, with the Exception of One Part

MIREYA NAVARRO

Pulitzer Prize–winning journalist Mireya Navarro has written numerous articles for several of the most prestigious newspapers and magazines in the country, including the New York Times, Latina *magazine, and the* San Francisco Examiner. *She won the Pulitzer Prize in 2001 for National Reporting. The following appeared in the* New York Times *on May 16, 2002.*

Pre-Reading

Reflect on your personal knowledge of television programs and films. Select one film or television program with a Latino character (for example, *Will and Grace*). How is the Latino character portrayed? Is he or she in a "low status occupation" (paragraph 7)? Does the episode reinforce or challenge stereotypes?

———————— ✦ ————————

Lupe Ontiveros's idea of a plum role is a Hispanic heroine, someone like the union organizer Dolores Huerta, a founder of the United Farm Workers, or perhaps the 17th-century Mexican poet and nun Sor Juana Inés de la Cruz, often viewed as the first feminist of the Americas.

But for most of her 25 years as an actor, Ms. Ontiveros has played mostly maids. She figures she has played a maid at least 150 times, in films like "As Good as It Gets" and NBC sitcoms like "Veronica's Closet" and, most recently, "Leap of Faith."

"It's their continued perspective of who we are," Ms. Ontiveros said of Hollywood and how it views Hispanics. "They don't know we're very much a part of this country and that we make up every part of this country." Indeed, to play a maid, she must put on an accent her family lost a generation ago.

"When I go in there and speak perfect English, I don't get the part," said Ms. Ontiveros, a college graduate from El Paso whose parents were immigrants from Mexico and owned two restaurants and a tortilla factory.

The role of maid has belonged to different ethnic groups at one time or another in the history of film and television, but these days it seems to be a niche for Hispanic actresses, especially on prime-time television. As maids, they are now featured on, or have made recent appearances on, "Will and Grace" (Rosario) on NBC, "Dharma and Greg" (Celia) on ABC and even in animation, with "King of the Hill" (Lupino) on Fox.   5

There was also "Pasadena," a prime-time soap on Fox that was broadcast four times this season; Ms. Ontiveros played Pilar, one of two Hispanic maids. (There was also one white maid.) Film and television typecasting of blacks in such roles once led to protests by groups like the National Association for the Advancement of Colored People, and today the black maid has all but disappeared from big screen and small.

But that sensitivity has not carried over to Hispanics. Ms. Ontiveros has become a sort of Hispanic Hattie McDaniel, who played variations of the smart-mouthed maid in dozens of movies in the 1930's and won an Oscar for best supporting actress for her portrayal of Scarlett O'Hara's mammy in the 1939 film "Gone With the Wind."

Children Now, a child-advocacy group in Oakland, Calif., that keeps track of diversity on prime-time television, says that Hispanics are the most significantly underrepresented ethnic group on prime time—given their 12 percent share of the nation's population—and that Latino characters, more than any other, tend to be concentrated in low-status occupations like service workers, unskilled laborers and criminals.

The group released a report yesterday taking NBC, ABC, CBS, Fox, UPN and WB to task for making "minimal progress" on diversity on prime-time television.

10   "The baton has been passed from black actors to Hispanic actors to play this kind of stereotypical role," said J. Fred MacDonald, a television and radio historian who runs a historical film archive in Chicago. The reasons for the pigeonholing were not clear, he said, but there did not seem to be enough of a united front among the Hispanic groups to pressure the industry as black groups did.

Others said the lack of variety in roles could also have to do with the fact that many writers and producers live in Los Angeles, where many maids, if not most, are indeed Hispanic: maids, gardeners, parking valets and restaurant workers may be the only Hispanics those in charge of the shows may know.

"It's not that some Hispanics are not maids," said Jeanine Basinger, chairwoman of the film studies department at Wesleyan University. "The issue is that not all Hispanic women are maids. And since some white women and black women and Asian women are maids, can we see maids other than that?"

In a study by the Tomas Rivera Policy Institute commissioned by the Screen Actors Guild in 1999, actors from Los Angeles, New York and Miami complained that the entertainment industry seemed stuck on the image of Hispanics as mostly poor, Spanish-speaking or of recent immigrant origin.

15   This week, at the preview of the fall season, NBC, the No. 1 network, introduced the comedy "Good Morning, Miami," featuring Tessie Santiago, a Miami native, as Lucía Rojas Miller, a scatterbrained co-anchor of a morning television show who sports tight red outfits and a heavy Spanish accent. In "Kingpin," a six-part limited series about a drug lord and his family, the main female Hispanic character also has an accent and works as a Drug Enforcement Administration agent.

Jeff Zucker, president for NBC Entertainment, says it is just a matter of time before Hispanic portrayals evolve into a fuller picture.

"As diversity increases, the span of roles increases," he said. "It's an evolution."

Officials at Fox played down the significance of Hispanic maids on "Pasadena" and "King of the Hill," noting that "Pasadena" also had a white maid and that the maid on "King" was a minor character that made only rare appearances.

"Can we also take a look at the other roles Latinos are being placed in?" said Mitsy Wilson, senior vice president for diversity development at Fox, speaking of lead roles like those played by

Jessica Alba on "Dark Angel." "We're moving in the direction of putting people in roles of leading characters."

In the fall season, WB plans to put on "Greetings From Tucson," a comedy about a Mexican-Irish family, and CBS is to add "C.S.I.: Miami," to feature a Hispanic character in the ensemble. 20

But typecasting seems entrenched even as the depiction of Hispanics in movies and television has improved noticeably, with increasingly versatile roles offered to Hispanic actors, thanks to an increase in Latin-themed projects made by Latinos and the mainstream success of Hispanic leads like Jennifer Lopez and Antonio Banderas.

Ms. Ontiveros has had some independent film standing of her own, winning a special jury prize for acting at this year's Sundance Film Festival for "Real Women Have Curves," an HBO movie that will have its premiere in September. The film is about generational conflict between a Mexican-American teenager (America Ferrera) who wants to go to college, while her mother, played by Ms. Ontiveros, wants her to work in a Los Angeles sweatshop.

Last year, she received excellent notices for her role as the maid Consuelo in Todd Solondz's "Storytelling." And in 2000, Ms. Ontiveros won the National Board of Review award for best supporting actress in the film "Chuck and Buck," in which she played a sympathetic theater manager without an accent.

On television, the Latin-themed "George Lopez Show" on ABC, "Resurrection Boulevard" on Showtime and "American Family" on PBS present other images of Hispanics. But Hispanic actors and media watchdogs argue that stereotypical roles loom disproportionately large because there are not enough alternatives to counteract something like the Hispanic maid in hit comedies like "Will and Grace."

"As long as Latinos are not a force in the writing and producing, the wait is going to be a lot longer," said Judy Reyes, who plays a no-nonsense nurse on NBC in "Scrubs." 25

In its report, Children Now said Latino characters in the 2001–2 television season inched up to 4 percent of the prime-time population, from 2 percent the previous year. But they remained stuck at only 2 percent of primary recurring roles. "We see a troubling picture," said Patti Miller, director of the group's program on children and the media. "Television may be entertainment, but what message does that send to a Latina girl about her place in the world?"

Lisa Navarrete, spokeswoman for the National Council of La Raza, a civil rights organization that puts on the annual American Latino Media Arts Awards to promote the Latino image in entertainment, said the problem of perceptions runs deep.

She noted that in the Oscar-winning film "A Beautiful Mind," based on the life of John Forbes Nash, the math genius and Nobel laureate, there was one factual lapse that received little attention but particularly rankled her. His wife, Alicia Nash, is from El Salvador, but the movie made no mention of her ethnicity and the part was played by Jennifer Connelly, a non-Latina, who won an Oscar for the portrayal.

Ms. Navarrete said the omission robbed audiences of the image of a Hispanic professional who helped her husband re-emerge from his mental illness. "They just changed it," she said of the real Mrs. Nash. "You'd think she's a Southern belle."

30   The film's director, Ron Howard, declined a request for comment. Akiva Goldsman, the screenwriter, did not answer a similar request.

For Ms. Ontiveros, being a maid is not her personal reality though it has become her signature role. Her middle-class parents sent her to Texas Women's University, where she majored in psychology and social work, and treated her to a month-and-a-half trip to Europe on graduation. At 4 feet 11 inches and admittedly not glamorous-looking, Ms. Ontiveros said she began being hired to play maids soon after she began as an extra in the 1970's, as she followed artistic leanings that came from childhood dance and piano lessons. Her maid résumé includes some memorable parts, and films including Steven Spielberg's "Goonies" and Gregory Nava's "Norte."

In 20 films she has also played other roles, like Selena's murderer in "Selena," and has also found varied parts in Latin-themed theater, most notably "Zoot Suit" on Broadway and cable shows like Nickelodeon's "Brothers Garcia" and "Resurrection Boulevard" on Showtime.

Ms. Ontiveros, who for a long time pursued an acting career while working as a social worker and bringing up three sons with her husband, a car-parts dealer, in Los Angeles, said she did not regret playing so many maids. It has given her steady work and allowed her to portray working people honorably, she said. She recently narrated the documentary "Maid in America."

"I'm proud to represent those hands that labor in this country," she said. "I've given every maid I've ever portrayed soul and heart."

35   And, she added, she has never hired one.

Questions for Discussion and Writing

1. According to Navarro, how are Latinos portrayed in entertainment? What specific forms of entertainment are mentioned in the article?
2. In what ways have organizations such as the National Association for the Advancement of Colored People challenged stereotypes in Hollywood?
3. Jeff Zucker, president for NBC Entertainment states, "it's just a matter of time . . . as diversity increases, the span of roles increases" (paragraphs 16–17). Why do you believe Navarro includes Zucker's statement? Is the article fair and balanced?
4. Select any one scene in any television show (*Will and Grace, Dark Angel*, etc.) or movie (*Selena, Real Women Have Curves*, etc.) and write an essay analyzing the extent to which it perpetuates the Latino stereotype as described by Navarro.
5. Two Latino heroines are mentioned in paragraph 1, Dolores Huerta and Sor Juana Inés de la Cruz. Conduct research on either one of the heroines and write an essay demonstrating whether or not you believe their life story represents a positive Latino image.

Different Stories

Chris Tucker

Comedian and actor Chris Tucker is best known for his outrageous comedy act and film roles, including the wildly popular Rush Hour 2 *(2001) and* Rush Hour *with action superstar Jackie Chan (1998),* Jackie Brown *(1997),* The Fifth Element *(1997),* Money Talks *(1997), and others. The following essay, written in a colloquial style, is from* America Behind the Color Line: Dialogues with African Americans *(2004), edited by the award-winning African-American scholar, member of the Pulitzer Prize board, and distinguished professor at Harvard University, Henry Louis Gates, Jr., who has been a tireless activist in expanding the literary canon.*

Pre-Reading

Write a list of three African-American actors and describe recent roles they played. Did the characters portray a positive or negative view of African Americans? Does the plot reveal "politically correct or incorrect" attitudes?

✦

I was the youngest of six children. My mother, Mary Tucker, is a missionary at a church. She's been a missionary all her life, helping people. My father, Norris Tucker, has a cleaning business. I've always been a business-minded person, because I watched my father run his own business, and before coming to California, I only worked for my father. That was it; I never had another job in my life before I went out to L.A. and started doin' comedy.

I was just a kid with a dream and a vision. I loved entertainment. I loved movies. I used to go see all the old movies with my daddy—like *Stir Crazy* with Richard Pryor. On the weekend my daddy would take us one of two places. We'd either go to the high school football game and go to McDonald's afterwards, or we'd go to the movies and then get some pizza.

We always saw the black movies. Every Eddie Murphy movie, every Richard Pryor movie, every black movie, we'd go see. I would sit in the movie theater and be fascinated and just feel so good. I used to look at the screen and say, I'm gonna do that one day—I'm gonna be up on that screen. I used to go home and sleep and dream about being in movies. So from a young age, I had a passion for entertainment and movies.

People know what's funny. When I'm in a movie, I'm a comedian before anything else. I know people, all people, and I make sure I can relate to everybody. I thought about this throughout my career. I said, I don't want to be a comedian that just gears toward black people or just gears toward white people. I want to be a universal comedian. I want to take my comedy and make it broad so everybody'll laugh and I'll never be just in a box. I thought about it when I was young. And to this day I say, when I do a movie, I want everybody to be able to enjoy it. I don't know how I do it, but it's part of my consciousness when I work.

5   I like a lot of comedians. Eddie Murphy is a genius. He can just laugh and be funny. One of my favorite movies is *48 Hours* 'cause he was real; he didn't do slapstick. That's my whole thing. I never wanted to be slapstick. Eddie Murphy wasn't slapstick; he was just straight funny. He was naturally funny, and that's what I always wanted to be. I modeled myself a lot watching Eddie Murphy, just the way he did it. You could feel that he was real. You thought you'd go out of the movies and he'd be standin' right there.

When you make films in Hollywood, you experience everything. I prepared myself for it and I maneuvered around it. Whatever you do, there's gonna always be somebody who don't like you or somebody saying you ain't good enough, or we want to do this or we want to use you for that. My whole thing is, try not to get caught into it. If you spend too much time in it, that means they got you. My thing is to just maneuver right around and step right over whatever it is and keep going, because you're gonna experience a little bit of everything, whatever you do, and not just in Hollywood.

You have to separate this entertainment business from your real life, because if you don't have your life right, and if you're not together, then it's gonna be real difficult to be creative and to make that creativity go over into movies. I knew from the start that when you get successful, when you get famous, you sometimes get unfocused. A lot of new people come into your life, a lot of big decisions. My thing was, okay, I knew it was gonna happen, so let me prepare myself for it. Let me separate myself so I can keep my creativity, so I can keep fresh ideas, keep my vision, keep renewing myself. So I live out of town, outside the star system. If you soak yourself all over in the Hollywood thing, then you just do whatever, because you listen to everybody. Especially because I'm younger, I knew I had to do something to keep myself focused.

I gotta thank God for my parents, because I've always been around spiritual people. My mother's very spiritual, and my father is very spiritual. My spirituality comes from my upbringing, and from Atlanta, Georgia. It comes from being raised in the church. Even though I was sleeping in the church half the time when I was young, it's still there in some way. It's a part of me, just who I am. I've met a lot of people in my life who come to me because I could tell them something, because I've been raised a certain way and can say, when times get hard, get on your knees and pray. I think before anything—before church and everything—you've gotta be spiritual and have a relationship with God. The higher you go, you're gonna have more decisions and bigger decisions to make.

What motivates me is people. I think that's why I know people, and I know what makes them tick. I know what makes them laugh, I know what makes them chuckle, and I love people. That's my thing, my shtick. I study a person in a minute. When I go to the movies, I don't watch the movie. I look to the side. I watch people and see what makes them laugh and what bores them. When they're bored, I say, well, I know I ain't gonna ever do that! And when they start laughing, I say, I can do that; I could take that to another level when I do a movie. I watch people, I listen to people, and then I just do it. People are my thing.

10   If I look at something and I know it ain't cool, because of the way my mama and daddy raised me, it hurts me more than I think it hurts other people, 'cause people just want to see me do movies. They're just like, do a movie! Do a movie! Do a movie! But I gotta think about the little kids—about all kids, 'cause I got little white kids come up to me, and Chinese kids, everybody comes up to me, and they're my fans, and I don't want to mislead them, no matter what. I don't think a movie is that important compared to these kids. I think movies are good. I love them. They're fun and they're entertaining. But I want to do something that's gonna motivate, and maybe even change people's lives. My expectations are big. I want to go to the next level. I don't just want to make movies. I want to do movies that change people's lives— movies that affect even my life, learning and traveling around the world. I'm always excited about the next thing I'm gonna do. Lots of times I don't know what the next thing is, and that's the good thing about it. That's the point of being alive: don't know.

    The movie companies have seen what works, so they keep doing it. What people gotta realize is—and I understand it, and it's fine—movie companies want to make a lot of money. People gotta understand, the studio heads can get fired. Any day! If they make a wrong move—make two, three bad moves—they're fired. Then they gotta go to another studio, or if that don't happen, they might not have work. So they're saying, okay, what works? If Chris Tucker opens big, get Chris Tucker. And they offer me anything, a movie doin' anything. They just want to know it's gonna open, it's gonna make money, and they're gonna look good on the balance sheets. And then there they go; they keep their job. They're fighting for their job, and we're fighting for our job.

    Seriously, I definitely see myself as having a particular responsibility for black people out there. I've got a responsibility and I'm real hard on myself, harder than anybody. We are blessed here in America, but that brings a lot of responsibility. If you're blessed, you have to help others. That's why we're put here on this earth—to help others, not just to be well off and not help others and say, that's not my problem. It is our problem, if that's our brothers and sisters. If we know about it, then we need to do what we can to help. Going to Africa changed my life, and it motivated me, 'cause it's more than just doing movies—more than just going to get an award. It's people.

    When I went to South Africa, that was special, but nothing like my trip to Ethiopia and Uganda, because I saw real Africa! Especially Ethiopia, because it was spiritual ground, the home of ancient history. The Ethiopian people claim descent from King Solomon and the Queen of Sheba, and Menelik was the Ethiopian son of King Solomon and the Queen of Sheba. There were originally lots of Jewish people in Ethiopia, then Muslims and Christians. The Bible was written there, or close by, and I'm like, whoa! That's like big, you know.

People looked up to me in Ethiopia like I never dreamed of. They thought I was Menelik comin' back home or something. The people I met are very spiritual, and they have dignity. Everybody there is royal—royal people. Be broke on the street, still royal! When I was in Ethiopia, they treated me like royalty, so I think I got some Ethiopian in me. I think it's my Ethiopian eyes. It was like, we just loving you all, keep doin' what you're doin'! And I felt that, 'cause in America we can get a little materialistic sometimes because we're a rich country, and that happens. In Ethiopia you could see that they were a loving people, but there was a lot of poverty. Fortunately, there isn't that level of poverty here in America. But the Ethiopians are just nice people, and they don't care too much about all that stuff. They care about other stuff because they have to live life, survive it. They're not materialistic people, 'cause there ain't too much material over there! It changed my life, seeing it.

They've watched my movies out there, and mostly all of them 15 said, I love you, Chris Tucker—with passion. In America most people come up and say, you funny, man, you funny! Rarely somebody says, I love you. Everybody in Ethiopia, that's just a natural thing—I love you. I love you, Chris Tucker. And I was like, man, these people are just nice, beautiful people, and the movie means the world to them; my coming there meant the world to them. It really affected me, 'cause they couldn't care less about me being a star; they just appreciated the fact that I was over there.

I was invited to go to Ethiopia and Uganda by Bono, who's a big activist on poverty and AIDS in Africa. We met in D.C. through a mutual friend. He said he was setting up a special trip with Treasury Secretary Paul O'Neill to look at poverty and AIDS in Ethiopia and Uganda and help publicize these problems to kids and grown-ups in America so more can be done to help. And I said to him, I would love to go when you get it set up.

So I went with the treasury secretary and Bono and a couple of college students. We toured villages; we went to people's homes and to hospitals where kids were being treated for AIDS and to orphanages with little babies left behind when their parents died of AIDS. We traveled in motorcades everywhere. We visited a lot of schools and we visited places where they were producing coffee, cotton, sugar, and other things they grow for export and for themselves. Paul O'Neill wanted to see what was making the economy so bad and why they weren't capitalizing on their natural resources. We saw a lot of bad stuff, a lot of sad stuff that I'll never forget, a lot of deep stuff. It changed my life, because it showed me not to take nothing for granted. I've seen a total difference from America. I've seen poverty at its worst, but I also saw a beautiful country. I saw beautiful people. Traveling to Africa let me get another outlook on life, another perspective. Everything ain't just glitz and glamour, and we take a lot for granted, like water and other basics.

I don't know that we're on the verge of great things happening for black people in Hollywood, though I'd like it to be so. For people who make it big, the paychecks keep getting bigger. And there's a broader audience now for black people in Hollywood. But Hollywood is still a tight niche. You flip in through the door to get a movie, and then getting a hit movie is like trying to get into heaven. Even to this day, I see movies that I would've liked to get. I sort of wonder, why didn't I hear about that? Maybe it just wasn't right for me; they didn't think about li'l old me. You gotta be faster and quicker and maneuver better, I guess, 'cause it's real narrow. That's why there's only a few black comedians you can name, a few black actresses you can name. You can name a few white actors at the top who are really making a whole bunch of money, really doing good. It's just tight, tight, tight, so you gotta be the best at what you do, and you gotta know exactly what you want to do.

20   It's hard for everyone but it's harder if you're black, 'cause there aren't that many good movies being offered. There's a lot of creative black stories out there, but it's hard to get to the studios. It's hard for the studios too 'cause they have to decide, is this gonna make money? That's a great story, but it's kind of sad, they'll say. But it's a true story, and it's uplifting and it's powerful. Well, yeah, we don't know, it might not make money. So it never gets done. And we never see it; the actors never see it. I put myself on the other side, on both sides. I'd like to be in a position where somebody could bring me a script and if it's good and I can do it, I would get it done, or take it to the studios and get it done. But it's hard.

We depend too much on the studios to bring us what we want. We've gotta start opening doors; we gotta open them for ourselves. But to begin with, you gotta get through a narrow door. Some of the black women here in Hollywood say that if you're black and female, you gotta look like Halle Berry to get a good part, but black men can be dark or have medium brown skin or be light-complexioned and still get a part. They're right! Hollywood likes certain looks and they only go with what works. But my thing is, people give Hollywood too much credit. Hollywood and the movie studios are made up of businessmen. There's a couple of creative people up top, and you have a lot of creative studio-head people. People who want to make it here have gotta understand, Hollywood is looking for *us* to be creative and for us to open those doors and to break through. We have to bring more ideas to the studios, or do it independent to get it out there, because we just can't look to the studios to produce projects for different-type people. The studios go with what works. People around the world like Halle Berry. She works. But we gotta stop depending on the studios.

It's time for us to look forward and start inspiring ourselves to greater heights—but never forget. We need to tell the stories from back then, but don't just tell the stories where we got lynched and we got killed. We know that happened—we know that. The movies have been done. Tell the story of Frederick Douglass. The guy came from nowhere and was one of the most brilliant minds of all time—became a great speaker and wrote his best-seller and became the most famous black man on the face of the earth. Put it on the big screen. Motivate me.

You got people like Dick Parsons, president of AOL Time Warner, the biggest media company in the world. That's a great story. You got Bob Johnson. He started BET, and a lot of people think he's the first black billionaire, but I heard he's not. I heard there's a lot of other black billionaires. They just don't say anything 'cause they don't want anybody messin' with them, asking them for money. They don't want to get in no trouble. Oh, man! There are lots of billionaires you'd never know about. There's so many different stories, success stories that we should tell. And the more black entertainment there is, the more black writers, the more different stories will be told.

Sadness and grief are part of our history. We've seen too much tragedy and sadness. Sometimes black people don't go to see a movie like *One True Thing* because it's too sad! It's time to move on, though not to forget. Without Martin Luther King and other heroes putting their lives on the line, we wouldn't have the opportunity to become an actor or a comedian.

25   The first time I ever watched the Academy Awards was when Halle Berry and Denzel Washington both won, and the only reason I watched was because they had been nominated. They're great actors, and there'd been a lot of political pressure about them getting the awards. I was surprised they both won, and I was happy for them. But I don't think that Halle and Denzel getting the Academy Award means anything significant has changed in Hollywood for our people. Maybe that's 'cause I don't judge awards to be giving you credibility. I think your fans give you credibility. I think your peers give you credibility. And I think when people come up to you and say, you changed my life, and man, I loved that movie—it was something, that one little thing you did, it made me think about something when I walked out and I'm still thinkin' about it—right there, that's the award you want. It don't matter how prestigious the award is. An Academy Award would be nice, but I'll take that other award too. That's the main award I want.

In the future of black America, and the future of black Hollywood, there's gonna be bigger and better stories. The story of Gettysburg, the story of the American Revolution, the stories of men like Frederick Douglass. There's gonna be black stories. We want to see the biblical stories of black people instead of just slavery, like that's all our history. That ain't all black history. History—black history—goes back thousands and thousands of years, and I think black America is gonna tell stories like those, stories that are on another level. We have a culture of our own here in America that's bigger than just doin' a cookout.

Questions for Discussion and Writing

1. Write one paragraph describing your impression of Chris Tucker as a person. What are his values and goals? What information is missing from Tucker's essay?

2. Why do you think Tucker repeatedly emphasizes "movie companies want to make a lot of money" (paragraph 11); "is this gonna make money?" (paragraph 20); "Hollywood and the movie studies are made up of businessmen" (paragraph 21)?

3. This excerpt was published in a book for popular audiences. Where does Tucker use slang in the text? What do readers gain from his "insider perspective"?

4. Imagine that you have been asked by a major studio to submit a proposal for a new movie project. In your proposal, include specific suggestions: the name of the movie, target audience, and potential for sales. Your goal is to persuade the executive to invest in this meaningful and successful venture.

5. Conduct research on changing attitudes toward African Americans as depicted in Hollywood. Select one or two films from any decade and compare the representation of African Americans with the way they are represented in one current film. In what ways have opportunities been made available, and in what ways are they still limited?

Sports, Media Culture, and Race—Some Reflections on Michael Jordan

DOUGLAS KELLNER

Douglas Kellner teaches social sciences and comparative education at the University of California. This essay from Sociology of Sport Journal *(vol. 13, 1996) explores the racial complexities reflected in this sports icon. His recent book publications include* Grand Theft *(2000),* The Postmodern Adventure: Science, Technology, and Cultural Studies at the Third Millennium, *co-authored with Steven Best (2001),* Media and Cultural Studies: KeyWorks, *co-edited with Gigi Durham (2001),* Toward a Critical Theory of Society *(2001), and* Film, Art and Politics: An Emile de Antonio Reader, *co-edited with Dan Streible (2000).*

Pre-Reading

Using part of Kellner's title, write a one-page description of any athlete. "Sports, Media Culture and Race—Some Reflections on [your athlete of choice]." In your response, consider the racial and cultural impact of the athlete. How is the athlete portrayed in the media? Is he or she considered a racially significant figure?

———————— ✦ ————————

Professional sports is one of the major spectacles of media culture. "Spectacle" is a complex term develop by French situationist Guy Debord (1967) that "unifies and explains a great diversity of apparent phenomena" (p. 10).[1] In one sense, it refers to a media and consumer society, organized around the consumption of images, commodities, and spectacles. Spectacles are those phenomena of media culture that embody the society's basic values, serve to enculturate individuals into its way of life, and dramatize the society's conflicts and modes of conflict resolution. They include media extravaganzas, sports events, political happenings, and those attention-grabbing occurrences that we call news. As I write in August 1996, the spectacle of the Olympics is coming to a close and the spectacles of the national political conventions and 1996 election are about to begin, but TV Nation will long remember the spectacles of the TWA flight 800 disaster that preceded the Olympics and the Atlanta Olympic Park bombing which generated spectacles of a Summer of Terror during the games.

Under the influence of a postmodern image culture, media spectacles fascinate the denizens of the media and consumer society, involving them in the semiotics of a new world of entertainment, information, and drama, which deeply influence thought and action. In Debord's words: "When the real world changes into simple images, simple images become real beings and effective motivations of a hypnotic behavior. The spectacle as a tendency *to make one see the world* by means of various specialized meditations (it can no longer be grasped directly) naturally finds vision to be the privileged human sense which the sense of touch was for other epochs; the most abstract, the most mystifiable sense corresponds to the generalized abstraction of present day society" (p. 18).

Experience and everyday life is thus mediated by the spectacles of a media culture that dramatizes our conflicts, celebrates our values, and projects our deepest hopes and fears (Kellner, 1995). For Debord, the spectacle is a tool of pacification and depoliticization; it is a "permanent opium war" (p. 44) that stupefies social subjects and distracts them from the most urgent task of real life—recovering the full range of their human powers through creative praxis. The concept of the spectacle is integrally connected to the concept of separation and passivity, for in passively consuming spectacles, one is separated from actively producing one's life. Capitalist society separates workers from the products of their labor, art from life, and consumption from human needs and self-directing activity, as individuals passively observe the spectacles of social life from within the privacy of their homes (pp. 25–26). The situationist project by contrast involved an overcoming of all forms of separation, in which individuals would directly produce their own life and modes of self-activity and collective practice.

The correlative to the spectacle is thus the spectator, the passive viewer and consumer of a social system predicated on submission, conformity, and the cultivation of marketable difference. The concept of the spectacle, therefore, involves a distinction between passivity and activity, and consumption and production, condemning passive consumption of spectacle as an alienation from human potentiality for creativity and imagination. The spectacular society spreads its narcotics mainly through the cultural mechanisms of leisure and consumption, services and entertainment, ruled by the dictates of advertising and a commercialized media culture. This structural shift to a society of the spectacle involves a commodification of previously noncolonized sectors of social life and the extension of bureaucratic control to the realms of leisure, desire, and everyday life. Parallel to the Frankfurt School conception of a "totally administered" or "one-dimensional" society (Horkheimer & Adorno 1972; Marcuse 1964), Debord states that, "The spectacle is the moment when the commodity has attained the *total occupation* of social life" (p. 42). Here, exploitation is raised to a psychological level; basic physical privation is augmented by "enriched privation" of pseudoneeds; alienation is generalized, made comfortable, and alienated consumption becomes "a duty supplementary to alienated production" (p. 42).

In contemporary media culture, sports is a major field of the spectacle. Whereas the activity of participating in sports involves an active engagement in creative practice, spectator sports involves passive consumption of images of the sports spectacle. One of the distinguishing features of contemporary postindustrial societies is the extent to which sports has become commercialized and reduced to a spectacle. During the industrial era, actually playing sports was an adjunct to labor that created strong and skillful bodies for industrial labor, and taught individuals both how to play as part of a collective, to fit into a team, and to display initiative and distinguish themselves, thus training workers for productive industrial labor. During the postindustrial era, by contrast, spectator sports is the correlative to a society that is replacing manual labor with automation and machines and requires consumption and passive appropriation of spectacles to reproduce the consumer society.

Modern sports, as Armstrong points out in this issue, was organized around principles of the division of labor and professionalism, celebrating modern values of competition and winning. Modern sports replicated the structure of the workplace where both individual initiative and teamwork were necessary and sports celebrated at once both competing values. Sports was part of an autonomous realm, however, with its own professional ethic, carefully regulated rules, and highly organized corporate structure. Postindustrial sports, by contrast, implodes sport into media spectacle, collapses boundaries between professional achievement and commercialization, and attests to the commodification of all aspects of life in the media and consumer society.

There are, indeed, many ways in which contemporary sports is subject to the laws of the spectacle and is becoming totally commercialized, serving to help reproduce the consumer society. For starters, sports is ever more subject to market logic and commodification with professional athletes making millions of dollars, and events like basketball games are increasingly commodified with the "Bud player of the game," "Miller Lite genuine moments," the "Reebok half-time report," the "AT&T time out," and "Dutch Boy in the paint," along with ads featuring the star players hawking merchandise. TV networks bid astronomical sums for the rights to broadcast live professional sports events and super events, like the Super Bowl and NBA championship games, command some of the highest advertising rates in television.

It appears that professional sports, a paradigm of the spectacle, can no longer be played without the accompaniment of cheerleaders, giant mascots who clown with players and spectators, and raffles, promotions, and contests which hawk the products of various sponsors. Instant replays turn the action into high-tech spectacles, and stadiums themselves contain electronic reproduction of the action as well as giant advertisements for various products which rotate for maximum saturation—previewing forthcoming environmental advertising in which entire urban sites will become scenes to promote commodity spectacles. Entire sports stadiums, like the new United Center in Chicago or America West Arena in Phoenix, are named after corporate sponsors. The Texas Rangers stadium in Arlington, TX, is as much a shopping mall and commercial area as a sports arena, with its office buildings, its stores, and restaurant in which for a hefty price one gets a view of the athletic events.

It probably will not be too long before the uniforms of professional sports players are as littered with advertisements as racing cars. In the globally popular sport of soccer, companies such as Canon, Sharp, and Carlsberg sponsor teams and have their names emblazoned on their shirts, making the players epiphenomena of transnational capital. In events like the Tour de France or Indianapolis 500, entire teams are sponsored by major corporations whose logos adorn their clothes and cars. And throughout the world, but especially in the United States, the capital of the commodity spectacle, superstars like Michael Jordan commodify themselves from head to foot, selling their various body parts and images to the highest corporate bidders, imploding their sports images into the spectacles of advertising. In this fashion, the top athletes augment their salaries, sometimes spectacularly, by endorsing products, thus imploding sports, commerce, and advertising into dazzling spectacles which celebrate the products and values of corporate America.

Among the spectacles of media culture, Michael Jordan is a preeminent figure. As an NBA superstar, Jordan is the very picture of grace, coordination, virtuosity, and all-around skill. Jordan will reportedly receive $30 million to play for the Chicago Bulls in 1997 (*Time*, 1996, July 29, p. 61), and he reportedly earned $43.9 million in 1995, including $40 million in endorsements and promotions, making him the highest paid athlete in the world (*The Guardian*, 1996, June 11, p. 6). Jordan epitomizes the postmodern spectacle both on the playing field and in advertisements and media spectacles, which implode athletic achievement with commercialization, his sports image with corporate products, making Jordan one of the highest paid and most fecund generators of social meaning in the history of media culture.

There seems to be nothing that Jordan cannot do on the basketball court. His slam dunk is legendary and he seems to defy gravity as he flies through the air toward the holy grail of the basket. His "hang time" is fabled and as Cole points out in this issue, designations like "Rare Air" "render him extraordinary . . . and even godlike," a figure of transcendence. Nike developed a product line, Air Jordan, around the flying mythology and a 1990 *NBA Entertainment* documentary titled *Michael Jordan. Come Fly With Me* describes the player as "the man who was truly destined to fly," and celebrates him as the very embodiment of professional excellence, morality, and American values. He is regularly described as "the best player ever," "the greatest basketball player who has ever lived," and even the "greatest athlete of all time." The phrase, "there is nothing he cannot do," is frequently used to inscribe Jordan's sign-value as superstar sports deity, and in Nike ads which star Jordan one reads the corporate logo "just do it," implying that you, too, can be like Michael and do what you want to do.

In a sense, Michael Jordan represents a highly successful marketing phenomenon and calls attention to the construction of the media spectacle by corporations, public relations, and the techniques of advertising. Just as Jordan marketed Nike, Wheaties, and other products, so did these corporations help produce the Jordan image and spectacle. Likewise, Jordan was used to market the NBA and in turn, its publicity helped market Jordan (Andrews, 1996). A vast marketing apparatus of television, radio, magazines, and other publications help market and manufacture the stars of sports and entertainment, indeed attesting to an implosion between sports and entertainment. As Cole demonstrates in this special issue, Jordan is part of the Nike P.L.A.Y. program designed to present a positive corporate image and promote its products to a youth audience.

Michael Jordan is, thus, a dazzling sports spectacle who promotes both commercial sports and the products of the corporations that market products to sports audiences. His distinctive image is often noted and Jordan's look and style is indeed striking. His shaved head, extremely long shorts, and short socks are frequently shown defining features that are highlighted in Spike Lee's Nike ad which, in a brilliant effort to get the Nike message across repeatedly insists, "It's the shoes!" (i.e., which make Jordan the greatest). In addition, his wrist band, jersey No. 23, and tongue wagging and hanging as he concentrates on a play are distinctive signs of the Jordan trademark image. Jordan is so handsome he has often been employed as a model, and his good looks and superstar status have won him countless advertising endorsements for products like Nike, McDonald's, Gatorade, Coca-Cola, Wheaties, Hanes shorts, and numerous other products. A Gatorade ad tells the audience to "be like Mike," establishing Jordan as a role model, as the very icon of excellence and aspiration. In antidrug ads, Jordan tells the nation to "just say no," to avoid drugs, to do the right thing, and to be all you can be, mobilizing the very stereotypes of conservative postindustrial America in one figure. As Andrews (1996) points out, Michael Jordan is a paradigmatic figure of the "hard body" (Susan Jeffords) that is the ideal male image of the Reaganite '80s, a model of the powerful bodies needed to resurrect American power after the flabbiness of the 1960s and 1970s.

Yet Jordan is a distinctively Black spectacle and his Blackness is clearly a central feature of his image. Yet as a cultural signifier, as the "universal singular" who represents more general social significance (see Denzin's use of Sartre's term in this issue), Jordan is a highly polysemic signifier who encodes conflicting meanings and values. Michael Jordan is both an example of what Berlant (1991) calls the "national symbolic" (see the discussion by Cole in this issue) and the "global popular" (see the discussion in Andrew et al. in this issue). Jordan embodies national values of hard work, competitiveness, ambition, and success. As a Black superstar, he presents the fantasy that anyone can make it in the society of competition and status, that one can climb the class ladder and overcome the limitations of race and class. As a national and global superstar, he represents different things to different people in different countries (see the studies by Andrews et al. in this issue). Indeed, as Wilson and Sparks remind us in this issue, different individuals and audiences are going to receive and appropriate the text of Michael Jordan in different ways according to their own race, gender, class, region, and other subject positions.

As a polysemic signifier, Jordan thus presents a figure who   15
mobilizes many fantasies (i.e., athletic greatness, wealth, success, etc.) for the national and global imaginary, providing a spectacle that embodies many desirable national and global features and aspirations. Yet Jordan is extremely Black and his race is a definite signifier of his spectacle, though his Blackness too has conflicting connotations. On one hand, as noted, he is a privileged role model for Black youth ("Be like Mike"), he reportedly helps mentor young athletes, and he is a symbol of the African American who has transcended race and who is integrated in American society, representing the dream of assimilation, wealth, and success (see Cole and McDonald in this issue). But as Andrews (1996) has demonstrated, Jordan's Blackness is overdetermined and also has served to signify Black transgressions, as when his gambling behavior became a subject of negative media presentation and his father's murder led to speculation on connections with organized crime. In these images, Jordan is presented as the threatening Black figure, as the negative fantasy figure of Black deviance from White normality. Jordan's physique, power, and dominance also might feed into the fear of Black bodies as Giroux suggests in his analysis of how contemporary media culture is characterized by a simultaneous fascination with the accomplishments of the Black male body while also fearing the threat it poses (1994).

Consequently, Jordan's "just say no" conflicts with his "just do it," creating an ambiguous figure, who at once represents restraint and control, and transgression and excess. Yet on the whole, I believe that Jordan is positioned in media culture as the "good Black," especially against the aggressiveness and visual transgressions of teammate Dennis Rodman, who with his bleached and undisciplined hair, earring, fancy clothes, and regularly rebellious behavior represents the "bad" Black figure. But media culture is notorious for destroying precisely the icons it has built up, especially if they are Black. Jordan has already received his share of bad as well as adulatory press, and during 1996 as Nike was sharply attacked in the media for their labor policies, Jordan was put on the defensive, frequently asked to comment on Nike's labor practices. In a carefully prepared public relations response, Jordan countered that it's up to Nike "to do what they can to make sure everything is correctly done. I don't know the complete situation. Why should I? I'm trying to do my job. Hopefully, Nike will do the right thing" (cited in Herbert, 1996). Yet the media continued to pester him and he was often portrayed in images during the summer of 1996 turning away from interviewers with a curt "No comment" when asked what he thought of Nike's exploitation of Third World workers, especially women, at extremely low wages.[2]

Behind the Nike spectacle, there is, of course, the unedifying reality of underpaid workers, toiling at below subsistence wages and under terrible working conditions to produce highly over-priced shoes for youth, many of whom cannot afford and do not need such luxury items. Indeed, Nike engages in superexploitation of both its Third World workers and global consumers. Its products are no more intrinsically valuable than other shoes, but have a certain distinctive sign value that gives them prestige value,[3] that provides its wearers with a mark of social status, and so it can charge $130 to $140 per pair of shoes, thus earning tremendous profit margins. Nike provides a spectacle of social differentiation that establishes its wearer as cool, as with it, as part of the Nike/superstar spectacle nexus: "Be Like Mike, buy the shoes he sells!" Yo, as Brother Spike puts it down: "it's the shoes!"[4]

Michael Jordan tries to present himself as the embodiment of all good and wholesome values, but he is tainted by his corporate involvements. His symbiosis with Nike is so tight, they are so intertwined with each other, that if Nike is tarnished so, too, is Jordan (and vice versa, which is one of the reasons that Hertz moved so quickly to sever its ties with O.J. Simpson after the discovery of the murder of his former wife, Nicole, and her friend, Ron Goldman). The fate of Nike and Michael Jordan are inextricably intertwined with Nike taking on Jordan to endorse their products early in his career, helping make him a superstar known to everyone, while the Air Jordan product line helped reverse declining sales and made Nike an icon of corporate America with a global reach that made Nike products part of the global popular culture (Andrews, 1996). Thus, whereas Jordan was no doubt embarrassed by all the bad publicity that Nike received in 1996, his involvement with the corporation was obviously too deep to "just say no" and sever himself from this symbol of a greedy and exploitative corporation.

The media figure of Michael Jordan, thus, has contradictory effects. While he is a symbol of making it in corporate America, he also is tainted with the scandals and negative qualities with which the corporations to whom he sells himself are tainted, as well as embodying negative aspects of excessive greed, competitiveness, and other capitalist values. Moreover, although it is positive for members of the underclass to have role models and aspirations to better themselves, it is not clear that sports can provide a means to success for any but a few. The 1995 documentary, *Hoop Dreams*, brilliantly documented the failed hopes and illusory dreams of ghetto youth making it in college basketball and the NBA. For most would-be stars, it is indeed a false hope to dream of fame and athletic glory; thus, it is not clear that Jordan's "be like Mike" is going to be of much real use to youth. Moreover, the widespread limitation of figures of the Black spectacle to sports and entertainment also might contribute to the stereotype, as Mercer suggests (1994), that Blacks are all brawn and no brain, or mere spectacular bodies and not substantive persons.

20

Yet, I believe that so far and on the whole, the threatening and transgressive features of the Black body are contained in the Michael Jordan spectacle and that he serves as an icon of positive representations of African Americans. Jordan's concentration is often remarked and his awesome skills are obviously mediated by intelligence. His "air-driven bullets" seem to be guided by a highly effective mental radar system and his trademarked "aerial ballets" represent grace and spiritual transcendence as well as brute force. And as remarked earlier, Jordan seems to embody central American values and serve as a role model for American youth and as the White fantasy of the good African American. Thus, while it seems wrong to claim, as is often done, that Michael Jordan transcends race, he seems to produce unusually positive representations of African Americans, thus undercutting racist stereotypes and denigration.

Indeed, the extent to which the spectacles of sports have promoted the interests of African Americans and people of color has not yet been adequately understood. As recently as the 1940s, professional sports were segregated and athletes of color were forced to toil in "colored" leagues, condemned in effect to the minor leagues. With the breaking of the color line in professional baseball in the 1940s with Jackie Robinson, African

American athletes could be part of professional sports and eventually icons of the sports spectacle. Indeed, during the 1950s and 1960s, prominent African American baseball players like Willie Mays and Hank Aaron were acknowledged as superstars of the spectacle.

Black and brown athletes succeeded in equally spectacular ways in professional football, boxing, and basketball. Sports, thus, became an important route for people of color to grab their share of the American Dream and cut of the great spectacle of "professional" sports. On the positive side, the American fascination with sports promoted racial equality, acceptance of difference, and multiculturalism. With the incorporation of Black athletes into professional sports, they entered mainstream media culture as icons of the spectacle, as role models for youth, and as promoters (often unaware) of racial equality and integration.

Indeed, I would argue that the prowess of Black sports heroes and the rhythms of rock music promote racial equality and the rights of African Americans and people of color.[5] Postindustrial America became more and more of a media culture and professional sports and entertainment became key features of media culture. Once African Americans were allowed to sparkle and shine in media culture, they were able to enter the mainstream—or at least major figures of the spectacle such as O.J. Simpson, Hank Aaron, and Michael Jordan were. In Spike Lee's *Do the Right Thing* (1989), Mookie, a pizza delivery man played by Spike Lee, confronts Pino, the racist Italian son of the owner of the pizzeria about his racist, but contradictory attitudes toward African Americans.

MOOKIE: Pino, who's your favorite basketball player?

PINO: Magic Johnson.

MOOKIE: Who's your favorite movie star?

PINO: Eddie Murphy.

MOOKIE: Who's your favorite rock star? Prince, you're a Prince fan.

PINO: Bruce!

MOOKIE: Prince!

PINO: Bruce!

MOOKIE: Pino, all you ever talk about is "nigger this" and "nigger that," and all your favorite people are so-called "niggers."

PINO: It's different. Magic, Eddie, Prince, are not niggers. I mean they're not Black. I mean. Let me explain myself. They're not really Black, I mean, they're Black but they're not really Black, they're more than Black. It's different.

MOOKIE: It's different?

PINO: Yeah, to me it's different.

But the elevation to cultural icons itself is a double-edged sword. On one hand, Michael Jordan is a spectacle of color who elevates difference to sublimity and who raises Blackness to dignity and respect. An icon of the sports spectacle, Michael Jordan is *the* Black superstar and his prominence in sports has made him a figure that corporate America can use to sell its products and its values. Yet, such are the negative representations and connotations of Blackness in American culture and such is the power of the media to define and redefine images that even the greatest Black icons and spectacles can be denigrated to embody negative connotations. As Michael Jackson, O.J. Simpson, and Mike Tyson have discovered, those who live by the media can die by the media and overnight their positive representations and signification can become negative. Media culture is only too happy to use Black figures to represent transgressive behavior and to project society's sins onto Black figures. Indeed, despite the endemic problem of sexual harassment, Clarence Thomas is the representative figure for this transgression; despite the troubling problem of child molestation cutting across every race and class, Michael Jackson is the media figure who represents this iniquity; despite an epidemic of violence against women, O.J. Simpson is the ultimate wife abuser; and although date rape is a deplorable, frequent and well-documented phenomena, it was Mike Tyson who became "poster boy" for this offense (see Dyson, 1993, and Hutchinson, 1996, on the demonization of Black figures).

Hence, such is the racism of American culture that African American figures are the figures of choice to represent social transgressions and tabooed behavior. Michael Jordan has had his bouts with negative media representations, though on the whole, I believe that, so far at least, his representations are largely positive and his figure has been used to represent an 25 ideal of Blackness that American society as a whole can live with. Since the figures and spectacles of media culture play such an important role in the culture, it is important to develop critical insight into how media culture is constructed and functions. The papers in this special issue help to theorize the role of the sports spectacle, and in particular Michael Jordan, in postindustrial America and to articulate the importance for media culture of sports and the representations of a Black superstar. They provide critical insights into the contradictory meanings and effects of the sports spectacle, the ways that sports provides figures and ideologies to reproduce existing values, and the complex meanings and effects of a superstar like Michael Jordan.

Insight into how media culture works and generates social meanings and ideologies thus helps make possible critical media literacy that empowers individuals and undermines the mesmerizing and manipulative aspects of the media spectacle. The sort of critical cultural studies found in this issue thus help demystify media culture and produce insights into contemporary society and culture. The studies suggest to me that ultimately Michael Jordan reminds us of the truth of W.E.B. Dubois' insight that "race is the dividing line of the 20th Century" and that the phenomenon of race is central to all aspects of American society, that it is constructed largely in media culture, and that media culture is the stage in which our social conflicts are played out and our social reality is constructed.

References

Andrews, D.L. (1996). The fact(s) of Michael Jordan's Blackness: An excavation in four parts. *Sociology of Sport Journal*, 13(2), 125–158.

Baudrillard, J. (1981). *For a critique of the political economy of the sign*. St. Louis, MO: Telos Press.

Berlant, L. (1991). *The anatomy of national fantasy: Hawthorne, utopia, and everyday life*. Chicago: University of Chicago Press.

Debord, G. (1967). *Society of the spectacle*. Detroit, MI: Black and Red.

Dyson, M. (1993). *Reflecting Black: African American cultured criticism*. Minneapolis, MN: University of Minnesota Press.

Giroux, H. (1994). *Disturbing pleasures*. New York: Routledge.

Goldman, R. (1992). *Reading ads critically*. London and New York: Routledge.

Goldman, R., & Papson, S. (1996). *Sign wars*. New York: Guilford Press.

Herbert, B. (1996, June 10). Nike's pyramid scheme. *The New York Times*, p. A19.

Horkheimer, M., & Adorno. T.W. (1972). *Dialectic of enlightenment.* New York: Continuum.

Hutchinson, E.O. (1996). *Beyond O.J., race, sex, and class lessons for America.* Los Angeles: Middle Passages Press.

Kellner, D. (1995). *Media culture.* London and New York: Routledge.

Lipsyte, R. (1996, July 14) Pay for play: Jordan vs. old-timers. *The New York Times*, p. B2.

Marcuse, H. (1964). *One-dimensional man.* Boston: Beacon Press.

Mercer, K. (1994). *Welcome to the jungle: New positions in Black cultural studies.* London and New York: Routledge.

Endnotes

1. Debord's *The Society of the Spectacle* (1967) was published in translation in a pirate edition by Black and Red (Detroit, MI) in 1970 and reprinted many times; another edition appeared in 1983 and a new translation in 1994; thus, in the following discussion, I cite references to the numbered paragraphs of Debord's text to make it easier for those with different editions to follow my reading. The key texts of the situationists and many interesting commentaries are found on various Web sites, producing a curious afterlife for situationist ideas and practices.

2. Nike's shoes are produced mostly in Asia where the average wage is below the subsistence level. It was widely reported that Nike workers in Indonesia toil in sweat shops for $2.20 a day and Nike is now moving to Vietnam where the minimum wage is $30 per month. Nike also has made goods in China, South Korea, Thailand, and Taiwan, moving production from country to country to gain ever lower production costs. Meanwhile, its CEO Philip Knight earns millions per year, his stock is worth an incredible $4.5 *billion*, and Jordan, Andre Agassi, and Spike Lee are paid staggering sums for their endorsements and advertisements; see Herbert, 1996.

3. On the concept of sign value, see Baudrillard, 1981; Goldman, 1992; and Goldman and Papson, 1996.

4. Another *New York Times* article raised the question: "Does being Mike entail any responsibilities beyond doing your best on the court?" And answered: Let's ask Inge Hanson, who runs Harlem RBI, a youth baseball and mentoring program. She was mugged earlier this year by a 14-year-old and his 10-year-old henchboys. After they knocked her down and took about $60, a mugger kicked

her in the face. The next day, the bruise that had welled up on her left cheek bore the imprint of a Nike swoosh. It lasted for three weeks and she felt sad thinking she was probably robbed to finance a fancier pair of Nikes.

"But I can't honestly answer your question," she said. "How could Michael Jordan possibly know that by endorsing sneakers—sneakers!—he was involved in a crime? And yet, one does wonder if he has any responsibility to his audience beyond just saying, 'Just Do It!'" (cited in Lipsyte, 1996).

5. Of course, Martin Luther King and the civil rights movement did more to dramatize the plight of African Americans, but I would argue that sports and entertainment helped and that the tremendous achievements of Black athletes and especially music performers, I believe, were essential in getting mainstream America to accept and respect Blacks and to allow them into the mainstream—in however limited and problematic a fashion.

Acknowledgments

My comments on the sports spectacle and use of Debord draws on work with Steve Best in our book *The Postmodern Adventure* (Guilford, 1997). Thanks to David Andrews for providing material and comments which have helped with the production of this Afterword.

Questions for Discussion and Writing

1. Describe in your own words what you believe is Kellner's strongest argument.
2. What evidence does Kellner use to support his statement "Yet Jordan is a distinctively Black spectacle and his Blackness is clearly a central feature of his image" (paragraph 14)?
3. Kellner is writing for an academic audience. Why do you think Kellner begins with an exploration of the meaning of the "concept of spectacle" (paragraph 1)? Does Kellner succeed in illuminating what the concept means?
4. "Although it is positive for members of the underclass to have role models and aspirations to better themselves, it is not clear that sports can provide a means to success for any but a few. . . . For most would-be stars, it is indeed a false hope to dream of fame and athletic glory; thus, it is not clear that Jordan's 'be like Mike' is going to be of much real use to youth" (paragraph 19). Write an essay challenging Kellner's conditional statement "although it is positive . . . it is indeed a false hope" (paragraph 19). In your essay, persuade

readers that sports role models can indeed "be of much real use." In your essay, be sure to include specific examples from your observations to support the argument.

5. In paragraph 16, Keller points out, "But the media culture is notorious for destroying precisely the icons it has built up, especially if they are Black." Select any celebrity or sports hero and write an essay about how his or her image was destroyed by the media. Let your readers know whether or not you believe the attack was justified. What do you believe were the motives behind the attack?

Editorial Observer: How Hip-Hop Music Lost Its Way and Betrayed Its Fans

BRENT STAPLES

Editorial writer for the New York Times, *culture critic Brent Staples is author of the critically acclaimed autobiography* Parallel Time: Growing Up in Black and White *(1994). As an outspoken political and culture critic, Staples has penned numerous articles for magazines and newspapers such as* Harper's, Ms., New Republic, New York Woman, New York, *and the* New York Times Book Review. *The following Op-Ed appeared in the* New York Times *on May 12, 2005.*

Pre-Reading

Write a one-paragraph description of the "ghetto stereotype." Which hip-hop artists perpetuate the image? Do you believe it has a negative impact on teenagers? Explain why or why not.

———————— ✦ ————————

African-American teenagers are beset on all sides by dangerous myths about race. The most poisonous one defines middle-class normalcy and achievement as "white," while embracing violence, illiteracy and drug dealing as "authentically" black. This fiction rears its head from time to time in films and literature. But it finds its most virulent expression in rap music, which started out with a broad palette of themes but has increasingly evolved into a medium for worshipping misogyny, materialism and murder.

This dangerous narrowing of hip-hop music would be reason for concern in any case. But it is especially troubling against the backdrop of the 1990's, when rappers provoked a real-world gang war by using recordings and music videos to insult and threaten rivals. Two of the music's biggest stars—Tupac Shakur and the Notorious B.I.G.—were eventually shot to death.

People who pay only minimal attention to the rap world may have thought the killings would sober up the rap community. Not quite. The May cover of the hip-hop magazine *Vibe* was on the mark when it depicted fallen rappers standing among tombstones under the headline: "Hip-Hop Murders: Why Haven't We Learned Anything?"

The cover may have been prompted in part by a rivalry between two rappers that culminated in a shootout at a New York radio station, Hot 97, earlier this spring. The events that led up to the shooting show how recording labels now exploit violence to make and sell recordings.

5   At the center of that Hot 97 shootout was none other than 50 Cent, whose given name is Curtis Jackson III. Mr. Jackson is a confessed former drug dealer who seems to revel in the fact that he was shot several times while dealing in Queens. He has also made a career of "beef" recordings, in which he whips up controversy and heightens tension by insulting rival artists.

He was following this pattern in a radio interview in March when a rival showed up at the station. The story's murky, but it appears that the rival's entourage met Mr. Jackson's on the street, resulting in gunfire.

Mr. Jackson's on-air agitation was clearly timed to coincide with the release of "The Massacre," his grotesquely violent and misogynist compact disc. The CD cover depicts the artist standing before a wall adorned with weapons, pointing what appears to be a shotgun at the camera. The photographs in the liner notes depict every ghetto stereotype—the artist selling drugs, the artist in a gunfight—and includes a mock autopsy report that has been seen as a covert threat aimed at some of his critics.

The "Massacre" promotion raises the ante in a most destructive way. New artists, desperate for stardom, will say or do anything to win notice—and buzz—for their next projects. As the trend escalates, inner-city listeners who are already at risk of dying prematurely are being fed a toxic diet of rap cuts that glorify murder and make it seem perfectly normal to spend your life in prison.

Critics who have been angered by this trend have pointed at Jimmy Iovine, the music impresario whose Interscope Records reaped millions on gangster rap in the 90's. Mr. Iovine makes a convenient target as a white man who is lording over an essentially black art form. But also listed on "The Massacre" as an executive producer is the legendary rapper Dr. Dre, a black man who happens to be one of the most powerful people in the business. Dr. Dre has a unique vantage point on rap-related violence. He was co-founder of Death Row Records, an infamous California company that marketed West Coast rap in the 1990's and had a front-row seat for the feud that led to so much bloodshed back then.

The music business hopes to make a financial killing on a   10 recently announced summer concert tour that is set to feature 50 Cent and the mega-selling rap star Eminem. But promoters will need to make heavy use of metal detectors to suppress the kind of gun-related violence that gangster artists celebrate. That this lethal genre of art has grown speaks volumes about the industry's greed and lack of self-control.

But trends like this reach a tipping point, when business as usual becomes unacceptable to the public as a whole. Judging from the rising hue and cry, hip-hop is just about there.

Questions for Discussion and Writing

1. Describe in your own words what Staples means by "dangerous myths" (paragraph 1). What is Staples implying about society's attitudes toward race?

2. Is the specific evidence Staples uses to support his argument convincing? What information do you imagine is missing from Staples' editorial?

3. In what ways do you imagine that both the audience of the *New York Times* and the length restrictions affected Staples' style of writing?

4. Use Staples' "Editorial Observer" column as a model. Write your own "Editorial Observer" column of similar length (743 words) about any issue (violence, misogyny, authenticity, licensing, merchandising, etc.) in any genre of music (hip-hop, punk, rock and roll, jazz, heavy metal, etc.).

5. Select any hip-hop CD cover. Does the color, design, symbolism, language, and the like reinforce the ghetto stereotype (paragraph 7)? Write an analysis of the CD artwork supporting, arguing, or modifying his claim.

Questions for Making Connections

1. "There's so many different stories, success stories that we should tell" insists Tucker (paragraph 23). His sentiment is echoed by Navarro that "there are not enough alternatives" (paragraph 24). Both Tucker and Navarro clearly lament the lack of availability of roles and raise important issues about the necessity of telling new and alternative stories. In what ways are the arguments presented by Tucker and Navarro similar? In what ways do they differ?

2. Several of the selections in this chapter mention the reality that the entertainment industry is first and foremost a business concerned with profits. Tucker states, "It's hard for the studios too 'cause they have to decide, is this gonna make money?" (paragraph 20). Staples uses stronger language in attacking the music industry: "That this lethal genre of art has grown speaks volumes about the industry's greed" (paragraph 10). Clearly, many entertainment decisions are driven by profits. Is it right to accuse entertainment executives for not producing more culturally diverse films, television shows, music, and the like? Or are consumers to blame for purchasing products and, in effect, creating a demand for precisely the types of films and television many lament? Select either the film, movie, or music genre, and write an essay assigning blame to executives, consumers, or both. Write a focused thesis and cite evidence to support your point of view.

3. Can you imagine a time when stereotyping will no longer exist on television, in sports, or in movies? If so, write an essay explaining why. If not, write an essay explaining why you believe stereotyping will always be a part of television, sports, and/or the movies. In your response, include reference to at least two of the writers in this chapter.

4. "Our images and understandings of immigrants, of subcultures, and of the human nature of diverse peoples are heavily influenced by what we receive through culture," notes Beck (paragraph 7). Select any immigrant group (Italian American, Asian, Latino, African American, etc.) and write an essay about how any form of media (film, music, television, advertising, etc.) affected your personal understanding of that group. In your essay, write the name of the group, the image you have (had) of the group, and the medium (film, music, television, advertising, etc.). Has your understanding changed?

5. "African-American teenagers are beset on all sides by dangerous myths about race" writes Staples, insisting "the most poisonous one defines middle-class normalcy and achievement as 'white,' while embracing violence, illiteracy and drug dealing as 'authentically' black" (paragraph 1). Kellner writes about Michael Jordan, "he seems to produce unusually

positive representations of African Americans, thus undercutting racist stereotypes" (paragraph 20). Re-read both Staples and Kellner. Has Michael Jordan escaped the "dangerous myths" that Staples observes? Do your observations, personal experiences, or reading support, refute, or modify their claims?

Education: Popular Culture and the Academy

Is it more challenging to study Dickens than *Harry Potter*? Is it more meaningful to study classical music than rock and roll? Is reading more mentally stimulating than blogging? What do we have to gain from studying popular culture?

Before reading, think about the following: What is the purpose of education? What courses does your college or university require you to take as part of the curriculum? Do you assign a higher value to certain courses? For example, do you believe a Shakespeare survey course is more valuable to your education than a course on "Popular American Film"? Have you ever taken a popular culture course? If so, what knowledge did you gain? If not, what do you imagine you would gain from studying popular culture?

The selections in this chapter explore issues related to education, popular culture studies, and the academy. The diverse mediums include books, television, film, and the like (Trussell); scholarly books, music (Ross); books (Warmbold); books, television, Internet (Franzen); Internet and television (Johnson).

According to Trussell, "In academic halls from Berkeley to Bowling Green, young scholars and their instructors spend as much time tackling the history of shopping, television and comic books—in other words, popular culture—as they do analyzing Homer, Shakespeare and Milton" (paragraph 2). According to the scholars interviewed by Trussell, despite initial "hostility," popular culture studies are finally receiving recognition. As Browne explains, "movies and 'new history' and music and fast foods . . . are the things that shape and define American culture. They may not be loved, but they have to be understood" (quoted in Trussell, paragraph 33). Indeed, they do need to be understood because they reflect who we are as a society. In "Rock 101," Alex Ross of the *New Yorker* agrees with Trussell, as Ross observes: "Those of us who write on classical music have a lot to learn from pop studies. It exposes the hard realities of how music is made, how it is paid for, and how it is consumed" (paragraph 26).

In "Harry Potter: Oliver with a Magical Twist," Marie Warmbold bridges the gap between what some would consider important high literary culture (Dickens's *Oliver Twist*) and what critics of popular culture would call mass popular culture (*Harry Potter*). Warmbold's well-documented essay in MLA style draws parallels between Harry Potter and Oliver Twist. Her analysis illustrates that there may be compelling similarities between characters in the literary canon (such as Dickens's *Oliver Twist*) and popular culture characters.

Harry Potter's phenomenal book sales are unique at a time when many critics lament that people are no longer reading novels as avidly as in the past. In "The Reader in Exile," Franzen admits "I gave away my television set . . . because as long as it was in the house, reachable by some combination of extension cords, I wasn't reading books" (paragraph 1). He continues, "I mourn the eclipse of the cultural authority that literature once possessed" (paragraph 31). Do you agree that literature is losing "cultural authority"? How often do you read? If you were to get rid of your television, would you read more? Or is it not practical? Are the virtues of reading overrated?

Johnson believes that the virtues of the intellectual challenge posed by the stimulating nature of the Internet are not appreciated enough. His persuasive argument is encapsulated in the title of his book, from which an excerpt is included in this chapter: *Everything Bad Is Good for You: How Today's Popular Culture Is Actually Making Us Smarter*. Johnson writes, "The rise of the Internet has challenged our minds in three fundamental and related ways: by virtue of being participatory, by forcing users to learn new interfaces, and by creating new channels for social interaction" (paragraph 3).

Maybe popular culture scholars have had it right all along—popular culture is not dumb at all; in fact, after reading the selections in this chapter, you may actually turn away with a new respect for popular culture studies.

Pre-Reading Chapter 5

1. In your journal, answer the questions posed in this introduction. After writing your responses, review what you have written. Do your responses

reveal any prejudice against the study of popular culture? What do you imagine are the benefits and drawbacks to popular culture studies?

2. Survey the titles and extract key words and phrases that capture your interest: "Scholars Spend as Much Time with *Love Boat* as with Shakespeare"/Robert Trussell; "Rock 101: Academia Tunes In"/Alex Ross; "The Reader in Exile"/Jonathan Franzen; "Harry Potter: Oliver with a Magical Twist"/Marie Warmbold; and "The Internet—Everything Bad Is Good for You"/Steven Johnson—for example, "Rock 101," "slang," or "everything bad is good for you." What do you already know about the topics? What associations do the words connote? What would you like to know more about?

3. In your journal and scrapbook, record the requirements of your curriculm. Obtain a college bulletin and survey the list of courses. Are any of them connected to popular culture? For example, your school may offer courses such as the following: "American History and Film," "Women in Popular Music," and "Commercialism and Advertising." Which of the courses are required? Which of them are electives? If a majority of the popular culture courses are electives, what does that reveal about the priorities of the curriculum? Does your school offer a degree in Popular Culture Studies?

Scholars Spend as Much Time with *Love Boat* as with Shakespeare

ROBERT TRUSSELL

Award-winning journalist, theater critic, and popular culture specialist Robert Trussell has written numerous articles on a variety of topics including jazz, movies, theater, and popular culture. Published on December 10, 2004, this article on popular culture was written for Knight Ridder Newspapers and printed in numerous newspapers across the nation. Recipient of the 1997 award for enterprise reporting covering African Americans and other people of color from the Kansas City Association of Black Journalists, he continues to work at the Kansas City Star, *where he has been a reporter for 20 years.*

Pre-Reading

Write a list of your favorite television programs, movies, sports figures, and musicians. What do you imagine you would gain from analyzing each of them? What do you imagine would be the most significant drawback?

—————————— ✦ ——————————

It was a long, hard slog, but Donald Duck has achieved parity with Prince Hamlet.

In academic halls from Berkeley to Bowling Green, young scholars and their instructors spend as much time tackling the history of shopping, television and comic books—in other words, popular culture—as they do analyzing Homer, Shakespeare and Milton.

"I read a paper the other day by an anthropologist, and he was doing a study of Donald Duck," said Ray Browne, the 82-year-old godfather of the academic popular culture movement. Anyone in touch with the real world, Browne said, should be able to "admit the importance of Donald Duck and Disney."

From his home in Bowling Green, Ohio, Browne looks out on American universities and sees the results of seeds he cultivated long ago: scholarship devoted to virtually every cranny of pop culture.

In the last couple of years respected universities have awarded doctorates for dissertations on an amazing range of cultural phenomenon. They include a study of "the figure of the murderous lesbian in 1990s film"; consumer response to pop-up advertising; the "iconography of Clint Eastwood"; Playboy magazine; "the making of modern American manhood" by novelist Edgar Rice Burroughs through his pulp hero Tarzan; teenage girls' shopping habits in the '50s; and "women's rights rhetoric" in country music videos in the '90s.

In September, 18 scholars gathered at Yale University to examine Michael Jackson's "iconic career and celebrity status." Called "Regarding Michael Jackson: Performing Racial, Gender and Sexual Difference Center Stage," the conference was co-sponsored by the department of African American studies and the Larry Kramer Initiative for Lesbian and Gay Studies.

FOUND LIBRARY

Every week or so Ray Browne ventures out to the secondhand bookstores in Bowling Green and spends about $100 on used books. He then donates them to the Browne Popular Culture Library at Bowling Green State University that he and his wife, Pat, founded in 1969. Today it's considered an invaluable resource for pop culture scholars, with vast holdings of material on popular religion, board games, etiquette and pulp fiction—including 50,000 mystery-detective titles.

Browne retired from the university 12 years ago, but he begins work at 8 each morning on multiple projects. He and Pat Browne have written, co-written or edited an estimated 70 books on pop culture, and he's working on a new one: Shakespeare as a propaganda tool during the Civil War.

The study of popular culture can be traced to the '50s, but many people point to 1970 as the watershed year. That's when Browne, an Alabama-born professor with a doctorate in English from UCLA, persuaded Bowling Green University to let him create a popular culture department with a bachelor's and master's degree program. To his amazement, school officials said yes.

10   Looking back, Browne says it was good timing, coming at the end of an explosive decade when political-minded students and faculty were challenging university curricula.

"I was really riding a wave," he said. "I know my colleagues and I have been instrumental in legitimizing the study of popular culture, but . . . there were a lot of closet popular culture scholars before we came along. As soon as we turned the light on, these people came out. . . . There are thousands of people now teaching popular culture subjects in various departments."

But Browne said in the early days, it could get pretty lonely.

He and Pat established the *Journal of Popular Culture* in 1967, "and you would be surprised at the hostility it aroused. One of the Bowling Green graduates who had a radio program in California derided me . . . and wrote to the Bowling Green president saying this had to be stopped, this man is evil. . . ."

The Brownes plugged along, subsidizing the book press with journal subscriptions. As far as the university was concerned, they were on their own.

15   "We have always been handcuffed to a certain extent because we had very little money, and we never received a penny from the

university," he said. "We kind of occupied an ambiguous position. The president was very proud of us, the faculty was ashamed of us, and neither one supported us."

POP CULTURE SCHOLAR

One night in the late 1970s, a young art history and political philosophy undergraduate at the University of Chicago got some fast food, took it back to the dorm and allowed himself a 30-minute study break to eat. He turned on his little black-and-white television, which could pick up only two local affiliates—NBC and PBS.

His viewing choice: the history of Western civilization told through its art and architecture and "CHiPs," a weekly show about studly highway patrol troopers.

"Behind closed doors, with no one watching, I always elected to watch 'CHiPs,' and that really bothered me," Robert J. Thompson recalled. "I was a cocky intellectual at the time, and the fact that I would be watching this incredibly stupid show instead of something much more enlightening is ultimately what took me away from art history and political philosophy and turned me into a television and later popular culture scholar."

Thompson has become the most frequently quoted pop culture expert in America, in part because he returns reporters' calls, but principally because he carries vast amounts of information in his brain. The one-time president of the Popular Culture Association directs the Center for the Study of Popular Television at Syracuse University.

To earn his doctorate from Northwestern University, Thompson 20 wrote a dissertation that would become his first book: "Adventures on Prime Time: The Television Programs of Stephen J. Cannell."

If Cannell's name rings a bell, it's because he was among the most ubiquitous producer-writers on television in the 1970s and '80s. His shows included "Baretta," "The Rockford Files" and "The A Team."

"I chose that very carefully," Thompson said. "I was interested in trying to demonstrate that this stuff we generally don't take seriously at all, that we kind of wrote off as highly popular but really just detritus—cultural trash—was in fact filled with secrets that serious academic scrutiny could reveal."

The first article Thompson published was submitted to the *Journal of Popular Culture*.

It was called "The Love Boat: High Art on the High Seas," Thompson said. "It was to answer the question: Why is it that smart people watch dumb television?"

25   This is the sort of thing that drives the country's best-known conservative intellectual curmudgeons to distraction. Cultural critic Roger Kimball has written often of the "corrupting" influence of 1960s radicals, whose legacy, he says, is the explosion of scholarship in such things as gender studies, ethnic studies and pop culture. And literary critic Harold Bloom lamented in a 1999 interview the "ideological" crusade to remove barriers between popular culture and high culture.

"It's not as though they were really talking about popular culture," he said. "They're not talking about folkways, or folklore, they're talking about commercial garbage, manufactured for a consumer society."

Even author Gerard Jones, who serves on the comparative media studies advisory board at M.I.T., says the complaints may be valid.

"I think there's an argument there," said Jones, whose new book is *Men of Tomorrow: Greeks, Gangsters and the Birth of the Comic Book*.

"I think you have to pull back and realize there's something in Tolstoy and Shakespeare that isn't in a Jerry Bruckheimer action movie," Jones said.

30   But Jones says the counterargument is inescapable: Ignore what millions of people are interested in at your own risk.

"Why shouldn't it matter to us if a comic book or a movie is seen by 15 million people or 50 million people?" said David M. Katzman, chair of the American studies program at the University of Kansas.

"Why shouldn't it be as important as a Shakespearean sonnet which was read by a few thousand people then and is only read today because it's assigned in class?"

Browne says the culture is what counts, not people's opinions of it.

"(People) are reading our material and realizing that movies and 'new history' and music and fast foods . . . are the things that shape and drive American culture. They may not be loved, but they have to be understood."

Questions for Discussion and Writing

1. Trussell states: "In academic halls from Berkeley to Bowling Green, young scholars and their instructors spend as much time tackling the history of

shopping, television and comic books—in other words, popular culture—as they do analyzing Homer, Shakespeare and Milton" (paragraph 2). According to Trussel, how did "popular culture" scholarship evolve? What assumptions about popular culture did scholars need to debunk?

2. Evaluate the arguments in support of and against the validity of popular culture courses. Which do you believe to be more persuasive? Do you think that the article is fair and balanced? Are both points of view presented equally?

3. In what specific ways would the style of writing differ if Trussell had been writing for a peer-reviewed academic journal rather than a newspaper? What is the value of Trussell's opportunity to deliver his message to a newspaper audience?

4. According to Trussell, the Browne Popular Culture Library at Bowling Green State University is "considered an invaluable resource for pop culture scholars" (paragraph 7). Think about materials that are part of the library collection. Imagine that you have been asked to submit a grant proposal requesting public funding to support the local popular culture library. What arguments would you make in support of the popular culture library? In your essay, try to anticipate and respond to the opposing argument.

5. Write an essay exploring the controversy over popular culture studies. Do you think that high culture (classical music, classical literature) has a higher value than popular culture (rock music, *The Simpsons*, etc.)? You may want to examine books, articles, and interviews by cultural critics such as Harold Bloom and Roger Kimbel (paragraph 25). Use evidence from your observations, views, and research.

Rock 101: Academia Tunes In
ALEX ROSS

This essay, by distinguished New Yorker *music critic Alex Ross, is from the July 14 and 21, 2003, issues of the magazine. Before his tenure in 1996, Ross was a critic at the* New York Times *and a contributor for numerous magazines and newspapers including the* New Republic, Slate, *the* London Review of Books, Transition, Spin, Lingua Franca, *and* Feed. *His essays and articles have been featured and reprinted in several books. He received two ASCAP-Deems Taylor Awards for music criticism and a Holtzbrinck fellowship at the American Academy in Berlin. His first book,* The Rest Is Noise: Listening to the Twentieth Century, a Cultural History of Music since 1900, *is forthcoming from Farrar, Straus & Giroux.*

Pre-Reading

Write the connotation of the title "Rock 101." In what ways do you imagine that your association(s) could differ from other people? What are your expectations of the essay? In your own writing, how much time do you spend on creating an attention-grabbing title?

———————— ✦ ————————

Duke Ellington once had to field a barrage of questions from an Icelandic music student who was determined to penetrate to the heart of the genius of jazz. At one point, Ellington was asked whether he ever felt an affinity for the music of Bach, and, before answering, he made a show of unwrapping a pork chop that he had stowed in his pocket. "Bach and myself," he said, taking a bite from the chop, "both write with individual performers in mind." Richard O. Boyer captured the moment in a Profile entitled "The Hot Bach," which appeared in this magazine in 1944. You can sense in that exquisitely timed pork-chop maneuver Ellington's bemused response to the European notions of genius that were constantly being foisted on him. He said on another occasion, "To attempt to elevate the status of the jazz musician by forcing the level of his best work into comparisons with classical music is to deny him his rightful share of originality." Jazz was a new language, and the critic would have to respond to it with a new poetry of praise.

Now Ellington is himself a classic, the subject of painstaking analytical studies. He occupies a Bachian position in an emergent popular pantheon, which is certain to look different from the marble-faced, bewigged classical pantheons that preceded it. That very idea of a canon of geniuses may be falling by the wayside; it makes more sense to talk about the flickering brilliance of a group, a place, or a people. In the future, it seems, everyone will be a genius for fifteen minutes. The past decade has seen the rise of pop-music studies, which is dedicated to the idea that Ellington, Hank Williams, and the Velvet Underground were created equal and deserve the same sort of scholarly scrutiny that used to be bestowed only on Bach and sons. Pop-music courses draw crowds of students on college campuses, and academic presses are putting out such portentous titles as "Instruments of Desire: The Electric Guitar and the Shaping of Musical Experience," "Rock Over the Edge: Transformations in Popular Music Culture," and "Running with the Devil; Power, Gender, and Madness in Heavy Metal Music."

Pop-music professors, especially those who specialize in rock, are caught in an obvious paradox, which their students probably point out to them on the first day of class. Namely, it's not very rock and roll to intellectualize rock and roll. When Pink Floyd sang, "We don't need no education," they could not have foreseen the advent of research projects with titles like "Another Book in the Wall?: A Cultural History of Pink Floyd's Stage Performance and the Rise of Audiovisual *Gesamtkunstwerk*, 1965–1994." (That comes from Finland.) Ever since Ellington, Armstrong, and Jelly Roll Morton struck up the soundtrack to the bawdy, boozy twenties, popular music has been the high-speed vehicle for youth rebellion, sexual liberation, and chemical experimentation, none of which yield willingly to the academic mind. The pop scholar is forever doomed to sounding like the square kid at the cool kids' party, killing their buzz with sentences like this: "From the start, hip-hop's samples ran the gamut of genres, defying anyone who would delimit hip-hop's palette."

Then again, maybe it's not a problem that so much pop-music scholarship sounds conspicuously uncool. For decades, jazz rhapsodists and rock poets were so intent on projecting attitude that they never got around to saying much about the music itself. The pioneering rock critics of the sixties, such as Lester Bangs and Greil Marcus, wanted to mimic the music in their prose, and they had enough style to pull it off. Bangs, whose writings have been collected in a new anthology from Anchor Books, lived the life of a rock star, or at least died the death of one. But his writings are a better guide to the mentality of smart people who went to rock shows in the sixties and seventies than they are a reliable record of music and musicians. Discussing the Rolling Stones in 1974, Bangs wrote, "If you think I'm going to review the new 'It's Only Rock 'n' Roll' album right now, you are crazy. But I am going to swim in it." Between prose poetry and academic cant there has to be a middle ground, and pop-music studies is searching it out.

INTERROGATING BRUCE'S BUTT

One weekend last spring, a few hundred scholars, journalists, musicians, and onlookers arrived in downtown Seattle for Pop Conference 2003, entitled "Skip a Beat: Rewriting the Story of Popular Music." The Pop Conference was created two years ago by Eric Weisbard, a former *Village Voice* rock critic, and Daniel Cavicchi, an assistant professor of American Studies at the Rhode Island School of Design. The decision to bring scholars and journalists together was unusual. It gave the critics an opportunity to drop arcane allusions instead of having to pretend to sound like teenagers, while the academics could loosen up a little. Weisbard and Cavicchi hope that the two worlds can cross-pollinate each other, breeding a sensibility that is scholarly but not stuffy, stylish but not frivolous.

The conference took place within the wavy-gravy walls of the Experience Music Project, a Frank Gehry culture palace, housing artifacts and bric-a-brac from a century of pop. The dress code was diverse to the point of incoherence: some of the older academics showed up in business attire, while younger ones wore T-shirts and jeans. (The divergence of styles became especially dissonant when sixties-generation scholars espoused radical political agendas while Gen X doctoral students sounded a neo-formalist, let's-just-talk-about-the-music tone.) For three days, participants hawked their wares in a tight twenty-minute format, taking persnickety questions afterward. At any given time, there were three different panels running in the various rooms of the E.M.P., meaning that the curious onlooker had to choose among equally tempting offerings. In order to attend the Bob Dylan panel— entitled The Dylan—you had to skip panels on art music (one paper was "Changing the System: Brian Eno, Sonic Youth, and the Combination of Rock and Experimental Music") and contemporary R. & B. ("Supa Dupa Fly: Styles of Subversion in Black Women's Hip-Hop").

Some of the presentations, a few too many for comfort, lapsed into the familiar contortions of modern pedagogy. Likewise, in the many pop-music books now in circulation, post-structuralist, post-Marxist, post-colonialist, and post-grammatical buzzwords crop up on page after page. There is a whole lot of problematizing, interrogating, and appropriating goin' on. Walter Benjamin's name is dropped at least as often as the Notorious B.I.G.'s. The French sociologist Pierre Bourdieu gets more props than Dr. Dre. At the Pop Conference, I made it a rule to move to a different room the minute I heard someone use the word "interrogate" in a non-detective context or cite any of the theorists of the Frankfurt School. Thus, I ducked out of a talk on Grace Jones's "Slave to the Rhythm" album when I heard a sentence that began with the phrase "Invoking Walter Benjamin." And I bailed on a lecture entitled "Bruce's Butt"—Bruce Springsteen's butt, as seen on the cover of "Born in the U.S.A."—when the speaker began to interrogate the image of the butt, which, under sharp questioning, wouldn't give anything away.

Scholars of this type always want to see pop music as the emanation of an entity called popular culture, rather than as music that happens to have become popular. As a result, songs and bands become fungible commodities in the intellectual marketplace. In the anthology "Popular Music Studies," the hip-hop scholar Ian Maxwell asks the significant question "How can our analyses avoid reducing the objects of those analyses to desiccated cadavers on a slab?" His solution—a "more rigorous understanding of what an ethnographically informed approach might offer the study of popular music, nuancing that approach through Bourdieu's reflexive criticality"—gets us only so far.

Roger Beebe, one of the editors of the "Rock Over the Edge" anthology, even looks at music as purely a media phenomenon, inseparable from image and marketing. Analyzing Kurt Cobain's appearances on television, he says that Cobain mattered to his fans mainly as a disembodied entity, not as an individual with a voice, and that he exemplified something called "the postmodern *dispositif.*" Such McLuhanesque musings have been rendered obsolete as MTV has more or less stopped showing videos in favor of frat-house documentaries. Meanwhile, the Internet has become the main avenue for the spread of music. The mania for downloading music may be wreaking havoc with artists' careers, but it is interesting to see how the ear trumps the eye when the computer takes over. Music is being consumed with no images attached—no videos, no TV appearances, not even album jackets. In the nineteenth century, the Viennese critic Eduard Hanslick dreamed of a world "purely musical," beyond politics and personality. Such a world now exists in the form of the MP3.

THE MATHEMATICS OF "SUPERBAD"

Despite minor infestations of Benjaminites, there was no shortage   10
of up-close musical discussion at the Pop Conference. I often had the happy experience of being held hostage by an informed fanatic who convinced me that whatever he or she was discussing was the most important music on earth. The presenters tended to avoid obvious mainstream figures—there was nothing on Elvis, the Beatles, or the Rolling Stones—focusing, instead, on the margins and subtexts of pop history. There were papers on the lo-fi ideology of nineties indie rock, the Filipino d.j. scene in San Francisco, and the trailblazing transsexual punk of Wayne/Jayne County, among a hundred others. You got a sense of music as a

world of jostling subcultures, each with its resident inventors and masters, its purists and populists. The conference conjured up the everlasting complexity of how songs are made, heard, and remembered.

Rock and roll has generated more self-serving myths than any other genre, and scholars have been busy dismantling them. Too often, pop history has been written as a march forward to a handful of utopian moments in the late fifties and the sixties: Chuck Berry recording "Maybellene," Elvis appearing on Ed Sullivan, the Beatles appearing on Ed Sullivan, and Bob Dylan plugging in his guitar at the Newport Folk Festival. These events have acquired an exaggerated importance, mostly because they had sentimental value for the baby-boom generation that dominated early pop-music writing. Younger writers are especially impatient with the rock narrative—the "rockist paradigm," they call it—and delight in cataloguing its contradictions and omissions. Consider Dylan's famous rebellion against the folkies. At the Pop Conference, the historian Michael J. Kramer presented a paper in which he defended the folk-music movement from the stereotype that prevails in Dylan studies—the image of humorless fanatics rejecting the visionary in their midst. Kramer pointed out that the singer took a great deal of his mocking, critical voice—"humorous impurity," he called it—from the very movement that he was supposed to have renounced. In a similar vein, Franklin Bruno, a doctoral student in philosophy who writes quirky, literate pop songs, noted that Dylan in his electric period relied heavily on the tricks of Tin Pan Alley songwriting, precisely the sort of mom-and-dad music that the singer was supposed to have left behind. "Blonde on Blonde," Bruno said, was "a head-first dive into pop-song formalism." Everybody must get stoned, but not before the bridge and the modulation.

Again and again, popular music has been described as a story of youth rebellion, in which each generation breaks free of the oppressive mediocrity of its predecessor. When you place these rebellion narratives end to end, they cancel each other out. Whatever is considered edgy and liberating in one generation is dismissed as bland and confining for the next. An aging genre invariably becomes a straw man against which a new genre defines itself. Dylan "plugged in" and defied the folkies. Chuck Berry sang "Roll Over Beethoven" to get the original rock-and-roll revolution under way, using classical music as a foil. The Beatles were said to have swept aside the prefab pop of the early sixties, which happened to include some of the great early Motown songs. Punk sneered at disco. Why should the love of one kind of music necessitate the knocking down of another? Schopenhauer may have had the answer when he observed that the listener is always fighting battles in his head which he can never win in life. "We like to hear in its language the secret history of our will and of all its stirrings and strivings," the philosopher said. Music at its most potent creates the feeling that the world is about to undergo a vague but tremendous change, which is how political energies become attached to it. When the world fails to change as promised, however, the music becomes an object of ridicule.

The ultimate pop-music myth is the one that scholars file under the rubric "authenticity," according to which only the rudest, rawest music—the primal scream of the outcast—qualifies as "real." African-American music is usually expected to supply the perfume of the primitive. Since the nineteen-twenties, white teenagers have used black music as the Muzak of their pubescence. Some pop historians still perpetuate this mythology, but others make a point of celebrating all that is rigorous, complex, and exalted in the African-American tradition. One of my favorite passages in pop-music studies appears in "Instruments of Desire," an erudite paean to the electric guitar, by Steve Waksman, of Smith College. It describes how Bo Diddley came to invent his tremolando sound. "Tremolo involved an oscillation of the electronic signal," Waksman writes, "transmitted from the guitar to the amplifier so that the volume level would fluctuate at regular intervals between extreme loudness and virtual silence." I don't really know what this means, but it certainly puts Diddley's "bump-a-bump bump" in a new light. Likewise, David Brackett, the author of "Interpreting Popular Music," lost me when he began to expound on James Brown's "Superbad" by way of the mathematical proportions of the Golden Section, positing that various parts of the song relate to each other by a ratio of 0.618 to 1. Bach has long been subject to this sort of arcane analysis, and there is no reason that the hardest-working man in show business shouldn't get the same treatment.

In a less pedantic vein, a paper by Portia K. Maultsby, who teaches in the department of Folklore and Ethnomusicology at Indiana University, dismantled the clichés attached to Motown's "hit factory," which for a long time was accused of purveying what critics called a "diluted blackness." She stressed Motown's profound connections with the African-American tradition, especially jazz, gospel, and rhythm and blues: James Jamerson's restless, all-over bass lines are electric bebop. Maultsby's paper went hand in hand with an essay by John Sheinbaum in the "Rock Over the Edge" anthology—a devastating account of how white rockers are routinely celebrated as enigmatic artists while their African-American counterparts are made out to be simpleminded conduits of energy and fun. "The Rolling Stone Illustrated History of Rock and Roll" once described Motown as a "wholly mechanical style and sound." The Beatles, by contrast, were hailed as mop-top Beethovens immediately after releasing "I Want to Hold Your Hand." The Beatles were great, but they did not save music from oblivion when they arrived in America in 1964. In fact, as Keir Keightley notes in "The Cambridge Companion to Pop and Rock," the blues-besotted British Invasion had the effect of putting a great many African-American session musicians out of work.

THE CRUCIFIXION MAMBO

15   By common consent, the tour de force of the Pop Conference was a lecture by the Cuban music scholar and producer Ned Sublette, which took place at the not very funky hour of 9:30 A.M. In the space of twenty minutes or so, Sublette conjured up the sweeping influence of Cuban music and Caribbean traditions on almost every popular form of the twentieth century. It was not so much a lecture as an all-out performance: Sublette, who also leads a Latin-country fusion band, sang, tapped, and danced the Cuban rhythms that have insinuated themselves into every breakthrough moment in American music, including ragtime (Scott Joplin's "The Entertainer" uses the *danzón* rhythm), New Orleans jazz, bebop, rock and roll (Bo Diddley's "hambone" beat is similar to the Cuban clave), and funk. Sublette called Cuban music "the elephant in the kitchen that pop-music historians have failed to see"; it was, he insisted, the site of the original marriage of African rhythm and European harmony.

By installing Cuban music as "the other great tradition," Sublette did the unthinkable: he questioned the primacy of African-Americans in pop history. There were murmurs of unease when he announced that African-American music was not originally polyrhythmic. Robert Christgau, the fiercely informed critic of the *Village Voice*, said in the question-and-answer period that blues singers implied polyrhythm in the interplay of voice and guitar. In a way, though, Sublette's Cubacentric reading—the book version of which will be published next year—relieves African-Americans of the burden of being the primitives of American music; they become the appropriators rather than the appropriated.

Sublette mentioned, in passing, the fascinating history of two old Spanish-American dances, the *zarabanda* and the *chacona*, which probably stemmed from the Afro-Caribbean melting pot. They spread to Europe in the sixteenth and seventeenth centuries and helped shape some of the masterpieces of the Baroque. In Seattle, I got to thinking about the tangled history of the *chacona*, or chaconne, which has appeared in so many diverse places in the past five hundred years that it could be considered one of the iconic images of the universal language. It is identifiable by its bass line: a constantly repeating, often downward-plunging figure, over which higher instruments and voices play variations. "A dance in the way of the mulatto's," Cervantes called it. The lyrics were bawdy and irreverent; the music was said to have been invented by the Devil. Once it reached Europe, it slowed down and took on more solemn connotations. In the hands of Monteverdi it led to the "Lamento" bass, which was well suited to the dying utterances of operatic heroines. In its most striking form, the "Lamento" proceeded down a grand, chilly staircase of semitones, or chromatic steps. You can hear this version of it in the heart-stopping final lament of Purcell's "Dido and Aeneas," and in the "Crucifixus" from Bach's Mass in B Minor.

At the beginning of the twentieth century, a *chacona*-style figure reappeared in the hands of African-American musicians in New Orleans, Chicago, and, notably, the Mississippi Delta, where the Devil was again said to be active. It sounded obsessively in Skip James's "I'm So Glad," one of the greatest of the Delta blues, and can be heard rumbling beneath Ellington's "Reminiscing in Tempo." Descending chromatic basses gave a slow-marching power to some of the more ambitious rock songs of the sixties and seventies—Dylan's "Ballad of a Thin Man" and "Simple Twist of Fate," Led Zeppelin's "Dazed and Confused" and "Stairway to Heaven." Somehow, four centuries after the lamenting bass surfaced, its meaning remained the same. It summoned up the dark comfort of heartbreak and depression: the heart descending step by step to the bottom and going back up to repeat the journey.

Universal figures such as the *chacona*—"memes," as musicologists call them, borrowing from sociobiology—reveal the interconnectedness of all musical experience. If you could bring together a few seventeenth-century Afro-Cuban musicians, a continuo section led by the Master Bach, and players from Ellington's 1929 band, and then ask John Paul Jones to start them off with the bass line of "Dazed and Confused," they would, after a minute or two, find common ground. And very interesting music it would be,

too. Purists of all genres can never stand the fact that the geneal-
ogy of music is one long string of miscegenations and mutations.

THE TIMBERLAKE PERPLEX

20 When, in 1943, Ellington presented his symphonic masterpiece
"Black, Brown, and Beige" at Carnegie Hall, he spoke of it in the
first-person plural, including his band in the creative process.
Scholars often point out that African-American genres, like their
West African antecedents, resist the European cult of personality:
they tend to take the form of a collective ritual, not of a declama-
tion by a charismatic star to a passive crowd. The problem with
the "genius" model is that it puts up a wall between performer
and audience; this is surely why so many pop musicians reject it,
even as they feed on the adulation that creates it. They look warily
on the archivists and commentators who crowd around any long-
lasting genre. If, as another old German dude said, the owl of
Minerva flies at dusk, rock critics are Minerva's vultures: when
enough of them take flight, it means that something is dying.

Still, we listeners want to talk about genius. We want a language that articulates and perpetuates our passions. What's bedev-
illing about pop music is that while we sense greatness in a song
we have trouble saying where it comes from. It is often difficult to
say who even wrote the thing in the first place. Some performers
exert such a powerful presence—Billie Holiday, Sinatra, Elvis—
that they seem to become the authors of songs that were actually
the work of schlumpy men in the Brill Building. Then there are
the rock songs that were written by committee, often in the middle
of the night, and under the influence of something other than the
muse Euterpe. Composers have the advantage of being shrouded
in myth: we can project fantasies of omniscience upon them. Pop
stars torment us with their inconvenient humanness—their tax
problems, their noisome politics, their pornography collections,
their unwanted comebacks. No wonder the greatest legends are
the artists who die young.

Call this the Timberlake predicament. In the past year, rock
critics found themselves in the faintly embarrassing position of
having to hail Justin Timberlake's "Justified" as one of the better
records of the year. Timberlake, for those who have let their sub-
scription to *Teen People* lapse, is the blond, curly-haired twenty-
two-year-old lead singer of 'N Sync. Encomiums from certifiably
heterosexual male critics such as Christgau have demonstrated
that Timberlake was not getting praised for his pretty face alone.

Granted, cynics may see all this as a rationalization on the part of writers who can't admit that music keeps getting worse; they eat a Hostess Twinkie and call it a gourmet meal. But it shouldn't be forgotten that many of the most imposing achievements in pop history had their origins in ditsy teenybopper fads. The Beatles were once a boy band, too. What happened to them in the middle and late sixties was a mysterious transfer of energy, in which disposable fame was transmuted into artistic power. The band found fame first, then it found greatness. So it would be foolish to write Timberlake off too quickly.

In any case, the songs on "Justified" aren't really Timberlake's. A dozen names appear in the credits, and it's anyone's guess how much of a song like "Cry Me a River," the album's best track, actually came from Timberlake's pen, if he owns one. Every bit of the song shows the fingerprints of the hip-hop producer Tim Mosley, a.k.a. Timbaland, who is the éminence grise behind half of what is great in the Top Forty these days. He has sampled every genre under the sun, from world music to austere electronica. He likes to leave yawning gaps of silence between his speaker-puncturing beats, which inspire new kinds of vehemence on the dance floor. (As Virgil Thomson observed long ago, we dance to syncopated music because our bodies like to fill in the missing beats.) Modernist ideology accustoms us to think that experimentation can take place on the margins of a culture, but hip-hop production is the site of some of the weirdest, wittiest thinking in pop music today.

"Cry Me a River" has no apparent relation to the 1955 standard made famous by Julie London, although a future analysis of internal structural ratios may show otherwise. The vocals are plaintive to the point of whining, but the inner voices have a cool, contrapuntal flow, creating the sort of muscular melancholy so characteristic of postwar rhythm and blues. There are at least seven layers of simultaneous activity in the song—it's as if Timbaland wanted to see how much he could pile on without creating atonality. First there is an arpeggiated keyboard figure, followed by male voices singing a bit of Gregorian-style chant. Next comes a steady, sombre pattern that sounds a little like the minor-key vamp in Ellington's "East St. Louis Toodle-Oo." Below it are four bass notes, recurring in *chacona* style. Now the angelic Timberlake enters, together with a more nasty-minded rhythm section, a vaguely Indian-sounding synthesized string orchestra, and, finally, sped-up versions of all the above.

In sum, "Cry Me a River" may be the most polyphonically complex teenybopper ballad in history. At the very least, it's not 25 something that any idiot could have done. It has the inward delight of a song that is better than it needs to be. Popular music is full of this sort of mad tinkering; in the background of even the most ostentatiously numskulled acts may be a music geek who stays up all night trying to find a single chord. Pop-music scholars spend a lot of time describing the messages that become attached to songs, and this is a necessary part of the history of listening. Yet, when music passes from one generation to another, it leaves most of its social significance peeling off dorm-room walls, and its persistence is best explained with reference to beats, chords, and raw emotion. Which is why pop writers have to find a new way to describe musical events, and not just by offering dopey imitations of classical musicology. No one would give much credence to a style of art criticism that alluded to paintings without mentioning their shapes and colors, or an architecture criticism that refused to say whether buildings were made of stone or metal.

It was disappointing to hear from attendees at the Pop Conference that they are still viewed with intense suspicion by their colleagues in classical musicology. Increasingly, leading colleges and universities have full-time pop specialists; the musicology department at U.C.L.A. is headed by Robert Walser, the author of books on jazz and heavy metal. Given the vast quantities of obscurantism that classical musicologists have churned out in the past fifty years—the impenetrable tautologies of Schenkerian analysis, the higher-math delirium of pitch-class set theory—classical scholars have no right to dismiss their pop counterparts as anything less than serious. They probably picture themselves fighting a last stand against the armies of ignorance, but any mode of teaching that promotes close, historically attuned listening can't be a bad thing. And those of us who write on classical music have a lot to learn from pop studies. It exposes the hard realities of how music is made, how it is paid for, and how it is consumed. To understand music only as art and not as entertainment, as classical scholars tend to do, is to dehumanize the past. For all we know, Bach may well have rolled his eyes and munched on a pork chop whenever someone asked him about his relationship with Palestrina.

Pop music is music stripped bare. It is like the haphazard funeral portrayed in Wallace Stevens's "Emperor of Ice Cream": a woman laid out with all her flaws intact, covered with a sheet from a chest of drawers that is missing three knobs, her horny feet protruding. Boys bring flowers in last month's newspapers, but she is noble to look upon. Twentieth-century music, the empire of ice cream, lies before us in all its damaged majesty.

Questions for Discussion and Writing

1. Why do you think Ross begins with the paradox "it's not very rock and roll to intellectualize rock and roll" (paragraph 3)? What benefits are to be gained from intellectualizing rock and roll?

2. In your own words, briefly describe the various myths Ross refers to in his essay. Why do you believe Ross includes them in his argument?

3. Look up the terms "post-structuralist," "post-Marxist," and "post-Colonialist." What do they mean? In what context do they appear in the article?

4. Ross writes, "Ever since Ellington, Armstrong, and Jelly Roll Morton struck up the soundtrack to the bawdy, boozy twenties, popular music has been the high-speed vehicle for youth rebellion, sexual liberation, and chemical experimentation" (paragraph 3). Write an essay examining any one of these themes (youth rebellion, sexual liberation, chemical experimentation). In order to narrow your topic, focus on one genre of music (rock and roll, jazz, punk, heavy metal, disco, etc.).

5. Ross mentions several titles of academic papers. Select the title that is most interesting to you and write an essay on a similar topic. For example, "Supa Dupa Fly: Styles of Subversion in Black Women's Hip-Hop" (paragraph 6) could inspire an essay entitled "Queen Latifah: Bodacious Liberating Style in Hip-Hop." Use evidence to support your thesis.

The Reader in Exile
Jonathan Franzen

Best known for his critically acclaimed and award-winning book The Corrections *(2001), for which he won the National Book Award, novelist Jonathan Franzen has received numerous honors, including a Whiting Writers Award (1988), a Guggenheim Fellowship (1996), and the American Academy's Berlin Prize (2000). A frequent contributor to the* New Yorker, *Franzen's book publications include* The Twenty-Seventh City *(1988)*, Strong Motion *(1992), and* How to Be Alone *(2002), a collection of essays from which this is an excerpt.*

Pre-Reading

For one day, document the various types of reading you do and your different ways of reading. For example, did you read the newspaper in a different way from your notes for class? The next day, evaluate your reading habits. Would you characterize yourself as a reader? In other words, do you read for pleasure or more out of necessity?

─────────────── ✦ ───────────────

A few months ago, I gave away my television set. It was a massive old Sony Trinitron, the gift of a friend whose girlfriend couldn't stand the penetrating whistle the picture tube emitted. Its wood-look veneer recalled an era when TV sets were trying, however feebly, to pass as furniture—an era when their designers could still imagine them in a state of not being turned on. I kept it in inaccessible places, like the floor of a closet, and I could get a good picture only by sitting crosslegged directly in front of it and touching the antenna. It's hard to make TV viewing more unpleasant than I did. Still, I felt the Trinitron had to go, because as long as it was in the house, reachable by some combination of extension cords, I wasn't reading books.

I was born in 1959, on the cusp of a great generational divide, and for me it's a toss-up which is scarier: living without electronic access to my country's culture, or trying to survive in that culture without the self-definition I get from regular immersion in literature. I understand my life in the context of Raskolnikov and Quentin Compson, not David Letterman or Jerry Seinfeld. But the life I understand by way of books feels increasingly lonely. It has little to do with the mediascape that constitutes so many other people's present.

For every reader who dies today, a viewer is born, and we seem to be witnessing, here in the anxious mid-nineties, the final tipping of a balance. For critics inclined to alarmism, the shift from a culture based on the printed word to a culture based on virtual images—a shift that began with television and is now being completed with computers—feels apocalyptic. In much the same way that Silicon Valley dreams of the "killer application" that will make PCs indispensable to every American, alarmists seek a killer argument that will make the imminence of apocalypse self-evident.

One recent attempt at a such an argument is a book called *A Is for Ox*, by the literary scholar Barry Sanders, who takes as his starting point two dismal trends: rising violence among youth and falling verbal SAT scores. In answer to the well-documented fact that children don't read and write the way they used to, Sanders refreshingly declines to give the explanation that Barney has murdered Mother Goose. TV still plays the villain in his cosmology, but it works its evil less by displacing reading than by replacing verbal interaction with parents and peers. No matter how high the quality of the programming, an excess of passive reception stunts a child's oral development and prepares her or him to be frustrated by the seemingly arbitrary rules of standard English. Computers and video in the classroom only compound the estrangement from spoken language. Frustration turns to resentment: kids drop out of school and, in the worst case, join violent gangs of what Sanders calls "post-illiterates." It's his thesis that without a literacy rooted in orality there can be neither a self, as we understand it, nor self-consciousness. Interpreting the past, entertaining choices in the present, projecting a future, experiencing guilt or remorse—these are all, according to Sanders, activities foreclosed to the soulless young gangsters of today and to the fully computerized society, neither oral nor literate, of tomorrow.

The problem with Sanders's argument, as a killer, is that he   5
has to finger too many culprits. He lays the blame for the national crisis in literacy as much on the decline in the quality time parents spend with their children as on the video input that has filled the vacuum. Young gangsters, he notes, not only are addicted to images but also come from impoverished, unstable homes. So are we facing a techno-apocalypse, or is it plain old-fashioned social dysfunction? Every mother I know restricts her children's TV intake and sows resistance to it by encouraging reading. Like the readers of this essay, my friends and I belong to that class of well-educated "symbolic analysts" which Labor Secretary Robert Reich believes is inheriting the earth. Sanders's generalizations about "young people today" apply only to the segment of the population (admittedly a large one) that lacks the money or the leisure to inoculate its children against the worst ravages of electronic media. What he describes as the self-immolation of civilization is in fact only a partitioning; and the irony of this partitioning is that those with the greatest access to information are the ones least tethered by the wires that bring it.

Anyone with a taste for such ironies will enjoy Nicholas Negroponte's *Being Digital*, a guide to Tomorrowland for those who believe that technology has created no problems that better technology can't fix. Negroponte is the director of the Media Lab at M.I.T., and *Being Digital* is a compilation of his monthly columns in *Wired* magazine, the graphically adventurous "bible" (as I've seen it called) of the cyberworld. *Wired* attempts to celebrate the in-ness of the in crowd while leaving the door open for newcomers, and it manages the trick by selling both vision and inside dope. Negroponte's specialty is vision. He's the in-house oracle.

Leaders of government and industry flock to Negroponte for advice, and as a consequence, much of *Being Digital* is about (how else to put it?) resource allocation. Should developers of virtual-reality equipment spend their finite computing power on heightening video resolution, or on improving the equipment's reaction time to a user's head and neck movements? Go with the speed, says Negroponte. Should Wall Street invest in high-volume electronic pipelines or in TV technology that uses existing pipelines more efficiently? Go with the smart, small machine, says Negroponte.

Perhaps because the title *Being Digital* seems to promise the articulation of a new way of being human, it took me a while to realize that the book is not about the transformation of a culture but about money. The first question Negroponte asks of a development like virtual reality is whether there's a market for it. If a market exists, someone will inevitably exploit it, and so it's pointless to ask "Do we need this?" or "How might it harm us?" "The consumer" is a cheerful omnipresence in Negroponte's book, a most-favored arbiter.

Being Digital is awash in references to a world of moneyed internationalism—to the luxury hotels the author stays in, to his lunches with prime ministers, to transpacific flights, Burgundian vintners, Swiss boarding schools, Bavarian nannies. The ease with which jobs and capital and digital signals now cross national boundaries is matched by the mobility of the new informational elite, those lucky symbolic analysts who, like many a ruling class before them, are finding that they have more in common with the elect of other countries than with the preterite of their own. It's a revelation, when you notice it, how free of nationalism *Being Digital* is, how interchangeable the locales. In a brief aside, Negroponte complains that people lecture him about life in the real world—"as if," he says, "I live in an unreal world." He's right to complain. His world is as real as the ganglands that Barry Sanders evokes. But the two worlds are growing ever more unreal to each other.

10   High above the clouds, the sun always shines. Negroponte paints a tomorrow of talking toasters, smart refrigerators, and flavorized computers ("You will be able to buy a Larry King personality for your newspaper interface") that is *Jetsons*-like in its retention of today's suburban values. To find clues to a deeper transformation, you have to read between the lines. Negroponte has a habit, for example, of reducing human functions to machinery: the human eye

is "the client for the image," an ear is a "channel," faces are "display devices," and "Disney's guaranteed audience is refueled at a rate that exceeds 12,500 births each hour." In the future, "CD-ROMs may be edible, and parallel processors may be applied like sun tan lotion." The new, digital human being will dine not only on storage devices but on narcissism. "Newspapers will be printed in an edition of one . . . Call it *The Daily Me*." Authors, meanwhile, as they move from text to multimedia, will assume the role of "stage-set or theme-park designer."

When Barry Sanders looks at young people, he sees lost, affectless faces. Negroponte sees a "mathematically able and more visually literate" generation happily competing in a cyberspace where "the pursuit of intellectual achievement will not be tilted so much in favor of the bookworm." He espouses a kind of therapeutic corporatism, defending video games as teachers of "strategies" and "planning skills," and recalling how his son had trouble learning to add and subtract until his teacher put dollar signs in front of the figures. The closest Negroponte comes to recognizing the existence of social dysfunction is in his description of the robots that in the near future will bring us our drinks and dust our empty bookshelves: "For security reasons, a household robot must also be able to bark like a ferocious dog."

Its easy to fault Negroponte's resolute ahistoricism; harder, however, to dislike an author who begins his book by confessing, "Being dyslexic, I don't like to read." Negroponte is nothing more and nothing less than a man who has profited by speculating on the future and is willing, like a successful stockbroker, to share his secrets. Apart from offering a few misty assurances ("Digital technology can be a natural force drawing people into greater world harmony"), he doesn't pretend his revolution will solve problems more serious than the annoyance of having to visit Blockbuster in the flesh to rent a movie.

In a culture of false perspective, where Johnny Cochran can appear taller than Boris Yeltsin, it's difficult to tell if the Internet is legitimately big news. Russell Baker has compared the hyping of the Net to the hyping of atomic energy in the fifties, when industry pitchmen promised that we would soon be paying "pennies" for our monthly utilities. Today's technology boosters can't offer ordinary consumers as measurable a benefit as cheap electricity. Instead, the selling points are intangible—conveyed through the language of health and hipness.

Digital technology, the argument goes, is good medicine for an ailing society. TV has given us government by image; interactivity will return power to the people. TV has produced millions of une-ducable children; computers will teach them. Top-down program-ming has isolated us; bottom-up networks will reunite us. As a bonus, being digital is medicine that tastes good. It's a pop-cultural pleasure we're invited to indulge. Indeed, some of the best television these days is funded by IBM: nuns in an Italian convent whisper about the Net, Moroccan businessmen sip mint tea and talk interfacing. This is both advertising and luscious postmodern art. Of course, the aim of such art is simply to make the giving of our dollars to IBM seem inevitable. But popularity has become its own justification.

15   If I were fashioning my own killer argument against the digital revolution, I'd begin with the observation that both Newt Gingrich and Timothy Leary are crazy about it. Somewhere, something isn't adding up. Douglas Rushkoff, in *Media Virus!*—his book-length exploration of the media counterculture—quotes a skeptical New Age thinker as offering this bright side to the rev-olution: "There's no longer a private space. The idea of literate culture is basically a middle-class notion—it's the gentleman in his book-lined study with the privacy for reflection. That's a very elitist notion." Robert Coover, writing in a similar vein in a pair of essays for the *Times Book Review*, promises that hypertext will replace "the predetermined one-way route" of the conventional novel with works that can be read in any number of ways, and thus liberate readers from "domination by the author." At the same time, Speaker Gingrich's own clutch of New Age authors advertise the electronic town meeting as the perfect antidote to tired Second Wave liberalism. Where Wall Street sees a profit for investors, visionaries of every political persuasion see empower-ment for the masses.

That news of this better future continues to arrive by way of print—in "the entombing, distancing oppression of paper," as a *Wired* columnist put it—may simply be a paradox of obsoles-cence, like the necessity of riding your horse to the dealer who sells you your first car. But Negroponte, in explaining his decision to publish an actual book, offers a surprising reason for his choice: interactive multimedia leave too little to the imagination. "By contrast," he says, "the written word sparks images and evokes metaphors that get much of their meaning from the reader's imagination and experiences. When you read a novel, much of the color, sound, and motion come from you."

If Negroponte took the health of the body politic seriously, he would need to explore what this argument implies about the muscle tone of our imaginations in a fully digital age. But you can trust him, and the hard-core corporate interests he advises, not to engage in sentimentality. The truth is simple, if unpretty. The novel is dying because the consumer doesn't want it anymore.

Novels are by no means dead, of course—just ask Annie Proulx or Cormac McCarthy. But the Novel, as a seat of cultural authority, is teetering on the brink, and in *The Gutenberg Elegies*, a collection of essays subtitled *The Fate of Reading in an Electronic Age*, Sven Birkerts registers his surprise and dismay that its decline has not been more widely mourned. Not even professional book critics, who ought to be the front line of the novel's defenders, have raised the alarm, and Birkerts, who is a critic himself, sounds like a loyal soldier deserted by his regiment. The tone of his elegies is brave but plaintive.

Birkerts begins his defense of the novel by recounting how, while growing up in an immigrant household, he came to understand himself by reading Jack Kerouac, J. D. Salinger, and Hermann Hesse. The authors as well as the alienated, romantic heroes of their books became models for emulation and comparison. Later, on the desolate emotional beach on which the wave of sixties idealism seems to have deposited so many people, Birkerts weathered years of depression by reading, by working in bookstores, and, finally, by becoming a reviewer. "Basically," he says, "I was rescued by books."

Books as catalysts of self-realization and books as sanctuary: 20 the notions are paired because Birkerts believes that "inwardness, the more reflective component of self," requires a "space" where a person can reflect on the meaning of things. Compared with the state of a person watching a movie or clicking through hypertext, he says, absorption in a novel is closer to a state of meditation, and he is at his best when tracing the subtleties of this state. Here is his description of his initial engagement with a novel: "I feel a tug. The chain has settled over the sprockets; there is the feel of meshing, then the forward glide." And here is his neat reply to hypertext's promise of liberation from the author: "This 'domination by the author' has been, at least until now, the *point* of reading and writing. The author masters the resources of language to create a vision that will engage and in some way overpower the reader; the reader goes to the work to be subjected to the creative will of another." Birkerts on reading fiction is like M. F. K. Fisher on eating or Norman Maclean on fly-casting. He makes you want to go do it.

Counterposed to his idyll of the book-lined study, however, is a raging alarmism. In the decline of the novel, Birkerts sees more

than a shift in our habits of entertainment. He sees a transformation of the very nature of humanity. His nightmare, to be sure, "is
not one of neotroglodytes grunting and wielding clubs, but of efficient and prosperous information managers living in the shallows
of what it means to be human and not knowing the difference."
He grants that technology has made our perspectives more global
and tolerant, our access to information easier, our self-definitions
less confining. But, as he repeatedly stresses, "the more complex
and sophisticated our systems of lateral access, the more we
sacrifice in the way of depth." Instead of Augie March, Arnold
Schwarzenegger. Instead of Manassas battlefield, a historical
theme park. Instead of organizing narratives, a map of the world
as complex as the world itself. Instead of a soul, membership in a
crowd. Instead of wisdom, data.

In a coda to *The Gutenberg Elegies*, Birkerts conjures up, out of
the pages of *Wired* magazine, the Devil himself, "sleek and confident,"
a "sorcerer of the binary order" who offers to replace the struggle of
earthly existence with "a vivid, pleasant dream." All he wants in
return is mankind's soul. Birkerts confesses to an envy for the Devil:
"I wonder, as I did in high school when confronted with the smooth
and athletic ones, the team captains and class presidents, whether I
would not, deep down, trade in all this doubting and wondering and
just be him." Yet, tempted as he is by the sexiness of the Devil's technology, a voice in his heart says, "Refuse it."

Technology as the Devil incarnate, being digital as perdition:
considering that contemporary authors like Toni Morrison have
vastly larger audiences than Jane Austen had in her day, something other than sober analysis would seem to be motivating
Birkerts's hyperbole. The clue, I think, is in the glimpses he gives
of his own life beneath the shallows of what it means to be
human. He refers to his smoking, his quarts of beer, his morbid
premonitions of disaster, his insomnia, his brooding. He names
as the primary audience for his book his many friends who refuse
to grant him the darkness of our cultural moment, who shrug off
electronic developments as enhancements of the written word.
"I sometimes wonder if my thoughtful friends and I are living in
the same world . . . Naturally I prefer to think that the problem
lies with them."

These lines are redolent with depression and the sense of
estrangement from humanity that depression fosters. Nothing
aggravates this estrangement more than a juggernaut of hipness
such as television has created and the digital revolution's
marketers are exploiting. It's no accident that Birkerts locates

apocalypse in the arch-hip pages of *Wired*. He's still the high-school loner, excluded from the in crowd and driven, therefore, to the alternative and more "genuine" satisfactions of reading. But what, we might ask him, is so wrong with being an efficient and prosperous information manager? Do the team captains and class presidents really not have souls?

Elitism is the Achilles' heel of every serious defense of art, an   25 invitation to the poisoned arrows of populist rhetoric. The elitism of modern literature is, undeniably, a peculiar one—an aristoc-racy of alienation, a fraternity of the doubting and wondering. Still, after voicing a suspicion that nonreaders view reading "as a kind of value judgment upon themselves, as an elitist and exclu-sionary act," Birkerts is brave enough to confirm their worst fears: "Reading *is* a judgment. It brands as insufficient the under-standings and priorities that govern ordinary life." If he had stopped here, with the hard fact of literature's selective appeal, *The Gutenberg Elegies* would be an unassailable, if unheeded, paean. But because books saved his life and he can't abide the thought of a world without them, he falls under the spell of another, more popular defense of art. This is the grant-proposal defense, the defense that avoids elitism. Crudely put, it's that while technology is merely palliative, art is therapeutic.

I admit to being swayable by this argument. It's why I banished my Trinitron and gave myself back to books. But I try to keep this to myself. Unhappy families may be aesthetically superior to happy families, whose happiness is all alike, but "dysfunctional" families are not. It was easy to defend a novel about unhappiness; everybody knows unhappiness; it's part of the human condition. A novel about emotional dysfunction, however, is reduced to a Manichaeanism of utility. Either it's a sinister enabler, obstructing health by celebrat-ing pathology, or it's an object lesson, helping readers to understand and overcome their own dysfunction. Obsession with social health produces a similar vulgarity: if a novel isn't part of a political solu-tion, it must be part of the problem. The doctoral candidate who "exposes" Joseph Conrad as a colonialist is akin to the school board that exiles Holden Caulfield as a poor role model—akin as well, unfortunately, to Birkerts, whose urgency in defending reading devolves from the assumption that books must somehow "serve" us.

I love novels as much as Birkerts does, and I, too, have felt rescued by them. I'm moved by his pleading, as a lobbyist in the cause of literature, for the intellectual subsidy of his client. But novelists want their work to be enjoyed, not taken as medicine. Blaming the novel's eclipse on infernal technologies and treasonous literary critics, as Birkerts does, will not undo the damage. Neither will the argument that reading enriches us. Ultimately, if novelists want their work to be read, the responsibility for making it attractive and imperative is solely their own.

There remains, however, the bitter circumstance that, as Birkerts puts it, "the daily life of the average American has become Teflon for the novelist." Once upon a time, characters inhabited charged fields of status and geography. Now, increasingly, the world is binary. You either have or you don't have. You're functional or you're dysfunctional, you're wired or you're tired. Unhappy families, perhaps even more than happy ones, are all identically patched in to CNN, *The Lion King*, and America Online. It's more than a matter of cultural references; it's the very texture of their lives. And if a novel depends on the realization of complex characters against a background of a larger society, how do you write one when the background is indistinguishable from the foreground?

"Fiction," according to Birkerts, "only retains its cultural vitality so long as it can bring readers meaningful news about what it means to live in the world of the present." He has in mind the broad-canvased, big-audience novels of Tolstoy and Dickens, of Bellow and Steinbeck, and indeed, there seems little doubt that the form is going the way of Shakespearean tragedy and Verdian opera. But the news of its passing is perhaps less meaningful than Birkerts makes it out to be. The audience may have collapsed in the last few decades, but cultural vitality has had to reconcile itself with silence, cunning, and exile throughout our technological century. Kafka told Max Brod he wanted his novels burned, Henry Green and Christina Stead fell into obscurity in their own lifetimes, Faulkner and O'Connor hid themselves away in the rural South. The most original and farseeing novelists of our own day not only accept the shadows but actively seek them. "Everything in the culture argues against the novel," Don DeLillo said in a *Paris Review* interview. "This is why we need the writer in opposition, the novelist who writes against power, who writes against the corporation or the state or the whole apparatus of assimilation."

30   The modern idea of the oppositional writer is a long-established tradition, and its modern variants have been around since at least the First World War, when the Austrian satirist Karl Kraus described himself as the "hopeless contrary" of the nexus of technology, media, and capital. Something that has taken longer to emerge, but is implicit in a work like *The Gutenberg Elegies*, is

the idea of the oppositional *reader*. The paradox of literature elitism is that it's purely self-selecting. Anyone who can read is free to be a part of it. And, as the informational elite continues to inoculate itself with literacy, a certain percentage of readers will inevitably, like the fabled marijuana smoker, get hooked on harder stuff. Likewise, as the ranks of the preterite swell with the downwardly mobile, restless souls will have ever greater reason to seek out methods of opposition—"to posit an elsewhere," as Birkerts describes reading, "and to set off toward it." The apparent democracy of today's digital networks is an artifact of their infancy. Sooner or later, all social organisms move from anarchy toward hierarchy, and whatever order emerges from the primordial chaos of the Net seems as likely to be dystopian as utopian. The possibility of terminal boringness looms particularly large. But even if the digital revolution evolves into a free-market version of the Stalinist totality to which the Bolshevik revolution gave rise, the perverse effect may be the elevation of reading's status. The world of samizdat, the flowering of a readership that memorized wholesale the poetry of Osip Mandelstam and Anna Akhmatova, ought to remind us that reading can survive, and even flourish, in exile.

Not just Negroponte, who doesn't like to read, but even Birkerts, who thinks that history is ending, underestimates the instability of society and the unruly diversity of its members. The electronic apotheosis of mass culture has merely reconfirmed the elitism of literary reading, which was briefly obscured in the novel's heyday. I mourn the eclipse of the cultural authority that literature once possessed, and I rue the onset of an age so anxious that the pleasure of a text becomes difficult to sustain. I don't suppose that many other people will give away their TVs. I'm not sure I'll last long myself without buying a new one. But the first lesson reading teaches is how to be alone.

Questions for Discussion and Writing

1. Franzen begins with an admission: "I gave away my television set . . . because as long as it was in the house, reachable by some combination of extension cords, I wasn't reading books" (paragraph 1). Do you think that if you did not have a television set that you would read more? If you do not have a television set, would you say that you read more than people who do own a television set?

2. In your own words, describe Franzen's key idea. What images, language, and examples most effectively illustrate his key idea? Explain whether or not you agree with his point of view.

derived from the French word *essai*, an "attempt" (*Online* , Academic Medical Publishing, 1998). What is Franzen personal essay? What is to be gained from reading a per-

ne when you felt, like Franzen and Birkerts, that you were "rescued by books" (paragraphs 18 and 26)? Write a personal essay about a time when you felt rescued by books. Alternatively, if books did not have the power to rescue you, then what, instead, has had the power to rescue you? (for example, music, television, comics, film, sports, a celebrity, a hero, a person, etc.)?

5. In paragraph 16, Franzen writes "The novel is dying because the consumer doesn't want it anymore." Imagine that you have been asked to write a letter to a major publisher recommending new titles for its upcoming list. What genre of books do you think the publisher should include? If you think that books are no longer profitable, then write a letter persuading the publisher to invest in another form of entertainment (television, movies, music, etc.).

Harry Potter: Oliver with a Magical Twist

Marie Warmbold

Marie E. Warmbold came to academics as a second career; she worked for 16 years in the claims department of an insurance company. Her undergraduate B.A. is from Fordham University (Bronx campus), and her Master's and Ph.D. are from New York University. She loves Victorian literature (her field of specialty) and has given several papers at conferences on popular culture. She has taught in the City University system for over 14 years. This article, originally given as a paper at the Mid-Atlantic Popular and American Culture Association Annual Conference in Pittsburgh, PA, on November 1, 2002, was updated in December 2004.

Pre-Reading

Are you a fan of the Harry Potter series? If so, explain what you enjoy about the series. If not, consult with someone who is a fan or conduct research on the series. What do you imagine accounts for the success of the series? What fantasies, desires, and emotions do you believe the series caters to?

—————————— ✦ ——————————

Some headlines a few years ago:

> From the *New York Times:* "Harry Potter and the Quest for the Unfinished Volume" (May 5, 2002)
>
> From *Newsweek:* "Why They're Harried in Pottersville" (June 10, 2002)
>
> From the *Washington Post:* "Where's Harry?; Rowling's Fans Wonder About Book 5" (May 27, 2002)

Oh, the perils of serialization! Sales have been stupendous; readers of all ages have been hooked by Harry and his adventures; everyone—the reading public, the media, the bookstores, the publishing and video industry—has been waiting for the next installment. Will Harry start dating? (He'll be 16 now.) What is going to happen to Ron and Hermione? Some fans have been making up their own stories and publishing them on websites. Could *Potter* author Rowling have come down with writer's block?

No, not at all. The fifth volume, *Harry Potter and the Order of the Phoenix* came out in June 2003 with record sales, and at the end of 2004, there is good news for the New Year. The sixth Harry Potter book, *Harry Potter and the Half-Blood Prince*, will be published on Saturday, July 16, 2005. Because of pre-orders, it is already a bestseller on Amazon.com's Canadian, U.S. and U.K. websites (*Toronto Star*). Although author Rowling will not reveal the contents, "one racing certainty is that at least one character will die, although the field is wide open for candidates" (Malvern). Bookmakers are already making bets, according to the London *Times*.

Charles Dickens would understand. He always favored part-issue publication. Not one of his novels appeared for the first time as a single complete work. *Oliver Twist,* for example, appeared in monthly segments in *Bentley's Miscellany* (Stephen Gill, "Introduction," *Oliver Twist,* viii). Dickens often complained about the problems of serial publication. Here, for example, is his comment to a contributor of *All the Year Round,* a magazine that he edited. "The difficulties and discouragements of such an undertaking [writing a serial novel] are enormous, and the man [sic] who surmounts them today may be beaten by them tomorrow" (Dexter

3: 184). Rowling almost from the beginning thought of *Harry Potter* as a series of seven books—for each year he was a student at Hogwarts School of Witchcraft and Wizardry. The fact that number five was delayed—it didn't come out until June 2003—illustrated all the problems of an extremely popular work that the public knows has a set number. The current enthusiasm over the coming number six also underscores the point. Although C. S. Lewis's *The Chronicles of Narnia* was also published in seven volumes (Rowling was a fan of these books in childhood), the amount of public concern and the anxious wait for her next "installment"—which is how reviewer Karl Miller refers to the fourth book—reminds one more of Dickens than Lewis. And all the speculation about the death of a character (Rowling has confirmed it is not Harry nor his chief nemesis, Voldemort, according to the London *Times*) recalls the excitement over Dickens's character Little Nell, in *The Old Curiosity Shop.* Eager American fans of that serialized novel greeted the boats carrying the latest installment from Britain with the anguished cry, "Does Little Nell die?" Unfortunately, in that case, the answer was yes.

5   It is not only the serialization aspect of *Harry Potter* that makes it comparable to Dickens. In his Introduction to *Oliver Twist,* Stephen Gill characterizes Dickens: "intricate plots embodied in an extraordinary large number and range of characters . . . has always been recognized as the hallmark of his genius" (xiii). His characters are vivid; Angus Wilson once described them as they "might be after three or four glasses of champagne" (quoted in Nelson 30). His imagination has been described as "intense" (32). One of the reasons Rowling's *Harry Potter* series has captured readers of all ages is she is "'a master storyteller' who is able to weave a complex plot with control of character and control of style" (Wallace). The first book of the series, *Harry Potter and the Sorcerer's Stone,* has fourteen important characters and takes place mostly at Hogwarts, with the beginning chapters at Privet Drive where the Dursleys—Harry's aunt and uncle—live. Book IV, *Harry Potter and the Goblet of Fire,* has more than forty characters and involves seven locations. Book V, *Harry Potter and the Order of the Phoenix,* is one chapter and around 130 pages longer than Book IV: 38 chapters and 870 pages. A truly Dickensian size—one thinks of *Nicholas Nickleby,* approximately 930 pages in paperback. Just as Dickens's later novels became more complex in plot as well as ideas, so have hers.

One character that has a Dickensian touch is the incredibly vain—and none too bright—"Defense Against the Dark Arts" teacher, Gilderoy Lockhart, who appears in Book II *Harry Potter and the Chamber of Secrets*. Dickens loved to deflate pompous people and Rowling gives this man his just deserts at the end, but not before making him a superb satire. When Harry and his close friends Ron and Hermione are in the book/supply store, Flourish and Blotts, to buy their school supplies for their second year, they see him signing copies of his autobiography *Magical Me*. He is "wearing robes of forget-me-not blue that exactly matched his eyes; his pointed wizard's hat . . . set at a jaunty angle on his wavy hair." As he sits there signing the books, he is surrounded by magical portraits of himself " all winking and flashing dazzling white teeth at the crowd" (59). For his class, the students have to buy copies of all his books. The first day of class, he gives them a quiz. The first question is: "What is Gilderoy Lockhart's favorite color?" And it ends with: "When is Gilderoy Lockhart's birthday, and what would his ideal gift be?" (100). He proceeds to teach them how to deal with "freshly caught Cornish pixies." He lets them loose from their cage, and they "[proceed] to wreck the classroom more effectively than a rampaging rhino" (101–2). But when he goes to show the class how to capture and contain them, "It had absolutely no effect; one of the pixies seized his wand and threw it out the window, too" (102). After this disaster, for the rest of the semester, all Lockhart does is "read passages from his books to them, and sometimes [reenact] some of the more dramatic bits (161). When Harry suffers a broken arm in a Quidditch match (Quidditch is sort of an airborne soccer), Lockhart offers to heal him—unfortunately. After Lockhart has twirled his wand, Harry's bones aren't mended. They've been removed. So Harry is forced to spend a night in the hospital having his bones regrown. (Many things are possible in Wizard school.) When the teachers and Harry enter Lockhart's office late one night, we learn about the magical self-portraits on his wall. ". . . [T]here was a flurry of movement across the walls; Harry saw several of the Lockharts in the pictures dodging out of sight, their hair in rollers" (141). Rowling always has him wearing different color robes every time he appears, from "sweeping robes of turquoise, his golden hair shining under a perfectly positioned turquoise hat with gold trimming" (89), "wearing robes of palest mauve today" (113), "resplendent in robes of deep plum" (189). However, he is indeed a coward and aware his magic powers are nil. Harry catches him trying to run away from Hogwarts in Chapter 16. Lockhart reveals he is a fraud; all the magic described in his books was done by others, not himself. In the end, a Memory Charm backfires on him, and he ends the book a clueless dithering idiot.

For another example of Rowling's creativity and imagination, take my favorite characters—the owls. While we Muggles (non-magic folk in the *Potter* books) have email and "snail mail," wizards have owl post. All mail is sent by owls, which is why Harry is required to bring an owl with him to Hogwarts. Even Rowling's owls have distinct personalities. First, there is the elegant and dignified Hedwig, Harry's beautiful snowy white owl, who loves her master but gives him a nip or a cold shoulder—maybe I should say cold wing?—when necessary. Errol, the frail and weary Weasley family owl, certainly deserves retirement. Near the beginning of the second book, he lands on the breakfast table in the milk, and collapses owl-belly up on the table with an important letter for Ron clutched in his beak. And there's the enthusiastic and peppy minute owl, Pig (pronounced pidge), who becomes Ron's personal owl and clearly loves his job.

According to Elisabeth McKetta, the owls illustrate an important point in the *Harry Potter* series. All things in the wizard world have life; ghosts return and "live" within Hogwarts. "Walls, pet owls and mice have distinct opinions and personalities of their own, dwarves, wizards, elves, cars and plants all possess human characteristics." So in addition to vivid human characters, Rowling creates a whole gallery of "non-human" ones: peevish and mischievous ghosts, irascible trees, and a flying Ford Anglia, just to mention a few.

Harry Potter himself, Rowling's popular hero, who has appealed to adults as well as young adults and children, being both "quirky and unlikely," (McKetta) is closest to Dickens' Oliver Twist. Oliver too is an orphan, so both Rowling and Dickens take up what Karl Miller has called "the ancient theme of the orphan hero, with his wounds and his ordeals," but it is interesting to see how each one interprets those "wounds and ordeals." Neither Oliver nor Harry has a very pleasant childhood. Dickens seizes the opportunity to make keen and trenchant comments on the 1834 Poor Law, while Rowling, in the beginning chapters satirizes "the self-satisfied suburban world of the Dursleys" (Roback et al.). "Mr. and Mrs. Dursley had everything they wanted . . . [and a] son called Dudley and in their opinion there was no finer boy anywhere" (*Sorcerer's Stone* 1). By Chapter 2 it is clear that Dudley is the one most overindulged. Photos of him growing up seem to be of "a large pink beach ball wearing different colored bonnets" (22).

10   Oliver as an infant is "farmed . . . to a branch workhouse . . . [with] twenty or thirty other juvenile offenders against the

poor-laws" (*Oliver Twist* 4). At nine, Oliver is moved to the work-house to pick oakum and be just barely sustained by miniscule servings of gruel. Harry, meanwhile, is a *persona non grata* in the Dursley household. They, his aunt and uncle, are "raising him": he sleeps in a dark cupboard under the stairs; he is made to cook their breakfast and wear Dudley's huge castoff clothes. Michael Maudlin refers to it as a "Dickensian childhood . . . watching his same-aged cousin Dudley being spoiled with food and presents galore." "Harry had a thin face [his aunt and uncle often punish him by depriving him of food], knobbly knees, black hair, and bright green eyes. He wore round glasses held together with a lot of Scotch tape because of all the times Dudley had punched him on the nose"(24). Oliver has his Noah Claypole, Harry has his Dudley.

But both Oliver and Harry are survivors. Oliver finally has enough of Sowerby's house as well as Noah Claypole and goes off to London. Harry has a similar escape at an early age. Voldemort, the embodiment of Evil in the *Potter* series, manages to kill both of Harry's parents, but not him. According to Professor McGonagall, Deputy Headmistress at Hogwarts, "'They're saying he tried to kill the Potter's son Harry. But—he couldn't. He couldn't kill that little boy . . . No one knows why, or how . . . '" (15).

In his Preface to the Third Edition of *Oliver Twist*, Dickens insists, "I confess I have yet to learn that a lesson of the purest good may not be drawn from the vilest evil. . . . In this spirit, . . . I wished to shew, in little Oliver, the principle of Good surviving through every adverse circumstance, and triumphing at last" (liii). Dickens, of course, here is explaining his inclusion of such diabolical characters as Fagin and Bill Sikes: "to shew them as they really are, for ever skulking uneasily through the dirtiest paths of life, with the great, black, ghastly gallows closing up their prospect" (liv). Rowling, in an interview with *TIME* maga-zine, discusses Voldemort and the death at the end of Book IV. "If you're choosing to write about evil, you really do have a moral obligation to show what that means. So you know what happened at the end of Book IV. I do think it's shocking, but it had to be. It is not a gratuitous act on my part. We really are talking about someone who is incredibly power hungry. Racist, really. And what do those kinds of people do? They treat human life so lightly. I wanted to be accurate in that sense."

Like Oliver, Harry has to make choices. As Catherine M. Wallace puts it in *The Christian Century*, "Rowling's abused young hero must learn how to trust and whom to trust. Although Harry obviously has what moralists call 'a fundamental option for the good,' he needs to learn that exercising this option fully requires cooperation with others. The virtuous life is necessarily social."

Oliver is first led into the "social life" of Fagin and his crew. At first Oliver doesn't understand about the pocketbooks and handkerchiefs ("He is so jolly green!"[67]). But when he sees Mr. Brownlow having his pocket picked: "In an instant the whole mystery . . . rushed upon the boy's mind" (73) and he makes a choice that this is wrong, and not to get involved with it—or at least, he tries to.

15 Here Harry Potter follows a different path. A gentle giant named Hagrid arrives to shepherd him away to Hogwarts School of Witchcraft and Wizardry, whose Headmaster is Albus Dumbledore, a man who is a type like the caring and concerned Brownlow. Indeed, later in Book II, Dumbledore gives Harry the classic moral comment: " 'It is our choices, Harry, that show what we truly are, far more than our abilities' " (*Chamber of Secrets* 333). At the beginning of Book I, Hagrid tells Harry the truth: " 'Harry—yer a wizard . . . an' a thumpin' good'un, I'd say, once yeh've been trained up a bit.' " This is also the first time Harry learns the truth about his parents— they were wizards—and how they died. Hogwarts becomes a place of immense happiness to Harry. Here he meets the two who will be his closest friends—Ron Weasley and Hermione Granger—as well as another bully—Draco Malfoy. Although various challenges, choices face Harry at Hogwarts, there are also tremendous successes there, such as his skill as a Quidditch seeker. (Quidditch has been described by some as soccer, by some as polo, but played on broomsticks.) Karl Miller is right, I believe, in saying that what Rowling has created here is a "portrait of a mildly progressive English public boarding school"—with, of course, magic and wizardry added. In any event, this is why Rowling planned seven books: one for each year of school Harry will have. And every book ends at the end of term, with Harry going back to the Dursleys with heavy heart, to await the end of another summer. While Oliver does get some companionship from Fagin's gang, it is clearly not as positive. However, in both the Broadway play and movie version, *Oliver* does create a more genial scene and Fagin becomes an odd and funny old man, with the group singing songs like "Consider Yourself One of the Family," and "You've Got to Pick a Pocket or Two."

But there is yet another element that Oliver and Harry share: a mystery surrounding their birth. In Chapter One, we witness Oliver's birth in a workhouse to an unmarried young woman who dies in the process. While details are dropped throughout the book—and, therefore, throughout the monthly segments—we don't learn the complete story of Oliver's parents and family until the very last installment, a device to keep the readers coming back. As mentioned above, Hagrid tells Harry that he is a wizard in Chapter Four of the first book. He also tells Harry how his parents died. "'You-Know-Who killed 'em [Hagrid is mortally afraid of saying Voldemort's name out loud]. An' then—an' this is the real myst'ry of the thing—he tried to kill you, too. Wanted ter make a clean job of it, I suppose, or maybe he just liked killin' by then. But he couldn't do it. Never wondered how you got that mark on your forehead? . . . an' that's why yer famous, Harry. No one ever lived after he decided ter kill 'em, no one except you'" (69). Harry has a scar on his forehead in the shape of a lightning bolt. The mystery of Harry's parents—yes, we know who they are, but not much other than what Hagrid just said—continues throughout the four books, and we learn details as Harry does. In Book One he sees them for the first time in the Mirror of Erised. In Book III we learn about James Potter's (his father's) school friends and that Harry has a godfather. So this mystery continues, and at the same time, the presence—and evil—of Voldemort becomes more and more pronounced. In addition, each of the four books has its own mystery to solve. For the first, it's who is trying to steal the Sorcerer's Stone. In the second, it's who has opened the Chamber of Secrets. The third is about Sirius Black who has escaped from the wizard prison of Azkaban. And in the fourth, the reader wonders who has put Harry's name in the Goblet of Fire. According to Dickens scholar Archibald Coolidge, Jr., "Dickens's monthly serials contained several incidents from several plot lines each of which was likely to have interesting results"(56).

So like Dickens in his monthly parts or monthly segments, then, Rowling in each book drops more hints and weaves the plot more complexly, and this was one of the reasons why the fifth book (*Harry Potter and the Order of the Phoenix*) was delayed. Rowling has apparently "explained to her agent and publishers that writing this next book is proving to be more involved than she initially expected." Plus, there are "even more delicate subjects in her next book . . . 'more deaths coming.'" ("Harry Potter and the Quest for the Unfinished Volume," *New York Times*). As far as Book VI, there have already been clues leaked, such as, "The first chapter was written 13 years ago and was originally designed to open the first, third or fifth books. . . . Chapter 6 is [entitled] Draco's Detour" (Malvern). (Draco is the Hogwarts nemesis of Harry.) Rowling has noted that "she has had the time 'needed to tinker with the manuscript to my satisfaction and I am happy as I have ever been with the end result.'" ("Potter Book is Cooked.") She, as Dickens did, has her readers coming back for more.

Just as it is impossible to convey the genius of Dickens in a short paper, I feel equally constrained in trying to explain what a wonderful treat *Harry Potter* is to read. I haven't even touched on Rowling's humor, which is one reason why, I think, her books appeal to adults as well as children. One critic calls the books "laugh-out-loud fun" (Maudlin), another cites her "effective dry humor" (Miller) and another "poetry and gentle wit" (Rosenberg), all of which can be phrases used to describe Dickens too. The *Potter* books have climbed the best seller lists in both America and England. As a matter of fact, Rowling's British publisher in 1998 issued "a second edition of the first book with a more grownup cover, so older readers wouldn't be embarrassed to carry 'Harry'."(Power) So don't wait to use an adolescent as an excuse to buy and read them. Enjoy them—but I warn you, you'll be hooked too—and waiting for the next "installment." Here's proof: I, an academic, preordered Book V and read 500 pages the day it was delivered to my door. While I was updating this article, I also joined the many fans that have pre-ordered Book VI.

Works Cited

Coolidge Jr., Archibald. *Charles Dickens as a Serial Novelist*. Ames: Iowa State UP, 1967.

Dexter, Walter, ed. *The Letters of Charles Dickens*. 3 vols. Bloomsbury: The Nonesuch Press, 1938.

Dickens, Charles. *Oliver Twist*. Oxford: Oxford UP, 1999.

———. "The Author's Preface to the Third Edition." *Oliver Twist*. Oxford: Oxford UP, 1999. 1iii–lvii.

Gill, Stephen. Introduction. *Oliver Twist* by Charles Dickens. Oxford: Oxford U, 1999. vii–xxv.

Malvern, Jack. "Plot Clue Is Chronicle of a Death Foretold." *The Times (London)* 22 Dec. 2004. *LexisNexis*. Hunter College Lib., NYC, NY. 28 Dec. 2004.

Maudlin, Michael G. "Virtue on a Broomstick." *Christianity Today*. 44:10. 4 Sept. 2000. *OCLC First Search*. New York University Lib., NYC, NY. 22 June 2002.

McKetta, Elisabeth. *Sparknotes on Harry Potter and the Chamber of Secrets* 11 Oct. 2002. *http://www.sparknotes.com/lit/potter2*

Miller, Karl. "*Harry Potter and the Goblet of Fire* (Book Review)." *Raritan* 20:3. Winter 2001. *OCLC First Search*. New York University Lib., NYC, NY. 20 June 2002.

Nelson, Harland. *Charles Dickens*. New York: Twayne Publishers, 1981.

"Next Potter Book Already a Bestseller." *The Toronto Star*. 23 Dec. 2004. *LexisNexis*. Hunter College Lib., NYC, NY. 28 Dec. 2004.

"Potter Book Is Cooked." *Nationwide News Pty Limited Herald Sun (Melbourne, Australia)* 22 Dec. 2004. *LexisNexis*. Hunter College Lib., NYC, NY. 28 Dec. 2004.

Power, Carla. "A Literary Sorceress." *Newsweek*. 7 Dec. 1998. *ProQuest*. New York University Lib., NYC, NY. 20 June 2002.

Roback, Diane, Jennifer M. Brown, and Cindi Di Marzo. "*Harry Potter and the Sorcerer's Stone*." *Publishers Weekly* 20 July 1998. *ProQuest* New York University Lib., NYC, NY. 20 June 2002.

Rosenberg, Liz. "A Foundling Boy and His Corps of Wizards." *Boston Globe*. 1 Nov. 1998. *ProQuest*. New York University Lib., NYC, NY. 20 June 2002.

Rowling, J. K. "A Good Scare." *TIME*. 30 Oct. 2000:108.

———. *Harry Potter and the Sorcerer's Stone*. New York: Scholastic Inc, 1997.

———. *Harry Potter and the Chamber of Secrets*. New York: Scholastic Inc, 1999.

———. *Harry Potter and the Prisoner of Azkaban*. New York: Scholastic Inc., 1999.

———. *Harry Potter and the Goblet of Fire*. New York: Scholastic Press, 2000.

———. *Harry Potter and the Order of the Phoenix*. New York: Scholastic Press, 2003.

Wallace, Catherine M. "Rowling as Moralist: Harry Potter and the Bullies." *The Christian Century*. 118:21, July 2001. *OCLC First-Search*. New York University Lib., NYC, NY. 20 June 2002.

Questions for Discussion and Writing

1. The debate between high culture and popular culture is often presented as an either/or argument. In what ways does Warmbold's essay bridge the debate between high culture (Dickens) and popular culture (Harry Potter)?

2. Make a list of the comparisons drawn between Oliver and Harry. Which comparison do you believe is the strongest?

3. The article is written as a comparison essay and is well documented with a list of Works Cited. Examine the structure of the essay. What transitional phrases are used to illustrate the connections? As a reader, how can you utilize the Works Cited?

4. Using Warmbold's essay as a model, write an essay comparing any character in a literary text to any character in a popular book. What parallels do you see?

5. Write a research paper about the marketing success of the *Harry Potter* series. Why do you think it has been so successful? What does your research reveal? Alternatively, write about the marketing success of another popular series in any medium, *Star Trek*, for example.

The Internet—Everything Bad Is Good for You

STEVEN JOHNSON

Named by Newsweek *as one of the "Fifty People Who Matter Most on the Internet," journalist Steven Johnson has written numerous books on technology and the popular culture including the national best seller,* Mind Wide Open: Your Brain and the Neuroscience of Everyday Life *(2004), the critically acclaimed* Everything Bad Is Good for You: How Today's Popular Culture Is Actually Making Us Smarter *(2005),* Interface Culture: How New Technology Transforms the Way We Create and Communicate *(1997), and* Emergence: The Connected Lives of Ants, Brains, Cities and Software *(2001). Johnson has written for the* New York Times, *the* Wall Street Journal, *and* The Nation. *He is currently cofounder and editor-in-chief of* FEED, *a contributing editor for* Wired, *and a monthly columnist for* Discover *magazine.*

Pre-Reading

Write a one-paragraph description of your initial reactions to the title and subtitle. Then, on a separate page, create two columns: in Column A list three different ways you believe popular culture can increase intelligence; in Column B, list three different ways you imagine popular culture detracts from intelligence.

———————— ✦ ————————

Viewers who get lost in *24*'s social network have a resource available to them that *Dallas* viewers lacked: the numerous online sites and communities that share information about popular television shows. Just as *Apprentice* viewers mulled Troy's shady business ethics in excruciating detail, *24* fans exhaustively document and debate every passing glance and brief allusion in the series, building detailed episode guides and lists of Frequently Asked Questions. One Yahoo! site featured at the time of this writing more than forty thousand individual posts from ordinary viewers, contributing their own analysis of last night's episode, posting questions about plot twists, or speculating on the upcoming season. As the shows have complexified, the resources for making sense of that complexity have multiplied as well. If you're lost in *24*'s social network, you can always get your bearings online.

All of which brings us to another crucial piece in the puzzle of the Sleeper Curve: the Internet. Not just because the online world offers resources that help sustain more complex programming in other media, but because the process of acclimating to the new reality of networked communications has had a salutary effect on our minds. We do well to remind ourselves how quickly the industrialized world has embraced the many forms of participatory electronic media—from e-mail to hypertext to instant messages and blogging. Popular audiences embraced television and the cinema in comparable time frames, but neither required the learning curve of e-mail or the Web. It's one thing to adapt your lifestyle to include time for sitting around watching a moving image on a screen; it's quite another to learn a whole new language of communication and a small army of software tools along with it. It seems almost absurd to think of this now, but when the idea of hypertext documents first entered the popular domain in the early nineties, it was a distinctly avant-garde idea, promoted by an experimentalist literary fringe looking to explode the restrictions of the linear sentence and the page-bound book. Fast forward less than a decade, and something extraordinary occurs: exploring nonlinear document structures becomes as second nature as dialing a phone for hundreds of millions—if not billions—of people. The mass embrace of hypertext is like the *Seinfeld* "Betrayal" episode: a cultural form that was once exclusively limited to avant-garde sensibilities, now happily enjoyed by grandmothers and third-graders worldwide.

I won't dwell on this point, because the premise that increased interactivity is good for the brain is not a new one. (A number of insightful critics—Kevin Kelly, Douglas Rushkoff, Janet Murray, Howard Rheingold, Henry Jenkins—have made variations on this argument over the past decade or so.) But let me say this much: The rise of the Internet has challenged our minds in three fundamental and related ways: by virtue of being participatory, by forcing users to learn new interfaces, and by creating new channels for social interaction. Almost all forms of online activity sustained are participatory in nature: writing e-mails, sending IMs, creating photo logs, posting two-page analyses of last night's *Apprentice* episode. Steve Jobs likes to describe the difference between television and the Web as the difference between lean-back and sit-forward media. The networked computer makes you lean in, focus, engage, while television encourages you to zone out. (Though not as much as it used to, of course.) This is the familiar interactivity-is-good-for-you argument, and it's proof that the conventional wisdom is, every now and then, actually wise.

5   There was a point several years ago, during the first wave of Internet cheerleading, when it was still possible to be a skeptic about how participatory the new medium would turn out to be. Everyone recognized that the practices of composing e-mail and clicking on hyperlinks were going to be mainstream activities, but how many people out there were ultimately going to be interested in publishing more extensive material online? And if that turned out to be a small number—if the Web turned out to be a medium where most of the content was created by professional writers and editors—was it ultimately all that different from the previous order of things?

The tremendous expansion of the blogging world over the past two years has convincingly silenced this objection. According to a 2004 study by the Pew Charitable Trust, more than 8 million Americans report that they have a personal weblog or online diary. The wonderful blog-tracking service Technorati reports that roughly 275,000 blog entries are published in the average day—a tiny fraction of them authored by professional writers. After only two years of media hype, the number of active bloggers in the United States alone has reached the audience size of prime-time network television.

So why were the skeptics so wrong about the demand for self-publishing? Their primary mistake was to assume that the content produced in this new era would look like old-school journalism: op-ed pieces, film reviews, cultural commentary. There's plenty of armchair journalism out there, of course, but the great bulk of personal publishing is just that, *personal*: the online diary is the dominant discursive mode in the blogosphere. People are using these new tools not to opine about social security privatization; they're using the tools to talk about their lives. A decade ago Douglas Rushkoff coined the phrase "screenagers"[1] to describe the first generation that grew up with the assumption that the images on a television screen were supposed to be manipulated; that they weren't just there for passive consumption. The next generation is carrying that logic to a new extreme: the screen is not just something you manipulate, but something you project your identity onto, a place to work through the story of your life as it unfolds.

To be sure, that projection can create some awkward or unhealthy situations, given the public intimacy of the online diary, and the potential for identity fraud. But every new technology can be exploited or misused to nefarious ends. For the vast majority of those 8 million bloggers, these new venues for self-expression have been a wonderful addition to their lives. There's no denying that the content of your average online diary can be juvenile. These diaries are, after all, frequently created by juveniles. But thirty years ago those juveniles weren't writing novels or composing sonnets in their spare time; they were watching *Laverne & Shirley*. Better to have minds actively composing the soap opera of their own lives than zoning out in front of someone else's.

The Net has actually had a positive lateral effect on the tube as well, in that it has liberated television from attempting tasks that the medium wasn't innately well suited to perform. As a vehicle for narrative and first-person intimacy, television can be a delightful medium, capable of conveying remarkably complex experiences. But as a source of information, it has its limitations. The rise of the Web has enabled television to offload some of its information-sharing responsibilities to a platform that was designed specifically for the purposes of sharing information. This passage from Postman's *Amusing Ourselves to Death* showcases exactly how much has changed over the past twenty years:

> Television . . . encompasses all forms of discourse. No one goes to a movie to find out about government policy or the latest scientific advance. No one buys a record to find out the baseball scores or the weather or the latest murder. . . . But everyone goes to television for all these things and more, which is why television resonates so powerfully throughout the culture. Television is our culture's principal mode of knowing about itself.[2]

No doubt in total hours television remains the dominant medium in American life, but there is also no doubt that the Net has been gaining on it with extraordinary speed. If the early adopters are any indication, that dominance won't last for long. And for the types of knowledge-based queries that Postman describes—looking up government policy or sports scores—the Net has become the first place that people consult. Google is *our* culture's principal way of knowing about itself.

The second way in which the rise of the Net has challenged the mind runs parallel to the evolving rule systems of video games: the accelerating pace of new platforms and software applications forces users to probe and master new environments.[3] Your mind is engaged by the interactive content of networked media—posting a response to an article online, maintaining three separate IM conversations at the same time—but you're also exercising cognitive muscles interacting with the *form* of the media as well: learning the tricks of a new e-mail client, configuring the video chat software properly, getting your bearings after installing a new operating system. This type of problem-solving can be challenging in an unpleasant way, of course, but the same can be said for calculus. Just because you don't like troubleshooting your system when your browser crashes doesn't mean you aren't exercising your logic skills in finding a solution. This extra layer of cognitive involvement derives largely from the increased prominence of the interface in digital technology. When new tools arrive, you have to learn what they're good for, but you also have to learn the rules that govern their use. To be an accomplished telephone user, you needed to grasp the essential utility of being able to have real-time conversations with people physically removed from you, *and* you had to master the interface of the telephone device itself. That same principle holds true for digital technologies, only the interfaces have expanded dramatically in depth and complexity. There's only so much cognitive challenge at stake in learning the rules of a rotary dial phone. But you could lose a week exploring all the nooks and crannies of Microsoft Outlook.

Just as we saw in the world of games, learning the intricacies of a new interface can be a genuine pleasure. This is a story that is not often enough told in describing our evolving relationship with software. There is a kind of exploratory wonder in downloading a new application, and meandering through its commands and dialog boxes, learning its tricks by feel. I've often found certain applications are more fun to explore the first time than they actually are to use—because in the initial exploration, you can delight in features that are clever without being terribly helpful. This sounds like something only a hardened tech geek would say, but I suspect the feeling has become much more mainstream over the past few years. Think of the millions of ordinary music fans who downloaded Apple's iTunes software: I'm sure many of them enjoyed their first walk through the application, seeing all the tools that would revolutionize the way they listened to music. Many of them, I suspect, eschewed the manual altogether, choosing to probe the application the way gamers investigate their virtual worlds: from the inside. That probing is a powerful form of intellectual activity—you're learning the rules of a complex system without a guide, after all. And it's all the more powerful for being fun.

Then there is the matter of social connection. The other concern that Net skeptics voiced a decade ago revolved around a withdrawal from public space: yes, the Internet might connect us to a new world of information, but it would come at a terrible social cost, by confining us in front of barren computer monitors, away from the vitality of genuine communities. In fact, nearly all of the most hyped developments on the Web in the past few years have been tools for augmenting social connection: online personals, social and business network sites such as Friendster, the Meetup.com service so central to the political organization of the 2004 campaign, the many tools designed to enhance conversation between bloggers—not to mention all the handheld devices that we now use to coordinate new kinds of real-world encounters. Some of these tools create new modes of communication that are entirely digital in nature (the cross-linked conversations of bloggers). Others use the networked computer to facilitate a face-to-face encounter (as in Meetup). Others involve a hybrid dance of real and virtual encounters, as in the personals world, where flesh-and-blood dates usually follow weeks of online flirting. Tools like Google have fulfilled the original dream of digital machines becoming extensions of our memory, but the new social networking applications have done something that the visionaries never imagined: they are augmenting our people skills as well, widening our social networks, and creating new possibilities for strangers to share ideas and experiences.

Television and automobile society locked people up in their living rooms, away from the clash and vitality of public space, but the Net has reversed that long-term trend. After a half-century of technological isolation, we're finally learning new ways to connect.

Endnotes

1. Douglas Rushkoff, *Playing the Future* (New York: Riverhead, 1999).
2. Postman, *Amusing Ourselves to Death* (New York: Penguin, 1985), p. 92.
3. One way to think about the cognitive challenge of digital media is through a framework that I outlined in my 1997 book *Interface*

Culture: (San Francisco: Harper, 1997). What makes these new forms uniquely stimulating is that they require the mastery of interfaces in addition to the traditional "content" of media, and those interfaces are evolving at a dramatic clip. To send an e-mail, you need to think about the process of writing, but also your physical interface with the computer via keyboard and mouse, the interface conventions that govern the e-mail program itself, and the larger interface conventions of the operating system. Compare those different cognitive levels with the more direct system of handwriting a note and you get an idea of the increased cognitive demands of the modern digital interface.

Questions for Discussion and Writing

1. This excerpt is from Johnson's book *Everything Bad Is Good For You: How Today's Popular Culture Is Actually Making Us Smarter*. Explain whether or not you believe this excerpt fulfills the promise of the subtitle. Include specific information in the text to support your response.

2. Johnson insists, "It's one thing to adapt your lifestyle to include time for sitting around watching a moving image on a screen; it's quite another to learn a whole new language of communication and a small army of software tools along with it" (paragraph 2). Do you agree with his observations of the complexity involved in learning how to navigate the Internet?

3. In what order does Johnson present his ideas? Explain whether or not you believe he could have effectively presented the ideas in another sequence.

4. Johnson writes, "The rise of the Internet has challenged our minds in three fundamental and related ways" (paragraph 3). What are the three fundamental ways? Write an essay in which you support, refute, or modify his claims. In your response, also consider any additional ways in which the Internet "has challenged our minds."

5. Write a narrative essay about your personal experience of blogging. If you have never blogged, try it for the first time. Begin with a brief description of blogging. Describe the first time you blogged. How does your personal experience compare with the experiences documented by Johnson?

Questions for Making Connections

1. Johnson writes: "The rise of the Internet has challenged our minds in three fundamental and related ways: by virtue of being participatory, by forcing users to learn new interfaces, and by creating new channels for social interaction" (paragraph 3). How do you believe Franzen would respond to Johnson?

2. Both Ross and Trussell write about popular culture studies. Imagine that you have been asked by a friend whether or not you would recommend that he or she attend Bowling Green State University (mentioned in Trussell) to pursue a "Bachelor of Arts Degree in Popular Culture." Write an essay in the form of a letter advising him or her whether or not to pursue the specialized degree. What types of careers would the degree prepare him or her for? In your letter, use evidence from both Ross and Trussell. What course of action should your friend take?

3. Write an essay in the form of a letter to the Chair of your English Department. In your essay, write an argument in support of adding popular culture courses to the curriculum. Be sure to add specific benefits that students can gain from popular culture courses.

4. "While technology is merely palliative, art is therapeutic" (Franzen, paragraph 25). Do you agree with Franzen? Conduct research on the therapeutic properties of art. For example, if you are interested in art therapy and children, then perhaps your research can include visiting the American Art Therapy Association web site (*www.artherapy.org*) and evaluating their mission statement, research, and case studies; alternatively, you could research music therapy. Select a topic you are interested in exploring. In your response, include research to support your argument.

5. Writing for the *New Yorker*, Ross shares his experience at the 2003 Pop Conference entitled "Skip a Beat: Rewriting the Story of Popular Music" in Seattle, WA. Warmbold's essay was originally given as a paper at the Mid-Atlantic Popular and American Culture Association Annual Conference in Pittsburgh, PA. Re-read both essays. In light of Ross's reactions to the various papers delivered at the conference in Seattle, how do you imagine he would respond to the topic of Warmbold's paper? Use evidence from both essays to illustrate your point of view.

CHAPTER 6

Consumerism

In William Wordsworth's poem, "The World Is Too Much with Us," the second line cautions: "Getting and spending, we lay waste our powers." As you read the essays in this chapter, examine the "power" that you have wielded (and lost) as a lifetime consumer.

Before reading, consider your own consumer history: What are the possessions that have brought you joy throughout the various stages of your life? What purchases have you made as gifts, intending to bring surprise and pleasure to others? Are there any items that you imagined would make you happy but did not? How much of your desire for goods and services is influenced by popular culture (advertising, films, movies, television shows, sports, celebrities)?

From innocent childhood pleas to attend a fair or amusement park and to obtain the hottest toys, to adolescent desires for music, clothing, and technological goods, to young adulthood dreams of a first car, people of all ages are driven by consumption and desire. From the ever so popular 1984 television show "Lifestyles of the Rich and Famous" to the 2005 release of Curtis "50 Cent" Jackson's film *Get Rich or Die Tryin,* there are literally thousands of films, television shows, advertising slogans, and music lyrics with the word "rich" in the title that cater to the desire for luxury.

Popular culture forms are driven by consumer demand, and the industry's bottom line is always profit. The writers in this chapter raise questions about materialism, consumerism, trash, shopping, simplicity movements, the mall, and Disney. The diverse mediums covered include books (Twitchell); space, advertising

(Mazur and Koda); space, mall (Farrell); music (Rojas); film, books, and the like (Lessig).

How do Americans really feel about consumption? Twitchell invites us to look in our trash for the answers. In an excerpt from his book *Lead Us Into Temptation: The Triumph of America Materialism*, he writes: "Trash is central to commercial culture. It is the remains of our incomplete love affair with stuff. While we claim to be wedded to responsible consumption, while we claim to abjure advertising, packaging, whimsical changes in fashion, and casual shopping, we spend a lot of our time philandering. Trash is lipstick on the collar, the telltale blond hair, cheek-smudge" (paragraph 12). He surmises that perhaps "Our concern about garbage is really, as the psychologists might say, a displaced concern about consumption" (paragraph 22). The guilt associated with consumption is keenly illustrated in the hallowed recommendations of leaders in the so-called Voluntary Simplicity (VS) movement—a movement warning consumers that "commercialism is suffocating your natural innocence" (paragraph 37).

It is precisely this return to innocence that corporations such as Disney have been able to use to conquer both the imaginations and wallets of consumers. As Mazur and Koda point out, Disney has elevated the act of consumption into the art of religious devotion: "Disney's products (tangible and intangible) fill many of the roles often filled by religion" (paragraph 11). It thus becomes a place of escape, an illusion of a world of innocence—and, it is available for all to participate—for a price.

Another space that corporations have designed for profit is the mall. In an excerpt from his book *Shopping for American Culture*, James Farrell insists: "We need to follow Americans to the mall and see what they're doing because shopping centers can reveal cultural patterns that we don't usually see" (paragraph 4). As you study popular culture, think about any patterns that emerge. As explored in Chapter 5, studying popular culture is a valid pursuit, especially because it helps us to examine our own motivations, drives, impulses, and culture. Farrell's excerpt contains a illuminating chart summarizing core values, general features, and relevance to consumer behavior. The core values are achievement and success, activity, efficiency and practicality, progress, material comfort, individualism, freedom, external conformity, humanitarianism, youthfulness, and fitness and health. It is no surprise that many of the core values have been referenced in a majority of the selections in this book.

What makes consumerism particularly alluring is the consumption—there is always more to be consumed. So many of the products we consume are disposable—even music. In "Bootleg Culture," Rojas states: "bootlegs are music fans' response to the current disposability of pop culture. Effortlessly easy to create, with an infinite number of combinations possible, bootlegs are even more perfectly disposable than the pop songs they combine" (paragraph 21).

What are the legalities concerning licensing fees? Will there ever be a time when stringent copyright laws will change? In "Protecting Mickey Mouse at Art's Expense," Lawrence Lessig effectively proposes a compromise that would "move content that is no longer commercially exploited into the public domain, while protecting work that has continuing commercial value" (paragraph 5). The compromise would provide freedom for individuals and corporations to use material for "artistic and educational use" while still protecting commercially valuable intellectual property.

Clearly, the bottom line for every facet of the entertainment industry is profit. This is often easily cloaked in the allure of "creativity." But what the selections really ask is for readers to penetrate a deeper level of consumerism. What are the values behind the psychological impulses of a purchase? What are our "motivations, drives, impulses"? What does this activity reveal about our culture? Do you agree with Twitchell that consumerism is indeed "our better judgment"?

Perhaps the paradox raised in Ross's "Rock 101" applies to all aspects of popular culture: "It's not very rock and roll to intellectualize rock and roll" (Ross, paragraph 3). Perhaps we may not want to understand the motivations and impulses. But turn away at your own peril because indeed "we have a lot to learn from pop studies" (Ross, paragraph 25). We need to examine popular culture because it reveals "cultural patterns that we don't usually see" (Farrell, paragraph 4). As Browne states, "movies and 'new history' and music and fast foods . . . are the things that shape and drive American culture. They may not be loved, but they have to be understood" (quoted in Trussell, paragraph 34).

Pre-Reading Chapter 6

1. Write down all your responses to the questions raised in this introduction about your own spending habits. Sincerely evaluate your desires for goods and the popular culture influences on your consumer habits.

2. As you survey the titles of the essays, consider key words that spark your interest: "Trash and the Voluntary Simplicity Movement—The Triumph of American Materialism"/James Twitchell; "The Happiest Place on Earth: Disney"/Eric Michael Mazur and Tara K. Koda; "Shopping for American Culture"/ James Farrell; "Bootleg Culture"/Pete Rojas; and, "Protecting Mickey Mouse at Art's Expense"/Lawrence Lessig—for example, "trash," "voluntary simplicity movement," "Disney," "bootleg," and "art's expense." What do you imagine the selections will reveal? What do the words connote for you? Brainstorm all of your ideas so that after reading you can see if the readings fulfilled your expectations.

3. In your idea journal and scrapbook, keep track of all instances you come across this week that have to do with consumerism and the issues in the chapter. For example, keep track of all your purchases in one week. Do not limit your observations to the specific mediums referenced. For example, although Rojas writes about bootlegging and music, document any other references to bootlegging and popular culture that you encounter. For example, you might observe a story about bootlegging and movies. Then, before class discussion and writing assignments, review your observations. This will provide you with a rich resource of your own ideas and observations.

Trash and the Voluntary Simplicity Movement—The Triumph of American Materialism

JAMES TWITCHELL

Educator, writer, and popular culture scholar James Twitchell is an alumni professor of English at the University of Florida. He has contributed articles to academic journals and is the author of numerous books, including Carnival Culture: The Trashing of Taste in America *(1991),* AdCult USA: The Triumph of Advertising in American Culture *(1996),* 20 Ads That Shook the World *(2001), and* Lead Us Into Temptation: The Triumph of American Materialism *(2000).*

Pre-Reading

Although many of us prefer not to think about trash, many people participate in the ritualistic act of "spring cleaning." How difficult is it for you to throw away items? Do you hold on to belongings even though you have not used them in years? Why do you think there is a reluctance to throw away items never even used? Alternatively, what does the contents of your "trash" reveal about your lifestyle?

———————————— ✦ ————————————

I don't care about losing the money, it's losing all this stuff.
—Mrs. Navin R. Johnson on filing for bankruptcy,
The Jerk, 1979

One of the most helpful ways to understand modern American materialism is to watch Steve Martin in *The Jerk*. In this movie by Carl Reiner, Mr. Martin plays a kind of idiot savant named Navin R. Johnson. The story is held together by the running joke that when Navin is being the most idiotic, he is really being the most savant.

After a series of misadventures, Navin amasses a fortune by inventing a way to keep eyeglasses from slipping down the nose (the "Opti-grab"). He wins the hand of his sweetheart, buys incredibly gauche gold chains, swag lamps, outrageous golf carts, and ersatz Grecian mansions. Surrounded by things, he is finally happy. But then—curses!—he loses his possessions as googleeyed Carl Reiner wins a class-action suit because the Opti-grab has made many wearers cross-eyed. Navin's wife (Bernadette Peters) is distraught. She bursts into tears. "I don't care about losing the money, it's losing all this stuff."

Navin, as innocent as he is honest, says he doesn't really care about these things, he knows who he is without possessions. His sense of self is certainly not tied to the material world. "I don't want stuff . . . I don't need anything," he says to her as he starts to leave the room in his pajamas. He sees an old ashtray. "Except this ashtray, and that's the only thing I need is this," he says, as he leans over to pick it up. Navin walks to the door. "Well, and this paddle game and the ashtray is all I need. And this, this remote control; that's all I need, just the ashtray, paddle game, and this remote control."

Navin is growing progressively more frantic in vintage Steve Martin fashion. He is in the hall now, pajamas down around his knees and his arms full of stuff. "And these matches. Just the ashtray, paddle ball remote control, and these matches...and this lamp, and that's all I need. I don't need one other thing. I need this [he picks up a kitchen chair], but I don't need one other thing... except this magazine." We hear him gathering more things as he disappears down the hall.

We next see Navin leaving the mansion, now under a mound of things, still repeating the litany of what he needs, and proclaiming he needs nothing more. He soon leaves our sight walking down the road and we hear him say, "I don't need anything except my dog [and we hear his dog growling], no, I don't need my dog, but I need this chair, but I don't need anything more than the ashtray, the paddle game, the remote control, the chair." 5

Navin, jerk enough to think he needs nothing, is sage enough not to leave home without a few of his favorite things. In doing so he opens up one of the central myths of consumerist culture: protestations of independence are loudest where things are paramount. Navin is Everyman for our times. No other culture spends so much time declaring things don't matter while saying "just charge it." The country with the highest per capita consumer debt and the greatest number of machine-made things is the same country in which Puritan ascetic principles are most pronounced and held in highest regard. In repeated Gallup polls, when respondents are asked to choose what is really important—family life, betterment of society, strict morals, and the like—"having nice things" comes in dead *last*. On the way to Walden Pond, we pack the sport utility vehicle with the dish antenna, the cell phone, the bread maker, the ashtray, the paddle ball.

Such a paradox has traditionally (and logically) been interpreted as an indication of the basic instability of modern materialistic societies. To the enough-already crowd, it is a sure signal of imminent decline, coming right around the next corner. Study after study appears in the daily newspaper to the effect that in this age of plenty, in which capitalism seems to have won the day, Americans have loaded up on angst. Critics conclude that we are working more and enjoying the fruits less. We are gagging on goods.

As Eugene Linden has argued in *Affluence and Discontent: The Anatomy of Consumer Societies*, ironically (and perhaps illogically), a broad look at consumer societies leads to the conclusion that individual discontents and their larger manifestation in countercultural movements are a necessary part of a consumer society. Expressions of material discontent, far from being an indication of decline, are the way a consumer society balances conflicting demands and indulges different behaviors. Another paradox unique to our time and place is that many people are dispirited with materialism not because they have too little, but because they have too much.

This is the "complain about farmers with your mouth full" syndrome. One can see this characteristic contradiction in many places, but let's look at just two: Our recent dread of garbage that is articulated in our passion to recycle regardless of costs; and our willingness to consume "self-help" programs that wean us from our willingness to consume.

WASTE MATTERS: THE TERROR OF TRASH

10   A telling characteristic about our relationship to trash is that while it is viewed by the rest of the world as a sign of economic success and well-being, it is viewed by us with disgust bordering on reverence. How we now handle garbage has become a mark of our ability to be humble and contrite and, simultaneously, good and virtuous. So we separate the bottles from the paper, the plastic from the glass, the glossy paper from the cardboard in a weekly ritual of mild self-righteousness. Just as kids used to learn the three Rs of reading, 'riting, and 'rithmetic, they are now taught the modern version, Reduce, Reuse, Recycle.

If you don't think that these Rs have become serious, try tangling with a tot over McDonald's clamshell containers, or a teenager over how paper companies are raping the rain forest, or think of how you yourself feel when confronted by the modern riddle of the Sphinx: paper or plastic?

Trash is central to commercial culture. It is the remains of our incomplete love affair with stuff. While we claim to be wedded to responsible consumption, while we claim to abjure advertising, packaging, whimsical changes in fashion, and casual shopping, we spend a lot of our time philandering. Trash is lipstick on the collar, the telltale blond hair, cheek-smudge.

Shame is what humans feel when the disparity between do and ought occurs. We know what we should do, we don't do it, we feel ashamed, and shame makes us meek about ourselves, and often harsh on others. If you say you like the simple life, then why are you generating mounds of garbage? People who would never dream of telling you not to have children out of wedlock, or who would never criticize you for filing for bankruptcy, will express eye-rolling dismay if you use a plastic fork or get your smooth cardboard mixed in with your egg cartons.

Garbage has become mythic. Remember the strange national fascination with the "Islip garbage barge," which left Long Island in the spring of 1987, sailing for 55 days, searching in vain for a place to dump its pungent 3,168 tons of cargo? Or what of the "P.U. choo-choo," which rumbled out of New York City in the summer of 1992, chugging around the Midwest, searching unsuccessfully for a place to unload what Christopher S. Bond (R-Mo.) denounced on the Senate floor as "forty cars of rotting, maggot-filled trash." That's our culture, we say to each other. We filled up those boxcars. These stories made their way to the front pages because they seemed such apt images of our times. It was not Sierra Clubbers who expressed flagellating dismay, it was all of us.

We no longer seem able to discuss trash without invoking protective euphemisms and refrains. We call it waste, or solid waste, or municipal solid waste, or, better yet, MSW (which confers upon the lowly sack of garbage the exalted status of a Master of Social Work). We don't take this stuff to the dump, we go to the landfill. This landfill usually has a name like Shady Grove or Piney Woods. It is hard to imagine Bette Davis's famous line, "What a dump!" being rewritten, but that is the goal of landfill-think. The stuff we don't take to "Overlook Park" is called recyclable and you must *never* refer to it as trash. We will gladly drive across town to put it in a bin where, chances are, it will be carted off to Overlook Park if the aftermarket for glass, paper, or aluminum is not sufficiently profitable that week.

How many times have we been told that we throw out enough trash in a year to spread 30 stories high over a thousand football fields; enough to fill a bumper-to-bumper convoy of garbage trucks halfway to the moon; that we produce far more garbage than wheat or rice, nearly the same tonnage as corn; that we generate enough rubbish to fill the World Trade Center's twin towers 187 times over; enough to fill five million trucks, which would circle the globe twice if stood end to end? And...well, you get the point.

Like our Puritan ancestors, who enjoyed seeing themselves in the hands of an angry God and then went on to gleefully catalog the horrors, we entertain the suffocating vision of all the landfills being full, all the incinerators churning out toxic fumes, a nation engulfed by its own filth. Move over Commies, garbage has become the evil empire.

15

The key to such quasi-religious thinking is that it practices the economy of the closed mind. Orthodoxy will abide no stray interpretations. From time to time someone tries to confuse our shame of incomplete consumption with the facts. Most recently, John Tierney wrote the June 30, 1996 cover story of the *New York Times Magazine*, the *vade mecum* of the We Have a Serious Problem Here crowd. His title was "Recycling Is Garbage" and the subhead read, "Rinsing out tuna cans and tying up newspapers may make you feel virtuous, but recycling could be America's most wasteful activity." Reader response was vitriolic. This news was not fit to print![1]

Ironically, Tierney, the newspaper's staff science writer, said nothing new. He is not Rush Limbaugh, nor is he an "environmental whacko." But his thesis—much recycling "squanders money and goodwill, and doesn't do much for the environment either"— drew more mail than anything the magazine had ever published. How could this heretic have made his way into the sacred temple? reader after reader asked. Few questioned his facts.[2]

20   I'm not so much interested in those facts as I am in the outrage. If hypocrisy is the tribute that vice pays to virtue, then is our passion about recycling perhaps the tribute shame pays to desire? Instead of trying to understand the deep pull of the material world, instead of coming to grips with the allure of commercial culture, instead of trying to learn about why American marketing is so powerful, we focus on what we take to be the results of human yearning gone amok. We can't really want—ugh!—disposable things. We must have been tricked.

Or, to put it in slightly different terms, I'm not being tricked. I'm consuming sensibly. But *they* are so profligate, so wasteful, so careless. Someone should talk to them.

Our concern about garbage is really, as the psychologists might say, a displaced concern about consumption. We sort milk cartons and pop bottles, we put slick paper here and newsprint there, we step over dollars to pick up a dime, we indulge in fuzzy feel-good thinking because we live at a time when meaning and purpose are hard to come by, and much of what we have for meaning resides in manufactured objects. We want these objects and, if the price we have to pay is the ritual of sacramental separation, then so be it. While our Christian ancestors may have comforted themselves thinking they had dominion over the birds that fly and the fish that swim, we can find surcease consuming what we want as long as we are sure that the blue box—the eponymous Big Blue—is properly filled each week.

THE VOLUNTARY SIMPLICITY MOVEMENT

If entering the recycling movement is possibly the penance we pay for the guilty pleasures of consuming, then alliance with the Voluntary Simplicity movement is the righteous renunciation of such sin. Both concerns represent a backhanded tribute to the power of materialism. Most of the world practices recycling and simplicity, but not voluntarily.

The Voluntary Simplicity (VS) movement is not to be confused with the back to nature, let's live off the land types, who tear up their social security cards, stop paying taxes, and pull the plug. The simplicity movement of today has no retrograde romance of nature about it, rather a passionate belief that we can live well for less . . . *if* we buy and use the right stuff. Let recyclers avoid styrofoam cups for their morning coffee, the simplicity people will tell you just put a cloth around the coffee grounds and squeeze hard.

VS proponents believe we suffer from a social disease. This disease is contracted by falling for the American dream. It is spread by advertising, packaging, fashion, branding, and all the base contagion of marketing. Its symptoms are swollen expectations, shopping fever, chronic stress, and broken-down families. The wretched malaise goes by any number of names: crass commercialism, blatant materialism, hollow consumption. The cure? Inoculate yourself by buying a how-to-stop-buying book, attend some meetings, practice meditation, buy other stuff.[3]

Recently, the movement received the ultimate accolade of Mother Jones culture. It was featured on two Public Broadcasting System specials. The disease, now sporting a new name— "affluenza"—was seriously discussed by a suitably dour Scott Simon from National Public Radio. We had the usual scolds, the usual psychologists, the usual reformed admen telling us what they know but what we haven't found out: Things Can't Buy Happiness, You Can't Have It All. If only the nasty marketers would lay off, if only greedy bankers would quit sending us those charge cards, if only Sears didn't have that softer side, if only . . . then we could quit being victimized by consumerism and get on with it.

But good news. Help is on the way. Go into any bookstore and you will see the booming industry of what in psychobabble is known as "decathection," the partial reversing of magnetic polarities from gathering things to refusing to gather things. These books are now the profit center of the flagging self-help industry. They adapt pop-addiction therapy to human desire—twelve baby steps to freedom.

What used to be a single shelf of self-help books by Dale Carnegie, Bishop Fulton J. Sheen, and Norman Vincent Peale has exploded into an entire subsection of books on building self-esteem. In the 1950s these books argued a variation of the Little Engine That Could. You can succeed. You can get to the top of the hill. Just keep at it. I think I can, I think I can, I can. The reason you wanted success was so you could buy a ton of stuff.

Now that we have so much stuff (and the debt that often comes with it) the modern version is dedicated to the concept of Recovery. Recovery is based on the romantic story of the Child Is Father of the Man. Want success? Just relax. Let your inner child out. I don't think I can, I feel I can. I feel okay. I am okay. I've just been trapped by advertising, fashion, packaging, and branding. I'll relax my way free.

30   What is interesting to the student of materialism is not the resurgence of object relinquishment but the profoundly commercial nature of letting go. The male form of Voluntary Simplicity, as it were, is more ancient than Ecclesiastes. It pops up in Marcus Aurelius, St. Francis, the Puritans, Quakers, Shakers, Henry David Thoreau, Gandhi, Ralph Nader, and even Jimmy Carter. The mantra of male asceticism is Thoreau's furiously famous advice in *Walden, or Life in the Woods:*

> I went to the woods because I wished to live deliberately, to front only the essential facts of life, and see if I could not learn what it had to teach; and not, when I came to die, discover that I had not lived. I did not wish to live what was not life, living is so dear. I wanted to live deep and suck out all the marrow of life.

These males may have hectored their neighbors about consuming too much, but they never offered to sell them advice, go on a lucrative lecture tour, hold seminars, produce videos, or merchandise their "unique vision."

The current VS movement is the female form of asceticism. When a woman feels overwhelmed by a flood of things, she really can't head out to the woods. But she can buy a guide to help her stop consuming and join a group.[4] These guides range from Duane Elgin's evangelical *Voluntary Simplicity* (first published in 1981 and rereleased in 1993); then the husband-wife Dominguez-Robin blockbuster, *Your Money or Your Life* (1992), which has sold almost half a million copies (despite their advice to save money by getting it from the library); and most recently Elaine

St. James's *Simplify Your Life* (1994) and its many sequels like *Inner Simplicity* and *Living the Simple Life*.

Take the case of Sarah Ban Breathnach. In 1991 she was depressed. She had been hit on the head by a ceiling tile at a fast-food restaurant and was feeling punk. So she sat at her dining room table determined to write down one hundred things for which she could feel grateful. No problem with number one. She was still alive. She went on to continue the list until she found herself on another list: the *New York Times* Bestseller List. She had some help along the way. As is becoming customary for recovery books (or books in general, for that matter) she did a stint with Oprah. Millions of women in that audience resonated to her plight.

Breathnach has now become what is known in media culture as a profit center. Her initial inventory of blessings, *Simple Abundance* ($18.95!), a collection of 366 daily "meditations" for women ("I didn't know how men think," she has confessed) has become a cottage industry. In fact, Simple Abundance is now a corporation, a registered trademark, and a nonprofit foundation, all headquartered in a simple townhouse in suburban Washington. It is also an imprint of Warner Books—Simple Abundance Press—issuing four books a year on the importance of frugal living.

The ethos of the Voluntary Simplicity movement is, appropriately enough, simple. It is also as inadvertently deceptive as recycling. In the 1980s, it holds, much of America went astray, indulging in frivolous luxury consumption, frittering away time and money in wasteful habits and services, toiling in lucrative but ultimately unfulfilling jobs to pay for things we only thought we needed. (Does this sound like more yuppie shame, or what?) In the revered American tradition of sin, guilt, and merchandised redemption, we now can escape the cycle of consumption in the 1990s.

But how? Here's the kind of advice the simplify-your-life 35 groups give to ward off the dreaded affluenza:

- Sell the boat
- Get rid of your car phone
- Pack your own lunch
- Buy only what you need
- Make your own entertainment
- Buy secondhand stuff
- Wear things out before replacing them
- Stop reading the newspaper

- Stop answering the door when the doorbell rings
- Cancel your magazine subscriptions
- Don't watch infomercials or the Home Shopping Network
- Dump household clutter
- Move to a smaller place
- Pay off your credit card balance
- Eliminate all but one credit card
- Opt out of holiday gift giving if it feels oppressive

As Dave Barry would say, "Honest, I am not making this up." My favorite: "Work less and enjoy it more." One is tempted to add, quit buying books to tell you how to quit buying, or, to turn the consumerist phrase a bit, Just Quit Doing It. Surely, it is a sign of our twelve-step times that one needs to consume a program before consuming less ("Today I will not buy another garment with a Ralph Lauren logo, even if it's at a factory outlet store.")

Admittedly, the Voluntary Simplicity movement seems appealing to those for whom simplicity is a preexisting mental condition. But it is part of a larger constellation that floats around the consumerist world. For instance, books like *Chicken Soup for the Soul, The Seven Spiritual Laws of Success,* or *Care of the Soul* have been atop the bestseller lists for well over a year and all repeat the same message: commercialism is suffocating your natural innocence and only I, Deepak Chopra (or whoever), can help (if you buy my book) return you to health (childhood).

WHAT'S TO COME

I have (perhaps too harshly) calumniated the Recycling and Voluntary Simplicity movements not because they are not well-meaning and right-thinking, but because they distort common sense about consumerism in the name of helplessness. Why must we invoke social movements to describe individual responsibility? Recycling means, if I remember my mother's words, "Pick up after yourself," and VS means, to quote my father, "Don't buy what you can't afford."

But these movements say more—especially if you listen to those on their militant edges. What I hear goes like this: You have been led astray by the material world and those who champion it. Your innocence has been betrayed. You have been led out of Eden into sin and waste, and you must struggle mightily to repent. You must promise to be good because the forces of evil are so powerful and tempting. You have been made materialistic. You have become addicted.

I also hear this: We are the solution and you who do not agree 40 are still the problem. We are saving the world from you, for you. Such movements are the civic religions of our times. In a way, recycling and downshifting are what we have for a modern potlatch. *Potlatch*, the voluntary dumping of personal goods, was once a sign of dominance and prestige for Indian tribes in the Northwest. When the chief divested himself he was delivering the double whammy: I got it, but I don't need it. Now potlatch is practiced as a way of middle-class coping: I can't really afford it, but I could have it if I wanted. You, however, shouldn't even want it.

A DIFFERENT VIEW

What is overlooked in our hand-wringing about commercialism is what Navin R. Johnson, the jerk, seems to know. Consumerism is not forced on us. It is not against our better judgment. It is (at least for much of our lives) our better judgment. We are powerfully attracted to the world of goods. Navin knows what we may forget: we call them goods, not bads. He also knows that our passion to amass is as perplexing as our confusion about what to do next.

American culture is often criticized for being too materialistic, for taking too much from the general store. We are forever reciting the meaculpa of capitalism that, although we are only 10 percent of the world's population, we consume 90 percent of its resources. While the percents may change, the shame remains. We are continually being told our bloated consumption comes from greed, and that greed results from our making wants into needs, and then making false needs into real ones.

I think there are no false needs. Once we are fed, clothed, and sexually functioning, needs are cultural. Furthermore, I will contend that we are not too materialistic; if anything, we are not materialistic enough.

Endnotes

1. This kind of demurrer has been written before. First, in the 1970s, William Rathje, an Arizona archaeologist, and Cullen Murphy, the essayist, wrote a sensible piece for *The Atlantic Monthly* and later expanded it into *Rubbish! The Archaeology of Garbage*. They argued

that rumors of our impending asphyxiation by trash were a little exaggerated. A few years ago the *Wall Street Journal* published a comprehensive article under the comparatively mild headline, "Waste of a Sort: Curbside Recycling Comforts the Soul, but Benefits Are Scant" (Bailey A1).

2. The arguments presented were not particularly new. Recycling's costs generally outweigh its benefits; it is not always necessary for resource conservation; it attacks a nonexistent shortage of landfill space; and it may, in some cases, create environmental problems instead of solving them.

3. Call it Voluntary Simplicity, Downshifting, or Simple Living, the Trends Research Institute of Rhinebeck, N.Y., claims it as one of its top ten trends of the 1990s and predicts that by the end of the decade, 15 percent of America's 77 million baby boomers will be part of a "simplicity" market (Brant 1995:6F). In a wonderfully mercantile term, the Trends Research Institute (holder of quite a name itself) calls this cashing out. Cha-ching.

4. Such books are not new but the mass audience is. Think only of Edith Wharton's *The Decoration of Houses* (1899), which argued for a less cluttered domestic existence, and Charles Wagner's *The Simple Life* (1901), which sold hundreds of thousands of copies in the New York area alone and made Wagner a celebrity. Both authors reprimanded their mainly upper-class female readers for reliance on material goods and abandonment of tradition. And both authors, of course, were deep in the material world—Wharton as a consumer and outfitter of sizable manses and Wagner as a fervent disciple and booster of the Philadelphia retailing baron John Wanamaker. The real shift in modern temper came in the mid-twentieth century with the publication of Anne Morrow Lindbergh's 1955 book, *Gift from the Sea*. Lindbergh wondered why she was so busy when technology had given her so many new simplification tools. Her argument was an intellectual one, a proto-ecological one: step back, wonder, and reconsider.

Questions for Discussion and Writing

1. Do you agree with Twitchell's correlation between shame and consumerism? Explain why or why not.

2. In your own words, write a brief summary of two of the subsections: "Waste Matters: The Terror of Trash" and "The Voluntary Simplicity Movement." With which section do you most agree?

3. What does the anecdote from the film *The Jerk* illustrate? What household items do you imagine others in a similar unfortunate situation would take?

4. Twitchell writes, "Our concern about garbage is really, as the psychologists might say, a displaced concern about consumption" (paragraph 22). Write a personal essay about your own relationship with trash. Do you recycle? Do you consider yourself part of the collective "we" invoked in paragraph 22: "We sort milk cartons and pop bottles, we put slick paper here and newsprint there, we step over dollars to pick up a dime, we indulge in fuzzy feel-good thinking because we live at a time when meaning and purpose are hard to come by, and much of what we have for meaning resides in manufactured objects"?

5. "Sell the boat. Get rid of your car phone. Pack your own lunch. Buy only what you need . . . " are several suggestions from "simplify-your-life groups" (paragraph 35). Write an argumentation essay supporting, modifying, or refuting the claims of the voluntary simplicity movement (VS) as presented in the excerpt. In your essay, consider whether or not the suggestions are too extreme. What, if any, benefits can consumers receive by following the principles?

The Happiest Place on Earth: Disney
ERIC MICHAEL MAZUR AND TARA K. KODA

Interdisciplinary educator and scholar Eric Michael Mazur has published numerous articles in academic journals, has contributed to anthologies, and is the author of The Americanization of Religious Minorities: Confronting the Constitutional Order *(1999). He co-authored the following essay (from* God in the Details: American Religion and Popular Culture *[2000], which Mazur co-edited with Kate McCarthy) with Tara K. Koda, a graduate student and teacher at University of California, Santa Barbara. She has published articles and presented papers on Japanese-American religions at academic conferences.*

Pre-Reading

For you, what is "the happiest place on earth"? Is there a location where you are virtually guaranteed to feel satisfaction and joy? Does your location cost money to visit? If so, is entry worth the fee?

✦

Our personnel sincerely sell happiness. Hell! That's what we all want, isn't it?

—Walt Disney

IT REALLY IS A SMALL WORLD, AFTER ALL

In a classic commercial, sports celebrities caught after a contest hear a list of their accomplishments and a question: "Now what are you going to do?" Invariably they respond in what seems to be the only way possible in contemporary, commercial America: "I'm going to Disney World!" (see Fjellman 1992, 160).

Indeed, how many millions have neither experienced nor dreamed of participating in "the middle-class hajj, the compulsory visit to the sunbaked holy city," Walt Disney World (Ritzer 1996, 4)? It is just one facet of a global corporation that produces movies and television programs, owns part or all of several other theme parks, television studios and networks, sports teams, housing developments, cruise ships, retail outlets, seminar centers, and training facilities that earned more than $20 billion in 1997 (Miles 1999, 15).[1] One million people visited the California park, Disneyland, in its first seven weeks, and more than four million visited there in 1955–56, its first year of operation (Weinstein 1992, 152). In Florida, ten million visitors in 1971–72 (its first year) placed Walt Disney World ahead of the United Kingdom, Austria, and the former West Germany as a vacation destination, and more popular than the Great Smoky Mountains National Park (seven million visitors), Gettysburg (five million), and Yellowstone National Park (two million). By the beginning of the 1980s, more people visited Walt Disney World than the Eiffel Tower, the Taj Mahal, the Tower of London, or the Pyramids (Fjellman 1992, 136–39). In 1984 alone, the Florida and California parks drew nearly twenty million customers (Lawrence 1986, 65). "Since the number of visitors to both parks together exceeds the number going to Washington, D.C., the official capital," notes Margaret King, the parks could be considered "the popular culture capitals of America" (1981, 117). Appropriately, the Walt Disney World logo depicts the globe as one of three spheres used to silhouette Mickey Mouse's face; it's a small world, after all, and Disney covers it completely. The American who can avoid contact with Disney must live in a cave; to reject Disney is to defy a major global force, and challenges much that is synonymous with contemporary American culture.

But what has this to do with religion? In contemporary America, many consider all elements of life, even intangibles, as things that can be bought, and religious leaders now find themselves financially burdened competing for congregants' attention. On television or in the pulpit, they offer salvation along with twelve-step programs and child care. They have developed sophisticated attitudes toward money and fundraising, and some have adopted businesslike attitudes toward their congregants. As George Ritzer notes, "religion has been streamlined through such things as drive-in churches and televised religious programs" (1996, 48). Not surprisingly, many people treat salvation like a product, pursue it for selfish reasons, and often purchase it in seemingly nonreligious forms for seemingly religious reasons. Americans can be found pursuing diverse activities—working out, exploring nature, or watching televison— and believing that they have obtained the same benefits that they could receive from traditional religious activities. The distinction between religious and commercial activities has blurred, and as one scholar notes, such developments have made "a member of the Jehovah's Witnesses who peddled religion door-to-door on a Sunday afternoon much the same as a vacuum cleaner salesman" (R. L. Moore 1994, 256). In other words, whether it is through eternal bliss or clean carpets, salvation for many Americans is a readily available commodity.

An odd situation to be sure. But even odder when commercial ventures, operating for profit rather than piety, create competion for traditional religion. They are not simply providing paraphernalia for religious devotion—votives, Bibles, or "Pope-on-a-Rope" soap—but are *competing* (if unintentionally) with religious communities by offering similar goods: mythologies, symbols, rituals, and notions of community by which consumers organize their lives. These corporations offer (at a price) salvation from the modern world of twentieth-century American capitalism. And while, as Michael Budde argues, such a situation presents "new and imposing barriers ... to the formation of deep religious convictions," he also recognizes that "[m]ore than any other set of social institutions, these industries collectively influence how people relate to the processes and products of economic activity." They are the "vectors and initiators for ideas regarding the valued, the innovative, the normal, the erotic, and the repulsive" (1997, 14–15, 32). In other words, these companies create the environment in which even religious ideas are communicated.

5

The Walt Disney Company is one such business marketing religious symbolism and meaning and providing strong—if indirect—competition to traditional religion in the United States. There are others who are also exploring this market, other purveyors of religious symbols and meaning. However, because of its market penetration, its integrated marketing, and its access to many levels of culture through its corporate network, Disney is uniquely suited for the "religification" of its commodity. And as Margaret King suggests, because a coincidence of factors unique to post–World War II America makes possible, "even obligatory—for Americans, adults as well as children, at least one pilgrimage to Disney Land [sic] or World as a popular culture 'mecca' of nearly religious importance" (1981, 117), this corporation is able to capitalize on its commodity in a way that is distinctly suited for this time and place.

THE MARKETPLACE AND COMPETITION IN CONTEMPORARY AMERICAN RELIGION

Once firmly committed to the idea that religion would fade from society as that society became more sophisticated, sociologists have come to use an economic model to explain the continued religiosity of the American citizenry (see Warner 1993). This model argues that religious communities—free of government intrusion or control—benefit from a "free market," and in competition with other religious communities ("producers") offer to religious adherents ("consumers") "products" they can compare and select rationally. These "products" (comfort, identity, community, but usually some form of salvation) are like items in a supermarket and compared in terms of their desirability, "market share," and general consumer appeal.

Though this model has its critics, it seems to explain in a more satisfying manner the continued vitality of religion in contemporary America. However, it means nothing if the "consumers" in the model—religious participants—aren't free to pick from religious options; market economies depend on consumers who are free to choose. Thus, over the past decade, scholars have examined the freedom individuals have enjoyed to "go shopping" for religion, and the loss of loyalty to specific religious communities that has resulted. Phillip Hammond argues that restrictions on religious identity have virtually disappeared, and "the social revolution of the 1960s and '70s wrought a major change: a near absolute free choice in the religious marketplace" (1992, 168). Similarly, Wade

Clark Roof notes that among members of the "baby boom" generation, "religion was whatever one chose as one's own" (1993, 244, emphasis omitted). The loss of a cultural monopoly by any one religious tradition, matched with the growing role of the individual (rather than the community) as the locus of identity, has made Americans freer to pick from among the various religious options, and to mix and match as they please.

At its logical extreme, this suggests market forces so diverse, and competition between religious "producers" so fierce, that consumers may not only choose more varied and less traditional forms of religious participation (as seems to be the case currently), but might also turn to nonreligious "producers" for the same (or similar) "products." In such a climate Disney, as much as any other for-profit venture, might be understood as creating, maintaining, and even being depended upon for the images, ideas, and emotions that were once reserved for traditional religious communities. In other words, in a religious marketplace truly free of limits, competition to provide religionlike commodities might include organizations not traditionally understood as religions, and any institution with the wherewithal can compete equally with traditional religions, regardless of its financial or religious goal.

There is a great temptation to equate everything with religion, including Disney. Even a discussion of its founder, Walter Elias Disney, suggests Christlike comparisons: a man with a vision, lifelong innocence, a message to be shared with the world, and a special affinity for children, envisions a new kingdom of heaven on earth and leaves his vision with his disciples, who build cathedrals in his honor while he awaits resurrection. The myth of his cryogenic preservation and postmortem corporate participation suggest a continued presence and guidance from beyond (see Fjellman 1992, 418, n. 33; Ritzer 1996, 174–75). One author describes meetings with "the spirit" of Disney in attendance; anticipating his company's future, Walt had himself filmed for screening at meetings after his death, asking questions of participants and commenting on the status of scheduled events (Fjellman 1992, 117).

However, it would be fruitless to suggest that Disney is the same as a traditional religion, or that it is consciously designing its business for religious competition. The first claim would be foolish to make, the second impossible to prove.[2] Instead, Disney's products (tangible and intangible) fill many of the roles often filled by religion. They have entered the market at a time when many people are not only searching for alternatives to traditional religion, but are also flexible with what they find. They have also entered the market at a time when religious institutions are in competition with "global culture industries" (Budde 1997) over the construction and maintenance of meaning at the end of the twentieth century.

Endnotes

1. A commission of the Southern Baptist Convention lists more than 200 subsidiaries connected to Disney. (Thanks to Shawn Rapp for locating "The Disney Family Tree" at http://www.ERLC.COM/Culture/ Disney/1997/famtree.htm.) Michael Budde notes that, according to Disney, "on an August weekend in 1990, 30 percent of all movie theaters in the United States and Canada were screening a feature produced by one of Disney's production companies" (1997, 30).

2. For quasi-religious analyses of Disney, see Brockway 1989; King 1981; Knight 1999; Moore 1980. We are thankful to the "Religion and Popular Culture" panel and audience at the Popular Culture Association meeting (Orlando, March 1998) who heard an earlier version of this chapter. We are particularly grateful to one participant who exclaimed that, though she lived near the park and visited often, she did not consider it religious. We are reminded that many residents of Jerusalem—the focus of major religious traditions for centuries—consider it simply another city, but we are grateful for the reminder that sometimes the sacred becomes mundane and needs re-clarification.

References

Budde, Michael. 1997. *The (Magic) Kingdom of God: Christianity and Global Culture Industries*. Boulder, Colo.: Westview Press.

Fjellman, Stephen M. 1992. *Vinyl Leaves: Walt Disney World and America*. Boulder, Colo.: Westview Press.

King, Margaret. 1981. "Disneyland and Walt Disney World: Traditional Values in Futuristic Form." *Journal of Popular Culture* 15, 1 (summer): 116–40.

Lawrence, Elizabeth A. 1986. "In the Mick of Time: Reflections on Disney's Ageless Mouse." *Journal of Popular Culture* 20, 2 (fall): 65–72.

Miles, Margaret R. 1999. "Disney Spirituality: An Oxymoron?" *Christian Spirituality Bulletin* (spring): 13–18.

Moore, Alexander. 1980. "Walt Disney World: Bounded Ritual Space and the Playful Pilgrimage Center." *Anthropological Quarterly* 53, 4 (October): 207–18.

Ritzer, George. 1996. *The McDonaldization of Society*, revised edition. Thousand Oaks, Calif.: Pine Forge Press.

Weinstein, Raymond M. 1992. "Disneyland and Coney Island: Reflections on the Evolution of the Modern Amusement Park." *Journal of Popular Culture* 26, 1 (summer): 131–64.

Questions for Discussion and Writing

1. What do you believe are the authors' opinions about Disney? Support your answer with references to the text.

2. How do the authors respond to their own question raised in paragraph 3: "But what has this to do with religion?"

3. Where are statistics used in the text and what purpose(s) do the statistics serve? Explain whether or not you believe the statistics effectively support the argument.

4. Mazur and Koda write, "Disney's products (tangible and intangible) fill many of the roles often filled by religion" (paragraph 11). Write an essay in which you agree with, refute, or modify this claim. In your essay, consider the role that religion plays in life. Is it possible for a corporation like Disney to truly substitute for religion?

5. Conduct research on the practices of the Disney corporation. Write an essay comparing and/or contrasting your findings of the Disney corporation to the image promoted by their public relations department.

Shopping for American Culture
JAMES J. FARRELL

Historian, educator, writer, and popular culture scholar James Farrell has published several books, including Inventing the American Way of Death 1830–1920 *(1980),* The Nuclear Devil's Dictionary *(1985),* The Spirit of the Sixties: The Making of Postwar Radicalism *(1997), and* One Nation Under Goods: Malls and the Seductions of American Shopping *(2003), from which the following is an excerpt. James Farrell is currently teaching at St. Olaf College.*

Write a list of all the various motivations for shopping (for example, escape, need, enjoyment). How often do you shop? Is shopping a dreaded chore or a relaxing escape? If it relaxes you, try to explain why you find enjoyment and how you feel when you are shopping. If it is a dreaded chore, then explain why you believe so many people enjoy shopping.

———————————— ✦ ————————————

M alls are an American cultural phenomenon. The United States now has more shopping centers than high schools, and in the last forty years, shopping center space has increased by a factor of twelve. By 2000, there were more than forty-five thousand shopping malls with 5.47 billion square feet of gross leasable space in the United States. Currently, America's shopping centers (most of which are strip malls) generate more than a trillion dollars in annual sales. Not counting sales of cars and gasoline, that's slightly more than half of the nation's retail activity. The International Council of Shopping Centers (ICSC) reported that in 2000, America's shopping centers served 196 million Americans a month and employed more than 10.6 million workers, about 8 percent of the nonfarm workforce in the country. We go to malls 3.2 times a month and spend an average of $71.04 each time (a one-third increase in spending from 1995 to 2000). Shopping centers also support our state and city governments, generating $46.6 billion in sales taxes, almost half of all state tax revenue (see table 1).[1]

Shopping is such a common part of America's pursuit of happiness that we usually take shopping centers for granted. But although malls are usually places of consumer forgetfulness, they can inspire a sense of thoughtfulness. It's no particular problem if we come back from the mall empty-handed, but it should be a deep disappointment if we come back empty-headed.[2]

But why should we think about malls?

Quite simply, because Americans go to malls. We may not like the malling of America, but if we want to understand Americans, we have to look for them where they are, not where we think they ought to be. We need to follow Americans to the mall and see what they're doing because shopping centers can reveal cultural patterns that we don't usually see. In some ways, culture is what happens when we are not paying attention. When we are fully conscious of our choices, they are likely to express our individual

Table 1
Shopping Centers in the United States

	1970	1980	1990	2000
Number of shopping centers	11,000	22,100	36,500	45,000
Total leasable sales area (billions of square feet)	1.49	2.96	4.39	5.57
Retail sales in shopping centers (billions of dollars)	82.0	305.4	681.4	1,136.0
Employment in shopping centers (millions of people)	2.49	5.28	8.60	10.69

Source: Data from ICSC, *Scope.* (Scope is a publication of the International Council of Shopping Centers, Inc., New York, N.Y.; reprinted by permission.)

values and preferences, but when we're going about our daily business with little thought about what we're doing, we act according to the habits of our hearts, and those habits are shaped as much by culture as by character.[3]

Malls are a great place for the pleasures of shopping, but they're an even better place for the pleasures of thinking, in part because they help us think about the cultural contours of shopping. Shopping is, etymologically, the process of going to shops to purchase goods and services. According to Webster, a shop is a small retail store; the word comes from a root that denoted the booths or stalls of the marketplace. The verb *to shop* appeared in the late eighteenth century; by the late twentieth century, shopping had become a way of life. Measured in constant dollars, the average American of today consumes twice as many goods and services as the average American of 1950 and ten times as much as a counterpart from 1928. On average, we each consume more than one hundred pounds of materials a day. Shopping, it seems, might be more American than apple pie.[4]

Sometimes shopping is a utilitarian act. We need a shirt or a suitcase, and we go to the mall to get it. Sometimes, though, shopping is intrinsically pleasurable, and we go to the mall to just do it. Shopping itself can be therapeutic, even fun, whether or not

5

anything ends up in the shopping bag. So an exploration of malls can help us think about what we have in mind—as well as what we don't have in mind—when we are shopping.[5]

When we get home from the mall, we tell the family, "I was shopping." It sounds simple. Yet shopping is a complex act, or, more precisely, a complex interaction. It's not just a matter of choosing items and paying for them; it's an act of desire that is shaped individually and culturally, an interaction with shops and with a complex infrastructure of production and distribution. It's an act of conscience in which our own values interact with commercial and cultural values. Shopping requires a biological being to enter an architectural space outfitted with commercial art and designed to sell artifacts manufactured and distributed in a market economy. Shopping centers are built of solid materials, but the spaces are also socially constructed and regulated by political entities. Our malls reflect and affect personal perceptions, social norms, religious beliefs, ethical values, cultural geography, domestic architecture, foreign policy, and social psychology. And the artifacts within shopping centers are equally complex, synthesizing material form and symbolic meaning. Shopping is no simple task.

Malls are a good place to think about retailing and retail culture, an important subset of American commercial culture. Because we are consumers, we think we know how consumption works, but we don't usually pay attention to how consumption is *produced*. In malls of America, consumption is not just happenstance. It's carefully planned and programmed. To be informed consumers, therefore, we need information not just about the products we buy but also about the spaces—architectural and social—where we buy them.

Malls are America's public architecture, a primary form of public space, the town halls of the twentieth and twenty-first centuries. Sociologist Mark Gottdiener contends that the mall "has become the most successful form of environmental design in contemporary settlement space." The late nineteenth century was known for its train stations and department stores. In the early twentieth century it was skyscrapers and subways. Mid-twentieth-century Americans created suburban forms, including subdivisions, malls, and office parks. The late twentieth century was an era of malls and airports, and the airports increasingly looked like malls.[6]

10   Malls are also art galleries, carefully crafted collections of commercial art. To the connoisseur, they offer an unending display of artful design, including product design, package design,

retail design, visual merchandising, sculpture, and architecture. The artists we find in museums often challenge our conceptions of ourselves and unsettle our sense of society. The artists who exhibit their skills in the museums we call malls, on the other hand, tend to reinforce our sense of ourselves, producing a commercial art that makes malls more popular than museums in American culture. But even people who have taken courses in art appreciation don't always take time to appreciate the creativity of commercial art.

Malls are also outstanding museums of contemporary American material culture. In them, we find a huge collection of the artifacts that help us make sense of our world. And as in most museums, reading these artifacts can help us read the culture.

Indeed, as cultural institutions, malls perform what Paul Lauter calls "cultural work," a term that describes "the ways in which a book or other kind of 'text'—a movie, a Supreme Court decision, an advertisement, an anthology, an international treaty, a material object—helps construct the frameworks, fashion the metaphors, create the very language by which people comprehend their experience and think about their world." In short, malls help teach us the common sense of our culture. If we look closely at malls, we will soon be looking inside our own heads. So it is partly the purpose of this book to explain this social construction of common sense—the way we teach each other, both explicitly and implicitly, the common sense of our culture.[7]

Understanding a single act of shopping means understanding the culture in which it occurs. When we go to the mall looking for jeans, we find ourselves embedded in a cultural fabric that fits us like a pair of jeans. Shopping centers are constructed of steel and concrete, bricks and mortar, but they are also made of culture. Indeed, culture is about the only thing they *can* be made of. Retailers routinely use our cultural values to stimulate sales. Shopping centers reinforce these values even as they distract us from other American values—justice, equality, democracy, and spirituality— that might also animate our lives (see table 2).[8]

As this suggests, malls are a manifestation of popular philosophy. They're a place where we answer important questions: What does it mean to be human? What are people for? What is the meaning of things? Why do we work? What do we work for? And what, in fact, are we shopping for? Like colleges and churches, malls provide answers to these critical questions. Like colleges, malls are places where we make statements about the good, the true, and the beautiful. Like churches, they are places

Table 2
Summary of American Core Values

Value	General Features	Relevance to Consumer Behavior
Achievement and success	Hard work is good, success flows from hard work.	Acts as a justification for acquisition of goods ("You deserve it.")
Activity	Keeping busy is healthy and natural.	Stimulates interest in products that are time-savers and enhance leisure time
Efficiency and practicality	Admiration of things that solve problems (e.g., save time and effort)	Stimulates purchase of products that function well and save time
Progress	People can improve themselves, tomorrow should be better than today	Stimulates desire for new products that fulfill unsatisfied needs; ready acceptance of products that claim to be "new" or "improved"
Material comfort	"The good life"	Fosters acceptance of convenience and luxury products that make life more comfortable and enjoyable
Individualism	Being oneself (e.g., self-reliance, self-interest, self-esteem)	Stimulates acceptance of customized or unique products that enable a person to "express his or her own personality"
Freedom	Freedom of choice	Fosters interest in wide product lines and differentiated products
External conformity	Uniformity of observable behavior; desire for acceptance	Stimulates interest in products that are used or owned by others in the same social group
Humanitarianism	Caring for others, particularly the underdog	Stimulates patronage of firms that compete with market leaders

Youthfulness	A state of mind that stresses being "young at heart" and having a youthful appearance	Stimulates acceptance of products that provide the illusion of maintaining or fostering youthfulness
Fitness and health	Caring about one's body, including the desire to be physically fit and healthy	Stimulates acceptance of food products, activities, and equipment perceived to maintain or increase physical fitness

Source: Consumer Behavior, 5th ed. by Schiffman/Kanuck. © Reprinted by permission of Pearson Education, Inc., Upper Saddle River, N.J.

where we decide what is ultimately valuable and how we will value it. And malls are places where we act out, and institutionalize, our values.[9]

Endnotes

1. International Council of Shopping Centers (ICSC), "Scope USA," at the ICSC web site, www.icsc.org; John Fetto, "Mall Rats,"*American Demographics* 24 (March 2002): 10; Judith Ann Coady, "The Concrete Dream: A Sociological Look at the Shopping Mall" (Ph.D. diss., Boston University, 1987), 720; Ira G. Zepp Jr., *The New Religious Image of Urban America: The Shopping Mall as Ceremonial Center*, 2d ed. (Niwot: University Press of Colorado, 1997), 10.
2. As my colleague Eric Nelson says, malls "are the last place anyone would go to think seriously. There is nothing, however, that demands more serious thought." Eric Nelson, *Mall of America: Reflections of a Virtual Community* (Lakeville, Minn.: Galde Press, 1998), 152.
3. Zepp, *New Religious Image*, 10.
4. John C. Ryan and Alan Durning, *Stuff: The Secret Lives of Everyday Things* (Seattle: Northwest Environment Watch, 1997), 4–5.
5. Barry J. Babin, William R. Darden, and Mitch Griffin, "Work and/or Fun: Measuring Hedonic and Utilitarian Shopping Value," *Journal of Consumer Research* 20 (March 1994): 646–47.
6. Mark Gottdiener, "Recapturing the Center: A Semiotic Analysis of Shopping Malls," in *The City and the Sign: An Introduction to Urban Semiotics*, ed. Mark Gottdiener and Alexandros Ph. Lagopoulos (New York: Columbia University Press, 1986), 291.
7. Paul Lauter, *From Walden Pond to Jurassic Park: Activism, Culture, and American Studies* (Durham N.C.: Duke University Press, 2001), 11.

8. Leon G. Schiffman and Leslie Lazar Kanuk, *Consumer Behavior*, 5th ed. (Englewood Cliffs, N.J.: Prentice Hall, 1994), 437.
9. Jon Goss, "Once-upon-a-Time in the Commodity World: An Unofficial Guide to Mall of America," *Annals of the Association of American Geographers* 89 (March 1999): 47.

Questions for Discussion and Writing

1. How does Farrell answer the question posed in paragraph 3, "why should we think about malls?" Explain whether or not you agree with Farrell's response.
2. Enumerate the ways in which malls are "outstanding museums of contemporary American material culture" (paragraph 11).
3. Farrell includes a table listing a "Summary of American Core Values." Evaluate whether or not you think the information is useful and/or relevant. How frequently do you include charts and diagrams in your own work?
4. Visit the local mall and spend some time observing the design of storefront windows. Select one store and write a description of the window design: the products showcased, dominant colors, designs, photographs, and layout. What does your analysis of the storefront reveal about American material culture and American core values?
5. Farrell writes, "Shopping is a complex act, or more precisely, a complex interaction" (paragraph 7). Using your response to the Pre-Reading questions about shopping, write a personal essay about your own psychology of shopping. What do you believe are the specific positive and/or negative psychological effects of your own spending habits?

Bootleg Culture
PETE ROJAS

Guest speaker and freelance expert technology and digital entertainment journalist Pete Rojas wrote this article for Salon *magazine (August 21, 2002). He is editor-in-chief of* Engadget, *one of the most successful web-based technology magazines. His extensive publishing credits include the* New York Times, Popular Science, *the* Village Voice, Salon, Money, Fortune, Popular Science, Wired, *and many others.*

Pre-Reading

From the title of the essay, what are your expectations? Do we live in a "Bootleg Culture"? Write one paragraph describing what you already know about bootlegging and whether or not you believe it is acceptable.

─────────────── ✦ ───────────────

When the Belgian DJ duo 2ManyDJs were creating their own album of "bootlegs"—hybrid tracks that mix together other people's songs to create new songs that are at once familiar yet often startlingly different—they decided to get permission to use every one of the hundreds of tracks they mashed together. The result: almost a solid year of calling, e-mailing, and faxing dozens and dozens of record labels all over the world. (Creating the album itself only took about a week.) In the end about a third of their requests were turned down, which isn't surprising. Many artists and their labels have become reluctant to allow any sampling of their work unless they are sure the new work will sell enough copies to generate large royalty checks.

What is surprising are the names of some of the artists who turned them down: the Beastie Boys, Beck, Missy Elliott, Chemical Brothers, and M/A/R/R/S—artists whose own careers are based on sampling and who in some cases have been sued in the past for their own unauthorized sampling. For whatever reason these artists decided not to license their material, the net effect is that more entrenched, "legitimate" sampling artists are preventing lesser known, struggling sampling artists from doing what the legitimate artists probably wish they could have done years ago: sample without hindrance to create new works.

Typically consisting of a vocal track from one song digitally superimposed on the instrumental track of another, bootlegs (or "mash-ups," as they are also called) are being traded over the Internet, and they're proving to be a big hit on dance floors across the U.K. and Europe. In just the past couple of years, hundreds if not thousands of these homebrewed mixes have been created, with music fans going wild over such odd pairings as Soulwax's bootleg of Destiny's Child's "Bootylicious" mixed with Nirvana's "Smells Like Teen Spirit," Freelance Hellraiser's mix of Christina Aguilera singing over the Strokes, and Kurtis Rush's pairing of Missy Elliott rapping over George Michael's "Faith." Bootlegs inject an element of playfulness into a pop music scene that can be distressingly sterile.

While there have been odd pairings, match-ups and remixes for decades now, and club DJs have been doing something similar during live sets, the recent explosion in the number of tracks being created and disseminated is a direct result of the dramatic increase in the power of the average home computer and the widespread use on these computers of new software programs like Acid and ProTools. Home remixing is technically incredibly easy to do, in effect turning the vast world of pop culture into source material for an endless amount of slicing and dicing by desktop producers.

5   So easy, in fact, that bootlegs constitute the first genre of music that truly fulfills the "anyone can do it" promises originally made by punk and, to lesser extent, electronic music. Even punk rockers had to be able to write the most rudimentary of songs. With bootlegs, even that low bar for traditional musicianship and composition is obliterated. Siva Vaidhyanthan, an assistant professor of culture and communication at New York University and the author of "Copyrights and Copywrongs," believes that what we're seeing is the result of a democratization of creativity and the demystification of the process of authorship and creativity.

"It's about demolishing the myth that there has to be a special class of creators, and flattening out the creative curve so we can all contribute to our creative environment," says Vaidhyanthan.

The debate over what bootlegs are and what they mean is taking place within the wider context of a culture where turntables now routinely outsell guitars, teenagers aspire to be Timbaland and the Automator, No. 1 singles rework or sample other records, and DJs have become pop stars in their own right, even surpassing in fame the very artists whose records they spin. Pop culture in general seems more and more remixed—samples and references are permeating more and more of mainstream music, film, and television, and remix culture appears to resonate strongly with consumers. We're at the point where it almost seems unnatural not to quote, reference, or sample the world around us. To the teens buying the latest all-remixes J.Lo album, dancing at a club to an unauthorized two-step white-label remix of the new Nelly single, or even hacking together their own bootleg, recombination—whether legal or not—doesn't feel wrong in the slightest. The difference now is that they have the tools to sample, reference, and remix, allowing them to finally "talk back" to pop culture in the way that seems most appropriate to them.

The recording industry instinctively fears such unauthorized use of copyrighted materials. But instead of sending out cease-and-desist orders, it should be embracing bootlegs. In a world of constantly recycled sounds and images, bootleg culture is no aberration—it's part of the natural evolution of all things digital.

Bootlegs don't contain any specific audible element of originality in the track, in the sense that one can identify any specific original vocal or musical composition created by the remixer. The only original element of a bootleg is the selection and arrangement of the tracks to be blended into a new work. Scottish bootlegger Grant Robson, who goes by the name Grant McSleazy, responsible for such tracks as Missy Elliott versus the Strokes, readily admits this: "There is a creative aspect, because not all songs work well together, but all the lyric writing and music composition has been done for you. You may rearrange the segments of an instrumental/a capella, but that's just production work."

Even so, isn't production work what constitutes most of what goes into crafting most hip-hop, electronic music, and pop these days? Because of this, bootlegs highlight the increasing difficulty in distinguishing between musicians, DJs and producers. Is there really all that much difference, on a technical level, between Mc Sleazy, DJ Shadow, Moby and P. Diddy? Putting aside any qualitative judgments, on one level or another they are all just appropriators of sound. They are all combining elements of other people's works in order to create new ones, in effect challenging the old model of authorship that presupposes that the building blocks of creativity should spill forth directly from the mind of the artist.

Already we've seen that our notion of what makes a song "creative" has widened in the case of hip-hop. Early on, hip-hop—constructed largely with snippets of other songs—faced similar charges that it lacked a creative element. Eventually, because a great deal of arrangement is involved (usually a large number of samples are blended together to create just a single hip-hop track), and because the rapping itself contributes an original element, pop culture at large has found it easier to acknowledge some aspect of originality and creativity within hip-hop. Bootlegs challenge this notion even further, but it is almost inevitable that as they grow in popularity, something similar will happen, and our definition of creativity will expand to accommodate them.

Existing copyright laws mean that, for the most part, this movement will remain underground. Consequently bootlegs may be the first new genre of music that is almost entirely contraband, and most bootlegs now can only be found on a few Web sites or on file-sharing networks like KaZaA and Gnutella. The bootleggers behind these audio mismatches know they will never get permission from the artists they sample and haven't even bothered to try to get it. Though 2ManyDJs tried to go legit and get permission for as many songs as possible, they still were unable to get clearance for a significant number of samples they used on their album—and even the permissions and clearances they do have are so restricted that it will be impossible to release the album in the United States. Despite the tremendous amount of energy poured into these desktop productions, the fact remains that because the original works cut and pasted together are used without the original artists' permission, bootlegs have stayed, well, bootlegs.

While everyone (particularly the companies touting the technologies that make all this possible) predicted a flood of original movies and music spewing forth from the desktops of bedroom auteurs, no one anticipated that large numbers of people would be more interested in using their computers to combine, mash together, or remix other people's work. Sharing one's unauthorized creations via the Net is even easier. It's a dramatic change from just a few years ago, when a bootlegger's sole option would have been to have vinyl or CDs manufactured and then distributed, something that would risk arousing the attention, and legal action, of the record labels of the remixed artists.

This phenomenon hasn't been limited to music: Remixing has begun to infect film as well. Last year copies of a home-edited version of "Star Wars Episode 1: The Phantom Menace" began circulating on the Internet to widespread acclaim from fans who declared "Star Wars Episode 1.1: The Phantom Edit" the superior of the two versions. It's probably only a matter of time until someone creates a fan edit of "Attack of the Clones." Inspired by the "Phantom" edit, DJ Hupp, a freelance film editor in Sacramento, Calif., has created his own "Kubrick edit" of Spielberg's "A.I.," and it is unlikely that his will be the last fan edit we see of a major motion picture.

15   Such fan edits are also, technically, illegal, but from the perspective of the turntablists, remixers, and home editors at the forefront of the explosion of bootleg culture, copyright laws don't look like anything other than the means by which one group of artists limits the work of another.

Illegality can actually be a large part of the allure of bootlegs. Much underground cultural expression takes place at the margins of the law—rave culture, for example, has its origins in illegal warehouse parties. Using other people's music without permission used to be the point of mash-ups. Back in the '80s and early '90s, when culture-jamming sound collagists like Negativland and the Evolution Control Committee released their first works, mash-ups had a decidedly subversive edge to them. Mash-ups were typically created as statements about pop culture and the media juggernaut that surrounds us, not as fodder for the dance floor. Pasting together elements swiped from the top 40 and placing them together in a new form was supposed to snap us out of what these sonic outlaws saw as our media-induced trance and make a point about copyright in the process.

Traces of that element remain in the bootlegs being made today. One Australian bootlegger, a 26-year-old who goes by the name Dsico, and for legal reasons prefers that his identity be withheld, sees bootlegs as akin to the kitschiness and pastiche of pop art. "The reinterpretation and recontextualization of cultural icons like Britney Spears or the Strokes is fun and good for a laugh. But if I can grab an a cappella track of Mandy Moore and mix it with something like "Roxanne" by the Police, while that juxtaposition may be trite, it still works as a commentary on pop music today."

And at a time when it has become increasingly difficult for pop music to be shocking (witness the mainstream acceptability, however grudging, of Eminem), it may be that the only way to write a transgressive pop song is to flat-out steal it from someone else. In other words, the only way left to shock is not through controversial content, but by subverting the very form and structure of the song itself.

Even though making music out of other people's songs without permission may appear to pose a threat to the business model of the recording industry, killing off this nascent genre may not ultimately be in the industry's best interests. Radio stations in Britain that have played bootlegs have found themselves on the receiving end of cease-and-desist orders. Hip-hop got its start using pre-existing music in innovative and not always legal ways. It is arguable that had the music industry clamped down on sampling earlier than it did (it wasn't until a 1991 suit against rapper Biz Markie that sampling without permission was established as illegal), the industry's top-selling genre would never have gotten off the ground commercially. Now legendary hip-hop albums, such as Public Enemy's "It Takes a Nation of Millions to Hold Us Back," and the Beastie Boys' "Paul's Boutique," would be impossible to release today.

Just as with every other subcultural movement that has threatened the status quo, the music industry's best response may be to let the genre flourish online and on the margins. So far no one is really making any money from bootlegs—if anything, bootlegs stimulate demand for the original songs. Rather than

20

threaten bootleggers with legal action, a sounder strategy would be to co-opt the scene by skimming the best ones off the top and re-releasing them as "official" bootlegs. This has already produced one No. 1 hit, with Richard X's mash-up of new waver Gary Numan and soul singer Adina Howard. The track follows in the footsteps of DNA's bootleg dance remix of Suzanne Vega's "Tom's Diner," which Vega ended up authorizing and re-releasing to much chart success in 1990.

As computers and software programs get more and more powerful with each passing year, as file-sharing networks make it simple for anyone to share their work with the world, and as it is next to impossible to outlaw digital editing software (which has plenty of legitimate uses), bootlegs and remixes will likely be a part of the cultural landscape for years to come. Bootlegging may even evolve into something of a hobby for tens of thousands of desktop producers who will spend their free time splicing together the latest top 40 hits for kicks, like model-airplane builders. The record industry could even respond by selling its own do-it-yourself bootleg kits, complete with editing software and authorized samples. In a sense bootlegs are music fans' response to the current disposability of pop culture. Effortlessly easy to create, with an infinite number of combinations possible, bootlegs are even more perfectly disposable than the pop songs they combine—by the time the novelty and the cleverness have worn off there will always be new hit singles to mash together.

Eventually recombining and remixing is likely to become so prevalent that it will be all but impossible to even identify the original source of samples, making questions about authorship and origins largely irrelevant, or at least unanswerable. We're already seeing the beginnings of that, like the hip-hop song that samples an older hip-hop song that samples a '70s funk song. Some artists, most notably David Bowie, are already proclaiming the death of authorship altogether. Technology has not only expanded who can create; in blurring the distinction between consumers and producers, these new digital tools are also challenging the very ideas of creativity and authorship. They are forcing us to recognize modes of cultural production that often make it impossible to answer such once simple questions as, Who wrote this song? The cultural landscape that emerges will be a plural space of creation in which it may even become pointless to designate who created exactly what, since everyone will be stealing from and remixing everyone else. The results might be confusing, but it'll probably be a lot more fun and worth listening to than a world where only those with the financial resources to pay licensing fees (e.g., P. Diddy) get to make songs with sampling.

Questions for Discussion and Writing

1. At the salon.com site, this article carries the following lead-in: "Powerful computers and easy-to-use editing software are challenging our conceptions of authorship and creativity. As usual, the entertainment industry doesn't like this one bit." In what ways does the lead-in illuminate the material contained in the article?

2. Compare your expectations of the article from the Pre-Reading exercise to your post-reading assessment. In what ways did Rojas reinforce or challenge your views?

3. Do you think that the article presents a fair balance of both points of view? Explain whether or not you believe the counterargument is fairly represented.

4. Write a personal essay about the way you purchase music. What is your preferred genre of music? Do you purchase CDs, or do you go online and download songs? How has the Internet changed the way you consume music? If you download songs into your computer and/or I-Pod, do you pay a fee?

5. Rojas writes: "In a sense bootlegs are music fans' response to the current disposability of pop culture" (paragraph 21). Conduct research on the legal debate concerning bootleg music and copyright laws. Who is actually being injured? Are you for or against bootlegs? In your paper, be sure to include your own solutions to the issue.

Protecting Mickey Mouse at Art's Expense

Lawrence Lessig

Named as one of "Scientific American's *Top 50 Visionaries" and distinguished Stanford Law School Professor and founder of the school's Center for Internet and Society, Lawrence Lessig has received numerous accolades and awards, including the Free Software Foundation's Freedom Award. Lessig's passion for his work is evident in this persuasive Op-Ed for the January 18, 2003, issue of the* New York Times. *He has authored numerous articles for magazines and newspapers such as the* Los Angeles Times, *the* New York Times, *the* Wall Street Journal, Wired, *the* Industry Standard, Slate, *the* Boston Globe, *the* New Republic, *and others. His book publications include* Free Culture *(2004),* The Future of Ideas *(2001), and* Code and Other Laws of Cyberspace *(1999).*

Pre-Reading

Look up the following terms in a general dictionary and then a legal dictionary (such as www.law.com): *patent, copyright, intellectual property.* In what ways are the definitions similar and/or different?

——————— ✦ ———————

The Supreme Court decided this week that the Constitution grants Congress an essentially unreviewable discretion to set the lengths of copyright protections however long it wants, and even to extend them.

While the court was skeptical about the wisdom of the extension, seven justices believed it was not their role to second-guess "the First Branch," as Justice Ruth Bader Ginsburg put it. As I argued the opposite before the court for my clients, a group of creators and publishers who depend on public domain works, I won't say I agree. But there is something admirable in the court acknowledging and respecting limits on its own power.

Still, missing from the opinion was any justification for perhaps the most damaging part of Congress's decision to extend existing copyrights for 20 years: the extension unnecessarily stifles freedom of expression by preventing the artistic and educational use even of content that no longer has any commercial value. As one dissenter, Justice Steven G. Breyer, estimated, only 2 percent of the work copyrighted between 1923 and 1942 continues to be commercially exploited (for example, the early Mickey Mouse movies, whose imminent entry into the public domain prompted Congress to act in the first place).

But to protect that tiny proportion, the remaining copyrighted works will stay locked up for another generation. Thus a museum that wants to produce an Internet exhibition about the New Deal will still need to find the copyright holders of any pictures or sound it wants to include. Or archives that want to release out-of-print books will still need to track down copyright holders of works that are almost a century old.

5   This is a problem that the First Branch could fix without compromising any of the legitimate rights protected by the copyright

extension act. The trick is a technique to move content that is no longer commercially exploited into the public domain, while protecting work that has continuing commercial value. The answer is suggested from the law governing patents.

Patent holders have to pay a fee every few years to maintain their patents. The same principle could be applied to copyright. Imagine requiring copyright holders to pay a tax 50 years after a work was published. The tax should be very small, maybe $50 a work. And when the tax was paid, the government would record that fact, including the name of the copyright holder paying the tax. That way artists and others who want to use a work would continue to have an easy way to identify the current copyright owner. But if a copyright owner fails to pay the tax for three years in a row, then the work will enter the public domain. Anyone would then be free to build upon and cultivate that part of our culture as he sees fit.

None of the supporters of the copyright extension act should have any complaint about such a provision. All of them argued that they needed the term increased so they could continue to get revenue from their works that supported their other artistic endeavors. But if a work is not earning any commercial return, then the extension is pointless. Of course, there may be people who want to keep their work from passing into the public domain, even if it is not commercially exploited. That's why the tax should be low, and should apply only to work that was published. The privacy and control that copyright law gives authors would thus be assured for as long as Congress deems proper.

This compromise, of course, puts much less work into the public domain than my clients believed that the framers of the Constitution envisioned. But it would nonetheless make available an extraordinary amount of material. If Congress is listening to the frustration that the court's decision has created, this would be a simple and effective way for the First Branch to respond.

Questions for Discussion and Writing

1. Describe whether or not you believe the title of the editorial—"Protecting Mickey Mouse at Art's Expense"—is effective in capturing the author's main argument.

2. Do you believe the compromise to "move content that is no longer commercially exploited into the public domain, while protecting work that has continuing commercial value" is an effective solution (paragraph 5)? Explain why or why not.

3. Explain what you believe to be missing in Lessig's editorial.
4. Use Lessig's 667-word *New York Times* editorial as a model and write your own editorial on copyright protection from the opposing point of view. Conduct research so that you can support your rebuttal.
5. Conduct further research on the controversy surrounding the extension of copyright protection. Write an argument supporting, opposing, or modifying the extension.

Questions for Making Connections

1. Refer to the "American Core Values" list presented in Farrell. Select two or three values and show how they are relevant to one of the other essays in this chapter or book. For example, you could select "Progress and Youthfulness" and show how these values are relevant to consumers who attend Disney World and/or purchase Disney's products (Mazur and Koda); alternatively, you could select the value of Fitness and Health and show how it relates to one of the essays in Chapter 2 (for example, Dove, Smith, or Stibbe).
2. Twitchell writes, "Consumerism is not forced on us. It is not against our better judgment. It is (at least for much of our lives) our better judgment"(paragraph 42). Write an argumentation essay in defense of materialism. In your response, also include counterarguments and your response to them. You may want to include reference to any of the writers in this chapter (Twitchell, Farrell, Mazur and Koda, Rojas, Lessig).
3. Write an essay comparing Disneyland as a space to the therapeutic experience of the mall as a space. In what ways are both of them similar? How do they differ?
4. Both Rojas and Twitchell refer to different aspects of the disposability of consumer culture. Write an essay examining whether or not you believe popular culture is disposable. You may want to think about focusing on one medium (music, television, film) and one period of time (60s, 70s, 80s, 90s, etc.). What does the disposability of the medium you selected reveal about Americans? What do you believe are the short- and long-term consequences arising from the fickleness of American tastes?
5. Lessig writes about "the early Mickey Mouse movies, whose imminent entry into the public domain prompted Congress to act in the first place" (paragraph 3). What role do you believe Disney had in "prompt[ing] Congress"? How do you imagine Mazur and Koda would respond to Lessig's statement? In your essay, use evidence from both Lessig and Mazur and Koda to support your point of view.

American Civil Liberties Union (ACLU). "ACLU Comments to the Federal Communications Commission re: MB Docket No. 04-261, the Matter of Violent Television Programming and Its Impact on Children." September 15, 2004. Public Domain. Permission granted by American Civil Liberties Union.

Beck, Bernard. "The Myth That Would Not Die: *The Sopranos*, Mafia Movies, and Italians in America." *Multicultural Perspectives*. Volume 2 (2) © 2000, pages 24–27. Reprinted by permission of Lawrence Erlbaum Associates, Inc.

Deneen, Patrick J. "Awaking from the American Dream: The End of Escape in American Cinema?" from *Perspectives on Political Science*, Volume 31, Issue 2, p. 96 (8 pages), Spring 2002. Reprinted with permission of the Helen Dwight Reid Educational Foundation. Published by Heldref Publications, 1319 Eighteenth St., NW, Washington, DC 20036-1802. Copyright © 2002.

Donald, Ralph R. "From 'Knockout Punch' to 'Home Run': Masculinity's 'Dirty Dozen' Sports Metaphors in Amercan Combat Films." *Film & History*. Volume 35. Issue 1 (2005). Reprinted by permission of Ralph R. Donald, Ph.D. Copyright © 2005.

Ehrenreich, Barbara. "Why Don't We Like the Human Body?" Copyright © 1991 Time, Inc. Reprinted by permission.

Farrell, James J. "Shopping for American Culture" from *One Nation under Goods: Malls and the Seductions of American Shopping*. Copyright © 2003 Smithsonian Institution. Reprinted by permission of HarperCollins Publishers.

Franzen, Jonathan. "The Reader in Exile" from *How to Be Alone*. Copyright 2002, 2003 by Jonathan Franzen. Reprinted by permission of Farrar, Straus and Giroux, LLC.

Garrison, Eric. "*The Simpsons:* A Reflection of Society and a Message on Family." Copyright © Eric Garrison (tallents2@yahoo.com), November 12, 2001. Posted on *www.snpp.com*.

Gertner, Jon. "The Futile Pursuit of Happiness." Copyright © 2003 by The New York Times Co. Reprinted with permission.

Trussell, Robert. "Scholars Spend as Much Time with *Love Boat* as with Shakespeare." December 10, 2004 from Kinght Ridder/Tribune, represented by TMS Reprints. Used by permission.

Tsing Loh, Sandra. "Shopworn: Like the Valley Girls Who Made It Famous, the Suburban Mall Is Now on the Wrong Side of Forty." Copyright © 2004 by Sandra Tsing Loh. First appeared in the *Atlantic Monthly*

Tucker, Chris. "Different Stories" from *America Behind the Color Line* by Henry Gates. Copyright © 2004 by Henry Louis Gates, Jr. By permission of Warner Books, Inc.

Twitchell, James. "Trash and the Voluntary Simplicity Movement—The Triumph of American Materialism" from *Lead Us into Temptation: The Triumph of American Materialism*. Copyright © 1999. Reprinted with permission of Columbia University Press.

Warhol, Andy. "What's Great About This Country." Excerpt from *The Philosophy of Andy Warhol (From A to B and Back Again)*. Copyright © 1975 by Andy Warhol, reprinted by permission of Harcourt, Inc.

Warmbold, Marie. "Harry Potter: Oliver with a Magical Twist." Used by permission.

"Only Two Percent of Women Describe Themselves as Beautiful." Used by permission of Unilever.